V&R unipress

Transottomanica
Osteuropäisch-osmanisch-persische Mobilitätsdynamiken

Band 2

Herausgegeben von

Stefan Rohdewald, Stephan Conermann und Albrecht Fuess

Evelin Dierauff

Translating Late Ottoman Modernity in Palestine

Debates on Ethno-Confessional Relations and Identity in the Arab Palestinian Newspaper *Filasṭīn* (1911–1914)

With 24 figures

V&R unipress

MIX
Papier aus verantwortungsvollen Quellen
FSC® C083411

Bibliografische Information der Deutschen Nationalbibliothek
Die Deutsche Nationalbibliothek verzeichnet diese Publikation in der Deutschen Nationalbibliografie; detaillierte bibliografische Daten sind im Internet über https://dnb.de abrufbar.

Umschlagabbildung: Street vendor with newspaper "La Palestine" in Jaffa (1921–1923),
© The Netherlands Institute for The Near East (Leiden), Frank Scholten Collection,
www.nino-leiden.nl/collections/frank-scholten-legacy
Druck und Bindung: CPI books GmbH, Birkstraße 10, D-25917 Leck
Printed in the EU.

Vandenhoeck & Ruprecht Verlage | www.vandenhoeck-ruprecht-verlage.com

ISSN 2626-9449
ISBN 978-3-8471-1066-8

To Karl Dierauff (1901–1992), an example of *ṣumūd*,
and my parents, Lydia & Ernst (1935–2002).

Contents

Acknowledgements

This study is a revised version of my dissertation that I submitted to the Department of Oriental and Islamic Studies at Tuebingen University in 2018. Several people were extremely helpful in finishing this study and provided to me various kinds of support. I am grateful to my supervisors, Johann Büssow and Stefan Rohdewald, who both helped with practical advises and dedicated a lot of time to critically discuss and reevaluate the concepts of this work. I owe many thanks to Johann Büssow who has shared his notes of his former research on Ottoman Palestine, materials on Palestinian elites and his own evaluations of *Filasṭīn* with me and always helped to reframe this study and its methodological approach. Many thanks go to Emanuel Beška who was so generous to provide me with the digital issues of *Filasṭīn* of 1914 – without this it would not have been possible to complete my conclusions on the Orthodox Renaissance during the late Ottoman years. I also owe many thanks to the people who read pieces or even complete chapters of this work, corrected mistakes and improved the style; especially Johann Büssow, Stefan Rohdewald, Emanuel Beška, Martin Streibel, Franzi Dröscher, Petra Nendwich and Sarah Schmitz-Büssow. Special thanks also go to Carol Rowe who was extremely engaged, thorough and quick in co-editing the whole piece and who always supported me with practical advises.

Finally, my deepest and heartfelt gratitude goes to a circle of beloved and unique friends who have encouraged me, and accompany me in this life journey, or parts of it. You make my day.

Notes on the Transliteration and the Use of Terms

The transliteration system used for Arabic terms follows the regulations of the Deutsche Morgenländische Gesellschaft (DMG). Words in the Arabic text spelled in dialect mostly applies to names of persons and places. In these cases, I slightly adapted the pronounciation of the transliteration. For example, I used the feminine ending -eh instead of -a (*ta-marbūṭa*) when written accordingly in the original text. As for the transliteration of Hebrew words, I followed the norms in line with DIN-31636, however, with slight alterations.[1] I applied the discriticial sign ḥ for ḥa, ʿ for ʿayyin, ṭ for ṭet, ṣ for ṣameḥ, ts for tsade, q for quāf, and š for šin. In case of Ottoman Turkish terms, I followed the recommendations of the Redhouse Turkish/Ottoman-English Dictionary. The transliterations in Arabic, Hebrew or Turkish are in general given in small letters and italic script, or cursive writing; besides translitered names of persons and places which are in normal script. Capital letters are given only in case of translitered names of persons (for instance, Muḥammad) and places (al-Quds, ʿAǧamī, etc.), and for titles of magazines (*Filasṭīn*) taken from the original script. Regarding the first mentioning of proper names, the full name is spelled with the original article (Arab.: al-, Hebr.: ha-). This applied for instance to names of persons (Yūsuf al-ʿĪsā) and titles of magazines (*ha-Ḥerut, al-Karmil*). In the following, I omit the article (*Ḥerut*, ʿĪsā).

Some Arabic and Hebrew words that are in frequent use in the Arabic source or scholarly literature, are given in their original version; for example, terms deriving from the Ottoman administration that describe offices or institutions, such as *muḫtār*, *waqf*, or that define organizations, such as *šomrim*. This also applies for some key terms that often appear in the newspaper's jargon and therefor stand for itself in the frame of this study. For example, I will use the word *nahḍa* instead of "renaissance" and *milla* instead of 'religious community'. Importantly to note, I decided to spell terms deriving from Ottoman bureau-

1 For the revision of the DIN-norm for Hebrew transliteration, see the article of Heuberger (2006).

cracy, that are in frequent use in *Filasṭīn* in its Arabic transliteration and not in the Turkish version; for example, *mutaṣarrif*, *qaḍā'*, *qā'imaqām* or *ḥaḫāmbāšī*, but also the honorary title Bek (Tur.: Bey). For explanations, please consult the glossary of Hebrew and Arabic terms (Appendix IV). However, words that derive from other languages and made their way into English, are given in its common spelling. This applies to the terms mufti, rabbi, qadi, sheikh and lira, but also for Yishuv (defining the Jewish community in Palestine), or Tanzimat (as the period of Ottoman reforms, 1839–1876), etc.

Names of institutions, parties and associations are usually given in capital letters and will be fully spelled at the first mention. In the following, they might be shortened, for instance, I will use CUP instead of Committee of Union and Progress or WZO instead of World Zionist Organization. For this, please consult the list of abbreviations.

List of Abbreviations

AIU	Alliance Israélite Universelle
APB	Anglo-Palestine Bank
Ar.	Arabic
CUP	Committee of Union and Progress
CZA	Central Zionist Archives
Hebr.	Hebrew
ISA	Israeli States Archives
JCA	Jewish Colonial Association
JN	Jewish National Fund
LU	Liberal Union
Turk.	Turkish
WZO	World Zionist Organisation
ZAC	Zionist Actions Committee
ZCO	Zionist Central Office

Introduction

1. Historical Context and Definitions

This book explores how 'ethno-confessional relations' were negotiated in Palestine during the years before World War I as a particular 'translation of late Ottoman Modernity', linking the reconstitution of its group identities with greater mobility dynamics such as transregional migration and the appropriation of transottoman concepts in the local context.[1] Although situated in the Ottoman periphery, Palestine definitely played an important role in the Arab Middle East as a magnet for migrants, tourists, pilgrims and diplomats. Before the outbreak of the War, societies in the Arab East in general and in Palestine in particular, underwent far-reaching transformations.[2] From the nineteenth century, reforms and new institutions were introduced in the region that faced paradoxical circumstances: the beginning of secularization and civic equality, as well as the rise of sectarianism and inter-confessional strife, great technological change and integration into global markets but also economic crisis, migration, political disintegration and the emergence of nation states outside the imperial frame.

In the light of articles published in the local Arabic Palestinian newspaper *Filasṭīn* ('Palestine') in Jaffa from 1911–1914, this study analyzes local views on social cohabitation between different confessional and ethnic groups in Pales-

1 See Rohdewald, Fuess, Riedler, and Conermann 2019, 83–103, on 'Wissenszirkulation' in the transottoman context. The term 'ethno-confessional relations' used here implies a simplification, subsuming relations between certain confessional and/or ethnic groups. My analysis focuses on the intra- and inter-confessional levels of group relations. However, local debates about these relations may include arguments about ethnicity.

2 In this work, alternative terms for geographical spaces are used (Eastern Mediterranean, Arab Middle East, Arab Provinces, Palestine, Holy Land, Jerusalem District). None of these terms are neutral or 'innocent' as they are constructed by power relations and reflect political perspectives. The terms 'Middle East' and 'Orient' only make sense from the perspective of Europe situated west of the Mediterranean. The term 'Holy Land' defines Palestine from a Biblical point of view, marginalizing its Muslim history, which became the dominant European-historical perspective. See Krämer 2002, 11–13.

tine, the socio-economic integration of migrants into local society and ideals of civic participation and governance through the lens of selected case studies.[3] It looks at how these views were negotiated in *Filasṭīn* as a joint production or a 'pool of publishers', were diffused into the public space and contributed to the reconstitution of ethno-confessional relations in Palestine. While *Filasṭīn* has been the subject of studies before, it has been given simplistic labels as pioneer of anti-Zionism and Palestinian nationalism before World War I on the basis of random samples, without proper contextualization of its coverage during the years 1911–1914. Through a concise in-depth media analysis, this study tries to link the production of local discourses with the broader historical context: a local Palestinian society in the Ottoman periphery, affected by transottoman migration, urbanization and competing proto-national discourses; all of this accompanied by high expectations in the field of modernization according to the global *zeitgeist.*

Inter-Confessional Relations in the Context of Ottoman Reforms

The Ottoman Reforms, the *Tanzimat* (1839–1876) or *Tanẓīmāt-i Ḫayrīye* ('Beneficial Reorganization'), aimed at strengthening the central state and the military, securing the tax flow from the provinces and bringing about modernization in line with European standards. The reforms were implemented to gain European support, or ward off European intervention in Ottoman policies, but Zurcher points out that they were strongly motivated by the belief that only a European-style reformation could pave the way out of the financial, political and military crisis, the Empire was experiencing. Thus, the *Tanzimat* proclaimed the civic equality of Muslims, Christians and Jews, at least in theory and under European pressure to liberalize in line with the ideals of the French Revolution.[4] The Ottoman population had previously been divided into Muslims and non-

3 Articles from *Filasṭīn* will be quoted in the following format: *Filasṭīn*, date: number of issue/number of page/number of column on the page (from right to left).

4 In 1839, the first edict, the *Ḫaṭṭ-ı Šerīf of Gülhane*, was issued to gain British support in the 'Egyptian crisis', and to end the expansion of Muḥammad ʿAlī in Syria. It reformed judicial, tax and military structures and confirmed the equality of all subjects. The second edict, the *Ḫaṭṭ-ı Humāyūn* (1856), was issued under tremendous European pressure following the Ottoman defeat in the Crimean War (1853–1856) and focused on regulating relations between the Empire and non-Muslims so as to take a stand against European interference, and especially against a European appeal to Ottoman minorities under the pretense of offering them protection. The *Tanzimat* ended with the promulgation of the Fundamental Law (Tur.: *Qānūn-ı Esāsī*) in 1876, and the suspension of the Constitution by Sultan Abdülhamid (1878). However, a lot of civic and legal reforms were implemented only under the regime of the Young Turks (1908–1918). See Reinkowski 1995, 13, and Zurcher 2004, 50–70. For guidelines of the edicts of 1839 and 1856, see Matuz 1985, 224–231; and the German translation, Meier 1994, 54f., 60f. For its aims and effects, see Sonyel 1993, 147–155, and for its ambivalences, Davison, *Tanẓīmāt*. In: EI².

Muslims (*muslim wa-ġayr muslim*). According to the Sharia on minorities under Muslim authority (*ahl aḏ-ḏimma*), non-Muslim communities were granted an inferior legal status but were protected and given extensive autonomy in religious and civil affairs.[5] Here, the Ottoman *millet* system regulated relations between the state bureaucracy and the non-Muslim communities who were acknowledged as *millets* and had an official representative to the state; this applied, until the nineteenth century, to the Greek Orthodox and Armenian Christians and Ottoman Jews.[6]

The *Tanzimat* officially abolished traditional religious distinctions between Ottoman subjects. Instead of religious identity, the state now fostered secular concepts of citizenship and Ottoman patriotism (Tur.: *osmanlılık*; Ar.: *al-waṭanīya al-ʿuṯmānīya*) regardless of confessional ties, so as to unite the disparate segments of society.[7] The edict of 1858 reconfirmed civic equality and the abolition of by-laws and special taxes (*ǧizya*) for non-Muslims stipulated in Islamic law. It also made provision for recruitment to the military, regardless of faith or ethnicity, introduced mixed courts for legal issues between Muslims and non-Muslims, and confirmed participatory rights for non-Muslims in political bodies. The state also claimed that Muslims, Christians and Jews should have equal rights to representation in the Ottoman bureaucracy and the provincial administration on the basis of a proportional quota.[8] Public reactions in Arab cities to the declaration of civic equality were mixed. Many Muslims felt that it was a provocation that challenged their former superior status.[9] There were also Muslim

5 Sharia, often translated as 'Islamic Law', is not a fixed corpus but a legal and moral value system that constantly produces regulations. For non-Muslims under early Islamic rule, see Bosworth 1982, 37–51, and Braude 2000, 409–418.

6 *Millet* (Tur.) or *milla* (Ar.) means 'denomination' or 'religious community' or, in the modern context, 'nation'. See Öztürk 2009. There is a huge debate about the origins and historical meanings of this term, which is usually applied to non-Muslims. Braude states that, until the Islamic Middle Ages, *milla* referred to any religious community and the concept was transformed over time. In nineteenth-century correspondence, *millet* referred to acknowledged non-Muslim groups whose representatives were the Patriarchs for the Christians, and the Chief Rabbi for the Jews. Later, the *millet* status was extended to other groups, such as Catholics and Protestants. For the debate on concepts of *milla*, see Braude 1982, 69–73 f.; Ursinus 1989, 201 f., 206–207. For the traditional *millet* system, see Levy 1992, 42–44; Ágoston and Masters 2009, 382–384. For its extension to the Catholics, Protestants and others (Syriac Orthodox, Chaldeans, etc.), see Merten 2013, 52–91, 97–101.

7 Barkey classifies Ottoman patriotism as the 'management of diversity' in the Empire. It was especially espoused by the Young Ottomans (1867–1876) to attract non-Muslim elites who might otherwise be drawn to the West. Barkey 2006, 191. For the Young Ottomans, see Kayalı 1997, 22–24.

8 Krämer mentions that the quota system privileged Christians and Jews over Muslims in the provincial councils in terms of the number of seats. See Krämer 2002, 115–116.

9 Masters has investigated chronicles on Muslim-Christian relations in nineteenth-century Syrian cities following the declaration of equality. In Aleppo, when the imperial decree was

protests against military conscription, which was, by the way, only fully applied to non-Muslims under Young Turk rule (1908–1918).[10] Until then, Christians and Jews mostly paid, in lieu of military service, the *bedel-i askeri*, practically a modified *ǧizya*, according to Davison.[11]

In the context of the *millet* reorganization, communities were also restructured on the intra-confessional level. The formation of so-called 'Mixed Councils' was to grant lay participation in the administration of the Greek Orthodox, Armenian and Jewish *millets*. This created intra-confessional tension between the traditional clerical hierarchies and lay people who wanted to have a say in the decision running of their community.[12] Despite of Ottoman citizenship and the promotion of civic equality, and also as a result of the quota policy, confessional identities in the Middle East were strengthened rather than blurred, which contributed to increasing inter-confessional rivalries in the Arab Levant at the end of the nineteenth century.[13] The rise of sectarianism was further fostered through the 'Capitulations' (*imtiyāzāt*), bi-lateral treaties between the Empire and European powers that allowed the latter to intervene in Ottoman internal affairs. Originally, the *imtiyāzāt* secured privileges for foreign merchants and diplomats in the Empire, exempting them from taxes and the Ottoman legal system and making them accountable only to consular courts. Up to the nineteenth century, the Europeans expanded the treaties far beyond their original

announced before Muslim notables, it made their faces turn 'grey as ashes', wrote the Syrian Muslim historian al-Ustuwānī in his chronicle *Mašāhid al-Aḥdāṯ*. On the other side, the atmosphere was euphoric. Christian elites were celebrating and invited to receptions by the foreign consul, according to the Syriac Christian historian Baḫḫāš. See Masters 2013, 172f.

10 For instance, in Aleppo (1850) rumors about Muslim military registration gave rise to plunder and murder in Christian neighborhoods. This went on for several days until Ottoman and British forces intervened. About 1,000 were killed, and 500 injured. In Damascus too, Muslim resentment escalated from time to time into anti-Christian massacres. After riots between Druze and Christian factions in Lebanon, inter-confessional strife spread to Syria in 1860. Muslims looted Christian quarters in Damascus, causing hundreds, or according to other reports thousands, of deaths. This was a massive shock to the Ottoman government and caused a Christian exodus from the city and international diplomatic entanglements. Masters 2013, 169f., 174–182; and Ma'oz 2002, 108–118.

11 See Davison, *Tanẓīmāt*. In: EI².

12 In this context, Davison refers to "Millet Constitutions", which stipulated the formation of 'Mixed Councils' for the Greek Orthodox (1860–1863), Armenian (1863) and Jewish (1865) *millets*. Davison 1973, 114–134. For the rise of the Chief Rabbi or *Hakhambashi* (Ar.: *ḥāḫāmbāšī*) as representative of the Sephardi Jews to Ottoman bureaucracy and internal conflicts arising from this, see Levy 1992, 105–108, and Levy 1994, 425f. For the reformation of Jewish education, see Levy 1992, 108–115.

13 For the emergence of sectarianism in nineteenth-century Lebanon in the context of modernization and policies of diplomats and missionaries, see Makdisi 2000. For the transition of inter-confessional relations in Ottoman Syria and Palestine after the *Tanzimat*, see Ma'oz 1982, 92–95, and 2002, 108–118. For roots of sectarianism in Syria see Masters 2001, and on sectarian dissonance in the Arab "periphery", Masters 2013, 163f.

frame: diplomats passed on their privileges to Jewish and Christian minorities collectively, acting as the protectors of non-Muslims, or even granted citizenship to individuals.[14] Empire wide, these factors contributed to a growing gap between Muslims and Christians and challenged traditional patterns of interaction and segregation in inter-confessional and state–citizen relations, renegotiated in the light of Ottomanism and a new political culture.

Migration and Nationalism in the Age of 'Global' Modernity

During the *Tanzimat*, the Middle East and late Ottoman Palestine faced the first stages of modern globalization and its transforming effect on local cultures. Globalization dynamics introduced new technologies, increased human mobility, accelerated the circulation of commodities and ideas, provided new access to knowledge, speeded up the dissemination of information and contributed to the establishment of trans-regional networks to an extent never seen before.[15] The Middle East became integrated into global markets and increasingly exposed to European imperialism and hegemony, linked with the idea of cultural 'civilization' and the 'elevation' of colonized societies.[16] In particular, late Ottoman Palestine became subject to foreign investment, transottoman and global migration in unprecedented forms; all the more since it was loaded with religious symbolism as the 'Holy Land' (Ar.: *al-arāḍī al-muqaddasa*) in Jewish, Christian and Muslim tradition and attracted people from all continents[17] and Jerusalem, the Palestinian coastal plain and the Galilee especially saw migration from all over the Levant and the Middle East, North Africa, the Balkans, the Russian Empire and Western Europe. These migrants, who transformed local ethno-confessional compositions, were farmers, Bedouins, soldiers, refugees, pilgrims, tourists, merchants, entrepreneurs, missionaries, diplomats and governmental

14 Campos 2011, 64f. For the development and extension of the *imtiyāzāt* to protect foreign communities and individuals from the fourteenth century until their abuse as capitalist instruments, see Wansbrough, İnalcık, Lambton, and Baer, Imtiyāzāt. In: EI². Also, Boogert 2005.

15 Kozma, Schayegh and Wishnitzer dedicated their volume to the exploration of the history of the 'first modern globalization' in the Middle East, understood as an "unprecedented intensification in the movement of people, commodities and ideas". See Kozma, Schayegh, and Wishnitzer 2015, 1. For concepts of globalization, see Osterhammel and Petterson 2003, 7–15.

16 For imperial policies, the industrial revolution and global capitalism, see Osterhammel and Petterson 2003, 50–70. For imperialism and 'civilizing missions', see Osterhammel 2005, 363–426; cf Buessow 2011, 427–430.

17 The idea of Palestine as a sacred space exists in Judaism, Christianity and Islam. In Muslim tradition, Jerusalem (Ar.: *al-Quds*, meaning 'the Holy' or *Bayt al-Maqdis*, meaning 'Sacred House') is the center of this space. The city was praised in Muslim *faḍā'il* literature, describing the 'virtues of Jerusalem' (*faḍā'il al-Quds*) to pilgrims. See Khalidi 1997, 29–30, and Ben-Bassat 2011, 1–14.

representatives.[18] A high number of foreign religious, educational and political institutions were concentrated in Jerusalem, capital of the District and a place of political and spiritual importance.[19] The vital interests of foreign investors contributed to Jerusalem's quick urbanization, which caused inter-European competition in building activity and 'hunting' for public works projects.[20]

Another center of quick demographic, agricultural and economic expansion in the District was the coastal city of Jaffa.[21] Despite being a minor town, Jaffa was considered the 'gateway of Palestine' because of its port,[22] and became *the* economic hub in Ottoman Palestine.[23] This development was accelerated by the rapid expansion of its citrus industry and rising exports to Europe. Thus, at the beginning of the twentieth century, the society of the late Ottoman Jerusalem District was a very heterogeneous 'kaleidoscope' of different confessions, ethnicities, languages and cultures.[24] However, increasing mobility led to the phe-

18 For nineteenth-century-migration from Egypt, Morocco, Tunisia, Algeria, Circassia, Chechnya and Bosnia to the Palestinian coastal plain, the central mountains and the Sharon valley, see Grossman 2011, 43–77.

19 For Ottoman reforms in the Jerusalem District, and the practical work and political activities of the Jerusalem municipality (Ar.: *baladīya*) to develop the public space, see Buessow 2014, 97–141.

20 For infrastructural developments and economic growth in Jerusalem and Jaffa through initiatives undertaken by the Ottomans in terms of roads, water, sanitation and public places, see Kark 1986, 46–58. Avcı has explored public works schemes to foster urban development in Jerusalem and Jaffa. The plans for an electric tramway system, electric light and drinking water, an extension of the Hijaz railway to Jerusalem via Haifa, a city plan for Jerusalem, infrastructure and customs facilities at Jaffa's port mostly stayed on paper but shed light on the dilemmas of Ottoman urban policy. See Avcı 2011, 81–102. For public projects and the Chamber of Commerce in Palestine and initiatives of the Jerusalemite Sephardi David Yellin in public projects, see Norris 2013, 39–46.

21 Kark has explored urban change in the Palestinian coastal cities of Acre, Haifa, Jaffa and Gaza during the *Tanzimat* under the influence of Ottoman administration and Western engagement. Kark 1990a, 69–90.

22 See Tolkowsky's (1924) account of Jaffa as 'gateway of Palestine'.

23 See Avcı 2011, 89, and the letter of the Ottoman Minister of Finance to the Minister of Interior on p. 95. On the rapidly growing importance of Jaffa's port, its citrus industry and transportation system during the late Ottoman period and the high interest of the Ministry of Public Works in its development, see Norris 2013, 36–38.

24 According to McCarthy, the Ottoman population in the districts of late Ottoman Palestine amounted to 657,000 Muslims, 81,000 Christians and 59,000 Jews in 1914. McCarthy 1990, 10. Schmelz has reported that in 1914, 121,000 Ottoman citizens lived in the Jerusalem District: 70,000 Muslims, 33,000 Christians of many denominations and 18,000 Jews of Sephardi and Ashkenazi origin. A considerable number of foreign Jews lived in Jerusalem. In 1914, Arthur Ruppin, director of the Palestine Office of the International Zionist Organization in Jaffa, estimated the total number of Jerusalemite Jews at 45,000. There were also numerous foreign Christians in Jerusalem, but their number is not known. Schmelz 1990, 25–26.

nomenon of international migration throughout the late Ottoman Empire, not only in Palestine.[25]

In the age of globalization, the Middle East had to contend with the demands of 'modernity', defined as a new 'set of practices, institutions and discourses' that emerged in nineteenth-century Europe, and characterized by movement towards global markets, industrialization, urbanization, representative political structures and new concepts of the 'public', superseding absolutist concepts of political rule. This transformation, referred to as modernization, went along with the production of new discourses about political liberalization and 'social questions'.[26] By the end of the nineteenth century, modernity standards had spread, more or less, around the globe but were received in different regions of the world at different moments and certainly not to the same extent. What, in the European context, was understood as the 'standard set' of modernity was received differently in other regions. Eisenstadt has called this phenomenon 'multiple modernities', while Schmidt has defined it as 'varieties of modernity'.[27] Asking 'whose modernity?', Pappé suggests exploring what modernity meant in different regions from the perspectives of *local* actors and *how* it changed their lives, rather than in comparison with European modernity.[28] At the beginning of the twentieth century, local varieties of modernity emerged in the Arab East that still need to be explored further in future research.[29]

The Palestinian intellectuals who discussed society and politics in *Filasṭīn*, were much engaged with this global *zeitgeist* of modernity. As is clear from *Filasṭīn*, a 'modernization imperative' was adapted by Palestinian elites of each confession. These authors were deeply convinced that only a comprehensive modernization from above *and* below would constitute the basis for a successful future in Palestine. They were inevitably confronted with a Euro-centric 'standard set' of modernity, which was articulated by European authors and much quoted in *Filasṭīn*, and which shaped their vision of 'being modern'.

As part of global modernity, nationalism became popular.[30] At the beginning of the twentieth century, the era of the multi-religious and multi-ethnic empires

25 For Ottoman immigration and settlement policies during the *Tanzimat*, see Başak 2014, 252–271.
26 Buessow 2011, 10–12, and Bayly 2004. For the definition of modernization as 'social change', see Bendix 1969, 510; quoted in Uhl 2001, 10–15.
27 Eisenstadt 2000, Wittrock 2000, and Schmidt 2006.
28 Pappé 2005, 1–13.
29 Freitag has investigated Middle Eastern intellectual thought on modernity during the *Tanzimat* and the terminology applied to describe modernization processes, such as *iṣlāḥ* (reform), *ḥaḍāra*, *madanīya* and *tamaddun* (civilization) and *taqaddum, taraqqin* (progress). See Freitag 2008, 89–117.
30 Smith equates the paradigm of nationalism with classical modernism. See Smith 1998, 1–4.

of Tsarist Russia, Austria-Hungary, and the Ottomans slowly came to an end.[31] Nationalist ideologies set out to design the modern 'nation state' that was to replace heterogeneous empires with smaller territorial units much more homogenous populations.[32] Multiple identity models, both overlapping and conflicting, circulated in the Arab East. In Palestine, supra-confessional Ottomanism existed side by side with local Arab identity, created variations of a 'Palestinian Ottomanism',[33] and faced a first flare-up of Arab proto-nationalism.[34] Since Zionist migrants from Eastern Europe outnumbered migrants from other regions and transformed local ethno-confessional patterns, political Zionism became a major factor in identity conflicts before World War I. In response to these phenomena, the urban and educated segments of Palestinian society sought to establish a 'public discourse' on group relations. 'Discourse' as a specific 'understanding of reality' as defined by Foucault, is expressed through language forms and produced by the selection, organization and channeling of knowledge according to certain rules. Based on power relations, an 'order' is set up concerning *what* and *how* something is to be said or *not* to be said in a debate. This shapes the *content* and *form* of the perception of reality. The term 'discourse', the production of reality through a 'structured and organized communication' that is linked to power, is used in this study to refer to the 'order of what to say or not to say' in a debate.[35]

31 For a comparison between Ottoman and Habsburg decline, see Barkey 2006, 167–197. For the definition of 'Empire' as political frame with reference to Charles Tilly, see idem, 173–175 and Kasaba 2006, 201.

32 For the definition of 'nations' as imagined and constructed communities, see Anderson 1996. Assuming that nationalism is constructed, its emergence as first an ideology and then a movement is a process that Hobsbawm divided into three phases. Phase A implies cultural, literary and folkloric activity without political or national implications. In phase B, activists engage in political propaganda to mobilize groups. Only in phase C does a nationalist program acquire mass support, at least to some extent. See Hobsbawm 1990, 12.

33 See Campos 2003, 16–18.

34 The origins of early Arab nationalism have been widely discussed in scholarly literature. In an early standard work 'Arab Awakening' (1938), Antonius saw the activities of literary societies in Beirut and Damascus during the second half of the nineteenth century as the beginnings of Arab nationalism and cultural resistance to Turkish policies. Zeine (1958) defined the era of the Young Turks (1908–18) as the critical phase in the emergence of Arab nationalism. Dawn (1973, 1991) has explored the ideological foundations of Arabism during the same era in Damascene elite politics. Khalidi (1977, 1984, 1991) has argued that socio-economic changes in Arab cities fostered the rise of a popular nationalism that reached the middle-classes during this era. Kayalı 1997, 11–16.

35 See Foucault 1991; Jäger 2004 and Ullrich 2008.

Public Debates between 'Freedom' and 'Cataclysm' (1908–1914)

In the negotiation of group relations, the Arab press of the Second Constitutional Era (1908–1914) played an important role. On its pages, a spectrum of Palestinian authors entered into passionate debates about coexistence in a transottoman society, the integration of migrants and conditions for political participation, trying to work out standards that were perceived as fitting 'the spirit of this age' (*rūḥ hāḏā l-ʿaṣr*), or 'the new age' (*al-ʿaṣr al-ǧadīd*), a slogan used by Palestinian journalists in *Filasṭīn*, and a synonym for progress and late Ottoman modernity.[36]

'The new age' signified the post-revolutionary era under the regime of the Young Turks; and 'the spirit' was the values of modernity and the Constitution that granted equal rights to Otttoman citizens regardless of their faith.[37] In the aftermath of the Young Turk Revolution (1908), the autocratic rule of Sultan Abdülhamid II (1876–1908) ended, the Ottoman Constitution of 1876 was restored, and three Palestinian delegates were elected to represent the Jerusalem District in Parliament in Istanbul.[38] On the agenda of the Young Turks were modernization, secularization, the abolition of the *millet* system, the fostering of Ottomanism, resistance to the European powers and the abolition of the *imtiyāzāt*.[39] The slogan of the 1908 Revolution, 'liberty, equality, fraternity' (*ḥurrīya, musāwāt, iḫāʾ*), picking up the principles of the French Revolution, was chanted by the urban elites in Jerusalem, Haifa, Jaffa, Nazareth and other cities, who exuberantly celebrated 'the age of freedom' (*ʿaṣr al-ḥurrīya*), adding a sacred dimension to the idea of freedom.[40]

The Young Turk era up to World War I (1908–1914) is very crucial in the exploration of Palestinian press debates. The official lifting in 1908 of censorship that had led to the dissemination of only official reports and the omission of 'bad' news, caused an explosion of private journalism in Palestine, more or less free from censorship, and enabled public debate. The press quickly picked up the political vocabulary of the Young Turk era: Arab newspapers euphorically celebrated the introduction of constitutional rights and a 'new age' that ended des-

36 See, for instance, *Filasṭīn*, 15 July 1911: 51/2/3–3/4. Here, the journalist Būlus Šiḥādeh from Jerusalem called for the modernization of Palestinian education in line with the 'spirit' of the age, the constitutional values.

37 On the typical press discourse on 'liberty, Constitution, brotherhood, equality' (*ḥurrīya, dustūr, iḫāʾ, musāwāt*), compare an article in *Filasṭīn*, 15 July 1911: 51/2/3–3/4.

38 The Young Turks, a group of opposition officers, organized a coup from Salonika, overthrew Abdülhamid and held the first governmental elections in 30 years. The delegates from the Jerusalem District were the Jerusalemite notables Rūḥī al-Ḫālidī and Saʿīd al-Ḥusaynī and the businessman Ḥāfiẓ as-Saʿīd from Jaffa. Fishman 2005, 7.

39 For the course and aftermath of the Young Turk Revolution, see Zurcher 2004, 93f., and Divine 1994, 143–168.

40 Campos defines this process as the 'sacralization' of freedom. Campos 2011, 20–58.

potic rule. The terms 'liberty' and 'equality' became slogans that were used to excess in the post-revolutionary press and, without fear of exaggeration or ambivalence, interpreted quite freely. A similar obsession is to be observed regarding the concept of Ottoman 'unity' which acquired a sacred dimension in the journalistic discourse of the Young Turk era.[41]

It must be stressed that the journalistic output of these years was surprisingly controversial and Palestinian journalists showed considerable self-confidence, presenting themselves as 'educators of the nation' in line with the constitutional spirit, and as creators of a 'new public' that was to act as mature citizens and stand up for their civic rights. A protest culture emerged in Palestine, unthinkable before 1908, generated through the foundation of civic and communal organizations, whose official purpose was to protect Ottomanism and educate their members in the spirit of the Constitution. Practically, these organizations promoted the interests of a certain groups to the state; this in the light of the quickly transforming imperial hierarchy and inter-communal rivalries, as Campos explains.[42] Moreover, the new protest culture was generated through countless 'open letters' and petitions in the press, which presented itself as the 'watchdog' of the government,[43] claiming to be the people's 'mouthpiece' (*lisān*). Contemporary intellectuals stressed the meaning of the press as an advocate of 'the public interest' (*al-maṣlaḥa al-ʿāmma*), 'civilizational interests' (*maṣāliḥ ʿumrānīya*),[44] and 'the public benefit' (*al-manfaʿa al-ʿāmma*) – terms that acquired tremendous popularity in the political discourse, as echoed in the press.[45]

However, the years 1908–1914 were marked by great ambivalence. Although Palestinian authors wort euphorically in the press about the new age, they experienced in the same measure a sense of insecurity. The Young Turks' regime was from the start on the defensive, overshadowed by internal fragility, rebellions

41 For the term 'Ottoman brotherhood' in contemporary intellectual discourse, see Campos 2003, 66–91.

42 As example, Campos discussed the agenda of the Jerusalemite Society of Ottoman Jews. Officially, it defined the patriotic education of Jewish citizens as its main goal. Practically, it acted as a lobby for Jewish interests in Palestine. Campos 2003, 297–307; and idem 2011, 145–148. See also Campos's discussion on bourgeoisie networks after 1908 through the Chamber of Commerce, Industry and Culture, the Anglo Palestine Bank (APB) and the Freemasons' Barkai Lodge in Jaffa. Campos 2003, 168–236. The Chamber of Commerce, Industry and Culture was founded in Jerusalem and Jaffa by local landowners, businessmen and merchants of Muslim, Christian and Jewish backgrounds to foster public works projects in Palestine, and it served as an intermediary between Ottoman ministries, local investors and European vendors. Campos 2003, 172–181.

43 See Campos 2015, 93f.

44 *Filasṭīn*. 17 April 1912: 128/1/1–3. Here, the editors underpinned their loyalty to the CUP and their support for Jaffa's development in the 'public' and 'civilizational interest'.

45 *Filasṭīn*, 6 September 1913: 269/3/4–4/2. Here, a reader passionately called for the development of the Palestinian economy, as the 'basis of civilization', for 'the public good'.

and repression, and Palestinian press debates revealed great fear. Up to this point, political decision-makers, community representatives and intellectuals had not seen an alternative to the Empire and, in the light of upheavals and territorial losses, they feared the breakdown of the existing order – a nightmare in their eyes.[46]

It was not yet time to take an Arab proto-nationalism seriously, and the preservation of the Ottoman framework was the goal of all the authors publishing in *Filasṭīn* until late summer 1914, as I shall show. Among the events that deeply shook the populations in the Arab provinces during the Young Turk era were the losses in Libya (1911) and the Balkans (1912–1913), after which the Empire had lost its last stand in North Africa to Italy and all its European territories to Bulgaria, Serbia, Montenegro and Greece. The loss of the Balkans was a major demographic, economic, cultural and political set-back. Its impact on Arab populations cannot be underestimated, and the Balkan rebellions and battle fronts received extensive coverage in *Filasṭīn*.[47]

The regime was also shaken by counter revolts and internal opposition.[48] In the aftermath of manipulated elections in 1912, the ruling party of the Young Turks, the Committee of Union and Progress (Tur.: *İttihad ve Terakki Cemiyeti*; CUP), was overthrown by the oppositional Liberal Union (Tur.: *Hürriyet ve I᾿tilaf Fırkası*; LU).[49] Internal friction between CUP followers, called 'Ittihadists' (Ar.: *ittiḥādīyūn*) and LU supporters, the 'Itilafists' (Ar.: *i᾿tilāfīyūn*), both meaning unionists, were hot topics in the Palestinian press and caused insecurity among local elites. With growing internal and external pressure, the regime encouraged

46 Recently, 'Ottoman Cataclysm' was introduced as a term at the Research Foundation Switzerland-Turkey, a research cluster exploring the 'Cataclysm', the end of the Ottoman world during the 1910s as a decade of "catastrophic change". See Kieser, Öktem, and Reinkowski 2015, 16. https://nahoststudien.unibas.ch/forschung/projekte/laufende-projekte/ottoman-cataclysm/ (accessed 17.08.2017).

47 First, it was a moral defeat as Salonika had been the heartland of the Young Turks and many leading Young Turks were originally from the Balkans. Second, the Empire forfeited nearly 60,000 square miles and four million people and it had to deal with Muslim refugees from the Balkans who had to be resettled elsewhere. Zurcher 2004, 108–109. After a period of two years of Albanian revolts, Albania withdrew from the First Balkan War as an independent state. For background and the course of the Albanian revolt (1910–1912) against the Young Turks, the Tripolitanian War (1911) and the First and Second Balkan Wars (1912–13), see Shaw 1977, 287–298, and Matuz 1985, 254–261. For internal friction and external pressure in a wider context, see Zurcher 2004, 99–109.

48 Soon after the Young Turks' rise to power, their regime was confronted with the Counter Revolution (1909), driven by conservative powers and supporters of the former regime of Abdülhamid. See Zurcher 2004, 95–99.

49 When the elections in 1912 were won by the CUP, the oppositional LU, supported by a group of officers, declared that they had been manipulated. In July 1912, the CUP cabinet was dissolved and its paper *Tanin* suspended, and the LU came to power. See Reinkowski 1995, 33, and Shaw 1977, 290f.

the Turkish element in state bureaucracy and, from 1913 onwards, increasingly embraced Turkish nationalism. Arab resistance to Ottoman centralization fostered the rise of an Arab Movement for Decentralization.[50]

This movement arose from the 'Arab Renaissance' (*an-nahḍa al-ʿarabīya*), hereafter *nahḍa*, a modernist movement that sought to revive the Arab cultural heritage, modernize Arabic as the language of Islamic literature and scholars (*ʿulamāʾ*), and secularize local education. Thus, it initiated the translation of modern sciences, European literature and political philosophy into Arabic. Importantly, the *nahḍa* was neither centrally organized nor a mass movement but driven by intellectual urban elite networks, both Muslim and non-Muslim, in Beirut, Damascus and Cairo. Its pioneers were mostly Syrian-Lebanese teachers, journalists and publishers who had received their education in foreign missionary schools, such as the Syrian Protestant College, predecessor of the American University of Beirut (AUB) and one of the 'think tanks' of the *nahḍa*.[51]

In contrast to the Arab *nahḍa*, the supporters of Arab decentralization also formulated a political agenda. In 1912, they established in Beirut the Arab Reform Committees and in Cairo the Decentralization Party (*ḥizb al-lā-markazīya*), and demanded administrative autonomy for the Arab provinces under the umbrella of the Empire. Their central demands were the introduction of Arabic as the official language, the replacement of Turkish officials by locals, a certain degree of political autonomy with an independent budget and the stationing of Arab soldiers near their provinces. Driven by a conflict in principle with the state, the Arab elites felt neglected by a central power that derived its legitimacy from the restoration of civic equality between all Ottomans but favored the Turkish element in state bureaucracy.

The decentralists were not very numerous and but ambitious. Their activities in Beirut and the First Arab Congress in Paris in July 1913 stimulated heated debates in *Filasṭīn* about the sense or nonsense of Arab administrative autonomy during the summer of 1913.[52] The Young Turks were already facing a 'national

50 Haddad and Kayalı have called for a distinction to be drawn between Turkification and Ottoman centralization. Haddad views Arab proto-nationalism merely as a consequence of opposition to Turkish nationalism, Young Turk centralization and European control over the Arab provinces. Haddad 1994, 213; Kayalı 1997, 13–14, n. 24. For a short discussion on the development of Pan-Turkism under the influence of internal and external political developments, see Kieser, Öktem, and Reinkowski 2015, 19–22.

51 For contributions to the *nahḍa* by Butrus al-Bustānī, publisher of the journal *al-Ǧinan* in Beirut, see Sheehi 2000, 2004, 2011. For the career of Ḫalīl Sarkis, publisher of *Lisān al-Ḥāl* in Beirut, see Ayalon 2008. For Ḫalīl al-Ḫūrī, publisher of *Ḥadīqat al-Aḫbār* in Beirut, see Zachs 2011. For the thought of Ǧurǧī az-Zaydān, publisher of *al-Hilāl* in Cairo, see Philipp 1971, 1973, 1979, 2010, 2011. For the achievements of Muḥammad Kurd ʿAlī, publisher of *al-Muqtabas* in Damascus, see Hermann 1990, and Seikaly 1981.

52 See *Filasṭīn*, 7 May 1913: 234/2/2–4; 5 July 1913: 251/3/1; 9 July 1913: 252/1/4–2/3; and 19 July 1913: 255/1/5–2/1.

question' in Anatolia and Zionist settlement was about to provoke another one in Palestine; they did not want to assist the emergence of a third national question in the Arab East and responded with fierce repression. Arab decentralists did not become separatists until 1914, but their persecution by the regime pushed the transition of Arab decentralization to become a proto-nationalist movement during World War I.[53]

Unfortunately, research literature has often missed the distinction between cultural Arabism, Arab decentralization as an elite movement with a clear political agenda and Arab nationalism as an ideology or a popular movement.[54] Kayalı has shown that Arab nationalism was not fully articulated under the Young Turks. Following Hobsbawm, in the emergence of nationalism, he equates the cultural activities of 'Arabists' in the nineteenth century with the first phase, and the second phase with the beginnings of political mobilization, when Arabism formulated a political agenda during the Young Turk era, spurred on by a political culture that would 'fit in with broader imperial patterns of political contestation'. Yet, this did not lead to Arab separatism and was without 'mass' support. Kayalı explains:

> Despite their denunciation of the Ottoman government, viewed as Turkish and Turkifying, most Arabists did not disavow the monarchy and lacked a clear conception of the territorial basis of a national Arab unit. Nevertheless, Arabism was closely connected to politics. Even if one does not subscribe to Dawn's instrumentalist representation of Arabism, its relationship to empire-wide political agendas needs to be appraised in addressing it as Arab proto-nationalism.[55]

Thematic, Social and Geographical Scope of the Study

This study investigates how relations between specific confessional and ethnic groups were negotiated and re-constituted on the ground in the Jerusalem District before World War I, considering local, regional and transottoman factors that made an impact in the local context. As I follow the debates mainly through the local newspaper *Filasṭīn*, my results are shaped by its coverage and the spectrum of its authors. In contrast to former research that saw *Filasṭīn* mainly as a private platform for its editors, the newspaper will be considered in this study as a publication with many contributors. *Filasṭīn* was used as a public forum for a 'pool of publishers' who established discourses on group identities and relations

53 The persecution of 'separatists' during World War I produced the first Arab 'martyrs'. The persecution of secret organizations, and the torture and public executions of Arab nationalists in Beirut, Damascus and Jerusalem in 1915 and 1916 by Camal Pasha, the Turkish military governor of Syria, made a deep impression on the collective memory of the Arab populations. On Camal Pasha, see Çiçek 2014, and Kayalı 2014.

54 For this critique, see Haddad 1994, and Reinkowski 1995, 42.

55 Kayalı 1997, 15.

through controversial debating and the appropriation of political concepts important in the Ottoman frame and beyond. They constituted the contemporary Palestinian elites (Ar.: *al-ḫāṣṣa*) ', that were, the notables or the 'efendiyya' (Ar.: *afandīya*) and holders of honorable titles, positions or social status who came from an urban context and were distinct from the majority (Ar.: *al-ʿāmma*) by reason of their education, political influence or property.[56] Since their contributions clearly represent the views of a Palestinian minority deriving from the urban, educated middle and upper classes, who were in the context of *Filasṭīn* journalists, pedagogues, intellectuals, doctors, merchants or scholars, this analysis naturally implies a certain bias. These authors came from different communities, towns and ethnic origins and were necessarily wealthy, but they shared similar educational backgrounds, and certainly a 'set of mental concepts and values' in line with 'modernity'.

This study follows how these authors discussed in the light of their 'set of values' 1. patterns of social cohabitation and exclusion in the urban fabric of Jaffa, 2. the participatory rights of Arab Palestinians in the administration of the Greek Orthodox Patriarchate of Jerusalem, and 3. the socio-economic integration of Zionist migrants from Eastern Europe into the Jerusalem District. As a micro study, it cannot cover the whole social, ethnic and confessional spectrum in pre-World War I Palestine but focuses on the re-constitution of selected group identities and relations that publishers in *Filasṭīn* considered crucial. Although the focus is on the inter- and intra-confessional level, the work touches on the ethno-social component of group relations in so far as the question of 'ethnicity' might be used as a political instrument in debates on distinctions between 'foreign' versus 'local'.

Geographically, the case studies of this work are settled in the Jerusalem District (*liwāʾ al-Quds*); especially the area between Jerusalem and Jaffa.[57] Despite the programmatic name *Filasṭīn* ('Palestine'), the two northern districts of Nablus and Acre, subordinated to the province of Beirut, were mostly excluded

56 In *Filasṭīn*, they were mostly called *aʿyān* (Sg. *ʿayn*) in the sense of dignitaries, a term applied to Muslim, Christian and Jewish eminent individuals. Apart from that, other terms in use were *wuǧahāʾ*, *ḏawāt*, *ašrāf*, *asyād*. Whatever they were called, these individuals constituted political decision-makers (government officials, delegates in communal councils), influential figures in economy (merchants, landowners, investors), intellectuals (journalists, teachers, poets, writers, thinkers), community representatives and oligarchs (muftis, imams, abbots, priests, rabbis), or tribal and village leaders (*muḫtārs*). They usually had established networks or access to political power or played a role as mediators (*wusaṭāʾ*) between the authorities and the populations they sought to represent. For the politics of notables, see Hourani 1968, for his definition of the term 'notable', 46–49; and Buessow 2011, 310–315.

57 See the maps of the coastal plains of Jaffa and its environs in Buessow 2011, 217, 228.

from the newspaper's coverage.[58] Instead, *Filasṭīn* focused on the Jerusalem District, cementing the already existent north–south division of late Ottoman Palestine. The Jerusalem District included the subdistricts (*qaḍāʾ*) of Jaffa, Gaza, Hebron and Beersheba in the Negev, but *Filasṭīn* was strongly oriented towards the capital through a regular correspondent and ties to Jerusalem notables.[59] Its second focus was the *qaḍāʾ* of Jaffa since the newspaper was based in that town and Jaffa was economically important for the District, as locals were very well aware. In 1913, Jaffa's municipality sent a telegram to the Grand Vizier in Istanbul, demanding that he 'make Jerusalem a province (*wilāya*) of its own and Jaffa an independent district (*mutaṣarrifīya*)'.[60] Finally, the editors had close ties with the *qāʾimaqām*, the Ottoman sub-governor in Jaffa, and initiated campaigns in the field of local politics several times.

2. Historiographical Context

This study is located in relational historiography and aims to contribute to existing studies on Palestinian group identities and social relations. Previously, studies rooted in the 'dual society paradigm' have explored confessional or ethnic groups in late Ottoman and Mandate Palestine as distinct societies and coherent 'national communities' without internal contradictions and have, for instance, presented 'Arabs versus Jews' as two completely separate cultural systems that were only linked by the national conflict that consolidated during the Mandate.[61]

---

58 In 1864, the administration of Ottoman territories was reorganized into the following categories: province (*wilāya*), county-district (*sanǧak*, synonymous with *liwāʾ*), subdistrict (*qaḍāʾ*), rural community (*nāḥiya*) and village (*qarya*). The *wilāya* of Beirut consisted of three *sanǧaks*; the *sanǧak* of Beirut (containing the *qaḍāʾs* of Beirut, Sidon, Tyre and Marj-Ayoun), the *sanǧak* of Acre (Acre, Haifa, Safed, Nazareth and Tiberias) and the *sanǧak* of Nablus (Nablus, Jenin and Tulkarem). On Palestine as a unit, see Schölch 1986, 17–24. On its bounderies and provincial reforms, see Biger 2004, 13f., and Zurcher 2004, 61.

59 In 1872, the *sanǧak* of Jerusalem was separated from the province of Beirut and became a district in its own (*liwāʾ*, *mutaṣarrifīya*), directly subordinate to Istanbul. In the north, it included Jaffa and stretched south to the Negev. Divided into the subdistricts of Jaffa, Gaza, Hebron and, since 1909, Beersheba, the Jerusalem District was now ruled by a governor (*mutaṣarrif*). Each *qaḍāʾ* was administrated by a district council (*maǧlis al-idāra*), headed by a sub-governor (*qāʾimaqām*; Tur.: *kaymakam*) who was subordinate to the governor. For the rise of Jerusalem as an independent District, see Buessow 2011, 41–58. For its restructuring during the *Tanzimat*, 60–100. For its political system under Abdülhamid II., 9.

60 See *Filasṭīn*, 11 June 1913: 244/3/4.

61 'Conflict' is the focal point in Gelvin's historiography, as is clear from his title (Gelvin 2005). In Kayyali's history of modern Palestine, the first chapter is entitled 'Setting for a Conflict: 1881–1908' and begins with Zionist migration. See Kayyali 1978, 11–21. Krämer confirms that it was typical for studies on modern Palestine to take Zionist migration as starting point, although this date had no political or economic relevance. See Krämer 2002, 122.

In fact, the 'dual society model' constitutes an excellent starting point for studying Palestinian heritage, the emergence of Palestinian nationalism and the constitution of the 'New Yishuv', the Jewish community in Palestine, a term that is associated with a modern national project.[62] However, this model leaves little space for differentiation and factors of unity and diversity that exist in societies. Thus, scholarship has increasingly embraced 'relational history', exploring reciprocal effects in inter- and intra-communal relations;[63] a concept that is crucial for my methodological approaches and treatment of *Filasṭīn*.

2.1. 'Dual Society' and Inter-Confessional Relations

Earlier studies with a 'Holy Land outlook' on the East, have shed light on Palestinian heritage and society in the modern era as described in travel accounts and guidebooks.[64] Alex Carmel has documented the life circumstances of the Templars, German-Protestant colonists in Palestine, and contributes valuable insights into general conditions and the infrastructural and political changes in the Jerusalem District before World War I.[65] Area photographs, taken in 1917–1918 by the German flying squadron and edited by Dalman, give an indication of Palestinian geography, especially the Jaffa region before World War I, as do the maps of the Templar architect Theodor Sandel.[66] Ethnographical works documenting the daily life, religious customs and tribal law of the Arab populations are valuable sources on popular culture in late Ottoman Palestine.[67] At the same time, they treat Palestine as the 'Holy Land', stress its Biblical character and address a European audience that was just discovering the 'East'.[68] These trav-

62 Literally, the Hebrew *yišuv* means 'population', deriving from the verb *yiššev*, 'to settle' or 'to colonize' I use 'Yishuv' in the following as a fixed term.

63 See Anderson 1986.

64 See Baedeker's *Handbook for Syria and Palestine*, the historical description of Jaffa by Tolkowksy (1924) and Salten's account *Neue Menschen auf alter Erde* (1986).

65 For difficulties faced by German settlers in Palestine, their relations with the Ottoman authorities and the Arab and Jewish populations, see Carmel 1973, 224–294. For articles in *Die Warte*, the magazine of the Templar community between 1853 and 1882, see Carmel 1978; and between 1882 and 1914, see Carmel 1983.

66 Dalman 1925, 3–5, 76–77.

67 See the work of the Palestinian politician ʿĀrif al-ʿĀrif (1892–1973) on the tribes of Beersheba (1934, 1974) and the ethnographies of the Palestinian medical doctor Tawfik Canaan (1892–1964) on Muslim sanctuaries (1927), magic practices and beliefs (1914, 1929), and family life (1960). Gustaf Dalman (1855–1941), a German theologian and scholar of Oriental studies who was very interested in all aspects of Palestinian socio-cultural life, accurately documented in seven volumes every day Palestinian customs, working practices and livelihood. See Dalman 1928–1941.

68 Philip Baldensperger concisely studied Palestinian clothing, religious practices, songs, proverbs, etc. He tended to link his observations to Biblical myths and saw the population as

elers, geographers and ethnographers framed local society within an 'East–West paradigm'.[69] Whether themselves of Western or Palestinian origin, they used a European 'standard set of modernity' as the benchmark. Applying it to the local populations, they contrasted an industrialized and 'enlightened' West with a traditional and 'backward', if not 'unchanging', Arab East.[70] These stereotypes of a West–East dichotomous worldview seem to have been accepted among Arab elites and were very much present in *Filasṭīn*, which will play a role in my analysis.

As for society building in late Ottoman and Mandate Palestine, Israeli and Palestinian national historiography was the starting point for the exploration of group relations. A corpus of studies has explored Zionist migration and settlement, and the formation of the New Yishuv, Jewish-national identity and state-building.[71] On the Palestinian side, studies with a strong local focus since the Mandate period have brought together biographies of notables and studied the urban history (Jerusalem, Haifa, Nablus, Gaza, Jaffa, etc.) of late Ottoman Palestine, such as Mannāʿ's work on Palestinian notables or Ṭarāwina's study on Jaffa. These are encyclopedic collections of data and valuable compilations of Arab sources that have never been systematically explored before.[72]

In the context of post-colonial studies, a branch of Palestinian national historiography emerged to counter Zionist narratives. In this context, Edward Said coined the term 'Orientalism' and criticized the image of the 'Orient' as a construction of Western scholarship that was deeply influenced by the colonial

'immoveable'. See Baldensperger 1913. The Palestinian author Kaleel described family life in Ramallah at the beginning of the twentieth century, drawing on his childhood memories. Clearly, he was accustomed to a European lifestyle and eager to present local customs in a likeable, if not romanticized, way to the Western reader. See Kaleel 1920.

69 Krämer called this the 'Orientalist outlook' on Palestinians through European 'spectacles', portraying them as backward and at the same time giving them a romantic air. Krämer 2002, 106–108. Doumani went further in his critique of the 'European Biblical discovery of Palestine'. He called it 'discovering the land without discovering the people', who were portrayed as 'living décor' and whose function was to confirm the Biblical character of the land. See Doumani 1992, 7–9.

70 Canaan addressed his book *Aberglaube und Volksmedizin im Lande der Bibel* to the 'friends of the Holy Land in the world' who were to contribute to the 'cultural rise' of Palestine through 'true science'. It treats popular Palestinian thought about the causes of diseases and traditional practices of healing, which he considered 'irrational', compared with the 'clarity' of modern science. See Canaan 1914, VII–IX.

71 On Jewish settlement patterns, see Ben-Artzi 1990, 1997. On the ideological approach of Arthur Ruppin (1876–1943), a leading figure in the coordination of the Zionist Yishuv, see Bloom 2011. For the Jewish citrus industry, see Karlinsky 2005. For the ideology and practices of the Jewish National Fund, see Katz 1994, 2005; Shapira 1992 and Shilony 1998.

72 Doumani, however, criticized the author's 'fetish' with documentation while they ignored contextualizing the information. Doumani 1992, 17. See for instance the works of ʿĀrif al-ʿĀrif on the history of Gaza (1943); the monumental historiography on Palestine in 11 volumes by Dabbāġ 1965–1976, the history of Nablus in four volumes by Nimr 1937–1975, and biographies of Palestinian notables in the Ottoman age by Mannāʿ 1995.

perception of the superiority of the 'self' and the inferiority of the Oriental 'other'.[73] This branch of historiography also sought to document the existence of the Palestinians and conserve their Arab heritage, which had been lost with the hegemony of the Israeli state.[74] These works focused on the emergence of a Palestinian nationalism as a counter to Zionist historiography and looked at society-building in Palestine mostly from the perspective of national conflict.[75] Inspired by an anti-colonialist outlook, several of these studies investigate early Arab opposition to Zionism, linking anti-Zionism with the emergence of Palestinian nationalism as its driving force.[76]

2.2. Plural Societies in Ottoman Modernity

Since the 1990s, a generation of 'New Historians' has re-evaluated the formation of the Yishuv, the wars of 1948 and 1967 and 'national myths' commonly accepted in Israeli society, providing new knowledge about the impact of the Yishuv on Arab populations and processes of state-building beyond earlier narrations.[77] Increasingly departing from the 'dual society paradigm', scholarship has shifted towards 'relational history', which explores patterns of reciprocal interactions between and within groups that reveal mutual interdependencies and internal contradictions. This makes sense in so far as the definition of the 'self' can only be given meaning through the demarcation from the 'other', and collective identity always needs another collective as a mirror.

73 Yet Said (1978) retains the East–West dualism, moving within the same categories that he criticizes.

74 These authors often present a nostalgic view of Ottoman and Mandate Palestine and portray the peasant as prototype of the 'authentic' Palestinian. This can be seen in the collection of illustrations in W. Khalidi (1984) and Sanbar (1994). See also R. Khalidi's documentation of (disappeared) Palestinian villages before 1948; a very valuable source for identifying places referred to in *Filasṭīn*. See Khalidi, Rashid 1992.

75 See Muslih 1988 and Porath (1974, 1977) for the emergence of the Palestinian-Arab national movement after World War I and under the British Mandate.

76 This dualist outlook of (Palestinian) victims and (Zionist) perpetrators molds Khalidi's work on early anti-Zionism and Palestinian identity (1980, 1982, 1997, 2001, 2009). See also Ḥağğū on the 'danger of Zionism' echoed in the Arab press (2007, 146–230) and Naǧǧār (2005) on Palestinian nationalism and the anti-Zionism in the Palestinian press as a shaper of nationalism.

77 This was possible through newly available access to Israeli military archives. See Morris 2007, 11–28; Pappé 2007; Segev 2007; Shlaim 1988; Sternhell 1998; and Zerubavel 1995. The 'New Historians' provoked polemic debates in Israeli scholarship which I shall not delve into. It is enough to mention here that the 'New Historians' were accused of 'fabricating' Israeli national history. See, for instance, the work of Karsh 2002.

Shifting from the history of political leadership to micro perspectives, Schölch and others went on to consider other levels of Palestinian social history.[78] Doumani has called for the writing of an 'alternative' history. Lockman and Bernstein have criticized the dual society paradigm as it reproduces discourses of separation between Arabs and Jews without looking at internal differences, and have explored shifting relations between Arab and Jewish workers. Stein and Swedenburg bring the perspectives of local actors and forgotten social groups into the play by exploring popular culture. Cohen explores Arab collaboration with Zionists, questioning national narratives that present a monolithic Palestinian nationalism.[79]

Scholars have also stressed the need for a better contextualization of Ottoman history and its effects on Palestinian society, which have been neglected by Western, Zionist and Arab studies.[80] For a long time, the Ottoman contribution to Palestinian modernity has been disregarded due partly to difficulties in accessing historical sources but also to a lack of scholarly interest.[81] In fact, Ottoman archives continue to provide striking perspectives on the history of modern Palestine and are still waiting to be explored.[82]

78 This approach was applied by Schölch (1986) in his history of Palestine during a time of change (1853–1882).

79 Doumani 1992, 22f.; Lockman 1996, and 1999, 93, 99–105; Bernstein 2000; Stein and Swedenburg 2004, 10. In an earlier work, Swedenburg (1995) investigated popular narratives about the Great Revolt *(aṯ-ṯawra al-kubrā)* of 1936–1939 and Palestinian farmers' views of it by tracing oral history. See also Cohen 2008. Concerning internal contradictions of nationalism in Mandate Palestine, Matthews (2006) has explored the changing discourse of the Independence Party (*ḥizb al-istiqlāl*) in the 1930s and its shifts between Islamic and Pan-Arab identities.

80 The fact that earlier historiography gave little attention to the effect of Ottoman policies and reforms has been criticized. Doumani (1992) has stressed the need to write Palestine's Ottoman past "into history". See also Pappé (1999, 1–7) and Abu-Manneh (1992) on the rise of the Jerusalem District; and Tamari (2011a) on a diary, written by a Palestinian soldier during World War I as a testimony to Jerusalem's "erased" Ottoman past.

81 Kark, who has studied the coastal towns of Acre, Jaffa, Haifa and Gaza under the paradigm of 'rise and decline', links their 'decline' with the era of Muslim and Mamluk rule, and sees its 'rise' as indirect outcome of the Industrial Revolution in Europe, while she is convinced of the "Ottomans' negative attitude" towards developing Palestinian cities. See Kark 1990a, 69–90.

82 In a lecture about Ottoman cartography on Palestine during the *Tanzimat* at Tübingen University (19.07.2017), Israeli scholar Yossi Ben-Artzi confirmed that historians teaching at Israeli institutions are still reproducing the paradigm of Ottoman inefficiency, insisting that their government had no interest in developing Palestine. However, Ben-Artzi has documented, by using a large number of Ottoman maps of Palestine, the vital interest of the government in 'mapping the area' so as to establish taxation categories and push infrastructural development.

Recent studies have explored variations of 'late Ottoman modernity' in a Palestinian society with 'multiple identities'.[83] The questions of how local elites in the very heterogeneous society of late Ottoman Palestine negotiated, altered, appropriated or modified and *localized* transottoman concepts on 'state order', 'political rule' and 'unity versus diversity', what were their visions on the 'integration versus exclusion' of migrants, strangers or local stigmatized groups, what models of 'citizenship', 'equality' and 'participation' they put forward, and how all of this affected local inter-confessional balances, are crucial for the present study. In this respect, inspiring publications have come from Der Matossian, who has looked at the impact of the Young Turk Revolution on the administration of the Jewish, Armenian and Greek Orthodox communities in Jerusalem and in the context of new public spheres.[84]

On the level of inter-communal relations, Ben-Bassat has investigated in his pioneering works early Arab-Zionist encounters through petitions to Istanbul, and how a Palestinian protest culture was translated into the Ottoman context and against the background of Ottoman policies.[85] Fishman has explored the development of Jewish and Palestinian national movements during the Second Constitutional Period (1908–1914), drawing, albeit selectively, on an impressive amount of Arabic, Hebrew and Ottoman sources.[86] Beška has explored very thoroughly early oppositional responses to Zionism among prominent Muslim and Christian Arab Palestinians, including politicians, intellectuals and the editors of *Filasṭīn* before World War I.[87] Gribetz's inspiring analysis traces intellectual debates and reciprocal influences on concepts of the Jewish/Arab 'self' and 'other'.[88] Klein has traced Arab–Jewish commonalities in the daily lives of

83 Studies on Ottoman Palestine under Young Turk rule have been published by Ben-Bassat and Ginio (2011).

84 Der Matossian 2009, 2011, 2012.

85 Ben-Bassat 2009, 2013a, 2013b, 2013c, 2013d, 2015.

86 Fishman claims that he challenges 'a pillar of Middle East studies', which is the paradigm that declared the 'emergence of a Palestinian identity and nationalism a post-World War I phenomenon'. At the heart of the work is his thesis that Palestinian nationalism emerged during the pre-World War I Young Turk era. His methods are to be criticized, however, since he does not distinguish the level of actors, uses quotations out of context and omits to conceptualize nationalist terminology. For instance, he quotes an Ottoman official, interpreting his claim as commonly accepted among 'the Palestinians' as a collective. See Fishman 2007, vi–viii, 39f.

87 Beška 2007, 2010, 2011, 2012, 2014, 2015, 2016a, 2016b, 2016c.

88 Gribetz has analyzed the Muslim-intellectual perspective on Zionism in an unpublished manuscript of the Jerusalemite notable Rūḥī al-Ḫālidī (1864–1913) and his historical contextualization of the 'Israelites', the contemporary jargon for 'Jews' in the late Ottoman context. Through the Arabic newspapers *al-Hilāl*, published in Cairo by the Christian intellectual Ǧurǧī Zaydān (1861–1914), *al-Muqtaṭaf* (Cairo) and *al-Manār*, published in Beirut by the Muslim reformer Rašīd Riḍā' (1865–1935), Gribetz analyzes Arabic discourses on 'being Jewish'; and through the Hebrew press, Jewish-Zionist discourses on 'being Arab'. Gribetz 2014.

Arab Muslims and Jews in Jerusalem, Hebron and Jaffa as 'mixed cities' during late Ottoman and Mandate times through the memories of Jewish authors, who, under the impression of the consolidated Jewish–Arab conflict, sometimes, in retrospect, projected nostalgic images on the Ottoman past.[89] Among these authors were Sephardi Jews or 'Sephardim', a term that describes Oriental Jews of various origins, and Ashkenazi Jews, Jews of European origin.[90]

On the Jewish intra-communal level, the works of Campos and Jacobson are the most enlightening. Campos explores the harmonization of Zionist and Ottoman identity concepts among Jewish Palestinian elites and their vision of 'Ottoman Brotherhood' as negotiated in the Hebrew press. Jacobson explores Ashkenazi–Sephardi relations in Palestine, and 'alternative' Jewish voices that sought to harmonize Zionism with a local Palestinian Arab imperial identity during the last years of the Ottoman Empire and in World War I Jerusalem.[91]

Relevant works investigating imperial-local interrelations in the context of transottoman modernity in Palestine have been published by Buessow, who analyzes how Ottoman political structures were translated into the Jerusalem District during the era of Sultan Abdülhamid II (1872–1909) and how this affected local society.[92] Tamari has investigated how a transottoman modernity was translated into the urban context of Jerusalem against the background of newly emerging public spaces during a period of transition from imperial to Mandate rule, and how this affected Jerusalemite inter-confessional relations.[93]

With regard to the translation of late Ottoman modernity in Palestine and the Arab East and changing notions of modernity in transition from imperial to mandate rule, future research is needed. This micro-study seeks to contribute to it by looking at Palestinian concepts of society-building during the last moments of Ottoman modernity and before the breakdown of the imperial order. In *Land of Progress* Norris has investigated infrastructural development in Palestine in the 'colonial age' (1905–1948) with a focus on Haifa. Dolbee has studied the links between modern physical culture and national education in Mandatory Syria, for instance, through national development programs for 'village recovery' that aimed to include the rural areas, and the scout movement as explored through

89 For instance, see the memoirs of Yonathan Cohen, Eliahu Eliyashar, Ya'akov Yehoshua, Yehoshua Yellin, Yosef Mehuya, Gad Fromkin, Mordechai Elkayam, S. Yizhar and others. Klein 2014, 19–109.

90 The term 'Sephardi' derives from the Hebrew word of Spain, 'Sefarad', and actually addresses the Jews who were evicted from Spain in the course of the Reconquista (ending with 1492), settled in North Africa or the Arab Levante and spoke Judeo-Spanish (Ladino) or Arabic as their mother tongue. See Campos 2003, 283f.

91 Campos 2003, 2005, 2011, 2015, 2016; Jacobson 2001, 2003, 2004, 2008, 2009, 2011a, 2011b.

92 Buessow 2010, 2011, 2012, 2014.

93 This through the memoir of the Jerusalemite 'storyteller' Wasif Jawhariyyeh, who described a shared communal life in the Old City. See Tamari 2009, 2011b, 2014.

the newspaper *al-Qabas*.[94] An important contribution on Middle Eastern modernities came from Watenpaugh, who explored conceptions of Arab modernities in Aleppo during the French Mandate period.[95]

2.3. Dialectics of Space, Communication and Society-Building

Considering relationalities of discourse and group relations, the dialectics of physical, mental and social spaces must be discussed. Social and cultural space is produced through forms of interaction and communication, as argued by Lefebvre. Here, urban space is of special importance as a zone of very concentrated interaction between people.[96] When urban space becomes 'occupied' through religious or cultural markers (mosques, churches, etc.), it constitutes a symbolic space for certain groups.[97] Thus, ethno-confessional coexistence in cities automatically includes dynamics of group integration *and* segregation, while both are natural in processes of urban socialization.[98] In the Israeli–Palestinian context, Monterescu, Rabinowitz, LeVine and Yacobi stress the relationality of space and society. Monterescu and Rabinowitz have studied Jewish-Arab 'mixed towns' as spaces with a mutual matrix in which people share 'elements of identity, symbolic traits and cultural markers'. LeVine explores the Jaffa-Tel Aviv region during the Mandate and after as a space for the production of collective memory and historical narratives.[99]

94 Norris 2013; Dolbee 2010, 2012.

95 Watenpaugh 2006.

96 Lefebvre defines social space as a 'set of relations between objects and products' and deals with *how* it is produced. Lefebvre 1991, 82–83. Löw explains that social space only emerges through links 'between social goods and people'. Löw 2001, 158f. For functions of urban space, see Gunn 2011, 9–11; Tonkiss 2005, 1, 59f.; Elden 2007.

97 Mißfelder argues that religious conflicts in cities are linked with and constituted through culturally marked spaces. He discusses as an example the conflict over a mosque in Cologne in 2007. Here, in a space of religious coexistence, conflict emerged at a moment when local Muslims started to demonstrate their presence in public space by building a representative mosque. Opponents rejected this as an occupation of territory by 'Islamic architecture as a symbol of power'. Mißfelder 2010, 10, 11. For forms and limits of coexistence and political culture with regard to Islamic symbols in German cities, see Mißfelder 2010, 7–20; and Hüttermann 2006a, 285–300. Regarding the Islamic presence in German cities during the 1990s, see Hütterman 2006b, 155–192.

98 Segregation as a method of 'complexity management' in urban spaces is negatively connotated while 'cultural assimilation' and the 'melting together' of differences is taken as the 'ideal' in society. For models of assimilation versus integration, see Oswald 2007, 93–104; and Mißfelder 2010, 12. For spatial segregation versus integration in urban sociology, see Häussermann and Siebel 2004, 139–195. In terms of conflict management in spatial coexistence, see a study on peace and conflict between Christians and Muslims in peripheral regions of Southeast Europe, based on narrative interviews. See Kahl 2009.

99 See Monterescu/Rabinowitz 2007: 3; Rabinowitz/Monterescu 2008: 198. LeVine 2005.

Yacobi unfolds processes of 'urban ethnocracy' in the Israeli-Palestinian town of Lod as a model for policies on the segregation of ethno-confessional spaces.[100] Jacobson has investigated the 'negotiation' of public space in World-War-I Jerusalem in three forms of urban space, suggested by Tonkiss: the park as a collective space accessible to all, the coffee house as a place of interaction and entertainment, and the street as the 'basic unit' of public life that enables interaction between all social segments that do not normally mix.[101] Tamari has discussed the 'confessionalization of public space' in Jerusalem through the division of Old and New City under British Mandate rule in terms of administration and architecture.[102]

The 'relationality of space' is relevant for my exploration of *Filasṭīn* from the point of view of the links between 1. media communication and the public, 2. media communication and identity production, and 3. media communication and discourse production through controversial press debates.

Concerning the first aspect, the category of space is relevant for my study in so far as it can be identified as a physical or mental platform of interaction between people that produces new forms of sociability. In cities, this process is more concentrated than in the countryside. Parks, streets, squares, government buildings, churches, mosques, coffeehouses, railway stations, schools, clubs and debating circles are physical platforms for interaction. The editorial office of *Filasṭīn* was such a physical space for human interaction. Situated in the busy commercial center of Jaffa, discussions and meetings between people, and of course, the writing process of *Filasṭīn*, took place there The spatial concept can also be applied to *Filasṭīn* as a medium for communication and a mental space for intellectual interaction between a pool of publishers and the readers. In this

100 Yacobi 2003. Yacobi also argues in a contribution on Israeli state policies in the Jerusalem neighborhood of Silwan, that 'urban ethnocracy' shifted towards a 'policy of apartheid'. See also Yiftachel and Yacobi 2016.

101 Jacobson applies this typology to Jaffa Gate, Jaffa Street and the Jerusalem city garden. Drawing on the diaries of Ḫalīl as-Sakākīnī and Iḥsān Turǧmān, she discusses 'how public space was contested and negotiated'. These sources are undoubtedly interesting evidence on World-War I Jerusalem, but I do not see how spatial theory has affected Jacobson's analysis of these sources. See Jacobson 2011b, 53–55, 60–79.

102 Under British town planning, Tamari has argued, the Old City as a religious-symbolic space was developed into an 'open air (Bible) museum' for pilgrims. The New City was expanded as its secular counterpart, designed to serve the needs of European modernity. In particular, the triangle between Jaffa Gate, Jaffa Street and King George Street was developed as a center for entertainment, business and communication through the construction of banks, hotels, post offices, bars, the railway, etc. Tamari 2009, 2011. Drawing on the memoirs of the Greek Orthodox Waṣīf al-Ǧawharīya about his 'vagabond years' in post-war Jerusalem, Tamari describes how the bourgeoisie of all confessional and ethnic backgrounds overcame the borders set by urban planning, and how they and shared the hedonistic culture of a scandalous night life in Jerusalem. See Tamari 2000, 2011b.

respect, *Filasṭīn*'s public function is crucial to this study in so far as the resonance of media debates in the public sphere becomes visible. Here, the relationalities between print media and the public have been demonstrated by Eisenstein, Herzog and Roper, who have explored the press as an 'agent of change'.[103]

Concerning the relationality of media communication and identity production, concepts applied by Stefan Rohdewald have been very inspiring. Treating Lithuania and Ruthenia as 'trans-cultural communication space', Rohdewald explores contacts between Armenians, German Lutherans, Ashkenazi Jews, Christian Lithuanians and Tartar Muslims.[104] Assuming that such a space has transparent borders rather than being sealed, it is open for interaction from outside.[105] Kießling has shown that space is always constituted through communication; that is social interaction. Kießling and Rohdewald deal with a concept of 'communication space' as a space in which communication is more condensed inside than outside.[106] The central aspect is that, in communication, constant negotiations about rapprochement and separation are already implied, and thus, media communication as a process of intellectual interaction helps to produce cultural identities and practices.[107]

Finally, regarding the links between media communication and discourse production, the controversial aspects and dialogical structures of press publications are to be explored. In an innovative approach, Glaß, in her pioneering work on the Egyptian literary magazine *al-Muqtaṭaf*, Glaß makes the 'dispute' (*munāẓara*) a key term of media communication. Glaß has criticized the fact that most studies treat the press merely as a pool of information in the sense of a monological channel transferring information in one direction, while she deals with the press as a dialogical 'medium' in the literal sense of the word. With reference to Luhmann's dialogical communication model, which includes the response of an addressee, Glaß stresses the interactive relation between the newspaper and the public by which it is consumed.[108] Glaß investigates the interaction between the editors and readers of *al-Muqtaṭaf* as a forum for dispute,

103 Eisenstein (1980) applies the concept to the European press, Herzog (1995) and Roper (2007) to print media in the Arab and Islamic world.

104 Rohdewald, Frick, and Wiederkehr 2007, 7–33. See also on Poland–Lithuania, Rohdewald 2005.

105 Compare concepts of cultural spaces in Osterhammel 2004, 50–65.

106 See Kießling 2001, 11–39, esp. 21–22; and Rohdewald, Frick, and Wiederkehr 2007, 15.

107 Hörning 2004, 139f.

108 Communication is not restricted to sending and receiving information but is a process of three elements: 1. transmitting information, 2. receiving information, 3. understanding and interpreting information. Communication is only fulfilled through 'understanding and interpretation' as the precondition for a response by the recipient of information. It is important to note that misunderstandings are included as normal in the process of understanding and interpreting. See Luhmann 1984, 193–200; and Glaß 2004, I, 53, 62f.

defining it as a 'debating club'. Here, she looks at the rules for participating in this dispute, which establish a controversial discourse on a subject and define the taboos: 'the order of what to say or not to say'.[109] Through disputing, the participants defend opinions and this consolidates a discourse on the topic discussed.[110]

Analyzing *how* authors disputed, by using the readers' letter (*ar-risāla*) as an instrument, Glaß was the first to show how the private press in the Arab *nahḍa* pushed debates to generate a public. However, Glaß focuses strictly on discourse formation, documenting the communication between readers in chronological order in dispute records ('Disputprotokolle') without considering the context of the debates. Here, her approach has been very inspiring in so far as *Filasṭīn*'s coverage is considered as a medium for communication with controversial and dialogical elements. This study, however, will abstain from producing chronological dispute records but will consider the press debates in their broader historical and social context.

3. Exploring *Filasṭīn* as a Medium

3.1. Research on the Palestinian Arabic Press and *Filasṭīn*

In the field of chronological compilations on Arabic print media in the Syro-Lebanese and Egyptian context, Ṭarrāzī's four extensive volumes are a standard reference as well as the works of ʿAqqād, Ḫūrī, Sulaymān und Yehoshu'a on the Palestinian Arabic press.[111] The concise history of the Arab press in the Middle East by Ayalon was the first to take an analytical approach, and treats very

109 For the definition of 'controversial discourse', according to which disputing participants claim conflicting versions of truth and reality, see Habermas 1981, I, 38; quoted in Glaß 2004, I, 14.

110 Glaß refers to dispute as a method practiced by scholars in the Islamic Middle Ages. Thus, dispute was not an invention of modernity. However, the activists and journalists of the Arab *nahḍa* tried to reach a new dimension by directing the dispute more to the outside so as to receive reactions. Glaß 2004, I, 15.

111 See Ṭarrāzī 1913–1914 and al-ʿAqqād 1967. Ḫūrī (1976) provides a chronology of Arabic, foreign and Palestinian magazines and newspapers, published in Palestine from the Abdülhamidian era until the British Mandate. Sulaymān (1987) highlights the role of the press in the *nahḍa*, providing a chronology of literary, academic and political magazines in Palestine. Yehoshu'a (1973, 1974, 1981) provides a chronology of press publications and gives background information about their editors and their lives. Šūmalī has compiled indices of literary contributions published in *Filasṭīn* between 1911and 1967 (1992) and the newspaper *al-Karmil* (1996).

practical aspects of the publication process, state censorship, the generation of readership and Arabic reading culture, especially with reference to Palestine.[112]

Since the Arabic press of the late Ottoman period is hardly accessible and *Filasṭīn* is one of the rare examples systematically collected, it has been the subject of several surveys, although often in a one-dimensional manner.[113] Since many studies on late Ottoman Palestine have been preoccupied with the 'national conflict paradigm', most of them frame *Filasṭīn* to this same paradigm, mainly evaluating it as anti-Zionist, Arab Palestinian nationalist and anti-Ottoman.

First, *Filasṭīn* was classified as *the* pioneer of anti-Zionism in the Arab press in the works of Mandel and Khalidi, who, however, did not conduct a systematic survey of its coverage.[114] Second, *Filasṭīn* has been presented as the pioneer of early Palestinian nationalism under Young Turk rule by Khalidi and Fishman;[115] and as a mouthpiece for the nationalistic views of Palestinian intellectuals by Shomali.[116] As Beška has shown, Bracy's discussion of *Filasṭīn* as a forerunner of Palestinian nationalism is in large parts 'borrowed' from other authors and is not reliable in terms of scientific standards.[117] Fishman quotes from *Filasṭīn* to prove his thesis about the existence of an early Palestinian nationalism before World War I, but his interpretation lacks proper contextualization and does not differentiate between actors' levels.[118] Third, *Filasṭīn* is classified by Tamari and Robson as anti-Ottoman; a simplification based on an autobiography of its director, ʿĪsā al-ʿĪsā (1878–1950), that he produced in retrospect and under the impact of Zionism during the Mandate era.[119] ʿĪsā's unpublished manuscript

112 See Ayalon 1995, 1998, 2002, 2004, 2010. For the historical development of Hebrew and Arabic print media in Palestine, Suleiman (2009) provides a good overview.

113 A lot of Arabic sources were destroyed in the War of 1948, and Arabic newspapers from this time are rarely available and mostly belong to private collections that are hard to access. Ayalon 2004, 15; and Mandel 1976, xix.

114 See Khalidi 1982, 1997, 2006, 2009; and Mandel 1976.

115 Khalidi 2009; Fishman 2007.

116 Shomali 1995, 229.

117 See Beška on 'too much borrowing' in the book by Bracy (2010). Beška 2012, 13–19.

118 At the heart of Fishman's work is his thesis that, during the period of the Second Constitution, a unique Palestinian identity, independent of Syrian identity, emerged and, before World War I, crystallized into the early stages of a 'full-blown nationalism'. Fishman 2007, 35. However, Fishman does not define his theoretical concepts nor does he contextualize the terms used by Arab authors, whom he quotes much out of context in order to support his theses. For instance, when analyzing petitions, Fishman attributes the political language used by Arab notables in official correspondence with the central government with that of other segments of Palestinian society to prove that 'the Palestinians' as a nation were of one mind, without being able to access the opinions of the social segments that he claims to speak of. Fishman 2007: 65–67.

119 See Tamari 2014b, 16–17. Robson refers to a statement by ʿĪsā al-ʿĪsā in which he defined the Orthodox cause, anti-Ottomanism and the battle against Zionist encroachment as his three major political causes from the beginning of his journalistic enterprise. Robson 2011a, 87, n. 35, 189. Her evaluation goes back to the work on Palestinian biographies by ʿAǧāǧ

'Memories from the Past' (*Min Ḏikrayāt al-Māḍī*) was written between 1938 and 1950 during his exile in Beirut; it has been edited and translated into French by Noha Tadros.[120] In this manuscript, ʿĪsā al-ʿĪsā defined his political stance during the late Ottoman period as anti-CUP because of the coalition of the Young Turks with the Zionists, and Tamari took up this view of ʿĪsā's position.[121]

Here, one should take into account that this manuscript was written after 1948, while ʿĪsā lived in exile, and it is likely that, in his reflections on the Ottoman era under the impact of the Palestinian defeat of 1948 against Israel, he made an effort to correct his personal past. A systematic reading of *Filasṭīn* during 1911–1914 has shown that the strong pro-Ottoman stance was never abandoned by its editors. Although *Filasṭīn* was shut down several times for its sharp criticism of the government before the War, the editors exercised their freedom to speak out as 'proud Palestinian Arab Ottomans' without seeing a contradiction between this and expressing criticism of the government and certainly not considering themselves anti-Ottoman in any way.[122]

Apart from Buessow's study on the political elites of Hamidian Palestine through *Filasṭīn* as a mirror, Beška's detailed documentation on the discursive shift in *Filasṭīn*'s coverage on Zionism from 1911 to 1914, and an online-article by Aṣleh on floating concepts between local identity and Ottomanism during the same period, *Filasṭīn* has not been explored systematically.[123] Rather, it has been studied on the basis of random samples without proper contextualization of its discourse, and it has thus been given simplistic labels. Campos and Kayalı have underscored the complexity in the construction of collective identities and the need for a broader contextualization of the Second Constitutional Era beyond the paradigms of Arab nationalism and so-called 'tyrannical' Turkish rule.[124] In order to frame group relations in the Jerusalem District before World War I in the light of contemporary press debates, I have limited the exploration of primary sources to *Filasṭīn* in order to carry out in-depth research of its coverage, which has not been done before.

Nuwayhiḍ (1981, 30), who extracted this statement from a speech given by ʿĪsā in an unknown context. However, this speech must be from a later point of time.

120 There, ʿIsā focused on the late Ottoman period and the interlude of the short-lived 'Faysal State' in Damascus up to ʿĪsā's return to Palestine in 1921, and only engaged to a minor extent (13 of 76 pages of the manuscript) with the Mandate period. For ʿĪsā's stay in Damascus with Faysal, see Tadros 2011, 9–10.

121 Tamari 2014b, 16–17. This claim, based on the translation of his memoirs, was taken up by Dolbee and Hazkani, who claim that ʿĪsā leaned towards decentralization, which was not the case. Dolbee and Hazkani 2015a, 247.

122 Campos 2015, 92.

123 See Buessow 2002 (unpublished MA thesis), Beška 2016c, and Aṣleh 2012.

124 Kayalı 1997, 10–11, 13. Quoted in Campos 2015, 92.

What is to be expected from an in-depth analysis of *Filasṭīn?* First, *Filasṭīn* is a rich source of information on how group relations that were of special interest in pre-World War I Jaffa and Jerusalem were negotiated and reconstituted. Second, its treatment of Zionism, Arab Palestinian nationalism and Ottomanism during the transitional years of 1911–1914 included complexities, shifts and ambivalences that have not yet been worked out. This survey of *Filasṭīn* will revise its simplified image as the pioneer of anti-Zionism, promoter of early Palestinian nationalism and opponent of Ottomanism before World War I, and instead work out commonalities, ambivalences and shifts in discourse and the reality of group relations. Here, a thorough reading of *Filasṭīn* shows that, during the years 1911 to 1914, multiple collective identity concepts overlapped, and political concepts were interpreted quite freely and could take on multiple meanings. The political terminology of the post-revolutionary period, especially with reference to 'constitutional rights', was extensively exploited in the press and sacralized so as to legitimate the cause of the disputing author. At the same time, striking inconsistency and fluidity in the use of nationalist terms can be observed.

Part I of this media analysis will explore the set of mental concepts conveyed through *Filasṭīn*, how they are reflected in its terminology, and how far they were stable or fluid, overlapping into different contexts and 'travelling' through time, place and content issue. Since this study strongly focuses on chronological developments in *Filasṭīn*'s debates, carving out its major shifts, transformations in selected group relations can be observed in slow-motion. Part II explores debates on local politics and cohabitation in the Jaffa *qaḍā*ʾ as the geographical focus of *Filasṭīn* and the socio-political context in which the newspaper was rooted. It carves out general commonalities and particularities regarding the coexistence of groups in the region, defines rules for interaction or segregation and sets out how they were implemented in local politics. Part III analyzes the agendas and instruments of the 'Orthodox Renaissance Movement' (*ḥarakat an-nahḍa al-urṯūḏuksīya*), an anti-clerical movement of Arab Palestinian of Greek Orthodox confession in the Jerusalemite Patriarchate, and the role of *Filasṭīn* in it. So far, research lacks proper evaluation of the Orthodox Movement in the post-revolutionary context. This is particularly surprising, since, in December 1910, a Mixed Council was established, instructed to work out reforms to end previous violence between the Orthodox Movement and the Patriarchate. *Filasṭīn* documented its bi-weekly sessions and is an excellent source on the intra-Orthodox conflict before World War I. Since its editor in chief, Yūsuf al-ʿĪsā (1870–1948), represented Jaffa's Orthodox in the Mixed Council, it is even more surprising that *Filasṭīn* has not been explored to investigate the Orthodox cause. Part IV analyzes the Palestinian debate on Zionism based on *Filasṭīn* articles. Beška has been working simultaneously on the same topic and has exhaustingly evaluated the same source. In his recently published concise analysis of the breaking shifts in *Filasṭīn* on Zionism from 1911 to 1914, he focuses on the shift from 'neutrality towards hostility' and an articulation of severe anti-Zionism since 1913, treating *Filasṭīn* mainly as the mouthpiece of its editors without giving much attention to its networks and socio-political context. This study, on the other hand, treats *Filasṭīn* as a 'joint production' by a pool of publishers and will pay attention to the actors' level. Regarding the debate on Zionism in *Filasṭīn*, the present work focuses on its controversial aspects, considers it as a dispute between actors from different backgrounds, and relates its discursive shifts to other debates and general local and regional developments.

3.2. Collecting and Evaluating the Coverage in *Filasṭīn*

The systematic documentation of newspaper articles from *Filasṭīn*, confronted me with a flood of data, which explains why the focus of this study is only on the Ottoman years. Regarding qualitative empirical survey of media, methods of content analysis have been introduced in cultural sciences by Brosius, Mayring and others, including the 'grounded theory'.[125] In my dealings with *Filasṭīn*, I have developed my own method of collecting, categorizing and filtering, and evaluating its coverage, which will be briefly outlined.

Collecting and Registering

Starting with issue number 51 (15 July 1911) and ending with issue number 345–348 (15 August 1914), I had 288 issues of *Filasṭīn* at my disposal,[126] and practically, I scanned every single issue available for the period.

1. I identified articles that concern the spectrum of social, ethnic and confessional groups present in Palestine, their forms of contact and interaction, and their shared practices and conflict patterns.
2. I looked at the focus of content in each section of the newspaper, singled out figures who published frequently, identified their main arguments and striking terminology used in the articles, and I sought to extract their views on collective identities, the integration or exclusion of groups, notions of nationhood, citizenship, social class, and their attitude ton government institutions and contemporary prominent figures.

125 See Mayring (2008) for methods of qualitative analysis of texts. See Altheide (2013), Ayaß (2006) and Brosius (2009) for qualitative analysis of media and media communication. See Hepp (2010) for qualitative media research in cultural studies; and Glaser (2010) for a summary of methods of 'grounded theory' in social sciences.

126 Copies of issues from July 1911 to December 1913 are held at *Tuebingen University* and the library of the *Hebrew University* in Jerusalem; and issues number 151, 172 and 183 were missing from both collections.

3. I gave close attention to articles on various subjects apart from my topic in order to carve out a catalogue of central concepts conveyed through the authors.

This method was conducted in my exploration of each issue until the concept analysis, as reflected in different topics and language forms, reached, in my view, a 'saturation point', and most thoroughly with regard to the years 1911 and 1912, which allowed me to work out major conceptual shift occurring in 1913. Because of time limits and since I have received the issues of 1914 only through a lucky coincidence towards the end of my study,[127] the analysis of media coverage in 1914 was limited to coverage on the Orthodox Movement, the Zionist question and general observations regarding major shifts in contents and designs.

From these 288 issues of *Filasṭīn*, I extracted and registered 1,895 articles or items that I found relevant concerning Palestinian group relations. In parallel, I summarized these items, which amounted to 1,000 printed pages of rough translations, and I entered these items simultaneously in a bibliographical data base, adding a content summary, translations of relevant terminology, and quotations. Although this was not a sophisticated data base, this method enabled me to assign multiple keywords to the items and produce qualitative categories of themes, language forms and mental concepts that seemed dominant in *Filasṭīn*'s coverage. This helped because the registered items, sorted under a set of key words, appear in chronological order, providing a concise picture of changes in the topics discussed and language forms.

Keyword Indexing

Simultaneously with the process of collecting data, I developed a keyword index of qualitative categories for each article or item in the newspaper. A keyword may define:

1. *content topics* that are treated, such as education, infrastructure and reform, Ottoman unity, nationalism, Orthodox matters, budget matters, property issues, Zionism, holy places and pilgrimage, ceremonial culture, clubs and societies, violence and security matters, health and hygiene, migration, Muslim–Christian relations, Muslim–Jewish relations, Christian–Jewish relations, commercial relations, agriculture, etc.
2. *central concepts and terminology*, such as, constitutionalist terminology, concepts on modernity and progress, nationalism, notions of the public and

127 Regarding the issues of 1914, I owe many thanks to Emanuel Beška, who shared with me those that he found in the library *Dār al-Kutub* ('House of Books') in Cairo. Accessing *Filasṭīn*'s coverage of 1914 contributed to new results of this work, especially with regard to the Orthodox Movement. Thank you, Emanuel!

civil society, definitions of political justice versus despotism, evaluations of religious fanaticism, European hegemony, anti-Semitism, freedom, masculinity, jihad, etc.

3. *places*, that is, indications about where or about which city the article was written: Jerusalem, Jaffa, Gaza, Bethlehem, Beit Jala, New York, etc.
4. *literary genre*, such as editorial, readers' letter, petition, open letter, protest letter, correspondents' reports, reprint, advertisement, etc.
5. *communicational scope and networks*, for instance, through the registration of notables or journalists who appear frequently because they have personal ties with the editors.

In the process of collecting and categorizing the data, every one of the registered 1,895 items extracted from the 288 issues was allocated several keywords as qualitative categories. As the number of categories grew to 162 keywords, the indexing of articles became increasingly consuming and fragmented; and especially with regard to 'mental concepts' applied in *Filasṭīn*, they were increasingly observed to overlap in different topics.

There follows only a small selection of categories that occurred frequently in *Filasṭīn* to give an indication of its focus regarding topics, central concepts and terminology, and communicational features.

1. Concerning *topics*, 527 registered items address Ottoman unity, 452 Arab Orthodox matters, 407 education and reform, 368 progress and development, 292 violence and security issues, 362 Zionism, 236 cultural issues or activities, 187 Jewish-Christian relations, 168 Muslim-Christian relations, and 83 Muslim-Jewish relations.
2. Concerning *concepts and terminology*, 341 items promote concepts of the 'public' and civil society, 262 items foster the emancipation of groups (mostly Arab-Orthodox), 260 items call for civil rights, 254 encourage Ottoman patriotism, 162 foster the concept of the 'public interest', and 131 criticize European hegemony in the Middle East.
3. Concerning *literary genres*, 348 items were registered as readers' letters, 218 as editorials, and 118 were reports of *Filasṭīn*'s correspondents.
4. Concerning the *communicational character* of articles, 520 items have the intention to educate the readers (with 397 items expressing direct appeals to the readership), 241 are appeals to the local government, 79 appeal to the central government, and 224 are protest letters.

4. Central Concepts and Methods

As a micro study, this work explores the 'order of what to say or not to say' in *Filasṭīn*'s debates on group identities and relations. Linking the content issues in its coverage to the language forms applied, positively or negatively connoted, provides an insight into the worldview of the contributing authors and their underlying 'mindset' of moral values and mental concepts that stand out as promoted ideal standards, and allows conclusions to be drawn as to how far this constituted a 'shared mindset' among contemporary Palestinian elites. Further, it is questionable how far these values and concepts that were promoted derived from a broader trans-Ottoman frame, how far they were localized to serve local needs, and how much they circulated between debates on different issues.

Further, I focus on *Filasṭīn*'s communicational range among the public. Since *Filasṭīn* was a space for intellectual interaction, I treat it not as the mouthpiece of its editors, but as a platform for a pool of authors who established identity discourses through controversial discussions and acted as 'agents of community building'. Here, *Filasṭīn* served as a 'medium' in several respects: it established communication between its editors and the readership, between readers and readers (readers' letters), and between the public and the government (open letters, telegrams, petitions, reprints of edicts, etc.). Further, the editors viewed civic participation as an important parameter of modernity and encouraged the readership to get involved in public debates.

In order to track the scope of communication, relevant actors will be identified. Here, it is important to treat authors who present themselves as the 'mouthpiece' of a certain community as individuals, and not necessarily as representatives of the collective groups in whose interest they claim to speak. Second, I track the flow of communication, that is, I explore how far the articles were designed as a dialogue, open to the exchange of controversial opinions; or as a *monologue*, a campaign not open to controversy. Third, I analyze the function of communication, that is, whether it was designed to strengthen alliances between groups or to stigmatize and exclude groups.

Finally, the 'relationality of discourse and reality construction' in Palestinian group relations is called into question in so far as it is possible to track this through *Filasṭīn's* coverage. Here, the practical impact of debates on group relations on the ground will be considered: how is what happened on 'the street' echoed in *Filasṭīn*, what does this say about alliances or segregation between groups, and what were the underlying reasons for these alliances or segregations?

By using the methods of in-depth media analysis and the theoretical approaches outlined above, this study touches upon Palestinian conceptual history during a moment of massive transition with regard to values, identity models and political visions before the Ottoman collapse. During the Second Constitutional

Period (1908–1914) and after World War I, the Middle East experienced a 'saddle period', as Kosellek calls it, a fundamental change with regard to social relations and concepts, which is reflected through semantic innovations, and is still unexplored.[128] For a better understanding of these processes, more in-depth surveys of contemporary Arab newspapers are needed in order to follow the change of agendas conveyed through press organs in Jerusalem, Jaffa, Haifa, Beirut and Damascus, and to unravel this 'saddle period in the Middle East', an era that can be called an 'Ottoman Twilight', since it is still half in the dark as far as historiography is concerned.

5. Content of Study

Chapter I discusses the emergence of *Filasṭīn* as an enterprise in the context of print media development in the Middle East. I explain the personal background of its editors and the local conditions experienced by the press in the Ottoman Second Constitutional Era. Then, I demonstrate how *Filasṭīn* as a medium was structured and arranged, and what its content focus was. Further, the central concepts advocated will be outlined, that is, the 'mindset' of moral values and political views that the authors publishing in *Filasṭīn* presented to the reader, and how this 'mindset' was reflected in language and terminology and overlapped in different debates.

Chapter II presents a brief history of the Jaffa region as an expanding 'ethno-confessional contact zone', addressing its major demographic and socio-economic developments since the *Tanzimat*, relations between the urban and the rural space, practices of power sharing and the constitution of ethno-confessional spaces. Further, I discuss local campaigns for the modernization of Jaffa and the implementation of public security, which included campaigns for the exclusion of stigmatized social and ethnic groups, and *Filasṭīn*'s perspective on that.

Chapter III explores the conflictual relations between the clerical hierarchy in the Greek Orthodox Patriarchate of Jerusalem and Arab Palestinian Orthodox activists in the Orthodox Renaissance Movement. The chapter traces how the movers of the Orthodox Renaissance negotiated local participation in the administration of their Patriarchate, and how they tried to access its financial and cultural resources. I identify the activist circles, and outline the language and political instruments they used to pressurize the clergy and the Ottoman authorities, and to mobilize the Orthodox congregation and the Palestinian public. Further, I track the controversies on reforms in the Mixed Council published in

128 See Koselleck 2006; Kollmeier 2011; and Wittrock, Heilbron, and Magnusson 1998, 7–10.

Filasṭīn, while highlighting the agendas of the parties to the conflict, and the role of the ʿĪsās in the Orthodox Movement.

Chapter IV analyzes controversial debates by a spectrum of contributors from different confessions on the 'Zionist question', and how they discussed through *Filasṭīn* the potential benefits and harms for Palestine that resulted from Zionist migration and settlement. The chapter explores how the socio-economic integration, or exclusion, of Zionist migrants into local society was negotiated, and its underlying conditions. It traces the rivalries between Arab Palestinians and Zionist settlers over access to economic resources in the Jaffa region in the context of local and transregional factors and how this affected Sephardi–Christian relations in the Jerusalem District. Finally, factors that led to the closure of the controversial debate and pushed an anti-Zionist campaign in *Filasṭīn* in 1914 will be outlined.

I. *Filasṭīn* and the 'Spirit of the Age': Educating the Nation

1. The Development of Arabic Print Media in Palestine

Print Media in the Middle East

Arabic block printing (*ṭarš*), for example on amulets, had been known in the Middle East since at least the tenth century,[1] but printing technology with moveable letters did not make an impact on the textual culture of the Arabic-Islamic world until far beyond the age of Gutenberg, in the second half of the nineteenth century; and then only in urban centers such as Istanbul, Cairo and Beirut.[2] One reason for this was that the production of texts was expected to be under the control of Islamic scholars, and the copying of text was limited to sacred texts and printing in Turkish and Arabic script was forbidden until Sultan Ahmet III permitted it by decree (Tur.: *ferman*) in 1726. Even then, this was limited to secular texts, and the printing of the Qur'an and Qur'an exegesis (*tafsīr*), as well as texts on Islamic tradition (*ḥadīṯ*) and jurisprudence (*fiqh*), was forbidden until 1803.[3] Printing in other languages was exempted from prohibition as it was not linked to the production of Islamic texts and the first printers in the Empire were non-Muslims who printed in various scripts: Armenian, Greek, Syriac and Hebrew.[4]

The first Ottoman printer in Arabic was Ibrahim Müteferrika, a Christian convert to Islam, who launched the first Arabic printing press in Istanbul after the 1726 *ferman.*[5] In the Arab East, Arabic printing was introduced in the eighteenth century through Syrian-Lebanese church and missionary institutions and was restricted to sectarian texts. The first press with Arabic fonts started

---

1 See Bulliet 1987, 435; and Schaefer 2006, 1–39.

2 Glaß 2004, 4; and Ayalon 2004, 1.

3 Schulze 1997, 41–44. See Roper on the printing press and change in the Arab East (2007, 250–267).

4 Ayalon 2016, 1–2. The first Hebrew printing press was founded around 1490 in Istanbul by Rabbi Isaac Garcon. See Suleiman 2009, 79f.

5 Ayalon 2016: 1–2. On Müteferrika's initiatives, see Ergınbaş 2014, 54–100, esp. 84.

printing in Aleppo in 1706,[6] producing liturgical texts and Arabic Bibles.[7] In Lebanon in 1610, a prayer book in Syriac was clearly printed in a monastery at Mount Lebanon. Yet, these were short-lived endeavors that produced only few copies.[8]

In Egypt, the situation was different, and printing was under the control of the Khedival regime. The first Arabic press was introduced by the French during the Napoleonic campaign (1798) to print pamphlets and explain the campaign to Muslim scholars. When the French left, however, they took their equipment with them. Soon after, Muḥammad ʿAlī Pasha, having gained independence from the Empire, and pursuing a policy of territorial expansion and the modernization of Egypt, established his own printing press in the Cairo Citadel in 1819. Named *The National Press* (*al-maṭbaʿa al-ahlīya*) and controlled by the Pasha, it circulated the Khedive's version of news among the Egyptian bureaucracy, informed officials about decrees and official state policy, and became the first Arabic newspaper.[9]

In Lebanon, a center of Arabic printing, such enterprises were initiated by foreign missionaries and Western agents, and supported by local partners.[10] Arabic printing in Lebanon was, in general, dominated by religious institutions and sectarian motives and the first Arabic press was 'The American Press' (*al-maṭbaʿa al-amrīkānīya*), a missionary enterprise, established in 1834 for the distribution of religious books.[11] Only after the second half of the nineteenth century did the printing of texts spread beyond church institutions and monasteries,[12] and was promoted by educational and literary societies and private publishers.

Print Media in Palestine

Especially because of the rather late adoption of print technology in the Ottoman Empire, the consumption of Arabic texts enforced spectacular changes in the twentieth-century Middle East. Palestine, Ayalon says, was catapulted within a

6 This was a printing press manufactured in Romania. See Suleiman 2009, 79.

7 Under the guidance of the Melkite Patriarch of Antioch, Dabbās, the Christian deacon and goldsmith ʿAbdallāh b. Zaḫarīyā Zāḫir (1684–1748) from Aleppo printed the psalter as the first book published by this press. See Ayalon 2016, 2.

8 Zāḫir's initiative in 1706 yielded only eight religious tracts in quite modest editions. Müteferrika produced 16 books and all together about 10,000 copies. See Ayalon 2016, 2.

9 This press also produced school books to educate the new bureaucratic elites serving under the Pasha and later became later the famous publishing house 'Bulaq Press' (*maṭbaʿat Būlāq*).

10 Ayalon 2016, 25–29.

11 This press was built in Malta and transferred to Beirut by Protestant missionaries, who translated the Protestant Bible into Arabic and spread it via their press. For the 'American Press', see Auji 2016.

12 It should be noted that the method of copying sacred texts by hand, as previously practiced by Christian monks, continued in the churches and monasteries. See Suleiman 2009, 80.

'brief historical moment' from almost total illiteracy into the 'massive reliance' on the written word.[13] While the conditions for Arabic text production in Palestine were quite similar to those in the Empire, the status of Palestine as the Holy Land imposed special conditions on the local printing market. As in the Syrian-Lebanese context, printing in Palestine was dominated by religious societies, which spread dramatically in the nineteenth century, and by Jewish and Christian entrepreneurs.

Until 1846, all texts in Palestine were printed by local Jews using Hebrew fonts. Jews also took a leading role in early local journalism and the first newspapers, printed in the 1860s, were in Hebrew.[14] The rapid rise of Jewish print media in late nineteenth-century Palestine was generated by Zionist migrants from Europe, who tried to spread Jewish nationalism and revive Hebrew as a language. The increase in Christian print media in Palestine arose from a high number of European societies, missionary institutions and schools in Jerusalem, Haifa and Jaffa, and competed with the printing activities of monasteries and private entrepreneurs. The 'London Society for Promoting Christianity among the Jews' maintained their own printing press from 1868 onwards in Jerusalem, and the Armenians did the same from 1848.[15] The Franciscans, starting in 1846, the Anglicans and the Greek Orthodox set up printing shops in their Jerusalem missions, producing educational and evangelistic materials, sometimes in Arabic.[16]

These initiatives met a response from local Palestinians, both Muslims and Christians. From the early 1890s, some private Arab printing presses existed in Jerusalem, Haifa and other towns, as is stated in an official Ottoman document. Yet, according to Palestinian scholar Muḥammad Sulaymān, there is no information on such places apart from scattered references to a few presses in Jerusalem.[17] What we know is that the Arab Palestinian Greek Orthodox Jerusalemite Ǧūrǧī Ḥabīb Ḥanānīyā (1857–1920), a pioneer of printing and journalism in Palestine, started a printing shop with Latin letters near Jerusalem's Jaffa Gate in 1894 and, from 1898 onwards, managed to secure a license to print in Arabic. According to his own account, he managed to print 281 publications,

13 Ayalon 2004, 1.

14 The first newspaper in Palestine was the Hebrew *Ha-Levanon* ('Lebanon'), published by Yael Broueil in Jerusalem in 1862. In 1870, Frumkin started the publication of *Ḥavazelet* ('The Lily'), and in 1890 Ben Yehuda started *Ha-Or* ('The Light'), which soon became the most popular Hebrew newspaper in Palestine. Suleiman 2009, 81–85.

15 Suleiman 2009, 79–85.

16 Ayalon, on the basis of an interview with Rasim Yousuf Jbara in Taybe, who has produced a bibliography of Arabic publications in Palestine, reports that the Franciscans printed 65 works prior to 1900. Ayalon 2004, 57, n. 53, 170.

17 Cited in Ayalon 2004, n. 54, 170.

including 83 in Arabic script, before the lifting of state censorship in 1908, although there is no evidence of titles.[18]

From the end of the nineteenth century, book shops, public reading rooms and libraries began to be opened in Jerusalem, such as the Khalidi Library (*al-Maktaba al-Ḫālidīya*). It was founded in 1899 by Rāġib al-Ḫālidī (1866–1952), member of the prominent Khalidi family, who traditionally held positions in the Jerusalem Sharia court, to collect his ancestors' manuscripts going back to the Mamluk era.[19] Apart from the al-Aqsa Library and the Budayriya Library, the Khalidi Library was among the first local endeavors in the modern age to preserve the Arab Palestinian cultural heritage and foster the status of Jerusalem as an Islamic place;[20] it also collected a great variety of Arab periodicals and contemporary newspapers, open for the public to read.[21] However, we have no data about literature consumption and the spread of print media, since hardly catalogues or reading lists have been preserved from the libraries.[22]

Accessing Knowledge, Generating Cultural Identity

The trend to preserve Islamic sciences and Arabic literature was interpreted by Rashid Khalidi (a member of the Khalidi family himself) as an indicator of intellectual change that fostered forms of modern identity, and encouraged the awakening of a local patriotism and a specific Palestinian identity, as he says. As part of this, he highlights the expansion of educational initiatives from the 1870s, among them a school, called the 'National Ottoman Islamic Garden of Knowledge' (*Rawdat al-Maʿārif al-Waṭanīya al-ʿUṯmānīya al-Islāmīya*), founded by a Muslim sheikh in 1906, and the famous 'Constitutional School' (*al-Madrasa ad-Dustūrīya*), established by the Orthodox journalist and teacher Ḫalīl as-Sakākīnī (1878–1953) in 1909.[23]

Increasing access to cultural knowledge helped to foster Arab identity, while the Arabic press served as a multiplier of ideas and cultural knowledge. Those who knew how to read and write could access this knowledge, which is why Glaß

18 As stated by Ḥanāniyā in a newspaper article in his newspaper *al-Quds*, 18 September 1908; quoted in Yehoshu'a 1974, 41–43. See Ayalon 2004, 57–58, n. 56, 170.

19 See Ayalon 2004, 46; and Khalidi 1997, 42–46, see also the website of the Khalidi Library http://www.khalidilibrary.org/indexe.html (14 May 2019).

20 The Khalidi Library collected more than 1,200 manuscripts, bought copies of traditional works in Islamic sciences and had them printed and, until today, it owns autobiographical works of modern Islamic scholars, such as al-Afġānī and Muḥammad ʿAbduh. See Khalidi 1997, 43–46.

21 Among them were *al-Ǧawāʾib*, published by Fāris Aḥmad aš-Šidyāq, *al-Ǧinan*, published by Buṭrus al-Bustānī, *al-Muqtaṭaf*, published by Fāris Nimr, *al-Hilāl*, published by Ǧurǧī Zaydān, *al-Manār*, published by Rašīd Riḍāʾ, and *al-Muqtabas*, published by Muḥammad Kurd ʿAlī. See Khalidi 1997, 54.

22 Ayalon 2004, 15.

23 For the expansion of schools, see Khalidi 1997, 46–51.

stresses the role of the press as 'custodian of knowledge'. Arab journalists, such as the editors of *al-Muqtaṭaf*, Yaʿqūb Ṣarrūf and Fāris Nimr, measured the 'civilizational grade of nations' (*miqyās li-ḥaḍārat al-ʿumam*) according to the spread of literacy, since reading and writing were still a privilege and the 'general people' were excluded from written platforms of communication and knowledge.[24] Thus, the press was *the* symbol of progress and an indicator for 'civilization and reform' (*tamaddun wa-iṣlāḥ*) in the eyes of many Arab intellectuals.[25] It is true that the ambitions of the Arab *nahḍa* to revive authentic cultural knowledge were expressed most in the rise of the Arab press. At the same time, it was an expression of manifested 'Westernization', as Glaß points out. Just as the magazine became the medium of European enlightenment in the eighteenth century, its Arabic counterpart, the *maǧalla*, became the major instrument for the initiators of the *nahḍa* during the nineteenth century as a didactic instrument to educate and to entertain.[26]

In general, educational societies such as the 'Syrian Society for Science and Art' (*al-Ǧamʿīya as-Sūrīya li-l-ʿUlūm wa-l-Funūn*) were the predecessors of modern Arab media communication, and the *maǧalla* in particular. In 1847, the Syrian Society was established in Beirut by Butrus al-Bustānī, a prominent Lebanese Christian pedagogue, intellectual and *nahḍa* pioneer, and by Cornelius van Dyck, an American missionary and translator of the Protestant Bible into Arabic. Private publishing during the *nahḍa* was driven by these educational societies, and intertwined with missionary activity. The 'Syrian Society' consisted of 42 members, mostly American missionaries, Arab Christians affiliated with missionary institutions and merchants from Beirut, and its goal was to educate the 'general people' (*al-ʿāmma*) in modern sciences by publishing 'sermons' (*ḫiṭābāt*), 'treatises' (*mufāwaḍāt*) or lectures.[27]

The Post-Revolutionary Press in Palestine

In Lebanon and Egypt, there had been a private press since the 1870s, initiated by *nahḍa* pioneers, although they did not have a deeper impact on the political culture, but the first Arabic news publication in Palestine was the newspaper *al-Quds aš-Šarīf* ('Sacred Jerusalem'), published in Turkish and Arabic as an official state bulletin from 1876. Under Sultan Abdülhamid, press censorship was strict but it was lifted in the aftermath of the Young Turk Revolution in June 1908, which created an outburst of creative energy in Arab journalism and a boom in press publications from Baghdad to Tripoli.[28]

24 Glaß 2004, 9.
25 Glaß 2004, 4.
26 Glaß 2004, 4–9, 122–124.
27 Glaß 2004, 124–131. For Arab identity in Bustānī's discourse, see Sheehi 2000, 2004, 2011.
28 Buessow 2010, 103, 107.

In Palestine, the first private newspaper was *al-Quds* ('Jerusalem'), published in 1908 by Ǧurǧī Ḥabīb Ḥanāniyā (1857–1920) in Jerusalem.[29] In the same year, Ḥannā ʿAbdallāh al-ʿĪsā (d. 1909) and Ḫalīl as-Sakākīnī (1878–1953) started the monthly magazine *al-ʿAṣmaʾī* ('The Solid') with the support of Ḥannā's younger brother Yūsuf al-ʿĪsā (1870–1948), who later founded *Filasṭīn*, all of them Greek Orthodox initiatives. However, *al-ʿAṣmaʾī* was a short-lived enterprise and came to a sudden end with the death of Ḥannā in 1909. In 1908, Naǧīb an-Naṣṣār (1865–1947) started the publication in Haifa of the newspaper al-*Karmil*, named after the mountain in Haifa, which became very influential in northern Palestine. In 1909, Ḫalīl Baydas (1874–1949), also an Orthodox Christian, started publishing the Haifa-based magazine *an-Nafāʾis al-ʿAṣrīya* ('Modern Treasures').[30] Further, the Jerusalemite *al-Munādī* ('The Crier'), published by the Muslim journalist Saʿīd Ǧārallāh, also became quite successful.[31]

In 1908, the sudden change from suppression to journalistic freedom led to a high number of private press enterprises. The seriousness with which the young press took the right to freedom of expression and even exploited it has been explained before. Accounts of the number of magazines vary but the quantitative output was tremendous. According to Ḫūrī, 15 newspapers were found in Palestine in 1908.[32] Suleiman mentions that the first weeks after the proclamation of the Constitution saw the publication of nine newspapers in Jerusalem, two newspapers and one magazine in Haifa and one magazine in Jaffa.[33] Buessow reports the existence of 25 new newspapers in the Jerusalem District between 1908–1911,[34] and Campos at least 34 Arabic and five Hebrew newspapers between 1908–1914 in Palestine.[35] The most permanent enterprises were *al-Quds*, *al-Karmil* and *Filasṭīn*, all published by Christians.

Limiting Factors for the Arab Press

In spite of the journalistic explosion between 1908 and 1914, many factors hampered Palestinian press development. The new freedom was limited as much as it was celebrated, and this also applied to freedom of expression, despite of the lifting of censorship. Many newspapers were shut down by the authorities when they were suspected of supporting the political opposition, especially during internal crises faced by the regime in 1909, 1912 and 1913, and the methods of the

29 See Ḫūrī 1976, 8; and Hanania 2007, 51–69.
30 Tamari 2014b, 25; Yehoshu'a 1974, 92–93. On Ḫalīl Baydas and his literary output, see ibid. 93–98.
31 For *al-Munādī*, see Yehoshu'a 1974, 54–60.
32 According to Ḫūrī, 13 newspapers were found in Jerusalem and two in Haifa. Ḫūrī 1976, 7–26.
33 Suleiman 2009, 88–89.
34 Buessow 2002, 39.
35 Campos 2003, 240.

Young Turks were in this respect no less oppressive than Abdülhamid's. Many newspapers were closed repeatedly, quickly received renewed licenses, which impeded regular publication. With increasing pressure on the regime from 1912, the journalistic flurry was soon strangled, and *Filasṭīn* too was subject to temporary closures, as we shall see.[36]

Other obstacles to local press development were its lack of professional experience, technological challenges and economic difficulties. Despite the considerable quantity of journalistic production, the gap between quantity and quality was large. Many newspapers were short-lived with tiny sales numbers; their editing was not professional and many of them quickly disappeared. Thus, there were never more than approximately a dozen papers available on the Palestinian market at the same time.[37] Many contemporary writers criticized the 'journalistic anarchy' (*fawḍa ṣiḥāfīya*) because of the frequent appearance and disappearance of papers like 'bubbles', or complained about the low ethical standards of their colleagues who mixed free debate with quarrelsomeness and the defamation of opponents.[38]

Apart from political factors and lack of experience, economic factors also prevented press development. Sales numbers were relatively low in the Middle East compared with Europe, and the Palestinian press market was still smaller than that in Egypt, Syria and Lebanon. High production costs made newspaper consumption an expensive habit, and thus a luxury enjoyed by the urban elites. In addition, high illiteracy rates meant that the Arabic press could only reach the tiny percentage of the population who had received some education, but not the majority of the middle class and certainly not the lower classes in society.

2. *Filasṭīn* in Context

2.1. The Background of *Filasṭīn*

Filasṭīn was first issued as a 'political, literary and illustrated newspaper' (*ǧarīda aḫbārīya siyāsīya adabīya muṣawwara*) on 14 January 1911 in Jaffa as a co-production of the Arab Palestinian cousins ʿĪsā Dawūd al-ʿĪsā and Yūsuf al-ʿĪsā,

36 The press law was changed several times: the first time during the Counter Revolution (1909) and further five times up to 1914. Government crises led to political oppression and, towards the end of the Young Turk era, newspapers were closed when there was only the slightest suspect of opposition. Ayalon 1995, 68, 69; and Ḫūrī 1976, 154–171.

37 For instance, newspapers would declare themselves to be 'dailies' but appeared irregularly for lack of professional experience. See Ilyās 1982–1983, 170–171, 298–355. Compare with Ayalon 1995, n. 60, 255; and Sulaymān 1987, 139–140.

38 Ayalon 1995, 67.

and appeared twice a week.[39] The ʿĪsā cousins belonged to Jaffa's rising middle class and one of its most prominent families; they were among the leading figures in the local Orthodox community, and they were both, particularly Yūsuf, political activists for local participation in the Greek Orthodox Patriarchate. Yūsuf's older brother, Ḥannā, was the community leader (*muḫtār*) of the Orthodox of Jaffa, and edited from 1908 to 1909 the short-lived magazine al-ʿ*Aṣmāʾī*, mentioned above. The ʿĪsā's were a family of oil and soap merchants but they also engaged in the orange trade, and one family member, Nadīm, had established commercial contacts as far away as Liverpool.[40] The ʿĪsās did not belong to the economic elite, however, and were not even well off, but they were definitely among the intellectual elite and the most prominent figures in the District.

The ʿĪsā Cousins: Biographical Details

ʿĪsā al-ʿĪsā (1876–1950), attended the Catholic seminary in Jaffa and the Syrian Protestant College in Beirut, which later became the AUB). After working for an Egyptian company, ʿĪsā returned to Jaffa and started publishing *Filasṭīn*. Being summoned before a military tribunal for 'seditious' articles,[41] ʿĪsā had to leave Palestine for the first time in 1915. Via Anatolia, he fled to Damascus where he became chief secretary at the Royal Court of Emir Faysal in 1918–1920. After the fall of Faysal in Syria, he returned to Jaffa and revived *Filasṭīn*. In 1938, he had to leave Palestine again, this time upon British insistence and following death threats from political groups in Palestine, and went to Beirut. There, he experienced the Palestinian *Nakba* and died in exile in 1950.[42] His son Raǧāʾ al-ʿĪsā (1922–2008) continued *Filasṭīn* in Jaffa until also he fled during the 1948 war. After a break, he moved the publication to Jerusalem until *Filasṭīn* ceased in 1967 and Raǧāʾ went to Amman following the Israeli occupation of East Jerusalem.[43] The journalistic career of ʿĪsā al-ʿĪsā during the Ottoman and Mandate years has been explored by Tadros, Tamari and Khalidi using an unpublished manuscript entitled 'Memories from the Past' (*Min Ḏikrayāt al-Māḍī*), which ʿĪsā wrote towards the end of his life in Beirut.[44] When evaluating *Filasṭīn*'s coverage of the Ottoman years through these

39 Ḫūrī 1976, 20.

40 Apart from this, it is known that one sister, Muḥība, studied at the Orthodox seminary in Beit Jala. One brother, Ǧirǧis, headed the Arab Broadcasting station in Palestine in the 1930s. See Sulaymān 1987, 83; Buessow 2002, 41; idem 2010, 104, 224, n. 15; and Yehoshu'a 1974, 117.

41 Tamari 2014b, 24.

42 Dolbee and Hazkani 2015a, 246. The information is originally from ʿĪsā's memoirs. Tadros 2009, 227.

43 Raǧāʾ al-ʿĪsā moved in 1967 to Amman, where *Filasṭīn* was finally merged with the publications *al-Manār* and *ad-Dustūr*. See http://cosmos.ucc.ie/cs1064/jabowen/IPSC/php/journal.php?joid=2079. (accessed 20.11.2017) For the publication history of *Filasṭīn*, see Yehoshu'a 1974, 116f.

44 See Khalidi 2009; Tadros 2009 and 2011; and Tamari 2014b.

memoirs, one should keep in mind that they are formulated in retrospect and under the strong impact of the *Nakba* and life in exile, circumstances that deeply affected ʿĪsā's presentation of the Ottoman period.

Figure 1: ʿĪsā al-ʿĪsā, director and co-editor of *Filasṭīn*, at unknown age. (Source: al-ʿĪsā Family Archive. With permission of PASSIA Jerusalem – Palestinian Academic Society for the Study of International Affairs)

About the younger cousin, Yūsuf al-ʿĪsā (1870–1948), we have less information. He was the author of most *Filasṭīn* editorials and the articles in the 'Local News' section (*Aḫbār Maḥallīya*), and an activist on many levels. As a pedagogue, he headed a Bible study group for Arab lay Orthodox (*iǧtimāʿ li-tafsīr al-inǧīl*).[45] On the level of politics, Yūsuf was a strict CUP supporter and a leading member of its Jaffa branch. However, his main interest was to foster the Arab Orthodox Movement in Palestine through *Filasṭīn*. From 1911, Yūsuf represented Jaffa in the Orthodox Mixed Council, which consisted of six lay Arab Orthodox and six clerics and was tasked with working out reforms in the Patriarchate. As we shall see, the conflicts between him and the Patriarch escalated in 1913 to such an extent that the Holy Synod tried to excommunicate him.[46] Like his cousin, Yūsuf left Palestine during World War I for Damascus. But unlike ʿĪsā, Yūsuf stayed

45 Buessow 2002, 40–41.
46 *Filasṭīn*, 10 July 1912: 152/1/1–3. See also *Filasṭīn*, 25 June 1913: 248/1/2–4; and 248/3/3–4.

there and gave up *Filasṭīn*. Instead, he started publishing *Alif Bā* in Damascus, which continued until his death in 1948 – a magazine that would later become the press organ of the Syrian Baath party, and still awaits exploration by historical research on the Arab press.[47]

Socio-Cultural Environment and Networks

Soon after its first publication in 1911, *Filasṭīn* became one of the most widely read papers and, in the opinion of Sulaymān, 'the mother of newspapers in Palestine' (*umm ǧarāʾid Filasṭīn*).[48] Under the British Mandate, it became the 'main daily', according to Khalidi.[49] First, the privileged position of Jaffa as an economic hub and connection point between the coast, Jerusalem and central Palestine helped to make *Filasṭīn* a successful enterprise. Second, the ʿĪsās had a passion for their profession and journalistic skills, and they knew how to generate attention. Third, the ʿĪsās maintained a wide social, cultural and political network across the District, with ties to officials, notables and intellectuals, regardless of religious affiliation, and they were known across Palestine.

As supporters of the Young Turks, they rented out space in their house for the CUP's Jaffa branch,[50] and they were also members of Jaffa's Freemasons' lodge Shafaq,[51] they supported Jaffa's cultural activities, and engaged in charitable and welfare projects initiated by the local Orthodox community. In Jaffa, they were involved with merchants and landowners and maintained close ties to the *qāʾi-maqām* and the police commander. They enjoyed well established contacts with Muslim notables and intellectuals from Jerusalem, such as the poet Isʿāf an-Našāšībī (1885–1948), the writer Rāġib al-Ḫālidī (1866–1952), founder of the Khalidi Library, and Rūḥī al-Ḫālidī (1864–1913), representative of Jerusalem to the Ottoman Parliament, and they were among the leading activists in the Orthodox Movement, together with the Jerusalemite pedagogue, journalist and activist Ḫalīl as-Sakākīnī (1878–1953). In contrast to the official reputation of *Filasṭīn* as the pioneer of anti-Zionism in Palestine, the editors also had personal relations with Ashkenazi migrants, such as Goldenberg, director of Jaffa's branch of the Zionist Anglo Palestine Bank, to which they rented out an office on the ground floor of their house, and to the Ukrainian Menashe Me'irovitch (1860–1949) from the Zionist settlement Rishon le-Tzion.[52]

47 Buessow 2002, 41.
48 Sulaymān 1987, 83.
49 Khalidi 1997, 126.
50 Buessow 2002, 39; and idem 2010, 104.
51 Campos has traced the establishment of the lodge, the Temple of Solomon, in Jaffa (1891), which was renamed L'Aurore ('Dawn') in 1904, and was called accordingly Barkai in Hebrew and Shafaq in Arabic. Campos 2005b, 43f.
52 Buessow 2002, 39.

Figure 2: The house of the ʿĪsās on ʿAǧamī Street where they rented out the ground floor to the Zionist Anglo Palestine Bank from 1903–22/23, and lived on the upper floor. (Source: Samuel Giler)

Content Focus and Central Agendas

How can the focus of *Filasṭīn* and its cultural and political agendas be summed up? In general, the ʿĪsās were passionate modernists and strongly promoted the imposition of the ideals of 'reform and modernization' on all levels of society. That overall agenda hovered over every topic reported on, promising that a Western-style modernization would be a comprehensive cure for local society from its 'social diseases' (*amrāḍ iǧtimāʿīya*), as the editors called the current state in Palestine.[53] As pioneers in Arab journalism, the ʿĪsās actively supported a revival of the Arab heritage and language in line with the *nahḍa*. In this respect, 'education' (*tarbiya*) was a field much discussed, and the reformation of local education was clearly a focal point in *Filasṭīn* that has not yet been explored. In terms of national politics, the ʿĪsās stuck strictly to the imperial discourse on 'Ottoman unity and brotherhood', a vision that had to be maintained by all means, especially against the background of political crisis prior World War I. However, their declared Ottomanism never hindered them from expressing fierce criticism of the government and, whenever they saw the development of Palestine neglected by the authorities, they did not hesitate to attack Ottoman officials.

With regard to content priorities, the focus of *Filasṭīn* was the Orthodox cause. The ʿĪsās headed a circle of Arab Orthodox activists engaged in a campaign against the clerical establishment in the Patriarchate. In this respect, the ʿĪsās used *Filasṭīn* as a platform to generate public support for the Orthodox cause and declared *Filasṭīn* 'the mouthpiece of this community' (*lisān ḥāl hāḏihi al-milla*).[54] The Orthodox cause cannot be underestimated as *the* driving force for the establishment of *Filasṭīn* in January 1911, as a result of the Arab Orthodox rebellion that broke out against the Greek clergy in the Orthodox Patriarchate in Jerusalem in 1910. Another focus in the 'Local News' section was Zionist migration to Palestine, including controversial debates about its risks and its potential benefits for local society, brought up by the ʿĪsās in November 1911.[55] 'Public security' was also a content focus in the Local News. This was a particularly sensitive issue with regard to Jaffa and Bethlehem, because of high crime rates and high expectations of the authorities to improve public security by using the armed forces.

Filasṭīn: a Medium for Mental Transfer and a 'Joint Enterprise'

Despite the Arab printing business's difficulty in accessing markets, *Filasṭīn* was very successful. It accessed and distributed information rather professionally and initiated public debates; it cannot be regarded simply as a private enterprise of the ʿĪsās but in practice functioned as a 'collective enterprise', with the ʿĪsās depending on their networks and a circle of publishing authors. As mentioned above, the editorials were mostly written by the editor-in-chief, Yūsuf. The Local News, which focused on events in the Jaffa *qaḍāʾ*, were mostly covered by the ʿĪsās as well, and it also served to disseminate the official news, orders and announcements of Jaffa's government authorities. However, the editors heavily

53 For instance, see *Filasṭīn*, 19 July 1911: 52/3/1–2.
54 *Filasṭīn*, 15 July 1911: 51/1/2–3.
55 *Filasṭīn*, 4 November 1911: 83/2/1.

depended on reports from other local and international newspapers, which were printed on the first two pages, and they also relied on a network of correspondents, who reported from inside and outside the District, and on readers' letters.

In what follows, I shall indicate how *Filasṭīn* worked as a 'collective enterprise' and public 'communication channel'. It carried frequent reprints from the Jerusalemite *al-Munādī* ('The Crier'), *al-Quds* ('Jerusalem') and ar-*Ra'y al-ʿĀmm* ('Public Opinion'), from the Egyptian *Fatāt an-Nīl* ('Young Woman of the Nile') and *al-Ahrām* ('The Pyramids'), from the Beiruti newspapers *Lisān al-Ḥāl* ('Mouthpiece of the Current Situation') and *al-Mufīd* ('The Beneficial'), and from the Syrian press, such as the Damascene *al-Muqtabas* ('The Quoted'). Of course, there were frequent reports from the Turkish press to cover events at the center of the Empire, which were widely quoted from the Istanbul-based CUP organ *Tanin*. The ʿĪsās also reprinted from Jewish newspapers such as the English *The Truth* and the Hebrew *ha-Ḥerut* ('Freedom'), both published in Jerusalem, from the international and European press, such as French, English, German and Italian newspapers or magazines, whose titles could often not be identified because of the missing vowels in the Arabic script, and from leading press organs such as the London based *The Times* and *The New York Times*.

Another source of information was news agencies through which 'official news' and, of course, the latest news from the war fronts in Libya and the Balkan were reported. The most important agencies were the London based *Reuters*, and the Ottoman *Havas* and *Lloyd Ottoman*, which transmitted international news and developments in Istanbul by telegraph.[56]

The other main information source was a significant network of correspondents. They regularly reported from numerous cities in the Jerusalem District (Ramla, Lod, Gaza, Jerusalem, Bethlehem, Beit Jala), the Arab provinces (Beirut, Tripoli, Damascus, Hama, Aleppo, etc.), and rather rarely from the northern Palestinian districts. *Filasṭīn* heavily relied on an anonymous correspondent from the District capital Jerusalem and from Lod in the Jaffa *qaḍā'*. There were also anonymous correspondents who reported more or less regularly from provincial cities; such as from Kerak that belonged to the Orthodox Patriarchate.[57] The New World was reported through Palestinian migrants who described the benefits of a modern Western-style life and the griefs of a life in exile. Only a few of the regular correspondents can be identified since their names were usually not given. The correspondents from Beit Jala were Iskandar Niqūlā Badar,

56 There were also agencies sponsored by foreign powers to shape the public opinion in the Empire. For instance, the *Lloyd Ottoman* was paid by the German government. See Buessow 2010, 106, FN 29, 224.

57 See a literary piece, praising the Kerak region and Syria. *Filasṭīn*, 25 November 1911: 89/3/2–3.

a Latin Christian, and Ǧibrān al-Maṭar, an activist in the Orthodox Movement. *Filasṭīn* also maintained correspondence with distant cities. A Muslim resident of Jerusalem, ʿĀrif al-Muwaqqat, about whom no biographical information is available, regularly reported from Medina on pilgrimage and groups traveling from all Muslim lands to Saudi Arabia. In 1914, there was also a correspondent from the port city of Jeddah, Saudi Arabia.[58] Ḥanāʾ Buyūk, a Palestinian Christian and member of the Buyūk family from Bethlehem, was the 'official agent' (*al-wikāla al-ʿāmma*) for *Filasṭīn* in Chile, La Calera.[59] All of these mentioned figures are well known in the environment of *Filasṭīn* but no other biographical information on them can be found.

Apart from publishing local, regional and international news, *Filasṭīn* also functioned as a 'communication channel' between government and citizens through which government telegrams from Istanbul to the Jerusalem District were distributed, notifying the introduction of laws, the military service and tax issues. Decrees of the Jerusalem governor that were passed on to the Jaffa *qāʾi-maqām* were published, as well as announcement from the *qāʾimaqām* to the population in Jaffa. In each issue, the Jaffa and Gaza land registry offices, the *ṭābū*, gave information about land sales and auctions, and police news reported on criminal cases.

Apart from acting as this 'channel', *Filasṭīn* published other information and personal opinions. First, the editors published interviews with public figures, such as the Jerusalem governor, Jewish rabbis and Muslim sheikhs, and foreign diplomats in the District. There were articles on contemporary icons of modern Arab art and culture, such as George Abyaḍ (1880–1959), an Egyptian actor of Lebanese origin,[60] and on Ǧūrǧī Zaydān (1861–1914), the Syriac-Christian editor of the Egyptian magazine *al-Hilāl* ('The Crescent'), when he visited Jerusalem in 1913.[61] Plenty of telegrams, sent by local citizens, were published, addressing Ottoman authorities and state officials in form of 'open letters' (*kitāb maftūḥ*) and 'petitions' (*ʿarīḍa*, pl. *ʿarāʾiḍ*). In this respect, *Filasṭīn* worked as a 'protest channel' between citizens and the government, and I have located 224 items that were published between 1911 and 1914 as protest letters, protest telegrams, open letters or petitions. Here, the Orthodox Christians of Jerusalem and Bethlehem were outstanding and published numerous letters of protest to the governor complaining against the Patriarchate, as will be demonstrated in chapter III.

58 See for instance *Filasṭīn*, 01 April 1914: 320/2/5f.

59 *Filasṭīn*, 27 April 1912: 131/3/1. Once, *Filasṭīn* reminded 'our subscribers in South America' to pay the annual fee to Ḥanāʾ Buyūk in La Calera. *Filasṭīn*, 4 December 1912: 194/4/3

60 See Seleiha 2011, 153f. For the editors, Abyaḍ was the 'genius of the East' (*nābiġat aš-šarq*), and in 1913, they covered his performances in Jaffa in a series of articles; see e.g. *Filasṭīn*, 16 July 1913: 254/1/1–4.

61 For instance, see *Filasṭīn* 6 August 1913: 260/2/5–3/2; *Filasṭīn*, 9 August 1913: 261/3/4–4/1.

Last but not least, *Filasṭīn* was widely used as a communication channel between a pool of readers who debated over controversies through letters (*ar-risāla*) but were not necessarily personally linked to each other. For the period 1911–1914, I have identified 350 readers' letters that refer to my topic only, without paying attention to letters on other subjects, which proves the relevance of *Filasṭīn* as a platform for dispute and made the newspaper a 'collective enterprise', as will be seen in the case studies. To this pool of publishers in *Filasṭīn* belonged local prominent figures, journalists, notables, poets, teachers and political activists from different confessions but similar who had social backgrounds, educational standards and modernist views. Outstanding among them were the above-mentioned Orthodox teacher Ḫalīl as-Sakākīnī, the Muslim notable Rāġib al-Ḫālidī, founder of the *Khalidi Library*, who published on the reformation of Islamic education and the *awqāf* in Jerusalem, the Muslim poet Isʿāf an-Našāšībī and the Muslim correspondent ʿĀrif al-Muwaqqat, all from Jerusalem. The reformer and teacher Ḥabīb Ḫūrī Ayūb wrote from Gaza, and the Christian migrant Ḥanāʾ Buyūk, originally from Bethlehem, from his new home in Chile, La Calera.

In addition, a large number of contributions in every issue came from the anonymous Jerusalem correspondent; his identity is unknown, but it is clear he was an Orthodox Christian. Other frequent contributors belonging to the Orthodox networks of the ʿĪsās will be introduced more fully, as far as further data on them is available, in chapter III on the Orthodox Renaissance Movement: Ǧūrǧī al-Ḫūrī Yaʿqūb from Beit Sahour, and Ǧibrān al-Maṭar and the teacher and poet Iskandar al-Ḫūrī al-Baytǧālī (1888–1973), both from Beit Jala. The Ashkenazi migrant Menashe Me'irovitch (1860–1949) from Rishon le-Tzion and the Sephardi Jew Shimon Moyal (1866–1915) from Jaffa also published regularly in *Filasṭīn*; both will be introduced in chapter IV on Zionism. From Jaffa, members of the influential merchant family, the Bayrūtīs, especially Naḫleh and Naǧīb, wrote in *Filasṭīn* on tax issues and Jaffa's orange trade.[62]

2.2. Accessing Readership and Markets

The journalistic boom of 1908 and its controversial character expanded the accessibility of information and drove a change in readership.[63] However, newspapers were *not* a mass media, but were consumed by only a tiny part of the population and could not reach readers *en masse*.

62 See for instance *Filasṭīn*, 13 September 1911: 68/1/1–3; 14 December 1912: 197/2/3–5; and 4 November 1911: 83/3/4.

63 Buessow 2010: 107.

The Readership

First, illiteracy rates in Palestine were high, as was the case in the rest of the Middle East. There was a very wide gap between a small segment of urban, very well educated elites, who enjoyed a cosmopolitan education, and the vast majority of Palestinians, who had no access to basic education and could not read or write, a dividing line between the urban and the rural elements of society.[64] In spite of private and state educational initiatives, there were 20,000 children in Palestinian schools in 1914, equal to three percent of school-age children, and research estimates a total illiteracy rate of 95 percent in Palestine during these years.[65] There are, of course, various stages of literacy to consider. For example, in 1913, 30 percent of men were able to write their name, according to the 'Friends School' in Ramallah.[66] People with basic education could read display boards and advertisements, and many might have been able to recite from the Qur'an and prayer books.[67]

However, accessing newspaper articles demanded a much higher level of literacy, which is what Yūsuf al-ʿĪsā defined as a sufficient level of education. In an editorial summarizing the first six months of *Filasṭīn*'s publication, he complained about a phenomenal illiteracy rate of 98 percent in Palestine and thought that the cultural state of the nation was disastrous. According to him, 'the ignorance of the uneducated class embraces all spheres of life comprehensively. This is the state of the nation, which has overall two percent of educated people.'[68]

Yūsuf obviously considered as 'fully literate' only the two percent in Palestine who had received an international education like himself and he was not alone in these complaints. These views form part of a wider elite discourse on the 'lethargy' (*ğumūd, ḫumūl*) of the Palestinians, and 'Eastern people' (*aš-šaʿb aš-šarqī*) in general, in the jargon of the press. This negative image was contrasted with ideals of Western-style reforms and modernization, promoted in *Filasṭīn* as an educating tool.

On the other hand, there were private initiatives that tried to bridge the gap between the illiterate and educated populations. There was a culture of 'collective reading' and newspapers were read aloud in public places and coffee houses, so that anyone interested (among the males) could listen to local and international news, open letters, poetry and so forth. Newspapers were read aloud in social

64 For the possibilities of Palestinian children at that time to gain education through private and state initiatives, and for school enrollment rates, see Ayalon 2004, 19–24.

65 Ayalon 2004, 22; and Buessow 2002, 51.

66 Buessow 2002, 51.

67 The first records of literacy in Palestine were made by the British authorities. They published an estimate that in 1931, 20 percent of the Arab population, at that time 970,000 people, could read and write. Ayalon 2004, 16–19, 40.

68 See *Filasṭīn*, 15 July 1911: 51/1/1–2.

gatherings to family, relatives and neighbors. Also, the press called for private commitment to 'educate' the masses 'for free'. In 1908, the Jerusalemite Hebrew paper *ha-Zvi* ('the Deer') pleaded for regular evening gatherings during which an 'educated Arab' should read aloud from the daily press to the people.[69] *Filasṭīn* warmly welcomed such initiatives and the editors often pleaded with Jaffa's population to make use of free education and evening lectures, offered by intellectuals or priests.[70] The ʿĪsās considered themselves entitled to *educate* the population and explained that this 'mission' was linked to their profession. They also got practically engaged in bridging the gap between the urban and the rural. Each *muḫtār* in the *qaḍāʾ*, heading a village with over 100 inhabitants was among the 'natural subscribers' (*muštarikūn tabīʿūn*) tf *Filasṭīn* and received an issue for free, delivered by the the *qāʾimaqām*'s gendarmerie patrol. The ʿĪsās declared that they did this

> with the intent that the farmer can, on the one hand, be informed about what happens in the Empire, and, on the other, understand his rights (*yafqahu ḥuqūqahu*), so he will not leave a space for those who do not fear God or his prophets to control him and take possession of his means of livelihood.[71]

The Local Market and Sale Numbers

The local print market was very limited not only because widespread illiteracy but also because production costs were high, which made newspapers a luxury good for the upper classes and severely limited the possibilities of accessing a bigger market. This made Arabic printing a risky business that did not yield income but demanded passion and access to financial capital. Newspapers were often only able to survive through sponsors and advertisement and most of them were tiny enterprises that could not employ permanent staff. In the late Ottoman era, the annual subscription for a newspaper in Palestine amounted up to 70 piasters, or *qurūš*. When a worker made up to eight *qurūš* a day and a teacher had a monthly salary of about 150 *qurūš*, a newspaper subscription was quite expensive for

69 Campos: 2003, 241–243.

70 *Filasṭīn* regularly announced 'free lectures' (*durūs maǧānīya*) by a priest called Gregorius, offered in his home in ʿAǧamī to those interested in universal history, science, political 'questions', and lessons in German and English. See *Filasṭīn*, 23 December 1911: 97/4/1–2; 27 December 1911: 98/4/2; 30 December 1911: 99/4/2; 3 January 1912: 100/4/2; and 6 January 1912: 101/4/2.

71 *Filasṭīn*, 11 June 1913: 244/3/4–5. Fishman cites the same paragraph from *Filasṭīn*, quoted from Khalidi, who indicates the wrong *Filasṭīn* issue (Khalidi 2006, 93, n. 69, 247). Of course, *Filasṭīn* was interested in raising the interest of the rural population in politics, but Fishman took this quotation as a 'prime example' out of context as to prove his thesis about the existence of Palestinian nationalism before World War I, and to show that the educated urban elites worked to create a 'national bond' between elites and peasants. Fishman 2007, 47–48.

them, and so it was a custom to share annual subscriptions collectively.[72] In 1913, Ǧurǧī Ḥanāniyā, the editor of *al-Quds*, complained bitterly that one single issue was shared by 'up to 50 men'.[73] Thus, newspaper sales at that time were modest, but one issue probably reached a significant number of readers.

Filasṭīn also struggled with these conditions because it was a two-man-company. In 1967, ʿĪsā al-ʿĪsā reported in retrospect about its modest starting point. In the winter of 1910–1911, he had a savings of 70 francs. When a second-hand printing press was for sale in Jerusalem, he bought it on the spot for 74 francs, spending all his savings. He bought new print fonts had them fitted to the machine and launched the first publication in January 1911 in a store that he rented on Bustrus Street, Jaffa's new commercial center, in a building near the post office.[74] The issues announced the prices: *Filasṭīn* cost ten francs in Jaffa and in the other provinces three riyals (*riyālāt maǧīdīya*), Ottoman silver coins.[75] For comparison, *al-Karmil* was sold for two Ottoman silver coins in Haifa and other provinces, and for half a franc in Egypt and abroad.[76]

In order to survive, the ʿĪsās had to access other sources of income. Yūsuf, for example, worked as an Arabic teacher for Jewish students in Jerusalem.[77] As was typical for Arab publishers at that time, the ʿĪsās were multi-tasking and functioned as authors, editors, printers, publishers and distributors in one.[78] ʿĪsā al-ʿĪsā recalled how he travelled through the Jerusalem District on the back of a donkey or a camel to enlist new subscribers and collect the fees from villages and Bedouin tribes.[79] Apart from subscriptions, issues of *Filasṭīn* were distributed by street sale in Jaffa, Jerusalem and other cities; and in shops for whose owners the editors provided free advertisements in return. They included Ibrahīm Ġandūr's shop on 'Iskandar Street', situated at Bustrus Market, Jaffa's commercial center,

72 Campos 2003, 243, see n. 15.

73 Ayalon 1995, 158; and Buessow 2002, 53.

74 Ayalon 1995, 225; and Tamari 2014b, 26. For a description of Jaffa's Bustrus Street as Nodal Point of Modern Culture before World War I and some information on the history of Bustrus Street, see my article 'Performances of Late Ottoman Modernity: Culture, Entertainment and Leisure Activities in Pre-World War I Jaffa' (forthcoming 2020).

75 See *Filasṭīn*, 2 August 1911: 56 (see front page, top right).

76 See *al-Karmil* 6 January 1914: 396 (see frontpage, top right).

77 Yehoshua 1974, 23; compare with Ayalon 1995, 197.

78 Ayalon pointed out what private publishing during the *nahḍa* meant. Portraying the career of Ḫalīl Sarkis, publisher of the Beirut newspaper *Lisān al-Ḥāl*, he demonstrated the efforts, risks and passion of Arab printers who functioned as editors, publishers, journalists and booksellers at the same time. Ayalon 1998, 258–280; idem 2008, 563–569; and idem 2010, 73–93.

79 See Buessow 2002, 52; idem 2010, 107; Yehoshua 1974, 18–19; and Campos 2003, 243. For ʿĪsā's remark, see Ayalon 1995, 197, 225 (quoted from *Filasṭīn*, 21 March 1967).

which traded in the 'finest sorts of English tea',[80] and Mikhāʾīl Salfītī's shop in Jerusalem, about which there is no more information.[81] There were also offices selling *Filasṭīn* outside the Arab provinces and the newspaper had subscribers in New York and various cities in South America.[82]

Figure 3: Young Street Vendor of the newspaper *Filasṭīn* in Jaffa. Photo made by Frank Scholten, ca. 1922. (© The Netherlands Institute for The Near East (Leiden), Frank Scholten Collection; www.nino-leiden.nl/collections/frank-scholten-legacy)

Filasṭīn sold more than any other Palestinian newspaper during the Ottoman years, although the number of issues sold is not precisely known. Once, the editors reported about 1,121 registered subscribers, including 20 Jews[83] but daily street sales are not included in this number and so the actual spread of *Filasṭīn*

80 See *Filasṭīn*, 13 November 1912: 188/4. 'Iskandar Street' was the first part of Bustrus Street, named after Iskandar ʿAwād (Engl.: Howard), dragoman of Thomas Cook's travel agency in Jaffa. The second part of the street was named after Najib Bustrus who had properties there, and in *Filasṭīn*, the whole area is referred to as 'Bustrus Market' (*Sūq al-Bustrus*). For a description of the area, see my article 'Performances of Late Ottoman Modernity: Culture, Entertainment and Leisure Activities in Pre-World War I Jaffa' (forthcoming 2020).

81 See *Filasṭīn*, 9 January 1913: 206.

82 The agent for *Filasṭīn* in Chile was Miḫāʾīl Ḥannā Buyūk. For instance, see *Filasṭīn*, 27 April 1912: 131/3/1.

83 See *Filasṭīn*, 18 December 1912:198/3/1f.

must have been much wider. *Filasṭīn*, *al-Quds* and *al-Karmil* were all successful enterprises but *Filasṭīn* probably had the highest sale numbers.[84]

Ayalon estimates that there were about 6,000 newspaper readers in the Palestinian market during late Ottoman times, which was far below newspaper production in the centers of Arabic journalism: Cairo, Damascus, and Beirut.[85] Leading Arabic newspapers before World War I usually reached a distribution of 1,000–1,500 copies daily, and the highest numbers were reached by the Lebanese press with about 2,000–3,000 daily. The Beirut daily *Lisān al-Ḥāl* with a sale of 3,500 issues daily had the highest circulation rates of any Arabic newspaper in the Ottoman Empire.[86] Still, newspaper consumption was extremely low compared to European circulation numbers, which was noticed by Arab journalists: in 1912, *Filasṭīn* reported that the London *Times* sold up to 40,000 copies every day.[87]

2.3. Structure of Press Communication

The Front Page of Filasṭīn

Until 1911–1913, the newspaper consisted of four pages, and from 1914 onwards of six pages and extended advertisements, which were divided into five columns. On top of the front page, the logo was printed in Arabic (*Filasṭīn*) and French (*La Palestine*), the names of its editors ʿIsā al-ʿĪsā as official director (*mudīr mas'ūl*) and Yūsuf al-ʿĪsā as editor-in-chief (*ra'īs taḥrīr*), the address of the editorial building and price of the copy. The cosmopolitanism of the editors required it to give the date according to three calendars: the Gregorian, the Orthodox, and the Islamic calendar.[88]

The editorials, mostly signed with *Yā* for Yūsuf, discussed a broad spectrum of local, regional and international affairs. As 'evergreens', they discussed Ottoman unity and internal political crises in Istanbul, but also external crises and Ottoman military operations with a focus on the Balkan crisis, international diplomacy issues, the dismantling of Ottoman integrity through European imperialism and colonialism, juridical and educational reforms in Palestine, local cultural heritage, the development of infrastructure in the Jerusalem District and the Jaffa

84 Buessow 2010, 101, 107.
85 Ayalon 1995, 152; Buessow 2002, 51; and idem 2010, 107, n. 154.
86 The numbers are taken from Ilyās but quoted in Ayalon 1995, n. 63, 255; cf. Khalidi 1997, n. 44, 250.
87 See *Filasṭīn*, 25 September 1912: 275/1/4–2/1.
88 The Gregorian calendar was marked by the letter *ġayn* for *ġarbī* ('Western'), the Orthodox calendar with a *šīn* for *šarqī* ('Eastern'); the Islamic calendar followed last. I use the European (Gregorian) calendar to specify the date of the issues of *Filasṭīn* quoted, as this was the calendar listed first.

فلسطين
LA PALESTINE

Figure 4: Frontpage of *Filasṭīn* from 20 April 1912.

region, local agriculture, the orange trade and international exports, etc.[89] The editorials were also a platform on which the ʿĪsās demonstrated their pro-CUP agenda throughout the Ottoman years. They strictly refused any kind of ethnicity

89 In an editorial in 1911, summarizing their first six months of publication, Yūsuf al-ʿĪsā defined public security issues, elections, juridical reforms, tax issues, the orange trade and local agriculture as central themes. Editorials focused on events in Istanbul and throughout the Empire. See *Filasṭīn*, 15 July 1911: 51/1/1f.

policies, frequently condemned the separatist aspirations of Christian 'elements' in the Balkans and widely adapted the CUP's political terminology.[90]

After the editorial, there were reprints from the international press. Having enjoyed a cosmopolitan education, the ʿĪsās spoke Turkish and French, appreciated European literature and often quoted from English and French literature, philosophy and the press; but also from Lebanese, Egyptian and Damascene newspapers, and from the Turkish press, to provide information about events that took place at the center of the Empire, especially from *Tanin*, the CUP organ. After the editorials and the reprints, a number of regular sections followed that will be briefly introduced to demonstrate *Filasṭīn*'s role as a channel between editors, government and readers.

Monological Sections

After the editorial and reprints from foreign newspapers on the front page, several sections followed that were monological in character, to use Glaß's term. The 'Telegrams' section (*Teleġrāfāt*) printed the news from agencies, transmitted by telegraph, mostly on the second page, covering the events in Istanbul, the war fronts and international diplomacy. Then, the 'Various News' section (*Aḫbār Šattā*) reported on international politics in a short telegram style, and covered Greece, Serbia, Albania, Italy and so forth. Special attention here was given to Salonika and its Jewish population, but also to European and American cities, such as Vienna, Rome, New York, Chicago, Santiago de Chile and others.

After 'Telegrams' and 'Various News', 'Provincial News' section (*Aḫbār al-Ǧihāt*) followed, with information about the Middle East and Palestine. In terms of the Jerusalem District, the news focused on Gaza, Jerusalem, Bethlehem and Beit Jala, covering all fields of communal politics, police news, court judgments, and so on. Hebron and Beersheba, although part of the District, were rarely mentioned. 'Provincial News' covered Palestinian cities outside the Jerusalem District, such as Acre, Haifa, Nablus, Safed, Tiberias and Nazareth, much more briefly, and developments in northern Palestine were mostly completely omitted from the coverage. This reflects the north–south division between the Jerusalem District and the northern Sanjaks Nablus and Acre, which were commercially, administratively and culturally oriented towards South Lebanon and Syria. 'Provincial Newscovered all important centers of the Eastern Mediterranean: Beirut, Tripoli, Sidon, Zahle and Mount Lebanon, Damascus, Aleppo, Hama, Homs, the Hawran, Port Said, Alexandria, Cairo, etc. Occasionally, there were

90 For example, *Filasṭīn* adopted a clear anti-Albanian stance in the Albanian revolts, calling the Albanian 'rebels' *(ṯuwwār)*; in contrast to Naǧīb an-Naṣṣār's position in *al-Karmil*. See Campos 2015, 22, n. 22.

short notes about Baghdad, Mosul, Sanaa, Mecca, Medina or Jeddah, but the focus was on Lebanon, Syria and the Eastern Levant from Tripoli to Alexandria.[91]

Afterwards, the 'Local News' section (*Aḫbār Maḥallīya*) followed on *Filasṭīn*'s third page which covered the Jaffa *qaḍā*ʾ and was mostly written by the ʿĪsās and regular correspondents from Lod and Ramla. 'Local News' covered communal elections, cultural activities, educational institutions, religious foundations, infrastructure, commerce, reports of the land registry office, the *ṭābū*, including sale announcements for real estate and agricultural land, exports, Jaffa's port, Jewish migration into the District and male (illegal) emigration from the Jerusalem District through Jaffa's harbor to escape military conscription, hygiene and health issues, police news and security issues, such as reports on burglaries, robbery, brawls and murder. There were also extensive reports about welfare activities driven by local societies, such as those by Jaffa's Muslim Society for Piety and Welfare (*Ǧamaʿīyat al-Birr wa-l-Iḥsān*), and the donation campaigns that took place in solidarity with the Ottoman troops during military crises.[92] Extensive space was reserved in this section for 'Orthodox Matters' (*Šuʾūn Urṯūdūksīya*). Under 'The Orthodox Renaissance' (*an-Nahḍa al-Urṯūdūksīya*) and 'The Mixed Council' (*al-Maǧlis al-Muḫtalaṭ*), came regular reports about the state and strategies of Orthodox reform policies.[93]

Dialogical Sections

The dialogical potential of *Filasṭīn* as a communication channel unfolded through 'the letter' (*ar-risāla*) as a frequently used instrument for readers' participation. In this respect, *Filasṭīn* offered specific dialogical sections in which readers' contributions appeared. One of them was 'Products of Others' (*Baḍāʾiʿ Ġayrinā*), a column in which readers commented on the coverage, expressed personal positions or addressed Ottoman officials with demands. In the editors' words, 'Products of Others' was open to those who wanted to complain, 'regardless of whether this opinion or complaint is in compliance with or contrary to our ideas', they declared.[94]

Other dialogical sections were 'Another Speaks' (*Ġayrunā Yatakallam*), 'The Right Thing' (*aṣ-Ṣaḥīḥ*), and the 'Section of the Addressee' (*Bāb al-Ilā*) and the 'Section of the Sender' (*Bāb al-Min*), that *Filasṭīn* had explicitly opened, the editors claimed, to collect statements on the Zionist question and open a debate

91 Buessow has also identified the Arab Levant as its geographical focus. Buessow 2010, 100–127.

92 *Filasṭīn*, 13 June 1914: 327/5/3–4.

93 See also fields of communal politics represented in *Filasṭīn* as defined by Buessow 2002, 64–66, 74–85.

94 '*Siwāʾ kāna hāḏā r-raʾy aw tilka š-šakwā muṭābiqīn aw muḫālifīn li-afkārinā*'. *Filasṭīn*, 23 August 1911: 62/1/3.

between readers on that issue.[95] In general, the 'question-answer-dialogue section' (Ar. *masāʾil*), was extensively used in Arabic magazines as a didactic method to present knowledge and demonstrate principle cases.[96] In *Filasṭīn*, the sections *Bāb al-Ilā* and *Bāb al-Min* were designed to foster interaction, not as a method of presenting, but this section did not appear on a regular basis and most readers' letters on Zionism and other topics were published under 'Products of Others' and 'Another Speaks'.

The Evaluation of Readers Contributions in Press Analysis

Scholarship has addressed the question of the extent to which readers' contributions in the Arabic press during the late Ottoman period are to be considered a reliable source for press analysis. Glaß and Bucher considered the letter as important instrument in *public* communication.[97] On the contrary, Ayalon evaluated letters in the Arabic press as a 'non-authentic' source, since they underwent a process of selection and modification before publication or were even fabricated by the editors.[98]

I do recognize the editors' potential to modify, correct, reject or even 'fake' letters. However, it would not be appropriate to treat *Filasṭīn* as its editors' private club, and readers' contributions are central to my analysis since the ʿĪsās relied to a great extent on interaction with the public and welcomed readers' interventions. In dealing with the journalist's public responsibilities, they told readers when they published a modified version of a letter because of 'bad language' or when they shortened a letter that was unacceptably long. Sometimes they also announced reasons for refusing to publish a certain letter that was considered too provocative. At other times, they picked up a current incident with the justification that a considerable number of letters had asked them to cover the issue. From this it is clear that interaction with the public was a *central* reference for the editors' decisions on what to publish.

The letters published in *Filasṭīn* are an indicator of political networks and alliances between relevant actors, as will become evident in the case studies for the debate on Zionism and the Arab Orthodox Movement, which both show evidence of readers' participation on a large scale. While previous studies have

95 *Filasṭīn*, 4 November 1911: 83/2/1.

96 The question-answer-dialogue helped the Arab reader during the *nahḍa* to get used to the press as a new medium. During the Middle Ages, it was a traditional teaching method in the Islamic context, and was used in juridical sciences. European missionaries in the Middle East also used this form to teach the catechism and the Bible. In its nature, it was a faked dialogue with little freedom for dispute. Glaß 2004, 260–270.

97 Bucher 1986, 145; and Glaß 2004, 47–48. Glaß investigates the shape and structure of the 'readers' letter' in her survey of *al-Muqtaṭaf*. See Glaß 2004, 270–282.

98 Ayalon 1995, 159.

treated *Filasṭīn* as the ʿĪsās' private stage, the readers' letters treated in this study open a window onto the worldview of the upper segments of Palestinian society, which does not necessarily match the editors' political positions.

Advertisements and Global Consumption

The last page of *Filasṭīn* served as a section for illustrated advertisements of all kinds, used by local, regional and international trading companies and craftsmen of all denominations, which the editors depended on as an essential source of income.[99] Among regular advertisers from 1911 to 1914 were local shop keepers and owners of restaurants; such as the 'Restaurant of the Beautiful View' (*lūkanda al-manẓar al-ǧamīl*).

Apart from local entrepreneurs, *Filasṭīn* was a platform for advertizing a globalized consumption culture. From 1911 onwards, the London Grisham Company regularly offered life and health insurance. The distributor of Tuborg in Palestine and Syria was presented in every issue during the Ottoman period with a large logo of the Danish beer. The Swiss company Nestle occupied considerable space on the advertisement page, which gives a hint of the consumption culture of Western industrialized commodities in the Arab Provinces of the Ottoman Empire. Nestle milk, for instance, was promoted through the illustration of a well-fed baby boy, wearing a Tarzan leopard-skin costume and lifting an oversized tin of Nestle milk powder. A picture of a noble woman with a Roman hair style, wearing a tunic and holding up a Nestle chocolate placard was also often found on the ads page.

A Middle Eastern globalized consumption culture before World War I is also seen in *Filasṭīn*'s promotion of international health products and, from 1914 onwards, the major part of the advertisements page was occupied by medical and hygiene products. Local pharmacists promoted fish oil, cod liver oil and other medications that allegedly strengthened the nerves and the blood. On a regular basis, a medicine against migraine was advertised that supposedly strengthened the heart, and the picture of a woman contorted in pain demonstrated the product's targeted customer group. A Dr. Brawn, a Jewish dentist, regularly advertised false teeth.

In 1914, the space was opened up to a wider range of medical and luxury products produced in Europe, including Pilules de Blancard, French iron and iodine pills to encourage activity of the thyroid gland, and some kind of a 'beef extract' (*ʿuṣālat laḥm aṯ-ṯawr*) promoted to combat anaemia. There were advertisements for stimulating fluids, expensive mineral water, vitamin juices and restorative tonics such as the French Quina Laroche, which contained wine with quinine to prevent malaria and fever.

99 Ayalon reports that a banner advertisement for a French shipping company yielded 20 *qurūš* per issue. Ayalon 1995, 205.

Figure 5: Advertisement page in *Filasṭīn*.

Figure 6: Enlarged advertisement in *Filasṭīn* for milk powder of the Swiss company Nestle.

Figure 7: Filastin's advertisement for the Danish beer label Tuborg.

3. Central Concepts and Terminology in *Filasṭīn*'s Discourse

3.1. Missions and Priorities

Among *Filasṭīn*'s most outstanding priorities were the mission to 'educate the nation' as part of the new controversial political culture after the Young Turk Revolution, and the claim of the Arabic press to mediate between the government and the public, and act as the 'mouthpiece' of the people.[100] *Filasṭīn* was a child of this atmosphere. It became an important political actor in the District and, in 1912, *Filasṭīn* was praised by the newspaper *al-Iḫāʾ* ('Brotherhood') as 'progressive' (*rāqiya*) and 'the only newspaper that the Palestinians (*al-filasṭīnīyūn*) should accept and be proud of'.[101]

For the ʿĪsās, journalism was not a mere profession; they also saw themselves as on a moral mission as *educators* of local society. This tendency is also to be observed among the other publishing authors who used *Filasṭīn* as an 'educating forum' and saw themselves as 'soldiers through the pen' for the sake of 'enlightenment' (*tanwīr*), 'progress' (*taqaddum*) and 'civilization' (*tamaddun*), terms that were frequently promoted. Ǧurǧī Ḥannā Ḥazbūn, a Palestinian Christian from Bethlehem who had migrated to Chile and from there frequently contributed in *Filasṭīn*, stressed the role of newspapers as *agents of change*, 'movers of ideas' (*muḥarrik li-afkār*), the 'greatest obstacle against ignorance' (*aʿẓam rādiʿ li-l-ǧihāl*), and the 'most useful reminder for the people' (*anfaʿ muḏakkir li-n-nās*) to measure reality. While it was common in Chile to read newspapers on buses and people seriously discussed news and literature in public places, in Palestine, people read newspapers for entertainment or found them too expensive. If Palestinians only changed their reading culture, Ḥazbūn argued, they would understand that it was through the press that 'peoples were liberated' (*šuʿūb ḥurrirat*).[102] This view on the press as an agent of social and political change was shared by Yūsuf al-ʿĪsā, who stressed that the 'mission of the journalist in our country' (*waẓīfat a ṣ-ṣiḥāfī fī bilādina*) was not 'merely the spreading of the news' but to raise awareness for issues of public concern, and 'to create a public opinion and cause a subversion of moral values and habits' (*an yaḫluq raʾyan ʿāmman wa-yuḥdiṯ inqilāban fī l-aḫlāq wa-l-ʿādāt*).[103]

100 Campos has emphasized the impact of the post-revolutionary press on the emergence of civil identities and believes that the effect of the Revolution on the concept of an Ottoman-Palestinian society was much deeper than had previously been realized. Campos 2003, 237–279; and idem 2011, 133–165, 224–244.

101 *Filasṭīn*, 7 February 1912: 109/3/5.

102 *Filasṭīn*, 8 June 1912: 143/2/4–5.

103 See *Filasṭīn*, 15 July 1911: 51/1/2.

The Mindset of Modernist Values

The ʿĪsās took their educating mission very seriously and tried to impose a set of modernist values promoted as compatible with the 'spirit of this age' (*rūḥ hāḏā l-ʿaṣr*). In this respect, the concepts of 'modernization and reform' were identified as *the* supra-dominating element in *Filasṭīn*'s discourse imposed on every topic, be it with respect to education or migration to Palestine. On the second level of most propagated concepts was the imperial discourse on Ottomanism as the only national model considered acceptable in the present age. In contrast, other national models based on confessional, linguistic or ethnic bonds were viewed extremely negatively in *Filasṭīn* and portrayed as fanaticism. On the third level of the newspaper discourse was a significant notion of the 'public' and concepts of active citizenship. In this respect, the existence of 'public opinion' (*ar-raʾy al-ʿāmm*) was defined as an important feature of modernity, and 'public benefit' (*al-maṣlaḥa al-ʿāmma*) as the ideal motive for action. These three major concepts were commonly accepted by a circle of Palestinian modernist authors who used *Filasṭīn* as an 'educating forum', and they seem to have constituted a shared 'mindset' that was obviously considerably shaped by European standards of modernity. They promoted ideals and produced a set of arguments, a 'terminological corset', that one simply had to apply in any debate in order to follow the commonly accepted 'order of what to say or not to say' and which were imposed on negotiations of ethno-confessional relations in Palestine too, as the case studies will show.

Rhetoric and Language

Speaking of language forms and terminology, the rhetoric applied in *Filasṭīn* and its sharp controversial style will be briefly addressed. As was typical for the press of the Second Constitutional Era, there was a passion for dispute and combat in *Filasṭīn*, and a tendency towards polarization in debates so as to make texts attractive and entertaining to the reader. This also included the provocation of government officials and prominent personalities, who were often bluntly attacked, which seems to have been a reaction against the previous decades of strict censorship under Sultan Abdülhamid II that had strangled Arab journalism from the first 'Ottoman Law of Printing and Publishing' (1857) and the 'Law of Journalistic Publications' (1865). From the late 1870s, Arabic print production was under intensifying repression, the 'stick' of the central state, as Ayalon has expressed it, calling the Arabic press between 1878 and 1908 'impotent'.[104]

---

104 After the Ottoman defeat in the Russian War (1877–1878), the Empire lost Serbia, Bulgaria, Romania and Montenegro, which became independent, and the Caucasus to Russia. Sultan Abdülhamid reacted with severe centralization measures, dissolved the Parliament, abolished the Constitution (1878) and imposed strict censorship on Arab publishers. See Ayalon

A growing list of censored terms and issues suspected of presenting a challenge to the authority of the regime included words such as 'rebellion', 'independence', 'republic', 'liberty' and 'constitution' and were banned from newspapers, as were any terms related to rulership.[105] When, after the Revolution, censorship was lifted and concepts of liberty acquired a sacred dimension, the downtrodden creativity of Arab publishers led to the opposite: a very polarizing way of reporting that culminated in the practice of 'defaming' government officials and institutions – a phenomenon that Ayalon calls the 'beaten-angel-syndrome' of the Arabic press, which took the form of aggressive verbal beating and released the aggression of Arab intellectuals that had been hidden for over 30 years.[106] Be that as it may, in *Filasṭīn*, polarization was a central rhetorical device used to make texts appealing. This study cannot systematically explore the language styles of the modern Arabic press which has been so far a neglected field of research.[107] I shall only briefly mention typical stylistic devices commonly applied in *Filasṭīn* to prepare the reader for the translations from *Filasṭīn* that will be quoted in the coming sections.

Authors in *Filasṭīn* often used rhetorical questions or directly addressed the reader in other ways, and applied dichotomies to suggest to the reader what was to be considered as ideal or abominable, a strategy that I might call the 'praising-or-defaming-syndrome' as a typical style in the press of the Second Constitutional Era. Most authors applied a very emotional style with a passion for drama and a tendency to exaggeration that was supposed to entertain the reader and provoke his reactions. Authors applied figurative language and used countless examples of hyperbole, parallelisms as repetitions, biological metaphors, and

---

1995, 113. For 'stick and carrot' approach as a government strategy imposed on the press, see idem, 110–112.

105 In this respect, state censorship often distorted the context of press articles. For instance, the term mulk, written without vowels in Arabic as *m-l-k*, was forbidden in the Ottoman press since it can be interpreted to mean either *mulk* in the sense of 'political rule', or as *malik* in the sense of 'king'. In general, m-l-k was replaced with 'imperator', a term that defined foreign rulers. However, in Arabic, *mulk* also means 'private property', but Ottoman censors did not always understand the context of the Arabic text. So when the land registry office announced the sale of a piece of land, classified as 'private property' (*mulk*), the censor changed it to 'the sale of the imperator', which was an absurd distortion of the context. Ayalon 1995, 113f.

106 Many respected Arab intellectuals, such as Ǧurǧī Zaydān, editor of *al-Hilāl* in Cairo, and Rašīd Riḍāʾ, editor of *al-Manār* in Beirut, severely criticized this phenomenon in Arab journalism as an abuse of the freedom of expression and 'anarchy'. Zaydān spoke in this respect of freedom as being 'like a sword in the hands of a baby', reminding his colleagues to observe the limits of politeness in journalism. See Ayalon 1995, 132–134.

107 For standard references with regard to classical Arabic rhetoric (*balāġa*), see Mehren 1853, and on the development of rhetoric as a theory in classical Arabic sciences, see Bauer 2005, 2016. On rhetoric and persuasive style in modern Arabic texts, such as advertisements, and on the varieties of Arabic text, see Stock 1997, 2005.

allusions, referring to religious narratives and weaving into their arguments famous quotations from Qur'an and the Bible that the readership must have been familiar with, so as to give them a sacred aura.

The ʿĪsās were themselves known for hostile sarcasm and their passion for provoking prominent figures. They would use biological metaphors to portray certain political actors or social groups as collectively damaging local society, comparing them to dangerous diseases or microbes. They favored introducing their editorials with fables that carried a moral message before they led into the article's subject. The controversial element in their texts was *essential* to their intention to communicate with the readership and address 'public opinion'. This obvious pleasure in controversy and the 'aesthetics of controversial dispute' was a phenomenon in the modern Arabic press and was well reflected in *Filasṭīn.*

3.2. Modernist Discourse

3.2.1. The Sacred Mission of Modernization

At the top level of *Filasṭīn*'s discourse was clearly a 'modernization imperative', as I call it, with the 'mantra of reform' as an overall slogan and the omnipresent element in the newspaper coverage. This was a phenomenon in line with the *zeitgeist* of modernity on a global scale but also an expression of a particular form of Ottoman Arab-Palestinian modernism.

With regard to my topic of investigation, I have extracted 407 items on 'education and reform', and 368 items on 'progress' in *Filasṭīn*'s coverage from 1911 to 1914. Here, the terms of 'reform' (*iṣlāḥ*), 'enlightenment' (*tanwīr*), 'progress' (*taqaddum*), 'growth' or 'rise' (*tarqiya, tarraqin, raqy*) and 'civilization' (*tamaddun*) had acquired a sacralized meaning among Palestinian intellectuals, as becomes clear from their extensive application in the articles by editors and authors of letters alike. In line with the euphoria linked with the idea of progress, reform and modernization were seen as *the* means to transform local society comprehensively and push it towards modernity, which was articulated as the ultimate goal. It was believed that innovative technologies and economic and educational reforms would not only improve living standards but also advance the collective morals of society and lift it to a higher form of existence. Authors in *Filasṭīn* frequently called for infrastructural development by governmental authorities, and called upon Palestinian teachers and parents to educate the 'new youth' (*an-nāšiʾa al-ǧadīda*) in line with the values of 'the new age' (*al-ʿaṣr al-ǧadīd*), the Constitution and Ottomanism.

The field of 'educational reforms' constituted a central element in *Filasṭīn* before World War I and in its overall discussion of how to modernize Palestine, as will be outlined below. In the field of education, the West was clearly taken as benchmark for modernity standards. However, Palestinian authors created their own expressions of modernity that made sense in their local context, a form of 'glocalized' Arab-Palestinian trans-Ottoman modernism, I say. As an integral part of globalization, the circulation of modernity concepts gained momentum, creating 'hybrids' of local modernities in different environments.[108] With regard to these overlapping expressions of modernity, more in-depth research into the Arabic press is much needed in the future. What is certain is that the 'mantra of reform' was not limited to *Filasṭīn* but was discussed all over the Arab East, which fostered an Arab Ottoman discourse on 'progress' that was heavily espoused by state officials and the political and intellectual elites, as Norris notes, particularly after the 1908 Revolution.[109]

Apart from the field of educational reform, the 'modernization imperative' was also echoed in the debate on Zionist migration into Palestine, although, in *Filasṭīn* prior World War I, much more attention was given to 'education' as a content field than to Zionism. However, the question of whether Zionist migration was beneficial or damaging the development of Palestine was the central measurement for its approval or opposition. In the local press of the pre-World War I era, as seen in *Filasṭīn*, Zionist migration was supported where it was interpreted to be a driving force for civilizational progress, technical modernization and economic growth in Palestine, and it was opposed where it was interpreted as an exclusivist movement competing for local resources and seen as an obstacle to regional development. As will be outlined in detail in chapter IV, opponents of Zionism in Palestine also acknowledged with bitterness the progressive potential of the Zionist Movement, and Arab intellectuals sometimes used *Filasṭīn* to call upon Palestinians to work with the same discipline for the progress of Arab society that they observed among the Zionists as an awaking Jewish national movement, working as a 'vital and ambitious community' (*al-umma al-ḥayya wa-r-rāqiya*) for its own revival.[110]

Scope of Modernist Publishers

In *Filasṭīn*, apart from its editors, a range of mostly Muslim and Christian, but also Jewish, authors appeared as strong advocates of progress and modernization in Palestine. Often, these were teachers or intellectuals from Jerusalem, Ramallah, Bethlehem, Beit Jala or Gaza, who viewed the modernization of local education at lying at the heart of any other level of modernization. Among them

108 This 'heterogeneity effect' of globalization has been called 'glocalization'. See Robertson 1995, 25–44.

109 Norris 2013, 22–23, 34, 44–46. Aspects of the debate on modernization in the Arab East have also been explored by Watenpaugh, Shayegh and Dolbee (2010, 2012).

110 *Filasṭīn*, 9 August 1913: 261/2/2.

were the Protestant journalist Būlus Šiḥādeh (1882–1943) from Ramallah,[111] the Greek Orthodox Ḫalīl as-Sakākīnī, director of the Jerusalemite Constitutional School and *Filasṭīn*'s anonymous Jerusalemite correspondent. The Orthodox activists Ḥannā Ḥazbūn and Ǧibrān Maṭar from Beit Jala and the teacher Ǧurǧī al-Ḫūrī Ya'qūb from Beit Sahour frequently wrote on educational reform, as did Dimītrī Tādrus from Jaffa, a doctor named Ilyās Ṣawābīnī, about whom no data was found, and the Protestant director of the Friends School in Ramallah, Ḫalīl Ṭūṭaḥ (1877–1955).[112] The teacher and poet Iskandar al-Ḫūrī al-Baytǧālī (1888–1973) from Beit Jala, who strongly promoted female education, regularly published a column of moralist articles entitled 'Lilies of the Field' (*Zanābīq al-Ḥaql*), which will be introduced in chapter III. The Jerusalem notable Rāġib al-Ḫālidī frequently wrote on the reformation of Muslim institutions in Palestine,[113] and articles on educational reforms in Gaza were published by the teacher and reformer Ḥabīb Ḫūrī Ayūb.[114] These are only the tip of an iceberg of articles treating educational reform that appeared in *Filasṭīn*.[115]

Apart from that, a circle of modernist authors in *Filasṭīn* were Palestinian emigrants, mostly Christian, from the Bethlehem and Beit Jala region, who lived in North America, Chile and Mexico. As readers of *Filasṭīn* and frequently contributing to it with letters, they stayed in close contact with their home country and were well informed about local developments. They were Palestinian patriots and at the same time Ottoman modernists, and demonstrated in *Filasṭīn* the close connection of Palestinians in the New World to their homeland, documenting the establishment of patriotic activities.[116] In the New World, they pursued their fortune and reported on urban lifestyles in New York, Chicago,

111 Editor of the Jerusalemite newspaper *Mir'āt aš-Šarq* ('Mirror of the East') from 1919 onwards. See Norris 2013, 72f. and the entry for *Mirat al-Sharq* at the website of Jrayed – Arabic Newspaper Archive of Ottoman and Mandatory Palestine, hosted at the National Library of Israel in Jerusalem. https://web.nli.org.il/sites/nlis/en/jrayed/pages/Mirat-al-Sharq.aspx (accessed 15.08.2019).

112 For biographical data, see Hawārī 1979, 155, n. 485.

113 For information on his published books, see Hawārī 1979, 166, n. 514.

114 For biographical information, see Hawārī 1979, 131, n. 392.

115 See examples in *Filasṭīn*, 2 August 1911: 56/3/1–3; 23 September 1911: 71/2/2–3; 27 September 1911: 72/2–73/1; 1 November 1911: 82/3/5–4/2; 29 November 1911: 90/1/1–3; 13 March 1912: 119: 1/1–3; 16 March 1912: 120/1/3–2/1; 22 June 1912/147/2/5–3/2; 20 July 1912: 155/3/4–5; 3 August 1912: 159/3/1; 7 August 1912: 160/1/3–2/1; 31 August 1912: 167/1/4–2/1; 31 August 1912: 167/2/4–3/1; 2 October 1912: 176/3/4–5; 16 November 1912: 189/3/2–4; 7 June 1913: 243/1/5–2/2, and other issues.

116 *Filasṭīn*, 8 June 1912: 143/2/4–5. One Ilyās Miḫā'īl and Iskandar Šiḥādeh reported on the activities of the 'Palestinian Patriotic elites' (*nuḫbat riǧāl al-ġayra wa-l-ḥumīya al-waṭanīya*) and the foundation of the Palestinian Welfare Association in Chicago (*ǧama'iyat Filasṭīn al-ḫayrīya*). *Filasṭīn*, 1 February 1913: 209/3/2–3; 10 May 1913: 235/2–3. For another report on the progress of the Palestinians in Chicago, see *Filasṭīn*, 11 April 1914/323/2/4–5; and 15 April 1914: 324/3–4 (page not clear).

Santiago de Chile and Mexico City. Among them were Ḥannā Miḫā'īl Buyūk and other members of the Buyūk family, who reported about living conditions in Chile, and on the tense security situation in their hometown Bethlehem. This circle of emigrants elaborated on the need for reforms in Palestine, which they perceived as 'backward', comparing it with the 'advanced' standards in America.

Arab authors from Egypt also contributed to *Filasṭīn*'s modernist vision through editorials or reprints. For instance, the article 'Equality' (*al-Musāwāt*) by a female author, Ḥamīdeh Ṣabrī, treated the emancipation of women and was reprinted from the Egyptian *al-Ǧarīda* ('The Newspaper').[117] The ʿĪsās highly appreciated female literary contributions and favored publishing articles by 'the female Egyptian intellectual' (*al-adība al-miṣrīya*) Sārah al-Muhaybīh, who wrote in *Fatāt an-Nīl* ('Young Woman of the Nile') in a strongly anti-colonial tone and in favor of the Ottoman Porte on political issues.[118] Sabrī and Muhaybeh were not exceptions; in pre-1919 Egypt, a range of female intellectuals were active in journalism and wrote on the liberation of the Egyptian woman, as well as on the National Movement.[119]

The Centrality of Modernist Education and the Youth as Target Group

Educational reforms were at the top of the agenda of Arab Palestinian modernists in Filasṭīn, since, in the words of a local author, 'knowledge is the only medicine to heal our social diseases' (*al-ʿilm huwa ad-dawā' al-waḥīd allaḏī lā dawā' ġayrihi fī šifā' amrāḍinā l-iǧtimāʿīya*).[120] In line with this view, the Jerusalemite Muslim sheikh, writer and journalist ʿAlī ar-Rīmāwī defined 'the growth of science and education' (*taraqqī l-ʿilm wa-l-maʿārif*) as the essence of reform,[121] the precondition for progress in terms of civilization (*al-ʿumrān*), agriculture, industry and trade, and a new mentality in Palestinian inter-confessional relations. Rīmāwī argued that, 'if we really achieve this growth' (*taraqqaynā taraqqiyan ṣaḥīḥan*), Muslims, Christians and Jews will become 'one and the same thing' (*šay'an wāḥidan*), and that is so 'because we have understood the value of

117 *Filasṭīn*, 26 March 1913: 224/4/1.

118 *Filasṭīn*, 12 June 1912: 144/1/5–2/3; 22 June 1912: 147/1/4–2/1; 4 September 1912: 168/1/5–2/3. See also the article 'Words of a Woman' *(Ḫiṭāb Nisā'ī)* by a female Egyptian in *Filasṭīn*, 11 December 1912: 196/3/4–4/1.

119 For women's involvement and the links between gender and early Egyptian nationalism, see Baron 1991, 271–188; and idem 2005.

120 See *Filasṭīn*, 19 July 1911: 52/3/1–2.

121 In this article, Rīmāwī responded to a statement by ʿUṯmān Našāšībī published in *al-Munādī* under the title 'The Jerusalemites and Reform' (*al-Qudsīyīn wa-l-Iṣlāḥ*). Našāšībī opposed the *Beirut Reform Committees* who had criticized in the press the lack of engagement of Jerusalemite elites for Arab decentralization and warned against incitement to Arab–Turkish conflicts, which would only benefit European interests in the Middle East. See *Filasṭīn*, 22 March 1913: 223/1/5f.

the homeland, affection and unity'. Rīmāwī contined: 'As soon as we rely on these [values], the greed of the Europeans will disappear at our end.'[122]

The Egyptian nationalist Amīn ar-Rāfiʿī (1886–1927) from Zaqaziq, who frequently wrote in the national newspaper *al-Liwāʾ* ('The Standard')[123] and promoted Arab decentralization and Arab Muslim–Christian unity, stressed in *Filasṭīn* that history held evidence that nations only progressed if they took good care of the educational sector, and 'stretched out hands' to each other 'in favor of the education of our umma' (*fī sabīl tarbiyat ummatinā*). He was convinced that 'the social diseases' (*al-amrāḍ al-iǧtimāʿīya*) could be healed 'only through good education' (*illā bi-t-tarbiya aṭ-ṭayyiba*). This could come true, he stressed,

> if we ourselves take over tolerance and indulgence as a principle (*ʿalā mabdaʾ at-tasāhul wa-t-tasāmuḥ*) and if we cease to see the differences, and the Muslim calls the Christian 'my brother', and the Christian refers to the Muslim in the same way. But this can only happen through loyalty and if one understands the common interest of life (*fahm al-maṣlaḥa al-ḥayātīya*).[124]

Inter-confessional 'unity' was typically promoted in the Arabic press of the Second Constitutional Era as *the* precondition for the progress of society. Only through progressive education could 'the new youth' (*an-nāšiʾa al-ǧadīda*) be built who was to accomplish this vision; this was agreed among Palestinian authors. They defined the 'new youth' as the main target group to modernize Palestinian in a 'bottom-up-approach'. Apart from the 'new age', the notion of 'new youth' also became a popular slogan in the pre-World War Arabic press, as seen in *Filasṭīn*. 'Youth' was a feature in line with the global trend towards 'young movements', and it was also attributed to the 'Young Turks'. In Palestine of the Young Turk era, the youth became a 'resource for political activism', as Buessow has stressed.[125] Concepts of vitality and 'youthfulness' became central values among Arab urban elites, in contrast to the tradition in the Middle East to honor the elders. In 1911, Yūsuf al-ʿĪsā confirmed this, arguing that it was no longer enough to 'be proud of one's ancestors and content with the reputation of one's name and honor' as in the old days, since this could no longer represent what was needed in 'the age of hard work and running' (*ʿasr al-kadd wa-r-rakḍ*).[126] The notion that only a new and disciplined generation could create a powerful society,

122 *Filasṭīn*, 22 March 1913: 223/1/5–2/3. On ʿAlī ar-Rīmāwī, his Ottoman agenda and an Ottoman campaign against Arab separatism in 1916, see Tamari 2013–2014, 8–11.
123 Goldschmidt 2000, 163–164.
124 *Filasṭīn*, 18 June 1913: 246/1/4–5.
125 See Buessow 2011b, 61.
126 See *Filasṭīn*, 16 December 1911: 95/1/3. See also the section on a modern body culture in pre-World War I Palestine in my article 'Performances of Late Ottoman Modernity: Public Culture, Entertainment and Leisure Activities in Pre-World War I Jaffa' (forthcoming 2020).

capable of coping with the new age, was a central motive in *Filasṭīn* from 1911 to 1914, and most put forward by the Arab Palestinian Orthodox Movement.[127]

Western Educational Models

The above-mentioned modernist authors in *Filasṭīn* saw it as their mission to plant the spirit of modernity in the new youth through progressive schools, including education for females, and 'free classes' (*durūs maǧānīya*) for adults;[128] Western educational models were considered as the benchmark of progressive education in contrast to local schools, which were viewed as backward. *Filasṭīn*'s editors, for instance, particularly propagated the didactic methods of American institutions. In contrast to the 'enslavement of children' (*istiʿbād al-awlād*) in Palestinian schools, Yūsuf al-ʿĪsā propagated the liberal educational style followed in American schools as *the* raw model that would create mature thinking among individuals, and he fostered an understanding of universal children's rights, such as the right to free time, and mental and physical recreation. The American understanding of 'total freedom' (*al-ḥurrīya al-muṭlaqa*), ʿĪsā explained, sought to implement freedom for 'men, women, children and even animals' and in the schools, it had 'liberated the pupils from the bond of cowardliness, shame and fear'. Instead of intimidating students, teachers made them 'hold the head up high' so pupils would 'fear nothing but God and their duty'.[129] A boy was accepted as 'partner' (*rafīq*) in a conversation with an adult,[130] which stimulated his 'mature thinking' (*al-fikr al-muṭlaq*) and introduced him to 'manhood' (*ruǧūlīya*), ʿĪsā explained.[131] On the institutional level too, American associations defend students' interests and 'provide them with the same rights' to physical and mental recovery enjoyed by adult men, ʿĪsā explained,

127 One of the key strategies of this movement was to mobilize the youth in line with the spirit of the new age as to reform the Orthodox Church, as is visible in the writings of the activist Ḫalīl as-Sakākīnī from Jerusalem, who appropriated major political concepts of the Second Constitutional era, including proto-nationalist terminology, to promote the Orthodox renaissance in Palestine. For this topic, see my article 'The Appropriation of Political Concepts in Ḫalīl as-Sakākīnī's Discussion of the 'Orthodox Renaissance' (1908-1914)' in which I have discussed a political pamphlet published by Sakākīnī in 1913 through which he tried to mobilize the Orthodox youth (forthcoming 2020).

128 For example, in Jaffa, a priest called Gregorius regularly offered in his home for free lectures covering all kinds of scientific, historical and religious topics, such as 'the global history of revolutions' and apocalyptic ideas, and contemporary political issues such as the 'Oriental Question' (*al-masʾala aš-šarqīya*). *Filasṭīn* regularly advertized these classes under 'Local News'. *Filasṭīn*, 23 November 1911: 97/4/1–2; 27 December 1911: 98/4/2; 30 December 1911: 99/4/2; 3 January 1912: 100/4/2; and 6 January 1912: 101/4/2.

129 *'Qad fakkū talāmīḏatahum min ribāṭ al-ǧubn wa-l-ḫaǧl wa-l-ḫawf wa-ǧaʿalū minhum ruʾasāʾ murtafiʿa lā taḫšā illā llāh wa-l-wāǧib'*. See *Filasṭīn*, 22 February 1913: 215/1/1.

130 *'ar-Raǧul hunāka iḏā ḥādaṯa waladahu ẓanna annahu rafīquhu'*. See *Filasṭīn*, 22 February 1913: 215/1/1.

131 *Filasṭīn*, 22 February 1913: 215/1/1.

for he [the student] arrives at ease and with a clear mind [from school] and without thoughts keeping him busy and exhausting his little body with work. For he can spend his evening totally free as a sparrow out of its cage … and so he can, on the [next] day, return to his nest and get on with all the duties of school he is obliged to do. … They said that man rests at night in his house; so how can the child not rest as he does when his body is weaker than a man's body.[132]

In contrast to this, ʿĪsā criticized, local traditions degraded students through punishment and thus, in Palestinian schools, the fear of punishment prevented them from studying well.[133] In *Filasṭīn*, the 'Constitutional School' (*al-Madrasa ad-Dustūrīya al-Waṭanīya*), established in 1909 in Jerusalem by the famous Palestinian Orthodox activist, pedagogue and humanist Ḫalīl as-Sakākīnī was basically seen as the only local positive role model for modern education and will be briefly referred to here.[134] *Filasṭīn* emphasized that this school accepted students from any confession and 'teaches each pupil the roots of his confession' (*tuʿallim kull tilmīḏ uṣūl maḏhabihi*).[135] Being devoted to multi-confessional Ottoman patriotism in line with the 'spirit of the age', Sakākīnī's institution was most appealing to local elites of all faiths during the late Ottoman era. *Filasṭīn*'s Jerusalemite correspondent praised Sakākīnī's 'effective service for the progress of the youth in this homeland' (*al-ḫidma al-fiʿilīya fī sabīl raqy nāšiʾat haḏā l-waṭan*),[136] and it was hoped that this would raise 'the spirit of Ottoman education' (*rūḥ at-taʿlīm al-ʿuṯmānī*) and 'the sense of patriotism among the new generation' (*rūḥ al-waṭanīya fī an-nāšiʾa al-ğadīda*).[137]

Indeed, Sakākīnī's pedagogical approach was unconventional, if not radical, and it was portrayed as *the* counter-model to local schools. Sakākīnī was among the first pedagogues in Palestine to ban physical punishment in school. He presented interactive didactic methods and secular education, providing lessons in Arabic, Turkish, English and French language, in photography, music and sports.[138] According to *Filasṭīn*, the liberal teaching style at the Constitutional School lifted the 'good morals' (*al-aḫlāq al-karīma*) among the young people, and strengthened their 'self-confidence' (*taqwiyat an-nafs*) instead of 'humiliating them' (*lā iḏlālahā*). It promoted their talents instead of fighting them, and finally fostered 'the spirit of independence, bravery and manliness' (*rūḥ al-*

---

132 *Filasṭīn*, 22 February 1913: 215/1/2.
133 *Filasṭīn*, 22 February 215/1/3–4.
134 For the life of Sakākīnī and his activities in various cultural and political fields, see my article 'The Appropriation of Political Concepts in Ḫalīl as-Sakākīnī's Discussion of the 'Orthodox Renaissance' (1908–1914)' (forthcoming 2020).
135 *Filasṭīn*, 2 October 1912: 176/3/4–5.
136 *Filasṭīn*, 2 October 1912: 176/3/4; 11 May 1912: 135/3/4.
137 *Filasṭīn*, 31 January 1912: 107/2/5.
138 *Filasṭīn*, 2 October 1912: 176/3/4.

istiqlāl wa-aš-šuǧāʿa wa-ar-ruǧūlīya) through sports and 'military exercises' (*tamārīn ʿaskarīya*), ʿĪsā explained.[139]

3.2.2. The Other Side of the Coin: Palestinian 'Backwardness'

The 'modernization imperative' promoted in *Filasṭīn* included, as becomes clear from ʿĪsā's discussion of educational models, a negative image of the Palestinian reality, presented as the other side of the coin in part of the discourse on 'modernization and progress'. Palestinian modernists evaluated local conditions according to a 'standard package' of modernity, with the West as measure, presenting a dichotomous view commonly accepted among local elites, according to which the image of an 'enlightened' West was contrasted with a narrative influenced by a colonial outlook on the world: the narrative of an underdeveloped and 'erratic' East living in 'darkness', in a state of 'backwardness' (*taḫalluf, taʾaḫḫur*), 'standstill' (*ǧumūd*), 'lethargy' (*ḫumūl*) and 'apathy' (*futūr, wahn*), to apply the jargon of *Filasṭīn*. This lethargy, as it was seen by Palestinian authors, penetrated both society and individuals' minds. Apart from merely introducing new technologies and accomplishing and economic growth, the Palestinian state of mind had to be reconstructed through progressive school and social education – so thought the authors from the elite segment of local society who had themselves mostly enjoyed a cosmopolitan education and felt uncomfortable with the developmental gap between 'West' and 'East'.

The Mental 'Decline' of 'Easterners' as a Motive

To demonstrate how Palestinian modernists interpreted the so-called 'decline of Easterners' (*inḥiṭāṭ aš-šarqīyīn*), which was, in their perception, a collective mental symptom, somehow rooted in the Eastern mentality, I present some selected examples from *Filasṭīn* that reveal the emotional discomfort of the authors, who seemed to suffer from an inferiority complex as a result of the constant comparison with the (Western) form of modernity that the East, in their view, was so far away from.

The anonymous author of an article in 1912 saw Palestine as 'in decline to the lowest point' (*munḥaṭṭa ilā ḥaḍīḍ aṣ-ṣaġāra*). He not only defined its agriculture, economy and trade as undeveloped, but also viewed its society as completely corrupted: children were brought up according to the principles of 'fawning' (*tazalluq*) and 'selfishness' (*anānīya*), teachers were liars, and the country on the whole was in need of 'light and guidance' (*nūr wa-hudā*). The author saw the solution in the implementation of 'the modern educational styles and new regulations that requires this age' (*muḥtāǧa ilā asālīb at-tarbiya al-ḥadīṯa wa-l-*

139 *Filasṭīn*, 2 October 1912: 176/3/4.

qawānīn al-ǧadīda allatī taṭlubuhā haḏā l-ʿaṣr).[140] Another author, a Christian Palestinian emigrant from Beit Jala, expressed his disappointment after his return. Although he had quickly got used to the improved standards of hygiene and a 'system that runs exactly' (*an-niẓām sāʾiran bi-kull daqqa*) and felt treated well abroad, he was always homesick for 'Palestine, my Homeland' (*waṭanī Filasṭīn*). Returning on the 'wings of hope' following the restoration of the Constitution, he had expected to find the 'light of freedom' (*nūr al-ḥurrīya*), but complained that he ended up very disappointed to see his hometown in a state of dirtiness, cultural backwardness and apathy, with people hanging around 'killing time'.[141]

Ǧurǧī al-Ḫūrī Yaʿqūb on the Need for Positive Raw Models in Society

The writings of Ǧūrǧī al-Ḫūrī Yaʿqūb in *Filasṭīn*, a teacher from Beit Sahour and an activist in the Orthodox Movement, reflect the dichotomous 'Western'–'Eastern' worldview that was influenced by the 'colonialist perspective' on the East and was presented by local authors in the pre-World War I Arabic press. In his editorial 'Morals and Traditions' (*al-Aḫlāq wa-l-ʿĀdāt*), he defined the East as synonymous with 'ignorance' (*ǧahl*), and the 'the Orientals' (*aš-šarqīyūn*) as lazy and lacking ambition. According to Yaʿqūb, the local youth had no positive role models to inspire them since Palestinians systematically destroyed the quest for knowledge in their children. Addressing 'especially parents and teachers', Yaʿqūb called for a change from below.[142] Relying on pedagogical and psychological insights, he elaborated:

> Whenever mankind climbs the ladder of humanity (*kullamā tadruǧ al-insān fī sullam al-insānīya*), his mind rises with him… Every day, there is new evidence bearing witness to his progress (*yašhad bi-taqaddumihi*) and his intellectual radius broadens (*tawassuʿ dāʾirat ʿaqlihi*)… except among our Eastern people (*illā šaʿbunā aš-šarqī*)!… Whenever they climb the ladder of humanity, their minds degenerate (*kullamā tadruǧ fī sullam al-insānīya yanḥaṭ ʿaqlahu*)… and their ability to comprehend narrows (*yaḍīq idrākahu wa-tataqayyadu*)… Here, I intend to explain the backwardness of man in the East through observation and education, not philosophy (*aqṣid … aš-šarḥ taʾaḫḫur al-insān fī š-šarq ʿan ṭarīq an-naẓar wa-t-tarbiya lā ʿan ṭarīq al-falsafa.*)… since learning through observation… and… the observation of role models… has a greater influence on the student than the reading of dozens of books… ever could… The difference between Europeans and Easterners [in this respect] is tremendous… Here, I want to reveal to the Easterner the harmfulness of his actions in the education of the new youth through [cognitive] observation (*aradtu an ubīn li-š-šarqī sūʾ aʿmālihi fī tarbiyat an-nāšiʾa al-ǧadīda ʿan ṭarīq an-naẓar*).

140 *Filasṭīn*, 27 March 1912: 123/3/4.
141 *Filasṭīn*, 19 April 1913: 231/3/1–3.
142 *Filasṭīn*, 11 October 1913: 279/1/5–2/2.

...And so, I say that parents have the greatest responsibility since they are the only instrument (*al-āla al-waḥīda*) through which the child climbs the ladder of the social body (*yatadarrağ bihā l-walad fī sullam al-hay'a al-iğtimā'īya*). As soon as the infant is alive, its endeavor awakes to linger on every little thing in his environment... and to observe everything that is happening in front of him (*yuḫlaq ma'ahu al-mayl an-naẓarī ilā kullamā yağrī amāmahu*)... Although the child does not understand the things that his parents do out of habit ... he imitates everything in [their] language, general behavior and morals...

As soon the child is out of the cradle... he will notice that older children look down on him. Older people chase him away as they deem themselves superior to him and they make fun of him if [he as] a child sits with his father. The man [the father] is embarrassed when the child follows him and caresses him... and chases him away, saying: 'Stupid, get lost and play with your own sort...' So, the child is left in charge of himself (*taḥta ri'āyat nafsihi*). Yet, the soul constantly urges evil. So he spends the days roaming around. He learns only laziness and apathy (*yata'allam al-kasl wa-l-baṭāla*); and above all, impertinence and brutality (*fawqa ḏālika al-qiḥa wa-širāsat al-aḫlāq*)... They [the children] destroy olive groves and plantations, they pluck out the branches and steal... Just for fun and to pass the time, they destroy birds' nests, without empathy or regret (*bidūna šafaqa wa-lā ḥanān*).

Then, when a boy enters school, he is already afraid as he imagines the teacher is brutal executioner who wants to tear him apart (*yataṣawwar fī šaḫṣ al-mu'allim ğallādan qāsiyan yurīd an iftirāsahu*). He takes in the teacher's every move and with every movement, he says [to himself]: 'He will beat me.' When the student comes to school in the morning... the teacher receives him with a sharp look that shows the extent of his contempt and plants fear and horror into the student's heart... and he is not aware that, by this, he makes the student developi an aversion [to the teacher]... and dreariness instead of affinity (*al-waḥša 'iwaḍ al-ulfa*)... The father is not interested in his son's aversion to school and thinks that his son does not have an inclination to school (*yaẓunn anna waladahu lā yamīl al-madrasa*) and that knowledge is not necessary (*lā yağib al-'ilm*). He criticizes his stupid mind (*yantaqid ġilāẓat 'aqlihi*) and throws him into one of the factories and under the burden of the... worker in the workshops.

By this, he wipes out the sense of patriotism and his desire for knowledge... and distances him from enlightenment and progression (*bi-ḏālika yuṭfī' fīhi rūḥ al-waṭanīya wa-r-raġba fī ntiqā' al-'ulūm wa-l-ma'ārif wa-yub'iduhu 'an at-tanawwur wa-l-irtiqā'*). It is no secret that damage is caused as he spends his days in idleness, strolling around in the streets, coffeehouses and taverns caring for nothing but his worldly pleasures (*yaqḍī nahār al-baṭāla fī t-tağawwul fī aš-šawāri' wa-l-qahāwī wa-l-ḥānāt lā yahtamm bi-ġayr mulaḏḏātihi ad-dunyawīya*)...

Having outlined the lack of appreciation for learning that he saw in the local culture of private education and teaching, Ya'qūb's judgment on Palestine was severe. He concluded:

Considering these observations, it is no wonder that our Eastern people (*ša'bunā aš-šarqī*) are doomed to humiliation and decline (*aḏ-ḏall wa-l-inḥiṭāṭ*). They do not know the path of right guidance or understand the meanings of reform (*lā ya'rif ilā ṭarīq al-hudā sabīlan wa-lā yafham min al-iṣlāḥ ma'nāhu*). Our morals are degraded, our ideas confused.'[143]

Internal Division and Lacking Collective Solidarity

Another motive that was presented by Palestinian authors when complaining about what they felt to be an element in local backwardness was a lack of communal solidarity (*taḍāmun*) and patriotic feeling (*'āṭifa waṭanīya*) as a mental symptom among 'Easterners' they hindered them from working towards common progress. This was a sensitive issue since these authors compared the Palestinian 'failure' with the 'effectiveness' of the Zionist Movement in Palestine, which, as they saw it, was rooted in the Zionists' strong sense of community. For instance, a secondary school teacher from Jerusalem, Muṣṭafā Tamar, complained in his article 'The Disorder of the Social Body in the East' (*Iḍṭirāb al-Hay'a al-Iǧtimā'īya fī š-Šarq*) about internal fragmentation and discord as a general feature of Eastern societies.[144] Yūsuf al-'Īsā expressed a similar view about the lack of a sense of community among the Arabs. While Europeans were never satisfied in their striving for knowledge, he declared, the Arabs never got enough of grasping for money and property.[145] He saw a sense of mutual solidarity among Zionists that he missed among Palestinians and commented on the election of Jewish delegates from Jerusalem, Jaffa and some settlements to represent the Yishuv in Palestine at the International Zionist Congress, saying:

> We can only be fascinated by this vital and advanced community (*hāḏihi al-umma al-ḥayya wa-r-rāqiya*) for the sake of its individual members, and is miraculously persisting in its existence and frightening in its mutual solidarity. We wish we could see such a sense for cooperation and solidarity at our end too; not only... between one city and another, or between one family and another, but between one brother and another.[146]

Yūsuf missed not only a sense of community among Palestinians but also interest in their own cultural heritage, even 'among the intelligent' (*fī qulūb al-aḏkīyā'*). In contrast, he mentioned the 'brilliant success' (*naǧāḥan bāhiran*) of the 'Hebrew *nahḍa*' through the efforts of the Zionist Movement, which had achieved the revival of Hebrew as the language of Jewish education and daily life, and as a modern language that 'had risen from the grave thanks to the cooperation and unity of its people' (*qad qāmat min qabrihā bi-faḍl ta'āḍud wa-ttiḥād abnā'i-hā*).[147]

143 *Filasṭīn*, 23 August 1913: 265/1/2–2/1.
144 *Filasṭīn*, 20 March 1912: 121/3/3–2/1.
145 *Filasṭīn*, 13 March 1912: 119: 1/1–3.
146 *Filasṭīn*, 09 August 1913: 261/2/2.
147 *Filasṭīn*, 27 July 1912: 157/1/3–5.

In this Arab-Palestinian discourse, as becomes clear, the image of the 'activist' Zionist with a Western mentality was set in contrast to the 'laziness' of Palestinians as those who lacked a sense of discipline. Ǧibrān al-Maṭar, an Orthodox activist from Beit Jala, defined 'unity' as a condition for progress, which he missed in a Palestine that he saw in 'stagnation' (*ǧumūd*).[148] The cultural awakening that was recently occurring was accomplished through the contribution of the 'active migrants' and what Palestinians took over from 'European civilization' (*at-tamaddun al-awrūbī*), he lamented. He identified European and Zionist migrants as those who were about to wake Palestine up 'from its deep sleep' (*hum allaḏīna ayqaẓūhā min subātihā l-ʿamīq*), commenting especially on the lively Hebrew press and effective Jewish organizations:[149]

> Do you know, dear reader, that there are today no fewer than 30 settlements or villages owned by these hardworking migrants (*fī ḥawzat haʾulāʾ al-muhāǧirīn an-našīṭīn*) who have many ways, be it on the ideational, material or artistic level… And do you also know that this migration is making rapid, astonishing and strange progress and that Hebrew will become after a while the official language of this country? And do you know that those [migrants] have progressive schools (*madāris rāqiya*) and many important newspapers? And do you know that they have strong associations (*ǧamaʿīyāt qawīya*) supporting them? …[150]

Maṭar presented a counter-image of the 'scattered' Palestinian who, in his view, was incapable of working out a united agenda. He set out an appeal to the reader:

> Knowing all of this, rise from your sleep and stand there as a dam (*saddan manīʿan*) preventing the flood. Your peoples are divided, oh Palestine (*iḫtalafat šuʿūbuki yā Filasṭīn*). Their … principles have diverged (*tabāyanat … mabādīhim*), their languages and confessions multiplied, their [individual] circumstances are diverse; manifold are their schools and there is no common word. So, it is bound to be a wonder if you progress (*iḏā taqaddamti*) while you remain in this state.[151]

Ḫalīl as-Sakākīnī also missed local potential for innovations and applied a colonialist outlook on the Middle East, speaking of the East as a 'sick man' (*marīḍ*). The East, he complained, only 'borrowed' concepts and did not develop an authentic versions of them, and the local understanding of reform was 'fantasies and pipe dreams' (*aḍġāṯ al-aḥlām wa-awhāman*):

> The concept of reform itself is not a local one and is not something that would come to the Eastern mind unless it came to him from outside. And before, the Constitution was nothing but a borrowed costume because the Easterner lost his strength a long time ago.

148 *Filasṭīn*, 31 August 1912: 167/1/4.
149 *Filasṭīn*, 31 August 1912: 167/2/1.
150 *Filasṭīn*, 31 August 1912: 167/2/1.
151 *Filasṭīn*, 31 August 1912: 167/2/1.

> He has become weak in his opinions and decisions and indifferent ... and he is like a sick man babbling into his mattress.[152]

Referring to the motif of the 'sick man', Sakākīnī picked up the image of the Ottoman Empire as the 'sick man of Europe' that was circulating in the Western press and was brought up by the Russian Tsar Nicholas I in the context of the Crimean War in Russian-British correspondence in 1853.[153] This statement demonstrates how much the worldview of Palestinian modernists was shaped by the East–West dichotomy and deep identity conflicts. Torn between a passion for reviving Arabic literature and an authentic Palestinian culture, the local elites felt alienated from the traditions of their society, which caused them permanent internal discomfort, as seen from the texts.

3.3. Imperial Discourse

3.3.1. Ottoman Constitutionalism versus Despotism

At the second level of *Filasṭīn*'s discourse were the principles of 'Ottoman patriotism' (*al-waṭanīya al-ʿuṯmānīya*) and 'Constitutionalism' (*ad-dustūrīya al-ʿuṯmānīya*), presented as untouchable foundations of late Ottoman-Arab modernity. In the aftermath of the Revolution of 1908, the slogan 'liberty, equality, fraternity' (*ḥurrīya, musāwāt, iḫāʾ*) was chanted in Arab cities and reflected the high hopes of the local elites for political change. The Arabic press quickly adapted a dichotomous discourse according to which Ottoman Constitutionalist rule was equal to 'justice' (*ʿadl*) and legitimate governance while the pre-revolutionary era of Sultan Abdülhamid was presented as political 'oppression' (*ẓulm*) and 'despotism' (*istibdād*) through arbitrary rule.

Filasṭīn integrated this dichotomous political discourse and imposed its arguments on the debate on Palestinian group relations. Especially in terms of the minority rights of Ottoman Christian and Jews, the protection of the 'the spirit of the Constitution' (*rūḥ ad-dustūr*) was made the central argument. Specifically,

152 *'Bal fikrat al-iṣlāḥ nafsuhā laysat waṭanīya ayy laysat mimā yaǧūl fī fikr aš-šarqī wa-lā mimā yaḫṭur lahu fī bāl bal hiya wārida min al-ḫāriǧ kamā anna ad-dustūr qablahā lam yakun illā ḥulla aǧnabīya mustaʿāra li-anna aš-šarqī qad zāyalathu quwwatuhu al-ḥayyawīya min ān baʿīd fa-aṣbaḥa ʿāǧiz ar-raʾy mutaḫāḏil al-ʿazm ... wa-huwa ka-l-marīḍ yatamalmal fī far-āšihi.' Filasṭīn*, 16 April 1913: 230/3/2.

153 British ambassador Sir Hamilton Seymour reported in a letter to Lord Russell in 1853 that the Tsar had referred to the Ottoman Empire as a 'sick man' and as a man 'who has fallen into a state of decrepitude'. *The New York Times* picked up this label in an article on 12 May 1860 and it stuck and became a popular reference. See Hughes 2017, 546f; and de Bellaigue 2001. http://www.nybooks.com/articles/2001/03/08/turkeys-hidden-past/#fnr1 (accessed 28. 10. 2017).

the discourse on constitutional rights and civic equality was systematically applied by Arab Orthodox activists in their anti-clerical campaign in order to legitimize politically the cause of the Orthodox Movement in the Jerusalemite Patriarchate, establish a discourse on Arab 'Orthodox rights' (*ḥuqūq al-milla al-urṯūḏuksīya*), and generate public support for this local movement.[154] The Arab Orthodox case demonstrates that the discourse on Ottoman patriotism and Constitutionalism spilled over into local debates and was instrumentalized to boost local reform movements. The emergence of the Arab Orthodox rebellion was rooted in the aftermath of the 1908 Revolution and adopted its political arguments and terminology. Its supporters presented this rebellion as a 'constitutional revolution' on the local level, whereas the privileges of the Patriarch, granted in the imperial *berat*s, were portrayed as an outdated relic from the time of Sultan Abdülhamid's 'despotic rule'. Picking up the discourse on Abdülhamidian despotism, which was widespread in the Ottoman press, Arab Orthodox activists defined the clerical hierarchy as a 'despotism of the monks' (*istibdād ar-ruhbān*) that was incompatible with the Ottoman Constitutionalist government since

> it is difficult to maintain a kingdom of priests within a democratic Empire (*min aṣ-ṣaʿb ibqāʾ mamlaka ruhbānīya ḍimna mamlaka dīmūqrāṭīya*); especially since obviously the monks have decided that the Constitution will not enter the gates of their monastery (*ar-rahbana qarrarat ʿadam duḫūl ad-dustūr abwāb dayrihā*).[155]

3.3.2. Overlapping Ottomanism, Arabism and Palestinian Patriotism

Apart from presenting the dichotomy of Ottoman constitutionalism versus Abdülhamidian despotism, the pre-World War I Palestinian Arabic press typically promoted multiple collective identity models. As seen from *Filasṭīn*, multi-confessional Ottomanism existed alongside an Arab identity and local Palestinian patriotism, which created its own alterations to an Arab Palestinian Ottomanism. These different identity models were still fluid during 1911–14 – sometimes overlapping each and sometimes in rivalry. Without going too much into detail, I shall outline below how and in what context Arab identity and Ottomanism were fostered in *Filasṭīn*, what function these identity models had in the thinking of individual authors, and what concept of 'Palestine' was presented between 1911 and 1914.

154 For instance, see *Filasṭīn*, 4 May 1912: 133/3/5–4/1.
155 *Filasṭīn*, 19 August 1911: 61/2/2–4.

Separation of Ottomanism and Arabism

In *Filasṭīn*, an Arab revival on the *cultural* level and the 'Arab Renaissance' (*an-nahḍa al-ʿarabīya*) were passionately supported. The ʿĪsās were very aware of their 'Arabness', strongly identified with Arab history and language, and, despite being Christians, they felt strong bonds with the Islamic tradition of the Arab East. Here, the Arab cultural affiliation of *Filasṭīn* must be distinguished from its Ottoman identification and a multi-confessional Ottomanism, which was the only acceptable *political framing*; other forms of national organization were strictly rejected in *Filasṭīn*. The ʿIsās were active supporters of the CUP, and whenever a political crisis arose in Istanbul, they feared a coup against the Young Turks. For them, and other Christians and Muslims publishing in *Filasṭīn*, the integrity of the Empire was an imperative, and the only guarantee that 'order' and 'equality' between the different 'elements' (*ʿanāṣir*) of society could be maintained, especially during the years of instability and military crises before World War I. In this sense, The ʿĪsās strictly avoided using the term 'minorities' (*aqallīyāt*) in reference to confessional groups in the Ottoman Empire, and refused to adopt European conceptions of non-Muslims as 'minorities'. In their view, it was part of the imperialist powers' agenda to interfere in Ottoman internal affairs in order to break traditional Christian–Muslim bonds in the Arab East. In sharp contrast to their approval of Western-style modernization in the fields of technology, education, etc., the ʿĪsās responded with a very hostile anti-Europeanism to the European press's discourse of 'Muslim fanaticism' towards non-Muslim groups in the Arab East, which was, as they saw it, an 'invention' of European politicians.[156]

Instrumental Ottomanism

It also should be stressed that the notion of Ottomanism presented in *Filasṭīn* was quite an 'instrumental nationalism'. As the ʿĪsās explained it, the central government was the executive power that could secure the political integrity of the Empire. In 1912, they declared that

> it [the central government] is nothing but an executive committee (*laysat illā hayʾa iğrāʾīya*) to govern the nation and consider its affairs. And it is tasked with two things: the protection of security in its territories and the defense of the homeland's borders.[157]

From the perspective of the authors publishing in *Filasṭīn*, there was no authority other than the Ottoman state that could guarantee public order and security, and implement reforms to boost the modernization of Palestine! Once an anony-

156 See *Filasṭīn*, 3 February 1912: 108/1/1–3.

157 *Filasṭīn*, 6 December 1912: 92/1/2.

mous Jewish author who signed himself as 'a free Ottoman' (*ʿuṯmānī ḥurr*) set 'unity' as precondition for 'progress', demanding that

> we harshly oppose all those who spoil the purity of the people (*yuʿakkirūn ṣafāʾ al-ahālī*) during a time when what we need most is harmony (*al-iʾtilāf*) and solidary (*aš-šuġl al-mutaḍāmin*). Only on this is the progress of the country based (*bi-hi waḥdahu taraqqī l-bilād*).[158]

This is not as to claim that the loyalty to Ottomanism declared by the authors in *Filasṭīn* was hypocritical. The Palestinian elites simply could not see that there were any other political alternatives in the light of contemporary military crises, separatist movements and the interference of the imperialist powers. It is important to note that the discourse on Ottoman unity in *Filasṭīn* was primarily designed to protect stability in a heterogeneous Palestinian society and to serve the development of Palestine. The Ottomanism presented by so many contributors in *Filasṭīn* was *instrumental* but for the time being also *unconditional*, and, until 1914, Arab proto-nationalism was not seen as an alternative to Ottomanism by Palestinian actors.

How Much Decentralization for Palestine?

In *Filasṭīn*, it was warned from Arab separatism and political decentralization. The editors repeatedly confirmed that they defended equality between Muslims and Christians as well as between Arabs and Turks. They expressed strong opposition against the preference for Turkish over Arabic in administration but also declared that a strong power (*sulṭa qawīya*) at the center was needed as a 'point of reference' (*marǧaʿ*). The Ottoman homeland, the ʿĪsās stressed, was the protector of equality rights to 'prevent that the majority from swallowing up the minority' (*yamnaʿnā ʿan akl baʿḍinā baʿḍan wa-btilāʿ al-akṯarīya al-aqallīya*), and 'so that minority rights might not be violated' (*la ʾilā yaṣīr al-iḥǧāf bi-ḥuqūq al-aqallīya*). This was exactly what the European states were waiting for, the ʿĪsās said, and would provide them with the excuse to interfere in the Empire's affairs.[159]

In an editorial, titled 'Is Decentralization Good for Palestine?' (*Hal Taṣluḥ al-Lā-Markazīya fī Filasṭīn*), the ʿĪsās evaluated the policy of the Arab Reform Committees in Beirut that became active in 1913 and were also discussed in Palestine. What might be beneficial for the urban context of Beirut was not suitable for Palestine, as a province with an agricultural character, they argued, and they concluded that the agendas of the Reform Committees were not applicable in the Palestinian context.[160]

158 *Filasṭīn*, 16 September 1911: 69/2/2.
159 *Filasṭīn*, 22 March 1913: 223/1/1–4.
160 *Filasṭīn*, 19 April 1913: 231/1/1–4.

The question of 'how much decentralization' was useful or damaging for Palestine was a topic of lively discussion in *Filasṭīn* during the summer months of 1913. The activities of the Lebanese-Syrian Arab Reform Movement were observed with keen interest by Palestinian modernists, and the First Arab Congress, held in July 1913 in Paris, was covered extensively in *Filasṭīn*, which commented critically on the demands Arab delegates made of the government.[161] The ʿĪsās, although refusing Arab decentralization and always warning that the road to reform had to pass through the center, published controversial views on the topic. Some prominent figures called for the establishment of Arab Reform Committees in Palestine. This can be seen in reform letters from Gaza and Jerusalem, or in a statement by the businessman and politician Ḥāfiẓ Bek as-Saʿīd from Jaffa, who was a delegate in the Ottoman Parliament for the Jerusalem District.[162]

In June 1913, the Egyptian journalist and nationalist ar-Rāfiʿī, a passionate reader of *Filasṭīn*, forcefully promoted Arab decentralization in his article 'Forwards not Backwards' (*Ilā l-Amām lā ilā l-Warāʾ*).[163] The editors' response to his letter reveals a very pragmatic political agenda. They confirmed that it was essential that the highest political rule in the Empire was concentrated at a central point (*nuqṭa markazīya*). Their firm support for the CUP derived from their belief that only the 'unionists' would maintain the Constitution and political stability:

> We have to let the author know that we are only 'unionists' because we understand the term 'union' (*ittiḥād*) as [equal to] 'Constitution' (*dustūr*), and we have no trust that the Constitution will be maintained if it arrives to other hands ... However, when the war [in the Balkans] is over and things in the Empire have calmed down again, and when we see then, that the unionists have not learned from this example and do not turn to reforms .... then, we will be the first to turn against them and declare them our enmity (*fa-naḥnu awwal man nuqallib ʿalayhim wa-yuǧāhiruhum bi-l-ʿadāʾ*).[164]

The above quotation clarifies the overall goal presented by the editors throughout the whole Ottoman period, which was the preservation of political stability between the various groups, and the implementation of reforms in Palestine that would develop it. The Ottoman patriotism that was clearly demonstrated in

161 For instance, see *Filasṭīn*, 28 June 1913: 249/3/2–3; 05 July 1913: 251/2/1–2; 5 July 1913: 251/3/1; 9 July 1913: 252/1/4–2/3; 19 July 1913: 255/1/5–2/1; 23 July 1913: 256/2/3–5; and 13 August 1913: 262/1/1–4.

162 *Filasṭīn*, 12 March 1913: 220/3/3; 26 March 1913: 224/3/107; 7 May 1913: 234/2/2–4. See also an interview with the Jerusalemite Šukrī al-Ḥusaynī on the 'Arab question' (*al-masʾala al-ʿarabīya*) on 24 May 1913: 239/1/5–2/1.

163 *Filasṭīn*, 18 June 1913: 246/1/1–5.The letter was in response to an editorial by the ʿĪsās on 'The Three Powers in Palestine' (*Quwā Filasṭīn aṯ-Ṯalāṯ*), which the ʿĪsās defined as 'the governor' (*al-mutaṣarrif*), 'the sayyeds' (*al-asyād*) and 'public opinion' (*ar-raʾy al-ʿāmm*). *Filasṭīn*, 28 May 1913: 240/1/1–4.

164 *Filasṭīn*, 18 June 1913: 246/1/5–2/2.

Filasṭīn was subordinated to this 'development agenda' and was a very practical, instrumental patriotism that was promoted as long as the central government stood for 'stability' and 'reform'.

Yet, despite their strict loyalty to the CUP, the ʿĪsās faced confrontations with the regime and *Filasṭīn* was shut down a couple of times in 1913 and 1914 accused of 'propaganda against the government'.[165] These years marked turning points in the Arab East in many ways. In the context of the Balkan crisis, the debate on Arab decentralization, the Armenian question in Anatolia and the gradual alienation of the Ottoman center from its non-Turkish elements during 1913, new concepts were introduced in the Palestinian press. Under the impact of the debate on the 'Arab question' (*al-masʾala al-ʿarabīya*) during spring and early summer 1913, new terminology on 'Turks' (*atrāk*) versus 'Arabs' (*ʿarab*) started to appear in *Filasṭīn*;[166] and the term 'minority' (*aqallīya*) was reluctantly introduced at the same time, despite the newspaper's strict 'equality discourse'.

Since concepts of 'minorities' appeared at the Ottoman center in the context of rising proto-national questions, they 'travelled' through the press to the Arab East, for example through translations from Turkish newspapers, and started to be discussed in Ottoman Palestine, although without doubting that the principle of Ottoman integrity was untouchable. In *Filasṭīn*, the term 'minority' was used in 1913 when the editors appealed to the government to integrate a regulation on 'minority rights' (*ḥuqūq al-aqallīya*) into the new provincial law of the Jerusalem District, which would make he demands of Arab decentralists null and void, with reference to a quota for Christians and Jews in the Provincial Council.[167] However, the exact application of new minority concepts in the Arab press during 1913–1914 needs further contextualization in future research.[168]

How Much 'Palestinianism'?

In addition to their Ottomanism on the national level and Arabism on the cultural, the ʿĪsās were Palestinian patriots on the local level. How was this 'Palestinianism' demonstrated? The programmatic title of the newspaper *Filasṭīn*

165 In November 1913, the ʿIsās harshly criticized the Governor and Jaffa's *qāʾimaqām*, Māǧid Bek, who temporarily closed down *Filasṭīn*, a move that was probably initiated by the Patriarch, who had been attacked by the ʿĪsās. In April 1914, it was shut down again because of an anti-Zionist article, according to Mandel 1976, 180.

166 See for example the debate between the Jerusalemite journalists ʿUṯmān an-Našāšībī and ʿAlī ar-Rimāwī in the press on the issue. See *Filasṭīn*, 22 March 1913: 223/1/5–2/3.

167 *Filasṭīn*, 19 April 1913: 231/1/1–4. See also the debates between the ʿĪsās and Ḥāfiẓ Bek as-Saʿīd about minority rights, on 28 May 1913: 240/1/1–4; 31 May 1913: 241/1/4–2/3.

168 For minority concepts in French Mandate Syria during the 1920s in the context of colonial policies, see the White (2011), who claims that this concept was a phenomenon that only appeared after the early Mandate period. However, it has been shown that it started to circulate before World War I in the Arab East.

('Palestine') reflected the local editors' affiliation and shows that a concept of Palestine as a geographical unit existed before World War I. The choice of the title and the frequent use in the newspaper of the terms 'Palestinians' (*al-filasṭīnīyūn*) and the 'Palestinian lands' (*al-bilād al-filasṭīnīya*) as an Ottoman province shows that a concept of Palestine was commonly understood among the population, although Palestine did not exist as a political unit.

However, multiple meanings of 'Palestine' were presented, and the territorial boundaries of late Ottoman Palestine were somewhat flexible. In *Filasṭīn*, the geographical concept of 'Palestine' was mostly equal to the Jerusalem District, while in the context of Orthodox matters, 'Palestine' was equal to the Patriarchate of Jerusalem.[169] In an article on the modernization of Jaffa's port, 'Palestine' was set equal to the Jaffa *qaḍā'*.[170] Only once did the editors of *Filasṭīn* include the districts of Acre and Nablus in their geographical concept of 'Palestine', which, together with the Jerusalem District, largely coincided with the borders of later Mandate Palestine, when they indicated the number of inhabitants of Palestine to be 650,000.[171]

Fluidity of Nationalist Terminology

With regard to nationalist ideology presented in *Filasṭīn*, Fishman has interpreted specific terms in line with political meanings that consolidated in the region after World War I to support his thesis that an early Palestinian nationalism existed, although he does so without a systematic approach or proper contextualization. For instance, he has taken the use of the terms 'Palestinians' (*ahālī Filasṭīn, al-filasṭīnīyūn*) and 'Palestinian community' (*al-umma al-filasṭīnīya*) in *Filasṭīn* as evidence of a Palestinian nationalism before World War I that reached all social classes.[172] A systematic reading of *Filasṭīn* from 1911 to 1914, however, has shown that the contemporary concept of *umma* took on multiple meanings. It could stand for 'nation' in a political sense, for religious 'community', or simply for 'society'. The fluidity of political concepts and inconsistency in the use of political terms was a typical phenomenon in Arabic journalistic discourse before World War I. The terms 'Palestine' and 'Palestinians' were mostly applied in *Filasṭīn* to the population of the Jerusalem District without reference to the northern Palestinian districts, but they were also used flexibly in different geographical contexts. The term *umma* was used extensively

169 See *Filasṭīn*, 12 June 1912: 144/3/5–4/1; 24 May 1912: 156/3/5.

170 Asking the government *When will the Turn Come for Palestine (Matā ya'tī ad-dawr li-Filasṭīn)?*, an anonymous letter referred to the rivalry between Jaffa and Haifa which was about to surpass the importance of Jaffa; such feared Jaffa's population. See *Filasṭīn*, 07 August 1912: 160/1/3–2/1.

171 See *Filasṭīn*, 27 July 1912: 157/1/3f–2/1.

172 Fishman 2007, 65–67.

for the 'Orthodox community' (*al-umma al-urṯūḏuksīya*) and the 'Israeli community' (*al-umma al-isrāʾīlīya*), and as an equivalent to *milla. Umma* was also applied to the population of cities, for example when referring to the residents of Jaffa as a 'vital community' (*umma ḥayya*) and was used in this context as an equivalent to 'local citizens'.[173] *Umma* was applied as well to the 'Ottoman population' (*al-umma al-ʿuṯmānīya*) as citizens of the Ottoman 'homeland' (*al-waṭan*).[174]

Usually, the concept of *waṭan* was only used for the Empire while *bilād* ('country') was usually applied in the regional context. However, there is one quotation from June 1914, the only time in the pre-World War I coverage in which Palestine was equated with the 'beloved homeland', in which ʿĪsā refers to the various confessional groups as being 'branches of one tree'. He stressed: 'This is the tree of Palestine, the beloved homeland' (*furūʿ šaǧara wāḥida hiya šaǧarat Filasṭīn al-waṭan al-maḥbūb*).[175] We see from this that political and geographical terms in the years prior to World War I were fluid and were used inconsistently in Arabic public discourse; and it seems that, for the authors, there was no contradiction in harmonizing Ottoman nationalism with Palestinian patriotism.

3.3.3. Ottoman Brothers

This section will outline the central characteristics of the concept of Ottoman brotherhood and the *millet* discourse as it appeared in *Filasṭīn*, and the terminology and topics typically linked with this concept, while considering the practical motivations that underlay its promotion by the authors. Their presentation gives an impression of how Ottoman brotherhood was demonstrated by Palestinian notables and associations in times of political crisis, and how relevant the protection of Muslim–Christian relations was for *Filasṭīn*. Here, the authors, and especially the ʿĪsās, fostered a Muslim–Christian alliance in Palestine and linked this to an anti-imperialist discourse, as will be demonstrated in the 'Ramla incident' in 1911, an act of violence against the Christians of Ramla in the context of the Italian conquest of Tripoli.

Advocating Impartiality, Judging Fanaticism

The authors in *Filasṭīn* strictly imposed the imperial *millet* discourse like a 'corset' the debates about local group relations. The strong notion of 'Ottomans brothers' (*al-iḫwān al-ʿuṯmānīyīn*) was non-negotiable, and the discourse of 'unity between the different elements' (*ittiḥād al-ʿanāṣir al-muḫtalifa*) in Pales-

173 *Filasṭīn*, 01 May 1912: 1912: 132/3/1.
174 *Filasṭīn*, 05 June 1912: 142/3/3.
175 *Filasṭīn*, 20 June 1914: 329/4/2.

tine was also a strategy of conflict management. Impartiality towards any confession was the guiding principle, and national affiliations based on denomination, such as Zionism, or ethnicity, such as Arab separatism, were stigmatized as 'partisanship' (*taḥazzub*). The fear of 'bias' (*taḥāmul*), 'fanaticism' (*ta'assub*) and 'extremism' (*taṭarruf*) was ever-present in *Filasṭīn*, and it increased during times of political crisis in Libya and the Balkans and when anti-Christian hostilities popped up in various cities in the Arab East.

In this respect, the 'Īsās were almost paranoid. They were terrified when they saw conflicts sliding into 'religious dispute' (*ǧadal dīnī*), and felt obliged to interrupt debates when they feared the authors were sliding into 'extremism'. In 1911, the editors intervened in a dispute in *Filasṭīn* between the Sephardi Jew Shimon Moyal and a Muslim pharmacist from Jaffa, Muḥammad Ṣihyūn, which centered around the agenda of the 'Ottoman Patriotic Party' (*al-Hizb al-Waṭanī al-'Uṯmānī*) regarding the Ottoman Jews at a moment when it was becoming increasingly polemical, and declared that both had become 'extremist' (*yataṭarrafā*), which 'we forbid them both as well as the newspaper [*Filasṭīn*]'.[176] Once, the 'Īsās even declared extremism to be 'our national disease' (*dā'unā l-waṭanī*).[177] The teacher Muṣṭafā Tamr from Jerusalem also lamented that 'cleavages' (*šiqāq, tafrīq*) unfortunately belonged to the 'social body in the East' (*al-hay'a al-iǧtimā'īya fī š-šarq*).[178]

The The 'Īsās' motivation to support the 'unity of the elements' was surely connected with the fact that they were Christians and themselves belonged to a minority. In line with their understanding of impartiality, they also judged anti-Semitism, harshly, strictly differentiating it from anti-Zionism. While anti-Zionism was legitimate, anti-Semitism was a 'disease' from the Middle Ages and not appropriate in the age of modernity, knowledge and science; this was the stand of the 'Īsās.[179] Prominent Muslims were also exposed to criticism when the 'Īsās sensed discrimination. Once, they harshly attacked a sheikh from Gaza when he called upon 'the Sultan of the Muslims' during an official celebration in the Gazan branch of the CUP, and referred to the Ottoman lands as the 'Muslim Empire'. This Islamic national rhetoric was unacceptable to the 'Isās, and they objected that, while the CUP stood for unity, the Sheikh had 'thrown away the other groups'.[180] On another occasion, a high-ranking Ottoman minister visited Jerusalem and was received by Mayor Ḥusaynī and Jerusalem's Muslim notables while the Christian and Jewish notables were been invited to the reception. The

176 *Filasṭīn*, 23 September 1911: 71/3/1.
177 *Filasṭīn*, 10 May 1913: 235/1/1f.
178 *Filasṭīn*, 20 March 1912: 121/3/3–2/1.
179 *Filasṭīn*, 25 October 1913: 283/1/1f.
180 *Filasṭīn*, 2 August 1911: 56/2/4–5.

ʿĪsās were outraged that the minorities were excluded from this event.[181] They felt that Ḥusaynī had acted as if the Christians and Israelis were not 'sons of this Homeland' (*abnāʾ hāḏā l-waṭan*) and were 'no longer registered as subjects' (*lā yazālūn fī daftar al-ʿubūdīya muqayyadīn*).[182] Moreover, rumors circulated that the minister allegedly appealed to the Muslim notables to be 'wary of the Christians' (*iḥtarisū… min an-naṣārā*) and to 'avoid the Jews' (*taǧannabū l-yahūd*). Allegedly, he had appealed to the Muslim notables to 'be a united Islamic community' (*milla islāmīya muttaḥida*) 'standing up to these two communities' (*qāʾima fī waǧh hātayni l-millatayn*).[183] These rumors were a scandal to the ʿIsās, fabricated by the Jerusalemite gossip factory. Nevertheless, they made Mayor Ḥusaynī personally responsible for the confusion and showed solidarity with the 'Israelis', whose political rights as an Ottoman community they saw as being discriminated against.

Demonstrating Brotherhood in Times of Crisis

Public demonstrations of Ottoman unity particularly increased in times of political and military crisis, as is clearly seen through *Filasṭīn*. During the Tripoli and the Balkan Wars, communal and welfare associations in Jaffa and Jerusalem initiated fundraising campaigns to collect money for the Ottoman army. The ʿĪsās and other notables associated with *Filasṭīn* called upon the citizens' 'patriotic enthusiasm' (*ḥumya, ġayra waṭanīya*) and encouraged them to enroll in the military or donate to the army. The *Local News* section was full of reports about solidarity initiatives by local associations under the section 'Aid Funds' (*iʿānāt*), which published lists of donations collected for the army, the Red Crescent Society and widows and orphans affected by the war. These lists included the names of Jewish, Christian and Muslim donors and the sum given by each of them to motivate others to follow their example.

During the Tripoli crisis, *Filasṭīn* published such lists for weeks. At the end of October 1911, the 'fourth list' announced that Jaffa's residents had collected a total of 650 francs. The list included the names of 57 donors who had given an average of 1–5 francs.[184] During the Balkan War of 1912, *Filasṭīn* published that a sum of 491 francs had been donated so far. The highest donation by far came

181 *Filasṭīn*, 31 January 1912: 107/1/1.
182 *Filasṭīn*, 31 January 1912: 107/1/1–2.
183 *Filasṭīn*, 31 January 1912: 107/1/3.
184 The highest sum, 15 francs, was donated by the head of the Latin monastery, followed by Yaʿqūb Abū l-Hudā and Saʿīd Bek an-Nābulsī with 10 francs each. See *Filasṭīn*, 25 October 1911: 80/3/3–4. It was probably also in the context of the Tripoli War that a couple of emigrants from Bethlehem donated considerable sums from the 'diaspora' (*al-mahǧar*) to the local Orthodox community to 'support them in their jihad' (*musāʿadatan ʿalā ǧihādihā*): Nikola Mūsā Zarzar and Bišāra Ḥanā Zarzar each gave 30 francs, Sābā Qasṭeh Farīḥ and Yūsuf Ḥanā ʿAṭā Allāh each gave 20 francs. See *Filasṭīn*, 25 October 1911: 80/3/2–3.

from Shimon Moyal, a Jewish doctor from a prominent Sephardi family in Jaffa, who gave 25 francs, and the Sephardi Chelouche family from Jaffa also stood out for its high level of donations.[185] Apart from communal associations of Palestinian Muslims, Christians and Jews and wealthy individuals, Zionist institutions also participated in these demonstrations of loyalty. In 1911, the Hebrew Gymnasium in Tel Aviv conducted a 'music night' (*layla musīqīya*) as a charity event as to collect money for the Ottoman navy.[186] Committees were established to raise funding for army uniforms or in support of poor families whose sons were at the front. Notables also gave material donations, such as horses.[187]

This public engagement in support for Ottoman unity was also a sign of crisis on the local level. During the Tripoli war, sectarianism and hostilities between Muslims and Christians flared up in Jaffa, Ramla and Beirut. *Filasṭīn*'s correspondent from Ramla appealed to stop the public instigations of a certain Sheikh Fayḍī, who had insulted the Patriarch in the Ramla market place and called for the 'destruction of church bells and the Church and the eviction of the [community] head' (*bi-luzūm taḥṭīm al-aǧrās wa-hadm al-kanīsa wa-ṭard ar-raʾīs*).[188] Another author complained about a new jihad discourse applied by Muslim individuals who had 'lost the righteous path' (*ḍallu as-sabīl*), used religion 'as a weapon' to provoke 'strife' (*fitna*) between Christians and Muslims.[189] Muslim and Christian elites and scholars condemned these incidents as political factionalism and called upon community leaders to silence the 'fanatics', whom they stigmatized as 'ignorant people' (*ǧuhalāʾ*), and to engage in patriotic education to cure the 'confused' of their 'hallucinations'.[190] A Muslim Sheikh Muḥyī, in an article reprinted from the Beirut newspaper *Al-Barq* ('The Telegram'), stressed the patriotism of Ottoman Christians and interpreted civic equality among all citizens as a universal law advocated by all religions, saying:

> It is important for every pious person to know that all the religions … state in their teachings that the sons of one and the same Homeland are equal (*sawāsiya*) in all worldly matters and civil rights and that it is forbidden (*ḥarām*) from the theological point of view to attack those who disagree with religion…
>
> The Islamic religion… has postulated that it is the same to hurt Christians and Jews (*al-mūsawīyīn*) among the fellow citizens as to hurt a Sharia follower himself (a Muslim). To harm a Christian or a Jew is like hurting the Prophet, prayers and peace be upon him. The same applies to our lord Jesus, peace be upon him, who commended loving enemies

185 *Filasṭīn*, 2 November 1912: 185/3/5–4/1 and 6 November 1912: 186/3/5–4/1.

186 *Filasṭīn*, 13 December 1911: 94/3/4.

187 *Filasṭīn*, 30 October 1912: 184/3/2–3; 30 October 1912: 184/3/3 and 3/4; 2 November 1912: 185/3/5; 6 November 1912: 186/3/3–4.

188 *Filasṭīn*, 22 July 1911: 53/3/1.

189 *Filasṭīn*, 6 December 1911: 92/3/3–4.

190 *Filasṭīn*, 13 December 1911: 94/1/5–2/2.

> more than friends and fellow citizens. Moses, peace be upon him, did the same and he did not make this up, either. Because the source of these religions is one and the same (*maṣdar hāḏihi l-adyān wāḥid*) and dissent over it concerns legal aspects and 'if your lord wanted, he surely would have made mankind one united community (*umma wāḥida*)'.[191]

In the above quotation, Sheikh Muḥyī legitimized the concept of Ottoman unity by citing religious narratives. Here, the sacralization of political concepts on the one hand and the re-interpretation of religion in the light of secular political philosophy on the other was part of a phenomenon of Arab modernity that appeared in various contexts. Muslim modernists and the supporters of the *nahḍa* declared human benefit or the common 'interest' (*maṣlaḥa*) to be the essence of religion and equated Islam with the spirit of modernity, as did the Egyptian reformer Muḥammad ʿAbduh. As Schulze, Buessow and others have deduced from their investigations, bourgeois discourse had an impact on religious thought worldwide, which demarcated religious borders and facilitated an abstract, universal concept of religion that focused on practical ethics and separated 'history' from 'belief', the latter increasingly interpreted as individual experience.[192] Muslim scholars with a cosmopolitan education aimed to reform the understanding of Islam in line with the requirements of the present: they interpreted this as 'progress'. The Muslim reformer Rašīd Riḍāʾ, called the 'father' of the *salafīya*, a reform movement that sought to modernize Islam by returning to its essential roots, largely stressed in his texts the goal of religion as being to implement *maṣlaḥa*, the common good, in society.[193]

The fusion of religious traditions and modern political narratives was also practiced by Ottoman Jewish community leaders. In a speech addressing the Vice-President of the High Chamber, Ǧaʿfar Pasha, who visited Jaffa in March 1912, the rabbi, *ḥāḫāmbāšī* in the imperial jargon, emphasized not only Jewish loyalty to the Empire but stated that a correct understanding of Judaism must imply loyalty to the Ottoman political framework; a statement that he based on the Jewish experience during the Islamic Caliphate. He argued that history had taught the Jews that their fortune and their 'protection as a people' (*ḥafẓ qawmīyatihi*) were based on the integrity of the Ottoman Empire, and Islam had

191 Quotation from the Qur'an (*Sūrat Hūd*, 11:18). See *Filasṭīn*, 23 December 1911: 97/3/5.

192 Buessow investigates modern concepts of religion in Muḥammad ʿAbduh's *Risālat at-Tawḥīd* ('The Theology of Unity', 1897). Following Reinhard Schulze, he argues that there was a 'Protestant template for religion' transmitted to Middle Eastern thinkers through European publications. Instead of studying these phenomena within the 'Westernization' paradigm, he suggest a 'globalization perspective' for a better understanding of the transfer of such concepts. See Buessow 2015, 273–320.

193 Hamzah 2012, 90–127. For the *salafīya* in the early twentieth century, see the first two chapters in Lauzière 2016.

proven to be 'the most tolerant of all religions' (*akṯar ad-daʿwāt ad-dīnīya tasāhulan*), and he stressed that Islam was respected and loved by the Jews and, for the Jewish believer, it was impossible to be hostile towards descendants of the pious caliphs and the Ottoman sultans.[194]

These arguments of the Jaffa rabbi should also be seen in the light of the ongoing debate about the political aspirations of the Zionist movement in Palestine and the fact that Jaffa was the center of the World Zionist Organization (WZO) in the Yishuv, which put Palestinian Jews under considerable pressure from their fellow citizens. It became an established pattern of conflict management during the post-revolutionary period that representatives of minorities in general, and the Sephardi communities in specific, took public celebrations as an occasion to demonstrate their loyalty as a *milla* to the Empire, even basing it on Jewish tradition and historical experience.

Addressing the Muslims, Narrating Muslim-Christian Harmony

As part of the discourse on 'Ottoman brotherhood and unity' and since the ʿĪsās were Greek Orthodox Christians, Muslim–Christian relations in Palestine were of special importance in *Filasṭīn*. The editors were very much interested in making *Filasṭīn* a medium consumed by the Muslim majority and tried to make it attractive to them. Here, the choice of the newspaper's title *Filasṭīn* ('Palestine') addressed a wider circle of readers than it would have if it referred to 'Orthodox matters' although this clearly was its local political focus, or merely to the Jaffa *qaḍāʾ* as the geographical focus of *Filasṭīn*'s coverage. With Muslims in mind, the ʿĪsās proudly announced the opening of *Filasṭīn* as a forum for Muslim reformers who intended 'to make the values, morals and traditions compatible with the spirit of this civilized age without infringing the limits of the honored Islamic law'.[195]

I did not find many articles on modernist Islam in *Filasṭīn* but many Muslims used the newspaper as a regular platform. A Jerusalemite Muslim, ʿĀrif al-Muwaqqat (about whom nothing else is known), frequently reported from Saudi Arabia on pilgrimage to Mecca and Medina.[196] In the *Local News* section, Muslims were regularly congratulated on the occasion of their feastdays and holidays,

---

194 *Filasṭīn*, 30 March 1912: 124/3/5f.

195 '*Ǧaʿl al-ʿawāʾid wa-l-aḫlāq wa-t-taqlīdāt muǧāriya li-rūḥ hāḏā l-ʿaṣr al-ʿumrānī bi-mā lā yaḫruǧ ʿan ḥudūd aš-šarīʿa al-ġarāʾ*.' See *Filasṭīn*, 15 July 1911: 51/1/3.

196 In his column 'Medina, the Enlightened' (*Madīna al-Munawwara*), he regularly relayed his observations of pilgrim groups from around the world in Saudi Arabia, ceremonies, and interactions between pilgrims and local Bedouins and traders. In the Jerusalem District, Muslim pilgrims usually took the train from Jerusalem to Jaffa, and continued by boat from Jaffa to Haifa, where they changed on to the Hijaz Railway that took them (with stop-overs in Der'aa) on a four-day train trip to Medina. See *Filasṭīn*, 24 July 1912: 156/3/1–2.

as were the Jews. Prominent Muslims, such as Rāġib Efendi al-Ḫālidī and Isʿāf an-Našāšībī, contributed on the reformation of Muslim education and holy sites. Al-Ḫālidī in particular wrote ambitious articles on the meaning of the Holy Land for Muslim culture, declared science to be an indigenous part of Islam and stressing the need to reform the Islamic institutions and endowments (*awqāf*) in Jerusalem; but he also emphasized the civilizational achievements of Islam during the classical era and highlighted the historical Muslim attitude of tolerance towards other religions.[197]

The ʿĪsās, although they were Christians, closely identified with Islamic history as part of their cultural heritage, and did not make themselves an exception.[198] Thus, it was not very surprising that Yūsuf al-ʿĪsā wrote about Islamic cultural topics, such as the historical and spiritual meanings of fasting during Ramadan, calling on (Muslim) readers to respect the principles of the holy Islamic law and follow the fasting regulations.[199] While in the Arab Orthodox case the Ottomanist discourse was instrumentalized to discredit the Greek element in the Patriarchate, the discourse on Ottoman brotherhood was brought into play here to preserve an alliance between Palestinian Muslims and Christians, and a strong notion of Muslim–Christian harmony was promoted in *Filasṭīn*. I should stress that this narrative was mostly promoted by the Christian contributors, above all the ʿĪsās themselves, but also by Muslim intellectuals and modernists such as Rāġib al-Ḫālidī, who addressed the historical good relations between Muslims and Christians in Jerusalem.[200] Thus, the coverage on the issue in *Filasṭīn* was not a Muslim–Christian dialogue but to a great extent a *monologue* by Christian authors who, especially in the context of crisis, addressed the Muslim majority, reaffirming their loyalty.

This narration was directly linked with anti-European arguments against imperialist aspirations in the Empire. The contemporary anti-imperialism was a factor that especially nourished a narrative of peaceful Muslim–Christian coexistence since the early times of Islam in the Arab East, which flourished in the Arab press. In *Filasṭīn*, this narrative functioned as a defense to ward off internal

197 See for instance *Filasṭīn*, 19 July 1911: 52/1/1–4; 22 July 1911: 53/1/3; 6 December 1911: 92/2/2–3; 25 January 1913: 207/1/1–5; 2 April 1913: 226/1/1–4; 10 May 1913: 235/1/3–2/3; 4 June 1913: 242/1/3–2/1; 26 July 1913: 257/1/4–2/2; 10 July 1912: 152/3/5–4/1; 20 July 1912: 155/3/4–5.

198 It was typical for Christian supporters of the Arab *nahḍa* to portray early Islamic culture as a positive role model. The Syriac Christian Ǧurǧī Zaydān, for instance, did so extensively in his literary-cultural magazine *Al-Hilāl* ('The Crescent'), published in Cairo; its title addressed the Muslim majority in Egypt. For information, see the articles on Zaydān published by Thomas Philipp.

199 *Filasṭīn*, 30 August 1911: 64/1/1f.

200 See his article 'Citizenship in Palestine' (*al-ǧinsīya fī Filasṭīn*) in *Filasṭīn*, 4 June 1913: 242/1/3–2/1.

and external voices that questioned inter-confessional unity and civic equality in the Ottoman Empire. In this respect, the anti-Europeanism demonstrated by the ʿĪsās and other authors was in contrast to their pro-European modernist discourse. As much as European modernity was promoted as role model for the reformation of local education, and as much Palestinian modernists suffered from a minority complex due to the constant comparison of their environment with the West, the Arab press articulated even more strongly its protest against European hegemony in the East and attacked Western regimes and press organs.

The ʿĪsās also closely monitored the Western press's coverage of the East and its stance towards international politics. They regularly condemned statements in European journals about 'Eastern despotism' and the 'suppression of minorities' in the Empire as 'intrigues' designed by Western governments and scholars to break Muslim–Christian unity in the East. According to the ʿĪsās, the Western press was full of 'exaggerations and fabrications' (*mubālaġāt wa-taḥrīf*) about Muslim fanaticism, and they complained that the Havas and Reuters news agencies, although widely quoted in *Filasṭīn*, were a 'market of lies' (*sūq al-akāḏīb*).[201] During the much covered Balkan Wars (1912/13), anti-Europeanism became a paradigm in *Filasṭīn*. When the Western press reported the victories of the allied Balkan armies over the Ottomans at the end of October 1912, the ʿĪsās attacked it for the fabrication of news. Since there was speculation about European support in the war, the ʿĪsās compared Europe with a 'sick man' whose microbes and germs were scattering, as a counter-polemic to the image of the Ottoman Empire as a 'sick man' in the European press, constructed by Arab modernists.[202] Biological metaphors were frequently used in *Filasṭīn*, and it was a personal preference of the ʿĪsās to compare their opponents (the imperialists, the Greek Orthodox clerics, the Zionists, etc.) to insects, parasites or highly infectious germs to demonstrate the damage that, in their view, they caused society.

The Ramla Incident: 'Who is the Extremist?'

The narrative of Muslim–Christian harmony gained special importance in the context of the international military crisis. When in October 1911 and in the context of the Tripoli War and while the Italians were conquering Libya, anti-Christian riots occurred in Haifa and Jaffa, foreign consuls in Palestine protested at Muslim violence against minorities. According to the ʿĪsās, these were 'bugbears of the politicians' (*buʿbuʿ as-siyāsīyīn*) constructed to break Muslim–Christian unity. The ʿĪsās complained that the myth of 'Muslim fundamentalism' (*at-taʿaṣṣub al-islāmī*) was fabricated in the West to justify the European penetration of the Arab East. In the light of European 'aggression against the nations'

201 *Filasṭīn*, 19 October 1912: 181/1/1–3.
202 *Filasṭīn*, 30 October 1912: 184/1/1–3.

(*al-iʿtidāʾ ʿalā aš-šuʿūb*) and the fact that 'more than 100,000 Italians' still lived in the Empire without being harmed, the ʿĪsās wondered 'how Europe cannot recognize that, in this respect, our civilization surpasses theirs and that our tolerance is greater than theirs and our feelings are more progressive then theirs', since, they declared, the so-called peaceful intentions of the West in the East were hypocrisy and were really motivated by 'profit' (*kasb*) and 'colonization' (*istiʿ-mār*).[203] They turned around this argument under the title 'Who is the Extremist?' (*Man Huwa al-Mutaʿaṣṣib*), they denounced the bloody crushing by the British military of rebellions in Egypt against the Libyan war as European 'extremism'.[204]

In November 1911, the so-called 'Ramla incident' (*ḥādiṯat Ramla*) gave further reason to pick up the issue. In the city of Ramla, Muslims had attacked Christian inhabitants during demonstrations against the Italian attack on Tripoli. While Ramla's Christians initially participated in the parades, they later refrained when Bedouin thugs (*ʿurbān*) and a 'mob' (*ar-ruʿāʿ*) from outside joined the evening demonstrations. 'The mob' started to carry a dog, dressed up and painted with a cross as a symbol of 'Christian' imperialism, which was shot at the end of the parade. During the night, these 'outsiders' entered the Christian neighborhoods of Ramla, chanted slogans, shot in the air and started knocking on the doors of the houses. Some of the Christians, scared by the noise and shooting, fled from their homes and took shelter at the Franciscan monastery. When the news spread in town, Muslim notables and the shaykh proceeded to the monastery to calm feelings (*taskīn al-ḫawāṭir*), declaring this incident a 'great shame' (*ʿār kabīr*) for their town.[205]

According to the editors, the incident was a single slip-up committed by outsiders from the hinterland who were too ignorant to understand to concept of Ottoman brotherhood. The ʿĪsās' main concern here was to preserve the narrative of Muslim–Christian harmony and what they feared most was the 'falsification' (*taḥrīf*) of the incident in the foreign press and that the consuls would 'blow it up'. They declared that no fanaticism existed in Palestine. Here, they stated, 'one is connected to the other' (*yartabiṭ … al-wāḥid bi-l-āḫir*), and if certain hostilities occurred, it was only 'among the ignorant segment' (*bayna aṭ-ṭabaqa al-ǧāhila*). In Palestine, they declared, 'The Christian is like the Israelite [meaning: Jewish] citizen, and they are equal to the Muslim citizen. All are Ottomans and only to be distinguished by religion; and religion belongs to God.'[206]

---

203 *Filasṭīn*, 21 October 1911: 79/1/1–4.

204 *Filasṭīn*, 8 November 1911: 84/1/1–3.

205 *Filasṭīn*, 8 November 1911: 84/2/5–3/3.

206 *Filasṭīn*, 8 November 1911: 84/3/1. Please note the term 'Israelites' was used for 'Jews' in the contemporary jargon of the Arab press during the late Ottoman period, and I will use this term in this study accordingly.

The ʿĪsās had their own interpretation of what happened in Ramla: 'Both parties, Muslims and Christians, are to be blamed for this incident' (*al-farīqayn min muslimīn wa-masīḥīyīn malūmān*), they said, and made the Ottoman representative and the major responsible for the outbreak of hostilities as they had permitted or even encouraged night-time demonstrations, and they blamed the police forces, who had actually clamped down on the instigators.[207] Under the title, 'What is the Governor Waiting for?' (*Māḏā yantaẓir ʿuṭūfatuhu*), the editors bitterly complained about the Ottoman jurisdiction (*al-ʿadlīya*) that had allegedly randomly imprisoned 'innocents' (*abriyāʾ*). Taking the side of the latter, the ʿĪsās addressed the governor: 'By God, it is injustice (*ẓulm wallāhi*) that the jurisdiction is stretching out its hand to some of the stupid ignorant (*biḍʿa min al-ǧahala al-aġbiyāʾ*) who do not understand what they are doing'.[208]

What deserves attention here is that the ʿĪsās put the lion's share of guilt on Ramla's Christians. In their interpretation, the Christians had 'offended' their Muslim brothers (*asāʾū aẓ-ẓann bi-iḫwānihim*) by feeling threatened by them which was, the ʿĪsās declared, a 'misunderstanding' (*sūʾ at-tafāhum*). The Christian reaction to flee their houses was hysterical according to the ʿĪsās, and based on the 'delusion' (*wahm*) that they were going to be attacked. This was offensive to Ottoman Muslims, the ʿĪsās thought,[209] and they criticized the police who did not prevent the Christians from taking refuge in the Franciscan monastery as 'foreign' territory. The ʿĪsās asked, how the police could only

> watch with frozen eyes Ottoman wearers of the Tarbush (*ṭarābīš ʿuṯmānīya*) how they… escape out of fear into a foreign monastery (*dayr aǧnabī*); and this in a town that is ruled by them as Ottomans?[210]

Obviously, the 'Ramla incident' found considerable resonance among the public and gave rise to many readers' letters. However, the editors were too afraid that the subject would become a matter of religious conflict and decided in this case to abandon their declared function as a medium for public debates! They published none of the letters, declaring that the Muslims and Christians of Ramla meanwhile had returned to their 'life in brotherhood' (*aʿīšat al-iḫwa*), interacting in the markets during the day and sitting together during the evening as usual.[211] Surprisingly, what concerned the ʿĪsās in this context was not the security of local Christians but whether their behavior would be interpreted as a treachery and a 'crime' towards the Ottoman Homeland! In their opinion, the police forces should not have hesitated to prevent Ramla's Christians from fleeing their homes:

207 *Filasṭīn*, 8 November 1911: 84/3/2–3.
208 *Filasṭīn*, 15 November 1911: 86/1/1.
209 *Filasṭīn*, 8 November 1911: 84/3/3.
210 *Filasṭīn*, 15 November 1911: 86/1/2.
211 *Filasṭīn*, 15 November 1911: 86/1/1.

> Why did they [the police forces] not oppose the escapers and why they did not shout at them 'stop it, you people'. If there is death [waiting], we will die before you. But we cannot allow you to commit this crime towards the Homeland (*al-ǧināya al-waṭanīya*). You will have to step over our bodies and our blood before we allow you to enter the gates of this monastery and bring this shame (*hāḏā l-ʿār*) upon us.[212]

The treatment of this incident in *Filasṭīn* demonstrates that the real addressees of the coverage were not the Christians but the local Muslims and that the aim was to demonstrate solidarity with them and to preserve the narrative of Muslim-Christian harmony in Ottoman Palestine against 'foreign' influences. Here, the ʿĪsās clearly suspended the dialogical function of *Filasṭīn* to protect the Muslim-Christian alliance in times of crisis as fundamental principle.

3.4. Civic Discourse

Apart from the modernist and imperial discourse, notions on the civic public as a political actor were outstanding in *Filasṭīn*. In an editorial in May 1913 entitled 'The Three Powers in Palestine' (*Quwā Filasṭīn aṯ-talāṯ*), 'public opinion' (*ar-raʾy al-ʿāmm*) was even defined as the 'third power' in Palestine, along with the governor (*al-mutaṣarrif*) and the sayyeds (*al-asyād*).[213] What follows here is a brief presentation of concepts of the 'public sphere' in Palestine before World War I, the images of civic society and citizenry presented in *Filasṭīn*, and the terms linked with it – an issue, that needs much more investigation in future studies and can only be touched on here.[214]

The Public as a Power in Palestine

The concept of 'civic society' presented in *Filasṭīn* from 1911 to 1914 was ambivalent. On the one hand, the press presented itself as 'the voice of the people' (*lisān al-ahālī*) and a natural public authority that safeguarded the people's rights vis-à-vis the state. Indeed, it contributed to a new 'protest culture' in Palestine, which is also seen in the many petitions that were sent to Istanbul, as investigated by Ben-Bassat in *Petitioning the Sultan*.[215] The function of the Arab press as

212 *Filasṭīn*, 15 November 1911: 86/1/2–3.

213 See *Filasṭīn*, 28 May 1913: 240/1/1–4.

214 For a study on the development of 'public space' and the place of the 'street' in late Ottoman Damascus, see Grallert 2012, 327–359.

215 Apart from letters in the Arabic press, sending petitions to Istanbul became a frequent political instrument in the Arab East during the Second Constitutional Era. However, petitioning the ruler for special treatment or to complain about unjust treatment and abuse of power is not special to the Ottoman context or the age of modernity but is a universal phenomenon, as Ben-Bassat (2013) has pointed out. Petitions can be found in archeological artefacts, ancient documents, and even the Bible, and of course throughout the Islamic

'voice' of the public becomes clear in the publication of countless readers' letters on *Filasṭīn*'s pages as well as open letters to local authorities and state officials, protest letters and the reprinting of petitions. In 288 issues from 1911 to 1914, I identified 348 readers' letters, among them 224 protest letters concerning my research topic alone. This gives an idea of the extent of *Filasṭīn*'s contribution to a culture of controversial debate and its public resonance.

On the other hand, the majority of Palestinians were not reached by the press, and of course, only members of the upper social classes participated in press debates; thus, when we speak of the 'public' we refer only to a certain segment of Palestinian society that could access these debates because of the level of their education or social position. These participants mostly came from an urban environment, shared similar educational backgrounds and modernist world views, and assumed the right to speak for the interests of a certain group or community, as pointed out previously. This social gap between the urban and the rural is well expressed in *Filasṭīn*, where authors frequently distinguished between the 'educated' or the 'elites' (*an-nuḫab, al-udabāʾ*) and the 'simple-minded' (*al-busaṭāʾ, al-ǧuhalāʾ*) who remained largely invisible in textual communication.

Nevertheless, the elites did present the concept of a 'civic sphere' and thought that the 'public' should have an impact on politics. Many authors claimed to speak on behalf of the 'public interest', as a counterpart to state and government, and thus the terms 'common interest', 'public good' or 'public benefit' (*al-maṣlaḥa al-ʿāmma, an-nafaʿ al-ʿāmm, al-manfaʿa al-ʿāmma*) occurred frequently in *Filasṭīn*. The editors defined 'common interest' as main motivation for their journalistic engagement since 'we have always pursued the public benefit in our writings' (*kunnā dāʾiman nataḥarrā fī kitābātinā an-nafaʿ al-ʿāmm*).[216] Authors of readers' letters also used to claim to speak only in 'the service of the people' (*fī ḫidmat aš-šaʿb*), distancing themselves from 'personal interests' (*ġāyāt šaḫṣīya*). I identified 341 items on the topic of my research only, published between 1911

world. See Ben-Bassat 2013, 20f. 'Petitioning the Sultan' was an important Ottoman institution that was made wide use of on the provincial and imperial level. Petitions were often submitted by collective groups, and with the *Tanzimat*, they took a new level of importance (33f). This was fostered through legal changes and technological innovations, such as the introduction of the telegraph, which lifted the restrictions of geographical distance after the 1860s. This led to a 'flood' of petitions to Istanbul from the Jerusalem District; but the number of petitions to local authorities also rapidly increased after reforms introduced councils on the levels of district, subdistrict, community and city (42f). Petitioners were mostly representatives of a community: village *muḫtār*s, sheikhs or clerics who spoke in the name of groups' interests (48f). There were petitions by individuals in telegram style, but most were written by a professional petition-writer (Tur.: *arzuhalcı*) who offered his service in public places and applied specific jargon and official formulas (50–61).

216 *Filasṭīn*, 15 July 1911: 51/1/1.

and 1914, that addressed notions of the public interest. Unfortunately, I am unable to compare this with the coverage in other Arabic newspapers of the time, but it seems that it was common for the Arabic press of the Second Constitutional Era to underpin all kinds of reform demands with the claim that they served the 'public interest'.

Public responses were eagerly sought but the editors also established discursive rules for literary participation: protest letters had to be 'objective' and contain verifiable arguments. When letters were judged to be 'provocative' or not in line with the common interest, they were sometimes refused from being published. In the case of Mağdal, the editors announced that the population (of this town) 'has to excuse us if we stop reporting about it'. They asked 'the authors from Mağdal' (*kuttāb al-Mağdal*) to direct their 'flood of readers' letters to another newspaper' as it was 'easier to know if the fetus in the womb of a pregnant woman was male or female' than to know the truth behind contradictory contents in the letters arriving from Mağdal, and concluded that 'unfortunately, it is not possible for us to rely on a correspondent from your town who would report without pursuing [personal] interests (*ḫālī l-ġāya*)'.[217]

In terms of public awareness, there was a lot to be done in Palestine, thought the ʿĪsās. Much as they celebrated the resonance of their newspaper, they were just as pessimistic with regard to the cultural state of the Palestinians. In an editorial in 1911, Yūsuf al-ʿĪsā declared that the Jerusalem District was in a state of apathy and inertia. It was impossible to activate the great majority of the people since they could not read, and, in his opinion, the educated elites were disappointingly passive, as he reveals in the following statement:

> Possibly we were not (always) right in our views. But unfortunately, we have not found anybody among the citizens who stood up as to contest us and dispute with us, or to prove that our positions were weak. Sometimes we would even provoke public opinion in our writings (*nastaṯīr fī kitābātina ar-raʾy al-ʿāmm*) just to test how strong it is … Yet sadly, we have not found any proof that it even exists in this District. The best witness [to that] is our article titled 'The Nation Shall Prove its Existence' (*Fa-la-yuṯbit aš-šaʿb wuğūdahu*). In it, we said what can be named in one word: We noticed that dullness (*al-futūr*) has already seized the population of our city (Jaffa). Lethargy (*ḫumūl*) has been infiltrating their souls and cowardliness has been planted into their hearts. They neither oppose nor pretend to do so. They do not even write (to us) so that we could publish their protest letters with a signature and so the persons criticized would know that what is written is the opinion of the people. But, the response to our words was just silence…
>
> From that, two things have become clear to us. First, that the mission of the journalist (*waẓīfat aṣ-ṣiḥāfī*) in our country is much more difficult than in foreign countries. Because there, the journalist has merely to spread the news. But here, he has to create

217 *Filasṭīn*, 5 July 1913: 251/3/3.

> public opinion and cause a subversion of moral values and habits. Second, that the educated class accept what has been offered to them through their status without making the effort to think [critically] or be bothered to expressing criticism; while the ignorance of the uneducated class comprehensively embraces all spheres of life. – This is the state of the nation, which has an average of 2 percent of educated people.[218]

The ʿĪsās were not alone in this view. Many contemporary intellectuals complained of the lack of education and of apathy in Palestinian society. Rāġib al-Ḫālidī saw local Muslims imprisoned in 'despair and poverty'; and the Jerusalemite newspaper *Al-Munādī* attested in 1912 to the 'death of culture in Palestine' (*mawt aṯ-ṯaqāfa fī Filasṭīn*).[219]

Citizenry and Civic Participation

In the light of the perceived desolate state of the nation and in line with the 'educating mission' promoted in *Filasṭīn*, the authors gave importance to introducing to readers the potential of the public as a political actor. They elaborated on the meanings of 'civil rights' (*ḥuqūq aš-šaʿb*) and addressed the notions of the 'accountability' (*muḥāsaba*) and 'responsibility' (*masʾūlīya*) of state authorities towards the citizens.[220] The population should not be perceived as a ruler's obedient 'subjects' (*raʿīya*) or as a flock of sheep, as if it were under 'despotic rule' (*ḥukm mustabidd*), the authors claimed, referring to the period before the restoration of the Ottoman Constitution, which they called the 'age of despotism' (*ʿaṣr al-istibdād*). Authors of letters and editors alike regularly addressed the Palestinians as 'citizens' (*al-muwāṭinūn*), 'nationals' or 'locals' (*al-waṭanīyūn*) who should develop *and* express an opinion. They should understand the meaning of 'citizenship' (*al-muwāṭana*) and act as patriots. As mature citizens, they should stand up for their rights and actively demand them from the state authorities, which were to be held accountable for the rights promised in the Constitution.

In this respect, concepts such as 'participation in government' (*al-ištirāk fī l-ḥukm*) also were addressed. For example, Jaffa's imam Muḥammad Rāġib, a candidate in the parliamentary elections in 1912, pleaded in his *Filasṭīn* article entitled 'The Right to Vote and ' (*ḥaqq at-taṣwīt wa-l-intiḫābāt*) for the lowering of the age of the (male) voters from 30 to 25 or even 21 years. He elaborated on equality rights for citizens, guaranteed in the Constitution through indirect participation in political rule by the election of representatives. He confirmed that, according to the Fundamental Law (*al-qānūn al-asāsī*),

218 *Filasṭīn*, 15 July 1911: 51/1/1–2.
219 Yehoshua 1974, 171f; cf Ayalon 2004, 16.
220 See the discussion on the accountability of political institutions to the people, in *Filasṭīn*, 13 August 1913: 262/1/1–4.

'equality in essential rights' (*at-tasāwī fī l-ḥuqūq al-asāsīya*) is guaranteed to individuals of every (religious) community; and the most important (right) is the participation of all classes in (political) rule (*ištirāk ǧamīʿ ṭabaqātihā fī l-ḥukm*); and without differentiation (*lā mīza*) between rich and poor, the investor and the worker, the trader and the planter.

As direct participation of each individual in the rule is impossible (to implement) – and if it were, it would lead to chaos – civilized nations (*al-umam al-mutamaddina*) have agreed to enable the participation of the individuals in (political) rule through representatives (*wukalāʾ*) they appoint from among them ... and we can consider a government that rules through representatives as [exercising] honorable rule.[221]

Public Law and Order

Regarding concepts of the 'public' presented in *Filasṭīn*, there was a strong authoritarian notion of public space as a space of 'law and order'. The population of the Jerusalem District was much concerned with the security situation, and this was echoed in *Filasṭīn*. The general need for stability was immense, and the ideal that 'public order and security' (*al-amn al-ʿāmm*) should be guaranteed by state power was much emphasized. People wanted a strong state power able to protect the public space and frequently called for the strong presence of armed forces. The fear of chaos during the years before World War I dominated the elites. Given ethno-confessional diversity, international migration and the outbreak of Arab proto-nationalism, they were aware that Ottomanism was an artificial construct at risk. Groups suspected of destabilizing the fragile ethno-social coexistence in the urban space or endangering public security were to be severely sanctioned by state power, and there were demands for the expulsion of 'dangerous elements'.

In petitions to Jaffa's *qāʾimaqām* and the police commander, readers' letters demanded the building of more prisons, the organization of more street patrols, more effective criminal prosecutions, the imposition of the death penalty, the control of nomads and 'vagabonds' (to use *Filasṭīn*'s term) in town, and the construction of military compounds on Jaffa's perimeter. As the government failed to meet citizens' needs in this respect, authors complained about the authorities' carelessness and incompetence and reminded functionaries of what they claimed to be their central function: citizens' protection.

Security problems were obviously outstanding in the Bethlehem and Jaffa region. The *Local News* section in *Filasṭīn* was full of police reports about theft and robbery, murder, shootings, wanton destruction of agricultural land and blackmail of merchants; and I have documented 292 items on security issues and crime related to the topic of my investigation. The Bethlehem correspondent reported on bomb attacks on wealthy families' houses, arsen attacks on olive

221 *Filasṭīn*, 17 February 1912: 112/2/1–3.

groves, felling of trees and the wanton destruction of vineyards. In Jaffa, merchants and landowners involved in the citrus industry were victims of organized crime. In connection with this, migrants from the Maghreb countries and Afghanistan who were employed in the security sector were perceived as a security risk and a danger to local businesses, especially since they were armed and known for their short temper; a topic I shall pick up again in the latter part of the following chapter on the Jaffa region as an ethno-confessional 'contact zone'.

II. The Jaffa Region as an Ethno-Confessional Contact Zone

1. Historiographical Context and Relevance

This chapter explores the Jaffa region in the late nineteenth and early twentieth century as an expanding space and 'ethno-confessional contact zone' to illustrate the cultural, demographic and socio-political setting in which *Filasṭīn* emerged and which had an enormous influence on the views of the ʿĪsās and other publishing authors. Jaffa's geographical situation at the coast as the 'gateway to Palestine', to use Tolkowsky's words (1924), gave it much potential as did its strategic position as the economic hub of late Ottoman Palestine, as pointed out by Avcı and Norris, and a 'crossroads' for transport that connected Jaffa's port, travelers and trade with the rest of the District and created close links between Jaffa and Jerusalem. Late Ottoman Jaffa, though a provincial town, was the economic center of the Jerusalem District, and a kaleidoscope of cultures, ethnicities and confessions that lived together, side by side, or segregated. The special setting of this region, shaped by expansion, diversity and mobility, had a major effect on the range of topics presented in *Filasṭīn*. Since Jaffa's infrastructural, urban and economic development, its social problems and public security situation were a focal point of *Filasṭīn*'s coverage and the ʿĪsās' personal networks that were concentrated there, this chapter is dedicated to the conditions particular to this region at the turn of the twentieth century.

Jaffa and Tel Aviv in National and Relational Historiography

The region has a special place in the collective memory of Israelis and Palestinians, and scholarly production on Tel Aviv-Jaffa has been shaped by and reproduced in national narratives. Tel Aviv has a key position in Zionist historiography as a symbol of European modernity in the Middle East and has become the subject of glorifying descriptions. Zionist historiography has described the development of Tel Aviv as self-reliant, feeding the myth of a city that emerged autonomously 'out of the barren sand', as Gabriele Tergit, a German-Jewish journalist from Berlin, put it during the 1930s.[1]

Historically, Tel Aviv developed during the final years of the Ottoman Empire as part of Jaffa, and out of the Jewish quarter Aḥuzat Bayyit as the eleventh Jewish quarter that emerged outside the Old City walls since the second half of the nineteenth century. Tel Aviv, called in *Filasṭīn* a 'neighborhood' (*maḥalla*) of Jaffa, was one of more than 20 other new Christian and Muslim residential quarters that spread as part of Jaffa's urban expansion within a few decades north, east and south the Old City.[2] The interconnectedness of Tel Aviv and Jaffa lasted until the 1930s, when the 'daughter' Tel Aviv surpassed the 'mother' Jaffa, to use the words of LeVine. Receiving municipal status in 1934 and opening its own port in 1938, Tel Aviv had cemented its independence from Jaffa. Meanwhile, the discourse on Tel Aviv as a 'Hebrew city', the city of Jewish workers and pioneers, and a counterpart to Jewish exile consolidated in Zionist historiography and Hebrew literature, where Tel Aviv was the 'white' counterpart of Arab Jaffa, which became marginalized as Tel Aviv's 'back yard', described as a town of black houses, dirt, disorder and crime.[3] The fact that Tel Aviv in 2003 was declared a UNESCO World Heritage Site contributed to the myth of the 'White City' (Hebr.: *ha-ʿir ha-lewana*) of Bauhaus architecture, based on the urban planning of Patrick Geddes.[4]

In response to Zionist historiography, Palestinian literature nurtured a contrasting narrative on late Ottoman and pre-1948 Jaffa as a progressive and cosmopolitan Palestinian city. Like Tel Aviv in Israeli historiography, Jaffa became central in the Palestinian narrative as 'the Bride of the Sea' (*ʿarūs al-baḥr*) and 'a sad reminder of a glorious national past and a symbol of dispossession', as Monterescu has put it.[5] In Palestinian national historiography, late Ottoman and Mandate Jaffa was presented as the secret Palestinian capital, the 'greatest among the Arab cities of Palestine' (*kubrā l-mudun al-ʿarabīya fī Filasṭīn*) that lost the battle to Tel Aviv.[6] Thus, in Palestinian literature, Jaffa was a subject of nostalgic

1 See Tergit 1996, 70. Tergit migrated to Mandate Palestine in 1933. Looking through the eyes of an intellectual from a German urban environment, she described Jerusalem, Tel Aviv and Haifa against the background of local ethnic and cultural diversity in contrast to the consolidating Zionist Yishuv. Indulging in the 'Holy Land' perspective on the local population, she described the 'new' European modernity in Tel Aviv and Jewish settlements as its counterpart. For her account of Jewish opinions on life in Tel Aviv in 1936, see pp. 70–82. For Tel Aviv as the Zionist 'dream', see Schlör 1996.

2 LeVine 2005, 155–156.

3 LeVine 2005, 121, 122f.

4 See http://whc.unesco.org/en/list/1096 (consulted: 2 August 2017.)

5 Monterescu 2005, 13; see also Monterescu and Rabinowitz 2007, 12; and Rabinowitz and Monterescu 208, 206.

6 Daǧǧānī 1991, 74.

research and ideological rather than analytical interest. These studies were personal memories and poetry, describing Jaffa's houses, gardens, vineyards and 'fragrance' (*'iṭr*),[7] or biographical data collections of famous personalities, and urban studies mixed with poetry. All of them were motivated by the nationalist outlook, mourned the loss of Arab Jaffa and sought to conserve its heritage.[8]

Later, inter-relational studies on Jaffa-Tel Aviv as a multi-functional space, applying the dialectics of space and sociality, challenged both Zionist and Palestinian narratives. Monterescu and Rabinowitz studied Jewish-Arab cities as 'mixed towns' in terms of ethnic, social and professional diversity and an exchange of commodities and ideas, without implying harmony in Arab–Jewish relations.[9] Space production automatically includes segregation and conflicts, though without excluding cohabitation.[10] What interested the authors was the correlation between 'modernity, national concepts and dynamics of urban growth' and its impact on demographic interaction versus segregation in different towns of Ottoman and Mandate Palestine and Israel.[11] However, I find the theoretical categorization of space in the essays of Monterescu and Rabinowitz of little help in understanding the reciprocal impact of space production and social relations on the ground.[12] LeVine explored reciprocal architectural developments in Jaffa and Tel Aviv during the British Mandate and after, taking the urban space as a ground for the production of collective memory and historical nar-

7 For instance, see Fawzi Ḥāǧǧ's book *Yaffa. An Orchard of Perfume and Poetry: An Anthological* Documentation (*Yāfā. Bayārat al-'iṭr wa-š-ši'r. Tawṯīq antūlūǧī*). Ḥāǧǧ 2004.

8 See Bawwāb 2003. For Arab resistance to the British and the Jews during the Arab revolt (1936–1939) in Jaffa, see Daǧǧānī Aḥmad Zakī 1989; Daǧǧānī Sa'd 1991; Ġarbīya 1987; Ḥūt 2007. For biographies of Jaffa families, see Malak 1996; Qalyūbī 2006. There is also a historiography, which was unavailable at the time of my research (Rantīsī 1995–). For the architectural planning of Jaffa during the Mandate, see Mas'ūd 1946. For personal memories of Mandate Jaffa, see Heikal and Imad 1984; Tamari and Hammami 1998.

9 On 'Arab-Jewish mixed towns', see Monterescu 2005, 11–16; Monterescu and Rabinowitz 2007, 3; Rabinowitz and Monterescu 2008, 198.

10 National narratives that contradict each other are still interrelated, as one helps to create the identity of the other. See Monterescu and Rabinowitz 2007, 2, 6; Rabinowitz and Monterescu 2008, 196–198.

11 Monterescu and Rabinowitz explicitly distanced themselves from bipolar categories in urban studies, such as the 'colonial city' (Algiers in the 1950s), the 'holy city' (Mecca), the 'dual city' (Rabat in the post-colonial era) or 'divided city' (post-1967 Jerusalem). See Monterescu and Rabinowitz 2007, 1–2; Rabinowitz and Monterescu 2008, 196.

12 For instance, they categorized nineteenth-century Ottoman Jaffa as a 'proto-national, mercantile mixed town', which produced through its spatial expansion new kinds of public space and ethno-national competition. In 1921, they saw this period end with the massacre in Jaffa, when militant Palestinians killed 43 Jewish migrants, and Jaffa became what they called a 'bifurcated national capitalist mixed town'. See Rabinowitz and Monterescu 2008, 202–207; Monterescu and Rabinowitz 2007, 8–14.

ratives.[13] Rotbard has shown a more radical approach, criticizing not only Tel Aviv's physical hegemony over Jaffa but also the discursive erasure of Arab Jaffa from the collective memory through the dominant Zionist narrative on Tel Aviv as the 'White City' and Jaffa as the 'Black City'.[14]

For my study on late Ottoman Jaffa, the works of Kark and Ṭarāwina were of central importance. Both studies, rooted in the 'dual society outlook', provide valuable collections of data, although they lack analytical concepts. Kark comprehensively investigates the transformation of Jaffa from the nineteenth century up to the end of Ottoman rule. Based on an impressive selection of archive material, travelers' accounts, consular reports and population censuses, Kark traces its demographic, spatial, socio-cultural, economic, infrastructural, administrational and architectural development during that period. Assessing Jaffa's historical development through documents almost entirely written by Europeans (pilgrims, diplomats, scholars and Zionists, such as Abraham Moses Luncz and Moshe Smilansky) and the Hebrew press (*Havazelet*, *Ḥerut* and *Ha-Po'el ha-Za'ir*), Kark's study reproduces Zionist-European perspectives on Palestine. Kark almost completely ignores Arab and Ottoman perspectives on local developments, and the absence of Arab and Ottoman sources in her analysis is significant.[15] Kark's selection of sources led her to identify European migration as the main factor in Jaffa's transformation from a small harbor into *the* boom town of late Ottoman Palestine. Relying on foreign nineteenth-century reports that compared Jaffa with the 'standard package' of European modernity and viewed Arab Jaffa as a miserable place, Kark broadly reproduces this outlook.[16]

In her presentation, the modernization of Jaffa was carried out through Ashkenazi migration and embodied in the Jewish suburbs.[17] Kark sees Jaffa's development as driven by foreign powers and indulges in the narrative of Palestinian decline under 'Turkish' rule. She hardly considers the various effects of the Ottoman *Tanzimat* and marginalizes local contributions to Jaffa's develop-

13 In chapter five, LeVine (2005, 121–151) explores contrasting images of Jaffa-Tel Aviv in Palestinian and Israeli literature. In chapter six (152–188), he tackles architectural plans for urban developments derived from national identities, exploring the ideological implications in the urban design of Tel Aviv and Jaffa in the examples of the early plans of Tel Aviv as Garden City, in the later Bauhaus style of the 1930s and in the urban designs in Aǧamī.

14 Rotbard 2015.

15 Kark indicates several times that there were no reliable local sources to investigate. Although sources on the development of Jaffa during the late Ottoman times are limited, Arabic and Ottoman documents certainly exist. Kark did not consider them supposedly because of language barriers. The Sharia court files, for example, shed light on Christian–Muslim socio-economic interaction and legal issues, as explored by Layish (1970 and 1975). See also Agmon (2004 and 2006) on Jaffa's Sharia records regarding legal and family matters.

16 Kark 1990b, 53–61.

17 Kark 1990b, 118–34.

ment.[18] In terms of social cohabitation, she focuses on Jewish life as described from the perspective of Zionist migrants. Other parts of the demographic spectrum are hardly considered; very little is reported about the Muslim majority and Muslim–Christian relations are in general categorized as unstable.[19]

A valuable study on the development of the Jaffa *qaḍāʾ* between 1864 and 1914 is the Ṭarāwina's comprehensive work, which is much based on Arab sources. He has made extensive use of Jaffa's Sharia court records, the *siğillāt*, the land registry office, the *ṭābū*, the Ottoman population censuses, Arabic press from Palestine, Syria and Lebanon, and travelers' accounts, and thus has produced an encyclopedic collection of data and lists.[20] For instance, Ṭarāwina enumerates 110 Arab villages in the *qaḍāʾ*, giving information about their geographical situation, number of inhabitants and the size of cultivated areas,[21] including the Jewish settlements and German colonies in the region.[22] He lists Ottoman administrative bodies, religious offices with the names of office holders, security forces, juridical institutions, taxes, transport and communication services, trading companies and currencies. In addition, Ṭarāwina lists a variety of crafts and industries, presents demographic data on ethnic and confessional groups including names of community leaders and educational institutions.

Reframing Jaffa: Port City, Agricultural Agglomeration, Globalized Space

This study explores the expansion of late Ottoman Jaffa from the late nineteenth and early twentieth century in the context of Jaffa's features as a 'port city', an 'agricultural agglomeration', a 'globalized city' and a 'showcase model' of a well-developed region with close links to the capital, Jerusalem. Here, Kark's accounts and Ṭarāwina's numerical and statistical evaluations were extremely helpful for visualizing the spatial urban and demographic expansion of Jaffa. The chapter on the coastal plain in Buessow's work on Jaffa (2011) further contributed to this understanding, as did the maps of the Jaffa region drawn by the German Templar architect Theodor Sandel, reprinted in Kark, and Gustaf Dalman's 1917/18 area photos. Another aspect, the Jaffa *qaḍāʾ* as a 'showcase model of Ottoman-Palestinian modernity', became clear from the reading of *Filasṭīn*, which revealed its representative function in the Jerusalem District.

As a Mediterranean port city, Jaffa was characterized by a very high degree of mobility. Although it did not have a deep-water port but only a shallow harbor,

18 For example, see Kark 1990b, 29–30.
19 Kark's judgment on Jaffa's inter-confessional life cannot be taken as reliable since she does not consult local accounts. Regarding socio-economic interaction between different groups in Jaffa, Kark only mentions Arab employment in Tel Aviv. See Kark 1990b, 200 n. 203, 201.
20 Ṭarāwina 2000, 29–45.
21 Ṭarāwina 2000, 100–129.
22 Ṭarāwina 2000, 129–133.

there was a high level of seaborne comings and goings of people and commodities. The network of routes leading to and from Jaffa, especially over land and the Jaffa-Jerusalem railway link, made Jaffa *the* crossing point in late Ottoman Palestine. Basically, all tourists and pilgrims, merchants and diplomats traveling to or leaving Palestine passed through the city of Jaffa via the overland roads and its harbor. While Jaffa town in the 1840s was a harbor surrounded by a fortress, extensive cultivation from the 1850s fostered its expansion into an extended agricultural agglomeration, until, at the end of the nineteenth century, Jaffa extended over a considerable area, uniting features of urban modernity and agricultural space. Suburbs and garden villages emerged between the fields and connected the hinterland with the commercial centers and the harbor.

The vital plantation economy and rising exports led to Jaffa becoming the town with the most vital economy in late Ottoman Palestine. Agricultural expansion and the export boom stimulated migration. From the late 1820s, Egyptians started to settle on the coast, and the 1840s saw the beginnings of Jaffa's Sephardi community. From the 1850s, Muslims migrated from Morocco, Tunisia, Algeria, Afghanistan, Iran and India. From the late 1860s, German Protestants arrived and, from the 1880s, Ashkenazis came from Eastern Europe. These groups made Jaffa into a multi-cultural kaleidoscope and the most cosmopolitan place in Palestine. Jaffa integrated dozens of nationalities, ethnicities and religious communities, including Muslims, Greek Orthodox, Roman Catholics, Protestants, Armenians, Maronites, and Sephardi and Ashkenazi Jews, each of which maintained places of worship, monasteries, educational services, charities and administrative institutions. Although the confessional groups had enormous influence on shaping the town's transformation, Jaffa was known for cultural cosmopolitanism and religious moderation; at least, the town was presented as such in *Filasṭīn.* In contrast, Gaza was presented as a backward and remote city on the sandy periphery, cut off from civilization and a place where the government would not invest in reforms.[23] This was certainly an exaggeration. However, Jaffa had a representative function that Gaza did not. Jaffa was a channel for government officials who traveled to or left from Palestine via the port and viewed the *qaḍāʾ* as a positive role model for development.

23 In an editorial, Yūsuf al-ʿĪsā declared it the duty of journalists to know the state of his country's cities in terms of their civilizational progress. He traveled to Gaza, the third largest city in the *liwāʾ* after Jerusalem and Jaffa, to inspect it, and drew a quite depressing picture. He described its infrastructure as neglected, its architecture as boring and just like the other 'Eastern cities' (*al-mudun aš-šarqīya*), with its narrow alleys and 'miserable, intertwined buildings'(*al-abniya al-ḥaqīra al-mutarākiba*). The only positive thing he mentioned about Gaza was the new hospital, situated on a hill, and the good water quality. *Filasṭīn*, 31 August 1912, 167/1/1–4.

The following sections illustrate Jaffa's development as a port city, an expanding agricultural agglomeration and a globalized city, and a crossing point for people and goods with a tight connectedness between the urban and rural spaces and the various confessional groups, and between governmental institutions and local 'pressure groups' that were able to articulate a political agenda. The last part explores how urban politics were negotiated with a focus on the modernization of Jaffa's infrastructure and on ethno-social cohabitation and conflicts.

2. From 'Fortress' to 'Boom Town'

This section outlines the transition of Jaffa from a fortified harbor and fishing village to an expanding agricultural agglomeration and a boom town during the *Tanzimat* until it was the second largest city of Palestine after Jerusalem at the eve of World War I.

At the beginning of the nineteenth century, Jaffa was inhabited by less than 3,000 people.[24] Consisting of the harbor and a tiny city, it had the size of a village of about 108 *dunam* (or 25 acres). At the end of the Ottoman period, its population had increased to 50,000 inhabitants of various origins; its built-up area covered about 1,550 *dunam* (almost 400 acres), plus another 1,447 *dunam* outside the former city wall.[25] Under Abū Nabbūt, a Mamluk appointed governor of Jaffa from 1800 to 1818, the small harbor was turned into a fortress to guard the sea route to Jerusalem from Western attacks. Abū Nabbūt constructed a sea wall to protect the warehouses on the shore and a gated city wall with towers, and placed his artillery on top of the walls.[26] During the short period of Egyptian rule over Palestine and Syria (1831–1840), Jaffa was the headquarters of the ruler, Ibrāhīm Pasha, and developed further to serve the needs of Egyptian troops as the Jaffa port linked the coast of Syria and Palestine with Egypt.[27]

24 After the Napoleon conquest, the numbers of Jaffa's inhabitants ranged between 500 according to Buessow (2011, 216) and 2,500 or 2,750 people according to Kark (1990b, 10, 291).

25 Kark 1990b, 291.

26 Apart from the fortification of Jaffa, Abū Nabbūt restored the Maḥmūdīya Mosque in Jaffa, and built public fountains (*sabīl*) and the cotton and wool markets. It is said that he discriminated against Christians and under his rule, Christian children were converted to Islam and taken into his service. See Kark 1990b, 16–20.

27 On the 'centralized' rule of Ibrāhīm Pasha over Palestine and Jaffa, see Kark 1990b, 21–26.

Reforms and Security

Figure 8: General View at Jaffa's Old City from the Sea around 1920 (Courtesy of American Colony). (Source: National Photo Collection of Israel; Photography dept. Government Press Office)

With the restoration of Ottoman rule over Palestine and the imposition of technological, juridical and administrative reforms during the *Tanzimat*, the security situation on the Palestinian coast improved.[28] This had major effects on Jaffa, which was now ruled by an appointed *qāʾimaqām* subordinate to the governor of Sidon. With Ottoman provincial law, Jaffa became a *qaḍāʾ* of the Jerusalem District. Its *qāʾimaqām* was subordinate to the Jerusalem governor and advised by a District Council (*mağlis idāra*) composed of various sects. In 1871, the Municipality (*al-mağlis al-baladī*, or: *al-baladīya*) was set up to work on infrastructure, cleanliness and security.[29] Public safety was improved, so that the

28 Kark 1990b, 26–32.

29 The municipality council was elected by the males of the population who paid a certain amount of annual tax. At its inception in 1871, it was composed of four Muslims and four Christians, but no Jews. At the municipal election in 1913, it is known that there were about 700 electors, Muslims and non-Muslims. The Jews had at this time 25–30 electors, an under-

city gates did not have to be closed all night, the landward wall was torn down, and guards were posted along the Jaffa-Jerusalem road. Gradually, the trench around the Old City wall was filled in and the stones from the fortifications were used to build residential areas, shops and markets. A new lighthouse was constructed and access to the harbor and the streets of Jaffa was widened. By the middle of the 1870s, Jaffa's fortified appearance had disappeared.[30]

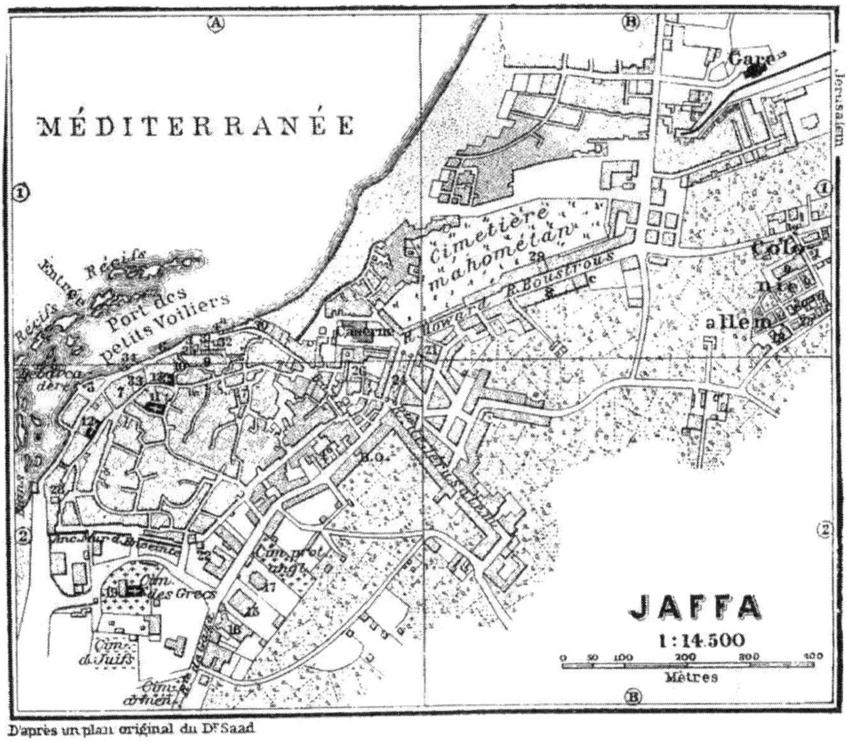

Figure 9: Map of Central Jaffa as printed in Baedeker, Karl. 1906. Palestine and Syria: with the Chief Routes through Mesopotamia and Babylonia: Handbook for Travelers. Leipzig: Karl Baedeker. London: T. Fisher Unwin. New York: Charles Scribner's Sons, 121.

The 'original' Old Jaffa, the fortified harbor and gated Old City on a rounded hill overlooking the sea, was a tiny area of narrow alleys. It twisted between the New Gate with the former moat to the east and the harbor to the west and, apart from

representation of the proportion of the Jewish population, according to Kark (1990b, 204–205). The municipality derived its income from real-estate holdings, taxes on property, wine production, import duties and highway tolls; and between 1904 and 1912, from a tax on urban development. The report of Cuinet states that in 1892, the municipality had an income of 169,813 piasters. See Kark 1990b, 46.

30 Kark 1990b, 32–36, 61–63.

Figure 10: Bazaar in central Jaffa between 1898 and 1914 from the G. Eric and Edith Matson Photograph Collection. (Source: Library of Congress)

Muslim, Christian and Jewish residential compounds, contained public institutions, markets, crafts, khans, bathhouses, coffee shops, mosques, synagogues, churches, the Greek convent, the Latin church and hostel, the Franciscan hostel, the Armenian church and convent, the Maronite church, a quarantine building (erected in 1835), foreign consulates and foreign post offices, schools and hospitals.[31] As a result of demographic growth in the latter half of the century, the 1880s and 1890s were decades of tremendous building activity and, at the beginning of the twentieth century, there were several new commercial and residential complexes outside the walls. The new business center was 'Bustrus Market' (*Sūq al-Bustrus*) on Bustrus Street, situated outside the Muslim cemetery on the roads to Nablus and Jerusalem on the way to the German Colony.[32] There,

31 Sandel marked the cemeteries of the various confessions on his 1878/79-map; among them the Muslim cemetery to the north, the Protestant cemetery to the east, and to the south-east the Greek Orthodox, Armenian, Roman Catholic and Jewish cemeteries. See Kark 1990b, 64–70; cf. the map on pp. 68–69.

32 According to 'Palestine Remembered', Bustrus Market is named after the wealthy Lebanese Bustrus family, and Iskandar ʿAwād. See http://www.palestineremembered.com/Jaffa/Jaffa/ (accessed 20 November 2017).

most Muslim and Christian shop owners leased to Jewish immigrants. The Greek convent purchased land outside the Muslim cemetery and built nearly 200 shops there, and the Greek Orthodox Church was one of the biggest owners of real estate in Jaffa, gaining enormous income from leasing shops.[33]

Land Reforms

The improved security situation and the Ottoman Land Reforms (1858, 1867) opened the way for rapid agricultural cultivation along the coast between Jaffa and Gaza. The Land Law of 1858 allowed individuals for the first time to acquire title deeds on land, and kept the categories that had been fixed in the Ottoman Law, the *kanūnnāme*, since the fifteenth century: state land (*mīrī*), private and absolute property (*mulk*), land that was not regularly cultivated or waste land (*mawāt*), property registered as a religious and pious endowment (*waqf*), and community land (*matrūk*), meaning land available for public use, e.g. streets, public places in villages, cemeteries, etc. The reform addressed mostly *mīrī* and *mawāt* land, which could now have individual title deeds. *Mawāt* land could be purchased as *mulk*, which was not limited to agricultural use. The ownership of *mīrī* land included the right to usufruct, was restricted to cultivation and the land reverted to the state after three years if it was not being cultivated. Categorized then as 'released' (*maḥlūl*), the land could be purchased by a new owner.[34]

The land reform was intended to foster the privatization and cultivation of land and make property rights more transparent so that the state could guarantee a steady flow of levies to the center. Property tax (*wīrkū*) was imposed on land or real estate classified as *mulk* while a tithe (*ʿušr*) was imposed on *mīrī* land. Title deeds on *mīrī* land guaranteed the owner the right to agricultural usufruct for a period of years, after which the land reverted to the state. There was a newly introduced right to acquire individual title deeds for *māwāt* land, mostly desert, sand dunes in coastal areas and swamps, which was intended to speed up the cultivation of waste land and limit communal land use (*mušāʿ*), a practice that was widespread on grazing land, for example, but also on agricultural land, and divided areas into tiny units whose cultivation rights circulated within a group of owners or tenants. The second land law of 1867 provided foreigners in the Empire with the right to acquire title deeds on landed property, which opened the way for European investors in the Arab provinces.[35]

33 Kark 1990b, 260–262.

34 LeVine 2004, 100f. For the categories, see also the Ottoman Land Code, translated from the Turkish by F. Ongley of the Receiver General's Office in Cyprus in 1892, 8–56. https://archive.org/stream/ottomanlandcode00turkuoft/ottomanlandcode00turkuoft_djvu.txt (accessed 27 October 2017).

35 For the land reform and its consequences, see Krämer 2002, 100–112; Gerber 1987, 67–82; Mundy 2007, 44–48. For the impact of the land reform during the *Tanzimat* and British era on

Krämer has pointed out that the land reforms did not quite achieve their aims and, in 1925, three-quarters of the land in Palestine was still neither surveyed nor registered in the cadasters.[36] Further, the law had unintended consequences, since in practice strengthened the role of the local effendis and opened the way for massive 'land grabbing'. Farmers and cultivators of leased land feared the taxes and military conscription that a property title would entail. Thus, they tended to transfer their rights of cultivation or ownership, which sometimes circulated within a community, to local strongmen, tribal and village leaders, urban notables or tax collectors. In practice, the farmers continued cultivating the land according to their traditions and often lived on it, but in law they became tenant farmers without registered property rights. The practice of registering land in the name of local notables created overnight a new class of large-scale landowners, and agricultural land became the favorite target for capital investment. Since it was possible to acquire large plots as property, the cultivation of the coastal area sped up, introducing monocultures. Wheat and barley were grown in the Gazan area, citrus fruit and grapes in the Jaffa region. Large areas of land and real estate were also acquired by churches, merchants, foreign diplomats and settlers.[37] This process opened the way for rivalries between the traditional Muslim elites, a rising middle class and Europeans, who mobilized large sums to buy land and real-estate.[38] The effect of rapid cultivation and 'land grabbing' was a dramatic price rise in the Jaffa region from the 1890s, with a tenfold increase in prices for agricultural land.[39]

Within a few decades, the Jaffa environs became an agricultural agglomeration with a large area of gardens (*bayārāt*) that were intertwined with the urban space and linked through a network of streets to its commercial centers and the harbor.

land ownership in Palestine from the first reform of 1858 until the end of the Mandate period, see Fakhr Eldin 2008. For changes of land ownership categories in the Jaffa-Tel Aviv region and the conversion of legal categories, see LeVine 2004, 100–146.

36 Krämer 2002, 102.

37 Wealthy merchants from Lebanon and Syria acquired land in northern Palestine and the coastal area, which created a new role, that of the 'absentee landowner', who usually came for the harvest season without permanently residing on the land or having social ties in the local context. See Krämer 2002b, 100–105.

38 This created intra-European competition for real estate and building activity, which was most evident in Jerusalem. Each nation enforced the erection of representative buildings and missionary institutions, such as the Russian Compound outside the Old City. Avcı also describes this in the 'hunting' for concessions to modernize Jaffa's port, which was never realized. See Avcı 2011, 93–96; Kark 1990b, 31–32.

39 Relying on the census of Luncz (1910/11), Divine reports that land in the Jaffa region that had previously been sold for 300–500 francs per hectare (10 *dunam*) was sold two decades later for 3,000–6,000 francs. See Divine 1994, 127. Smilansky documents similar prices for the 1880s–1890s (30–50 francs per *dunam*) and the first decade of the twentieth century (300–600 francs). Farmland for citrus plantation could even reach 1,500–2,500 francs per *dunam*. Prices for building land were lower, but varied in different reports. See Kark 1990b, 248, 249.

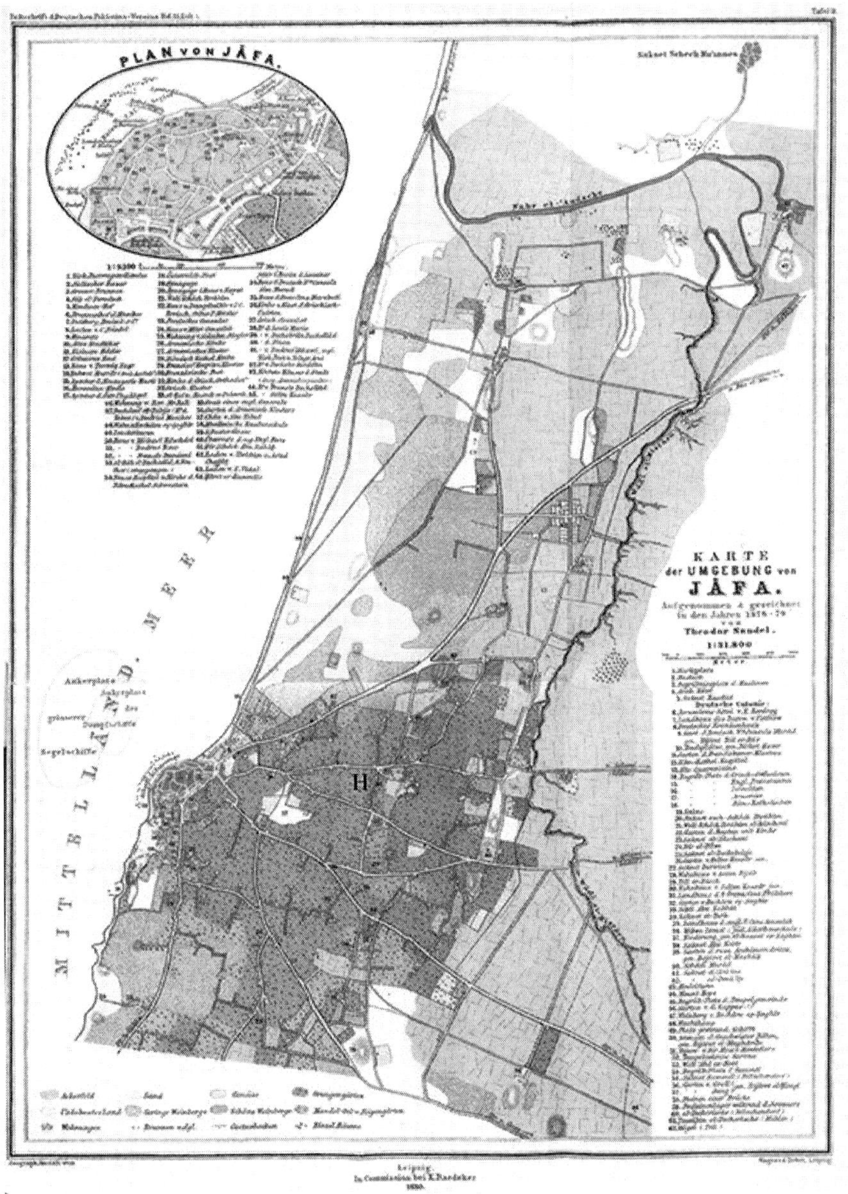

Figure 11: Map of Jaffa and environs as drawn by the German architect Theodor Sandel, 1878/79.

The map drawn by the German Templar and engineer Theodor Sandel in 1878/79 shows that the Jaffa hinterland at this time had been largely cultivated and plantations extended over a considerable area.[40]

The gardens were connected by watercourses and, given the high level of groundwater, irrigated by wells, from which water was extracted by animal-driven waterwheels, later to be powered by kerosene motors and pumps, filled into pools and distributed to the gardens. The fastest expansion of agricultural land took place from the 1890s until the beginning of World War I.[41] Around 1908, the coast was completely cultivated apart from a stripe of sand dunes and the swamps on the east side of Jaffa.[42]

Finally, one feature in the region that should be briefly mentioned, was the frequent confusion over tax categories and classifications of agricultural land.[43] After the Ottoman land registry office started documenting ownership, Jaffa's entrepreneurs often bribed officials to have their property registered as *mulk* instead of *mīrī* land, to avoid the annual tithe (*ʿušr*), which was, according to the German Vice-Consul in 1895, 12.5 percent of income from crops. Kark states that most of the land in the Jaffa region was classified as *mulk*, which led to the resistance of Ottoman authorities and foreign diplomatic intervention.[44]

Cash Crops, Export Boom and Industries

The preferred capital investment in the Jaffa region were citrus monocultures as cash crops (citrons and lemons, but especially oranges), and the citrus industry became Jaffa's largest and most profitable sector. Areas previously planted with other fruits or olives were replanted with citrus to the extent that Jewish agronomists of the early twentieth century judged the 'planting fever' in Jaffa as 'irrational'.[45] This development fostered the economic rise of Jaffa into a boom

40 The maps were originally published in G. Schwarz 1880. See also Kark 1990b, 63–65, 68–69.

41 Reilly mentions that, between 1895 and1915, the cultivated area expanded from 6,600 *dunam* to 30,000, (quoted in Divine 1994, 121). Kark states that, between the 1880s and 1916, cultivated land in the Jaffa region increased 'tenfold'. Kark 1990b, 244.

42 For water consumption and costs of cultivating a citrus grove of 25 *dunam* at the beginning of the twentieth century, see Kark 1990b, 242–244. The British consular report from 1906 documented 200 kerosene motors in the Jaffa area for irrigating gardens and operating mills. Kark 1990b, 245. Although as early as 1891, the Ottoman government had planned an irrigation project to supply the gardens with water from the Yarkon River (Ar.: *nahr al-ʿAwǧāʾ*) – among the promoters of the concession were the Sephardi Jew from Jaffa Joseph Navon, the French-Lebanese merchant Phillipe Efendi and the later major of Tel Aviv, Me'ir Dizengoff – the central government had not granted the concession by 1916. Avcı 2011, 89.

43 For the conversion of land categories in the region, see Le Vine 2004, 100–146.

44 For example, the German colonies in the region eventually had their land registered as *mulk* thanks to the intervention of the German chancellor. Kark 1990b, 246–248.

45 The main types of citrus fruit were two sorts of oranges; the thin-skinned *baladī* and the thick-skinned and seedless *šamūṭī*, developed by Arab Palestinian farmers for export. Also, citrons,

town, surpassing the other cities in late Ottoman Palestine, and Jaffa's commerce apparently multiplied about 50 times between 1890 and 1906.[46] Its economic significance was underlined by the fact that the Commercial Court for the entire Jerusalem District was opened in Jaffa in 1901, affiliated with the Chamber of Commerce, which handled all business affairs for Palestine.[47]

The citrus industry employed a lot of people. The growing, harvesting, the packing of the fruit in the fields and transporting it to the city, and shipping it out from the harbor was in the hands of the residents. The profits went back to the city. Although sesame, olive oil, cotton, wheat, wool, soap, wine, leather and other products left Jaffa's port,[48] citrus fruit was the major export. The 'Jaffa Orange', the *šamūṭī* type, became the most famous single export, and citrus fruits were exported to Europe from the 1850s.[49] The economic importance of citrus fruit for Jaffa is obvious: In 1880, it amounted to up to 20 percent of all of its exports, and in 1913, 40 percent, most of it going to England, Turkey and Egypt.[50] An editorial in *Filasṭīn* compared trade statistics for imports and exports via Jaffa in 1885 and 1911 to stress the importance of the harbor for urban growth.[51] An article reprinted in *Filasṭīn* from the Beirut newspaper *an-Naṣīr* stated in 1912 that tourists passing through Jaffa and its commercial vitality had now made Jaffa 'more important than Beirut' (*aʿẓam ahammīyatan min Bayrūt*). While Beirut's trade depended on foreign industrial output, Jaffa had an annual income of 'one million in foreign currency' from its own agricultural land, the article argued, which was the most profitable target for investment and attracted 'foreign money' (*al-māl al-ağnabī*).[52]

lemons, mandarin oranges and Indian oranges were grown, but in less quantity. Apart from this, grapes grew in the gardens along with olives, figs, almonds, pomegranate, peaches, apricots, sugar cane, water melons, vegetables and tobacco. During the 1850–1870s, there had been attempts to introduce mulberry trees for silk production and cotton as a cash crop, but they were dropped when artificial silk began to be manufactured in Switzerland and the cotton market declined. Kark 1990b, 220–242.

46 Kark 1990b, 262.

47 Jaffa lost this outstanding status after the reopening of the Jerusalem Commercial Court. Kark 1990b, 45.

48 Kark 1990b, 276–279.

49 British consular reports for that time mentioned exports of 171,000 boxes (valued at 50,000 pounds sterling). In 1909, 774,000 boxes were exported (200,000 pounds), and in 1913 1,609,000 boxes (300,000 pounds). Issawi 2006, 127. For more information on Jaffa's international trade and import and export numbers, see Buheiry 1981; Issawi 1988a; Ṭarāwina 2000, 393–421.

50 See Kark 1990b, 251; Buessow 2011, 221; Divine 1994, 213.

51 Revenues from imports amounted to 3,025,000 francs in 1885, and 15,954,000 francs in 1911. Revenues from exports amounted to 4,375,000 francs in 1885, and 11,855,000 francs in 1911. See *Filasṭīn*, 6 January 1912: 101/1/4–5. For a list on the monetary value of Jaffa's trade between 1800 and 1912 in pounds Sterling, see Kark 1990b, 277–278.

52 *Filasṭīn*, 20 January 1912: 104/4/1–2.

Figure 12: Picking the fruits in the fields. Photo made by Frank Scholten, ca. 1922. (© The Netherlands Institute for The Near East (Leiden), Frank Scholten Collection; www.nino-leiden.nl/collections/frank-scholten-legacy)

Figure 13: Packing the fruits. (Source: ibid.)

Figure 14: Transporting the fruits. (Source: ibid.)

Figure 15: Loading the fruits on little boats at the harbor. (Source: ibid.)

Figure 16: Bringing the fruits to the steamship that lies at anchor the shore. (Source: ibid.)

Figure 17: Shipping the fruit. (Source: ibid.)

Figure 18: Soap production in Jaffa. (Source: ibid.)

Apart from citrus fruit, other flourishing businesses were food and soap manufacture, and the water wheels along the Yarkon River that drove presses, grain mills and machines.[53] Arthur Ruppin, German director of the Zionist Palestine Office in Jaffa, estimated the number of sesame presses in the Jerusalem District before World War I to be around 40 and, according to the *siǧillāt*, there were 12 sesame presses in the *qaḍā'*, including nine in Jaffa.[54] In 1909, 22 grain mills were powered by water on the Yarkon River. Among them were five owned by the local notable and merchant Ḥāfiẓ Bek as-Sa'īd, and three by the municipality on the river north of Jaffa at al-Ǧarīša, al-Maḥmūdīya and al-Fārūḫīya.[55]

There were also factories producing soap from olive oil. The *siǧillāt* reveal that in 1871 there were around 25 soap factories in the *qaḍā'*: 15 in Jaffa, six in Ramla and four in Lod.[56] Jaffa was also known for perfume production and tanneries.[57]

53 According Ṭarāwina, 36 olive oil presses were operating in the Jaffa *qaḍā'*, nine of them in Jaffa, 14 in Lod and eight in Ramla. I do not know the year to which Ṭarāwina refers. The numbers seem to be taken from reports in the British 'Hand Book on Syria (Including Palestine)', published in 1920. See Ṭarāwina 2000, 314–315.

54 Ṭarāwina 2000, 315.

55 See *Filasṭīn*, 28 August 1912: 166/3/1; 18 December 1912: 198/3/3. There were three more grain mills powered by coal or petrol, one owned by Jewish settlers in 'Arṭūf, one in Jaffa itself and the third in the German colony of Sarona. See Ṭarāwina 2000, 316.

56 Ṭarāwina 2000, 318–319.

The German and Jewish settlements in the hinterland introduced wine growing in the region, at Rishon le-Tzion and Zikhron Yacob in 1885, for example. This became economically so successful that the District Council decided in 1912 to raise the annual wine tax from 1,000 to 1,500 lira.[58] *Filasṭīn* reported in 1911 that the German colony of Sarona had 300 hectares of vineyards and also produced high quality cognac for the export to Europe.[59]

3. Demographic Diversity and Migration

The following chapter illustrates how these developments, which massively stimulated migration from various regions during the second half of the nineteenth century, transformed Jaffa within a few decades into a 'globalized city'. Arab Muslims and Christians from other parts of Palestine and the Arab provinces, Arab Muslims and Sephardi Jews from North Africa, and Protestants and Ashkenazi Jews from Europe all came to Jaffa, and made its society tremendously diverse.[60] Here, international migration to Jaffa should also be explored in the context of migration movements that the Arab East in general saw during the second half of the nineteenth century. Grossman estimates the number of refugees migrating to various parts of the Ottoman Empire to be between two and three million. There were Muslim refugees from Algeria (after the French conquest in 1850), the Caucasus and Circassia (annexed by Russia in 1864) and Bosnia (lost to Serbia in 1878), who settled in Greater Syria (*bilād aš-Šām*) and Palestine. These movements made a deep impact on rural regions in Palestine and their interrelations need to be explored more in future research.[61]

Overall, Jaffa experienced for decades very high migration rates that exceeded those in other cities in Palestine. In 1917, Baldensperger stated that more than 25 nationalities were represented in Jaffa, each of which had its own leader to deal with the authorities[62] and, according to Jewish scholar and activist Zionist Moshe Smilansky, there were 18 doctors from different ethnical and religious back-

57 Ṭarāwina 2000, 320–322.

58 Ṭarāwina 2000: 322–323. See *Filasṭīn*, 25 December 1912: 200/3/3–4; *Filasṭīn*, 28 December 1912: 201/3/2f; *Filasṭīn*, 1 January 1913: 202/3/3–4.

59 *Filasṭīn*, 6 July 1911: 52/2/2–3; 19 July 1911: 52/2/2–3. From 1910 onwards, the colonists of Sarona also tried to cultivate cotton but soon gave it up again. *Filasṭīn*, 24 May 1913: 239/2/5.

60 For a very brief discussion of the reception of Jewish, Protestant and Maghrebi migration into the *qaḍā'* in *Filasṭīn*, see Dierauff 2015, 165–174.

61 Grossman 2011, 43–44. For migration from Egypt, Morocco, Tunisia, Algeria, Circassia, Chechnya and Bosnia to the Palestinian coastal plain, the mountains and the Sharon valley, see Dierauff 2015, 43–77.

62 Kark 1990b, 158; cf. Ṭarāwina 2000, 460.

grounds practicing in Jaffa in 1905.[63] The Ottoman population registers (*nufūs*) and the Jewish chronicler Ashkenazi document Palestinian migration to Jaffa from the early nineteenth century from Hebron, Jerusalem, Gaza, Nablus, Nazareth, Acre, Qalqilya and elsewhere in the Galilee and the highlands.[64] Muslims, and also Maronite Christians who migrated to Jaffa from outside Palestine came from Lebanon (Beirut, Tripoli, Sidon) and Syria (Aleppo, Latakia, Damascus, Hamah).

Indeed, these migrants became successful members of the local economic elite; the Christian Bayrūtī family, for example, was influential in the local orange trade and were among Jaffa's major landowners (*mallākūn*).[65] Members of this family, Naḫleh and Naǧīb Bayrūtī, frequently published in *Filasṭīn* on commercial issues, petitioned for tax relief and pleaded for the establishment of a trade union in Jaffa to create stable prices for oranges for the sake of the 'public good' (*aṣ-ṣāliḥ al-ʿāmm*).[66]

Muslim Migration from Egypt

The largest group of Muslim migrants in Jaffa were, according to Ṭarāwina, the Egyptians.[67] According to most sources, farmers or fellahin (from Ar.: *fallāḥīn*) came with the Egyptian military campaign following 1831. However, Ben-Zvi states that, by 1829, some 12,000 Egyptian fellahin had already 'infiltrated' the coastal area of Acre, Jaffa and Gaza to escape the control of the Khedival regime, military conscription and poverty.[68] And there is evidence that Egyptians were living in the *qaḍāʾ* even before that, since the 1820s. Ṭarāwina notes that, in 1824, Jaffa's *siǧillāt* listed Egyptian families from the village of al-ʿArīn in the Zaqāzīq region.[69] Others came as soldiers with the invasion by Ibrāhīm Pasha (1831–1840) and settled north of the Old City, and later the neighborhood of Manšīya.[70]

---

63 Kark 1990b, 283.

64 A report by Ashkenazi (1932) lists the Palestinian origins of 22 prominent Muslim families of Jaffa, probably based on oral testimony: Daǧǧānī (from Beit Daǧǧān); Bīṭār, Mustaqīm, Hafab, Ish Habar and al-Īmām from Jaffa; Dawwār and Šihāb ad-Dīn from Lydda; Abū l-Hudā from Ramla; Nābulsī and ʿAšūr from Nablus; Zayn ad-Dīn and Abū Ramaḍān from Gaza, Yāfā from Jerusalem; and Ḥamāma, ʿAzūnī, Bambiya, Dār al-Baral and Abū Ḫaḍrāʾ from Egypt (there was also the al-Ḫaḍrāʾ family of Gazan origins). See Kark 1990b, 158–159, who took the information from Layish (without reference date).

65 Ṭarāwina 2000, 462–464.

66 *Filasṭīn*, 23 December 1911: 97/1/1; 14 December 1912: 197/2/3–5.

67 Ṭarāwina 2000, 460. On Egyptian migrants and their spatial distribution in Palestine, see Grossman 2011, 45–62.

68 According to some scholars, Egyptian migration to Palestine and the refusal of Jaffa's governor ʿAbdallāh Pasha to evict these migrants was one reason for the invasion of the Levant by Muhammad ʿAlī. See Kark 1990b, 25–26, n. 48 and 49.

69 Ṭarāwina 2000, 459. There was also a 'courtyard' (*ḥūš*) inside Jaffa inhabited by Egyptians before Ibrāhīm Pasha's invasion, identified by Tobler in 1853, who also refers to a Coptic

However, most Egyptians who migrated to Jaffa were attracted by the agriculture on the coastal plain, where they worked as hired laborers during the grain and grape harvests, in the plantations or as packers of orange boxes.[71] The Egyptians lived in mud brick neighborhoods, the so called *sakināt* (pl. of *sakina*; Ar.: 'residential area') that stretched south and north of the Old City between the orchards.[72] They founded the Sakinat Ḥamād, Sakinat Darwīš and Sakinat Abū Kabīr, to name just a few.[73] The names of some indicated the regional origins of their inhabitants, such as Abū Kabīr in the Nile Delta, as did Egyptian family names in the *siǧillāt:* ad-Dumyāṭī, al-ʿArīšī, as-Swīsī, al-Būr Saʿīdī, al-Būlāqī, al-Fayūmī, ad-Damanhūrī, etc.[74]

In some of Jaffa's *sakināt*, Egyptians lived together with black Muslims, as in Sakinat al-ʿAbīd, 'neighborhood of the slaves'. It could be that they were descendants of former slaves; however, ʿAbīd means in certain contexts simply 'black', and many Egyptians of Nubian or Sudanese origin bear the family name ʿAbīd until today without necessarily deriving from black slaves. Anyway, in Jaffa, these black Muslims worked as agricultural laborers and in the packing industry or as craftsmen.[75] They had their own representative (*muḫtār*) to deal with the government, and the *siǧillāt* reveal that they were originally Nubians who had been freed by their masters but kept the addition *az-Zanǧī* ('the black') to their name. Ṭarāwina stresses that they enjoyed full citizens' rights after release and were also employed in the civil service.[76]

Muslim Migration from the Maghreb

The next largest group of Muslim migrants in Jaffa were from Maghreb countries – Libya, Algeria, Tunisia and Morocco. They were generally called 'Maghrebis' (*al-maġāriba*) by the locals, and the *siǧillāt* listed their names as al-Ǧazāʾirī al-Maġribī, at-Tūnisī al-Maġribī, al-Marākšī al-Maġribī, al-Miknāsī al-Maġribī, al-

village north of the Old City, which was called the 'Egyptian Colony'. See the 1863 British Admiralty map in Kark 1990b, 35, 72.

70 Agmon 2006, 15.

71 Buessow 2011, 213f. Ṭarāwina finds from the *siǧillāt* that some Egyptians became cattle breeders and owned bakeries in Jaffa; a few were employed in the security sector. See Ṭarāwina 2000, 460–461.

72 For the evolution of new quarters after the wall was demolished, see Kark 1990b, 73.

73 Ṭarāwina 2000, 460. There is a list of further *sakināt* in Kark, compiled from the maps by Schwarz (1880) and Yodfat (1925): Danāʾiṭe, Rašīd, at-Turk, al-ʿArāʾina, Šayḫ Ibrāhīm, al-ʿAǧamī, al-Ǧabalīya, al-Miṣrīya (Copts), Abū al-Ǧubayla, as-Sabīl, ad-Dawla. Kark 1990b, 110.

74 Ṭarāwina 2000, 359–360.

75 Kark 1990b, 160.

76 He mentions names of former slaves serving as officials in the Jaffa post office, the Ottoman forces and as officers. Ṭarāwina 2000, 476–477; Avneri 1984, 14.

Binġāzī al-Maġribī, etc., to indicate their origin.[77] Among them were also Algerians, who probably came after the French put down the rebellion of the Emir ʿAbd al-Qādir al-Ǧazāʾirī, who left for Syria in 1856 with some of his followers, but some of them are said to have settled in Palestine.[78] Other motivations for migration from the Maghreb to the region are not known. According to Baldensperger, Maroccans who came as pilgrims stayed in Jaffa on their return from Mecca out of poverty. Running out of financial resources, they settled in the Old City around the mosque.[79]

Although Ṭarāwina finds through the *siǧillāt* that the Maghrebis worked in retail and as barbers, teachers and farmers who owned land, it seems that the majority of them were employed in the security sector as guards (*nawāṭīr*), personal escorts or watchmen in the plantations. Several contemporary local sources, such as *Filasṭīn* and travelers' accounts refer to the Maghrebis only in their capacity as guards. They had a particularly bad reputation and were considered extraordinarily violent. In 1907, the Beirut newspaper *Al-Bašīr* reported that Jaffa's *qāʾimaqām* had expelled more than 30 Maghrebis from town because of complaints about them.[80] In *Filasṭīn*, they appeared in relation to theft, murder, blackmail and gang crime, and there were several attempts in 1912 and 1913 to have them evicted from the city, as will be outlined in the last section of this chapter.

Other Groups: Afghans, Indians, Iranians, Kurds and Gypsies

There were also Muslim migrants from Afghanistan and India with the *nisba* of al-Afġānī or al-Hindī added to their name, showing their origin. Most of them were engaged in retailing metal, precious stones and other items, herbs and perfume, which they sold in the streets, and some were guards in the orange groves.[81] They were rather poor, depended on donations and did not live in a distinct neighborhood in Jaffa. Some lived in *waqf* poor houses.[82] From the early nineteenth century, there were also some Iranians in Jaffa, such as the Ǧabar family, who had settled in Jaffa on returning from pilgrimage to Mecca. Some Iranians were successful in trade and one, ʿAṭā Allāh Bek b. Anis aṣ-Ṣabrī at-Tabrīzī, owned 375 *dunam* of orange groves.[83] Kurds who came with Ottoman

77 Ṭarāwina 2000, 461–462.

78 Apart from the Algerians in Jaffa, there were Algerian villages in northern Palestine, in the lower Galilee, Tiberias and Safed. See Avneri 1984, 16–17.

79 See Kark 1990b, 160.

80 From the newspaper *Al-Bašīr* (18 March 1907/3). Quoted from Ṭarāwina 2000, 462.

81 Kark 1990b, 160.

82 Ṭarāwina found that a member of the wealthy Daǧǧānī family, Ḫadīǧa Bint Salīm ad-Daǧǧānī, put six rooms in a house owned by her at the disposal of poor Afghans. See Ṭarāwina 2000, 473–474.

83 Ṭarāwina 2000, 474–475.

forces and stayed after leaving the military had also settled in the *qaḍā'*, and some occupied ranks in the local gendarmerie or other security forces.[84] Finally, there were a number of 'gypsies' (*sayyārīn, ṭawwāfīn*) of unclear origin who were also called *nawar* (sing.: *nūrī*), 'vagabonds'. They lived in tents, frequently moving on, and mostly worked as metalsmiths making small metal items or tools.[85] According to the Ottoman census of 1893, there were 1,107 gypsies (631 males, 475 females) in the *qaḍā'*.[86]

German-Protestant Migration

From the late 1860s onwards, Christian migrants arrived in Palestine from Baden-Württemberg, a region in southern Germany. In 1869, the German Templar Society, a pietistic movement of Swabian Protestants from the northern Black Forest, founded the German Colony in Jaffa. It was situated north-east of the Old City where the Germans benefitted from the structures of the former American Colony, which had been founded a few years earlier but was soon abandoned. There, the Templars acquired several buildings erected by the American settlers, including a hospital, a pharmacy, a saw mill, an olive press and a steam mill. They added European-style houses, churches, commercial buildings, schools and hostels to accommodate pilgrims.[87]

In 1871, they bought approximately 60 hectares of land further north-east of Jaffa on the road to Nablus and built the colony of Sarona according, following the plans of the architect Theodor Sandel.[88] In 1888, the Templars erected Walhalla on the eastern outskirts of Jaffa; and in 1902 the agricultural settlement of Wilhelma.[89] The Templars started industrial enterprises and were economically very successful. In Jaffa, they were the first to engage in a professional transport business and offered transport services for tourists from Jaffa to several places of pilgrimage. The settlers of Sarona maintained 300 hectares of agricultural land, plus 150 hectares of vineyards and 24 hectares of orange groves, and they kept 200 dairy cows, as reported in *Filasṭīn* in 1912.[90] In Walhalla, the Wagner Brothers ran

84 Ṭarāwina 2000, 474–475.

85 Kark 1990b, 160.

86 Ṭarāwina 2000, 475.

87 In 1866, messianic Christians from Maine had bought some land and erected a small colony, but it was a brief episode for the Americans in Jaffa. According to Ṭarāwina and Kark, they left only one year later due to internal conflicts and because they suffered from disease and hardship. See Ṭarāwina 2000, 465–466; Kark 1990b, 84–89.

88 Kark 1990b, 89–91, 99–100; and Glenk, Blaich, and Haering 2005, xviii.

89 See Glenk, Blaich, and Haering 2005, 43, 49; and Ṭarāwina 2000, 129–130. For the history of German settlement in the *qaḍā'*, see Carmel 1973, 25–79; and idem 1975, 442–446. For the achievements of the Templars in the Jaffa region, see Eisler 1997; for the German colony in Haifa, Yazbak 1999, 40–54.

90 *Filasṭīn*, 30 November 1912: 193/1/4–2/2; here 2/1.

a machine factory and Hugo Wieland established a cement factory. In 1904, the Sarona winery expanded into the Wilhelma-Jaffa-Sarona Wine Growers Cooperative, which later produced high quality Cognac for export.[91] The Templars were also the first to introduce pumps, powered by coal or petroleum, in Jaffa.[92] They imported Deutz motors and introduced new methods of agricultural production. In 1871, they first planted eucalyptus as to drain water from swamps and marshy land to stop the breeding of mosquitos carrying malaria;[93] and *Filasṭīn* mentioned that German and Jewish doctors started a research project in Palestine to find cures for the virus.[94]

Demographically, the Germans did not make a significant impact. *Filasṭīn* reported in 1912 that there were about 8,000 German-speakers in Palestine.[95] In the Jaffa region, there were about 630 Germans in 1907, according to Smilansky; and Carmel notes that some 800 Templars lived around Jaffa before World War I.[96] German colonization was observed by the locals with ambivalence. *Filasṭīn* reported that the road from Haifa to Nazareth was lined with German villages and that, in 1907, the German Colonization Assoziation ('Deutsche Kolonisierungsverein') had tried to bribe the authorities in order to buy land in Bethlehem.[97] Referring to successful German enterprises, *Filasṭīn* predicted in individual cases that the Germans would establish 'a state within a state', although the Germans did not have demographic weight. In 1911, only some 3,500 Germans lived in the Ottoman Empire; and in Haifa almost 400.[98]

What is certain is that the Templars kept themselves and lived in exclusive communities. They did not mix with the locals, and their presence in the Holy Land was not of philanthropic interest; at least, this was the official agenda of the Templar Society, which recommended the settlers to keep their distance from the 'lazy Orientals' and warned them against adopting local customs. Their magazine, *Die Warte* ('The Observation Point'), reported hostile actions on the part of locals, both Muslims and Christians, against the settlers and several attacks on them, until they built a wall around Sarona.[99]

91 *Filasṭīn*, 19 July 1911: 52/2/2–3.
92 Ṭarāwina 2000, 467.
93 Glenk, Blaich, and Haering 2005, xix, 48–50.
94 *Filasṭīn*, 11 September 1912: 170/3/2.
95 *Filasṭīn*, 27 July 1912: 157/1/3–2/1.
96 Buessow 2011, 214; Ṭarāwina 2000, 466; cf. Carmel 1973, 7–24, and the map on 300.
97 *Filasṭīn* 30 November 1912: 193/1/4–2/2. For the ambivalent relations between German colonists and Palestinians, see Carmel 1973, 238–258; and idem 1975, 446–455.
98 *Filasṭīn*, 6 September 1911: 66/2/2.
99 Carmel 1973, 238–244, 255f.

Jewish Immigration and Jaffa's Emergence as a Center of Zionism

The exact beginnings of Jaffa's Jewish community in the nineteenth century remain unclear because Jewish travelers give contradictory accounts, but it can be traced back to the 1830s, since Moses Montefiori's census in 1839 counted 122 Jews in Jaffa. According to various reports, the starting point of this community seems to have been the shipwreck of a sailing vessel from North Africa, after which its survivors stayed in Jaffa. Be that as it may, from the 1840s onwards, the number of Jewish inhabitants in Jaffa rose dramatically since they obviously attracted North African Jews from Jerusalem. In 1875, about 650 Jews were living in Jaffa and, in 1891, the local community contained 2,700 Jews.[100] From the 1870s onwards, Ashkenazi Jews from Eastern Europe, motivated by a messianic form of Zionism, immigrated to Palestine; and from the 1880s, Ashkenazi Jews surpassed German-Protestant immigrants in number. Up to the 1880s, 80 percent of Jaffa's Jews were of North African origin. However, from the 1890s, European Jews, the Ashkenazis, overtook the presence of Jaffa's Sephardim, the Oriental Jews. From the end of the nineteenth century, the Ashkenazi Jews had reversed the ethnic composition of its Jewish community.[101]

In 1870, the French Alliance Israélite Universelle (AIU), a Jewish philanthropist but non-Zionist organization, established a model farm with an agricultural school, the colony of Miqve Yisraʾel, south-east of Jaffa. It was intended to become a prototype for other Jewish farms in the region that depended on donations from associations abroad and the help of philanthropists, such as Baron Edmond de Rothschild.[102] Soon after, Jewish migrants from Russia and Ukraine founded the first Zionist colonies of Petaḥ Tikva (1878), Rishon Le-Tzion (1882) and Reḥovot (1890) in the Jaffa hinterland. These settlements were economically successful and innovative. They maintained training facilities and attracted labor. The Jewish settlements in the *qaḍāʾ*, apart from clusters of settlements south-east of Haifa and the Galilee, became the focus of Jewish activity in Palestine.[103] Ṭarāwina lists nine Jewish colonies in the *qaḍāʾ* for 1908, doc-

100 It is not known exactly when the shipwreck occurred, but it was between 1830 and 1840. See Kark 1990b, 180–183. In her travel account of Palestine in the 1930s, Gabriele Tergit dates the origins of Jaffa's Jewish community, founded by 'shipwrecked Moroccan Jews', to 1820, but she does not reveal her source. Tergit 1996, 70.

101 In 1891, according to the census carried out by Luncz, the Jewish community was made up of 2,700 people: 1,600 Ashkenazi and 1,100 Sephardi Jews. See Kark 1990b, 185.

102 See Buessow 2011, 201; Ṭarāwina 2000, 468. For the foundation of Miqve Yisarʾel, see Kark 1990b, 91–93.

103 For the spatial distribution of Jewish colonies in Palestine established between 1882 and 1908, see Ben-Bassat 2013d, 164 (map 5); and 2009a, 44–46. For the 'settlement bloc' of the 'Judean colonies' south-east of Jaffa, see idem. 2009a, 50–53.

umenting their Arab and Hebrew names and date of foundation.[104] At the end of the Abdülhamidian Era, Buessow finds that around 1,000 settlers were living in the *qaḍāʾ* in nine colonies.[105] Ṭarāwina presents higher numbers for the pre-World War I period, when he says 1,300 settlers living in Rishon le-Tzion alone, and 4,100 in Petaḥ Tikva.[106]

The Ashkenazi Jews made Jaffa the center of Zionist activity in the New Yishuv in Palestine. Before World War I, the bulk of Zionist institutions that 'pulled along' the Old Palestinian Yishuv, as Kark puts it, were concentrated in Jaffa. Kark defines Ashkenazi migration as the main reason for the urban and economic rise of Jaffa and its transformation from a traditional town into a 'piece of Modern Europe'. She supports this argument exhaustively by citing contemporary Jewish accounts that contrast the 'desolate land' of Arab Ottoman Palestine with the 'cleanliness, order and greenery' of civilized Europe, as, for instance, when they enthusiastically describe the new Jewish suburbs north of Old Jaffa.[107] Kark describes the 'renaissance' of Jaffa as initiated solely by Jewish activity, which brought the city to a new level of institutional and political organization, administration, lifestyle, professional cooperation, economic productivity, cultural achievement and literary activity.[108] In contrast, Kark dedicates a short note to local Muslim institutional and cultural activity, which, according to her, was mainly 'limited' to mosques and religious schools (*kuttāb*), and 'generally speaking, there was little cultural-social activity in Jaffa among the Muslims'.[109]

Although Kark assigned more cultural innovations to the Christians of Jaffa, her book limits the information given about local Christian cultural activities to the foundation of the Jaffa newspapers *al-Aṣmāʿī* and *Filasṭīn* and the foundation of the local YMCA-club, before she moves on to describe foreign Christian missionary and religious activities.[110] There is no doubt that foreign migration tremendously increased the vitality of Jaffa's institutional and political life, but Jaffa's urban and cultural development was driven by both foreign *and* local engagement. As briefly treated in the section on the modernist discourse pre-

104 1. Biʾr Yaʿqūb/Beer Yaqov (1907); 2. Pen Schemen (1906); 3. Dārān or Dayrān/Reḥovot (1890); 4. ʿAkkarūn/Mazkeret Bety (1883); 5. ʿUyūn Qāra/Rishon le-Tzion (1882); 6. Qaṭrat Yehūdā (1884); 7. Mulabbis/Petaḥ Tikva (1878); 8. Netter/Mikveh Yisra'el (1870); 9. Wādī Ḥanīn/Nes Tziona (1885). Ṭarāwina 2000: 130–133. See also his map of German and Jewish colonies on p. 134.

105 Buessow 2011, 215, n. 25.

106 Ṭarāwina 2000, 132.

107 For the accounts of Solomon and Ben Zion, see Kark 1990b, 53, 100. For a list of Jewish suburbs, see pp. 110–111.

108 Kark 1990b, 189–199.

109 Kark 1990b, 162–163.

110 Kark 1990b, 171f.

sented in *Filasṭīn*, its editors closely observed and documented developments in Jaffa. In the *Local News* section, they enthusiastically advertised the initiatives of local associations working for education, welfare, culture, art and entertainment – a field that needs more future research.

Confessional Composition and Demographic Allocation

Little information is available on the exact demographical composition inside Jaffa town as most Ottoman population registers (*nufūs*) are lost.[111] Ṭarāwina presents the demographic diversity of the *qaḍā'* by relying on consular reports and registers but correctly stresses that the numbers were often based on estimates since people tried to avoid registration for reasons that have been explained above.[112] The Ottoman census of 1914 reported that about some 70,000 citizens were living in the *qaḍā'*, of whom 86 percent were Muslims, nine percent were Christians and only five percent were Jews. However, if foreign citizens are included, a total of about 91,000 people were living in the *qaḍā'*, of whom had come with Zionist immigration, about 20,000 people. This means, that about 95 percent of all Jews residing in the Jaffa *qaḍā'* were Ashkenazi Jews who were not of Ottoman citizenship. If these foreign Jews are included, the population of the *qaḍā'* consisted of about 66 percent Muslims, 11 percent Christians and 23 percent Jews.[113] This shows that the presence of European Jews dramatically changed the demographic composition in the *qaḍā'* within a few decades, and most obviously in Jaffa town and its commercial centers.

On the eve of World War I, Jaffa had in total about 40,000–50,000 inhabitants, according to *Filasṭīn* in 1912.[114] The census carried out by Luncz in 1913 states that, among them were about 30,700 Muslims, mostly Hanafis. This makes a

111 Buessow notes that, in the Israeli State Archives (ISA), there is only one *muḫtār* book from 1884, and five Ottoman basic registers about Muslim population in ʿAǧamī, Naqīb, Sabīl and Sakinat Danāʾiṭa. Buessow 2011, 224.

112 However, he neglects Jaffa's Jews, despite listing all the Christian family names. He describes Jewish life on a little more than one page, giving numbers for the Jewish inhabitants as stated by the Damascene *al-Muqtabas* in 1911 and 1913, and names their community leaders. Ṭarāwina 2000, 458–459.

113 In 1913, a correspondent of *al-Muqtabas*, Naʿīm Ḥusām, estimated the total number of inhabitants of the Jaffa *qaḍā'* as 91,000, of whom 60,000 were Muslims, 10,000 Christians and 1,000 Jews, plus, about 20,000 Jews of foreign nationality. The census carried out by Me'ir Zamir, based on Ottoman statistics from 1914, reports the (Ottoman) population of the *qaḍā'* to be 72,206 persons. 62,758 of them were Muslims, 7,251 Christians, and 3,197 were listed as 'other groups' (*ʿanāṣir mutafarriqa*), without explicitly listing the Jews. This amounts to 87 percent Muslims, 9 percent Christians, and 4 percent others. See Ṭarāwina 2000, 443–444. See also statistics from various consular archives and Ottoman yearbooks between 1847 and 1893: ibid., 339–442; cf. Buessow 2011, 234–235.

114 *Filasṭīn*, 6 January 1912: 101/1/3.

Muslim proportion of 61 percent in the town, which roughly coincides with the Muslim percentage in the *qaḍāʾ* when considering foreign residents.[115]

While Muslims were present in all segments of the population, the Christians of the *qaḍāʾ* mostly lived in the urban contexts of Jaffa, Ramla and Lydda, and belonged to many denominations.[116] Ṭarāwina has tried to list their numbers according to various censuses and family names as recorded in the *siǧillāt.* Most of them were Greek Orthodox: 3,897 in 1893 according to the Ottoman census.[117] The second largest group were Roman Catholics, who numbered, according to Luncz, 639 people in Jaffa town in 1898.[118] In addition, 1,200 Latins were documented for the same year.[119] Jaffa was also inhabited by a few hundred Maronites from Mount Lebanon who were still under the jurisdiction of the spiritual head in Lebanon.[120] There were also some 150 Armenian Christians in Jaffa, and a few Coptic households in Jaffa and Ramla, but not amounting to more than 30 people.[121] Finally, there were around 109 Protestants, according to the 1893 Ottoman census.[122]

Little is known about ethno-confessional cohabitation in the urban context of Jaffa. Ṭarāwina claims that, under late Ottoman rule, relations between Muslims and Christians in the region were characterized by 'mutual respect' (*al-iḥtirām al.mutabādil*) and 'a spirit of peaceful coexistence' (*rūḥ at-taʿāyuš as-silmī baynahum*). Indeed, the *siǧillāt* reveal shared companies and vital economic cooperation and the Sharia records document Christian claims against Muslims and vice-versa.[123]

However, Jaffa faced the typical challenges of a 'migration society'. Despite a high degree of economic interaction between the various segments of society,

115 Kark 1990b, 158.

116 Only one Christian village is listed: Dayr Salāma situated at the suburbs of Ramla. Ṭarāwina 2000, 449.

117 Ṭarāwina lists Jaffa's Greek Orthodox family names from the *siǧillāt* (between 1895 and 1909) as: As-Sūsī, aš-Šāmī, al-Bartaqš, Batšūn, Kardūs, Handīleh, Harīš, Ġarbīlī, Ṣafadī, Munīr, Ṭanūs, Mudbak, Ḥabaš, Ḥakīm, Zakkāk, ʿĪsā, ʿAriḍeh, Ḫūteh, Dabbās, Daḫāḫīnī, al-Malik, Zarīfa. See Ṭarāwina 2000, 451–452.

118 Roman Catholic family names as recorded from the *siǧillāt* (1868–1875) were as follows: aṣ-Ṣabbāġ, al-Ǧabǧī, Šīmā, Ṣūfīh, Bārūdī, Aǧdā, Afnān, Ġarġūr, Naḥḥās, Ṭalāmās, Qālūš, Muṣulī. See Ṭarāwina 2000, 453.

119 This according to German consular reports. However, another census recorded many fewer Latins. Their family names were Dumānī, al-Bīṭār, al-Kassār, al-Qaṣīr, Būzeh, Qasṭeh, Zanīrī, Mītā, Rūk, Ǧibǧī. Ṭarāwina 2000, 454.

120 One census estimated their number in 1898 to be 210, while the census carried out by the German consulate gave an estimate of 400 people. See Ṭarāwina 2000, 454–455.

121 Here, there were only two names found in the *siǧillāt:* al-Fallāḥ and al-Qibṭī. See Ṭarāwina 2000, 455–456.

122 Their names were listed in the *siǧillāt* (1901–1906) as: Kālīs, Zabbāneh and Ṭāniyūs. Ṭarāwina 2000, 456.

123 Ṭarāwina 2000, 457.

people were socially rather divided and usually lived in groups defined by their affiliation to a clan (*ḥamūla,* pl. *ḥamāʾil*), ethnicity or confession.[124] Moreover, there was a high degree of fragmentation within confessions. Jewish communities shared neighborhoods and synagogues according to their country of origin – Yemen or Iran, for instance. Limited information is available about the geographic locations of the various communities, but there was no ethno-confessional ghettoization in Jaffa.

The Maghrebis lived around the mosque and the Egyptians in the *sakināt* outside town and in the Sakinat al-ʿAbīd, together with black Muslims.[125] Muslims lived in many neighborhoods, such as Manšīya, Ǧabalīya, ʿAǧamī, Naqīb, Sabīl and others. Christians had a neighborhood in the Old City, Ḥārat an-Naṣārā, but lived outside the Old City in mixed neighborhoods with Muslims and Jews, in ʿAǧamī, Naqīb and others. The *siǧillāt* reveal that Christians were strongly represented in Jaffa's economic and public life and cultural associations. They were active as merchants and landowners, the owned factories, and were employed in various crafts, administration and as attorneys.[126] With regard to the 'local Jews' (*al-yahūd al-maḥallīyīn*), Ṭarāwina mentions in reference to the *siǧillāt* that they lived in the mixed neighborhoods of Naqīb, al-Qalʿa and ʿAǧamī together with Muslims and Christians, not in separate quarters, and numbered up to 970 people, according to the Syrian editor Kurd ʿAlī, who visited Jaffa in 1911 and published an article about it in his newspaper *al-Muqtabas.*[127] Ashkenazi Jews made their presence felt in Jaffa's commerce and, at the end of the nineteenth century, most shops and flats in Sūq al-Bustrus were leased to Jews. However, Jews did not play a significant role in the citrus industry and Jewish accounts complained that the citrus orchards were mostly owned by Arab Muslims and Christians.[128]

4. Relationalities between the Urban and the Hinterland

This chapter outlines the interrelation between Jaffa and its environs, which was characterized by four main factors. First, the building boom and an extended road network quickly made new suburbs into integral neighborhoods of the town. Second, the expanding citrus industry linked new villages built in the fields for the workers with the urban center of Jaffa. Third, the economic boom fostered a tight connection between the city, its surrounding agricultural villages and

124 Also stressed in Kark 1990b, 190f.
125 Kark 1990b, 158f.
126 Ṭarāwina 2000, 450–451.
127 Ṭarāwina 2000, 458.
128 See Kark 1990b, 244, 268–269.

Bedouin tribes in the hinterland. Finally, the interrelation between Jaffa and its broader environs was intensified by its position as a crossroads for transport, e.g. the Jaffa-Jerusalem connection by road and railway.

Relationality of the City Center, Suburbs and Garden Villages

The economic and the demographic rise caused the town to spread beyond its early boundaries. Between the 1870s and 1917, its area multiplied about 30 times and Jaffa grew from a village of 100 *dunam* to a built-up area of almost 3,000 *dunam*. The building boom of the 1880s and 1890s led to the rapid incorporation of newly built suburbs north and south of Old Jaffa as integrated neighborhoods (*maḥallāt*).[129] South of the Old City and near the road to Gaza, the large neighborhood of al-ʿAǧamī emerged. It was one of the better residential areas and had a mixed, but mostly Christian, population. Reliable information about its beginnings could not be verified but it apparently began as a Maronite settlement. It is uncertain when exactly, but a Maronite church seems to have been built there in 1855. The Maronite-Lebanese Order owned real estate in Jaffa and by the beginning of the twentieth century it had a community of about 600 people.[130] At this point, al-ʿAǧamī was inhabited by Christian Arabs of various origins and stretched southwards, where it merged with the neighborhood of al-Ǧabalīya.[131] On the other side of town and north of the Old City, the former 'Egyptian Colony' of the nineteenth century had grown into the al-Manšīya quarter and a large Muslim neighborhood which, at the beginning of the twentieth century, extended in a long stripe northwards along the coast.[132] About its beginnings, it is only known that it was started by Egyptian workers.[133]

Apart from al-ʿAǧamī and Ǧabalīya to the south and al-Manšīya to the north, Jewish building activity spread north-east of town from the 1880s. There, Jewish migrants established Neve Tzedek (1887), Neve Shalom (1890), Mahane Yehuda (1896), Yefe Nof (1897), Aḥva (1899), and other neighborhoods.[134] Sephardi elites from Jaffa were the influential investors, such as Aharon Chelouche, Ḥaim Amzalek and Yosef Moyal. They purchased land, which was then leased or sold to

129 See the map in Kark 1990b, 112.

130 https://now.mmedia.me/lb/en/reportsfeatures/546588-maronites-of-the-holy-land (consulted: 6 June 2017).

131 https://archnet.org/sites/3552 (consulted 6 June 2017).

132 Situated in what is today the center of Tel Aviv, Manšīya was demolished to make room for a commercial center. The only remaining structures today are the mosque of Ḥasan Bek and a building that houses the Irgun Museum.

133 Dumper 2007, 201.

134 Kark 1990b, 100–104. See also the map of Jaffa's Jewish neighborhoods in 1914 on pp. 112–113, and descriptions of Neve Tzedek and Neve Shalom on pp. 114–116).

Jewish migrants or Zionist institutions and turned into new residential areas – a development that caused a rapid rise in the price of land.[135]

Jewish building activity took a new turn when the Jewish Aḥuzat Bayyit Society purchased land further to the north-east to found Tel Aviv (1909), which was constructed in the style of a European 'Garden City'.[136] Tel Aviv was meant to be the first 'Hebrew City' of the New Yishuv and was intended to cement the spatial separation from Arab Jaffa.[137] However, until the Mandate era, Tel Aviv was in practice tightly interwoven with Jaffa commercially and depended on its harbor until Tel Aviv opened its municipality in 1934 and built its own port in 1938.[138]

Apart from the quick integration of suburbs through the building boom, the interconnectedness between urban and agricultural spaces should be stressed as another feature of the expanding Jaffa. With the cultivation fever, all the land eastwards of the city was turned into gardens (*bayārāt*), attracting labor from various regions. The agricultural land extended over a considerable area and as the harvesting, packing and boxing of the citrus fruit took place on the spot, new housing was made available for workers in the fields. Entrepreneurs and landowners built summer houses on their property to be close to the crops and observe the harvesting and marketing of their produce during the season. Villas, 'garden villages' and *sakināt*, the mud-brick villages of Egyptian workers, such as Sakinat Abū Kabīr to the east and Sakinat Darwīš south of Jaffa, appeared within the orchards. They gradually turned into residential areas, making the Jaffa environs a mixed urban-rural space. A road network spread between the fields, connecting the gardens and the *sakināt* with the city markets and the port for shipping the fruit.

135 During the 1880s, one *dunam* in Jaffa would cost 30–40 francs. From 1906–1914, land sold to Jewish migrants by wealthy Sephardi families yielded 5,600–8,000 francs. See Kark 1990b, 126, 248–249.

136 The name Tel Aviv (Hebr.: 'Spring Hill') was inspired by Herzl's novel *Altneuland*. Krämer 2002b, 141.

137 Kark 1990b, 107, 118f.–134.

138 Dumper 2007, 201.

Figure 19: Area Photography of Jaffa in 1917, with the Old City and the half-rounded harbor at the center, and the beginnings of ʿAǧamī south of the harbor. At the other side, the road leads to the northeast (towards Nablus) with Bustrus Street, the commercial center of Jaffa, that is cut by the Jamal Pasha Boulevard (constructed during World War I). A bit further northeast, this road leads to the German Colony (note the church tower in the image). (Source: Dalman, Gustav. 1925. Hundert deutsche Fliegerbilder aus Palästina. Gütersloh: Bertelsmann, 77.)

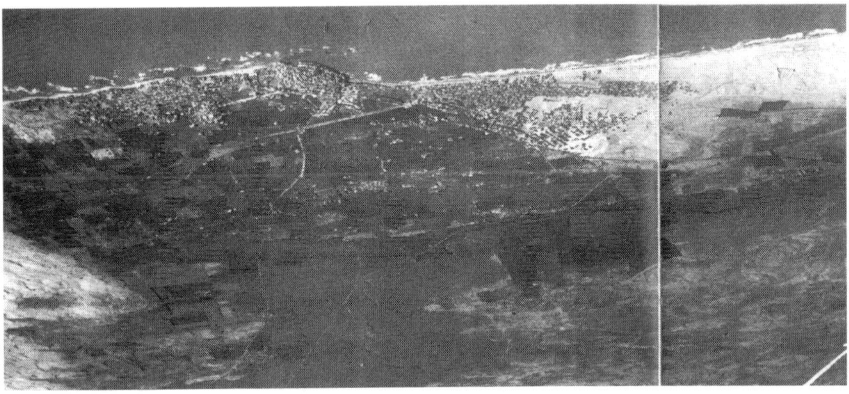

Figure 20: Extended Jaffa-Tel Aviv region in 1917 with the Old City and the harbor at the center, ʿAǧamī and Ǧabalīya in the south, Manšīya and Tel Aviv in the north, stretching along the Mediterranean coast. (Source: ibid.)

Interrelations between Villagers, Bedouins and Settlers

Jaffa maintained intense commercial ties not only with the inhabitants of the garden villages but also with the Arab farmers of its wider surroundings, the coastal plain and the Sharon plain, and Bedouin tribes of the hinterland. They all sold their agricultural products, animals and wool in Jaffa and stocked up with kerosene, sugar, oil, tobacco, clothing and other needs in town.[139] Unlike in the Palestinian highlands of Jabal al-Quds, Nablus and Hebron, where fortified villages, the so-called 'throne villages' (*qurā l-karāsī*), served as seats of power for sheikhs and local strongmen, there were no such villages in the Jaffa region.[140] Neither was Jaffa fortified in protection from Bedouin raids. Bedouin tribes (*ʿarab*, or *ʿurbān*) settled particularly in the further hinterland north-east of Jaffa. According to Ṭarāwina, there were predominantly good relations between the nomads and Jaffa's residents.[141] In *Filasṭīn*, there were very few accounts of clashes. In my period of investigation, there was one incident when the Arab villagers of Yāzūr suspected the Ḫaṭāṭira Bedouin tribe of having killed two people because their camp was close to the village.[142]

The biggest tribes were the ʿArab Abū Kišk and the ʿArab al-Ǧamāssīn ('buffalo raisers'), who settled near the Yarkon River (Ar.: *Nahr al-ʿĀūǧā*). The Sawālimeh and the Tarābīn tribes who had migrated from the Beersheba region, and the ʿArab as-Sūṭrīya settled in the area south-east of Jaffa. The tribes depended on grain farming or animal farming and were sedentary (*mustaqirra*) or semi-sedentary and partially nomadic.[143] However, they did not necessarily own title deeds to the land they cultivated or settled on. There is evidence that the Bedouins, often described in literature as an uncontrollable threat, had to fight for their ownership, as Ben-Bassat has pointed out in his investigation of Bedouin petitions from the Jaffa region to Istanbul. This correspondence, written by professional petition writers and signed by representatives of the tribe, is a rare

139 Kark 1990b, 263–265.

140 On the throne villages of Dayr Ġassāna, north of Jerusalem and family seat of the noble Barġūṯī family, see Buessow 2011, 113–117. On the childhood memories of ʿUmar Ṣāliḥ al-Barġūṯī, grandson of the last lord of Dayr Ġassāna, about the life of an aristocratic family against a rural Palestinian background, see Tamari 2002, 27–42. On the architecture in Palestinian throne villages in the eighteenth and nineteenth centuries, see al-ʿĀmirī 2003, and the website http://www.riwaq.org/qura-al-karasi-throne-villages-palestine (consulted 10 October 2017).

141 Ṭarāwina 2000, 449.

142 The villagers then attacked the Bedouin camp and, when their men fled, 'were content to steal the animals and beat the women and children', *Filasṭīn* reported on 13 January 1912: 102/3/2.

143 Ṭarāwina lists a number of other tribes settled in the hinterland of Jaffa. Some had preserved their nomadic traditions (the tribes of the as-Sūṭrīya, aṭ-Ṭuyūr, al-ʿAnūz, as-Sawārika, al-Ḫaṭāṭira and an-Nafaʿīyāt). Others had sedentarized (the al-Qarʿān, al-Hanādī, as-Sawālimeh Bawādī Ḥanīn). Ṭarāwina 2000, 447–449.

voice from the rural population during the late nineteenth century that belonged to the illiterate part of Palestinian society and are considered to have usually avoided government contacts.[144]

The Abū Ḥaṭaba Bedouin, a group of the Ṣūṭrīya tribe who cultivated agricultural land in Ḫirbat Dūrān, where they also lived, petitioned the Porte as early as 1890 against the sale of that land, which was situated east of Reḥovot, to the Jewish settlers. The group, consisting of about 200 people, had clearly occupied that land for generations. As they saw it, they were its legitimate owners by inheritance from the forefathers. However, they did not own title deeds and, legally, leased the land as tenants from an Arab landowner. When foreign settlers bought the land from him and became its legal owners, the Bedouins were asked to leave and, after some disputes, were chased away.[145] In another petition from 1884, the ʿArab al-ʿAuǧāʾ, a group of the Abū Kišk, complained that plots of land classified as *mīrī* that 1,500 people of their tribe had been occupying for many years and for which they claimed they paid the tithe (*al-ʿušr*) was classified as a *waqf* (religious endowment) by its new absentee landowners. This meant that the Bedouins were required to pay more taxes and were merely tenants. Also in this case, the conflict arose from the fact that the Bedouins did not own official title deeds for that land.[146] About the Abū Kišk, there is at least evidence in *Filasṭīn* that they had title deeds for land registered as their private property (*mulk*).[147]

In terms of ties between Jaffa, its outskirts and the hinterland, 'interrelation' should not be confused with social mixing or harmony. The principle of cohabitation in the Jaffa region was interconnectedness on the commercial level while social divisions between the groups, and even different legal systems, were maintained. Zionist settlements, for example, established their own by-laws. In 1911, Jewish community representatives from Tel Aviv ordered the main road leading from Manšīya to Tel Aviv to be closed to traffic with iron chains on Saturdays.[148] Zionist organizations also sought to enforce the principle of 'Hebrew labor' and Zionist youth clearly carried out boycott against Jaffa's Jews who ignored this principle and employed Arab construction workers. Goldenberg, director of the Anglo-Palestine Bank (APB) in Jaffa, for example, had his new

144 On petitions from rural segments of the Jaffa and Gaza region, see Ben-Bassat 2013d, 86–115; and idem, 2015, 135–162.

145 See Ben-Bassat 2013d, 101–103, 165–166, 195–198; Ben-Bassat 2015, 143–146.

146 Ben-Bassat 2013, 218–222; Ben-Bassat 2015, 147–149.

147 A landowner of the Abū Kišk leased to Christians: part of the private land (*mulk*) of Šayḫ Abū Kišk Hāšīm b Šayḫ Asʿad Abū Kišk al-ʿUṯmānī was leased on a 'temporary warrant' (*wikāla dawrīya*) and for a period of four years to Dāwud b Rufāʾīl Ṣābūnǧī and to Anṭūn b Ilyās at a public auction. See *Filasṭīn*, 3 October 1911: 74/3/3.

148 *Filasṭīn* reported that traffic in the 'settlement of Tel Aviv' (*mustaʿmarat Tel Abīb*) was blocked on Saturdays by iron chains and asked the Jewish community the reason for this. *Filasṭīn*, 20 January 1912: 104/3/4.

house in Tel Aviv built with Arab labor, *Filasṭīn* reported.[149] Further, it was reported in 1913 that the Zionists maintained their own House of Government (*dār al-ḥukūma*) with a separate court in Tel Aviv, while the Ottoman court was in the Jaffa House of Government.[150]

On the other hand, Jewish suburbs and settlements were economically closely interrelated with Jaffa and paid substantial taxes to the government: Rishon le-Tzion's success in wine production led to an increase in the settlement's annual wine tax in 1912/13 from 1,000 to 1,500 lira.[151]

A Transport and Communications Crossroads

Jaffa was also a significant *crossroads* for transport and communications, and was closely connected with Jerusalem. All the comings and goings of people and commodities in Palestine passed through Jaffa's port: foreign goods consumed by the inhabitants of Jerusalem, Bethlehem, Hebron, Gaza and Nablus, and all the travelers coming to Palestine. Every pilgrim, official or diplomat arriving from overseas went ashore in Jaffa, and from there most went on to Jerusalem.[152] The Jerusalem-Jaffa connection is also stressed in contemporary travelers' accounts, which refer to Jaffa as the 'port of Jerusalem'.[153]

Jaffa was not only the city for commerce and travelers but also the center of modern communication technologies and among the first Palestinian cities connected to Turkish and foreign postal services and telegraph networks, which were introduced in the Empire from the mid-1850s. Post offices provided these communications services and, in Jaffa, several foreign post offices, the Turkish, French, Austrian, Egyptian, Russian and German, operated near Sūq al-Bustrus.[154] From the beginning of the 1860s, the first line provided communication between Istanbul and Alexandria, Acre, Jaffa and Beirut. In 1865, a line was established between Jaffa and Jerusalem.[155]

Parallel with rising shipping activity from the 1870s, especially since the opening of the Suez Canal in 1868, which increased shipping traffic between Jaffa

149 *Filasṭīn*, 20 September 1913: 273/2/4.

150 Since the house of government in Tel Aviv maintained its own prison with armed forces, it was criticized in the press as 'a government within a government' (*ḥukūma fī ḥukūma*). See *Filasṭīn*, 18 October 1913: 281/1/5.

151 See *Filasṭīn*, 25 December 1912: 200/3/3–4; and 28 December 1912: 201/3/2f.

152 Buessow 2011, 216–220.

153 However, Kark also stresses the dependence of Jaffa, as well as Tripoli, Sidon, Damascus and Haifa, on the port of Beirut in terms of international imports. Only on the eve of World War I, did Jaffa, Haifa and Damascus begin to negotiate directly with European companies. Kark 1990b, 265–266, 271–272.

154 Kark 1990b, 217–219.

155 Much later, telegraph lines between Jerusalem and Jericho (1895), and Jerusalem and Hebron (1902) were installed. Kark 1990b, 219.

and Egypt, overland transport from and to Jaffa expanded dramatically. In 1869, the overland road to Jerusalem prepared for wheeled carriages opened, guarded by seventeen watchtowers and street patrols. In 1875, the Templars of Jaffa opened the first professional transport company in Palestine, operating with 23 horses and 40 carriages, soon to be followed by Arab entrepreneurs. Later, bridges over the Yarkon River and new roads to the north linked Jaffa with Nablus (1888), Haifa (1898) and Acre.[156] Finally, after receiving a concession in 1889, a French company built the first Palestinian railway, which operated between Jaffa and Jerusalem from 1892.[157] This explains why Jaffa, through its port, communications services and transport system, was much more interconnected with the capital Jerusalem than Nablus, Hebron or Gaza, which also had considerable economic resources but were much less connected with their hinterlands.

In *Filasṭīn*, Jaffa was proudly described as the most dynamic hub in Palestine. A reader's letter described the vitality of the town in an amusing anecdote. The anonymous author felt so stressed by the traffic, the noise, the crowds of people and caravans of camels rushing through Jaffa that he decided to take a day off in the quiet town of Ramla, where he planned to relax and finally read his newspapers in peace and solitude.[158] Although this was a sarcastic side swipe at the smaller Ramla, the busy atmosphere in Jaffa as described in the letter is not very exaggerated. In the *Local News* section, *Filasṭīn* regularly documented the arrivals and departures of Ottoman officials, prominent politicians and foreign diplomats who had government business in Palestine and headed to Jerusalem via the Jaffa port, stressing Jaffa's representative function.[159] Many press accounts also documented extended visits by Jerusalem governors in the *qaḍāʾ*, which served as a 'showcase' of Ottoman modernity and a 'draught horse' for Palestine. Here, the foreign colonies in the *qaḍāʾ*, the German colonies and Jewish model farms and training centers in the countryside and Tel Aviv, were given preference by visiting government officials, who considered them as positive role models for the locals, as was expressed by Ottoman Governor Muhdī Bek.[160]

156 Kark 1990b, 221–224. However, Palestine was still far from having motorized transport. The Templar magazine *Die Warte* ('The Observation Point') reported in 1914 that the German Wagner Brothers, who ran a machine factory in Jaffa, owned the only automobile in Palestine in 1913. Kark 1990b, 230.

157 Kark 1990b, 225–227.

158 *Filasṭīn*, 31 January 1912: 107/3/2–4.

159 *Filasṭīn*, 8 May 1912: 134/3/4.

160 *Filasṭīn*, 17 August 1912: 163/1/3–2/1.

5. Ethno-Confessional Cohabitation and Power Sharing

Apart from the principle of economic interaction and ethno-social or ethno-confessional division, how peaceful or conflicted in reality was the cohabitation between groups in Jaffa and its environs? Ṭarāwina speaks of good harmony in relations between the various groups but does not go into detail. The demographic and ethno-confessional diversity contributed to a vital cultural life but also caused conflicts in Jaffa, and the town had 'social hotspots' where violence occurred. Tension also existed on the inter-confessional, intra-confessional and ethno-confessional level.

Inter-Confessional Conflict Patterns and Tensions

In Jaffa's public ceremonies, feastday celebrations and official receptions, the local elites hailed the vision of 'Ottoman unity and brotherhood', the Arab press declared inter-confessional brotherhood to be the foundation of society, and Muslim, Christian and Jewish community leaders made countless appeals for solidarity between the religious groups, as outlined in the previous chapter. However, the social climate between the various groups in the region was rather fragile on the ground. The customary peace was from time to time interrupted by violent clashes between residents of town neighborhoods, or Arab villagers and foreign colonists in the hinterland. While occasional inter-confessional tension in the Empire occurred, usually between Muslims and Christians, and in general, sectarian violence between Muslims and Christians increased in the Arab East from the end of the nineteenth century, this conflict pattern was gradually reversed in Palestine under the impact of Zionist migration. In pre-World War I Palestine, violence occurred mostly between Jewish migrants and Arab Palestinians, sparked by rivalries for economic resources. Local Muslim–Christian relations moved towards an alliance while Christian–Jewish hostilities grew – a tendency that intensified with the emergence of Arab nationalism after the war.[161]

In Jaffa, Jewish–Christian relations were in general more hostile than Jewish–Muslim relations,[162] though inter-confessional tension occurred on various levels. In 1908, riots broke out between Russian-Zionist migrants and Muslim youths during the Jewish feast of Purim. This was followed by diplomatic wrangling between the Russian consul and the *qā'imaqām*, Asaf Bek, which ended with the removal of the latter from office.[163] Anti-Christian riots in Ramla

161 See Ma'oz 2002, 108–118.

162 Smilansky states that, in 1907, the atmosphere in Jaffa was openly hostile against Jews. This applied especially to the Christians, he said, while Jewish–Muslim relations were better, although he attested that the Muslims treated Jews in a patronizing way. Kark 1990b, 201f.

163 Buessow 2011, 236; Mandel 1976, 27f.

in the context of the Italian military action in Libya in 1911 have already been outlined above, where it was noted that *Filasṭīn*'s editors interpreted the incident as an untypical slip-up initiated by an 'ignorant' mob from the Jaffa hinterland, and blamed Ramla's Christians for having 'provoked' their Muslim brothers. This case demonstrates how essential it was in the view of local Christians, as a minority, to protect the narrative of Muslim–Christian harmony in the Ottoman Arab East during a time of political crisis. In addition, the interpretation of the incident is an indicator of growing political Muslim–Christian alliances in Palestine, also in the light of Jewish migration. It can be seen through *Filasṭīn* that, by 1912, relations between Jaffa's Christian elites and Jewish migrants were tense. First, the Christian merchants felt that they were being driven out of business by Ashkenazi Jews, who were rather dominant in urban commerce. Second, tensions between Jaffa and Jewish settlements also increased, arising from rivalries over land, as will be outlined in the chapter on Zionism. In the latter half of 1913, violent clashes in the hinterland between Arab farmers and Zionist settlers, the so-called 'Zarnuqa affair', also to be discussed in the chapter on Zionism, had a deep impact on an anti-Zionist discourse that was emerging in Palestine before the outbreak of World War I.

Intra-Confessional Conflicts and Tensions

Tension in the urban space also manifested itself on the intra-confessional level, since confessional groups were in general rather fragmented internally. For instance, Jaffa's Jewish community was ethnically very heterogeneous: the Jews used places of worship on the basis of their ethnic origins and, in general, relations between Sephardi and Ashkenazi Jews in Jaffa were ruled by rivalries over community leadership. This rivalry manifested itself in the Jewish 'Town Committee' (Hebr.: *va'ad ha-qehilla*), which was dominated by European Jews. There were boycott actions, enforced by Zionist youth organizations in Jaffa against Sephardi and Ashkenazi Jews who employed Arab laborer, as *Filasṭīn* discussed. There were also conflicts between Ashkenazi Jews in Jaffa over a Hebrew culture policy. Both these subjects will be picked up in the chapter on Zionism.

There was also intra-Christian tension. The atmosphere between Roman Catholics and Greek Orthodox in Jaffa was characterized by rivalry. When a local Orthodox welfare association registered the construction of a public bathhouse for the poor, a Catholic welfare association protested in court against the initiative.[164] Catholic clerics were mocked sarcastically in *Filasṭīn*,[165] and the Jerusalem correspondent commented on the 'national politics' (*as-siyāsa al-ǧinsīya*) of the Franciscan convent in Jerusalem, whose head had to be Italian, its rep-

164 *Filasṭīn*, 3 April 1912: 125/4/1.

165 *Filasṭīn*, 23 September 1911: 71/3/5–4/1; 7 October 1911: 75/4/2; 9 July 1913: 252/1/1–4.

resentative French and the treasurer Spanish.[166] Another time, *Filasṭīn* published a pamphlet that had previously been distributed by Franciscan monks in the churches of Jaffa in which they called their followers to abstain from 'the cardinal sins' (*al-ḫaṭāyā l-maḥfūẓa*): to marry outside of one's denomination, to enter the church of a heretic and to send one's children to a school run by other communities; and the editors were outraged by this 'ban' (*ḥirm*).[167] Relations between the Arab Palestinian Greek Orthodox and their Patriarchate, to be treated in the next chapter, were even more conflicted. This was seen in Jaffa when the local community locked the abbot, sent by the Patriarch of Jerusalem, out of the church that belonged to the Greek Orthodox convent, where he was to celebrate mass.[168]

On the ethno-social level, there was tension between Jaffa's merchants and landowners, and private armed security forces in the urban space and the garden area, who were of North African origin and had a reputation for violence. In *Filasṭīn*, a tremendous amount of police news was about this group, to be treated in a case study in the last part of this chapter.

Institutional Power and Local 'Pressure Groups'

Apart from the typical conflict patterns outlined above, established practices of 'power sharing' and 'pressure groups', who had an effective level of organization and were able to articulate their agenda in local politics, had an impact on cohabitation in Jaffa. The role of the local government and 'institutional power' was rather strong, as is shown in *Filasṭīn*. The full range of governmental institutions was concentrated in town as the center of the *qaḍāʾ*. Besides the Civil Court (*maḥkama niẓāmīya*), the Commercial Court (*maḥkama tiǧārīya*) for the Jerusalem District, the District Council (*maǧlis idāra*), and a municipality (*maǧlis baladī*), governmental security forces and the gendarmerie of the *qāʾimaqām*, whose role was quite strong in Jaffa, also operated in town.[169] In addition, the mufti, an office held by the Daǧǧānī family, took an important ceremonial role in the town.[170]

The ʿĪsās maintained a close relationship with the *qāʾimaqām* and *Filasṭīn* was regularly distributed by his gendarmerie to the rural areas and villages in the hinterland, and communication between government and citizens was channeled through the *Local News* section. There, the ʿĪsās passed on to him concrete

166 *Filasṭīn*, 22 February 1913: 215/3/5–4/2; 29 March 1913: 225/1/3.
167 *Filasṭīn*, 21 February 1912: 113/3/5.
168 *Filasṭīn*, 18 June 1913: 246/3/4–5.
169 Although the *qāʾimaqām* was usually not a local, Jaffa did have once an Arab *qāʾimaqām*. In 1905, Mūsā Kāẓim al-Ḥusaynī, a born Jerusalemite and descendant of the prominent Muslim Jerusalemite family, governed Jaffa. See Kark 1990b, 44; Pappé 2010, 111–112.
170 See Buessow 2011, 230f.

requests that they had allegedly received in oral conversations or letters from the population, and they published the telegrams from the *qāʾimaqāmīya* that informed citizens about laws and official government policies and decisions.

Apart from the strong role of government institutions in Jaffa, political and cultural activities were organized by the town's elites, the local branch of the CUP, the freemasons' Barkai Lodge, and communal associations. Each community had an elected representative (*muḫtār*), or a committee, to be responsible for dealing with the authorities and with the government in the interests of his community,[171] and each confessional group maintained its places of worship and organized welfare provision and school education. In 1895, there were eight monasteries and convents, several Christian schools and pilgrim hostels, clinics and orphanages; in 1896, there were in total 21 schools.[172] Communal associations, such as the Muslim 'Society for Piety and Welfare' (*Ǧamaʿīyat al-Birr wa-l-Iḥsān*),[173] the 'Orthodox Welfare Association' (*al-Ǧamʿīya al-Ḫayrīya li-r-Rūm Urṯūḏuks*),[174] the 'Association of Orthodox Women for the Support of Orphan Girls' (*Ǧamʿīyat as-Sayyidāt al-Urṯūḏuksīya li-ʿAḍd al-Yatīmāt*),[175] and the 'Israelite Women's Association' (*al-Ǧamaʾīya as-Sayyidāt al-Isrāʾīlīya*),[176] as well as secular platforms such as Jaffa's 'Sports Club' (*al-Muntadā ar-Riyāḍī*),[177] and the 'Society for the Prevention of Drugs' (*Ǧamʿīyat al-Imtināʿ ʿan al-Musakkirāt*),[178] initiated cultural and leisure activities and arts events, and organized donation campaigns for several purposes.[179]

Concerning Jaffa's institutional life, it must be stressed that it was the center of Zionist activity in Palestine, where the bulk of Zionist institutions were concentrated and the building of the New Yishuv was intended to be coordinated. In 1890/91, the Jewish Town Committee was elected to represent all the Jews of Jaffa in dealings with the authorities. It was open to all Jews but was by Ashkenazis and had considerable influence on local Zionist organizations, supporting the settlements around Jaffa and maintaining contacts with other Jewish societies. Jaffa also saw the foundation of the Jewish Artisans' Union (1893), the Workers'

171 This was also the case for specific ethnic groups or neighborhoods, such as the black Muslims of Sakinat al-ʿAbīd who could have been socially somewhat marginalized but did present their own *muḫtār*. See Ṭarāwina 2000, 476–477.

172 Eight Muslim schools, two Greek Orthodox, one Armenian, six Catholic, two Protestant and two Jewish. For 1912, Baedecker lists four Jewish and 11 Christian schools, leaving out the Muslims. See Kark 1990b, 172, 284.

173 *Filasṭīn*, 8 March 1913: 219/3/4.

174 *Filasṭīn*, 25 May 1912: 139/3/3; 18 June 1913: 246/3/5.

175 *Filasṭīn*, 15 February 1913: 213/3/5.

176 *Filasṭīn*, 6 November 1912: 186/3/4.

177 *Filasṭīn*, 12 March 1913: 220/1/3–5.

178 *Filasṭīn*, 5 June 1912: 142/3/3.

179 For this topic, see my article 'Performances of Late Ottoman Modernity: Public Culture, Entertainment and Leisure Activities in Pre-World War I Jaffa' (forthcoming 2020).

Society (1900) and others. At the beginning of the twentieth century, it was the ideological center of the WZO and Hebrew culture. In 1903, the first branch of the Anglo Palestine Bank, a Zionist credit institution, and in 1907, the Palestine Office, the WZO instrument for colonization in Palestine, opened in Jaffa. In 1914, 29 Hebrew newspapers were published, among them the Socialist-Zionist newspapers *Ha-Aḥdut* and *Ha-Poʿel ha-Tzaʿir*. There was also Hebrew and Yiddish theatre and the Hebrew Gymnasium of Tel Aviv.[180]

Apart from government institutions and confessional organization in Jaffa, there were professional 'pressure groups' able to present their agendas to the municipality or exert pressure on the government. The first group with considerable influence was the merchants (*at-tuǧǧār*) and the landowners (*al-mallākūn*) as the powerful economic elites of Jaffa. In 1912, a petition issued to the municipality signed by six merchants and, among others, 33 landowners successfully prevented the sale of water mills on the River Yarkon into private hands, and the mills were declared public property, a case to be illustrated in detail in the chapter on Zionism. Another professional group in local economics was the guild of boatmen (*al-baḥrīya*) consisting, according to consular reports, of 400–500 members in 1908.[181] The third group able to exert pressure in local politics were the guards (*an-nawāṭīr*) stationed in the urban area and the gardens. These guards were strongly stigmatized, known for gang crime and for dividing the area into spheres of their control, as will be seen at the end of this chapter.

6. Negotiating Urban Politics in Jaffa

This section introduces two 'hot topics' discussed in Jaffa's local politics that were at the top of the town elites' agenda, as can be seen in *Filasṭīn:* the modernization of local infrastructure and the improvement of public security (*al-amn al-ʿāmm*) in the *qaḍāʾ*. In a typical quotation, the Jaffa landowner and merchant Naǧīb Bayrūtī addressed Rūḥī al-Ḫālidī, elected chair of the Provincial Council, in a telegram to *Filasṭīn*, calling on him to engage in the implementation of 'useful projects' (*mašārīʿ mufīda*) such as the construction of a new port and public security.[182]

180 Kark 1990b, 190–199.

181 This according to the German consul. See Buessow 2011, 222, n. 46.

182 See *Filasṭīn*, 4 November 1911: 83/3/4. The Provincial Council (*al-maǧlis al-ʿumūmī*) was the supreme body of the province, composed of deputies from all subdistricts elected by members of the municipality and electors for parliamentary elections. It was convened by the governor for only a 40-day period each year to review the draft budget of the local government before it was sent to Istanbul. Although provincial administration was reorganized in the 1870s, the provincial council of Jerusalem only started to function after the

6.1. Modernization of Infrastructure: Roads and Port

Concerning the modernization of local infrastructure, the most urgent demands of *Filasṭīn*'s readers, in line with the spirit of reform outlined above, focused on the modernization of infrastructure. Here, the improvement of the road network was a central issue and many reports complained about the poor condition of carriage roads leading north and south of town, which were clearly either not or badly sealed. When it rained, the roads turned to mud and were hardly accessible, or when it was dry they would be so covered by sand blowing from the coast that vehicles could hardly find them.[183] The state of the road to Nablus was so bad that, according to *Filasṭīn*, it turned into a 'swamp' full of holes during winter, and the local government did not have the budget to repair it. German Templars who operated professional carriage services on the Jaffa-Haifa and Jaffa-Jerusalem routes had a vital interest in the maintenance of the roads. The Templar and Jewish colonies around Jaffa offered to repair the Nablus road at their own expense, as a 'donation' (*tabarruʿan*), according to *Filasṭīn*. However, the government clearly did not approve the initiative and the editors sarcastically asked about the hidden 'wisdom' (*ḥikma*) underlying this decision.[184]

Even more central was the constant demand in *Filasṭīn* for the construction of a deep-water port to support Jaffa's commercial development, which was relevant for local merchants and landowners, especially in the light of Jaffa's rivalry with the northern port city of Haifa. The importance of Jaffa's port had grown since the end of the 1860s as the number of steamships in the eastern Mediterranean rapidly increased, especially after the Suez Canal opened in 1868, and several foreign regular shipping companies started operating in Jaffa during the 1870s.[185] Rising steamship traffic connected Jaffa with the urban centers of Europe and the Arab East and, before World War I, its harbor was the most important on the eastern Levant coast between Beirut and Alexandria.

Filasṭīn stated that 766 steamships and 1,065 sailing boats passed through Jaffa's port in 1911.[186] For 1913, the Austrian consul-general of Alexandria, Anton

---

Hamidian period. See Buessow 2011, 79, 81–82. Although Gerber (1985) states that the first Provincial Council was established in 1913, *Filasṭīn* reported in 1911 concerning its election that it met several times and consisted of 20 members from the subdistricts. See *Filasṭīn*, 4 November 1911: 83/1/1; and 6 December 1911: 92/1/1-4.

183 *Filasṭīn*, 3 February 1912: 108/2/1.

184 *Filasṭīn*, 17 January 1912: 103/3/1–2.

185 German Vice-Consul Murād reported that five regular shipping lines were operating from Jaffa in 1870: the French Messageries Imperiale, the Lloyd Companies of Austria, Russia and Egypt, and the British Anglo-Asian Steamship Company. In addition, there were steamships and sailing ships from Egypt, Turkey, England, France and Greece. See Kark 1990b, 272.

186 *Filasṭīn*, 6 January 1912: 101/1/4–5.

Laurin, reported about 636 steamships and 676 sailing boats.[187] With regard to passengers passing through Jaffa, in 1895, the French Vice-consul in Jaffa reported that 5,000 tourists and 15,000 pilgrims had traveled by rail that year from Jaffa to Jerusalem, most of whom had entered the town via the port.[188] Reports in 1905 mention that there were numerous shipping companies, travel agencies, hotels, carriages and wagon services operating from the port area, as well as hundreds of guides and escorts, 23 khans, 64 restaurants and 81 cafes.[189] Between June 1911 and May 1912, *Filasṭīn* reported that 4,896 tourists were channeled through the Jerusalem District, handled by established tourist agencies, such as Thomas Cook's, Tādrus, Clark, Hamburg, Barakāt and Naṣīr, and Faraǧallāh.[190]

Despite of its significance in the eastern Levant, the much used Jaffa port was little more than a small basin not capable of meeting modern demands. The basin could only take small boats, while larger ships had to anchor far out in the open sea. Then, small boats would transfer cargo and passengers to the beach. This was not easy as the boats had to maneuver between the reefs, which was problematic especially when the sea was rough. Often, cargo was damaged and passengers injured. In stormy weather, the situation was too dangerous for mooring, forcing ships to wait, sometimes for days, on the open sea or to continue north to Haifa or Beirut or south to Egypt.[191] Winter storms flooded the harbor area and damaged goods stored for export, which caused severe losses, as reported *Filasṭīn.*[192]

From the 1860s onwards, there were already proposals from engineers of various countries for the modernization of Jaffa's port, which became the subject of imperialistic rivalries, as Avcı has documented.[193] Nevertheless, Jaffa was not to get a modernized sea port during Ottoman times, which caused countless complaints by locals to Ottoman delegates and the central government,[194] and the priority of the project was a topic of lively discussion in *Filasṭīn.* In 1912, it was reported that the government had finally decided to construct a new port basin 3,000 meters long ready to take 60 steamships.[195] However, the tender came to a halt despite the protests of Jaffa's residents.[196] *Filasṭīn* criticized the local gov-

187 For international maritime activity at the Jaffa port, see Kark 1990b, 273–274.

188 Kark 1990b, 286.

189 Kark 1990b, 288.

190 Among them 1,321 Americans, 992 English, 851 Germans, 465 Italians, 386 French, 215 Spanish, 208 Austrians, 177 Russians and 99 Indians. See *Filasṭīn*, 29 June 1912: 149/3/2.

191 Kark 1990b, 230–238.

192 *Filasṭīn*, 27 December 1911: 98/2/5–3/3; 6 January 1912: 101/1/1ff.

193 Avcı 2011, 93f.

194 *Filasṭīn*, 27 December 1911: 98/2/5–3/3.

195 *Filasṭīn*, 1 June 1912: 141/3/2–3.

196 Several articles sent bitter reminders to the central government in Istanbul, now the LU cabinet, complaining about the 'Eastern habit' of forgetting promises. See *Filasṭīn*, 11 September 1912: 170/3/4.

ernment for investing only in the railway and in an article titled: 'We Want a Port!' (*Nurīd Marfaʾ*),[197] Jaffa's merchants and notables (*tuǧǧār wa-ḏuwwāt al-balda*) called for the establishment of a 'special commission' (*qūmisyūn maḫṣūṣ*) to channel local petitions and requests concerning the port and direct them to the central authorities.[198] Another letter called for the founding of a joint-stock company by merchants, landowners and banks to obtain the concession with the help of European investors. *Filasṭīn*'s editors protested that the central government made three million francs a year in customs revenue via Jaffa's port and should construct the port at its own expense, and so citizens should continue petitioning Istanbul.[199] When in 1913, Governor Māǧid Bek's ship, on its way to Palestine, could not dock in Jaffa due to stormy weather and had to continue south to Port Said, the editors sarcastically mocked Māǧid Bek:

> What we hope is that the steamship … also will not be able to take anchor [there] and return him back to Haifa so he would be forced to come to us over land. Then, he personally could experience the dangers travelers are suffering from by land and by sea. Then he would strive with us in demanding a port for Jaffa and repairs to the roads in the first place.[200]

Appeals in *Filasṭīn* made by local notables to the government became more vehement in the light of the rivalry between Jaffa and Haifa over the construction of a new port. Haifa, situated north of Jaffa on the Mediterranean, was the most used harbor between Jaffa and Beirut. It seemed that Istanbul was showing more interest in modernizing Haifa's port, which would isolate Jaffa from its close connection with Beirut. South of Jaffa, the harbor of Gaza was a reloading point for wheat and barley in Palestine, but not a serious rival to Jaffa.[201] A letter published in *Filasṭīn* by Menashe Me'irovitch, a Zionist from Rishon Le-Tzion, who shared the ʿĪsās' passionate concern for the modernization project with regard to Palestinian agriculture and infrastructure,[202] complained about the 'ruin and destruction' (*al-ḫarāb wa-d-damār*) at Jaffa's port, and in an alarming voice, warned that a future modernization of Haifa's port would pose a serious

197 *Filasṭīn*, 6 August 1913: 260/1/1–3.
198 *Filasṭīn*, 7 August 1912: 160/1/4–5.
199 *Filasṭīn*, 6 September 1913: 269/1/1–4. The French Railway Company in Jaffa also discussed applying for the concession. See *Filasṭīn*, 10 September 1913: 270/3/1; 24 September 1913: 274/3/2.
200 *Filasṭīn*, 15 March 1913: 221/3/3.
201 The sandy coast of Gaza was not as dangerous as the Jaffa harbor but there too, ships had to anchor far from the city on the open sea. In 1912, Gaza's municipality invested 2,000 lira in a fleet of wooden boats but the future prospects for grain merchants in Gaza were not very encouraging, said *Filasṭīn* on 31 August 1912: 167/1/1–4.
202 From 1911 to 1912, Me'irovitch published his column 'Letters of a Farmer' (*Rasāʾil Fallāḥ*) in *Filasṭīn* under a pseudonym; this will be treated later in detail in Chapter IV on Zionism.

threat to Jaffa's urban development.[203] Frequent petitions to Istanbul from representatives of Jaffa's steamship companies for the construction of a new port was unfortunately, Me'irovitch lamented, nothing but 'drumming in the ears of the deaf' (*kull ḏālika ṭabl ʿinda ṭuršān*).[204] Istanbul ignored the fact that Jaffa was one 'of the most important port cities in the Ottoman Empire' (*min ahamm ṯuġūr al-mamlaka al-ʿuṯmānīya*), and the gate through which up to 20,000 visitors a year spread into Palestine, he stated. The development of the last three decades proved that Jaffa had accomplished an important 'step towards civilization and progress' (*ḫaṭwa fī sabīl al-madanīya wa-t-taqaddum*), Me'irovitch claimed and reported as a proof that the annual revenues from imports amounted to 15,954,000 francs, and from exports up to 11,855,000 francs.[205] While the government enjoyed the increase in tax revenues from the region, it did not invest in its development, Me'irovitch complained, and compared Jaffa with a dairy cow about which the government thought: 'May God bless the people of Jaffa. Their cow drops plenty of milk while it does not need a lot of food.'[206]

It is very obvious from *Filasṭīn* that Jaffa's residents constantly feared that Haifa would preempt them in the construction of a port. Local merchants seriously worried for their future if trade to and from Palestine across the Mediterranean were to be handled via Haifa, given the anticipated losses in terms of international trade, pilgrims and tourists.[207] These worries were justified. From 1905, Haifa was connected by rail with Deraa and Damascus in Syria and thus on a branch line of the Hejaz Railway, a prestige project of the Ottoman government.[208] Now, in 1912, time was pressing since an extension of the railway was currently under construction, connecting Nablus via Afula with Haifa in the north. After its completion, Jaffa would be cut off from the trade lines from the Palestinian highlands to the Jaffa port. In this situation, an anonymous letter ended with the question: 'When the turn will come for Palestine (*matā yaʾtī ad-dawr li-Filasṭīn*)'? The ʿĪsās, frustrated that the *qaḍāʾ* would be handicapped and by the government's silence, despite all the letters that had been sent, responded:

> Poor Palestine (*maskīna Filasṭīn*). Its turn has not yet come. And in terms of the general reform schedule its turn is (always) at the very end … If the port of Haifa is finished

203 *Filasṭīn*, 6 January 1912: 101/1/1 f. and 101/4/1. In another article, Me'irovitch addressed the Palestinian delegates in the Ottoman Parliament with an urgent appeal to finally lobby Istanbul for the construction of the Jaffa port. See *Filasṭīn*, 1 January 1912: 141/1/3–2/3.

204 *Filasṭīn*, 6 January 1912: 101/1/1–2.

205 See *Filasṭīn*, 6 January 1912: 101/1/4–5.

206 '*Bāraka allāhu fī l-Yāfīyīn fa-inna baqratahum tudirr labnan ġazīran wa-lā taḥūǧunā li-ʿalaf kaṯīr.*' See *Filasṭīn*, 6 January 1912: 101/1/5.

207 *Filasṭīn*, 27 September 1913: 275/1–4; and 1 October 1913: 276/1/3–5.

208 For the development of Haifa as a port city in late Ottoman times and its connection to the Hejaz railway in line with colonial considerations, see Norris 2013, 47–54.

> before (Jaffa), then it will take over the economic vitality of the qaḍā᾽ and attract away from her (Jaffa) the trade (coming) from Nablus – especially after the railway tracks from the Afula branch are finished – and this will be soon.[209]

In 1913, *Filasṭīn* happily announced that the construction of the new Jaffa port would begin in 1914, on an area that would extend to 27,000 square meters and be 'three times as large' as the port of Beirut.[210] However, this did not come to pass and, during the Mandate, Jaffa lost the competition with Haifa. The British decided to make Haifa a crossroads for transportation via the Hejaz railway and the harbor in order to protect the Suez Canal and their zones of influence in the Arab East. The deep-sea port, built in 1933, made Haifa the major transport center in the eastern Mediterranean.[211]

On the subject of the modernization of Jaffa's infrastructure, sanitation and hygiene were also hot issues. The locals pressed for the construction of a sewage system and the implementation of quarantine measures to avoid cholera epidemics that broke out from time to time, as *Filasṭīn* reported,[212] and there was permanent fear of cholera and other infections.[213] When electric streets lighting was installed in 1912,[214] the editors mockingly challenged the municipality that Jaffa's 'enlightenment' would now force them to take better care of its 'cleanliness'.[215]

6.2. Establishing Security, Defending Public Space

Jaffa was also a social 'hot spot', and faced violence and crime. Sūq al-Bustrus was a known for gang crime,[216] and in the Old City, ʿAǧamī and Manšīya there were frequent thefts, street brawls, shootings and murders, and *Filasṭīn* stressed that theft and robbery in ʿAǧamī had increased dramatically after the neighborhood

209 *Filasṭīn*, 7 August 1912: 160/1/4–5.
210 *Filasṭīn*, 27 September 1913: 275/3/2.
211 Seikaly 2002, 100–103.
212 See *Filasṭīn*, 7 August 1912: 160/1/3–2/1; 17 August 1912: 163/1/1–3; 1 March 1913: 217/3/2; 15 March 1913: 221/3/4–5. From the 1870s, ships were held in quarantine if necessary in order to avoid plagues, there was a quarantine center at the harbor, but there were still cholera epidemics in Jaffa in 1865, 1883 and 1886, and worse in 1902, 1910, 1911 and 1912. See Kark 1990, 212–214. On hygiene, health conditions and medical services in Jaffa, see pp. 209–216. Again, Kark ascribed all improvement in health and medical services to foreign efforts.
213 *Filasṭīn*, 28 August 1912: 166/2/5; 14 September 1912: 171/3/2; 18 December 1912: 198/3/3; 23 August 1913: 265/4/1–2; 27 September 1913: 1913: 275/1/4–2/2; and 27 September 1913: 275/4/1–2.
214 *Filasṭīn*, 7 August 1912: 160/1/3–2/1. Kerosene lamps had already been installed by the municipality in 1897. See Kark 1990b, 208.
215 *Filasṭīn*, 7 August 1912: 160/1/3–2/1.
216 See *Filasṭīn*, 1 November 1913: 285/2/5–3/1; 23 September 1913: 273/2/5–3/1.

was guarded by a new troop of Maghrebi watchmen.[217] In the view of the local elites, public space should be strictly controlled by the state. The question, how 'public security' (*al-amn al-ʿāmm*) was to be maintained was extensively discussed on the Local News page and was at the top of the agenda of Jaffa's merchants and landowners. Thus, 'violence and security' was a dominant issue in *Filasṭīn*, and I recorded 292 items published between 1911 and 1914 on this topic. From 1912–1913 in particular, a serious increase in violence in Jaffa was noted, described by the editors as 'a disease compared to which our other diseases fade away' (*maraḍ taḫiff bi-ǧānibihi amrāḍunā*).[218]

Indeed, the situation was described as precarious by the local economic elites, and also the governor and foreign consuls. Countless appeals were directed by the editors and readers to the *qāʾimaqām* and the police commander, calling for an increase in the number of armed forces in town, street patrols and posts on the roads to and from the city. In 1913, during the Islamic Feast of Sacrifice, a knife fight occurred at night in the heart of Jaffa, causing several injuries and the death of one Christian, Anṭūn ʿĪsā Sābā; the attackers escaped as there was no police presence. People were outraged, and the funeral of the dead man, jointly organized by local Christians and Muslims, escalated into a demonstration protesting against the government's neglect of Jaffa's public security,[219] although the number of security forces in the *qaḍāʾ* was in fact rather large. In 1912, *Filasṭīn* reported that about 16 Ottoman police officials in addition to diverse security units were operating in town,[220] and the German consul mentioned that there were in total 1,500 forces personnel in the urban area.[221] In addition, Ottoman gendarmerie and soldiers were stationed in barracks on the outskirts. Even so, in the eyes of the population, the government was completely failing to defend public space.

Police, Gendarmerie, Soldiers and Vagabonds

As seen from *Filasṭīn*, state efforts to protect Jaffa's citizens were perceived as highly ineffective, and complaints were bluntly directed at local police officers, the *qāʾimaqām*'s gendarmerie and foreign militias stationed in town. One issue frequently cited was the lax behavior and 'laziness' of police officials, who were said to be slow and only reluctantly ready to fulfil their duties.[222] Once, the editors quoted from an (imaginary?) interview with a local citizen who had waited five years after filing a lawsuit before he received a summons to appear in court.

217 *Filasṭīn*, 13 September 1913: 271/3/3–4.
218 *Filasṭīn*, 4 October 1913: 277/3/2–3.
219 *Filasṭīn*, 12 November 1913: 288/3/–3.
220 *Filasṭīn*, 22 May 1912: 138/3/4.
221 This in a report in 1911. See Buessow 2011, 237.
222 *Filasṭīn*, 25 October 1911: 80/1/1–3.

When he was the victim of a robbery for a second time, he gave up filing a complaint as he would not live long enough to see the end of his case.[223] The ʿĪsās, who regularly went to the police station to collect first-hand information about the latest security issues, complained that, if one walked around in Jaffa, one would hear about daily shootings robberies of banks and shops and assaults on citizens. However, their engagement was not much welcomed by the officers, who used to downplay the situation, saying, 'Thank God, there are no incidents to report' (*lā tūǧad ḥawādīṯ wa-l-ḥamdu lillāh*).[224]

Another subject of fierce complaints to the local authorities was 'the foreign Gendarmerie' (*al-ǧandarma al-ġurabāʾ*) in Jaffa, such as the Circassians who patrolled the town.[225] These foreign militias, who 'infiltrate through the walls and scare people inside their houses', the editors complained, did indeed cause public unrest in Jaffa, as the *Local News* section showed.[226] Being of foreign origin, they could not speak Arabic and the locals did not trust them. They had a reputation for rude behavior, and were perceived as a danger to public security rather than as a protection, and *Filasṭīn* occasionally appealed to the military commander or the chief of the gendarmerie to 'educate' their men, because they harassed pedestrians and used disproportionate violence in public places. During Easter 1913, for example, foreign militias attacked with knives some young Christian men who were euphorically shooting into the air during the celebrations, which led to complaints being made to the military commander.[227] And there was an incident when a military unit burgled the building of the Orthodox school and vandalized its furniture.[228]

People also filed complaints on another occasion, when the Jaffa based battalion (*ṭābūr*) of the Bany Ṣaʿb, about which I have no information, harassed locals strolling on the beach and beat them up with wooden sticks.[229] After Jaffa's *qāʾimaqām* and the deputy commander communicated with Jerusalem, the the battallion was ordered to withdraw to Haifa and a reserve battalion, the *Ṭābūr Radīf Ǧamāʿīn*, was ordered to Jaffa. Even so, the editors feared that the soldiers' presence in town would always cause unrest (*iḍṭirāban wa-tašwīšan*) in Jaffa's residential areas and asked the *qāʾimaqām* to keep them outside of town in the suburbs (*ḍawāḥī*), 'for the sake of the (public) interest and peace' (*li-l-manfaʿa wa-ḥubban bi-r-rāḥa al-ʿumūmīya*) and 'to prevent many complaints'.[230]

---

223 *Filasṭīn*, 3 September 1913: 268/3/2–3.
224 *Filasṭīn*, 30 August 1913: 267/3/3–4.
225 *Filasṭīn*, 28 August 1912: 166/4/1–2.
226 *Filasṭīn*, 30 September 1911: 73/3/2–3.
227 See *Filasṭīn*, 26 March 1913: 224/3/3–4; 19 April 1913: 231/3/4; and 5 November 1913: 286/3/3.
228 *Filasṭīn*, 10 July 1912: 152/3/2.
229 .*Filasṭīn*, 18 June 1912: 146/*mulḥaq*/2–3; and 29 June 1912: 149/3/2–3.
230 *Filasṭīn*, 29 June 1912: 149/3/2–3.

Apart from police, foreign gendarmerie and soldiers, vagabonds, gypsies and traveling performers disturbed the local's vision of public order and security. For instance, it was positively received in *Filasṭīn* when the police prohibited female dancers (*rāqiṣāt*) from performing in Jaffa's public places and coffee houses for they led to 'immorality' (*ḥawādiṯ muḫilla*).[231] In March 1913, the ʿĪsās complained that, with the beginning of the tourist season in spring, the 'season of our beggars' (*mawsim aš-šaḥḥāḏīna*) had also started, the same as every year. From the villages and the hinterland, vagabonds and 'tramps' (*mutašarridīn*) came to Jaffa, where visitors arrived at the port, to make a living begging. This was a 'disaster' (*muṣība*) that Jaffa's population and the visitors suffered from every year, the ʿĪsās declared, especially since they did odd things, such as getting undressed before pilgrims while making the sign of the cross, although these beggars were Muslims.[232] Violence was also experienced by social outsiders such as Turkmen tramps, who were beaten up by the people 'wherever they were found' when they came to town. They were dragged to the House of Government with bloodied faces, although they had done nothing, because of rumors that they intended to kidnap children.[233]

The Maghrebi Guards and Problems of Organized Crime

A special issue in *Filasṭīn*'s debate about public security in Jaffa and its environs was the role of Muslim migrants of Moroccan, Algerian or Afghan origin, who received a huge amount of negative attention in the *Local News* section. Some of them were 'tramps' (*mutašarridīn*) but the great majority were employed in the security sector: they worked patrolling the town and on the roads and as watchmen in the gardens, particularly ing the orange groves (*nawāṭīr al-burtuqāl*). According to *Filasṭīn*, most of the men who guarded the fields in the Jaffa region were of Maghrebi origin.[234] These Maghrebis (*al-maġāriba*) were said to be reckless in their use of weapons, and they were notably involved in about -third of *Filasṭīn*'s police reports. Of the 192 police reports from *Filasṭīn* that I recorded concerning my topic of investigation, 60 were related to criminal acts committed by Maghrebis. Many incidents of gunfire between Maghrebi gangs and police in town and in the gardens were reported,[235] and some of the Maghrebis gained a reputation as repeat offenders and became the source of rumors.[236]

---

231 *Filasṭīn*, 29 June 1912: 149/3/4.

232 *Filasṭīn* 19 March 1913: 222/3/3.

233 The ʿĪsās actually took sides with the Turkmen, criticizing the people, who continued to spread rumors about 'child kidnapping' (*ḫaṭf al-awlād*) without reason or proof. *Filasṭīn*, 10 August 1912: 161/3/2–3.

234 This according to a note of the deputy *qāʾimaqām* of Jaffa. See *Filasṭīn*, 16 March 1912: 120/3/1.

235 *Filasṭīn*, 16 August 1911: 60/3/2; 3 April 1912: 125/3/4–5.

The criminal activities of Maghrebi migrants were also documented in other towns, especially Bethlehem and Beit Jala, where the Maghrebis were called a 'disaster' (*muṣība*), and said to be involved in cases of road hold-ups, plundering, vandalism, shooting in the street and kidnapping.[237] Sometimes, conflicts with Maghrebi gangs escalated into nights of 'bullet storms' or battles between the gangs and the gendarmerie, supported by the locals.[238] *Filasṭīn*'s Bethlehem correspondent, Ǧibrān Maṭar, reported frequent bomb attacks that affected wealthy families who had migrated to America but owned real estate in their home town. *Filasṭīn*'s Chile correspondent, Ḫanā Miḫāʾīl Buyūk, even stated that Bethlehem's famous security problem prevented many migrants in South America from returning to their homes.[239]

However, Jaffa was especially known for its Maghrebi problem and as a scene of organized crime that the government was unable to control.[240] Competing gangs controlled the town districts and were involved in violent night-time clashes that escalated in wild shooting and murder.[241] And it was not only Jaffa town that faced gang crime; the lack of security throughout the *qaḍāʾ* was described as a 'disease' (*dāʾ*). Armed groups stole livestock, robbed merchants' shops and attacked government forces stationed in the town. The Lod correspondent reported 'nights of murder' in 'a hail of bullets', which he compared to a 'battlefield' in the Tripoli war.[242] Although the *qāʾmaqām* set up guarded posts (*maḥāfira*) on the roads to Yāzūr and Gaza, street banditry was frequent, and *Filasṭīn* demanded that the road to (Wadi) Miṣrāra and Nablus should also be guarded.[243] The road between Jaffa and Ramla was particularly affected. Maghrebi 'gangs of thugs' (*ʿaṣābāt al-ašqiyāʾ*) ambushed travelers, transport and postal services and even brought their children with them for support.[244] In 1912, robberies on the Jaffa-Ramla road became so frequent that it threatened the operation of transport services.[245]

236 For example, the Maghrebi guard al-Ḥāǧǧ Ramaḍān al-Maġribī was held responsible for many crimes and managed to flee several times. See *Filasṭīn*, 24 January 1912: 105/3/5.

237 *Filasṭīn*, 11 September 1912: 170/3/3; 5 October 1912: 177/2/5.

238 *Filasṭīn*, 11 September 1912: 170/3/3.

239 *Filasṭīn*, 18 December 1912: 198/2/3–4.

240 *Filasṭīn*, 13 April 1912: supplement (*mulḥaq*) 127/1/4–5.

241 *Filasṭīn*, 17 February 1912: 112/3/4.

242 *Filasṭīn*, 28 August 1912: 166/4/1–2.

243 *Filasṭīn*, 1 June 1912: 141/3/3.

244 *Filasṭīn*, 27 March 1912: 123/2/4–5; and 30 March 1912: 124/3/2. Readers' letters also complained about robbery on the roads from Jaffa to Gaza. Abū Ḥatab, an author from Maǧdal, described how he became a victim of robbery on the road to Maǧdal, between Jaffa and Gaza. *Filasṭīn*, 13 January 1912: 102/3/1.

245 *Filasṭīn*, 3 April 1912: 125/3/2–3; 125/3/4–5.

In the urban area, merchants and notables were threatened by Maghrebi and Afghan guards, even out in the streets.[246] The Jaffan merchant Iskandar Rok, for example, was blackmailed by a Maghrebi, who shot his servant.[247] Owners of gardens and fields (*al-mallākūn wa-aṣḥāb al-basātīn*) in the surrounding area were particularly affected, including Arab landowners but also Jewish settlers and German colonists.[248]

The Maghrebi and Afghan guards in particular terrorized landowners with acts of widespread destruction in the fields and vandalism, which caused the landowners serious losses.[249] Another tactic of the Maghrebi gangs was extortion. They demanded taxes from landowners for the protection of their lives and estate, called *ǧizya* in *Filasṭīn*, which the landowners 'submissively payed' (*yadfaʿūna… ʿan yaddin wa-hum ṣāġirūna*) *Filasṭīn* wrote, quoting a passage from the Qur'an referring to the taxes that non-Muslims had to pay under Sharia law before the *millet* reforms.[250] The reference to this Qur'anic verse was meant to show the humiliation of Jaffa's landowners, the economic elite of the city, by Maghrebi guards, social outsiders not integrated into local society.[251] In other cases, Maghrebis forced landowners to employ them as guards and issue them with documents accordingly. In case of refusal, they cut down their trees, stole their fruit or threatened their lives.[252] The ʿĪsās concluded that Jaffa's landowners were 'at the mercy' of these guards (*taḥta raḥmatihim*) since most of them did not even dare to file complaints with the authorities, 'knowing how weak they [the authorities] were' (*li-ʿilmihim bi-ʿaǧzihā*) and fearing for their lives.[253]

Of course, this meant risks for investors. *Filasṭīn* stated in 1912 that Jaffa's landowners had started to think about selling their land and instead buying fruit from the better guarded Jewish settlements to avoid the risks.[254] The extent of the landowners' helplessness around Jaffa was demonstrated by the case of the

246 *Filasṭīn*, 24 February 1912: 114/3/3.

247 *Filasṭīn*, 21 February 1912: 113/3/4; 2 March 1912: 116/3/4.

248 In 1912, the German consul filed a complaint with Jaffa's *qāʾimaqām* about alarming incidents in the German colony of Sarona, where Afghan guards had uprooted 36 orange trees (*ḫalaʿ ašǧār*). *Filasṭīn*, 3 July 1912: 150/3/5.

249 For example, Afghan guards cut down 37 trees in one night in the orchard of one Muḥammad ʿAlī al-Kī (or Kay); and 57 trees in the orchard of one Dāwud as-Siksik. *Filasṭīn*, 29 January 1913: 208/3/4.

250 *Sūrat at-Tawba* in the Quran contains the command to 'combat' (*qātilū*) the 'people of the book' (*ahl al-kitāb*), the Christians and Jews, 'until they pay the jizya submissively and from their hand' (*ḥattā yuʿṭū l-ǧizyata ʿan yaddin wa-hum ṣāġirūna*). See *Sūrat at-Tawba:* 29.

251 See *Filasṭīn*, 17 February 1912: 112/3/3; 6 March 1912: 117/3/2.

252 *Filasṭīn*, 17 February 1912: 112/3/3.

253 *Filasṭīn*, 6 March 1912: 117/3/2. Only Dimitri Tadrus, a famous citizen of Jaffa, was courageous enough to demand the investigation of his case. See *Filasṭīn*, 7 February 1912: 109/3/3; 17 February 1912: 112/3/3.

254 *Filasṭīn*, 17 February 1912: 112/3/3–4; 13 November 1912: 188/3/4.

German Templar Laemmle, a member of the Laemmle family in the colony of Sarona.[255] He had 200 trees cut down on his land by the 'guards'. He transported the trees to Jaffa and set them up in a row in front of the House of Government to demonstrate his losses to the authorities, with their inability to handle the Maghrebi problem.[256]

Government Strategies for Security Improvement

The government faced tremendous pressure from the public because of the dire security situation. In 1912, the editors of *Filasṭīn* declared that the Maghrebi and Afghan guards had become the 'masters' (*aṣḥāb al-ḥawl wa-ṭ-ṭūl*) in Jaffa,[257] while the *qāʾimaqāmīya* watched them 'like a weakling and a coward' (*naẓar al-ʿāǧiz wa-l-ǧabān*), as if the state's authority 'cannot reach further than five minutes outside the city'.[258] Thus, they addressed the new *qāʾimaqām* Hāšim al-Atāsī with the demand: 'We need a ruler of deeds more than a man of words' (*ḥākim faʿʿāl akṯar min amīr aqwāl*).[259]

In response to the situation, the government appointed watch crews (*ḫafrāʾ waṭanīyīn*) for whom merchants and landowners were to pay a special 'watch tax' (*rusūm al-ḥirāsa*), an approach that was not effective because the landowners refused to pay.[260] Second, the *qāʾimaqāmīya* ordered landowners to register their Maghrebi employees, bring them to the House of Government for registration and have their weapons licensed. Guards who were caught without registration or license would be deported and their employers would face legal consequences (*taʿqīb*), the government announced. The editors mocked al-Atāsī, saying, it would it be hard to bring before the authorities guards who were in fake employment and forced their employers to pay them protection money.[261] The upshot was that this approach made no impact, and the expulsion of unregistered Maghrebis was not pursued either, apart from sporadic attempts. For instance, there was one *Filasṭīn* report in 1912 that eight Maghrebis were deported and put on a steamboat to Egypt.[262] Al-Atāsī and the forces under chief police commander

255 The Laemmle family had several members but I do not know which one is meant here. Glenk, Blaich, and Haering 2005, 46, 47.

256 It is interesting that in this case, people reacted with malicious pleasure since the victim was a foreigner. The editors had only mockery for Laemmle. Referring to the power of the foreign consuls, they sarcastically wrote, 'as there is no safeguarding for the property of the Ottoman citizens, at least the property of the foreigners must be protected (*fa-ʿalā l-aqall al-muḥāfaẓa ʿalā amwāl al-aǧānib*)… who will not excuse this.' *Filasṭīn*, 22 January 1913: 206/3/2–3.

257 *Filasṭīn*, 17 February 1912: 112/3/3.

258 *Filasṭīn*, 17 February 1912: 112/3/3–4.

259 *Filasṭīn*, 6 April 1912: 126/3/2–3.

260 *Filasṭīn*, 7 February 1912: 109/3/3.

261 *Filasṭīn*, 16 March 1912: 120/3/1–2; 20 April 1912: 129/3/2.

262 *Filasṭīn*, 5 October 1912: 177/3/3–4.

Ḫalīl Efendi did do some work on the prosecution of criminal guards, and in spring 1912, for instance, were able to catch 12 members of a bigger Maghrebi gang and have them imprisoned 'in chains', but these were only occasional successes.[263]

Police custody and imprisonment were not reliable, either. Readers asked the ʿĪsās to mediate and direct an 'open letter' (*kitāb maftūḥ*) to the *qāʾmaqām*, asking him to judge the Maghrebis according to 'customary law' (*muḥākama ʿurfīya*) since processes in the government court took a long time and were viewed as too lax. Meanwhile, it is clear that Maghrebi prisoners managed to break out of jail, press reports complained, since prison guards who were of Maghrebi origin helped their fellow countrymen to escape.[264] In other cases, detainees managed to escape 'by the prison window or drainpipe' *(min nāfiḏat as-siǧn aw min bālūʿatihi)*, *Filasṭīn* reported.[265]

Campaigning against the Maghrebis

Since government achievements in dealing with the 'Maghrebi problem' were sporadic and unable to break gang crime in Jaffa, several campaigns were initiated by various local actors to confront the problem. The ʿĪsās addressed the *qāʿimaqām*, Jaffa's police commander and the Jerusalem governor directly, pleading for stricter punishment and the expulsion of dangerous elements from Jaffa's social fabric. In an interview, ʿĪsā al-ʿĪsā asked Governor Ǧawdat Bek 'to impose the law on vagrancy' (*tuṭabbiq qānūn al-mutašarridīn*) on the Maghrebis and 'deport them to where they came from' (*wa-tubʿiduhum ilā ḥayṯu ātū*), a suggestion that was, according to ʿĪsā, also approved by the foreign consuls in the *qaḍāʾ*.[266] However, many Maghrebis were not Ottomans but had French citizenship and were thus foreigners, which made their legal prosecution under Ottoman law complicated.[267] Further, the vagrancy law could hardly be imposed on the Maghrebis because they were employed as guards, which was why the *qāʾimaqāmīya* tried to have them licensed. The governor was aware of the difficulties and suggested closer cooperation with foreign consulates and embassies in the registration of the names of the Maghrebis living in the district as to 'clean the city of them because it is wrong to leave a city like Jaffa in their stranglehold', *Filasṭīn* quoted him as saying.[268]

Filasṭīn criticized the Ottoman secular juridical system (*al-ʿadlīya*) explicitly for its ineffective prosecution. Juridical punishment was a 'picnic' (*nuzha*) for the

263 *Filasṭīn*, 13 April 1912: 127 – Supplement (*mulḥaq*): 1/4–5; and 11 May 1912: 135/3/4.
264 *Filasṭīn*, 13 April 1912: 127 – Supplement (*mulḥaq*): 1/4–5; and 15 May 1912: 136/3/4.
265 *Filasṭīn*, 7 June 1913: 243/1/1.
266 *Filasṭīn*, 6 March 1912: 117/3/2.
267 *Filasṭīn*, 19 February 1913: 214/3/1–2.
268 *Filasṭīn*, 6 March 1912: 117/3/2–3.

Maghrebis, ʿĪsā said. They went in and out of prison several times and 'play games with the government and the law'.[269] Thus, the Christian editors even called for the implementation of Islamic sharia in criminal prosecution (*al-ḥudūd*), and they claimed to be expressing public opinion in this matter. Otherwise, they warned the local government, people would establish a committee to monitor negotiations with the Maghrebi gangs about protection money in order to deal with the mafia-like structures in Jaffa. This was clearly aimed to wake up the authorities, as is illustrated a speech ʿĪsā made in which he addressed the local and the central government as well as the highest Muslim authority in the Empire, the Sheikh al-Islam in Istanbul.

> Admit your weakness, oh (local) government. If you are incapable (*ʿāǧiza*), then tell us: 'I do not have the power to protect your blood and your property.' Then we ourselves will send an intermediary (*wasīṭan*) to this gang that is haunting our sleep and say to them: 'Enough of the nasty deeds and the killing ... Impose on us as much money as you want. We will meekly pay it as a tax for protection (*ǧizya*) in order to live next to you in safety.[270] ...
>
> And to you, oh central government – who have taken thousands (of lira) from us in despotic ways... and left us (alone), exposed to the despotism of thugs who surround us on all sides – and to you, His Eminence, Sheikh al-Islam, to whom the Sharia of this Empire is entrusted – we say that the suspension of the (Islamic) penalties (*al-ḥudūd*) is a [unreadable word] to the criminals. The state that we are in now is the result of the suspension of the penalties of God, which declare that one who kills should be killed (*huwa natīǧat taʿṭīl ḥudūd allāh al-qāʾila bi-anna al-qātil yuqtal*).[271] ...
>
> What we said above, is the opinion of every one (*lisān ḥāl kull fard*) of the inhabitants of this despairing city, whose souls are possessed by terror and from whose neighborhoods safety has fled... None of them can go out of town any more to oversee his properties.[272]...
>
> If the government is too weak to catch the thugs and jail cannot keep them inside and justice deprives them of the death sentence and Istanbul refuses to confirm this sentence ... then why waste time and put the people at risk. Let the population elect a committee (from among them) to approach this gang and agree with them on a certain amount of protection tax ... so we can regain our (former) safety and peace of mind.[273]

269 *Filasṭīn*, 3 April 1912: 125/1/1 + 2.

270 *'Fa-nadfaʿuh ka-ǧizya wa-naḥnu ṣāġirūna wa-naʿīš bi-ǧiwārikum āminīn.' Filasṭīn*, 3 April 1912: 125/1/1.

271 *Filasṭīn*, 3 April 1912: 125/1/1.

272 *Filasṭīn*, 3 April 1912: 125/1/2.

273 *'Iḏā kānat al-ḥukūma ʿāǧiza ʿan al-qabḍ ʿalā l-ašqiyāʾ wa-s-suǧūn lā tastaṭīʿu ḥafẓahum wa-l-ʿadāla taḍinn ʿalayhim bi-ḥukm al-iʿdām wa-l-Istāna tarfuḍ al-muṣādaqa ʿalā hāḏā l-ḥukm fīmā law ṣuddiru fa-limāḏā iḍāʿat al-waqt wa-limāḏā l-muḫāṭara ʿalā l-arwāḥ fa-li-yantaḫib al-ahālī laǧna minhum taḏhab wa-nattafiq maʿ hāḏihi al-ʿaṣāba ʿalā ǧizya maʿlūma ... wa-narǧaʿ naḥnu ilā amninā wa-rāḥat afkārinā.' Filasṭīn*, 3 April 1912: 125/2–3.

Filasṭīn's editors explicitly criticized the juridical reforms contained in the reform edict of 1856 for including too much 'mercy for criminals' and the 'delay' (*muṭāwala*) of punishment, and they pleaded for the enforcement of the sharia in criminal law. Usually, the Ottoman Constitution was 'sacralized' in the discourse of *Filasṭīn*, and considered as the necessary foundation of government, equal to the concept of 'justice'. But with regard to the 'Maghrebi problem', the editors switched the argument and declared civil jurisdiction a violation of god's law. By authorizing the 'penal law of Hümayun' (*qānūn al-ǧazāʾ al-humāyūnī*), ʿĪsā said, 'the legal experts and judges have considered themselves more just then God' (*ẓannū anfusahum aʿdal min allāh).* However, 'the divine penal law is greater than the civil law' (*qānūn al-ǧazāʾ al-ilāhī huwa aʿẓam min qānūn al-ǧazāʾ al-humāyūnī*), ʿĪsā concluded, and went on to say that the juridical experts had forgotten the wisdom of this law that decreed 'a life for life' (*an-nafs bi-n-nafs*).[274] In dramatic words, ʿĪsā described the latest cases of murder in the *qaḍāʾ* as a 'warning from God' (*inḏāran min illāh*) to Istanbul, and as a sign that it should 'return to its divine sharia which decrees the execution of every criminal'.[275]

Jaffa's economic elites also joined public campaigns protesting about the security situation. In February 1913, *Filasṭīn* reported that the merchants of Jaffa's Sūq al-Balābisa had petitioned the municipality, announcing that they would refuse to pay the 'watch tax' (*rusūm al-ḥirāsa*) in the future.[276] They said it would be safer if there were 'no security forces at all' (*ʿadam wuǧūd ḥurrās*) installed by the municipality, and announced that they would appoint their own guards, a kind of civil vigilantes, to protect their goods.[277]

The situation still worsened: theft, extortion and cutting down trees regularly continued and *Filasṭīn* documented the names of the victims and the losses they suffered.[278] In October 1913, *Filasṭīn* announced that the battle against organized crime was lost in Jaffa. Competing gangs, each headed by 'leaders' (*zuʿamāʾ*), the three major ones being the Maghrebis, the Afghans, and gangs of local outlaws, had divided the city between them into territories:

> In Jaffa, there is a big group of Maghrebis and also a big group of Afghans who are constantly competing to guard the orange groves. Between them, there is a history of bloody incidents whose consequences mostly affect the owners of the orchards. This year, a third group is participating in it – the tramps and outcasts. Those three groups

274 *Filasṭīn*, 7 June 1913: 243/1/1.

275 '*Li-yarǧaʿū ilā šarīʿatihi al-ilāhīya al-qāḍiya bi-iʿdām kull ǧānin.*' *Filasṭīn*, 7 June 1913: 243/1/1.

276 'Palestine Remembered' notes that the merchants of Sūq al-Balābisa traced their roots back to Egyptian migrants from Balbees. See http://www.palestineremembered.com/Jaffa/Jaffa/ (consulted 20 November 2017).

277 *Filasṭīn*, 1 February 1913: 209/3/5.

278 *Filasṭīn*, 8 October 1913: 1913: 278/3/1.

> have reached an agreement to divide Jaffa into spheres of influence (*taqsīm Yāfā dawā ʾir nufūḏ*): this side belongs to the Afghans, that side to the Maghrebis, and the other to the sons of the country; for they would not challenge each other anymore.[279]

> The negligence of the central government in the past caused the division of the Empire into spheres of influence (*taqsīm al-mamlaka dawā ʾir nufūd*) as we saw; and the negligence of the local government in Jaffa has caused its division between those thugs in spheres of influence.[280]

The previous illustration shows that the inclusion or exclusion of groups from Jaffa's social fabric was *not* related to confessional or ethnic affiliation. Since the Maghrebi migrants were considered as a serious threat to Jaffa's trade and tourism, and a risk to security in the urban space, they were clearly to be distinguished from the 'local' population of Jaffa as a 'migrant society' and were portrayed as 'foreigners', regardless of whether they held French citizenship or Ottoman. As they were a factor in economic instability, the Maghrebis could not be integrated into the concept of 'Ottoman unity', although had they lived as long in the *qaḍā ʾ* as other groups of migrants from Africa or Asia, and were Muslims like the majority of Jaffa's population.

279 *Filasṭīn*, 18 October 1913: 281/1/2–3.
280 *Filasṭīn*, 18 October 1913: 281/1/3.

III. The 'Arab Orthodox Renaissance' in the Greek Orthodox Patriarchate of Jerusalem: Conflicts about Participation

1. Framing the Topic

Short Chronology of the Arab Orthodox Conflict in Palestine (1908–1914)
Through *Filasṭīn*'s coverage from 1911 to 1914, this chapter explores the conflictual relation between the local Arab Palestinian Orthodox and the Greek Orthodox Church, called 'Rum Orthodox' (*rūm urṯūḏuks*), in the Patriarchate of Jerusalem (*al-kursī al-uwrūšalmī*);[1] specifically, how a circle of Arab Orthodox activists from the Jerusalem District negotiated the participation of locals in the administration of their Church. These negotiations included various escalations of tension between the clerical hierarchy and local communities and led to the Ottoman authorities being extensively entangled in the intra-Orthodox conflict. At the core of the problem was the fact that power in the Patriarchate was exclusively concentrated in the hands of Greek clergy, all of them members of the 'Fraternity of the Holy Sepulcher' (*aḫawīyat al-qabr al-muqaddas*),[2] or as it was also called in *Filasṭīn*, the 'Convent of the Holy Sepulcher' (*dayr al-qabr al-muqaddas*), the 'Orthodox Convent' (*dayr ar-Rūm*),[3] or simply, 'the monks' (*ar-rahbana*).[4] This powerful monastic order based in Jerusalem, owned extensive assets and real estate in Palestine, controlled the Patriarchate's institutions and economic resources, and defined its cultural agenda and its liturgical character, while the local Orthodox were excluded from decision making.

In the aftermath of the 1908 Revolution, a new generation of local Orthodox called for reforms to the power structures in the Patriarchate, then under Patriarch Damianos (1897–1931).[5] They called their movement the 'Orthodox Ren-

1 *Filasṭīn*, 6 November 1912: 186/4/1–2.
2 *Filasṭīn*, 9 September 1911: 67/3/5; 10 August 1912: 161/2/5; 30 October 1912: 184/4/2–3.
3 See, for instance, *Filasṭīn*, 21 June 1913: 247/3/2.
4 *Filasṭīn*, 19 August 1911: 61/2/2. In this study, it will be referred to as 'the Fraternity' or 'the Convent'.
5 For the reign of Damianos, see Dowling 1913, 27f; and Kildani 2010, 169f. For his treatment of the Arab Orthodox issue after the restoration of the Constitution in 1908, see ibid., 171–206.

aissance' (*an-nahḍa al-urṯūḏuksīya*),[6] and defined it as a 'popular movement' (*ḥarakat aš-šaʿb*),[7] and as a 'national reform renaissance' (*nahḍa iṣlāḥīya waṭanīya*).[8] The movement, referred to hereafter as the 'Orthodox Movement', was driven by a circle of activists from Jerusalem, Bethlehem and Jaffa with a very rebellious spirit, who were committed to modernist values and the Arab *nahḍa*, motivated by the political culture of the Second Constitutional Period. Their central aim was to access the Patriarchate's financial resources, and specifically, to participate in the administration of the Patriarchate's revenues from Orthodox institutions, properties and pious endowments (*awqāf*) through councils elected by the local people of each *qaḍāʾ*, the so-called 'local councils' or 'trustees' councils' (*maǧālis al-mutawallīn*). Finally, they aimed at cultural reforms in the dioceses, including the Arabization of Orthodox education.

Since these demands received no response from the Patriarchate, riots broke out against the clergy in Jerusalem, spread to other dioceses and escalated into a circle of violence from 1908 to 1910. To settle the conflict, a government commission from Istanbul issued the '1910 Resolution', as it will be referred to in this work, which stipulated the enactment of the Orthodox 'Mixed Council' (*al-maǧlis al-muḫtalaṭ*). The Council consisted of equal numbers of Greek clergy and Arab Orthodox lay delegates and was supposed to negotiate and supervise the reformation of Orthodox educational, social and welfare institutions in the dioceses. For this, it was to receive one-third of the Patriarchate's annual revenues, at least 30,000 lira.[9] This was a considerable sum. On the other hand, the 1910 Resolution did not touch Patriarchal privileges and did not provide the Mixed Council with far reaching legal competences that would make a change in the status quo possible. Even so, the Orthodox community had high expectations of the Mixed Council. It met bi-weekly from December 1910 until 1914, and its meeting minutes were regularly published in *Filasṭīn*.

However, the Council became the stage for a dispute between its lay and clerical delegates. Important to note is that Patriarch Damianos, as head of the Council, had the right of veto. Since the Patriarchate was in financial crisis and so Damianos blocked every reform demanded by the lay delegates, the Mixed Council's debates did not lead to solutions but went round and round in a circle of escalations and de-escalations. Orthodox activists mobilized the laity, organized demonstrations, occupied churches and Orthodox schools, boycotted ceremonies and sent petitions to the authorities. By 1913, intra-Orthodox conflicts had reached a peak and the Council underwent a crisis of legitimacy. A

6 *Filasṭīn*, 23 September 1911: 71/3/3–5; 27 September 1911: 72/4/1–2.
7 *Filasṭīn*, 9 April 1913: 228/1/4–2/2.
8 *Filasṭīn*, 7 October 1911: 75/3/5.
9 For the 1910 Resolution, see Ḫūrī 1925. For a translated summary of the resolution, see Appendix I.

Filasṭīn editorial in 1912, entitled 'That was the Last Drop that Makes the Barrel Overflow' (*Laqad ṭafaḥa al-kayl*), illustrated the Council's history as a sequence of failures, gives insight about the first experiment of the Arab Palestinian Orthodox with democracy, and recalls the central complaints against the Patriarchate:

> They [the government] told us: 'Be tolerant (*tasāhalū*) with the Patriarchate', and we were. They advised us to consider them as fathers, not as enemies, and we did ... Yet, this increased their [the clergys'] arrogance and tyranny (*ġaṭrasa wa-ṭuġyānan*) ... In this session, they reject what they decided in the last session. They postpone sessions, they waste time and use excuses ... What shall we do with this nation, oh people (*fa-mā l-ʿamal maʿ hāḏā l-qawm yā nās*)!? For the past two years, they have been playing with this Council as the cat plays with the mouse just to swallow it ... They made delay, suspension and nullification the basis of their policy (*ǧaʿalū rukn siyāsatihim at-taṭwīl wa-t-taswīf wa-n-naqḍ*) ... They lit the fire of rivalry between the dioceses (*nār at-tanāfus bayna al-abrašīyāt*) until ... the Council lost its credibility in the eyes of the nation...
>
> We came with good intentions to at least lay the corner stone for the Council's activities. However, we did not succeed. All the time, we said: 'Hand over to the Council its rights, let it work practically and not on paper (*sallimū l-maǧlis ḥuqūqahu wa-daʿūhu yaštaġil ʿamalīyan lā ʿalā l-waraq*) ... lte it have its budget ... let it supervise the [Orthodox] schools, churches and hospitals, protect the honor of the teachers and priests who are begging at the gates of your convent to grab the overdue payments of their salaries! Assign all of this to the Council to end this prevailing chaos. Let us know the invoices of the Council and what they are for'....
>
> Their [the clergy's] answer was always: 'After we have finished [calculating] the [annual] budget.' And when we came to [see] the balance sheets, they placed obstacles in our way and demanded that the budget be allocated ... in advance. As if we saw anything of this money!...
>
> There is no interest in reforms, the people are being ridiculed, the lay delegates are being mocked, the government and its resolutions are being disregarded. We shall see if the Ottoman government will tolerate this mockery, this laughter and the disregard of its orders.[10]

When Yūsuf al-ʿIsā wrote this, he was representing Jaffa in the Mixed Council and had become Damianos's main opponent; the Council's reputation was in tatters.[11] In summer 1913, the Patriarch shut down the Council's sessions. At the end of 1913, a commission was sent from Istanbul to settle the conflict and, under pressure from the head of the commission, the former Jerusalem Governor ʿAzmī Bek, the Council was reopened in January 1914. It took some quick decisions and

10 *Filasṭīn*, 28 September 1912: 175/1/1–4.
11 See, for instance, *Filasṭīn*, 22 October 1913: 282/4/2; 29 October 1913: 284/4/1–2.

continued its sessions until World War I but failed to implement substantial reforms.[12]

Nevertheless, the claim underlying this chapter is that the years between 1910 and 1914 were decisive for the Arab Orthodox Movement regarding the articulation of political arguments, the mobilization of the laity, and the establishment of a public discourse on the 'Orthodox cause' in pre-World War I Palestine, which was carried on into the Mandate period.[13]

Filasṭīn as a Source for the Investigation of the Arab Orthodox Cause

Filasṭīn is a most valuable but unexplored source through which the intra-Orthodox conflict in Palestine prior to World War I can be explored. In January 1911, in the aftermath of the enactment of the Mixed Council, ʿĪsā al-ʿĪsā launched *Filasṭīn* mobilize the Palestinian public for the Arab Orthodox cause, and I propose that this was the decisive factor in his journalistic initiative. From the beginning, the ʿĪsās devoted the major part of the newspaper's coverage to this cause; they designed *Filasṭīn* to be *the* central public forum for Orthodox activists and Yūsuf al-ʿĪsā defined it in July 1911 as the 'mouthpiece' (*lisān*) of the Orthodox *milla* in Palestine.[14] His cousin ʿIsā al-ʿĪsā confirmed in his memoirs, *Min Ḏikrayāt al-Māḍī* in retroperspective that his motivation was 'to serve the Orthodox cause above anything else' and that the Orthodox movement 'predominates on its pages' from the start 'until the present'.[15]

I have identified 452 items or articles on the Orthodox cause published in *Filasṭīn* in the period between July 1911 and August 1914. In almost every issue in the *Local News*, a couple of regular, extended columns were published, entitled 'The Orthodox Renaissance' (*an-Nahḍa al-Urṯūduksīya*), 'Orthodox Matters' (*Šuʾūn Urṯūḏuksīya*), or 'The Mixed Council' (*al-Mağlis al-Muḫtalaṭ*), in which the debates in the Mixed Council's bi-weekly sessions were documented in detail by printing the record of speeches of each speaker in chronological order.

These 'speakers' records' are very relevant to an exploration of the Arab Orthodox Movement since they provide a deep insight into the negotiations between the clergy and the lay Arab Orthodox during the Second Constitutional period. The Mixed Council was the first public forum to debate the Patriarchate's accountability and the participatory rights of Arab Orthodox, and was of high symbolic value for the local faithful. Being the only official institution that represented Arab Orthodox rights to the Patriarchate, its sessions aroused great interest among the public. Further, these speakers' records deliver a

12 *Filasṭīn*, 17 January 1914: 299/1/1–2.

13 For the Orthodox Movement in Mandate Palestine, see Robson 2011a, 2011b.

14 *Filasṭīn*, 15 July 1911: 51/1/3.

15 The quotation is taken from Tamari, who clearly had access to the manuscript. See Tamari 2014, 6, n. 49, 35.

micro-perspective on the first experiments with democracy and political participation in the Patriarchate of Jerusalem. Never explored before, they give insights into the process of parliamentary debates during the last years of Ottoman rule, and say a lot about intra-Orthodox power policies and the practical work of 'Mixed Councils' in the aftermath of the *millet* reorganization in the Empire. Pursuing The debates that took place in this Council may also reflect the negotiating processes that were taking place in other councils, which in turn may prepare the ground for exploring the overarching dynamics in transottoman and Arab debating culture of that time. Apart from these speakers' records, petitions and readers' responses on the intra-Orthodox conflict published in *Filasṭīn* also help to reflect the scope of the Orthodox Movement in the public sphere in Palestine.

Arab Christians in Palestine: Research Context

This study contributes to the 'relational' history of Arab Christians from a transottoman perspective during the Second Constitutional Period. Till now, studies have portrayed the various Christian communities in the Holy Land, the variety of sects and the history of their patriarchs, their demographic and ecclesiastical structures and institutions.[16] O'Mahony has documented the history, democracy and institutions of Christian communities in the Holy Land and considered relations between the Church and the Ottoman state.[17] Quḍāh has investigated the presence of Arab Christians in Jerusalem through a study of Ottoman documents, and Çolak has investigated relations between the Ottoman administration and the Orthodox Patriarchates of Antioch, Jerusalem and Alexandria, and the privileges of their patriarchs up to the eighteenth century.[18]

Earlier, the status of Palestinian Christians was mostly explored by treating them *en bloc*; as a monolithic group with *united* interests, and isolated from Palestinian Muslims. Tsimhoni, for example, investigated the legal marginalization of Arab Christians as a religious minority under the Mandate, contrasting them with Arab Muslims, through a study of British files.[19] An innovative study is that by Robson, who tackled Christian–British relations during the Mandate, arguing that the 'reinvention of the *millet* system' in Palestine by the Mandate power echoed British colonial practices in India and Africa, which

16 Fortescu (1920) portrayed the history of the Orthodox Patriarchates in the East, and Luke (1927) presented sketches of Christian sects in Palestine; Cragg (1992) recalled the history of Arab Christians in the Middle East, and Abujaber (2012) studied the Christian presence in Jerusalem.
17 O'Mahony 2000; 2003a; 2003b; 2004; 2009.
18 Quḍāh 2007; Çolak 2012.
19 Tsimhoni 1984.

aimed at organizing societies according to denomination. They did this by establishing of the Supreme Muslim Court (SMC) in 1921 and the Office of the Grand Mufti, held by Amīn al-Ḥusaynī – two Muslim institutions that represented all Arab Palestinians vis-à-vis the British Mandate government. Robson sought to portray the shift towards a 'sectarian political system' in Palestine by the implementation of colonial policies, which led to the marginalization of Arab Christians in national institutions.[20] However, Robson's analysis of Palestinian Christians is based only on British records.[21] She also tackles the Arab Orthodox Movement in the Patriarchate of Jerusalem, relying on official British correspondence and the reports of the Bertram-Luke commission, appointed by the British in 1921 to settle the conflicts between the Arab Orthodox and the Patriarchate, and she thus mostly reproduces the perspective of the British Mandate power on the intra-Orthodox conflict.

A study on Palestinian Christians during the Mandate that does consider the *intra-communal level* has been made by Haiduc-Dale, who explored controversial national agendas among Christian communities and their changing national loyalties during the 1920s and 1930s. Through Zionist archives, British records and the Arab press, he outlines the various national positions of the Greek Orthodox, Melkite and Latin Christian elites. For instance, the Greek Orthodox supported the Muslim-Christian Associations (MCA), a political network constituted by the former Ottoman Muslim and Christian elites, which unsuccessfully sought recognition by the Mandate power as the national representation of the Palestinians. The Melkite Bishop Hajjar was anti-Zionist, anti-British and supported the MCA only in so far as it was opposed to the British, while the Latin Bishop Barlassina subordinated the Palestinian national cause to a confessional agenda, and preferred a protective millet system.[22] While Robson accepts the (British) assumption that, after the introduction of the SMC in 1921, Palestinian Muslims *automatically* shifted to the 'Ḥusaynī-bloc' while local Christians shifted to the 'Našāšībī-bloc' in opposition to Amīn al-Ḥusaynī,[23] Haiduc-Dale has shown that prominent Christians switched their loyalties only very gradually from the second half of the 1920s.[24]

20 Robson 2011a, 6–14.

21 See Robson 2011a, 44–66.

22 Haiduc-Dale 2013, 29–38. For the rise and fall of the MCA in 1917–1923, see pp. 39–52.

23 Robson 2011a, 75–99; and idem 2011b, 6–23.

24 Haiduc-Dale based his study on the newspapers *Filasṭīn*, *Mirʾāt aš-Šarq* ('Mirror of the East'), published in Jerusalem by Būlus Šihāda, *Ṣawt aš-Šaʿb* ('Voice of the Nation'), published in Bethlehem by ʿĪsā al-Bandak, and others. While ʿĪsā al-ʿĪsā remained affiliated to the Ḥusaynī-bloc until it established its own press organ in 1925 and changed his allegiance to the Našāšībī-bloc in 1927, ʿĪsā al-Bandak applied Islamic nationalist terminology and defended an Islamic cultural dominance in Palestine until the end of the 1920s. Haiduc-Dale 2013, 61–90.

Studies on the Arab Orthodox Movement in Palestine

Previous studies on the intra-Orthodox conflict in Palestine, such as those by Roussos and Kuruvilla, mostly relied on British reports during the early Mandate era by British arbitrary commissions, such the Bertam-Luke commission in 1921 and the Bertram-Young commission in 1925, reflecting the colonial perspective on the conflict.[25] Studies on the Arab Orthodox Movement during late Ottoman times by Kechriotis, Vatikiotis and Der Matossian have explored the effect of the restoration of the Ottoman Constitution on Greek Orthodox policies in the aftermath of the 1908 Revolution by studying Greek sources or the British reports by the Bertram-Luke commission.[26] Katz and Kark studied the acquisition of land and the control of property in the Orthodox Patriarchate under Ottoman and British rule using Greek sources from the Patriarchal archives and correspondence between the Patriarchate and the Greek government.[27] Papastathis and Kark, Kuruvilla, Roussos and Der Matossian investigated intra-clerical power struggles which led to the 'Patriarchal crisis' from 1908 to 1910.[28]

The valuable account of Niqūla and Šaḥḥāda al-Ḫūrī from 1925 gives essential insights into the emergence of the Arab Orthodox Movement in Palestine, the prelude to the conflict during the Abdülhamidian era, the Patriarchal crisis in 1908, the eruption of violence against the clerical establishment in the aftermath of the 1908 Revolution and the spread of the rebellion from 1908 to 1910, the release of the 1910 Resolution and the establishment of the Mixed Council in December 1910,[29] with which their account ends.

The Ḫūrīs' account was extremely important for my analysis of the intra-Orthodox conflict from 1911 to 1914, since it provides the text of the 1910 Resolution as the legal basis for the Mixed Council's competences. Their report was essential for an understanding of the debate in the Mixed Council, which needs to be contextualized in the light of the crisis of 1910. Without their study, it would not have been possible to understand the terminology applied to the intra-

25 See Roussos 2003, 2004, 2005; and Kuruvilla 2011, 2012.

26 Kechriotis (2005) and Vatikiotis (1994) explore political strategies of the Greek Orthodox after 1908, and Der Matossian (2009, 2011, 2012) highlights the effect of the 1908 Revolution on the Armenian, Jewish and Orthodox *millet* in Jerusalem.

27 Kark and Katz 2005, 2007.

28 Papastathis and Kark 2014a; Roussos 2005; Kuruvilla 2011; Der Matossian 2009.

29 My reference here is the Arabic account of Ḫūrī and Ḫūrī 1992, a reprint of the original Jerusalem edition of 1925, edited by Abū Ǧābir. Abū Ǧābir also published an English translation of the demands of the Arab Orthodox after the Young Turk Revolution (Khoury and Abujaber 2002). However, it has been essential to use Ḫūrī's Arabic version as the basic text since the contributions on the Orthodox cause printed in *Filasṭīn* usually applied the Arabic terms from the original text, while the translation made by Abū Ǧābir (Abujaber), although being very helpful as a complementary reading, has shortened the text and changed its original wording. Compare the Arabic original text in the edition of Ḫūrī and Ḫūrī 1992 with the English edition of Khoury and Abujaber 2002.

Orthodox conflict, analyze the meeting minutes of the Mixed Council between 1911 and 1914 or interpret the arguments of the Arab Orthodox activists.

New Aspects on the Arab Orthodox Movement

This study fills a gap in the scholarship in several respects. All of the studies mentioned above end with the inception of the Mixed Council and provide is no insight into the development of the Arab Orthodox Movement during the Second Constitutional Period from December 1910 until the outbreak of World War I. In addition, apart from the Arabic account by Ḫūrī, the total absence of local sources in studies on the intra-Orthodox conflict in Palestine is remarkable. Scholarly research has considered British and Greek correspondence but has left out Arab Palestinian perspectives on the issue, including the Arab press. This is surprising since *Filasṭīn* was from its inception a leading supporter of the Arab Orthodox cause, and published the disputes that took place in the Mixed Council and local responses on the Orthodox Renaissance.

So far, research has labeled *Filasṭīn* as *the* pioneer of early anti-Zionism and Palestinian nationalism before World War I,[30] although *Filasṭīn*'s engagement for the Arab Orthodox cause after 1911 has been recognized in secondary literature. Although the engagement of the ʿĪsās on behalf of the Orthodox cause has been very briefly mentioned by Shomali, Robson, Tamari and Khalidi,[31] not a single study has consulted *Filasṭīn* on this matter in detail. The total absence of studies on intra-Orthodox disputes shifts *after* the inception of the Mixed Council in December 1910 until 1914 is remarkable, as is the fact that the activities of the Mixed Council have not received scholarly attention. This lack of research interest on the period between 1910 and 1914 is even more astonishing given that local faithful had great expectations of the Council and closely followed its activities. Scholarly literature unanimously states, however, that there is nothing to report on the Arab Orthodox Movement from 1910 to 1914 since the Council did not manage to implement anything substantial. Papastathis and Kark are contented to note that the Council 'never really functioned' and that there were 'only a few meetings between the two sides',[32] while, as *Filasṭīn* shows, it in fact met bi-weekly for a couple of years. Referring to the British reports of Bertram and Luke and Hopwood, Roussos also notes that 'in practice, the Mixed Council never functioned', and Kuruvilla took the same

30 See Khalidi 1997, 2009; Mandel 1976; Naǧǧār 2005; Tadros 2009, 2011; Tamari 2014b.

31 See Khalidi 2009: 89–90; Tamari 2014b, 17. Both Shomali and Robson note that the column *Orthodox Matters* was regularly published in *Filasṭīn* from 1911 – a tradition that ʿĪsā al-ʿĪsā continued during the Mandate. And Robson stresses that the Orthodox cause was still a focal point in *Filasṭīn* after World War I and quotes from three issues. Shomali 1995, 232; Robson 2011a, 87, n. 36, 189.

32 Papastathis and Kark 2014, 132.

line, both without consulting Arabic sources.[33] Niqūla and Šaḥḥāda al-Ḫūrī correctly noted in 1925 that the Council met for three years 'without implementing anything' and conclude that the Council's decisions 'remained ink on paper', that 'conflicts over the interpretation of points of the official resolution multiplied' and that 'chaos ruled' the Council.[34] This cannot be denied since there is no doubt that the Council could not solve the key issues in the conflict. They conclude that the conflict continued until 1913, when ʿAzmī Bek, Ottoman Minister of Justice, was sent to resolve it, and he did in fact manage to reconvene the Council, which had been suspended unilaterally by the Patriarch.[35] Bertram and Luke and Der Matossian wrongly interpret ʿAzmī Bek's visit as bringing about the 'final settlement' of the intra-Orthodox conflict. According to them, it ended the dispute between the Patriarchate and the locals and Der Matossian claims that 'all the tension dissolved'.[36]

The Articulation of an Arab Orthodox Agenda, 1910–1914

It is true that the Arab Orthodox Movement was not able to achieve anything substantial between 1910 and 1914. Although the Mixed Council met twice a week, produced reams of paper and came to public notice, it did not provide the lay delegates with the tools with which they could legally bring pressure to bear upon the Patriarchate. Nevertheless, this period was decisive for the development of the Arab Orthodox Movement since it was during 1910–14 that it articulated a political agenda and generated public support for it through the Mixed Council, through *Filasṭīn* and by using petitions to the government as political instruments. The Mixed Council served as a forum in which the lay delegates defended the interests of their local communities and it was thus of tremendous symbolic value. It met every Wednesday and Saturday in Jerusalem to negotiate reforms that should be implemented in the dioceses. Through the Council's speakers' records that were published in *Filasṭīn*, these negotiations were made *accessible* to the Palestinian public, and met with considerable resonance. This intense coverage of 'Orthodox Matters' and the campaign against the Greek clergy in *Filasṭīn* contributed to developing a controversial discourse on the Orthodox cause in Palestine, and spread the central arguments of the Orthodox activists

33 Bertram and Luke 1921, 264–273. Roussos 2003, 44. In two other articles, Roussos quotes Hopwood, claiming that the Mixed Council did not function effectively and ceased to convene in 1913 because of the 'fanaticism of both parties'. Hopwood also says that it never functioned effectively and was soon dissolved, because of intransigence on both sides. See Hopwood 1969, 199–200; Roussos 2005, 209; and Kuruvilla 2011, 60.

34 '*Lam yunaffiḏ šayʾan min muqarrarātihi fa-ẓallat ḥibran ʿalā waraq wa-taʿaddadat al-mašākil fī tafsīr faqarāt al-qarār ar-rasmī wa-sādat al-fawḍā*.' See Ḫūrī and Ḫūrī 1992, 278.

35 Ḫūrī and Ḫūrī 1992, 279.

36 Bertram and Luke 1921, 271; Der Matossian 2009, 28.

among the public and beyond the Jerusalem District. The arguments articulated during 1910–1914 were continued into the Mandate era and found expression in the Arab Orthodox Congresses of the 1920s, but they were rooted in the Second Constitutional Period.

Although the Orthodox Renaissance was a movement for cultural reforms, it nevertheless applied elements of nationalist terminology that were about to become popular to legitimize its cause, especially the Constitutional discourse of the post-revolutionary Ottoman years. In this respect, I a political pamphlet published by Ḫalīl as-Sakākīnī in 1913 deserves special attention in the context of new trends in the adoption of nationalist terminology during the years 1913–1914. What is relevant here is that these years marked a *cornerstone* in the articulation of an Arab Orthodox political discourse that was a turning point in the history of the Arab Orthodox Movement and carried on after the War and the break-up of the Ottoman world.

In what follows, Arab Orthodox activists' campaigns for participation in the administration of the Patriarchate of Jerusalem will be analyzed in several stages: first, the discursive and communicational features of the coverage of the Arab Orthodox cause in *Filasṭīn* will be analyzed, and the networks and leading actors in the Orthodox Movement will be identified. Then, the central motives, political arguments and instruments applied by the Arab Orthodox to access the Patriarchate's resources, will be outlined. In selected case studies, the controversial negotiations between the laity and the clergy in the Mixed Council will be explored in order to highlights points of escalation and de-escalation in its history, which should be seen in the context broader trends – a trend towards cultural Arabization and a new transottoman protest culture that fostered concepts of civic equality and participatory rights for the minorities, as guaranteed in the Constitution. Through this process, the main actors and power dynamics and the typical conflict patterns in the intra-Orthodox conflict and government involvement in it will be revealed, as well as the Council's activities as a history of escalations and de-escalations.

2. Historical Context

2.1. Features and Structure of the Jerusalemite Patriarchate

The Greek Orthodox Patriarchate of Jerusalem was established following the Council of Chalcedon in 451 AD and is, along with the Patriarchates of Constantinople, Antioch and Alexandria, one of the oldest patriarchates of the Orthodox Church.[37] It consisted of seventeen or eighteen dioceses and stretched to the eastern bank of the River Jordan, and its Patriarch bore the title: 'The most Blessed and Holy Patriarch of the Holy City Jerusalem and all Palestine, Syria, Arabia beyond Jordan, Cana of Galilee and Holy Zion'.[38] In Palestine, the Greek Orthodox constituted the largest group of Christians and the Greek Orthodox Patriarchate had a special status.[39] It was one of the most powerful institutions in the Holy Land and its center, Jerusalem, was the cradle of Christianity where the Fraternity of the Holy Sepulcher controlled pious endowments, holy sites and visitors' places, and most importantly, the Church of the Holy Sepulcher, usually called in Arabic 'the Church of the Resurrection' (*kanīsat al-qiyāma*).

Under Ottoman rule, the Greek Orthodox Patriarchate of Jerusalem was subordinated to the Ecumenical Patriarch in Constantinople as the official head of all Orthodox in the Empire.[40] From the first half of the seventeenth century until 1843, the Patriarch of Jerusalem resided in Constantinople and acknowledged authority of the Ecumenical Patriarch, who appointed his successor, who was then confirmed by the Fraternity in Jerusalem.[41] After the death of Patriarch Athanaseos in 1843, a conflict arose concerning a designated successor, and from then onwards, it was the Holy Synod in Jerusalem that elected the Patriarch, who took residence again in Jerusalem. The legal status of the Jerusalem Patriarchate was a matter of argument but, by 1909, it practically acted independently in

37 Der Matossian 2011, 223–224.

38 There are different reports about the number of dioceses in the Patriarchate. In 1912, Bliss listed Cesarea, Beisan, Petra, Acre, Nazareth, Lod, Gaza, Nablus, Samaria, Tabor, Jordan, Bethlehem, Tiberias, Philadelphia, Pella, Kerak, Sepphoris and Madaba – eighteen dioceses. Bliss 1972, 54, 55, 339. Ḫūrī and Ḫūrī say that the Jerusalem Patriarchate had seventeen dioceses. Ḫūrī and Ḫūrī 1992, 265. According to *Filasṭīn,* it had fourteen dioceses. See *Filasṭīn,* 22 October 1913: 282/4/1.

39 According to Schmelz, the Greek Orthodox constituted 60–61 percent of the Christians in Palestine. In 1914, among the total population of 32,462 Christians in the Jerusalem District, the Greek Orthodox numbered up to 19,717. See Schmelz 1990, 27–28. The total number of Christians in all provinces of late Ottoman Palestine is indicated in the census of McCarthy as 81,000 in 1914. See McCarthy 1990, 10. According to the British census of Mills from 1931, the Greek Orthodox constituted only 43 percent of Palestinian Christians. The other denominations were Latin Catholic (20 %), Melkites or Syrian Catholic (14 %), Anglicans (5 %), Maronites (4 %), and smaller groups, such as the Armenians, Syriac Orthodox, Lutherans, Abyssinians, Copts and others. See Mills 1932, 8.

40 Bliss 1972, 43. Bliss's work goes back to lectures from 1912 on the historical constitutions of the Orthodox Patriarchate of Jerusalem, their hierarchic features, liturgies and rituals. Bliss 1972, 39–74, 113–116.

41 Since the time of Theophanes (1608–1643), the Patriarch of Jerusalem had resided in a palace at the Golden Horn. He appointed his successor, to be approved by the Fraternity of the Holy Sepulcher, whose headquarters were at that time also in Constantinople, without consulting the Holy Synod in Jerusalem. The Ecumenical Patriarch merely transmitted the edict of the Porte that confirmed the new Patriarch. Bliss 1972, 43–45, 47, 53, 54.

internal matters and was recognized by the sultan, but not by the Ecumenical Patriarch, as an independent patriarchate.[42]

Hierarchical ranks in the Greek Orthodox Church included metropolitans, or archbishops, and bishops, both given the title of a *muṭrān*. Then there were archimandrites, priests and deacons. The rank of archimandrite was below that of bishop, and was also given to an abbot in charge of a group of monasteries, or to a priest who was a monk, a promotion, on the way to episcopal office.[43] The patriarch in Jerusalem was assisted by the Holy Synod by which he was elected, and which included, apart from himself, nine metropolitans, ten archimandrites and one archdeacon.[44] Lay people were excluded from participation in the elections and bishops hardly ever resided in the dioceses to which they were appointed.[45]

The Patriarchate controlled all the Orthodox holy sites and churches, monasteries, shrines, pilgrim hostels, pious endowments (Ar.: *waqf*, pl. *awqāf*) and landed properties in Palestine, and the revenues deriving from them. It actually owned more land than any other church in the Holy Land, and continues until today to be the largest non-governmental landowner in Israel and Palestine.[46] The Fraternity, which was in charge of all these assets, also maintained educational, social and welfare institutions for the local people: schools, hospitals and poor houses. The dominance of monks in the ecclesiastical hierarchy has shaped the historical relationship between the Patriarchate and the local Orthodox for centuries and dates back to the establishment of the Convent in the fourth century, together with the erection of the Church of the Holy Sepulcher by the Emperor Constantine, as the ecclesiastical tradition states. According to Bliss, access to the Convent was restricted to 'Greeks in race and language'. The head of the Fraternity was the patriarch, who was, together with the bishop, chosen from

42 Bliss 1972, 47–49.

43 Plank 1999, 118.

44 Following the death of a patriarch, the Holy Synod would elect a *locum tenens*, to hold temporary authority as his successor, who was nominated by an assembly. This assembly consisted of a delegation of married priests from the dioceses, members of the Holy Synod and the archimandrites, including the priests of the Fraternity of the Holy Sepulcher. See Bliss 1972: 49, 50, 54, also n. 2.

45 Bliss states that, of 18 dioceses, only the metropolitans of Nazareth and the bishops of Bethlehem and Acre lived in their dioceses. Bliss 1972, 54, and 339f. for a list of the dioceses in the Patriarchate of Jerusalem.

46 The Patriarchate owned extensive properties in and outside Palestine. Katz and Kark investigated the distribution of Greek Orthodox property in Palestine and its acquisitions during the nineteenth and twentieth centuries, although there are difficulties identifying the total area of properties. They were able to locate 355 properties amounting up to at least 36.779 *dunam*, but were only able to locate about half of Greek Orthodox properties. See Katz and Kark 2007, 385. The British commission report by Bertram and Luke named 631 individual Greek Orthodox properties in Mandate Palestine. Bertram and Luke 1921, 195f.

among the Fraternity, which ensured the exclusion of natives from the episcopacy.[47]

Although, in theory, the 1910 Resolution guaranteed to local Orthodox access to the Fraternity, until today, most of the monks in it are Greek.[48] Native Arab Orthodox were worshippers, parish priests and church servers but could not occupy powerful positions in the hierarchy of the Orthodox Church. Most of these local priests had received elementary schooling but not a higher theological education, for two reasons. First, parish priests did not require Greek language skills, apart from a few liturgical phrases, and church service books were translated to Arabic. Further, parish priests were married and priesthood was inherited in the family, which ran against the possibility of an 'educated priesthood', especially in rural areas.[49] Thus, an observer wandering around Jerusalem in 1909 would find clusters of convents, 'swarming with priests and monks' who spoke in Greek, so, according to Bliss, one could 'get the idea of a Greek Church' in control while many parish churches were closed.[50]

The headquarters of the Patriarchate was a complex of buildings near the Church of the Holy Sepulcher in the Old City.[51] There, it maintained an extensive infrastructure of institutions, such as a boarding school for boys and a theological college, both exclusively for students of Greek origin. The Faternity's school, founded in 1845 and called 'Nephews of the Monks', was for Greek students only, while local schools were shut down, which made the Arab Orthodox dependent on foreign education. For example, Russian initiatives in local Orthodox education marked an important 'transottoman link' between Russia and Palestine. The Fraternity ran a city hospital and a printing press and, from 1904, they published the magazine *The New Zion*.[52] The annual revenues of the Patriarchate from pilgrimages, and payments from Constantinople, Moscow, Athens and Crete were estimated at the end of the nineteenth century to be more a million Turkish lira. According to Bliss, this amounted to about 240,000 dollars, of which one-quarter was spent on the maintenance of holy places, one-third on

47 Bliss ascribes its organizational structures to the seventeenth century and the reign of Patriarch Dositheos (1669–1707). Bliss 1972, 61, 62, 64.

48 Based on interviews undertaken between 23 October 1994 and 4 May 1995, Panzer says that only six monks of the 90 brothers of the monastic order were of Arab origin. See Panzer 1998a, 26, n. 44; and idem 1998b, 235–249.

49 See Bliss 1972, 61f.

50 Bliss 1972, 61.

51 Bliss states that 138 persons lived in the convent, including 8 bishops and 9 archimandrites who were members of the Holy Synod, plus 21 other archimandrites, 26 ordinary priests, 19 deacons and 55 lay brothers. See Bliss 1972, 114, 115. For a description of other monasteries in Syria, Palestine, Lebanon and Sinai, see pp. 113–122.

52 In 1909, the number of students in the college was about 60; the hospital could accommodate 40 patients. Bliss 1972, 55, 56, 63.

the see; and about 68,000 dollars on the Orthodox of Jerusalem (free bread feedings, housing rents and schools).[53]

2.2. Factors in the Arab Orthodox Awakening

Several transottoman phenomena stimulated the Arab Orthodox awakening in Palestine from the second half of the nineteenth century: the Arab Renaissance Movement, the legal changes stipulated by the Tanzimat, Russian influence in Palestine, the rebellion of Arab Orthodox in the Patriarchate of Antioch against their Church and, most importantly, the 1908 Revolution and the restoration of the Ottoman Constitution under the Young Turks.

In general, the Arab Renaissance Movement for a revival of the Arab cultural heritage, the *nahḍa*, driven by intellectuals in the urban centers of the Arab East, inspired the Orthodox in Palestine to go for reforms. Naming their movement the 'Orthodox Renaissance', they embedded their cause into the broader trend towards the cultural Arabization of the region. More importantly, the re-organization of the hierarchies of the *millets* during the Tanzimat and the short-lived Constitutional era of 1876 stimulated the Arab Orthodox because it aimed at increasing lay participation in *millet* organization. The edict of 1856, the *hatt-ı hümayun*, had formally ordered the formation of Mixed Councils to administer the finances of the Orthodox Church, and the Constitution of 1876 further allowed local participation in the election of the Patriarch and the administration of *waqf* properties. Since the 1860s, the Porte in Istanbul had already been pressuring the Greek Orthodox Church to implement the new regulations. Finally, from 1860 to 1863, a Mixed Council was established in the Patriarchate of Constantinople, though not in the Patriarchates of Antioch, Alexandria and Jerusalem, where the laity continued to be excluded from higher ranks and decision-making.[54]

This reformation of intra-communal hierarchies at the center of the Empire encouraged the Arab Orthodox in Palestine to call for participatory rights in the administration of the Patriarchate's properties, which led to the 'Patriarchal

53 Bliss 1972, 62, 63, 73.

54 Roussos 2003, 216. For the reorganization of the Greek Orthodox, see Davison 1968, 93–108 and idem 1973, 114–134; especially 126–129. For the laws on the Mixed Councils, see Young 1981. For the privileges of the Patriarch of Constantinople, see Papadopoulos 1924, 245f, 252. For the evolution of the *berats*, granted privileges, for the Patriarchate of Jerusalem during the eighteenth century, see Çolak 2012, 165–169. For economic activities encouraged through the *berats* and their expansion outside Palestine, see Çolak 2012, 225–241. For historical relations between the Porte and the Greek Orthodox as Ottomans and Greeks before and after the Tanzimat, see Clogg 1982, 185–207.

crisis', during the last years of the reign of Kyrillos (1845–1872).[55] Under imperial pressure, the new patriarch, Ierotheos (1875–1882), issued the so-called Katastikon in 1875,[56] which formally permitted locals to enter ecclesiastical ranks, the Fraternity and the Holy Synod, establish a 'general committee' (*hayʾa ʿumūmīya*) of clergy and lay delegates under the chairmanship of the patriarch to watch over the finances for the schools in the dioceses, *waqf*s excluded, and to appoint local representatives (*wukalāʾ al-ahālī*) to manage the churches belonging to the local people, apart from the revenues from the holy places. These concessions were not implemented, however, and Arab Orthodox reform demands in Palestine were left without response.[57]

Russian support was another historical factor that encouraged the Arab Orthodox Movement in Palestine. In the aftermath of the Ottoman defeat in the Russo-Turkish War (1768–1774), during which the High Porte lost Crimea to Russia, Russian protection of Orthodox Christianity in the Ottoman Empire was formalized in the Treaty of Küçük Kaynarca (1774). The Russian Empire received the right to open consular agencies everywhere in the Empire and the same privileges in trade as France and England, and from then on, positioned itself as protector of Orthodox Christianity in the Ottoman realms.[58] In Palestine, the Russian Orthodox Church competed with the Greek Orthodox Church for control of the holy sites and sought to strengthen their position in the Holy Land by supporting the local Orthodox. To gain influence on the Greek Orthodox Patriarchate, Moscow paid money to the patriarch and interfered in the internal affairs of the Orthodox Church, such as the patriarchal elections.[59] The Russians also maintained schools, associations and journals in Palestine. In 1847, the first Russian missionary institution was opened in Palestine, and the foundation of the Russian Imperial Orthodox Society in St Petersburg (1882) was an important milestone in the emergence of Russian influence in Palestine.[60] The Russians also influenced the election of the patriarch during the crisis of 1872 through diplomatic pressure and by cutting off payments from Russia.[61] The Russian Imperial Orthodox Society maintained a Teachers' Training Seminar in Nazareth and Beit Jala for the local Orthodox, and the Russians built and restored Or-

55 On the reign of Patriarch Kyrillos, see Kildani 2010, 57f, 78–95.
56 On the reign of Ierotheos, see Kildani 2010, 109–113.
57 On the *Katastikon*, see Ḫūrī and Ḫūrī 1992, 221–227; Kark 2005, 517; Kildani 2010, 100–108; Kuruvilla 2011, 59.
58 See Matuz 1985, 200–203.
59 For Orthodox Christianity as a factor in Russian foreign policy, see Taki 2015.
60 For its development, goals and relations with the Jerusalemite Patriarchate, see Kildani 2010, 124–139.
61 Roussos 2005, 104–107. On Russian interests in Palestine and Russian influence, see Hopwood 1969; and idem 1975, 394–407; Kildani 2010, 40–57, 60–95.

thodox churches, provided local people with medical services, undertook research projects and organized pilgrimages from Russia to Palestine.[62]

Moreover, the impact of a reform movement led by native Orthodox in the Patriarchate of Antioch during the last years of the nineteenth century further encouraged the aspirations of the Arab Orthodox in Palestine. Inspired by the *millet* reforms and the Constitutional Period of 1876, Arab Orthodox in Syria revolted against their clerical establishment and successfully generated their Orthodox 'Renaissance'. In 1899, Metropolitan Meletios of Latakia was enthroned in the Patriarchate of Antioch; for the first time in over 160 years, a native Arab Orthodox was elected as patriarch; and the clergy, including bishops and priests, were 'Arabized', in what Bliss calls a 'truly national church'.[63]

The final trigger for the rise of the Arab Orthodox Movement as an oppositional movement against the clergy took place at the beginning of the twentieth century in the 1908 Revolution and the restoration of the Constitution on 11 July 1908, which inspired the local Orthodox to actively demand their participation in the administration of Orthodox assets in the Patriarchate through Orthodox councils, elected by local people, as will be outlined below.

2.3. The Patriarchal Crisis and the Arab Orthodox Rebellion

The first document that pointed to local protest was a tract published after the 1908 Revolution, entitled 'A Historical Glance at the Greek Brotherhood of the Holy Sepulcher' (*lamḥa ta ʾrīḫīya fī aḫawīyat al-qabr al-muqaddas al-yūnānīya*) and attributed to one ʿAbd al-Aḥad aš-Šāfī. He dates the exclusion of local people from the administration of the Patriarchate back to the reign of Patriarch Germanos (1537–1579), who had filled all the important positions in the Church with his fellow countrymen, although he claims that Islamic rulers had previously confirmed the rights of the native church.[64] In the aftermath of the Revolution, a generation of young Arab Orthodox had seen how Abdülhamid was deprived of power. They openly compared the Fraternity with his absolutist rule and initiated protest actions that turned into a violent rebellion of locals against their Church, which lasted for two years and led to an internal crisis between the patriarch and the Holy Synod.

62 For their initiatives, see Kildani 2010, 140–168.

63 Bliss 1972, 58–60. For the power struggle in the Orthodox Church in late Ottoman Syria, the rebellion of natives in 1891/92 and the opposition against the clerical hierarchy ending with the 'Arabization' of the Greek Orthodox Patriarchate in Syria, see Allen (2000). For the Arabization, see also Kildani 2010.

64 Bliss 1972, 62.

The Fundamental Law and Conflicts over 'Communal' versus 'Universal' Waqfs

At the core of the intra-Orthodox conflict were contradictory interpretations of the status of *waqf* properties in Jerusalem. After the 1908 Revolution, Orthodox notables approached the patriarch and demanded a say in the administration of these assets, which they based on article 111 in the Ottoman Fundamental Law (Ar.: *al-qānūn al-asāsī*, Tur.: *kanūn-e esāsi*) of 1876.[65] Article 111 of the Fundamental Law regulated the administration of 'local' or 'communal' *waqf*s and stipulated the formation of a local (Orthodox) council in each *qaḍā'*, assigned to supervise 'the administration of revenues from immovable property and capital subject to *waqf* according to the directions of the founders and in conformity with the customs observed of old', and also the 'use of properties appointed for philanthropic objects in conformity with the conditions prescribed in the testaments relating thereto', and the 'administration of the property of orphans in harmony with the special regulations on this subject'.

These local councils were to be elected by the communities of each *qaḍā'* according to 'special regulations to be drawn up' in the future.[66] Importantly, since the 'special regulations' were not yet drawn up, these local councils, called in *Filasṭīn* 'trustees' councils' *(mağālis al-mutawallīn)*, did not exist in law but were established in practice by the Jerusalemite community to gain influence over Orthodox *waqf* properties and holy places in Jerusalem.

The contradictory interpretations of article 111 remained among the fundamental conflicts between the local people and the Patriarchate and would also dominate the debates between the laity and the clergy in the Mixed Council. At the heart of the problem was the conflict between the Jerusalemite Orthodox notables and the patriarch. While these notables pressed for the implementation of article 111 concerning *waqf*s and holy places in Jerusalem as local property, the clergy considered article 111 as completely irrelevant, since, as they saw it, *waqf* properties in the Patriarchate belonged to Ottoman Orthodoxy as a whole and were universal property and thus subject to control of the Convent.[67]

The Outbreak of Riots and the Coup against Damianos

In summer 1908, a commission of Jerusalemite Orthodox priests and notables announced the election of a local council of 40 members, ignoring the fact that the 'special regulations' mentioned in article 111 had not yet been enforced. Patriarch Damianos criticized the formation of such a local council for Jerusalem

65 For an English translation of the Ottoman Fundamental Law issued on 23 December 1876 and reaffirmed in 1908, see http://www.anayasa.gen.tr/1876constitution.htm (consulted 17 November 2017).

66 Article 111 stipulates that these councils were subject to the local authorities and provincial councils. Bertram and Luke 1921, 250–251.

67 Ibid., 253–254.

but agreed to discuss reforms and had a number of meetings with the commission. On 1 October 1908, the commission officially submitted eighteen demands, among them a demand for the formation of a Mixed Council of six clergy and six lay members, analogous with the Council in Constantinople. On 19 October 1908, the Jerusalemite notables handed in an ultimatum to the patriarch and, when he rejected it, serious turmoil occurred in Jerusalem. In the Old City, local Orthodox demonstrated, occupied the Church of St James, or *Mār Yaʿqūb*, a small but strategically important church as it connected directly with the Convent with the Holy Sepulcher and was used by the patriarch as a shortcut when he went to celebrate the liturgy.[68]

On 15 November, the Holy Synod officially rejected the demands of the laity and decided to limit the annual rents that the Patriarchate paid to Jerusalemite Orthodox to 3,000 lira. There are different narratives about the origin of the custom that the Fraternity would pay housing rents for Orthodox families, which was a permanent source of conflict in the Mixed Council between Jerusalem and the other dioceses, as will be seen later.[69] The limit on this rent allowance triggered the outbreak of violence, which spread from Jerusalem to Jaffa and Bethlehem and gave rise to a long correspondences between the governor, Grand Vizier Kamil Pasha and Damianos. Members of the Fraternity and the Holy Synod took the rebellion as an opportunity to intervene against Damianos, and an internal power struggle broke out. A leading figure in this struggle was Archimandrite Meletio Metaxakis, Damianos's Chief Secretary, who made a deal with Photios, an old opponent of Damianos, and prepared a coup in Jerusalem to overthrow him.[70] Claiming that Damianos treated local reform demands with too much goodwill, was unable to put down the rebellion and incompetent in the conduct of his office, the Holy Synod announced his deposition *in absentia* in December 1908.[71] This patriarchal crisis interrupted Arab Orthodox negotiations

68 Bertram and Luke 1921, 252–253.

69 In some cases, free housing was made available by the Patriarchate. When no houses belonging to the Patriarchate were available, Orthodox families received an allowance for the houses they rented. Bertram and Luke reported that this was a very old custom in Jerusalem. Orthodox inhabitants of Jerusalem supposedly wanted to save their houses from confiscation by the Ottoman authorities and transferred property to the Convent, believing that it would be held in trust for their families. Another narrative claims that the annual rent allowance was granted by the Patriarchate in order to counter the propaganda of Romanist organizations who granted the members of their community similar financial aid. See Bertram and Luke 1921, 253.

70 The history of this internal opposition is documented in Papastathis and Kark 2014, 126–130.

71 In the night before 13 December 1908, monks went around the cells of the convent to stir up the brothers against Damianos as he was a 'danger to the Convent'. The Synod required Damianos to resign the next day. Although admitting he had health problems and, according to his own comment, was 'suffering from fatigue', Damianos refused to resign, left the meeting and was declared deposed in absentia. See Betram and Luke 1921, 255–256.

with the Patriarchate. Since Damianos was deposed, he could not conduct the Christmas services in Jerusalem and Bethlehem and, when his deposition became known, the behavior of the Orthodox crowds was 'very threatening' at the Christmas procession in Bethlehem, Bertram noted.[72]

In Jerusalem, the Orthodox held mass rallies and occupied the patriarchal headquarters, and the level of violence reached a new peak. Public opinion rose up against the Synod, especially Meletios Metaxakis and Chrisostomos Papadoulus, Chief of the Department for Education, two leading figures in the coup, and attempts were made on their lives. The Ottoman military in Jerusalem refused to fire on the demonstrating crowd, and the security situation was out of control and required governmental intervention. A delegation sent from Istanbul by the new Grand Vizier Hilmi Pasha to investigate arrived in Jerusalem on 26 January 1909 and was approached by Damianos, who was accompanied by a cheering crowd with flags,[73] made up of Orthodox laity and Muslim notables who petitioned in favor of the Arab Orthodox cause.[74]

The Suspension of the Coup

The delegation feared that Damianos's deposition would cause more bloodshed. Nazim Pasha, Governor of Syria and head of the delegation, declared he would not guarantee the safety of the Fraternity and the Holy places unless Damianos was reinstalled. The Synod feared for its rights in the holy places and gave in. On 16 February 1909, it issued a resolution suspending the deposition of Damianos and the leader of the coup, Metaxakis, was exiled.[75] The Synod declared, 'considering the extraordinarily critical circumstances', the 'disturbance of public order amounting to positive anarchy on account of the rebellious attitude of the mobs throughout nearly the whole of Palestine', the 'evident danger threatening … the very ownership of the holy places and the landed property of the Holy Brotherhood, and … the precious and immemorial rights in the sanctuaries of our pious nation in Palestine', and due to the 'intense struggle in which the strong and the weak … are united as enemies against our Holy Fraternity' and 'for the

72 Incidentally, the deposition of Damianos led to embarrassing diplomatic dilemmas between the local government, the Synod and Istanbul. The Ecumenical Patriarch in Istanbul recognized the deposition, and the governor of Jerusalem recognized the *locum tenens* elected by the Fraternity, the Archbishop of Tiberias, in January 1909, although without having instructions from Istanbul. In any case, the central government did not recognize the deposition and did not give any directions in the crisis. See Bertram and Luke 1921, 256–258.

73 Bertram and Luke 1921, 258–260.

74 Kuruvilla 2011, 62.

75 Papastathis and Kark 2014, 128; Bertram and Luke 1921, 260. It was only after a flood of telegrams, petitions and deputations arrived in Istanbul on behalf of the Jerusalem Synod to Istanbul that, in July 1909, the Ecumenical Patriarch and the Synod in Istanbul accepted Damianios's restitution without new elections. See Bertram and Luke 1921, 262–264.

sake of our national rights in the holy sanctuaries', it regarded the 'unanimous decision' to depose Damianos as 'suspended and unimplemented'.[76] This shows that the 'Arab Orthodox question' was a decisive factor in the suspension of the coup since the rebellion threatened the status quo of the Fraternity.

The Spread of the Rebellion and Negotiations with the Government

The rebellion in Jerusalem continued, despite the reinstallation of Damianos. On 23 February 1909, the Synod reversed its previous decision to reduce the rent allowances paid to the Jerusalemites in order to calm the people. The laity maintained their central demands and rebellion spread beyond the Jerusalem District. Locals occupied monasteries in Ramla, Lydda and Nablus. The Church of St James was still occupied by Arab Orthodox activists, and the clergy could not conduct services. The locals pressed for responses and the Synod transferred the matter to the High Porte. On 13 July 1909, a lay delegation from the Jerusalem District arrived in Istanbul and handed in their demands to the government. When they returned on 12 October 1909, the people gave them a 'glowing reception' (*istiqbālan bāhiran*) in Jerusalem, and Yūsuf al-ʿĪsā, who had been among the delegates, gave enthusiastic speeches in St James's about the victorious representation of the local Orthodox in the capital, although no response had yet been issued.[77]

Enthusiasm died fast and, in November 1909, turmoil spread again due to rumors that the Porte was favoring the Convent.[78] Moreover, the Fraternity's control over the Holy Sepulcher, the Church of Gethsemane and a third unidentified church, became a conflict issue. The government considered these churches public places while the rebels considered them local *waqf* and they occupied four convents in Jerusalem. The governor removed the occupiers out by force (*bi-l-quwwa al-ǧabrīya*). In response, the Orthodox of Jerusalem occupied the cemetery on Mount Zion, where they held a funeral procession 'to grieve for the rights of the constitution' (*li-yuǧannizū al-ḥaqq fī ʿahd ad-dustūr*). The governor promised to investigate the matter of the churches and the local councils, referred to in article 111.[79]

76 Bertram and Luke 1921, 260–261.

77 Among the other delegates were Ǧurǧī Zaḫariyā and Ilyās Ḥalabī, later delegates in the Mixed Council for Jerusalem, and Ḫalīl Qazāqiyā, later a delegate in the Mixed Council for Bethlehem. Ḫūrī and Ḫūrī 1992, 260; Tamari 2014b, 26.

78 Meanwhile, the exiled Meletios Metaxakis, much hated in Jerusalem, published from Istanbul press articles against Arab Orthodox reforms, that contributed to the protests and rumors in Palestine. Ḫūrī and Ḫūrī 1992, 261.

79 For the description of the turmoil of 1909, see Bertram and Luke 1921, 264–265; and Ḫūrī and Ḫūrī 1992, 259–261.

The Issue of the 1910 Resolution and Its Local Responses

Finally, a government resolution was issued on 17 May 1910, referred to hereinafter as the '1910 Resolution' and called in the press the 'resolution of the Ministers' Council' (*qarār maǧlis al-wukalāʾ*),[80] since it had been worked out already in November 1909 by a commission set up by the Council of Ministers (Ar.: *maǧlis al-wukalāʾ*, Tur.: *Meclis-i Vükela*),[81] the main executive and legislative coordination body in Istanbul that included ministers and directors of all departments from the police, the military and religious offices, and acted rather independently from the Grand Vizier.[82] The Resolution responded on six fundamental and five supplementary demands of the laity. Mainly, it aimed to reconfirm and supplement the rules in the *Katastikon* of 1875 regarding local participation and stipulated the formation of a Mixed Council in Jerusalem, consisting of six lay and six clerical delegates to negotiate reforms in the dioceses of the Patriarchate. Its content was documented in Arabic by Ḫūrī (see Appendix I), and was to remain a subject of debate in the Mixed Council from 1910 to 1914.[83] Governor Ṣubḥī presented the Resolution to the parties to the conflict, the clergy reacted with 'great relief' (*bi-mazīd al-irtiyāḥ*) and Malatios, *muṭrān* of Jordan and deputy of the patriarch, declared acceptance of the resolution on the Patriarch's behalf.[84]

The laity initially rejected the Resolution since it did not provide the Mixed Council with much legal authority and did not touch on the patriarchal privileges or the status quo in Jerusalem and its holy sites, as Ḫūrī and Ḫūrī have pointed out. The government had expected that the occupied monasteries and churches would be returned but the Resolution gave an opportunity for a new dispute since the Arab Orthodox felt 'deceived by the Ottoman Constitution' (*ḫudiʿū bi-d-dustūr al-ʿuṯmānī*). Activists, among them Yūsuf al-ʿĪsā, went to the governor's house[85] and handed in a protest letter, declaring that the resolution 'ruins our denominational

80 *Filasṭīn*, 1 October 1913: 276/3/4.

81 Ḫūrī and Ḫūrī 1992, 261.

82 For more information, see Shaw 1977, vol. II, 81f; and Somel 2010, 100f.

83 For the Arabic text, see Ḫūrī and Ḫūrī 1992, 262–277. For an analysis of it, as far as it concerns the intra-Orthodox conflict from 1911 to 1914, see my own translation in Appendix I at the end of this chapter. For an English summary of the Resolution, see Bertram and Luke 1921, 265–270, and for an evaluation see Kark and Papasthatis 2014, 131–132.

84 Ḫūrī and Ḫūrī state that the content of the Resolution favored the Convent since the monks 'bought the conscience of the rulers and the freedom of the press' (*fa-btāʿū ḍamāʾir al-ḥukkām wa-štarū ḥurrīyat al-ǧarāʾid*) and as a result of pressure from powerful Phanariotes and Greeks in the government in Istanbul. Ḫūrī and Ḫūrī 1992, 275.

85 Among them were Yaʿqūb Simʿān (for Nazareth), Naḫleh Ǧarīs/Ǧaryas Kattan (for Jerusalem), Ḥanā Malik and Yūsuf al-ʿĪsā (for Jaffa, Acre, Haifa and Gaza), Ḫalīl Yūsuf (for al-Ḥiṣn), Miḫāʾīl ʿAbd an-Nūr (for Nablus), Rūfā Ǧibrān Šabīṭeh (for Ramla), Iskandar Ilyās al-Ḥabš (for Lydda) Yaʿqūb Yūsuf (for Ṭaybeh) and ʿĪsā Yūsuf Ḥazbūn (for Beit Jala and Bethlehem). See Ḫūrī and Ḫūrī 1992, 275–276.

rights' (*muğhif bi-ḥuqūqinā l-millīya*), that it 'is contradictory to the spirit of the constitution' (*ʿadam muwāfaqatihi rūḥ ad-dustūr*), 'against the spirit of the Orthodox faith' (*muḫālafatuhu li-rūḥ ad-dīn al-urṯūḏūksī*), and 'not compatible with the spirit of the current age' (*ġayr mağārin li-rūḥ al-ʿaṣr*), and that it 'contradicts the Pact of Omar' (*muḫālifatuhu li-l-ʿahda al-ʿumarīya*).[86] However, after fruitless negotiations with the government and for lack of any alternative, the laity eventually accepted the Resolution. Basic regulations for the Mixed Council were decided, and it met for the first time in December 1910.[87] Its symbolic status was as high as it legal powers were limited, and the Orthodox teacher, journalist and teacher Iskandar al-Ḫūrī al-Baytǧālī from Beit Jala called the Mixed Council 'a pious endowment' (*waqf milla*) that 'we will not leave' (*lā natrukuhu*).[88]

3. *Filasṭīn* and the Arab Orthodox Cause

3.1. *Filasṭīn* as the 'Mouthpiece' of the Arab Orthodox Movement

Like the earlier newspaper, *Al-Inṣāf* ('Fairness'), published by Bandalī Ilyās Mušahwar and Iskandar al-Ḫūrī in Jerusalem in the aftermath of the 1908 Revolution,[89] *Filasṭīn* was the main defender of Arab Orthodox interests in Palestine from 1911 onwards, and the ʿĪsās saw themselves as on a mission of liberation from the 'despotism' of the Patriarchate, as the accusation was frequently made. In almost every issue, the ʿĪsās advocated the Arab Orthodox cause in the *Local News* section in the columns dedicated to 'The Orthodox Renaissance' (*an-Nahḍa al-Urṯūduksīya*), 'Orthodox Matters' (*Šuʾūn Urṯūduksīya*), and 'The Mixed Council' (*al-Mağlis al-Muḫtalaṭ*), where they published the Council's speakers' records, and lot of space was given to letters of protest from the dioceses. In July 1911, the ʿĪsās proudly declared *Filasṭīn* to be the only 'mouthpiece' of the Arab Orthodox cause while other newspapers had betrayed it:

> We shall not forget that our newspaper is the only one that protects the principle of the Orthodox Renaissance. ... So, it has become the mouthpiece of this community and has become worried about a circle of shilly-shallying individuals who are being blinded by the smile of a master [the Patriarch] and the threats of a ruler make them shiver. So, they have turned their weapons away from their enemies to stab their nation... so as to flatter this ruler and become close to that master.[90]

86 Ḫūrī and Ḫūrī 1992, 275–276.
87 Ḫūrī and Ḫūrī 1992, 277.
88 *Filasṭīn*, 27 June 1914: 331/4/1.
89 Yehôšuaʿ 1974, 69–72; Tamari 2014b, 23.
90 '*Wa-lā yağib an nansā anna ğarīdatanā hiya al-waḥīda allatī ḥāfaẓat ʿalā mabdaʾ an-nahḍa al-urṯūḏuksīya... fa-aṣbaḥat lisān hāḏihi al-milla wa-šağiya fī ḥalaq baʿḍ al-afrād al-muta-*

It is not known who was the betrayer addressed here, but the ʿĪsās also demonstrated their role as a 'mouthpiece' of the Orthodox as members of protest delegations and Orthodox associations. Yūsuf al-ʿĪsā participated in the delegation that went to Istanbul in the summer of 1909 to present the Arab Orthodox demands to the government, and gave enthusiastic speeches upon their return.[91] He was a member of the protest delegation after the release of the 1910 Resolution,[92] and Yūsuf al-ʿĪsā also preached in the occupied Church of St James.[93] In November 1911, he was elected to represent Jaffa as a delegate in the Mixed Council, by which time he had observed the first year of fruitless discussions in the Council. Determined to work, he appealed to the Council not to waste precious time, and demanded of the Orthodox in Jaffa that they convey the 'orders' (*awāmir*) of the local faithful to him so that he would be able to represent them.[94] Through his position, Yūsuf al-ʿĪsā was able to access the speakers' records of the Mixed Council, either through its secretary, or by recording sessions himself. He published this chronological documentation of each speaker's statement as a *dialogical* text, revealing the opposing positions of the disputants. From *Filasṭīn*, I have documented 114 speakers' records between 1911 and 1914 that constitute an important source on the nature of the Arab Orthodox Movement.

Functions and Authenticity of the Council's Speakers' Records

There are difficulties concerning the analysis of speakers' records. Their literary style is verbose and the speakers got lost in details and personal hostilities. The debates sometimes occupied up to one-third of *Filasṭīn*'s coverage, they going round and round in circles of escalations and de-escalations and sessions often ended without definite conclusions. As a result, it is hard for the reader to extract the essence of the debate. This raises the question of the extent to which the publication of the speakers' records were meant to make the intra-Orthodox debate transparent or simply to discredit the Patriarchate. Why did *Filasṭīn* dedicate so much space to reproducing the speakers' positions? How far can they represent authentic dialogues between the delegates, or were they constructed by ʿIsā to persuade the reader to join his opposition to the Patriarchate? At the end of the day, it is difficult to judge how far the Council's records were completely authentic or and how far they were constructed, although Yūsuf al-ʿIsā vehemently affirmed their authenticity. He documented each session carefully so

ḍabḍibīn allaḏīna taġurruhum ibtisāmat raʾīs wa-yurǧifuhum tahdīd ḥākim fa-yaḥūlūn silāḥahum ʿan aḥṣāmihim wa-yaṭʿanūn bi-hi ummatahum tazallufan ilā hāḏā l-ḥākim wa-taqarruban min ḏāka ar-raʾīs.' *Filasṭīn*, 15 July 1911: 51/1/3.

91 Tamari 2014b, 26.

92 Ḫūrī and Ḫūrī 1992, 275–276.

93 *Filasṭīn*, 30 August 1911: 64/3/4–5; and 2 September 1911: 65/3/4.

94 *Filasṭīn*, 18 November 1911: 87/3/4–5; 22 November 1911: 88/3/5; 15 May 1912: 136/4/1.

even the secretary[95] used to consult his transcripts since they were the 'best record for everything that happened in it [the Council]' (*tārīḫ li-kullimā ǧarā fīhi*), as Yūsuf himself stated.[96] However, ʿĪsā, journalist *and* activist, played different roles and oscillated between mediating and initiating campaigns.

On the one hand, political accountability was a topic in *Filasṭīn*, and ʿĪsā repeatedly stressed the Council's obligation to make its activities transparent to the public.[97] When in 1913, the Council underwent a legitimacy crisis and the patriarch stopped the secretary from recording its sessions, a dispute over the Council's obligation of transparency escalated between the clergy and the laity in the Council. According to ʿĪsā, this was unacceptable for a political body in the age of the Constitution, and he declared that he would take over the function of secretary, record the sessions as he remembered them, and to inform the Orthodox abroad.[98] On the other hand, ʿĪsā used the Council as a stage on which to present himself as a spearhead of the Arab Orthodox Movement, and he undertook his role as a delegate egotistically, his own speeches taking the most space in the speakers' records. Putting himself at the center of the dialogue meant either that he was the leading figure among the lay delegates or that he manipulated the records reprinted in *Filasṭīn* so that his own statements would dominate. Be that as it may, ʿĪsā exploited his position as a delegate, in one way or another, to produce extended monologues and put himself in the spotlight as a defender against Greek despotism, and the publication of the Council's records was a tool to generate public support for his position. ʿĪsā's main purpose here was not to implement transparency but to ridicule the clergy and make a fool of the patriarch. Often enough, he actively contributed to the escalation of sessions in the Mixed Council, and he documented his extended battles with the patriarch or his deputy so that, by 1912, the patriarch had brought three cases against him to the government.[99]

Discursive and Communicational Scope of the Coverage on the Orthodox Cause

The leading actors in the anti-clerical campaign in *Filasṭīn* were the ʿĪsās and a circle of activists and fellow combatants from Jerusalem, Bethlehem, Beit Jala and Nablus, who used *Filasṭīn* as an instrument to mobilize the public for the Orthodox cause. Their demands were underpinned by the modernist agenda that dominated *Filasṭīn* in general. In line with this, the modernization of Orthodox

95 The Mixed Council had a succession of secretaries, which are only known to me as far as they are documented in *Filasṭīn:* that the secretary in spring 1911 was one Ǧarīs Saʿīdeh, and in fall 1911, one Īsīdrūs aš-Šammās. *Filasṭīn*, 14 February 1914: 307/4/2; 6 September 1911: 66/3/4–5.

96 *Filasṭīn*, 11 June 1913: 244/4/2.

97 *Filasṭīn*, 4 December 1912: 194/4/2–3; 29 March 1913: 225/4/1–2; 5 April 1913: 227/4/1–2.

98 *Filasṭīn*, 11 June 1913: 244/4/2.

99 *Filasṭīn*, 10 July 1912: 152/1/1–3.

education was a focus of their reform agenda, and a lot of the Arab Orthodox activists were pedagogues and journalists, as will be seen. They quickly adapted to the new political culture of the age and embedded the post-revolutionary constitutionalist discourse into their speeches and writings so as to add legitimacy to the Arab Orthodox cause. Just as the aims of the Movement were economic, so were their arguments political, and tailored to fit the political rhetoric of the Young Turks' regime. They portrayed their movement as a repeat of the Constitutional Revolution on the micro-level of the Jerusalem District, where the networks of the Movement were concentrated, as an apocalyptic battle between Ottomanism and Greek despotism (*istibdād*). In this quite radical and combative rhetoric, the Arab Orthodox Movement was an emancipatory struggle of indigenous locals *and* Ottoman citizens against the rule of 'the Greek monks' (*ar-ruhbān al-yūnān*),[100] portrayed as foreigners and oppressors who 'violate the rights of the *milla*' (*iġtiṣāb ḥuqūq al-milla*),[101] and undermined the Constitutional principles. Underpinning political agendas with the constitutionalist discourse was, incidentally, the strategy of both parties to the conflict, who extensively referred to the Fundamental Law or the 1910 Resolution in their petitions.

Concerning the coverage of the intra-Orthodox conflict in *Filasṭīn*, most of the contributing authors belonged to the Arab Orthodox activist spectrum and wrote in support of the Orthodox *nahḍa*. Thus, the communicational structure on the Arab Orthodox cause in *Filasṭīn* is a *monologue* of its supporters and not a dialogue. This can also be applied to the speakers' records as a record of dispute. They nevertheless deliver a perspective on the intra-Orthodox conflicts from within, since they illustrate the poisonous atmosphere in the Council and reveal the central conflict lines, the terminology underlying the arguments and the main opponents and alliances.

The geographical scope of the press communication on the Orthodox cause in *Filasṭīn* focused on Jerusalem, Jaffa and Bethlehem, where the networks of the Orthodox activists were concentrated, but also included Nablus, Acre and Nazareth, and Kerak and Jerash since the dioceses of the Orthodox Patriarchate extended as far as present-day Jordan.

100 *Filasṭīn*, 26 June 148/3/3.
101 Here in a very polemical letter, in *Filasṭīn*, 23 September 1911: 71/3/3–5.

3.2. Arab Orthodox Networks

Opponents of the Arab Orthodox Movement

Apart from the statements of the clerical delegates in the Mixed Council's records, who were the Archimandrites Yūsuf, Dosithios, Eftimios and Makarios, and the *muṭrāns* Sofronios and Malatios, the supporters of the patriarchal circle stayed in the shadows. Only a few authors who opposed the Arab Orthodox circle responded to the anti-clerical campaign in *Filasṭīn*. Among them was a nephew of Damianos, Yūnus Fāyānūs, who protested in a letter against his defamation in *Filasṭīn*.[102] The other protesters were parish priests who feared that the Arab Orthodox Movement threatened their positions. An opponent of the Arab Orthodox Movement was a priest in Jaffa, one Ḥanā Ġaṭṭās al-Harīš, about whom no further information could be found. In *Filasṭīn*, he sharply attacked the Orthodox reformer Bandalī al-Ḫūrī, who had called for the exclusion of the salaries of parish priests from the social budget of the dioceses.[103] Another priest from Jerusalem, one Niqūlā Ġaṭṭās, attacked the leaders of the Orthodox Renaissance in the Muslim magazine *al-Manār* and the Egyptian *al-Muqaṭṭam*.[104] Another pro-clerical statement in *Filasṭīn* came from a 'lowly priest' (*al-ḥaqīr fī l-kahana*) from Nablus, whose letter was written in strange Arabic and published with all its mistakes.[105] Another opponent was Bišāra Ṭāsū, an Orthodox merchant from Jaffa, who was affiliated with the patriarchal circle and filed complaints with Jaffa's *qā'imaqām* against Yūsuf al-ʿĪsā.[106]

In 1912, Yūsuf addressed the circle of patriarchial supporters, emphasizing that they had been waiting for responses from the pro-clerical fraction in vain since 'they are still not responding to Filasṭīn when we criticized ... the Patriarchate's actions in our paper', and he confirmed that 'our paper does not belong to us but to the readers and subscribers' (*taḫuṣṣ al-qurrā' wa-l-muštarikīn*).[107] It is to be assumed that *Filasṭīn* would have published letters from the pro-clerical faction if they had sent some. Indeed, such statements would have been an occasion for the ʿĪsās to expose the clergy to ridicule. But it is obvious that the pro-clerical faction did not accept *Filasṭīn* as a forum for debating the intra-Orthodox conflict.

102 The Jerusalem correspondent had stated that Fayānus had usurped Orthodox property situated near the Hotel Kaminz in Jerusalem that was classified as *waqf*, and that he held a title deed (*mulkīya*) on it. *Filasṭīn*, 7 September 1912: 169/3/3f; 28 September 1912: 175/1/4–2/1.

103 *Filasṭīn*, 15 May 1912: 136/3/5; 22 May 1912: 138/3/2.

104 *Filasṭīn*, 23 September 1911: 71/3/3–5; and 27 September 1911: 72/3/5–4/1.

105 *Filasṭīn*, 2 October 1912: 176/4/3–4.

106 *Filasṭīn*, 10 July 1912: 152/3/3; 19 October 1912: 181/3/3.

107 *Filasṭīn*, 10 July 1912: 152/1/1–3.

Supporters of the Orthodox Movement

As has previously been made clear, *Filasṭīn*'s coverage of the intra-Orthodox conflict was designed by the supporters of the Arab Orthodox Movement. Apart from Yūsuf al-ʿĪsā, the lion's share of anti-clerical articles came from the (anonymous) Jerusalemite correspondent, who published weekly anti-clerical news from the center of the Patriarchate, so to say, and stood out for his very polemic rhetoric. He was one of the main actors in the production of *Filasṭīn* in general, including with regard to the Zionist movement, local government activities, official ceremonies, and so on. His focus however, was the defamation of the 'monks of the Convent' (*rahbanat ad-dayr*).

Apart from him, a circle of supporters of the Arab Orthodox Movement, who were associated with the ʿĪsās, contributed to the anti-clerical campaign in *Filasṭīn*. Among them was Iskandar al-Ḫūrī al-Baytǧālī (1888–1973), who was was originally from Beit Jala and was also a member of the Orthodox delegation to Istanbul in 1908. Baytǧālī was a teacher and held a degree from the Faculty of Law in Jerusalem. Later, he held various positions as director of Orthodox schools, and during the Mandate as a lawyer. He also became famous as a poet, introduced a new prose style to Palestinian poetry and published literary contributions in Arab newspapers.[108] In *Filasṭīn*, he regularly published his column 'Lilies in the Field' (*Zanābīq al-Ḥaql*) during the years 1912–1913, which stood out for its very metaphorical, moralistic and sentimental style.[109] In poetic prose style, Baytǧālī adapted religious symbols supported with allegories from the Bible to educate the readership. He was a passionate supporter of 'enlightenment' (*tanwīr*) and the modernization of education, and specifically, the education of girls, but he was also notable for his conservative moral values. He frequently called for female participation in public life and politics, but also mourned the loss of women's feminine characteristics under the influence of the West.[110] In addition, he saw himself as on a mission for Orthodox cultural reform and called upon the 'free heroes of the light' (*aḥrār an-nūr*), the Arab Orthodox activists, to defend their movement against 'treachery' (*al-ḫiyāna*) and agents of partisanship (*taḥazzub*). In every revolution, he said, there were traitors in the midst of the nation, who sought to break its unity and sell the 'public good' (*al-maṣlaḥa al-ʿāmma*), and he called for endurance in the Arab Orthodox struggle.[111]

The Orthodox Ḫalīl as-Sakākīnī (1873–1953), director of the Constitutional School in Jerusalem, was another frequent publisher on the Orthodox cause in *Filasṭīn*. As one of the movement's most rebellious spirits, he had been among the

108 Embaló, Neuwirth, and Pannewick 2001, 195–198.

109 *Filasṭīn*, 31 August 1912: 167/2/4–3/1; 9 November 1912: 187/3/1–2; 27 November 1912: 192/3/5–4/2; 11 December 1912: 1912: 196/4/1; 22 January 1913: 206/4/2; 16 April 1913: 230/4/1–2.

110 *Filasṭīn*, 12 October 1912: 179/3/1–2; 5 July 1913: 251/2/2–3.

111 *Filasṭīn*, 22 June 1912: 147/2/5–3/2.

initiators of anti-clerical demonstrations and gave passionate speeches in the occupied Church of St James.[112] In *Filasṭīn*, he was defined as 'one of the leaders of the Orthodox renaissance' (*wāḥid zuʿamāʾ an-nahḍa al-urṯūḏuksīya*),[113] and became, together with ʿĪsā, one of the fiercest enemies of the patriarch, who successfully forced him out of a school board that was to work out educational reforms in the Orthodox dioceses under the supervision of the Mixed Council.[114] After a series of escalations between him and the clergy, priests affiliated to the patriarch prevented his wedding in Jerusalem, and, with the active support of ʿĪsā al-ʿĪsā, the marriage ceremony was conducted by an Orthodox priest in Jaffa.[115]

Another frequent combatant for the Arab Orthodox Movement in *Filasṭīn* was ʿĪsā Yūsuf Ḥazbūn from Bethlehem. He was one of the earliest activists and had protested with Yūsuf al-ʿĪsā in front of the governor's house after the release of the 1910 Resolution.[116] He was from an Orthodox family in Bethlehem in which there were also priests.[117] From 1910 until 1912, he represented Bethlehem and Beit Jala as a lay delegate in the Mixed Council, and usually acted in coalition with Yūsuf al-ʿĪsā in the Council. After he left the Council in the autumn of 1912, he emigrated to America,[118] from where he commented in *Filasṭīn* on each of the Council's steps until 1914.[119]

Ǧurǧī Ḥanā Ḥazbūn, also a member of the Orthodox Ḥazbūn family from Bethlehem, who had migrated to Chile, was another contributing author on the Arab Orthodox cause.[120] He was a *Filasṭīn* subscriber in Chile, and one of the active promoters of modernization and Ottomanism in *Filasṭīn*. He reported on the progress of Palestinian migrants in Chile and demonstrated that their Ottomanism was still alive. Although being proud of living in America, which he regarded more civilized, Ḥazbūn considered Palestine his home. He commented on the failures of the Mixed Council, which he called 'shameful' (*ʿār*) and historically unforgettable, accused its members of dullness (*tawānin*) and sluggishness (*ḫumūl*),[121] and directed wake-up calls to the Orthodox laity on the

112 *Filasṭīn*, 2 August 1911: 56/1/1–4; 30 August 1911: 64/3/4–5; 2 September 1911: 65/3/3–4; 30 September 1911: 73/3/4; 13 April 1912: 127/3/2.
113 *Filasṭīn*, 17 January 1912: 103/3/2.
114 *Filasṭīn*, 28 September 1912: 175/3/5; 23 October 1912: 181/3/4–4/3.
115 *Filasṭīn*, 17 January 1912: 103/3/2; see also Tamari 2014b, 28–29; cf. Sakākīnī 2003, I, 351–352.
116 Ḫūrī and Ḫūrī 1992, 275–276.
117 A priest or monk of the Ḥazbūn family from Bethlehem was al-Ab Yūḥannā Ḥazbūn. Yehoshu'a 1974, 8, 50.
118 *Filasṭīn*, 2 November 1912: 185/4/3.
119 Later, he clearly moved to Chile. See *Filasṭīn*, 11 June 1913: 244/3/5–4/2.
120 Other members of the Ḥazbūn family migrated to El Salvador, among them ʿAbdallāh Ḥazbūn and Ḥarīs Ḥazbūn with his brothers. On the National Day of the Republic, there were reports about the participation of the Palestinians in the celebrations in the capital San Salvador. *Filasṭīn*, 13 December 1911: 94/3/1–3.
121 *Filasṭīn*, 21 February 1912: 113/3/1–2.

Council.[122] Reforms in Palestine, he said, consisted of papers circulating 'from committee to committee' to be finally just stored in cupboards, and he lamented: 'The reform is locked inside these cupboards' (*al-iṣlāḥ maḥṣūr ḍimna haḏihi al-ḫazāʾin*).[123] In contrast, Ḥazbūn portrayed Chilean society as progressive and praised the state of education,[124] law and order there.[125]

Another frequent author on the Orthodox cause in *Filasṭīn* was Ǧibrān Maṭar from Beit Jala; a passionate modernist, Ottoman patriot and Orthodox activist.[126] He strongly encouraged the use of Arabic in Orthodox institutions,[127] and wrote on the modernization of Palestine and Ottomanism, but the critical security situation in Beit Jala and Bethlehem also concerned him.[128] He called upon Palestinian migrants in the New World to maintain their links with their country and subscribe to *Filasṭīn* to stay informed.[129] Like other intellectuals, he considered 'unity' (*ittiḥād*) to be *the* precondition for progress, and complained that he did not see that there was a feeling for unity in Palestine, which made progress impossible, 'and the closest witness to this is the Mixed Council'.[130]

Another frequent author in *Filasṭīn* on the Arab Orthodox cause was Ǧurǧī al-Ḫūrī Yaʿqūb from Beit Sahour, an Orthodox pedagogue who wrote in favor of the modernization of education. He criticized the 'decline' (*inḥiṭāṭ*) of the 'Orientals', which he attributed to their lack of discipline,[131] and specifically lamented the backwardness of Orthodox education. He feared that it would cause many Young Orthodox to convert to other confessions, for they received better education in foreign schools. Another author was Iskandar Niqūlā Badar, *Filasṭīn*'s agent (*wakīl*) in Beit Jala and the correspondent from there.[132] Although he was a Latin Catholic, he reported on Orthodox affairs 'as a patriot in favor of reforms' (*ka-waṭanī muḥibb li-l-iṣlāḥ*).[133]

Among the supporters of the Arab Orthodox Movement were a circle of Palestinian migrants residing in Latin America: Ḥanāʾ Miḫāʾīl Buyūk, originally from Bethlehem, published from the diaspora on the Orthodox cause and was

122 *'Nabbih ʿuqalāʾ al-umma kīlā yanāmū ʿan ḥuqūqahum wa-ḥarrik ġayr al-muktariṯīn bi-n-nahḍa inna kāna yanfaʿahum at-taḥrīk wa-anḏir al-ǧamīʿ bi-anna taqṣīrahum yūriṯuhum al-ʿār wa-laysa lahum min ʿaḏīr.' Filasṭīn*, 21 February 1912: 113/3/2.

123 *Filasṭīn*, 27 November 1912: 192/4/2–3.

124 *Filasṭīn*, 8 June 1912: 143/2/4–5.

125 *Filasṭīn*, 13 November 1912: 188/3/2–3.

126 *Filasṭīn*, 30 March 1912: 124/2/5–3/1.

127 *Filasṭīn*, 17 April 1912: 128/4/1–2; 24 September 1913: 274/3/4–5; 4 July 1914: 333/5/2.

128 *Filasṭīn*, 22 May 1912: 138/3/4; 4 July 1914: 333/5/2; 8 July 1914: 334/5/3.

129 *Filasṭīn*, 25 May 1912: 139/3/2.

130 *Filasṭīn*, 31 August 1912: 167/2/1.

131 *Filasṭīn*, 23 August 1913: 265/1/2–2/1.

132 *Filasṭīn*, 12 November 1913: 288/3/3; 4 July 1914: 333/5/2.

133 *Filasṭīn*, 1 July 1914: 332/3/2.

Filasṭīn's agent in Chile.[134] Another supporter was Salīm Buyūk, also writing from Chile, and probably a relative.[135] Ḥanā Abū ṣ-Ṣawf, a migrant in Mexico, sent passionate letters, calling upon his brothers to keep the combative spirit of the renaissance. In 'A Cry from the Pacific Coast' (*Ṣarḫa min šawāṭī' al-Bāsīfīk*), Ṣawf complained to the patriarch that Orthodox schools could not compete with 'modern Arabic teaching methods' (*asālīb at-tadrīs al-ʿarabīya al-ḥadīṯa*) practiced in the foreign schools, explicitly naming the Russian Orthodox college in Beit Jala. He sharply attacked the clergy in the Mixed Council as follows:

> So, work together with the lay delegates for educational reforms and collect the dispersed Orthodox youth together who are waiting for you to implement reforms so impatiently. Otherwise, shut down your (Mixed) Council and your schools and bury them. And then, let the rest of the Orthodox children go to the foreign schools too, which will doubtless receive them with open arms and teach them the true sciences (*al-ʿulūm al-ḥaqqa*)...
>
> Know, you masters, that you live [now] in an age of freedom (*ʿaṣr ḥurrīya*) in which your outdated principles, like the strategy of 'divide and rule' (*farriq tasud*), do not fit. The people (*aš-šaʿb*) will not obey you blindly anymore but want to take from you all their legitimate rights (*ḥuqūqahu aš-šarʿīya kullahā*), whether you like it or not. And it would be good for you to contemplate and to pull out the plug of your ethnic fanaticism (*at-taʿaṣṣub al-ǧinsī*), which is not befitting (*lā yalīq*) to the heads of the Church of Christ.[136]

Other responses supporting the Arab Orthodox Movement came from Būlos Šahādeh, a Protestant who from 1918 onwards published *Mirʾāt aš-Sarq* in Jerusalem,[137] Bandalī al-Ḫūrī from Bethlehem, who published regularly in *Al-Quds*,[138] and other Palestinian Orthodox about whom I did not find any biographical information, including Salīm Ǧurǧī al-Ḫaml, a teacher at the Orthodox Mār Ǧirǧis School for boys in Jerusalem,[139] Miḫāʾīl Aṭlīl from Jerusalem, who was closely associated with Ḫalīl as-Sakākīnī,[140] Yūsuf ʿAṭā Allāh from Bethlehem,[141] and finally, Ḫalīl Naṣr, a combative writer for the Orthodox Renaissance from Haifa.[142]

---

134 *Filasṭīn*, 27 April 1912: 131/3/1.

135 *Filasṭīn*, 9 August 1911: 58/3/2–3.

136 *Filasṭīn*, 18 October 1913: 281/3/5–4/2.

137 Yehoshu'a 1974, 28.

138 Yehoshu'a 1974, 27.

139 *Filasṭīn*, 23 April 1913: 232/3/3–4.

140 *Filasṭīn*, 13 December 1911: 94/4/1–2.

141 He was an Orthodox beadle (*šammās*) who served before in Beirut and the monastery of Mar Saba until he was relocated by the *muṭrān* back to Bethlehem where he was refused to become a priest (*kāhin*). The issue caused a scandal in Bethlehem. ʿAṭā Allāh announced his emigration to Chile and his clan obviously converted to Catholicism. See *Filasṭīn*, 9 April 1913: 228/4/1; and 3 May 1913: 233/3/5–4/2.

142 *Filasṭīn*, 12 November 1913: 288/3/5–4/2.

The reputation of Arab Orthodox activism spread in the foreign press. In February 1913, the Beirut newspaper *Lisān al-Ḥāl* confirmed that the disputes in the Mixed Council were discussed in the 'Arab clubs' and societies of Beirut since the Greeks 'had deprived the Syrian Orthodox Palestinian people of their rights'.[143] In contrast, the Russian Orthodox implemented 'real reforms' and 'took the mask from the eyes' (*tarfaʿa al-qināʿ ʿan aʿyun*) of the Orthodox, *Lisān al-Ḥāl* claimed, receiving a rebuke from the ʿĪsās, for 'such rumors are the capital of the Patriarchate'.[144]

It is to be stressed that *Filasṭīn* strictly avoided asking for Russian support, and the ʿĪsās particularly did not want to give the impression that they relied on a foreign power to represent their case or that they were promoting Russian interests in Palestine. However, there was diplomatic Russian support for the Arab Orthodox Renaissance, which was welcomed by local communities, as is indicated by individual reports. For instance, an Orthodox delegation from Ajloun (Jordan) prepared a petition, signed by 160 persons from their home town, in which they protested against a priest who had been sent by the Patriarchate and demanded the salaries for their own priests, trustees and Orthodox schools. They handed this to the Russian Consul Kruglow in Jerusalem, who promised the support of the Russian Imperial Orthodox Society in the matter.[145]

4. Language and Themes Used in the Arab Orthodox Campaign

This section will identify the central language, terminology and themes applied by the Arab Orthodox activists that served to legitimize the Arab Orthodox in the eyes of the government and the Palestinian public, and to impart to the cause a sense of the sacred, as will be demonstrated by selected examples from *Filasṭīn.*

Constitutional Rights versus Despotic Rule

The Arab Orthodox activists particularly embedded their cause to the political discourse of the Second Constitutional Period, marked by the 1908 Revolution and the restoration of the Constitution, in order to portray their Renaissance as a repetition of the Revolution on the intra-communal level: a constitutional revolution of *locals* and *Ottomans.* Thus, the leading activists of the Movement integrated the omnipresent notions of reform (*iṣlāḥ*), Ottoman patriotism (*al-waṭanīya al-ʿuṯmānīya*) and Constitutionalism (*dustūriya*), and civil rights

143 *'al-Yūnān al-urṯūḏuks yurīdūn an yubqī aš-šaʿb as-sūrī l-urṯūḏuksī l-filasṭīnī maḥrūman ʿan ḥuqūqihi'*. *Filasṭīn*, 5 February 1913: 210/4/3.

144 *'Hāḏihi al-išāʿāt hiya raʾsmāl al-baṭrīarkīya kullamā ṭalab al-waṭanīyūn minhā iṣlāḥan'*. *Filasṭīn*, 5 February 1913: 210/4/3.

145 See *Filasṭīn*, 21 September 1912: 173/3/5.

(*ḥuqūq aš-šaʿb*) into their discussion of the Orthodox Renaissance. In reference to the officers of the Young Turk Revolution, they defined the activists as 'the free Orthodox' (*al-urṯūḏuksīyūn al-aḥrār*).[146] They claimed that the movement was grounded on 'free principles' (*mabādiʾ ḥurra*),[147] and 'constitutional rights' (*ḥuqūqunā mašrūʿa*),[148] and portrayed the Renaissance Movement as a patriotic project in solidarity with Ottomanism, which, as the Orthodox Miḫāʾīl Aṭlīl from Jerusalem put it, was to be seen as a confirmation of 'our Ottomanism' and 'our love for the homeland'.[149]

Creating a counter-image, they equated patriarchal rule with despotism (*istibdād*) – an absolutist rule without representative structures, maintained by 'the usurping monks' (*ar-ruhbān al-muġtaṣibīn*), the members of the Convent. This rule was portrayed as an outdated relict from ancient times that did not fit with the 'spirit' of the 'new age' and modern concepts of citizenship, but it represented in the Arab Orthodox activists' argumentation, a foreign hegemony in the Ottoman realm: a rule of 'strangers' (*aġrāb*) from the (Agean) 'islands'.[150]

In *Filasṭīn*, these themes are reflected in the writings of Sakākīnī, who argued that the clergy were 'tyrannous despots' (*mustabidd ǧāʾir*) who 'represent a government within a government' (*yumaṯṯil ḥukūma fī ḥukūma*) and 'oppress the nation' (*aš-šaʿb maḍġūṭ ʿalayhi*), which 'is exposed to humiliation and degradation' (*yasām al-ḫasf wa-ḏ-ḏull*).[151] Another passage by an anonymous Orthodox activist in *Filasṭīn* demonstrates how the concept of citizenship was instrumentalized. He lamented that 'despair and distress are upon the Orthodox citizens in Palestine because of the suppression from some of the alien monks' (*ar-ruhbān al-aġrāb*) who ' have adopted lies and slander about Ottomanism to usurp the rights of the people' (*li-iġtiṣāb ḥuqūq al-umma*).[152] The 'local priest' (*al-kāhin al-waṭanī*), he demanded, must be in the 'vanguard of those who defend the rights of the nation' (*fī muqaddimat al-mudāfiʿīn ʿan ḥuqūq aš-šaʿb*) and was assigned 'before each citizen to defend the rights of the people who are his sons',[153] until the people observed that their rights were 'implemented according to what the constitutional government decided' (*tanfīḏ mā qarrarathu … al-ḥukūma ad-dustūrīya*).[154]

146 *Filasṭīn*, 29 July 1911: 55/2/1–5.
147 *Filasṭīn*, 15 November 1913: *al-Aḫbār* – 495/3/5–4/2.
148 *Filasṭīn*, 14 August 1912: 162/4/1–2.
149 *Filasṭīn*, 13 December 1911: 94/4/1–2.
150 *Filasṭīn*, 25 December 1912: 200/3/2.
151 *Filasṭīn*, 29 July 1911: 55/2/5.
152 *Filasṭīn*, 23 September 1911: 71/3/4.
153 *Filasṭīn*, 23 September 1911: 71/3/4.
154 *Filasṭīn*, 23 September 1911: 71/3/4–5.

The paradigm of the 'constitutional rights' of Ottoman 'citizens' versus the 'foreign usurpation' of the Greek clergy was applied by the supporters of the Arab Orthodox cause whenever the public or the authorities were addressed in letters, petitions, speeches and newspaper reports. For instance, when Orthodox notables petitioned to complain about the privatization of *waqf* property by the Convent, they did so in the name of the 'Ottoman national *milla* of the Rum Orthodox' (*millat ar-rūm al-urṯūḏuks al-ʿuṯmānīya al-waṭanīya*).[155] While in earlier reports, the terms *milla* or *ṭāʾifa* in the sense of 'denomination' were applied to the Orthodox community in Palestine, the activists' rhetoric increasingly started borrowing proto-national terms from 1913 onwards, calling the the people 'the Orthodox nation' (*aš-šaʿb al-waṭanī l-urṯūḏuksī*).[156] Here, the favored terms *umma* and *šaʿb*, meaning 'people' or 'nation', were used interchangeably with *waṭanīyīn* or *muwāṭinīn*, 'locals' or 'citizens' to refer to the Orthodox community; and the Orthodox Movement was even defined as a 'national renaissance' (*nahḍa qawmīya*).[157]

The intention here was to stress that local citizens, as the *natural* collective of this place, were ruled by non-Ottoman elements. However, the application of this proto-nationalist vocabulary should not be misunderstood as 'ethnic nationalism', since the activists of the Second Constitutional period always based the legitimacy of their cause on the Constitution and their equal rights as Ottoman citizens. To express the gap between the clerical rule and the Constitution, they even defined the Fraternity as a 'monastic kingdomin a democratic Empire' (*mamlaka ruhbānīya ḍimna mamlaka dīmūqrāṭīya*).[158] Since political 'unity' (*ittiḥād*) was, in *Filasṭīn*'s perception, the precondition for progress, the clergy was portrayed as an element undermining this unity by implementing the imperialist principle of 'divide and rule' (*farriq tasud*) in order to 'split' (*taqsīm*) the *umma*, and sow 'schism' (*šiqāq, fitna*).[159] Portraying clerical rule as a kind of imperialist invasion in the Ottoman realms, the activists used drastic images and even openly called the clergy 'the internal enemy' of the Empire that is 'gnawing off its bone' (*al-ʿadu ad-daḫilı allaḏı yanḫiru ʿaẓamahā*).[160]

Another facet of the exploitation of Ottomanism in the Arab Orthodox discourse was the instrumentalization of the external Ottoman political crisis. In the face of national movements in the Balkans and military defeats and territorial losses in North Africa and Europe, the patriarchal leadership was equated with the 'traitors' of the Aegean, who deceived the homeland with the help of the

155 *Filasṭīn*, 2 August 1911: 56/2/4 – *mulḥaq* (supplement).
156 Here, in an article by Ḫalīl as-Sakākīnī in *Filasṭīn*, 19 March 1913: 222/3/5–4/1.
157 *Filasṭīn*, 17 May 1913: 237/4/1.
158 *Filasṭīn*, 19 August 1911: 61/2/2–4.
159 *Filasṭīn*, 8 March 1913: 219/3/4–4/1.
160 *Filasṭīn*, 1 January 1913: 202/4/1.

imperialist states. In 1912, when confrontations between the Ottomans and the allied armies in the Balkans were about to reach a new escalation point, the Jerusalemite correspondent, known for his polemic style, integrated this argument into his anti-clerical writings:

> Our Ottomanism is inside and outside, your Excellency, the Patriarch ... We are not like the people of Rhodes who burnt the uniforms of the Ottoman army and we are not like your fellow countrymen, the people of Samos, who were applauding and cheering the Italian army. We are also not like the rest of the Greek islands, whose people are now holding conferences to betray their homeland and exchange the flag of the crescent with another one! The monks have already opened this chapter... to show what kind of nation this is who plays tricks on our Porte.[161]

Motives of Jihad and Combat

Arab Orthodox reformers applied very combative vocabulary and borrowed religious terminology to equate their efforts with a spiritual struggle. They called the Renaissance a 'blessed movement' (*ḥaraka al-mubāraka*),[162] and even a 'jihad' (*ǧihād*). Jihad, in classical Islamic thought 'the struggle on the righteous path for the sake of God' (*al-ǧihād fī sabīl illāhi*), was used as a theme by Christian Orthodox authors in various contexts so as to give their struggle a sacred aura. For instance, Ǧibrān Maṭar praised Yūsuf al-ʿĪsā for his efforts for the Orthodox 'jihad' and called him 'the great fighter for the *milla*' (*al-muǧāhid al-kabīr fī sabīl al-milla*).[163] As mentioned before, the Arab Orthodox preferred a rather combative rhetoric, and especially fond of this style was Sakākīnī, who asserted that the 'Orthodox nation' was 'enflamed' and eager to 'strive for a heroic jihad' (*ǧāhada fī ... ǧihād al-abṭāl*).[164] Ḥanā Abū aṣ-Ṣawf, a Palestinian Orthodox living in Mexico, also wrote very combative letters to *Filasṭīn* to motivate the brothers at home, and called upon them to

> Continue to struggle, oh people (*la-nuǧāhidu yā qawm*), with souls that do not know boredom and do not surrender to despair... The Orthodox milla has ... shown to the world that it is a living nation (*annahā umma ḥayya*). It shall not consider itself too noble to give its fortune, and to sacrifice its men on the way of its renaissance and listen to Filasṭīn [that calls them] to unite, to work together and continue.[165]

In contrast to the positively connotated Orthodox 'jihad', religious terminology was also borrowed to compare the Fraternity with devil's rule; for instance, Yūsuf al-ʿĪsā wrote in an article that the Patriarchate was 'on the way of the cursed

161 *Filasṭīn*, 26 June 1912: 148/3/3.
162 *Filasṭīn*, 23 September 1911: 71/3/4.
163 *Filasṭīn*, 21 January 1914: 300/3/2–3.
164 *Filasṭīn*, 29 July 1911: 55/2/5–3/2.
165 *al-Aḫbār*, 15 November 1913: 495/4/1.

Satan' (*fī sabīl aš-šayṭān ar-rağīm*), a phrase that he borrowed from the Qur'an.[166] Another facet of the combative language applied by Arab Orthodox activists was the popular use of biological metaphors to discredit the members of the Convent, such as comparison of the Greek monks to insects, parasites and 'microbes'[167] that had 'spread' and 'polluted the air' of Jerusalem.[168]

Mismanagement, Falsification, Delay

A frequent accusation presented by Arab Orthodox activists against the patriarchal establishment was on the theme of 'mismanagement' (*su' al-idāra*), falsification and 'delay' (*mumāṭala*) as a tactics to prevent reforms. The clergy did everything to boycott reforms, the activists claimed: bribing governmental officials, creating 'defamations' (*iftirā'āt*) to twist the 1910 Resolution,[169] and putting 'falsifications, revisions and thousands of obstacles' in the way of Orthodox reforms.[170]

The standard charge was that the clerical delegates in the Mixed Council and the patriarch boycotted regulations stipulated in the 1910 Resolution; and the patriarch did indeed reverse decisions taken in the Mixed Council, cut off debates or dissolved sessions when he felt provoked by the lay delegates, and, as *Filasṭīn*'s Jerusalem correspondent dramatically put it, 'chased away' the delegates 'in the way people would say shoo to a goat' (*miṯlamā qālū li-l-ʿanaza: irḥalī*). Often, the Mixed Council's lay delegates would proceed to the governor after such an interrupted session to complain about 'this hocus-pocus' that the clergy 'invent' to suspend the sessions.[171]

Corruption, Usurpation, Greed

Other frequent theme used by the Arab Orthodox activists was 'corruption' (*fasād*), the usurpation (*istīlā'*) of Orthodox property and 'greed', laid as standard accusations against the patriarchal establishment. For instance, many letters in *Filasṭīn* cited cases of the privatization of *waqf* property by the Convent. The financial state of the Patriarchate came close to bankruptcy before World War I and so the Patriarchate sold real estate to private investors, foreign consulates and increasingly to Zionist organizations which, of course, provoked a lot of criticism from the local people. *Filasṭīn* claimed that, in this way, the Orthodox

166 *Filasṭīn*, 1 November 1913: 285/1/3.
167 *Filasṭīn* 2 September 1911: 65/1/2–3; and 25 November 1911: 89/3/1.
168 '*at-talawwuṯ bi-l-mikrūb al-aklīrīkī l-muntašar fī ğaw al-Quds.*' *Filasṭīn*, 23 September 1911: 71/3/2 and 3/3.
169 *Filasṭīn*, 27 September 1911: 72/4/1–2.
170 *Filasṭīn*, 14 August 1912: 162/4/1–2.
171 *Filasṭīn*, 12 August 1911: 59/3/4.

monastery of Bethlehem had lost all its *awqāf*.[172] This topic was never openly debated in the Mixed Council, and will not be treated here in length since *Filasṭīn* does not provide enough details about the cases cited, but complaints about the sale of *waqf* were published several times.[173]

For instance, the Archimandrite Eftimios, head of the Church of the Holy Sepulcher (*ra'īs al-qiyāma*), was accused of having transformed and divided *waqf* land in Katamon, situated south-west of Jerusalem's Old City and next to the road to Bethlehem, into 90 plots, apparently selling each one for 20 francs as 'small colonies for Greece' (*mustaʿmarāt ṣaġīra li-l-yūnān*). Another case that raised protests in Jerusalem and embroiled the governor and the Grand Vizierate, dealt with the privatization of *waqf* land in Nakfūrīya, which the author claimed was turned into a 'Greek colony' (*mustaʿmara yūnānīya*).[174] Apparently, it was sold off and registered in the names of individual members of the Fraternity who received 'title deeds' (*qawāšīn mulkīya*) for it from the land registry office in Jerusalem since the monks had bribed its 'corrupt' director.[175] Comparing property belonging to or acquired by the Convent to 'Greek colonies' should suggest to the reader that this was equal to the usurpation of Ottoman citizens' property by non-Ottomans. In the context of the Nakfūrīya case, Orthodox notables raised a petition demanding that the District Council in Jerusalem recognize properties registered in the name of the Convent as collective property of the Orthodox *milla*, but without success.[176]

Many readers' letters also used the motif of the 'greedy monk' and blamed the Patriarchate for a policy of financial deceit,[177] cheating in tax issues,[178] and evicting poor Orthodox families from their homes by force because the real estate they resided in was needed for other purposes by the Convent, while 'our honorable fathers were watching [the scene] … from behind the silk curtains,

172 *Filasṭīn*, 9 April 1913: 228/4/2.

173 To give an example from *Filasṭīn*, in 1914, a Jerusalemite complained that a Jewish quarter beside the Jerusalem railway on the road to Bethlehem had been Orthodox *waqf* until the Holy Synod sold off 22,000 cubits (*ḏirāʿ*) of it for 6 francs per cubit to the Zionists years ago. *Filasṭīn*, 24 June 1914: 330/4/1–2.

174 *Filasṭīn*, 2 August 1911: 56/1/4–5 – *mulḥaq* (Supplement).

175 *Filasṭīn*, 25 October 1911: 80/4/1.

176 *Filasṭīn*, 25 October 1911: 80/4/1.

177 In one case, Ḫalīl Anasṭās from Bethlehem, a carpenter, had built a bridge for the Greek Orthodox monastery in Wadi Qelt near Jericho, and the monastery owed him 40 francs for his work. After he was brushed off by the abbot, he approached Patriarch Damianos several times but without success. See *Filasṭīn*, 3 January 1912: 100/2/4–5. Another example was the case of an artisan in Jerusalem who had painted a portrait of Damianos without being paid and filed a court case against his dragoman. The court estimated the price of the portrait at 600 lira and imposed a considerable fine on the dragoman. See *Filasṭīn*, 2 September 1911: 65/1/2–3; 25 November 1911: 89/3/1.

178 *Filasṭīn*, 25 December 1912: 200/3/2.

smiling', *Filasṭīn*'s Jerusalem correspondent claimed.[179] Another author complained that the Convent, despite the financial crisis, erected new buildings 'high as towers' financed by donations, instead of investing the money for the poor,[180] and another called upon the Convent to give up the habit of pompous celebrations that would cost thousands of dirham and reduce the 'Maghrebian army' (*ǧayš al-maġāriba*), forces of Maghrebi origin, stationed at the Convent, who were accused of being violent.[181]

5. Political Instruments of the Arab Orthodox Movement

During the Second Constitutional period, the Arab Orthodox Movement developed their decisive ideological arguments and political rhetoric, which included, as demonstrated in the previous section, the contemporary discourse on 'Constitutionalism' versus 'despotism', and on 'civic rights' (*ḥuqūq aš-šaʿb*), and the usual claim that it was working 'for the sake of the public good' (*li-l-maṣlaḥa al-ʿāmma*) and 'to serve the nation's interest' (*ḫidmatan fī maṣlaḥat aš-šaʿb*).[182] Apart from discursive paradigms, they also established very practical political instruments to present their case to the authorities and the Palestinian public, as will be outlined here. The political instruments presented by the Orthodox activists included, first of all, the intensive involvement of the Ottoman government in the intra-Orthodox conflict by sending open letters, petitions and delegations. Second, they actively worked for the politization and mobilization of the Orthodox laity through demonstrations, and boycott actions against individual clergy and the ceremonial status quo of Orthodox celebrities.

Government Involvement

In response to the patriarch's policy to block Orthodox reforms, Orthodox activists, community representatives and notables proceeded in delegations from Jerusalem and the dioceses to the Jerusalem governor and handed in petitions or addressed him in 'open letters' published in the press, in which they complained that they did not see any progress with reform.[183] Orthodox representatives or the lay delegates of the Council sent protest telegrams to the Grand Vizierate in Istanbul, and their standard demand was for the implementation of the 1910 Resolution.[184] Typically, they applied the dichotomous discourse of 'con-

179 *Filasṭīn*, 16 October 1912: 180/1/5.
180 *Filasṭīn*, 26 February 1913: 216/4/1–2.
181 *Filasṭīn*, 25 December 1912: 200/3/3.
182 *Filasṭīn*, 18 October 1911: 78/4/1.
183 For example, see *Filasṭīn*, 5 November 1913: 286/3/5–4/2.
184 For instance, see *Filasṭīn*, 1 October 1913: 276/3/4.

stitutionalism versus despotism' and 'Ottoman citizens versus foreign usurpation' as is demonstrated in the example of a petition presented in September 1911 by the Orthodox of Bethlehem to the Ministry of Justice and the Grand Vizierate in Istanbul:

> We have had enough of the despotism of the monks …, enough of the intrigues and tricks they use to usurp our rights. We, the Orthodox citizens of Palestine who have no refuge apart from Ottomanism, which is the only bond we are proud of, unfortunately consider ourselves forced to protest as our ongoing complaints concerning the government order (the 1910 Resolution) … has not been implemented … We believe that a constitutional government that holds firm to its position must send strict and definitive orders to the responsible authorities for the above-named order to be implemented as the hardship of the population … increases each day and people are waiting impatiently for your wise measures.[185]

While responses from Istanbul took a long time, the Arab Orthodox concentrated on involving the local government. Every year, a new governor was sent to the Jerusalem District with no instructions from the center on how to deal with the intra-Orthodox conflict and without being familiar with the internal conflict issues. As soon as he arrived, Orthodox delegations would go to him, presenting their case and portraying Arab Orthodox demands as a 'Constitutional movement' that was constantly blocked from progressing by the policy of the patriarch as head of the Mixed Council to use his right of veto in every vote. Orthodox representatives alleged to every new governor that the former governor ʿAzmī Bek had promised the Arab Orthodox that the lay delegates would have a two-thirds majority on the Council but had disappointed their hopes.[186]

For the governors, receiving Orthodox delegations was time-consuming and nerve-wracking. Furthermore, Orthodox leaders organized ongoing Sunday demonstrations during which the Orthodox congregation processed after the sermon through Jerusalem's Old City to the House of Government at Jaffa Gate, where people chanted their reform demands and Orthodox activists gave combative speeches and stirred up the crowd. All of this put considerable pressure on the governors, who tried various strategies to calm people's emotions, just to prevent another rebellion. An example of what I have called, the 'pressure of the street' on the Jerusalem governors, took place one Sunday at the end of July 1911. While the people were was waiting outside, Orthodox delegations from Jerusalem, Bethlehem and Lod approached the new governor Ǧawdat Bek, presenting their case, and the activist Ḫalīl Ibrāhīm Qazāqiyā from Bethlehem reminded him of the unfulfilled promise of a two-thirds lay majority

185 *Filasṭīn*, 27 September 1911: 72/4/2.

186 *Filasṭīn*, 2 August 1911: 56/1/3 – *mulḥaq* (Supplement). For a review of the history of the Mixed Council, see *Filasṭīn*, 1 November 1913: 285/1/1–2/1.

on the Council. After more than five hours of meetings, the Governor gave in, giving assurance that he would inspect the Resolution and 'resolve the issue within four or five days'. He stepped out the House of Government, addressing the crowd:

> I am not like the former governors and I will walk on the one and only path. You [Orthodox], take up your rights and the government will be with you! ... It knows that the clergy have cultivated despotism and has understood their goals and aims. But they [the clergy] have forgotten that the government is watching them (*al-ḥukūma la-hum bi-l-mirṣād*). Be certain that not one letter of the Resolution will be changed! They may send their delegations to Istanbul and do what they please, but they will not gain what they wish for. I say to you now: the [coming] days will soon make it a reality for you.[187]

Of course, the 1910 Resolution did not promise a two-thirds lay majority, and Ǧawdat Bek never addressed the issue. Soon, he even tried to prevent the Sunday rallies and calm Orthodox activism by using the security forces. The Orthodox decided to intensify their efforts and sent more protest telegrams to Istanbul calling for 'the renewal of the renaissance in Jerusalem' (*taǧaddud an-nahḍa fī l-Quds*).[188] One year later, nothing had happened in terms of Orthodox reforms and Qazāqiyā reminded the new governor, Muhdī Bek that

> It pains us, the Orthodox nationals, very much to see that nothing concerning the [1910–] Resolution has been implemented ... Our general demands are in accordance with law and justice (*muṭābaqa li-l-ḥaqq wa-l-ʿadāla*) ... and the implementation of the government order is within the frame of the Constitution and justice (*ḍimna dāʾirat ad-dustūr wa-l-ʿadāla*). That is why we ask our just and constitutional governor to meet our demands .... in accordance with the necessities of [his] obligations and in the name of public security and peace (*bi-sm al-amn wa-ar-rāḥa al-ʿāmma*).[189]

On the other side, also the Patriarchate sent complaints about the local Orthodox to Istanbul, and they involved the local government in various ways. Traditionally, the patriarchs maintained close relations with the Jerusalem governors, who were provided with a residence in a house in Katamon that belonged to the Convent and was called in *Filasṭīn* the 'mousetrap of the rulers' (*miṣyada li-l-ḥukkām*).[190] Obviously, the Patriarchate also made gifts to the governors, and

187 *Filasṭīn*, 2 August 1911: 56/1/1 – *mulḥaq* (Supplement).
188 *Filasṭīn*, 12 August 1911: 59/3/4–4/1.
189 *Filasṭīn*, 14 August 1912: 162/4/1–2.
190 The ʿĪsās claimed that the 'Katamon house' was furnished by Albert Antébi, a Jerusalemite Jew of Damascene origin with excellent links with Ottoman officials, Muslim notables and Zionists. He was disliked by the ʿĪsās for his engagement in Zionist land purchases, an issue to be addressed in detail in chapter IV, and the editors advised the governor to 'refuse the house completely'. See *Filasṭīn*, 22 March 1913: 223/3/4. When Muhdī Bek allegedly refused to take the Katamon House in 1912, ʿĪsā triumphed. *Filasṭīn*, 31 July 1912: 158/3/3.

Filasṭīn claimed that Governor Māǧid Bek had received a car from the Orthodox Church.[191]

In general, the Arab Orthodox suspected that the Jerusalem governors were bribed by the monks,[192] and it was typical for their speeches and writings to complain about 'Jerusalem's corrupted rulers' (*al-Quds mufassadat al-ḥukkām*),[193] or 'the microbes of Jerusalem that corrupt the rulers' (*mikrūbāt al-Quds al-mufassida li-l-ḥukkām*).[194] In fact, the governors tried to maintain good relations with the Patriarchate as a powerful actor and the biggest landowner in Palestine and, for instance, the governor attended Orthodox festivals and official celebrations. However, they did not know how to interpret certain legal aspects of the 1910 Resolution that were presented to them in contradictory ways by the parties to the conflict. They tried various strategies to deal with the problem, sometimes, trying to reconcile the parties, sometimes asking for advice from Istanbul, sometimes sending security forces to resolve Orthodox demonstrations, or playing 'deaf', as *Filasṭīn* complained.[195]

Boycotting the Ceremonial Status Quo

The Arab Orthodox Movement did not limit their efforts to involving the government and the local elites but also sought to mobilize the Orthodox public. Arab Orthodox activists called upon the faithful to boycott religious services conducted by the members of the Fraternity and to stay away from ceremonies presided over by the patriarch, thus boycotting the ceremonial status quo of the Greek Orthodox Church.

For instance, Arab Orthodox representatives stopped attending the Easter processions during which they usually received the 'holy fire' on Easter Saturday, the 'Saturday of Light' (*sabt an-nūr*) in Arabic, during a ritual conducted by the patriarch.[196] According to the tradition, the patriarch would take fire from Jesus's grave in the Church of the Holy Sepulcher and carry it on two great candles through the church, accompanied by priests changing. According to custom, he would sit on a throne, carried by local Orthodox notables and proceed from the church into the outer yard, where he was awaited by a crowd of locals and

191 *Filasṭīn*, 21 June 1913: 247/3/1.

192 See for instance, *Filasṭīn*, 2 August 1911: 56/1/3 – *mulḥaq* (Supplement).

193 Here in a statement by Sakākīnī to Ǧawdat Bek. *Filasṭīn*, 2 August 1911: 56/1/3 – *mulḥaq* (Supplement).

194 *Filasṭīn*, 1 February 1913: 209/1/2. Muslim notables were not immune to this suspicion either. When the Jerusalem delegate in Parliament ʿUṯmān an-Našāšībī went on a trip to Jericho with the patriarch's dragoman and dined with him in a restaurant of the Orthodox *waqf*, he was attacked by the ʿĪsās and defended himself by saying that he had paid for the car and the restaurant. *Filasṭīn*, 7 May 1913: 234/2/1–2.

195 *Filasṭīn*, 1 November 1913: 285/1/1.

196 *Filasṭīn*, 13 April 1912: 127/3/2; 3 May 1913: 233/2/4–5.

pilgrims. The patriarch would then pass the 'holy fire' to the priests of the various confessions and local Orthodox representatives, who lit candles with it and carried it to their community churches. During the Arab Orthodox rebellion, however, local Orthodox priests stayed away the ceremony and made their congregations stay away too, thus enforcing a change in ceremonial traditions, as will be demonstrated in a few examples.

During Easter 1912, *Filasṭīn*'s Jerusalem correspondent reported that the patriarch had to pass the fire to the Greek bishops (*maṭārina*) since there was no local Orthodox priest to receive it.[197] During the Easter procession of 1913, the traditional flags of the Orthodox, traditionally carried through the Old City alleys were now carried by 'young Greeks' instead of locals. The young Arab Orthodox attended wearing uniforms to respond to local resistance 'in a military manner', the correspondent reported and, on Easter Saturday, there were no Orthodox notables present to carry the patriarch on the throne outside into the yard and no Arab priests to receive the fire. When the patriarch handed it to a Greek monk, turmoil broke out and the police had to stop the violence.[198] At the Feast of St James, too, during which the patriarch usually led a procession from the now occupied Church of St James and distributed round loaves to the poor and pilgrims, representing the blessing of Apostle James, 'not a single one of the sons of the community' attended the ritual of the blessing (*tafrīq al-baraka*), which was described by the correspondent as a disaster with 'punching, yelling and beating' by the patriarch's Maghrebi forces.[199]

The Arab Orthodox also boycotted clergy sent by the patriarch to the communities. For instance, in 1911, when Damianos sent abbot Basilios to the monastery of Jaffa without approval of the local Orthodox, the *milla* bluntly rejected him.[200] To express their protest, local people occupied a church belonging to the monastery by blocking the gate that connected it with the monastery and only opening it for the local people during prayer services, so the abbot could not conduct the liturgy there.[201] The dispute went on for two years until abbot Basilios handed a petition to Governor Māğid Bek, who, in liaison with the patriarch, eventually forced the church key to be handed over to Basilios.[202]

197 *Filasṭīn*, 13 April 1912: 127/3/2.
198 *Filasṭīn*, 3 May 1913: 233/2/5–3/2.
199 *Filasṭīn*, 9 November 1912: 187/4/5.
200 *Filasṭīn*, 26 July 1911: 54/3/4–5.
201 *Filasṭīn*, 18 June 1913: 246/3/4–5.
202 The article was reprinted in *Filasṭīn*, 21 June 1913: 247/3/1–2 from the Jerusalem newspaper *al-Munādī*.

Public Mobilization and the Occupation of the Church of St James
Another mobilization strategy of the Arab Orthodox Renaissance activists was the occupation of Orthodox institutions, such as schools and churches, belonging to the Patriarchate and closing them to members of the Fraternity. Of great importance for the movement was the Church of St James in Jerusalem, which was occupied in the course of the Orthodox rebellion in autumn 1908 and held until the beginning of 1914.

It was a rather small church, situated in the center of the patriarchal headquarters, but of strategic significance since it connected the Convent with the Church of the Holy Sepulcher and was used by Damianos as a short cut on his way to celebrate the liturgy.[203] After its occupation, the patriarch's corridor was cut off and he had to pass through the Old City alleys to enter the church via the yard as did all visitors – a humiliation. From 1908 to 1914, Orthodox activists controlled the opening of the Church of St James for the congregation and did not allow Greek clergy to conduct prayers there. Instead of the Convent's priest, Orthodox lay people led the church services at St James's and activists politicized the Sunday liturgy in support of the Arab Orthodox cause. Yūsuf al-ʿĪsā conducted Bible exegesis and, after the sermon, Orthodox activists, including among them Ḫalīl as-Sakākīnī, Ǧurǧī Yaʿqūb al-Ḥalabī, Iftīm Mašbak and others, read aloud the latest news of the debates in the Mixed Council and gave anti-clerical speeches.[204] Motivated by the speeches, the congregation would process from St James's via the Old City to the House of Government near Jaffa Gate where they continued chanting anti-clerical slogans until the gendarmerie called the governor in his private home, and he came, received delegations and tried to calm the crowd.[205]

The reaction of Governor Ǧawdat Bek to this kind of activism was to observe. During a Sunday service in August 1911, police entered the Church of St James with a government order 'to be present and listen to the preaching' in order to 'to protect order and peace' because, in the words of Ǧawdat Bek, the clergy 'have informed me that your sessions raise tension and uncomfortable outcomes'. The congregation was outraged by this 'act of aggression', the Jerusalem correspondent wrote; they marched to the police station at Jaffa Gate and then to the governor's residence, including the 'all the Orthodox youth' (*kull šubbān aṭ-ṭāʾifa*).[206]

The police intervention at St James's led to a series of protests by the Orthodox of Jerusalem, Bethlehem and Jaffa. In cooperation, they announced in Jerusalem

203 See Bertram and Luke 1921, 252f; *Filasṭīn*, 16 March 1912: 120/3/5–4/2.
204 See *Filasṭīn*, 2 August 1911: 56/1/1–4; 30 August 1911: 64/3/4–5; 2 September 1911: 65/3/3–4; 30 September 1911: 73/3/4; 13 April 1912: 127/3/2.
205 *Filasṭīn*, 2 August 1911: 56/1/1–4.
206 *Filasṭīn*, 16 August 1911: 60/3/4–5.

'a great demonstration to protest against the police entering the church during prayers'.[207] A special train was to bring 100 Orthodox from Jaffa, while the Jerusalemites promised to accommodate their brothers in their homes.[208] At the same time, the Jerusalem Orthodox handed to the police commander and the governor a protest letter, signed by 'the general public of the sons of the Orthodox' (*'umūm abnā' al-milla al-urṯūḏuksīya*), in which they condemned police intervention in the church as a 'breach of law'.[209] Delegations from Jerusalem and other dioceses repeatedly approached Ǧawdat Bek and, by promising support, he eventually managed to persuade the Orthodox notables to cancel the great demonstration.[210]

However, the occupation went on, although there was disagreement within the congregation as to whether the closure of holy places was in accord with the spirit of Christian Orthodox belief. In *Filasṭīn*, an Orthodox Jerusalemite published an appeal to the clergy and justified the occupation of St James's, mingling religion with modernism:

> Places of worship are made to proclaim the servitude to God. If the intention is to proclaim [in it] the servitude to tyrannical and despotic men, it is a prayer and an act of worship to close them ... To reopen them in the old state would be a blasphemy against God...
>
> If you [clergy] want to open the church, let it be by approval and choice of the people, for you deserve [through that] the affection of the nation (*aš-ša'b*)... What should be the benefit to reopen the church while the sons of the community are scattered in foreign schools where they are not brought up in compliance with Orthodox values. Before you initiate the reopening of the church by splitting the nation you [clergy] must collect the sons of the nation in your schools to teach them the roots of their belief and the principles of their religion.
>
> It is not in compliance with religion to open [the church] and celebrate liturgies and splendid festivals. Religion lies in the love for the nation (*maḥabbat aš-ša'b*), the service of humanity (*ḫidmat al-insānīya*)... and pure actions (*al-a'māl al-mabrūra*) ... Otherwise, your passion for religion is a lie (*kāḏiba*) ... On one hand, you [clergy] call for the opening of the church in protection of church law. On the other, you trample the nation under your feet, and destroy its rights .... Know that the nation is no longer apathetic and ignorant (*lam ya'udd ḏālika aš-ša'b al-ḫāmil al-ǧāhil*) but the nation of today knows more about the roots of its religion than you; and its passion for it is deeper than yours.[211]

207 '*Muẓāhara kabīra iḥtiǧāǧan 'alā duḫūl riǧāl al-būlīs ilā l-kanīsa aṯnā' aṣ-ṣalāt.*' *Filasṭīn*, 16 August 1911: 60/3/5.
208 *Filasṭīn*, 23 August 1911: 62/3/5.
209 See *Kitāb maftūḥ ilā mudīr al-būlīs fī liwā' al-Quds*, in *Filasṭīn*, 19 August 1911: 61/3/5–4/1.
210 *Filasṭīn*, 19 August 1911: 61/2/3; 26 August 1911: 63/3/5.
211 *Filasṭīn*, 6 November 1912: 186/4/3–5.

Thus, from 1908 to 1914, St James's was a symbolic forum for the activists to mobilize the public for the Arab Orthodox cause, and a political stage for an anti-clerical campaign that greatly aroused the emotions of the people against the Patriarchate. Second, Orthodox activist circles considered the occupation of St James's, due to its strategic position, an important means by which to press the patriarchal leadership for reforms. From 1908 to 14, the Patriarchate tried a lot to reopen the church for the clergy by negotiating, petition writing and involving the governor in the issue. Before Easter 1912, the governor's deputy and police commander tried to make the community leaders of the Jerusalemite Orthodox reopen the church for the services, and supporters of the Patriarchate tried to persuade the governor to have the police open it by force.[212] But the Orthodox refused to open it and, on Easter Saturday, instead of crossing from the Convent to the Church of the Holy Sepulcher, Damianos had to walk round.[213] Orthodox notables discussed the issue with other community representatives in the Jerusalem CUP office, decided that occupied churches would not be reopened unless legal steps were guaranteed by the patriarch, and the Orthodox in other dioceses should be encouraged to occupy their churches as well.[214] This continued until ʿAzmī Bek pressed for the reopening of the Church of St James in 1914.

6. The Mixed Council as a Platform for Debate

This section briefly outlines the set-up and practical function of the Mixed Council as a legal forum for the Arab Orthodox to negotiate demands for reform, as stipulated in the 1910 Resolution. It further defines the general culture of decision-making that ruled the Council's debates and the key issues of debate from 1910 to 1914.

Set-Up and Function of the Mixed Council

The Mixed Council consisted of six clergy and six lay delegates, each representing a diocese. The Council was headed by the patriarch, who was usually accompanied by his dragoman since he did not speak Arabic, as becomes clear from the Councils' speakers records that were published in *Filasṭīn*. Importantly, the patriarch, as president of the Council, held the casting vote. Thus, he could boycott the Orthodox laity's demands and block decisions that were against clerical interests, which had a profound impact on the Council's debates.

212 *Filasṭīn*, 6 November 1912: 186/4/3–5.

213 *Filasṭīn*, 13 April 1912: 127/3/2.

214 *Filasṭīn*, 7 August 1912: 160/3/5–4/2.

The Council did not really have relevant legal competences but it was to negotiate and supervise the reformation of Orthodox educational, social and welfare institutions in the dioceses, which were 'exposed to misuse' by the Patriarchate, as confirmed the 1910 Resolution.[215] For this, the Patriarchate was obliged to pay one-third of its annual revenues, or at least 30,000 lira, as a 'social budget' for the Council, which would then negotiate its distribution and transfer it to local communities. This means that, despite the high hopes of the Orthodox laity, the Council did not have the legal competences to resolve the key issues of the intra-Orthodox conflict since it had neither authority over the revenues from pilgrimage and *waqf* properties, nor could it influence the rules to access to the spiritual hierarchy in the Patriarchate, but was nevertheless to supervise the reform of Orthodox education, churches, hospitals and welfare institutions in the dioceses, which were classified as 'concerning the locals'.[216] In the dioceses, representatives elected by the local population, the so-called 'the local trustees' (*al-mutawallīn*) or the 'trustees councils' (*maǧālis al-mutawallīn*) were to supervise the administration of their budget share. The system for the election of these trustees, who were under the authority of the spiritual heads in the dioceses, the 'Ighoumenos', was to be set up by the Mixed Council, as stipulated in the 1910 Resolution.[217]

The Councils' records published in *Filasṭīn* identify the delegates. The six clerical delegates were appointed from the members of the Fraternity. From 1911 until 1913, these were the archimandrites Yūsuf, Dosithios, Makarios and Eftimios, *muṭrān* Sofronios and *muṭrān* Malatios, who was also the deputy (*wakīl*) of the patriarch. Each of the six lay delegates represented a diocese and they were elected in the local communities. In 1911, the six lay delegates in the Council were the doctor Ilyās al-Ḥalabī for Jerusalem, the journalist Ḫalīl Baydas for the diocese of Nazareth,[218] Šawqī al-Mulkī for Acre, the activist ʿĪsā Yūsuf Ḥazbūn for Bethlehem, *Filasṭīn*'s editor Yūsuf al-ʿĪsā for Jaffa and ʿAwdeh as-Sālim for Salṭ. The 1910 Resolution stipulated that, every year, 50 percent of the Council's delegates from each side were to be replaced 'by lot' (*bi-l-qarʿa*).[219] Thus, the representation of the dioceses rotated systematically, apart from Jerusalem, which held a permanent seat on the Council. However, the rotation was subject to contradictory interpretations, as will be demonstrated.

The Council usually met on Wednesdays and Saturdays from 9 am until 2 pm in Jerusalem, apparently inside the patriarchal headquarters. In 1914, the days

215 Ḫūrī and Ḫūrī 1992, 265.
216 Ḫūrī and Ḫūrī 1992, 266.
217 Ḫūrī and Ḫūrī 1992, 266.
218 Ḫalīl Baydas was the editor of the magazine *An-Nafāʾis al-ʿAṣrīya* ('Modern Treasures'). Shomali 1995, 229.
219 Ḫūrī and Ḫūrī 1992, 265.

seemed to have changed to Tuesdays and Fridays.[220] This entailed tremendous cost in time and money for the lay delegates. While Damianos received the Council in the patriarchal center, the lay delegates had to travel long distances twice a week to represent their community. Each time, they had to find accommodation in Jerusalem and, given the transport situation, it was quite an effort for them, while the clergy were in the comfortable situation of being based near the Council's meeting place. The delegates were reimbursed with a payment that Bertram and Ḫūrī say was 200 francs a year,[221] while *Filasṭīn* said it it was 180 francs.[222] Yūsuf al-ʿĪsā emphasized that his involvement in the Council even left him out of pocket since the salary for the position 'does not cover the round trip by train, not to mention the expenses for the guest house'.[223]

The Culture of Decision Making or, the 'Limits of Participation'

Although the Council was to have a substantial amount of money at its disposal, it failed to implement reforms because the parties to the conflict had contradictory interpretations of legal aspects in the Fundamental Law or the 1910 Resolution, they lacked experience of political participation and discipline in democratic decision-making, and, most of all, the patriarch adopted a strategy of blocking decisions by his right to veto.

First of all, the 1910 Resolution left room for flexible interpretations of laws, which both parties made use of, and *Filasṭīn* often complained about the government's 'elastic resolutions' (*al-awāmir al-lāstīkīya*).[224] It seems from the speakers' records published in Filasṭīn that neither the delegates nor the government were completely clear about the Mixed Council's legal mandate, but the general interest of the laity was to *expand* the authority of the Council in financial matters while the clerical agenda was to limit its authority, referring to the patriarchal privileges. Each party supported its agenda by citing contradictory regulations that were part of the Ottoman Fundamental Law. In particular, contradictory interpretations of article 111 led to endless complaints to the authorities, while the key conflict issues of were left unsolved. Frustrated, al-ʿĪsā wrote:

> Dozens of petitions reached the governor and the laymen consulted him many times. He also sent dozens of telegrams to Istanbul, whose authorities did not respond. And if [they did], it would be something like the latest document issued by the Ministry of Justice, which only makes things more complicated… Most [of the documents] are full of expressions flexible as gum: they may stretch and contract as you wish.[225]

220 *Filasṭīn*, 1 March 1913: 217/4/2–3; 26 March 1913: 224/4/1–2.
221 Bertram and Luke 1921, 269–270; and Ḫūrī and Ḫūrī 1992, 277.
222 *Filasṭīn*, 10 September 1913: 270/4/1.
223 *Filasṭīn*, 10 July 1912: 152/1/1–3.
224 *Filasṭīn*, 1 November 1913: 285/1/2.
225 *Filasṭīn*, 16 December 1911: 95/3/5.

Second, the lay delegates were inexperienced in political participation and democratic decision-making. Yūsuf al-ʿĪsā confirmed that the Council's formation was accompanied by total 'naivety of the people' (*saḏāǧat aš-šaʿb*) since 'the people did not have experience with such councils'.[226] The meetings seem unorganized, the items on the agenda were often not set in advance and often seemed to be selected randomly, and the course of the session seemed meandering. It was typical that one delegate would suggest discussing the authority of local councils in the dioceses, while the next would protest and declare it more important to determine the annual budget, and a third one would plead for discussion of the election of the Council's delegates.[227] Furthermore, since the exact process of decision-making was not defined in the Council's regulations, debates on key issues of conflict would continue until one of the disputants became hostile towards his opponent. Then, other delegates would jumped in to de-escalate the situation, quickly changing the subject of discussion, or the patriarch would simply 'adjourn' the session (*taʿṭīl al-ǧalsa*) and leave the room.[228]

In addition, the patriarch, who acted as chair of the Council, was absent from a considerable number of meetings without explanation. He would then be represented by his deputy, who refused to take decisions in his absence, and the Council lost precious time. Moreover, the patriarch made use of his 'right of veto' (*ḥaqq at-tarǧīḥ*), making a majority for the clerical position if votes were tied between clerical and lay members, which meant that the laity could not win the vote even if they stood united against the clerical members.[229] *Filasṭīn* blamed the government for paralyzing the Council in this way,[230] and a sense of powerlessness ruled the laity:

> After the opening of the Wednesday session, the Jerusalem delegate... called for the definition of... a general amount for the housing of the poor in all the dioceses. All the lay delegates agreed on this but the clerical members refused. As usual, arguments pread and the session ended as it had opened, without any outcome (*bidūn ǧadwā*)... It is already written in the book of fate that it [the Council] will not arrive at anything because the lay delegates have no majority. Until this day, the government has not addressed the issue of equality in voting (*masʾalat tasāwī l-aṣwāt*).[231]

Among the initial demands the Orthodox laity made of the government was a two-thirds majority of lay members in the Mixed Council – eight lay members

226 *Filasṭīn*, 1 November 1913: 285/1/2.
227 *Filasṭīn*, 18 November 1911: 87/3/4–5.
228 *Filasṭīn*, 12 August 1911: 59/3/4f.
229 *Filasṭīn*, 1 November 1913: 285/1/2; 2 March 1912: 116/4/1–2.
230 *Filasṭīn*, 1 November 1913: 285/1/2.
231 *Filasṭīn*, 16 December 1911: 95/3/5.

and four clerical members – which was rejected by the 1910 Resolution.[232] ʿAzmī Bek, the Jerusalem governor during the issue of the Resolution, promised the Orthodox that he would push through a two-thirds lay representation on the Council within a year, but failed to keep his word. All the governors that followed him were reminded by the Orthodox activists that they should keep this promise,[233] but they governors were unable to make any change to the equal representation of lay and clerical members and the patriarch simply played for time. With the Patriarchate in heavy debt, the Council's budget was a tremendous burden and Damianos always postponed payment. Furthermore, he usually did not transfer decisions taken in the Council to local decision makers, and unilaterally interrupted sessions as he pleased. The conflict was interrupted by World War I, when the Patriarchate was cut off from revenues from property outside Palestine and pilgrims ceased coming. Orthodox schools, charitable institutions and the Mixed Council were closed. At the beginning of the war, the debts of the Patriarchate amounted to 221,792 lira; at the end of the war, they stood at 555,887 lira.[234]

Key Subjects of Debate in the Mixed Council

The dominant key issues in the Council's debates were the status of *waqf* properties, the election of the 'trustees' councils', educational reforms, the rotation of the delegates in the Council, and the distribution of the social budget. First of all, the frustration of Orthodox lay demands concerning the administration of *waqf* properties in Jerusalem through local representatives critically contributed to the stagnation of Orthodox reforms. As already mentioned, the 1910 Resolution brought about the establishment of local councils in the various communities, elected by local people. These trustees' councils were to supervise Orthodox social and educational institutions and churches that were classified as being of local concern (which did not apply to the *awqāf* controlled by the Convent), and to supervise the distribution of their budget share. The functions of these councils were negotiated again and again from 1911 to 1914, which caused several escalations of tension between the clergy and the laity. In addition, the question of the trustees' councils also caused a rift between Jerusalem and the other dioceses represented on the Mixed Council since the patriarch prevented the activities of those local councils because there was an older conflict between the Patriarchate and Jerusalemite Orthodox notables who had sought to expand their authority to the administration of local *awqāf* via such a council.

232 See Ḫūrī and Ḫūrī 1992, 265.
233 *Filasṭīn*, 22 October 1913: 282/4/1.
234 Ḫūrī and Ḫūrī 1992, 279–280.

Second, the modernization of Orthodox education was on the central agenda of the Arab Orthodox Movement. In the context of the Orthodox rebellion of 1910, a number of Orthodox schools were occupied by activists in protest against their neglect by the Patriarchate. Others were simply closed by the Patriarchate because of financial shortages, and school reform was therefore a key issue in the Council. At issue was the composition of a new school board (*ʿumdat al-madāris*), the question of the Council as a supervisor (*niẓāra*) of educational reforms in the dioceses, and the role of the local trustees in the management of the schools.

Third, a major part of the debates in the Mixed Council was around the administration of the annual budget and its distribution to the dioceses according to proportional shares. As already mentioned, one-third of the Patriarchate's revenues, or at least 30,000 lira, was to be transferred to the Council annually.[235] The Patriarchate always postponed transferring the budget to the Council, while the local Orthodox communities were desperately waiting for their share, and the inability of the laity to enforce the transfer of the budged damaged their image in the eyes of the public. Finally, the system for rotating the Mixed Council's delegates continued to be a matter of heated dispute from 1911 to 1913. The 1910 Resolution stated that, by the end of the first year (end of 1911), the first half of the Council's delegates on each side, lay and clergy, should be replaced 'by lot' (*bi-l-qarʿa*), and the second half in 1912,[236] after the end of the administrative year in August.[237] Thus, each cluster of delegates would be members for two years, and each diocese would have a period of representation at its time. Only Jerusalem, as the center of the Patriarchate, occupied a permanent seat in the Mixed Council and simply rotated its delegate.

7. A History of Escalation(s): Case Studies on the Mixed Council

This section treats the debates that took place in the Mixed Council from 1911 to 1914 as a 'history of escalations'. It identifies the main issues at stake, the central actors involved in the debates, and the peaks of the intra-Orthodox conflict during the Second Constitutional period. The escalations will be illustrated by several case studies, and culminated in 1913 while the Council lost its legitimacy in the eye of the Orthodox public and was temporarily dissolved but reopened again after government intervention in January 1914. This section further analyzes the changing role of *Filasṭīn* and its editors in the course of these escalations

235 Ḫūrī and Ḫūrī 1992, 266.
236 Ḫūrī and Ḫūrī 1992, 265.
237 *Filasṭīn*, 2 March 1912: 116/3/5–4/3.

and the discursive turns that took place in *Filasṭīn* when Yusuf al-ʿĪsā was deprived of his role as a leader of the anti-clerical resistance in the Council in 1914.

7.1. Conflicts over the 'Trustees' Councils'

At the core of the intra-Orthodox conflict that overshadowed the debates between the laity and the clergy in the Mixed Council on all issues regarding Orthodox reforms, was the ambiguous definition of Orthodox institutions in the Patriarchate (schools, hospitals, holy sites, endowments, etc.) as *communal* or *universal* property. It was this question that had led in 1908 to the violent rebellion against the Patriarchate and the occupation of churches and monasteries that Arab Orthodox activists defined as 'local' (*mutaʿalliqa bi-l-waṭanīyīn*).

As stated above, the first demand handed to the authorities by Orthodox notables from Jerusalem in the aftermath of the 1908 Revolution was the establishment of 'local councils' (*maǧālis ǧamāʿa*) in each *qaḍāʾ*, entrusted with the administration of communal *awqāf* as stipulated article 111 of the Ottoman Fundamental Law.[238] While the Orthodox notables pressed for the implementation of this article concerning *awqāf* and holy places in Jerusalem, the clergy considered these properties as belonging to Ottoman Orthodoxy in general (*ʿumūm al-urṯūḏuks al-ʿuṯmānīyīn*), and thus, subject to control of the Convent.[239] They declared article 111 irrelevant, especially in Jerusalem as the center of the Patriarchate and the main source of its revenues. Concerning the administration of Orthodox *awqāf*, they insisted that articles 11 and 118 were relevant since they confirmed the imperial protection of patriarchal privileges according to former practices.[240]

The ambiguous interpretation of article 111 remained among the fundamental conflicts between the local people and the Patriarchate and would dominate the debates between the laity and the clergy in the Mixed Council; and at its core was the conflict between the Jerusalemite Orthodox notables and the patriarch over Orthodox institutions in Jerusalem, especially holy sites and visitors' hostels and monasteries, but also landed properties and real estate. This issue became the subject of extended conflicts in the Mixed Council from its inception. Ǧūrǧī Zaḫarīyā, the first Jerusalem delegate, who sat on the Council from 1910 to 1911, made fiery speeches, stressing the functions of the trustees (*waẓāʾif al-mutawallīn*) concerning the revenues from Jerusalemite *awqāf* that he classified 'local

238 Bertram and Luke 1921, 250–251; Ḫūrī and Ḫūrī 1992, 266, and my translated summary of the 1910 Resolution.

239 Ḫūrī and Ḫūrī 1992, 264; and Bertram and Luke 1921, 253–254.

240 Kark and Papastathis 2014, 124f.

in character'. He argued that the Jerusalem trustees were 'entitled to administer them and limit the benefits deriving from them' that would go to the other dioceses[241] – a position that also led to rivalries between the communities in Jerusalem and in the dioceses.

The 1910 Resolution and the Local Councils

The government's response to the first demand regarding the administration of Orthodox property though local councils was vague. The 1910 Resolution declared that the 'special regulations' regarding the election and duties of these councils were still to be enacted 'in the future' and would be drawn up in line with the 'special conditions' that applied to the *awqāf* in Jerusalem and other communities.[242] However, it specified that, in Jerusalem, there was practically 'no communal *waqf*' to administer.[243] It further stipulated that Orthodox institutions (schools, churches, hospitals, welfare institutions, etc.) that were situated 'in the villages' (*fī l-qurā*) and that 'concerned the locals' (*al-muta'alliqa bi-l-waṭanīyīn*) were to be 'transferred to trustees' (*min al-muqtaḍā iḥālatuhā ilā mutawallīn*) to supervise the administration of these assets under the authority of the bishop or spiritual head, the 'Ighoumenos'.[244] For the reformation of these institutions that had been 'exposed to misuse and waste' by the Patriarchate, confirmed the Resolution,[245] the trustees were to receive a share of the social budget transferred to the Mixed Council. Importantly, the Resolution referred to places outside Jerusalem and in the dioceses where the trustees were the key actors for the reformation of Orthodox institutions. Thus, the demand that these trustees be given their authority was the mantra of the laity in the Mixed Council.

The Orthodox laity interpreted the legal competences assigned to these trustees inconsistently. At times, they demanded the authorization of local trustees in compliance with article 111 of the Fundamental Law to underpin the right to local control over certain *awqāf*. They also preferred to argue with the Fundamental Law since it was issued by the central authority, while the 1910 Resolution was issued only by a government commission. At other times, they simply demanded 'the implementation of the governmental order' (*tanfīḏ qarār al-ḥukūma*),[246] the phrase under which they summarized the 1910 Resolution, although it only referred to sites outside Jerusalem.

241 '*La-hā ṣiffa maḥallīya fa-yuḥaqq li-l-mutawallīn idāratuhā wa-ḥaṣara manfa'atahā fī l-urṯūḏuksīyīn al-munḍawīn li-l-kursī l-awrūšalīmī.*' See Ḫūrī and Ḫūrī 1992, 279.

242 Ḫūrī and Ḫūrī 1992, 262–263.

243 Bertram and Luke 1925, 265; Ḫūrī and Ḫūrī 1992, 264.

244 See the sixth article of the governmental response on the Second Demand in Appendix I, and Ḫūrī and Ḫūrī 1992, 266.

245 Ḫūrī and Ḫūrī 1992, 265.

246 *Filasṭīn*, 15 July 1911: 51/2/5 – /3/1.

Regulations for the Election of Local Trustees

The centrality of the question of the local trustees' councils as a key issue cannot be overstated since the implementation of reforms depended on them. Collaboration between the Mixed Council, entrusted with the distribution of the budget share to the local communities, and the local trustees as *key actors* in the dioceses, was essential.

The 1910 Resolution had ordered the Mixed Council to work out a basic system of regulations for the election of these trustees in the dioceses. In spring 1911, during its 17th session, it set up the electoral system for the trustees' councils (*niẓām al-maǧālis*),[247] which *Filasṭīn* republished in February 1914.[248] Importantly, the set of regulations stipulated that the trustees' councils would only gain validity after the patriarch transferred a 'document' (*manšūr*) to the dioceses in which he authorized the communities to conduct elections.[249] Local priests and community leaders (*wuǧahāʾ aš-šaʿb*) would supervise the elections, and the number of trustees was not to exceed six persons in towns, and three in villages. As usual in the late Ottoman context, voting was in general restricted to the elites and males. The Council stipulated that only Ottoman nationals who were able 'to read and write', over the age of twenty and individually registered in the local Orthodox communities were entitled to vote and would elect the trustees for a term of two years.[250]

The patriarch did not enact the local council regulations for three years since he did not want to open the way for the local administration of any assets. The demands of the notables concerning Orthodox sites in Jerusalem made Damianos very sensitive and he feared the trustees in the dioceses would claim similar rights. For him, as he admitted, the trustees' councils were a 'stumbling block' (*ḥaǧr ʿaṯra*) and the 'cause of the plague' (*aṣl al-balāʾ*).[251] The patriarch's boycott of the trustees remained a key conflict until 1914 and made reforms impossible, since it cut off the local communities from money. The Orthodox lay delegates declared that this was 'despotism' (*istibdād*) that undermined the Ottoman Constitution.[252] Many letters called for the implementation of the 'trustees' councils' (*maǧālis al-mutawallīn*), and communities petitioned

247 This was stated in *Filasṭīn* in 1913. The first issue of *Filasṭīn* available is number 51, which documented the 30th session in July 1911. The 17th session must have been in April/May 1911, but the issues from that period were not at my disposal. *Filasṭīn*, 4 January 1913: 203/3/4–5.

248 For the regulations on the trustees, see 'The Functions of Trustees for the Churches in the Jerusalem Patriarchate' (*Waẓāʾif Mutawallī Kanāʾis al-Kursī l-Ūrušalīmī*) in *Filasṭīn*, 14 February 1914: 307/3/5–4/3.

249 *Filasṭīn*, 14 February 1914: 307/3/5.

250 *Filasṭīn*, 14 February 1914: 307/4/1–2.

251 *Filasṭīn*, 3 January 1912: 100/3/2–5.

252 *Filasṭīn*, 27 September 1911: 72/4/2.

against the 'paralysis' of the Orthodox *umma*, which was unable to act without these councils.[253]

In autumn 1911, the Mixed Council reached a point of high tension because of this issue. The Council had held 43 sessions and Damianos had been absent from the sessions for unknown reasons for some time.[254] Governor Ǧawdat Bek faced petitions and counter-petitions. Left without instructions, he declared the sessions 'invalid' until further orders arrived from Istanbul. The Council also failed to elect a school board, and schools stayed closed in autumn 1911. In Bethlehem, Orthodox notables pressed the community representatives to take steps until the *qā'maqām* intervened and prohibited the *milla* from further gatherings. In this context, the Bethlehem delegate in the Mixed Council, ʿIsā Yūsuf Ḥazbūn, addressed Damianos in an open letter. Referring to his obligation 'to serve the interest of the people' (*waẓīfatunā hīya ḫidma maṣlaḥat aš-šaʿb*), Ḥazbūn insisted that the trustees be appointed or otherwise, he would 'file a suit with the relevant authorities (*al-marāǧiʿ al-īǧābīya*) to protect the rights of the *milla*'.[255] Ḥazbūn also petitioned the Ministry of Justice, 'in the name of justice and the homeland' (*bi-sm al-ʿadāla wa-l-waṭan*).[256] In a new order, the Ministry of Justice admitted irregularities concerning the trustees' councils, stating:

> If these complaints are correct that, until this day, the election of the trustees for the schools and churches in the rest of the places [outside Jerusalem] has not taken place in accordance with… the resolution, this delay is harmful (*fa-yakūn hāḏā at-ta'ḫīr muḍirran*). As we understand from this situation and the consultations, there is still a misunderstanding (*sū' at-tafāhum*) concerning the resolution … between the local Orthodox and the Patriarchate, and it is obligatory for all sides to implement it.[257]

Despite this order, the patriarch still did not enact the trustees' councils. In May 1912, Bandalī al-Ḫūrī, a journalist from Bethlehem, addressed Damianos concerning the issue. He stressed that the *milla* 'complains to its creator about this despotism and the usurpation of its rights' and cried out:

> Your Excellency, the Patriarch! Almost two years have passed since the resolution has been issued. Since then, the milla has been awaiting any noticeable result. If you were guided by God, you would have acted in line with the resolution and ordered the formation of the trustees' council in our city … and for sure, you would have resolved the conflicts within the people and the interferences that weakened the local govern-

253 Here, written by two activists from Bethlehem, Ǧirǧis Abū Dīh and Yaʿqūb Daḥbūreh. *Filasṭīn*, 18 November 1911: 87/3/5.
254 *Filasṭīn* picked up rumors that the patriarch had been staying atn the Mt of Olives Hospital, speculating he might simulate health problems so as to avoid meeting the governor. *Filasṭīn*, 21 October 1911: 79/3/5–4/1.
255 *Filasṭīn*, 18 October 1911: 78/4/1–2.
256 *Filasṭīn*, 18 November 1911: 87/3/5.
257 *Filasṭīn*, 25 November 1911: 89/4/1.

> ment – during a time in which we Ottomans have to stay calm and have enough external disturbances! Our schools are shut down, our churches are closed, and our villages do not have anyone to take care of their affairs. All of this is the result of the absence of the formation of the trustees' council (*kull ḏālika natīǧat ʿadam taʾlīf maǧlis al-mutawallīn*)!
>
> Our children are hanging around in the alleys and streets where they pick up bad upbringing and the lowest principles (*sūʾ at-tarbiya wa-asfal al-mabādiʾ*) … Your Excellency, who is their spiritual father and shepherd, responsible for them to God, has left them in their state of despair. I know there are competent delegates in the Mixed Council. Yet, their screaming and begging is fading away between nagging and disputing…
>
> Our Council opens and closes its meetings without a result that could promise progress …. It is as if the delegates are shouting into a valley … That is why I plead to the Patriarch, speaking out for the needy and the weak and the poor of this milla, to order the formation of the trustees' councils. I guarantee that this Council is the best [remedy] to resolve the conflict and bring hearts together … and to establish adequate schools to educate and cultivate them (*li-taʿlīmihim wa-taṯqīfihim*) for their own benefit and the benefit of the High Porte, may God guide it. The new generation are the men of the future (*haʾūlāʾ al-aḥdāṯ hum riǧāl al-mustaqbal*). If they learn and go out, they will be the pride of the homeland and a resource for the state (*kānū li-l-waṭan faḫran wa-li-d-dawla ḏaḫran*).[258]

Despite these diplomatic involvements, the local trustees were not authorized by the patriarch since the question of the Jerusalem trustees and their financial demands occupied the Mixed Council from 1910 onwards, as will be explained below.

The Allowances for the Jerusalemites, the Social Budget and the Trustees

The conflict between the Jerusalem delegate in the Council and the clergy about the competences of trustees was also rooted in the question concerning the 'rent allowances' (*iǧārāt ad-dūr, uǧūr dūr*) for Jerusalemites, a payment that the Orthodox of Jerusalem traditionally received from the Patriarchate.[259] The core question was whether to exclude the rent allowances for the Jerusalemites from the budget that the Council should have at its dispersal, or to deduct them from their annual budget share. This question triggered ongoing confrontations between the Jerusalemite delegate, the patriarch and Yūsuf al-ʿĪsā. There are different narratives about the origins of this payment. In some cases, free housing was made available for (poor) families or flats were rented by the Patriarchate and assigned to Orthodox families, who received an allowance as support. It is also reported that, with the issue of title deeds during the *Tanzimat*, Orthodox Jer-

258 *Filasṭīn*, 4 May 1912: 133/4/1.
259 *Filasṭīn*, 16 December 1911: 95/3/4.

usalemites wanted to save their private property from confiscation by the authorities and transferred it to the Convent, believing it would be held in trust for their families. Another narrative claims the annual allowance was brought in by the Patriarchate to counter the propaganda of other Christian organizations who granted their communities a similar benefit.[260]

Doctor Ilyās al-Ḥalabī, the Jerusalem representative in the Council from 1911 after Ǧūrǧī Zaḫarīyā left following bitter conflicts with the patriarch, claimed that this payment was one of the 'old rights' (*min al-ḥuqūq al-qadīma*) of the Jerusalemites, approved from the time of Patriarch Gerasimos in the fourteenth century.[261] It is not known what percentage of the rent allowances was compensation for private property transferred to the Patriarchate, or how far it was part of the Convent's social welfare system, as the clergy claimed. The number of houses and where they were situated also remains unclear. The annual allowance paid to the Jerusalemites was said by Damianos to be 10,000 lira, but there is no other proof of this.[262] Whatever the case may be, the payment was a cornerstone of local resistance to the clerical establishment. When in November 1910, the Synod decided to limit the annual allowance to 3,000 lira, the Jerusalemites initiated riots.[263] Orthodox representatives in Jerusalem demanded that the allowance be excluded from their annual budget share and declared that this was a special agreement with the Patriarchate that was *not* related to the 1910 Resolution, which meant that the allowance should be paid *in addition* to the budget share for the Jerusalemites. Damianos feared that other dioceses would follow this example and invent their own privileges. He blamed the Jerusalemites for expand their legal competences and continued to boycott the formation of the trustees' councils.

Iyās al-Ḥalabī, Damianos and Resolution 139

In November 1911, the Mixed Council appointed a committee (*lağna*) to calculate the social budget for the new administrative year. It consisted of Ilyās al-Ḥalabī (Jerusalem), Ḫalīl Baydas (Nazareth) and Archimandrite Yūsuf. This committee was identical with the 'temporary' school board (*ʿumdat al-madāris*) that had been instructed to conduct a survey of Orthodox schools, and it was now to calculate the sum that the Patriarchate should pay a family for housing, reckoning four persons per household (*ḫān*), divided into various price categories between five and ten lira.[264]

260 See Bertram and Luke 1921, 253.
261 *Filasṭīn*, 29 November 1911: 90/4/1.
262 *Filasṭīn*, 25 November 1911: 89/3/5.
263 See Bertram and Luke 1921, 253.
264 *Filasṭīn*, 18 November 1911: 87/3/4–5.

The budget committee's star was not in the ascendant. Ḥalabī soon resigned and blocked its activities, arguing that the said amount was not high enough, and that the committee was undermining the role of the Jerusalem trustees.[265] He repeatedly insisted that the allowance for the Jerusalemites was *not* subject to the Council's social budget, included all the Orthodox of Jerusalem, and was not part of the Patriarchate's social welfare benefits for the poor.[266] The patriarch protested to the Ministry of Justice and Religious Affairs in Istanbul that the Jerusalemites were trying to usurp his privileges. In response, a new order, Resolution 139, was sent to the local government and reprinted in *Filasṭīn* in November 1911.[267] The Ministry rebuked Ḥalabī. Referring to the 1910 Resolution, it clarified that

> the participation of the public in the administration of the monasteries, visitors' hostels and pilgrimage revenues runs counter to the high berats and the Patriarchate's privileges;[268] ... and demanding money from the Patriarchate runs counter the amount decided for the Mixed Council to cover housing rents for the poor... All of this is incompatible with the spirit of justice and equality and the regulations of the resolution and the high berats.[269]

After the arrival of Resolution 139 from the Ministry of Justice and Religious Affairs, Ḥalabī did not stop campaigning for rent allowances for the Jerusalemites, inside and outside the Council. In polemical letters, he addressed the Patriarchate and claimed, in the registers of the Sharia court (*al-kašf ʿalā siǧillāt al-maḥkama aš-šarʿīya*) that it could be seen that the houses registered were *not* bought from the *milla*[270] and included property of wealthy families who were not in need of social welfare.[271]

Ḥalabī's campaign for the financial budget for the Jerusalemites also pitted him against the other lay delegates. They blamed him for 'blocking' the Council's business, and some of them became so bored with Ḥalabī's speeches on behalf of the Jerusalemites that they did not attend the sessions towards the end of 1911.[272] Ḥalabī became increasingly isolated in the Council, and Yūsuf al-ʿIsā in partic-

265 *Filasṭīn*, 25 November 1911: 89/3/5; 29 November 1911: 90/3/5.

266 *Filasṭīn*, 25 November 1911: 89/3/5.

267 For the whole text of Resolution 139, see *Filasṭīn*, 25 November 1911: 89/3/5–4/1.

268 '*Ištirāk al-ʿumūm bi-idārat al-adyīra wa-maḥallāt al-ziyāra wa-l-wāridāt al-ʿāʾida ilayhā huwa muḫālif li-l-baraāt al-ʿāliya wa-muḫill bi-imtiyāzāt al-baṭrīyarkīya.*' See *Filasṭīn*, 25 November 1911: 89/3/5–4/1.

269 '*Inna ṭalab darāhim min al-baṭrīyarkīya ḫilāf al-mabāliġ allatī taqarrarat li-l-maǧlis al-muḫtalaṭ li-iǧārāt dūr fuqarāʾ al-ahālī ... Wa-kull ḏālika munāfin li-rūḥ al-ʿadl wa-l-musāwāt wa-iḥkām al-qarār wa-li-taṣrīḥāt al-baraāt al-ʿāliya.*' *Filasṭīn*, 25 November 1911: 89/3/5–4/1.

270 *Filasṭīn*, 13 December 1911: 94/4/1.

271 *Filasṭīn*, 16 December 1911: 95/3/4.

272 *Filasṭīn*, 16 December 1911: 95/3/4–5.

ular accused him of pursuing personal interests (*masālih šaḫṣīya*) with his budget agenda and addressed him in annoyance:

> As I see that the dignified Council, knowing that matter of the Jerusalemites' housing rents is an unsolved Gordian knot, does not want to set it apart… and the Jerusalem delegate refuses to agree to compromise… and I excuse him for that because I noticed that the people he represents rose up against him… and as our Council has no legitimacy (*lā ṣalāḥīya*) to investigate… these rights… I call for the matter of the Jerusalemites' rents to be set aside so that the Council can turn to other things. If the Jerusalemites have rights, they are a matter for the Patriarchate, which must come to an agreement with them.[273]

At the same time, delegations pressed the governor to intervene. Ǧawdat Bek, confronted with different legal interpretations, hoped for instructions from Istanbul and acted ambivalently. A delegation of Jerusalem Orthodox told him they did not regard Resolution 139 as 'constitutional' and sent protest telegrams to the Grand Vizierate. The governor, under pressure, asked the delegation to wait for the Grand Vizierate's response, asked the patriarch to pay the allowances since he was 'under accusation',[274] and at the same time declared that the Mixed Council's sessions were no longer 'valid' since the election (*iqtirāʿ*) of the new delegates, which should have taken place in the autumn of 1911, had not happened.[275]

Debating the Trustees' Issue in the Mixed Council: an Example

Meanwhile, the atmosphere in the Council became extremely tensed. The patriarch accused the Jerusalemites of laying hands on the properties of the Church of the Holy Sepulcher and said that the trustees' councils would not be put in place before the budget issue with the Jerusalemites was resolved.[276] ʿĪsā announced he would resign if Damianos would not transfer the establishment of the local councils (*niẓām al-mutawallīn*) to the dioceses. Damianos played for time and asked that they wait for the response of the Grand Vizierate. The session in January 1912, quoted below, illustrates the course of two typical sessions in the Council:

> **His Excellency, the Patriarch:** Both, the housing rents and the trustees' issue have been hindering the work of the Mixed Council… We were forced to ask clarification from the Ministry of Justice about what the Jerusalemites did. The response from 30th of July says that, if the Jerusalemites have special assets, they can appoint trustees for them… and the government has prohibited any interference with the revenues and properties of the

273 *Filasṭīn*, 29 November 1911: 90/4/1.
274 *Filasṭīn*, 16 December 1911: 95/3/5.
275 *Filasṭīn*, 27 December 1911: 98/4/1–2.
276 *Filasṭīn*, 27 December 1911: 98/3/5.

(monastic) order of the Holy Sepulcher. The Jerusalemites still stated that their rents were compensation for assets they gave to the Patriarchate. But the government did not recognize that. The trustees that were appointed by the Jerusalemites and removed by us (*alġaynāhum*) … petitioned the High Authorities … and so the government took over this matter. We sent the required documents to the Council of Ministers, which transferred it to the State Council (*šūrā ad-dawla*) for investigation. And when the response of the State Council comes, all disagreement will be resolved and the Council can work accordingly.[277]…

Jaffa Delegate: … We, all the lay delegates, refuse any further discussion… or anything directed against the trustees. Nobody will think that with our persistence… we serve those who intend to shut down the Council (*taʿṭīl al-maǧlis*). No! We will not accept either [its] authorization (*ruḫṣa*) [to work] nor [its] closure (*taʿṭīl*). If the Patriarch seeks to authorize the Council, we will still come in spite of the authorization every Wednesday and Saturday. We will stand in front of that gate and say: 'Open up, so we can implement the governmental order (*li-nunaffiḏ qarār al-ḥukūma*)!'

His Excellency, the Patriarch: We cannot treat the Jerusalemites differently from the dioceses. The word 'trustees' is a stumbling block (*kalimat mutawallīn ḥaǧar ʿaṯra*) because, if we appoint trustees for the schools, they will act like 'supervisors' (*bi-ṣiffat nuẓẓār*). The term 'trustees' is a strange concept to the spirit of the Church and has (just) appeared accidently (*sahwan*) in the governmental order!

Archimandrite Yūsuf: Anyway, the last order of the Ministry of Justice (Resolution 139) says that, if there are places belonging to the local people (*iḏā wuǧida li-l-waṭanīyīn maḥallāt taḫuṣṣuhum*), there should be trustees appointed for them. So, let's examine the cities in which there are private assets (*amlāk ḫāṣṣa*) belonging to the local people in order to appoint trustees for them.

Jaffa Delegate: Yes, the Archimandrite will be blessed for mentioning this point. The document referred to (Resolution 139) only mentions the Jerusalemites and does not refer to the … meaning of the term 'trustees' because the appointment of trustees was ruled in the order of the Council of Ministers (the 1910 Resolution), which stands above the Ministry of Justice and is not bound by any restriction or condition.

His Excellency, the Patriarch: And what are we supposed to do if the trustees lay their hands on all the churches and assets of the (Convent of the) Holy Sepulcher?

Acre Delegate: The delegate of Jaffa asked his Excellency the Patriarch to act on one of the two issues by either implementing the (1910)-Resolution which enacted the Council… or… to introducing a new system in accordance with the government order.[278] I see that his Excellency claims to be waiting for instructions from Istanbul. Does he want to make us believe that we are not able to debate the 'trustee-issue' immediately? We ask for an explanation!

277 *Filasṭīn*, 3 January 1912: 100/3/3.
278 *Filasṭīn*, 3 January 1912: 100/3/3.

His Excellency, the Patriarch: The term 'trustees' is the origin of the plague (*aṣl al-balā'*)! This is what the Jerusalemites are counting on. They have laid their hands on some assets and refused to pay rents for the warehouses that are in their hands [i. e.: that they use]. That is why we have to wait for government instructions from Istanbul![279]

In the next session, the Patriarch again defended the delay of the 'trustees' issue':

His Excellency, the Patriarch: The trustees, they [the Jerusalemites] have appointed wanted to lay their hands on the assets of the Holy Sepulcher. This is what prevented me from sending the documents for the elections to the dioceses. So I asked the government to define the functions (*waẓā'if*) of the trustees. To be clearer, I say: It was neither I nor anybody else... who made the trustees' issue... so complicated. It was the Jerusalemites who sent petitions and telegrams signed by their trustees to the Grand Vizierate and the Ministry of Justice in which they insisted that the assets of the Patriarchate and the monasteries in general belong to them (a*nna amlāk al-baṭrīyarkīya wa-l-adyira 'umūman taḫuṣṣuhum*). By this, they opened the issue from the start. And because the government asked us [then] to inform it, we sent it [the documents]. And the Council of Ministers specified it and further sent it to the civic department of the State Council (*šūrā ad-dawla*)... who will soon publish its resolution... I repeat again that it is not we, the clerics, who set up obstacles; but the Jerusalemites... That is why I asked for the trustee issue to be postponed until... instructions arrive. If the Jaffa delegate does not attach importance to the claims of the Jerusalemites, I excuse him for his lack of interest. Because these allegations of the Jerusalemites will open the way for the other cities in Palestine, and abroad. All of them will lay their hands on the assets of the Holy Sepulcher, and then there will no longer be any need for the Patriarchates' existence, nor for the Mixed Council.[280]

Jerusalem Delegate: I don't have knowledge about the 'allegations' that his Excellency... mentioned. I only repeat once more that his Excellency seeks to revive disagreement.

Acre Delegate: What the government really intended from the formation of the Mixed Council is the reformation of the schools (*iṣlāḥ al-madāris*) ... With sadness, I see that the Council has returned to the 'trustee-issue' that we were already were engaged with during the first couple of months. I am begging to return ... to the school budget that the Patriarch promised to discuss in ... todays' meeting.

Jerusalem Delegate: But it is the trustees who form the administrative body to manage the schools (*al-hay'a al-idārīya allatī tudīr al-madāris*). It does not make sense to discuss the budget before their appointment.

Nazareth Delegate: We don't deny the significance of the trustees. But we have been drowning in that issue for twenty meetings! His Excellency has declared he will not set it down for discussion before the interpretation has arrived from Istanbul. I demand to return to the schools and the budget.[281]

279 *Filasṭīn*, 3 January 1912: 100/3/5.
280 *Filasṭīn*, 6 January 1912: 101/3/3–4.
281 *Filasṭīn*, 6 January 1912: 101/3/4–5.

Jaffa Delegate: The statement of his Excellency the Patriarch ... could not convince me... to postpone their appointment – you may call them trustees or representatives or supervisors (*man yadʿūhum mutawallīn aw wukalāʾ aw nuẓẓār*) – for the dioceses in general and Jaffa in particular ... As I see that my brothers delegates wish to return to the issue of the schools, I will not resign from the sessions as [I] announced but I will not participate in any other discussion than about the trustees, unless I find it necessary to interfere.

Bethlehem Delegate: I agree with what the Jaffa delegate said. I demand to apply his request. Not only for Jaffa but also for all the other dioceses, given that the Council has already decided in its seventh session to keep the term 'trustees'.[282]

The discussion documented here is a typical example of the course of a debate in the Mixed Council. It shows that that the patriarch suspected the trustees in the dioceses of expanding their functions concerning the schools, churches, hospitals and welfare institutions, classified as local to the Patriarchate's *waqf* properties. It also illustrates how the content of a debate oscillated from one topic to the other: from the Jerusalemites' rent allowances to the trustees' councils in the dioceses, the reformation of Orthodox education and the calculation of the social budget. It also reveals typical alliances: there was usually a coalition between the delegates of Jaffa and Bethlehem (Ḥazbūn), who in general opposed the Jerusalem delegate (Ḥalabī), and often the Nazareth delegate (Baydas).

The 1912 Resolution and Responses on it

The '1912 Resolution', as I refer to it, issued by the Council of Ministers, was sent by the Grand Vizierate to the governor in February 1912. It reconsidered a report of the State Council (*šūrā ad-dawla*) from December 1911 and Resolution 139.[283] The 1912 Resolution dealt with the electoral system of the Mixed Council, its competences in school matters, the social budget, the rent allowances and trustees for the Jerusalemites, and in general, decided in favor of the Patriarchate.[284] It argued that the 1910 Resolution did not assign a fixed amount as rent allowances and the Jerusalemites had no right to demand anything in addition to the annual budget assigned to the Council.[285] Concerning the six notables that the Jerusalemite Orthodox had appointed as 'trustees' in the course of the Orthodox rebellion of 1908, the 1912 Resolution also criticized their appointment.[286] The 1910 Resolution had instructed trustees to be assigned to administer Orthodox institutions concerned with the local people in the Patri-

282 *Filasṭīn*, 6 January 1912: 101/3/5.

283 'Resolution 139' (30 Hazayran 327/June 1911) referred to the local trustees. See *Filasṭīn*, 25 November 1911: 89/3/5–4/1; 17 February 1912: 112/3/4–5.

284 *Filasṭīn*, 2 March 1912: 116/3/5–4/3.

285 *Filasṭīn*, 2 March 1912: 116/4/2–3.

286 *Filasṭīn*, 6 March 1912: 117/4/2.

archate's *villages and towns*, but not in Jerusalem.[287] The new order of the Grand Vizierate specified again that this 'only referred to places outside Jerusalem' (*muḫtaṣṣan bi-l-amākina al-ḫāriǧa ʿan qaṣbat al-Quds aš-šarīf*) and that inside Jerusalem, 'no places were found' for which trustees should be elected.[288]

Ḥalabī agitated against the 1912 Resolution and ʿĪsā switched to his side. In the Council, ʿĪsā monopolized a session to declare the new resolution 'illegitimate' (*ġayr qānūnī*) and 'impossible to accepted as constitutional' (*lā yumkin qabūluhu dustūran*). This resolution was grounded on reports by the Patriarchate and the governor, who was not instructed to represent the case of the people, ʿĪsā declared, since no commission of inquiry had heard both sides.[289] ʿĪsā declared that the clerics had falsely stated that the Jerusalemites had demanded 30,000 lira as rent allowances and quoted the 'juridical rule' (*al-qāʿida al-fuqahīya*): 'What is grounded on false claim is [consequently] false' (*mā buniya ʿalā l-fāsid fa-huwa fāsid*).[290]

While ʿĪsā stood with Ḥalabī, the Acre delegate, Mulkī, took sides with the patriarch. He was critical of Ḥalabī, claiming that the new order was only the outcome of the constant provocations by the Jerusalemites, and pleaded with the lay delegates to cooperate with the Patriarchate in the public interest (*maḥabbat al-maṣlaḥa al-ʿāmma*) and not to follow the agenda of ʿĪsā and Ḥalabī, who were making 'a lot of trouble' for the Council.[291] Ḥalabī responded concerning the new order in *Filasṭīn*, summarizing the history of the Orthodox Movement as a complete failure since the government had decided it was in favor of the Patriarchal *berats*:

> The spirit of enthusiasm (*rūḥ al-ḥamās*) beat in their hearts, their rebellion bubbled up and this spirit spread to the dioceses. They closed the churches and claimed they would gain their rights within a few weeks. They sent their delegations to Istanbul… and presented their demands to Niẓām Bāšā. Every time they swore not to give up on any of them. After some standing and sitting, the waste of lots of money and the exhaustion of one and a half years… all we received was the Resolution (of 1910) by the Council of Ministers. Its outcome was very bad (*sayyiʾan ǧiddan*) so that old and young united in refusing it, and put clothed justice and the Constitution in a suit of armor (*labs al-ḥadād ʿalā l-ʿadāla wa-d-dustūr*). Yet, it is obvious that the government refused most of their demands, relying on the imperial berats, and explaining that they (the Jerusalemites) had no right to claim the endowments for themselves and that their participation in the

287 '*Fī l-qurā wa-l-qaṣbāt al-mansūba ilā l-baṭrīyarkīya yanbaġī l-iḥāla maṭali hāḏihi al-muʾassasāt al-mutaʿalliqa bi-l-waṭanīyīn ilā mutawallīn yantaḫibuhum al-ahālī l-maḥallīyūn.*' *Filasṭīn*, 2 March 1912: 116/4/3.

288 *Filasṭīn*, 2 March 1912: 116/4/3.

289 For the text, see *Filasṭīn*, 25 November 1911: 89/3/5–4/2.

290 *Filasṭīn*, 6 March 1912: 117/4/1–2.

291 *Filasṭīn*, 9 March 1912: 118/4/1–3.

administration of the convents, visitors' hostels and revenues deriving from them was against the Patriarchate's privileges (*muḫill bi-imtiyāzāt al-Baṭrīkḫāna*).[292]

According to Ḥalabī, the prohibition of trustees for the Jerusalemites by the 1912 Resolution was an 'extremist' position and he said that it was another extremist stance, represented by a faction of Orthodox activists, to demand that all Orthodox convents, holy sites and revenues deriving from them should be administered by locals.[293] Instead, the Jerusalemite trustees should administer only churches, hospitals, schools and welfare institutions that 'concern the nationals' (*al-muta'alliqa bi-l-waṭanīyīn*), he said, and named three churches in Jerusalem (Mār Ya'qub, al-Arba'īna Šahīdan and as-Salḥīya) as essential for 'the protection of the honor of the *milla* and its interests' (*ḥifẓan li-šaraf al-milla wa-maṣlaḥatihā*).[294] Ultimately, however, Ḥalabī could not achieve his aim. In the course of 1912, he switched to a more reconciliatory strategy until he seemed to be in coalition with the patriarch and, in 1913, he was isolated in the Mixed Council, as will be shown later in this chapter. On the trustees' issue, there was no movement until the intervention of a Royal Commission from Istanbul under the leadership of the former governor, 'Azmī Bek, which is discussed in the section 'From Escalation to Reconciliation'.

7.2. Debates on Educational Reforms

Education as a Central Topic

The reform of education was a key demand of the Orthodox Movement. A lot of Arab Orthodox activists were pedagogues and considered the modernization of education 'the crown of every reform' (*ra's kull iṣlāḥ*),[295] and as *the* basic element (*al-'unṣur al-awwal*) for the reformation of society.[296] Schools were seen a tool for the creation of a new generation in line with the spirit of the Orthodox Renaissance, the Arab *nahḍa* and Ottomanism. Many Orthodox activists also favored female education, and the 'Isās frequently called for support for the Orthodox Welfare Association (*al-ǧam'īya al-ḫayrīya li-r-rūm urṯūḏuks*),[297] and the Association of Orthodox Women for the Support of Orphan Girls (*ǧam'īyat as-*

292 *Filasṭīn*, 6 March 1912: 117/4/1.

293 '*Išrāk al-'awāmm fī idārat al-adyira wa-l-mazārāt wa-l-wāridāt al-muta'alliqa bihā muḫālif li-l-'awā'id al-qadīma wa-li-mā taṣraḥ al-barā'āt al-'ālīya wa-muḫill bi-mtiyāzāt al-Baṭrīyarkīya al-maḏkūra.*' *Filasṭīn*, 16 March 1912: 120/4/1.

294 *Filasṭīn*, 16 March 1912: 120/4/1–2.

295 *Filasṭīn*, 28 September 1912: 175/1/1–4.

296 *Filasṭīn*, 30 December 1911: 99/4/1.

297 *Filasṭīn*, 25 May 1912: 139/3/3; 18 June 1913: 246/3/5.

sayyidāt al-urṯūḏuksīya li-ʿaḍd al-yatīmāt), which was concerned for girls' education, and tried to raise funding for them.[298]

However, the current state of Orthodox schools was considered disastrous; the curriculum was outdated, and teaching was mostly conducted in Greek, a language that 'nobody can understand', the journalist Ǧibrān al-Maṭar complained.[299] Indeed, during the late Ottoman period, the number of Arab Orthodox in Palestine and the Levant diminished through emigration or the conversion of local Orthodox to Protestantism or Catholicism, and competition between Western Protestant and Catholic institutions in the Arab East also expressed itself through educational offers to local Christians.[300] The Syrian Protestant College in Beirut and the colleges that the Russian Orthodox Church maintained in Nazareth and Beit Jala, where many Arab Orthodox elites had received their education, became 'think tanks' of the Orthodox Renaissance activists in Palestine. According to them, the Patriarchate's neglect of education was a central factor in the increasing number of conversions of Orthodox youth to other congregations because they perceived that education there was much more progressive than in Orthodox schools. This argument was especially relevant since several Orthodox schools were closed during the 1910 crisis because communities were no longer provided with a budget or teachers. In remote areas, children were left without education.[301]

An Orthodox teacher, Ǧurǧī al-Ḫūrī Yaʿqūb, from Beit Sahour evaluated the state of 4,300 students in 85 Orthodox schools in Palestine, among them 63 schools for male atudents and 22 for females, who were taught by 861 teachers, as 'devoid of all progress and success' (*ʿāriya ʿan at-taqaddum wa-n-naǧāḥ*) and 'chaotic' (*aḥwāluhā fawḍā*). Education must 'elevate the habits and moral values of the citizens, Yaʿqūb pleaded, after 'oppression has been eating them for the past hundred years'.[302] Mismanagement in the faculties particularly bothered him.[303] He called for the school law to be reformed, predicting that, otherwise, more local people would turn to foreign schools.[304] Yaʿqūb clarified that it was not enough to change the text books; reforms should create a consistent curriculum and staff that were 'well trained in the profession of teaching according to pedagogical standards' and with a 'style of ethics that a skillful teacher could

298 *Filasṭīn*, 15 July 1911: 51/3/3.
299 *Filasṭīn*, 17 April 1912: 128/4/1–2.
300 For Protestant missionary efforts in Lebanon and Syria, see Makdisi 2008; Ferree 2014.
301 See *Filasṭīn*, 3 January 1912: 100/3/2–5; 4 May 1912: 133/3/5–4/1.
302 *Filasṭīn*, 30 December 1911: 99/4/1.
303 Here, he referred to the report of a former school inspector, Archimandrite Kaladion, published in the patriarchal magazine *New Zion (Ṣihyūn al-Ǧadīda). Filasṭīn*, 24 July 1912: 156/3/4/1.
304 *Filasṭīn*, 24 July 1912: 156/3/4/1.

use to impart knowledge in dealing with the pupils'.[305] In contrast, he said, the teachers graduating from the Orthodox college damaged the education of the Orthodox youth, concluding that the nation had the impression 'that we do not want the Orthodox community to succeed and progress'.[306] This was exactly what occupied the laity in the Mixed Council, was will be demonstrated in the following sections by illustrating its disputes on educational reforms.

The Competences of the School Board

From 1911 to 1912, the question of how the new school board (*ʿumdat al-madāris*) that was to supervise educational reforms in the dioceses should be constituted was a topic of extended quarrels in the Council. The issue was the role of the local trustees in the school reforms and the question of whether they should be members in the school board, or whether the board should consist of members of the Mixed Council, as the clerical faction wanted. The laity, on the other hand, wanted to separate the school board from membership in the Council. Since the Council acted as supervisory authority (*niẓāra*) over educational reforms, it was not possible, in the words of al-ʿĪsā, that 'the judge and the judged should be the same person' (*al-ḥākim wa-l-maḥkūm ʿalayhi wāḥidan*),[307] while the patriarch claimed the privilege of school management (*al-idāra*) for himself, since the Patriarchate would provide the finance for educational reforms.[308] The positions of individual delegates changed in the course of the debate, and the question of the composition of the school board was a subject of conflict not only between the laity and the clergy but also between Jerusalem and the dioceses. This rivalry caused particular confrontations between the Nazareth delegate, Baydas, and the Jerusalem delegate, Ḥalabī, during the summer of 1911.[309]

Ḥalabī insisted that at least four Jerusalemite trustees should be included in the school board since the Jerusalemites would not accept interference into their educational matters from 'outside'.[310] This was refused by the delegates of Acre and Nazareth and by Yūsuf al-ʿĪsā, who said, 'If the desired reforms in the dioceses depend on the tolerance of the Jerusalemites, the dioceses are not in real need of these reforms.'[311] It is clear that, in the spring of 1911, Ḥalabī and Baydas

305 '*Mutamarrinīn ʿalā mihnat at-tadrīs ḍimna dāʾirat al-bīdāġūǧī ayy al-uslūb al-adabī allaḏī yastaḫdimuhu al-muʿallim al-māhir li-talqīn al-ʿulūm wa-at-taṣarruf maʿ at-talāmīḏ.*' *Filasṭīn*, 24 July 1912: 156/3/4/1.

306 *Filasṭīn*, 24 July 1912: 156/4/1.

307 *Filasṭīn*, 15 July 1911: 51/3/2.

308 *Filasṭīn*, 29 July 1911: 55/2/1–5.

309 See *Filasṭīn*, 19 July 1911: 52/3/2; 26 July 1911: 54/3/2; 29 July 1911: 55/2/1–5; 2 August 1911: 56/2/1–4; 2 September 1911: 65/3/3.

310 *Filasṭīn*, 19 July 1911: 52/3/2.

311 '*Iḏā kāna kayān al-iṣlāḥ al-marġūb li-l-abrašīyāt mutawaqqifan ʿalā tasāhul al-Qudsīyīn fa-l-abrašīyāt fī ġanī ʿan hāḏā l-iṣlāḥ.*' *Filasṭīn*, 26 July 1911: 54/3/2.

had submitted to the Council a draft of the future composition of the school board, but the decision was postponed. Months later, Baydas accused Ḥalabī of having falsified his draft.[312] Ḥalabī, who was at that time apparently instructed to edit the text of the sessions' reports, claimed in a letter to *Filasṭīn* that Baydas had 'twisted' the truth and the texts had been checked by Ḫalīl as-Sakākīnī, director of the Constitutional School in Jerusalem.[313] The Council's fruitless debate on the school board aroused public anger. In a letter entitled 'Preferring the Essential over the Important' (*tafḍīl al-ahamm ʿalā l-muhimm*), Ḫalīl Qazāqīh from Bethlehem claimed that the delegates had no right (*lā ṣalāḥīya*) to get lost in 'scattered details' (*mutafarriqāt*),[314] and Būlos Šahādeh from Jerusalem warned the delegates not to spread the discord ruling the Council into the hearts of the population.[315]

In September 1911, the Council made a first attempt to elect the school board. When the delegates agreed on three candidates from outside the Council, the patriarch left in fury, but was brought back and asked to nominate the candidates himself. This was not accepted by Ḥalabī, who then declared the session 'illegitimate' (*ġayr qānūnīya*). Then, the laity indicated that Bandalī al-Ǧawzī, Ḫalīl as-Sakākīnī and ʿĪsā al-ʿĪsā should be appointed, all Orthodox activists, and the clerics 'changed their facial expressions' (*taġayyarat malāmiḥ wuǧūhihim*) in rage. Finally, the patriarch appointed two Greek clerics.[316] This was met with protests from the population. The Orthodox of Bethlehem sent a protest letter demanding that the board should consist only of 'nationals' (*ʿuḍwīyīn waṭanīyīn*).[317] The Council then appointed six 'nationals' from outside the Council: Bandalī al-Ǧawzī, ʿĪsā Iskandar al-Maʿlūf, Naḫleh Zurayq (all Orthodox reformers), Būlos al-Ḫawlī, Ḫalīl Bek Saʿd and Tawfīq Qazamā.[318] Suddenly, the sessions were interrupted and the patriarch declared the start of the Council's summer break to prevent the formation of the school board according along these lines since none of these candidates belonged to the clerical fraction.[319] Consequently, elections for the board were not conducted before the beginning of the new school year.

312 *Filasṭīn*, 2 August 1911: 56/2/1–4; 7 October 1911: 75/3/5.
313 *Filasṭīn*, 9 August 1911: 58/3/4–5.
314 *'Li-yaṣīr hāʾulāʾi al-mutawallīn wāsiṭat al-muwāṣala bayna al-umma al-urṯūduksīya wa-nawābihā allaḏīna fī l-maǧlis.' Filasṭīn*, 9 August 1911: 58/3/5 – /4/1.
315 *Filasṭīn*, 12 August 1911: 59/3/4–4/1.
316 These were Rīrbūr al-Afransī and Bandalmiyos. *Filasṭīn*, 6 September 1911: 66/3/4–5.
317 *Filasṭīn*, 9 September 1911: 67/3/4–5.
318 *Filasṭīn*, 9 September 1911: 67/4/1.
319 *Filasṭīn*, 7 October 1911: 75/3/5–4/1.

In October 1911, the candidates for the school board changed again, and the formation of a permanent board failed as a result of internal quarrels.[320] The Council appointed a 'temporary' board consisting of three members of the Mixed Council, who were to allocate the school budget for the dioceses: Archimandrite Yūsuf, and the opponents Ilyās al-Ḥalabī and Ḫalīl Baydas. Meanwhile, the Council was to look for 'competent men' (*riǧāl akifāʾ*) for a 'permanent' board.[321] The Jerusalemite Orthodox opposed the temporary board. Arguing for their 'national interests', a delegation approached the governor and protested 'against the reopening of the schools in the old state' and under 'Greek influence', calling for their schools in Jerusalem to be managed by local trustees:[322]

> As demonstrated, our respected clergy are determined to open the schools tomorrow in the same state as they were in the old days. This means that they still intend to poison the emotions of our youth (*yarmūn fīhā ilā tasmīm šuʿūr nāšiʾatinā*) and teach them their Greek language and literature, and the geography of their country (*tadrīs luġatihim al-yūnānīya wa-ādābihā wa-ǧuġrāfīyat bilādihim*) and other things through which they intend to spread Greek influence, to attack our Ottomanism and kill our national feelings (*našr an-nufūḏ al-yūnānī wa-mass ʿuṯmānīyatanā wa-qatl ʿawāṭifinā l-waṭanīya*). Their intentions have become known to the central government. That is why it decided that it is necessary to reform themt (the schools) and transfer their management to supervisors from among the nationals (*ilā l-mutawallīn min al-waṭanīyīn*) in order to repel this mistreatment. But the clergy still disdain the orders of our sublime government and continue their despotism (*mustamirran ʿalā istibdādihi*) ... We invoke the reform of your schools according to the content of the order, which means that local councils of supervisors should manage them and implement the curriculum and education as required by national interests (*ʿalā mā yaqtaḍīh al-maṣlaḥa al-waṭanīya*), and (furthermore) their closure until the government has implemented the order of the Council of Ministers [the 1910 Resolution].[323]

The governor could do nothing. In the autumn of 1911, negotiations between Archimandrite Yūsuf, Ḥalabī and Baydas over the distribution of the school budget failed and were interrupted.

Rivalries about the Composition of the School Board

In the summer of 1912, the debate over the composition of the school board took a new turn and became a feud between the patriarch and Yūsuf al-ʿĪsā. The patriarch argued that it was his privilege to nominate the members of the school board from the Council, who would then be confirmed by the Council. ʿĪsā

320 The Council appointed ʿĪsā Iskandar Maʿlūf as president, one clerical and one lay delegate, and Iftīm Mašbak from Jerusalem. When Maʿlūf refused, the Council declared the formation of a 'permanent' board had failed. See *Filasṭīn*, 7 October 1911: 75/4/1.

321 *Filasṭīn*, 7 October 1911: 75/4/1.

322 *Filasṭīn*, 7 October 1911: 75/4/1.

323 *Filasṭīn*, 07 October 1911: 75/4/2.

countered that, if the Council was to have the authority over the school board, it should vote for the candidates in free elections, and they should be from outside the Council as the laity had demanded by consent.[324] However, it emerged that, in the summer of 1912, the Jerusalemite delegate, Ḥalabī, was willing to cooperate with the patriarch since he was one of the persons nominated, and the delegates from Salṭ and Nazareth similarly changed sides. ʿĪsā was outraged:

> We all agreed on a secret selection by lot, provided that we select [the candidates] from outside the Council … It is not possible to unite the supervisor and the administrator in one person … Either it [the Council] has absolute legitimacy (*aṣ-ṣalāḥīya at-tāmma*) or no legitimacy at all! If his Excellency is privileged to appoint the board without considering our opinion, he should leave us out [entirely]. He cannot appoint candidates from the Council … and then tell us: I have already appointed [them], you just confirm (*antum faqaṭ ṣādiqū*)![325]

After long discussions, the delegates from Jaffa, Acre and Bethlehem stood against the delegates of Salt, Nazareth and Jerusalem and the clerical delegates. Muṭrān Sufrūnīyus declared that, since the 1910 Resolution did not give the Council the explicit right to appoint the school board, they had simply created a precedent. In dramatic words, ʿĪsā announced legal steps:

> I consider this … the death sentence for this Council (*ḥukm bi-l-iʿdām li-hāḏā l-maǧlis*) because the people (*aš-šaʿb*) will … notice … that nothing about the schools has improved. It will hold the Council responsible … and will no longer care if this Council is running or closed. I have said it before and I repeat that the responsibility to protection [the schools] imposes on us [the duty] to constitute a school board of specialists who are entirely dedicated to their work and from outside the Council. I consider your decision as illegitimate (*ġayr qānūnī*)… and as opposing the government resolution. I will not be content protesting … here. I and those of you who are with me will pursue legal steps with the Ottoman government to prove that this is against the [1910] Resolution.[326]

After being interrupted for a second time by the summer break of 1912, the dispute about the composition of the school board continued into the autumn due to continuing internal factionalism. During that summer, Ḥalabī resigned from the board. Then, the patriarch appointed the reformer and activist Ḫalīl as-Sakākīnī, since the Jerusalemite Orthodox opposed Ḥalabī's membership on the board.[327] The confusion went on. Sakākīnī soon resigned because of personal conflicts with the patriarch, but the efforts of mediators secured his return.[328]

324 *Filasṭīn*, 18 June 1912: 146/3/4–2/2.
325 *Filasṭīn*, 29 June 1912: 149/4/1–2.
326 *Filasṭīn*, 29 June 1912: 149/4/2–3.
327 *Filasṭīn*, 14 September 1912: 171/3/4–4/1; 28 September 1912: 175/3/4–4/1; 23 October 1912: 181/3/4–4/3.
328 *Filasṭīn*, 23 October 1912: 181/3/4–4/3.

Archimandrite Yūsuf resigned after being appointed financial supervisor of the Holy Synod and Archimandrite Dūsīṯīyus replaced him.[329] At the end of October 1912, Sakākīnī left the school board for good and Ḥalabī returned, declaring that he was accepting this post temporarily, and Archimandrite Yūsuf also returned.[330] Now, the board was back to its original composition of 1911: Archimandrite Yūsuf, Ḥalabī and Baydas.[331] Meanwhile, Ḥalabī was confronted with internal opposition in Jerusalem because he was pleading for reconciliation with the Patriarchate. Since Russia had cut 12,000 lira from its payment to Jerusalem, the Patriarchate was under pressure, and an Orthodox delegation from Jerusalem was to approach the Russians to ask for financial support for their schools. Ḥalabī was supposed to hinder the delegation, an anonymous author declared in *Filasṭīn*, stating that Ḥalabī had been reinstalled on the school board in place of Sakākīnī as Damianos's 'shield' (*daraqa*).[332]

From October 1912 onwards, Ḥalabī became increasingly isolated on the Council and the Orthodox activist scene because, for reasons that are unclear, he had become reconciled with the Patriarchate. In *Filasṭīn*, he responded to his opponents and presented himself as an intermediary between the Patriarchate and the people. Addressing the 'sons of the Orthodox *milla* in Jerusalem', he declared that he was seeking a balance between various interests by 'making myself a bridge' (*aʿmalu nafsī ǧisran*), and said:

> I served the interest of the milla with full loyalty and honor. And … I would have been able to accomplish a lot of things if there had not been people standing beside me as an observation post to demolish everything I built under the excuse of patriotic passion (*taḥta sitār al-ġīra al-waṭanīya*)… I would have spoken with even more honesty if I were not a person who hates sowing [internal] strife and obstacles in the way of the unity of the milla (*bazar al-fitan wa-ilqāʾ al-ʿaṯarāt fī sabīl ittiḥād al-milla*). Concerning the school board… I have not accepted it out of greed for income, as there is no income, or in ambition for personal glory… and I don't work for the goals of the monastic order… If time had allowed me, I would have been a teacher and a director. I have competences for this [position] and I am proud to offer my best expertise to our schools. I accepted this function temporarily till the Jerusalemites can agree on a permanent person… for [representing] the rights of the Jerusalemites on the school board… and I will be grateful to leave this position [again].[333]

329 *Filasṭīn*, 28 September 1912: 175/3/5; 23 October 1912: 181/3/4–4/3.
330 *Filasṭīn*, 23 October 1912: 182/4/1; 182/4/3–4.
331 *Filasṭīn*, 7 October 1911: 75/4/1.
332 *Filasṭīn*, 23 October 1912: 182/4/1–2.
333 *Filasṭīn*, 2 November 1912: 185/4/2.

The Reopening of the Mār Miṭrī School in Jerusalem: Fall 1912

Reports of the Council's sessions in September and October 1912 were dominated by conflicts over the agenda of the Orthodox school board; especially ʿĪsā's attacks on the members of the board, Archimandrite Yūsuf and Ḫalīl Baydas, about the case of the Mār Miṭrī School in Jerusalem. This was a boys' college situated near the Convent in Jerusalem's Old City, the majority of whose students were of Greek origin, and in October 1912, it was reopened unilaterally by the school board and the will of the patriarch.[334] ʿĪsā claimed that, although the Council previously decided on a budget of 4,000 lira for the opening of two other new boarding schools in Jerusalem, one boys' college and one girls' college, money had been spent on Mār Miṭrī without prior consultation of the Council, and without the Patriarchate handing over the school budget to the Council, which deprived it of its function as supervisory authority over schools. ʿĪsā said before the Council:

> As I see… that the Patriarchate has opened the schools in their old state with the same program and without our knowledge, and as we decided in the Council to open two colleges for which we calculated the expenses and appointed the number of students … and as the Patriarchate has not yet paid … its annual premiums … but it has started to spend money [from that budget], and as it claimed that it would hand it over to us in the new year … I demand that the Council be given its rights so that it can accomplish something… before entering the new invoices. Otherwise I will consider every dirham spent on the Mār Miṭrī School, which is NOT the school we decided on, as a donation (*tabarruʿan*) frrm the Patriarchate … The relevant authority (*marǧiʿ*) of the school board is the Council… As this committee did not consult the Council… I consider everything it has done illegitimate (*ġayr qānūnī*).[335]

ʿĪsā initiated a campaign against the reopening of Mār Miṭrī unilaterally by the will of the patriarch, who also appointed the teachers and limited the participation of students to certain towns so that the dioceses were disregarded. In his editorial 'That was the Last Drop that Makes the Barrel Overflow' (*Laqad Tafaḥa al-Kayl*), ʿĪsā claimed:

> We [the lay delegates] said: reformation of the schools is the head of each reform! Appoint a committee for it that will take them [the schools] out of their present disastrous state… They [the clergy] refused, appointed a committee of Council members and gave us holidays… We went away and returned, we sat and asked them what happened to the schools. They said: This is a curiosity from you! The authority of the Council is the patriarch and he is satisfied with what has been done in them [the schools] … And so it happened… what happened in the Mixed Council… We had decided to open two boarding schools… in Jerusalem and allocated 4,000 lira for that. We set them up for 60 students, divided between the dioceses… Now, we see nothing of that: no

334 *Filasṭīn*, 28 September 1912: 175/3/3–4.
335 *Filasṭīn*, 28 September 1912: 175/3/4.

> money, no schools, no curriculum… Yesterday, we found out that his Excellency has reopened the Mār Miṭrī School without informing the Council; and accepted 90 instead of 60 students according to his personal will. These students come from five or six towns without giving the rest of the dioceses their share. Concerning the [planned] girls' school, nothing has changed… Although the income that the Convent pays to those… teachers comes from the nation's assets (*min māl al-umma*), it does not want to show the invoices to the Council… There is no interest in reform, the milla is ridiculed, the lay delegates are mocked, the government and its resolutions disregarded. We shall see if the Ottoman government will tolerate this mockery, this laughter and the disregard of its orders.[336]

Supported by notables from Bethlehem and their delegate Ḥazbūn, ʿIsā petitioned the new governor Muhdī Bek on behalf of the schools, but without support from the rest of the laity on the Council.[337] Referring to the 1910 Resolution, Resolution 139 and the 1912 Resolution, ʿIsā demanded that the Council receive 'all its competencies' (*ǧamīʿ aṣ-ṣalāḥīya*), the annual budget for Orthodox schools, hospitals and welfare institutions, the formation of the trustees' councils (*maǧlis al-mutawallīn*) in the dioceses, and that the local government should control the Council. He reminded Muhdī Bek that, 'as a representative of the constitutional government, you are required to protect the dignity of this government; and the greatest protection of the dignity of this government is the implementation of its resolutions'.[338] ʿĪsā's intervention annoyed the patriarch. When Orthodox notables from Beit Jala inquired about why the school reforms were delayed, he shouted: 'Why do you ask me about that! Don't ask me, ask Yūsuf al-ʿĪsā as he is nowadays the patriarch!' The ʿĪsās responded to that get-out sarcastically casting Damianos as an 'absolute ruler':

> Why is his Excellency so outraged … and does not answer? Is it not he who is the president of the Council? Does the dignity of the Council not fall back to its president? Or does he want the absolute power (*al-ḥukm al-muṭlaq*) that he has pursued until now? Does he hate shared power (*al-ḥukm al-muqayyad*)…? This is another thing to be investigated![339]

Shortly after, ʿĪsā published a statistic concerning Mār Miṭrī after its reopening in its 'old state' in order to demonstrate the Patriarchate's 'absolutism' by the example of this school. It is not known from where ʿĪsā obtained the invoice, however, it revealed the dominance of the Greek element in the school: 334 of the 432 students were of Greek nationality while only 98 were registered as Ottomans.

336 *Filasṭīn*, 28 September 1912: 175/1/1–4.

337 The delegates of Nazareth and Acre refused to sign, and the Salṭ delegate abstained. Ḥalabī, now in alliance with Damianos, did not sign because 'he wanted reconciliation'. *Filasṭīn*, 2 October 1912: 176/4/2.

338 *Filasṭīn*, 2 October 1912: 176/4/1.

339 *Filasṭīn*, 2 October 1912: 176/4/3.

Furthermore, 13 teachers taught in Greek, earning 1,476 lira a year, and four teachers taught in Arabic, earning only 288 lira a year. Another two teachers taught in Turkish and earned 108 lira.[340]

It is important to note that, after the hasty reopening of Mār Miṭrī and ʿĪsā's protest campaign against it, the clergy declared that the patriarch was to appoint the board and act as the supervising authority over the schools in Jerusalem and the other communities through his own 'supervisors' (*nuẓẓār*).[341] The Jerusalemite Orthodox did not want the patriarchal supervisors, and approached Governor Muhdī Bek, who could not do anything about it.[342] Meanwhile, Damianos had sent abbots to the dioceses to appoint supervisors over the schools that suited him rather than the local trustees. An anonymous letter in *Filasṭīn* called for attention:

> Attention, attention, don't fall into that trap (*al-ḥaḏr al-ḥaḏr min al-wuqūʿ fī hāḏā l-faḫḫ*)! It is the obligation of every city if there are people in it who still have honor in their blood (*damm aš-šahāma*) to resist the head of the Convent (*yaqif fī wağh raʾīs ad-dayr*) and tell him: your schools are a shame (*madārisukum ḥarām*)! There is money … many teachers and who knows how many supervisors. We don't want school supervisors but the trustees that the government allocated so that they can perform their functions: the management (*idāra*) of the churches, schools, hospitals and poor houses belonging to the milla … This is what the population has to do if their leaders and notables fear God and care for their good reputation (*yuḥāḏirū ʿalā as-sumʿa al-ḥasana*).[343]

In January 1913, ʿĪsā published the 'Regulations for the Inspections of the Schools in the Dioceses of the Patriarchate' (*niẓām an-niẓārāt fī madāris abrašīyāt al-kursī*), according to which each town was to establish its own inspection authority (*niẓāra*) consisting of at least three lay members elected by Orthodox notables and approved by the metropolitan. This *niẓāra* was to be in charge of all administrational and educational matters in the schools, including the appointment of teachers and curriculums, and was to report annually to the patriarch. ʿĪsā gave a reminder that, according to the 1910 Resolution, it was the local trustees (!) who were to elect these inspectors, not the patriarch.[344]

At this point, in January 1913, disputes about the school inspectors were dropped because the Council became occupied with the rotation of delegates in

340 Among the subjects taught were natural sciences, bookkeeping, geography of Palestine, history, logic, psychology and religion, and also sport. *Filasṭīn*, 2 October 1912: 176/3/3; 176/4/2.

341 *Filasṭīn*, 19 October 1912: 181/3/4–4/3.

342 However, he gave permission to the Orthodox notables to use the Jerusalemite CUP office for their Sunday gatherings. *Filasṭīn*, 6 November 1912: 186/4/2–3.

343 *Filasṭīn*, 6 November 1912: 186/4/1–2.

344 *Filasṭīn*, 4 January 1913: 203/3/4–5.

the Mixed Council as will be documented later this chapter, and the Council ceased meeting in summer 1913. After its revival in January 1914, it took some quick decisions, including the appointment of a new school board, which will be documented in the section 'From Escalation to Reconciliation'.

The Reopening of the Orthodox School in Jaffa and Patriarchal Responses
Shortly after the campaign that ʿĪsā initiated against the reopening of Mār Miṭrī, the Orthodox community of Jaffa reopened their school, which had been closed down during the rebellion. In the Mixed Council, Yūsuf al-ʿĪsā tried unsuccessfully to gain the support of the other delegates and a share of the annual school budget. The clerical delegates refused to take any responsibility in the matter since the school had been closed down during the Orthodox rebellion and had now been unilaterally reopened by the locals but without the approval of the Patriarchate. According to the clergy, this violated the patriarchal privileges, especially since the school belonged to a *waqf*.[345] ʿĪsā replied in the Council with a furious outburst, affirming that 'the people of Jaffa can do without you and your schools and your money' (*ahālī Yāfā fī ġanī ʿankum wa-ʿan madārisikum wa-ʿan darāhimikum*).[346]

In spring, the Jaffans implemented a new curriculum, following the example of Sakākīnī's Constitutional School in Jerusalem, and started teaching at their own expense without receiving a budget from the Patriarchate but through financial support of Arab Orthodox activists and families. For instance, in Jaffa, they organized a 'family cinema festival' in support of the school,[347] and the Womens' Association for the Support of Female Orphans ran bazaars to raise money.[348] Orthodox migrants based in South America, Egypt and Lebanon also supported the campaign for Jaffa's Orthodox school and sent a total of 375 francs.[349] This represented a minor victory for the Orthodox Renaissance on the local level. In July 1913, a triumphant article in *Filasṭīn* testified that the pupils had passed their first-year exams in Mathematics, Geography, Arabic, English, Bookkeeping and Sport. The results were satisfying and *Filasṭīn* declared, 'This proves the huge difference between the former state of that school when it was run by the monks and its current state.'[350]

345 *Filasṭīn*, 10 May 1913: 235/4/1–2; 14 May 1913: 236/4/1–2.
346 *Filasṭīn*, 14 May 1913: 236/4/2.
347 *Filasṭīn*, 5 March 1913: 218/3/4; 12 March 1913: 220/3/5.
348 *Filasṭīn*, 7 May 1913: 234/4.
349 *Filasṭīn* published the names of the donors and amount of their donation. Among them were al-ʿĪsā Ḫalīl Dakart/Dakrat (100 francs); ʿĪsā and Sulaymān Ṣāfīh (20 francs); Yaʿqūb Ṣāfī (40 francs); Ḥanā Ǧirǧis al-Ḥalabī (30 francs); Ǧirǧis Manṣūr Iḫwān (40 francs); ʿAṭāʾallāh an-Naǧǧār (20 francs); Bernard Ḥamāmeh (25 francs) and Wahbeh al-ʿĪsā (50 francs). *Filasṭīn*, 14 May 1913: 236/3/4–5.
350 *Filasṭīn*, 19 July 1913: 255/2/5.

Following the reopening of Jaffa's Orthodox school and a series of minor clashes between the patriarch and ʿĪsā in the Council, the patriarch set about working towards ʿĪsā's excommunication, trying to remove him as the established leader of the opposition to the Patriarchate.[351] In June 1913, he forwarded a ban against ʿIsā, signed by a number of clergy, to the Holy Synod.[352] ʿĪsā explained that this ban had no practical consequences since his confessional affiliation was defined by his 'civic' status as a member of the Orthodox Church, confirmed by Ottoman law. Defining the intra-Orthodox conflict as 'civic not religious', ʿĪsā recalled all the central reform demands of the Movement that had occupied the Mixed Council since 1910:

> The excommunication is null and void (*al-ḥaram fāsid*) as the conflict between us and the monks is civic and not religious (*madanī lā dīnī*). It is impossible to put down the sacred religion of heaven to make it a tool for worldly desires ... So, let us talk in a civilized manner. Oh, you Masters: We are no longer living in the age of ignorance when the civil authority (*as-sulṭa al-madanīya*) submitted to the religious authority and implemented its orders ... I consider myself Orthodox by the mercy of the Ottoman sultanic census (*bi-niʿmat qūšān an-nufūs as-sulṭānī l-ʿuṯmānī*), which is in my hands and not by the mercy of your group, which is alien to us ethnically and strange to the (Ottoman) homeland (*ṭuġmatikum al-ġarība ʿannā ǧinsan wa-waṭanan*). I know, and you know, that your excommunication will change nothing about [my] civil status. The conflict between us is civic and not religious because it is the government of Istanbul that has set the criteria in it ...
>
> If you think, you can cut off my hands or my tongue ... and hinder me from defending the milla .... you are wasting your time and will be disappointed. We ask you to implement the government resolution: what has religion to do with it (*mā daḫlu d-dīn fī ḏālika*)? We ask you to hand over the schools to the experts, so our kids will receive a patriotic Ottoman education instead of being exposed to your influence ... What has religion to do with that? We asked you kindly and with humility not to disperse the fortune of the awqāf as that is not for the benefit of the umma. Is there a violation of religion in that? We asked you to appoint trustees in accordance with the government resolution and to hand over to them the schools, churches, hospitals and national endowments (*al-awqāf al-waṭanīya*), and we are not greedy for the institutions belonging to your ... monastery. Where is blasphemy in that (*ayyu kufr fī d-dīn fī hāḏā l-amr*)?...
>
> Be sure, you Masters, that an excommunication would concern me spiritually and emotionally more than your ban could ever do if it were issued by a simple, weak village priest.[353]

351 Damianos tried before to remove ʿĪsā from the Council and brought three legal cases against him in 1912. See *Filasṭīn*, 26 June 1912: 148/3/3; 29 June 1912: 149/3/5–4/2; 3 July 1912: 150/3/4–5; 10 July 1912: 152/1/1–3.

352 *Filasṭīn*, 25 June 1913: 248/3/3–4.

353 *Filasṭīn*, 25 June 1913: 248/1/2–4.

The situation between the Patriarchate and the Orthodox of Jaffa was about to escalate.[354] But ʿĪsā stayed triumphant. Māǧid Bek intervened on his behalf, and Damianos was forced to gather the Synod and 'lift the excommunication' (*rafaʿū al-ḥaram*), ʿĪsā wrote.[355]

7.3. Debates on the Social Budget

The social budget for Orthodox churches, health care, schools and welfare in the dioceses was, according to the 1910 Resolution, to be assigned to the Council at the beginning of the administrative year, which usually started in August. Due to rivalries between Jerusalem and the dioceses, the method for allocating the budget was a constant subject of disagreement in the Mixed Council. Some delegates thought that the budget for welfare should be distributed according to the size of the population (*ʿadad an-nufūs*). Others wanted to distribute it according to individual needs in each town. There were also arguments about which should be decided first – the amount of the social budget or the method for allocating it.

First of all, what made the debate difficult was the fact that the amount that the Council had to deal with was never made transparent by the Patriarchate, which neither presented receipts for revenues nor gave information on the budget negotiations that had taken place in the Holy Synod. Because the amount of the social budget was never revealed, and since the delegates could not agree on how to prioritize the allocation of the budget, the debate is difficult to follow. At some point the negotiations about the budget reached a point of tension and were interrupted. What makes it more difficult to evaluate the debate, is the fact that decisions on its distribution taken in the Council often seemed to contradict earlier agreements. In the following, the Council's debates on the social budget will be presented chronologically.

At the end of 1911, the Council agreed on a budget of 5,000 lira for social welfare, namely 'the housing of the poor and their other needs' in all the dioceses. To deal with the distribution, a committee was appointed, consisting of the delegates of Nazareth and Salṭ and Archimandrite Makarios.[356] The Orthodox of Bethlehem protested to the Council, asking for 5,000 lira for social welfare for them alone, which was rejected by the patriarch.[357] Then, budget negotiations were dropped and picked up again in June 1912.

354 *Filasṭīn*, 28 June 1913: 249/3/3; 2 July 1913: 250/3/1.
355 *Filasṭīn*, 2 July 1913: 250/3/1.
356 *Filasṭīn*, 27 December 1911: 98/3/4.
357 *Filasṭīn*, 31 January 1912: 107/4/1.

In June, before the new administrative year was to start in August, the laity pressed for the release of the budget to the dioceses. After negotiations, the Council assigned 14,000 lira for Orthodox schools, and *Filasṭīn* published the details of the method of allocation to the various cities. The largest share, 4,300 lira, was received by Jerusalem: 4,000 lira to be spent on an existing boys' college and a future girls' college for a total of 70 pupils, and 300 lira on kindergartens in Jerusalem.[358] The dioceses of Jaffa, Acre, Nazareth, Bethlehem and Salṭ were to receive a total of 3,150 lira: 610 lira each, plus 100 lira extra for a boys' and a girls' college and the kindergarten in Jaffa. Ramallah received 510 lira; the boys' college in Beit Jala 350 lira, and Kerak 300 lira. Also, Ṭaybeh receiveed 192 lira, al-Faḥīṣ 192 lira, Ajloun 192 lira, Bayt Sahour 170 lira, Ǧafnah 132 lira, Bir Zeit 132 lira, Nablus 120 lira and Kafr Kanā 120 lira, and Irbid 80 lira. The cities of Haifa, Madaba, Ḥiṣn, Lod, Ramla and Gaza were assigned 25 lira each, and 40 other villages received a total of 2,400 lira. The school board was to receive 520 lira, and 140 lira was to be held in reserve.[359] In addition, the sum of 1,500 lira was allocatedfor the maintenance of churches, 3,500 lira for health care and 2,500 lira for social welfare, in all the dioceses, including Jerusalem and 1,500 lira should be kept in reserve for Council expenses.[360]

In general, social welfare was a major cost to the Patriarchate, especially in Jerusalem where the bi-weekly provision of bread for the poor cost the Patriarchate more than 1,000 lira a year, and it was decided that half of it should be covered by the social budget.[361] As described earlier, the Jerusalemite Orthodox and the clergy disagreed about the classification of the rent allowances paid by the Patriarchate to the local people. While the Patriarchate classified them as welfare for the housing of the poor in Jerusalem, delegate Ḥalabī interpreted them as compensation for the property of Orthodox families that, in the past, had been registered in the name of the Convent. After a series of petitions and counter-petitions over whether or not the rent allowances should be separated from the social budget, the 1912 Resolution, issued by the Grand Vizierate, stated that the Jerusalemites had no claim to additional payments apart from their share of the social budget, and thus categorized the allowances as part of the social welfare budget. In the Council, it was suggested that the rent allowance for the Jerusalemites be reduced to 5,000 lira, and the delegates from Jaffa and Bethle-

358 The delegates from Jerusalem and Bethlehem, Ḥalabī and Ḥazbūn, refused this as they saw 4,000 lira as too little for the two schools and they pleaded for more to be invested more in girls' education. *Filasṭīn*, 29 May 1912: 138/4/1; 8 June 1912: 143/5–4/1.

359 *Filasṭīn*, 12 June 1912: 144/3/5–4/1. Ḥazbūn was offended by what he saw as the unjust treatment of Bethlehem and Beit Jala and refused to accept the results of the negotiation. *Filasṭīn*, 12 June 1912: 144/4/1.

360 *Filasṭīn*, 13 July 1912: 153/4/1–2.

361 *Filasṭīn*, 20 July 1912: 155/3/4–4/1.

hem, ʿĪsā and Ḥazbūn, protested. ʿĪsā demanded that they be reduced to 2,000 lira, and Ḥazbūn said lists of the poor in Jerusalem should be created first, since he feared the allowances were subject to misuse.[362] In July 1912, before the budget negotiations were finished, the Patriarchate unilaterally declared the beginning of the Council's summer holiday, so that minds could 'cool down'.[363] Ḥalabī complained to Governor Muhdī Bek, and delegates ʿĪsā, Ḥazbūn, Baydas and Mulkī petitioned the governor and sent delegations to Damianos to protest against the suspension of the sessions without 'permission' (*ruḫṣa*) from the Council.[364]

After the holiday, it was the beginning of the new administrative year and the quarrel in the Council over the budget took a new turn. The patriarch was often absent and represented by his deputy, Malatios, the Muṭrān of Jordan, who refused to take decisions in the patriarch's absence.[365] During the summer, none of the dioceses had received the money assigned to them but the Patriarchate meanwhile had paid the controversial rent allowances to the Jerusalemites. The dioceses were in a miserable financial situation and wrote protest letters to the Patriarchate. ʿĪsā, supported by all the lay delegates, now demanded that the allowances be excluded from the Council's budget and declared that every dirham of the budget spent on the Jerusalemites was to be considered a 'donation' (*tabarruʿan*) from the Patriarchate, and should not be paid from the Council's pocket. The deputy then left the Mixed Council session and, during the whole winter of 1912/13, the budget was not transferred to the dioceses.[366]

At the beginning of 1913, the clergy again postponed the budget transfer, arguing that giving money for social welfare in the dioceses was a new practice, and the budget should first be distributed according to the 'old practice'. If in the end, money was left over, it should then be sent for welfare purposes to the dioceses. ʿĪsā and the Acre delegate, Mulkī, protested and stressed that the Council had already decided on a budget of 5,500 lira for social welfare in the dioceses, where the 'poor are starving to death and naked'.[367] Even so, Archimandrite Yūsuf declared that 5,000 lira from the budget would be assigned to poor Jerusalemites since their rent allowances allegedly amounted to 10,000 lira and the Patriarchate would contribute the shortfall of 5,000 lira. ʿIsā countered

362 *Filasṭīn*, 20 July 1912: 155/3/4–4/3.
363 *Filasṭīn*, 27 July 1912: 157/3/5–4/2.
364 *Filasṭīn*, 31 July 1912: 158/3/4–4/2; 3 August 1912: 159/3/5–4/1.
365 Malatios had been Damianos's right-hand man for years and in May 1910 announced the Patriarchate's acceptance of the 1910 Resolution. Ḫūrī and Ḫūrī 1992, 275.
366 *Filasṭīn*, 21 December 1912: 199/4/1–3.
367 *Filasṭīn*, 1 January 1913: 202/4/2. It is not clear in what context the previously mentioned 2,500 lira, defined as the social budget, was changed to 5,500 lira, and *Filasṭīn* does not reveal it.

that the Council had 'nothing to do' with these allowances as they were a traditional compensation 'for hundreds of houses with which their forefathers had endowed the Patriarchate'.[368]

The reader is left ignorant of what eventually happened to the budget, if and when it reached the dioceses, and what amount was really paid to the Jerusalemites as their allowance. According to the speakers' records that were published in *Filasṭīn*, the Council's dispute over the social budget was interrupted at this point and no further information is given about its distribution.

7.4. The Rotation of Delegates and the Election Affair(s)

The 1910 Resolution stated that the Council should change 50 percent of the delegates from each party every year. Three new clerical delegates would be appointed by the Patriarchate, and lots would be drawn to decide (*bi-l-qarʿa*) which diocesan representatives would be replaced. There were many more dioceses in the Patriarchate than seats reserved for the laity (Ḫūrī and Ḫūrī refer to seventeen dioceses and *Filasṭīn* mentions fourteen)[369] so, every year, it would be the turn for two new dioceses while Jerusalem, which had a permanent seat, would replace its candidate every two years. Then, the new lay delegates would be elected by notables (*muʿtabarī l-milla*) in the three dioceses that were selected by lot.[370] To be precise, the replacement of the first half of the delegates had to take place after the end of the first year from the inception of the Council, in November 1911, and the replacements thereafter would take place each year in August, with the new delegates being installed at the beginning of the new administrative year in September. In this way, each delegate would represent his diocese for two years, while Jerusalem occupied a permanent seat.

Although the Mixed Council was an innovation in late Ottoman Palestine, its electoral system prevented it from advocating effectively for the interests of the local Orthodox since only a restricted number of communities were represented at any one time. What made the issue difficult was the fact that the rotation order among the dioceses was not defined, and there were irregularities about the election of new delegates in the dioceses. Moreover, the appointment of new delegates was not implemented on time: during 1911, the Council was fully occupied with the 'trustees' issue' until in March 1912, when the Grand Vizierate reconfirmed the rotation system in the 1912 Resolution.[371] In October 1911,

368 *Filasṭīn*, 1 January 1913: 202/4/2.
369 Ḫūrī and Ḫūrī 1992, 265; *Filasṭīn*, 22 October 1913: 282/4/1.
370 Ḫūrī and Ḫūrī 1992, 265.
371 *Filasṭīn*, 2 March 1912: 116/3/5–4/3.

Governor Ǧawdat Bek had declared the Council's sessions 'illegitimate' (*ġayr qānūnī*) since no new delegates had been appointed.[372]

The Elections in 1912: Dissent over Nablus, al-Ḥisn and Kerak

In January 1912, the patriarch finally ordered the election of new delegates.[373] The electoral system was established by delegations from the dioceses and re-confirmed by Damianos but opposed by the Jaffa and Jerusalem delegates, ʿĪsā and Ḥalabī. While the Council agreed to vote according to that system, ʿĪsā declared that he would not recognize the new delegates, arguing that the procedure was not based on 'the principle of free elections' (*laysa ʿalā ṭarīqat al-intiḫāb al-ḥurr*) as instructed by the government, which stipulated the choice of delegates by lot.[374] In an extraordinary meeting in February 1912, which ʿIsā did not attend, the Council still conducted the voting in the presence of a government observer. It was decided that Muṭran Sofronius, Archimandrite Eftimios and Archimandrite Makarios should leave the Council. From the laity, the representatives of the dioceses of Acre (Mulkī), Nazareth (Baydas) and Bethlehem (Ḥazbūn) were to be replaced in August 1912 by new delegates from Nablus, al-Ḥisn and Kerak (Jordan).[375] However, the process was interrupted. In July 1912, the patriarch unilaterally closed the Council for summer holidays without having ordered the elections in Nablus, al-Ḥisn and Kerak.[376]

ʿĪsā was deeply concerned for the Council's reputation and appealed to the laity 'not to expose themselves to the reproach of public opinion' (*kaylā yataʿarraḍū malām ar-raʾy al-ʿāmm*). If the new delegates were not elected during the holiday, there would be no new representatives in the autumn, while the old lay delegates would not be able to return to their posts! ʿĪsā called for a boycott of the Council's suspension for the holiday and pleaded for the sessions to continue and for a special committee to overview elections in the dioceses to be quickly established in the absence of the clergy.[377] The lay delegates promised their support and applied the usual political instruments to involve the government: A delegation of Orthodox notables, led by Ḥalabī, approached Governor Muhdī Bek and protested that the 1910 Resolution did not stipulate regular holidays for the Council.[378] ʿĪsā, Mulkī and Baydas petitioned Muhdī Bek, arguing that only the Council itself could give permission (*ruḫṣa*) for the sessions to be sus-

372 *Filasṭīn*, 7 October 1911: 75/3/5; 27 December 1911: 98/4/1–2.
373 *Filasṭīn*, 31 January 1912: 107/4/1–2.
374 *Filasṭīn*, 31 January 1912: 107/4/2; 3 February 1912: 108/4/1–2.
375 *Filasṭīn*, 3 February 1912: 108/3/5.
376 *Filasṭīn*, 31 July 1912: 158/3/4–4/2.
377 *Filasṭīn*, 31 July 1912: 158/3/4–4/2.
378 *Filasṭīn*, 3 August 1912: 159/3/5–4/1.

pended.[379] Muhdī Bek had to mediate between Damianos and various delegations and promised to consult the 1910 Resolution on the issue.[380] Eventually, the Council held a meeting in which it officially confirmed the 1912 summer holidays. Meanwhile, the patriarch was to order the election of new delegates in Nablus, al-Ḥiṣn and Kerak.[381]

However, the elections got stuck on the local level as well. In the first session after the summer break in September 1912, it turned out that only the diocese of al-Ḥiṣn had selected candidates for the elections.[382] In Kerak, the two leading families of al-Qasūs and aṣ-Ṣannāʿ quarreled about dividing the membership on the Council, failed to agree and did not select candidates. In Nablus, the Archimandrites Dosithios and Makarios declared the elections 'illegal' (*ġayr qānūnī*), claiming that the election results had been manipulated. The Council decided to repeat the elections in Nablus and send a monitoring committee consisting of Baydas and Archimandrite Yūsuf as observers.[383] Further, irregularities about the elections in al-Ḥiṣn leaked out. The candidate Sulṭī Ibrāhīm got the most votes (507), compared with his rival Salīm Farkūḥ, or Firkūḥ (316 votes), but only 616 people were entitled to vote in al-Ḥiṣn, so Sulṭī Ibrāhīm declared the votes for his opponent fraudulent. And suddenly, there was a third candidate, Sulaymān ʿAbdū, who also received votes. ʿĪsā demanded a recount in al-Ḥiṣn but protested against re-elections in Nablus.[384] In October 1912, the clergy unanimously decided to postpone sending the monitoring committee 'because of the current political situation', referring to the military crisis at the Balkans.[385]

Autumn 1912: Protest Reactions from the Dioceses

Meanwhile, the Orthodox of Nablus disputed the repeat of their elections and became active; *Filasṭīn* reported that the telegraph and postal services conveyed their 'protests and petitions', and ʿĪsā set himself up as the mouthpiece of the *milla* in Nablus by request of the local people.[386] In the Council, ʿĪsā presented the contents of a telegram he had received from Orthodox representatives in Nablus in which they asked for the committee to be sent immediately because they could not otherwise send their delegate to the Council. This provoked mockery from

379 *Filasṭīn*, 3 August 1912: 159/4/1.
380 *Filasṭīn*, 3 August 1912: 159/3/5–4/1.
381 *Filasṭīn*, 7 August 1912/160/4/1–2.
382 *Filasṭīn*, 14 September 1912: 171/3/4.
383 *Filasṭīn*, 14 September 1912: 171/3/4–4/1.
384 *Filasṭīn*, 21 September 1912: 173/4/1–2.
385 *Filasṭīn*, 19 October 1912: 181/3/4–4/3.
386 A priest from Nablus published a letter in *Filasṭīn* in which he complained about ʿĪsā's networks in his town and referred to a certain Ibrāhīm an-Nūr, someone unknown to me, on whom 'ʿIsā relies in his information service'. The poor quality of the copy makes his signature unreadable. See *Filasṭīn*, 2 October 1912: 176/4/3.

Muṭrān Sofronios, who responded, 'We all know how organized the reports from Nablus are.'[387]

During the winter of 1912/13, protests from Nablus and other communities nearby, such as Rāfidiyā and Tulkarem, continued be sent to the Patriarchate, the Council and the Holy Synod, lamenting the financial and spiritual neglect of their communities.[388] In the Council, ʿĪsā increasingly acted as the attorney of the people from Nablus who 'assigned me to investigate this case' (*kallafūnī an afḥaṣa ʿan hāḏihi al-masʾala*),[389] and he bewailed the fact that many other Orthodox communities were left without priests while the Protestants and Catholic were sending their missionaries and priests to every 'corner of the world', even to the 'wild men' (*al-mutawaḥḥišīn*), the Indians of Peru.[390] During this winter, ʿĪsā's rhetoric of became increasingly hostile and Archimandrite Dosithios accused him of 'tyrannizing' the Patriarchate.[391]

By December 1912, the new delegates from Nablus, al-Ḥiṣn and Kerak had still not arrived and the Council was incomplete. Arab Orthodox activists meanwhile found that the sessions had become a series of satires, which embarrassed the Movement. ʿĪsā printed a telegram from Nablus that announced that 'the Christians of the dioceses in Nablus and … the villages gathered and decided that, if the Patriarchate … won't send the committee, the whole population will submit a file to the district government … and inform the Grand Vizierate about this despotism'.[392] An anonymous author from Nablus also expressed his anger that the Balkan crisis was being used by the Patriarchate as an excuse for delaying Orthodox reforms:

> The last excuse that they have invented to postpone the [(electoral] committee was, that (it) must wait for the peace treaty (*ʿaqd aṣ-ṣulḥ*). Anyone who hears that would think that the Patriarchate was deeply involved in the war (*munhamika hiya ayḍan bi-l-ḥarb*) and

387 *Filasṭīn*, 30 October 1912: 184/4/2–3.

388 For example, from Rāfiḍiyā, the Orthodox complained about a Greek priest who was dividing the *milla* into 'groups and parties' (*fiʾāt wa-aḥzāb*) and intended to become the delegate on the Council. He went on campaign through the District to gain the support of local notables and took the only local priest with him, so an Orthodox from Rāfidiyā who died, had to be buried without a priest, which caused protests. See *Filasṭīn*, 13 November 1912: 188/4/3–5. Another author protested about the neglect of welfare in Nablus. As the *milla* had no financial means to support widows, orphans and poor, they depended on help from the local Muslim community, he claimed. *Filasṭīn*, 27 November 1912: 192/4/3–5. In this context, the Orthodox from Tulkarem also addressed the patriarch in a polemical telegram, reprinted in *Filasṭīn*, since their city was without a church or a priest as the Patriarchate would not send one and they could not celebrate the Christmas liturgy. See *Filasṭīn*, 15 January 1913: 204/4/1–2.

389 *Filasṭīn*, 16 November 1912: 189/4/3.

390 *Filasṭīn*, 15 January 1913: 204/4/1–2.

391 *Filasṭīn*, 16 November 1912: 189/4/3.

392 *Filasṭīn*, 11 December 1912: 194/4/2–3.

therefore not able to send two delegates of the Mixed Council to investigate the [election] results and solve the 'Oriental Question'![393]

At the end of December 1912, the Council finally appointed a new committee to monitor elections in Nablus, al-Ḥisn and Kerak: Archimandrite Dosithios and the delegate from Salṭ (Jordan), ʿAwdeh as-Sālim, who did usually not appear much in the Council minutes of meeting.[394] It took until June 1913 for this committee to actually arrive in Nablus because the Council was preoccupied with campaigns for and against its annulment during the spring of 1913, as will be treated elsewhere.[395] When Dosithios and as-Sālim returned in July 1913, their report was not ready to be presented before the Council. The patriarch seemed relieved and suggested breaking for the summer holidays and hearing the report after that. ʿĪsā appealed to the Council to 'get over this disease' (*nuḫallis min hāḏihi al-ʿilla*), so that the new delegates would be announced as legitimate members before the summer.[396]

Dissent over the Membership of Gaza, Ramallah and Beit Jala in the Council

In the last session before the summer holidays, the committee presented its report.[397] Damianos was absent, and his deputy, Malatios, suddenly suggested that the delegates from Jaffa and Salṭ should be replaced by delegates from Gaza and Ramallah in August/September 1913, while Jerusalem would elect a new delegate to replace Ḥalabī. This meant an exchange of 100 percent of the laity in autumn 1913 since the Nazareth and Acre delegates also had to resign, and the Bethlehem delegate had left Palestine in 1912. The delegates from Nablus, al-Ḥiṣn and Kerak were due to be replaced again in 1914, meaning that they would have lost one year of their two-year term on the Council. Malatios was supported by the clergy and Ḥalabī, and won the vote.[398]

ʿĪsā and Baydas fiercly complained that, if 100 percent of the laity was replaced, the rotation system would be 'permanently confused'. It was not the fault of Nablus, al-Ḥiṣn and Kerak that they had been put on hold since 1912 but of the clergy's 'delaying tactics', they both declared, and called for the year 1912–13 to be 'annulled' (*mulġāt*) as far as the rotation of delegates was concerned. They also suggested that the dioceses of Jaffa and Salṭ should then have their delegates replaced in the summer of 1914, although this would be their fourth year in office, and the delegates of Nablus, al-Ḥisn and Kerak should be replaced in summer

393 *Filasṭīn*, 28 December 1912: 201/4/2–3.
394 *Filasṭīn*, 21 December 1912: 199/4/1–2.
395 *Filasṭīn*, 11 June 1913: 244/2/5; 14 June 1913: 245/3/5; 25 June 1913: 248/4/2.
396 *Filasṭīn*, 12 July 1913: 253/4/1–2.
397 *Filasṭīn*, 23 July 1913: 256/3/4–5.
398 *Filasṭīn*, 23 July 1913: 256/3/5–4/1.

1915, after serving for two years, so as install a functioning rotation system for the future.[399] Tensions mounted. ʿIsā declared that the populations of Jaffa and Salṭ were not 'sheep' to be gambled with, and the Malatios shouted at ʿĪsā: 'So, send the population of Jaffa with rifles to kill me' (*iḏan arsil ahālī Yāfā maʿa banādīq li-yaqtulūnī*).[400] Then, the Council rose for the summer break.

During the summer holiday of 1913, the patriarch suddenly and unilaterally decided that Beit Jala should be represented on the Council instead of Ramallah and ordered the mayor of Beit Jala to prepare the *milla* for elections. The office of delegate was put to public auction and its price reached 215 lira – 35 lira more than a delegate's annual stipend, according to a *Filasṭīn* correspondent from Beit Jala.[401] A couple of ambitious candidates promised to donate their salary to their community in 'the service of the *umma*',[402] and were controversially discussed in Beit Jala. The reporter sensed the 'smell of intrigue' (*rāʾiḥat ad-dasīsa*) and predicted that 'the one who buys also sells', and that a delegate who buys his office, may later 'sell the Council' by 'making a deal with the patriarch as shut it down'.[403] In this context, ʿĪsā made criticisms of the electoral system. While in the late Ottoman context, voting was restricted to male citizen tax payers who were at least 25 years old and paid a minimum of 50 qurūš a year in property tax (*wīrkū*), which made political participation possible only for the urban elites and owners of real estate,[404] Damianos had obviously passed regulations concerning the election of delegates in the dioceses that opened up the voting to every male Orthodox over 20 years of age. ʿĪsā complained that, to let people vote 'randomly' instead of confining the vote to a number of 'electors' (*muntaḫabīyūn ṯānawīyūn*) would sew strife:

> It is a crazy idea to leave the elections first of all to the nation … which will cause hair-splitting… and schism, in contrast to [what would happen] if the matter were assigned to a fixed number of 30 electors, chosen in the dioceses, who would elect the six necessary delegates for the Council from inside or outside their circle, as we have demanded … And so, we … are harvesting now the results from this devilish system (*hāḏā at-tadbīr aš-šayṭānī*).[405]

399 *Filasṭīn*, 23 July 1913: 256/3/5–4/1.
400 *Filasṭīn*, 23 July 1913: 256/4/1.
401 *Filasṭīn*, 10 September 1913: 270/4/1.
402 *Filasṭīn*, 24 September 1913: 274/3/4.
403 *Filasṭīn*, 10 September 1913: 270/4/1.
404 See Buessow 2011, 73; Gerber 1985, 116.
405 *Filasṭīn*, 1 November 1913: 285/1/4.

After the 1913 Summer Break: the Incomplete Council

In September 1913, when the Council was reopened, it was still not complete. Meanwhile, the delegates from Acre, Nazareth and Bethlehem were replaced with newly elected delegates from al-Ḥiṣn (Sulṭī Ibrāhīm), Kerak (Yūsuf al-Madīnāt) and Jenin (ʿAwdeh ʿAṭāʾallāh),[406] although they had not received their official invitation (*daʿwa*) from the patriarch and so were not in attendance, and the Jerusalemites did not elect a new delegate to replace Ḥalabī. Therefore, the only delegates present were ʿĪsā from Jaffa and Sālim from Salṭ, and the Council, unable to take any steps in this form, was suspended. ʿĪsā and as-Sālim, now in coalition, petitioned Istanbul, and sent a telegraph to the newly elected delegates in the dioceses, informing them about Damianos's latest 'intrigue' (*dasīsa*).[407] In September 1913, they held a three-hour discussion with Damianos, which ʿĪsā called 'historical' and a 'death sentence' (*ḥukm al-iʿdām*) for the Council 'out of the patriarch's mouth'. Damianos said that ʿĪsā and as-Sālim had no right to speak for the Council since the clergy had decided that the term of the Jaffa and Ṣalṭ delegates had ended in August, and he insisted on adjourning sessions until elections in Gaza, Beit Jala and Jerusalem had taken place. ʿĪsā countered that the 1910 Resolution did not require the Council's suspension during the election of new delegates, so he and as-Sālim could not leave until the new delegates arrived. Damianos was not impressed and simply declared that he would 'not open the Council at all anymore unless the churches in Jerusalem and the schools in Jaffa were reopened'.[408]

This was the end of ʿĪsā's term as the Jaffa delegate on the Council. In fact, the first round in the rotation of delegates in the Mixed Council did not take place till the beginning of 1914, after government intervention by ʿAzmī Bek, which is documented in the later section below.

7.5. From Personal Feuds to the Council's Crisis

From the middle of 1912, disputes in the Council escalated into personal feuds between the patriarch and ʿĪsā, who positioned himself in the Council as the defender of the local Orthodox and was at the center of the published speeches given in the Council. After Ḥazbūn from Bethlehem left the Council in summer 1912 and the Jerusalem delegate, Ḥalabī, reconciled with the Patriarchate, ʿĪsā

406 The Nablus delegate was replaced by a delegate from Jenin. Nablus had asked to be split off from Jenin and to have its own delegate on the Council but the monitoring committee refused. Despite continuing protests from Nablus, ʿAwdeh ʿAṭāʾallāh from Jenin was elected. *Filasṭīn*, 23 September 1913: 273/3/4–5.

407 *Filasṭīn*, 10 September 1913: 260/3/5.

408 *Filasṭīn*, 23 September 1913: 273/3/4–5.

was, for Damianos, the only real troublemaker left in the Council and provoked him with statements, such as: 'We nationals will not be loyal to you Greek monks as long as this Empire is existing.' The patriarch responded with legal steps and tried to get ʿIsā out of the Council in several ways. He initiated several court cases against him at the *mutaṣarrifīya* in Jerusalem and the *qāʾimaqāmīya* in Jaffa, supported by a circle of largely unknown Orthodox notables from Jerusalem, notably Bišāra Ṭāsū, a member of the close patriarchal circle, who accused ʿĪsā at the *qāʾimaqāmīya* of 'betrayal' of the homeland (*ḫiyāna li-dawlatihi*).[409]

In articles seething with revenge, ʿIsā attacked the 'followers of the convent' (*aḏnāb ad-dayr*) who 'sell their nation' (*yabīʿūn ummatahum*), predicting that 'the one who betrays his nation and his homeland, will be judged by God and history'.[410] He stressed his leading position in the Orthodox Movement, proudly declared himself a major 'obstacle' in the patriarch's way, and called the enemies of the Orthodox cause 'swarms of insects' (*insiyāb al-hašarāt*) and 'birds of darkness' (*ṭuyūr aẓ-ẓalām*), who had hoped to deal the Movement a 'crushing blow' (*ḍarba muhlika*) by opening the cases against him. He declared:

> They [the traitors] are running behind the mentioned delegate... greedy to remove this obstacle in the way of his Excellency... First: the delegate of Jaffa did not move a hair's breadth away from his agenda during all this Renaissance despite all the measures undertaken by the Patriarchate... Second: he only entered the Mixed Council to meet the repeated requests of his community, in particular... 3,970 Orthodox out of 4,000 in Jaffa... Third: your and the Patriarchate's actions during the past four weeks have not shaken the communities' confidence in him. Remember that the sons of this milla elected him as a delegate at the last elections... with an absolute majority... and he only failed to gain 25 votes of all the community's votes. Fourth: the Jaffa delegate is proud that three cases against him have been directed to the government by the Patriarchate.[411]

ʿĪsā here strongly stressed his function as a representative serving Jaffa's Orthodox community to emphasize that his people stood behind him, and he repeatedly stressed the Council's responsibility towards the Orthodox public, presenting himself as the one who strove for transparency regarding its activities, and trying 'to cover what is happening in the council'.[412]

The Interruption of the Council's Sessions in 1913

With the turn of the year 1912–13, the Council approached a new level of crisis. After Orthodox Christmas in January 1913, the patriarch absented himself from sessions and did not reopen the Council, which had no consequences because the

409 *Filasṭīn*, 26 June 148/3/3; 3 July 1912: 150/3/4–5; 10 July 1912: 152/1/1–3.
410 *Filasṭīn*, 29 June 1912: 149/3/5–4/2.
411 *Filasṭīn*, 10 July 1912: 152/1/1–3.
412 *Filasṭīn*, 4 December 1912: 194/4/2.

Jerusalem District was without a governor during this period. Muhdī Bek had been removed from his post in November 1912, Governor Ṭāhir Bek arrived in the middle of January 1913 but resigned after only 13 days in office, and Jerusalem was left without a ruler until Governor Māğid Bek arrived in March 1913.[413] ʿĪsā's anti-clerical rhetoric during these months was especially sharp since there was no fear of censorship.[414] In February 1913, ʿĪsā gathered the lay delegates to petition the deputy governor, complaining that, after a series of petitions for two years and 120 sessions of the Council, the patriarch still did not recognize it as a legitimate body (*hayʾa niẓāmīya*) and intended to 'abolish the Council' (*ilġāʾ al-mağlis*).[415]

The laity, apart from Ḥalabī, gathered in front of the patriarchal 'club (*nādī*) to protest.[416] ʿĪsā had meanwhile become tremendously hostile towards Ḥalabī and accused him of leading a 'hidden movement' (*ḥaraka ḫafīya*), instigated by Damianos, working for the abolition of the Council.[417] A pamphlet, demanding this had been fixed to the gate of the Council chamber by an anonymous author, and ʿĪsā suspected Ḥalabī, the Jerusalem delegate. He pressured the patriarch's deputy, Malatios, to take a stand:

> **The Jaffa Delegate:** I would like to ask the deputy whether he is not willing to protect the honor of this Council given what was written at the door of the [Council] chamber and since it is situated inside the Convent? And whether he is not willing to deliver a report telling the governorate about the movement of those individuals … as their pamphlet is tantamount to an infringement (*šibhu t-taḥrīḍ*) of the government resolution? … Last, I am asking the honored deputy to tell us in complete sincerity … whether the Patriarchate is willing, if necessary, to defend the existence of the Council?
>
> **His Excellency, the Deputy:** I don't know what the Jaffa delegate is talking about. We think that every person is free to express his opinion as he sees fit.
>
> **The Jaffa Delegate:** The matter … is well known to everybody. Also his Excellency the deputy knows. So, what is his answer to my simple question?
>
> **His Excellency, the Deputy:** We are not responsible if the population rises up and demands the abolition of the Council since the government enacted its (1910) Resolution grounding it on the demand of the population (*bināʾan ʿalā ṭalab al-ahālī*).
>
> **The Jaffa Delegate:** The population has nothing to do with my question! I remind the Patriarchate that, when the resolution concerning the formation of the Council was issued, the population refused it as it did not meet their demands. Yet, on the second day

413 For more information, see *Filasṭīn*, 11 December 1912: 196/2/5–3/1 and 3/3; 15 January 1913: 204/1/1 and 3/2; 15 February 1913: 213/3/4; 15 March 1913: 221/3/3; 19 March 1913: 222/1/1–2.

414 *Filasṭīn*, 12 February 1913: 212/4/2f.

415 *Filasṭīn*, 12 February 1913: 212/4/2–3.

416 *Filasṭīn*, 26 February 1913: 216/4/2.

417 *Filasṭīn*, 1 Mach 1913: 217/4/2–3.

> after its arrival, the Patriarchate ran to the House of Government, accepted it like an awaited blessing ... and called for the wellbeing of the Porte. So, don't bring the population into play! We want to know if the Patriarchate is willing to defend this resolution that it was so grateful for; or if it is with those who work for its annulment?
>
> **His Excellency, the Deputy:** As usual, we follow the orders of the government.[418]

At the end of March 1913, the first session of the Council was conducted, and its course is documented in *Filasṭīn* by Yūsuf al-ʿĪsā like a satirical theatrical performance in which he exposed the Council to ridicule. The delegates of Jaffa, Salṭ and Nazareth, ʿĪsā, as-Sālim and Baydas, waited in the Council chamber for the opening of the session, but not a single clerical member was present. The Acre delegate, Mulkī, was asleep in his hotel room in Jerusalem and did not react to the knocking. Ḥalabī announced that he would not attend sessions since he felt threatened by ʿĪsā. Since the statute required a quorum of at least four delegates from each party, the session could not start. ʿĪsā, as-Sālim and Baydas proceeded to the patriarch who was 'drinking coffee, eating sweets and smoking a water-pipe', ʿIsā recorded. After this protest in the patriarch's room, the clerical members reluctantly arrived. Finally, the Acre delegate rose from his slumber and the meeting, which should have started at 8.30 a.m., began at 11 a.m. Damianos introduced the session with news from the Balkan Wars. Afterwards, he offered sweets and coffee to the delegates, which was unusual and led to informal chatter. Then, Damianos closed the session since 'time was over' (sessions usually lasted until 2 p.m.).[419]

The Council in the Crossfire of Public Criticism

The Council's credibility was irreparably damaged. Sakākīnī wrote in *Filasṭīn* that the last session was proof enough that this Council was a waste of everybody's time and was an instrument of Damianos. The delegates, he concluded, had ruined their bonds with the people and could no longer be considered their representatives.[420] Ḥazbūn, the former Bethlehem delegate, who had left Palestine for America, wrote in a very disappointed letter that his colleagues 'had sold the *milla*', while the government was too occupied with the Balkan War to assist.[421]

The Council's crisis led to a debate regarding its accountability. The laity insisted on transparency regarding all the Council's activities. They demanded through ʿĪsā, that each session should be recorded and released in the press or any independent publication, arguing that 'the Council will avoid wasting time if

418 *Filasṭīn*, 1 March 1913: 217/4/3.
419 *Filasṭīn*, 26 March 1913: 224/4/1–2.
420 *Filasṭīn*, 2 April 1913: 226/4/1.
421 *Filasṭīn*, 17 May 1913: 237/4/1. See also 11 June 1913: 244/3/5–4/2.

its members know that each movement they take will be uncovered'.[422] This was rejected by the patriarch, who argued that there 'can be no decision except with the approval of all delegates' (*ǧamīʿ al-aʿḍāʾ*). In *Filasṭīn*, the lay delegates were quoted to have responded that this 'does not happen in any Council of the world' and called for it to be 'put it to the vote. It is either yes or no. We are fed up with this way and our reputation has suffered among the people that we represent.'[423] Damianos refused a vote, and the laity unanimously boycotted the session with collective silence until the session was closed. ʿĪsā considered this a minor victory and the 'first important session' in the history of the Council.[424] Since the patriarch and his deputy had prohibited the publication of the Council's activities, ʿIsā recorded the sessions from memory and claimed that his accounts were usually so precise that even the secretary consulted him, as it was 'the best record (*aḥsan taʾrīḫ*) of whatever happened' in the Council.[425]

The 'Annulment Affair': Campaigns and Counter-campaigns

After the summer of 1913, the Council could not be reopened since there were not enough members because the patriarch had not officially invited the newly elected delegates from Jenin, al-Ḥiṣn and Kerak. ʿĪsā attacked the new delegates, saying they should have come to Jerusalem and forced Damianos to issue the invitation. He asked 'every Orthodox concerned with this issue' to send a statement 'so that we can publish it on the pages of our paper',[426] and he petitioned the governor, asking him to force Damianos to invite the new delegates and reopen the Council.[427]

Meanwhile, the public mood about the Council was fluctuating wildly. The Jerusalem correspondent reported that there was deep dissent about the future of the Mixed Council. Some petitioned the governor against its suspected abolition, and witnesses reported incidents of gunfire in Jerusalem, obviously to threaten the clergy.[428] On the other hand, 20–30 people, supported by Damianos, petitioned for the abolition of the Council.[429] An unknown Jerusalemite reported that 'the monks' were running a public campaign to annul the Council, approaching Orthodox shop owners, teachers and intellectuals to convince them of their case. Debates in Jerusalem were contagious. Some complained that the Council undermined the privileges of the Jerusalemites. Others countered that the Council

422 *Filasṭīn*, 5 April 1913: 227/4/1.
423 *Filasṭīn*, 5 April 1913: 227/4/2.
424 *Filasṭīn*, 5 April 1913: 227/4/2.
425 *Filasṭīn*, 11 June 1913: 244/4/2.
426 *Filasṭīn*, 23 September 1913: 273/3/5.
427 *Filasṭīn*, 1 October 1913: 276/3/4; 8 October 1913: 278/3/3–4.
428 *Filasṭīn*, 4 October 1913: 277/3/1.
429 *Filasṭīn*, 8 October 1913: 278/3/4.

also represented the interests of the other dioceses. Others feared that the Orthodox Movement was damaging the believers' devotion to God.[430] Leaflets were distributed to stir up the Jerusalemites against the dioceses.[431]

The 'annulment affair' spread beyond Jerusalem. Three individuals from Nablus forwarded a document (*maḍbaṭa*) that demanded the abolition the Council. Others sent a counter-statement to the Orthodox of Jerusalem, signed by the 'general public of the diocese' (*ʿumūm ahālī l-abrašīya*), claiming the document had been 'fabricated' by the monks and bore a 'forged seal' (*ḫitām muzawwara*). They also sent an official petition to Māǧid Bek, signed by the priests and community leaders of Nablus and Rafīdīya so as to represent the 'general Orthodox public'.[432] In Istanbul, the *Telegraf al-Istāna* ('Constantinople Telegraph') published a report that the laity had refused the revival the Mixed Council in Jerusalem. ʿĪsā suspected Ṭablāriyūs Efendi, Damianos's advisor, to be responsible for this and sent him an outraged statement in which he portrayed Damianos as a senile old man who signed every 'fabricated' paper.[433]

Meanwhile, the clergy initiated campaigns to convince representatives of different Orthodox communities that the Council was obsolete. The Orthodox of Bethlehem petitioned for the abolition of the Council through a document, forwarded by their new mayor, which showed that the intra-Orthodox conflict had entered the municipality.[434] The Bethlehem correspondent responded that the Orthodox of Bethlehem 'were not the Convent's' puppets' (*laysū ṣanīʿat ad-dayr*) and counter-petitioned for the reopening of the Council, confirming they were ready to elect a delegate.[435] The campaigns for and against the Council also spread outside the District, and in Nazareth, Archimandrite Dosithios tried to 'seduce' (*iġwāʾ*) the Orthodox to hand in a petition like the Bethlehemites.[436] Ḫalīl Naṣr reported on the issue from Haifa and concluded: 'These are the deeds of our spiritual heads as they throw stones in our way and split the nation apart' (*yuqassimūn al-umma baʿḍihā ʿan baʿḍin*).[437] Archimandrite Yūsuf went on a three-week trip to Salṭ, Kerak and Madaba in Jordan to collect petitions for the Council's abolition. But *Filasṭīn* reported that he failed to persuade the Orthodox

430 *Filasṭīn*, 8 October 1913: 278/3/4–5.

431 A leaflet signed by one Salīm al-Fārī warned the Orthodox of Jerusalem that they were losing their privileges to the dioceses. *Filasṭīn*, 15 October 1913: 280/3/3.

432 The petition was signed by the priests Ilyās and Miḫāʾīl and the *muḫtār* of the *milla*, speaking for the Christians of Nablus (*ʿumūm masīḥīyī Nāblus*); and by a priest called Ašrīdeh and the head of the *milla* in Rafīdīya, speaking for the Christians of Rafīdīya (*ʿumūm masīḥīyī ....*). *Filasṭīn*, 15 October 1913: 280/3/3.

433 *Filasṭīn*, 18 October 1913: 281/1/1–2.

434 *Filasṭīn*, 25 October 283/2/4.

435 *Filasṭīn*, 25 October 283/2/4.

436 *Filasṭīn*, 25 October 1913: 283/2/3.

437 *Filasṭīn*, 12 November 1913: 288/4/1.

of Jordan for 'the Arabs in these provinces are very strong souls' (*li-anna ʿarab tilka al-ǧihāt hum aʿzāʾ an-nufūs*).[438] In Beit Jala, the campaign took a special turn. A subscriber informed the readers that the 'seduction' (*iġwāʾ*) of the monks had driven some 'naïve people' (*busaṭāʾ*) to deliver a document demanding the Council's abolition and offered to withdraw from the Beit Jala seat on the Council in return for 200 lira from the Patriarchate to be spent on Orthodox reforms. The majority of the Orthodox in Beit Jala counter-petitioned. Īsā responded that the Beit Jalans must be naïve to think that their seat on the Council was a right that could be bought or sold while fourteen other dioceses were waiting to be represented.[439] When an anonymous author asked why the Council should be revived when it produced no results, the editors declared the Council a 'matter of national significance' (*masʾala qawmīya ḥayawīya*).[440] Referring to the fact that, in 1875, the so-called *Katastikon* had formally permitted the Arab Orthodox of Jerusalem to establish a mixed committee that practically did not work,[441] ʿĪsā reminded the reader that

> we were only able to revive it [the Council] after 50 years of violent struggle (*ǧihād ʿanīf*), after spending a lot of money and shedding blood. This is what makes us defend this Council and gather our strength for its reopening, by the will of God and through justice and the Constitution of Turkey.[442]

Meanwhile, a flood of petitions from various Orthodox delegations involved the local government in the public controversy throughout the autumn of 1913. Each petition tried to give the impression that it represented the will of the community. A petition 'by the majority of the Jerusalemites' (*bi-tawqīʿ akṯarīyat ahālī l-Quds*) asked for its immediate reopening.[443] A 'rush of telegrams' (*tadaffaqat al-barqīyāt*) from Jerusalem, Jaffa and other towns was directed to the Grand Vizierate and the Ministry of Justice and Religious Affairs in Istanbul.[444] In October and November 1913, Māǧid Bek was 'deluged' by delegations from Jerusalem, Jaffa and al-Ḥiṣn, all pleading in the name of the 1910 Resolution that the Patriarchate be forced to reopen the Council.[445] Damianos meanwhile played for time. At times, he admitted to the governor that he was tired of this Council and did not

438 *Filasṭīn*, 22 October 1913: 282/4/2.
439 *Filasṭīn*, 29 October 1913: 284/4/1–2.
440 *Filasṭīn*, 1 November 1913: 285/1/1.
441 On the *Katastikon*, see Ḫūrī and Ḫūrī 1992, 221–227; Kark 2005, 517; Kildani 2010, 100–108; Kuruvilla 2011, 59.
442 *Filasṭīn*, 1 November 1913: 285/2/1. Note that it is not the Ottoman Constitution that is mentioned here, but the 'Constitution of Turkey'.
443 *Filasṭīn*, 22 October 1913: 282/4/1.
444 *Filasṭīn*, 25 October 1913: 283/3/3.
445 *Filasṭīn*, 5 November 1913: 286/3/5–4/2.

want to revive it.[446] At other times, he declared the Council could not be reopened because the Beit Jalans were not ready to conduct the elections of the new delegate due to their internal rivalries. At yet other times, he declared that the communities themselves had demanded the Council's abolition.[447] In November 1913, when Damianos was about to leave for to his holiday residence in Caesarea, the delegations pressed harder on the governor to act. Māǧid Bek became weary and declared that he could do nothing for the reopening of the Council and recommended that they direct their complaints to Istanbul.[448]

7.6. Back to Square One? From Escalation to 'Reconciliation'

In the context of the Mixed Council's 'annulment crisis', the loyalty of the ʿĪsās to the local government and the High Porte began to crack. The editors were outraged that Māǧid Bek was not willing or able to enforce the reopening of the Council. They suggested:

> We think that the Orthodox Patriarchate is not Ottoman anymore. And if the central government thinks the same way [as the governor], we are begging it to let us know to which foreign country this Patriarchate belongs to (*ilā ayya dawla aǧnabīya tantasib hāḏihi al-Baṭrīyarkīya*), so we can complain about it [there] and beg [there] for [the implementation of] these resolutions that are issued by a government that is not able to implement them (*aṣdarathā ḥukūma lā tastaṭīʿ an tunaffiḏahā*)![449]

Māǧid Bek's reluctance to engage in the Orthodox cause made him a target of the ʿĪsās, which led to the temporary suspension of *Filasṭīn* in November 1911 after it published an editorial entitled 'What is seen and what is not seen' (*Mā yurā wa-mā lā yurā*), which addressed the gap between official government orders and actual government practices. In it, the new *qāʾimaqām* of Jaffa and the local security forces were openly blamed, and especially Māǧid Bek who could, as they quoted him, 'not do a thing if the Patriarch is not willing to', regarding the implementation of government orders.[450] This had consequences. The vice governor of the *qāʾimaqām*, ʿAlī Riḍāʾ Bek declared *Filasṭīn* suspended because of 'bias (*taḥāmul*) against the government' and 'articles against the central government' (*maqālāt ḍidda l-ḥukūma as-sanīya*).[451]

446 *Filasṭīn*, 25 October 1913: 283/3/3.
447 *Filasṭīn*, 1 November 1913: 285/4/2–3.
448 *Filasṭīn*, 5 November 1913: 286/4/1.
449 *Filasṭīn*, 5 November 1913: 286/4/2.
450 *Filasṭīn*, 12 November 1913: 288/1/1.
451 *Al-Aḫbār*, 15 November 1913: 495/3/2; *Al-Aḫbār*, 19 November 1913: 496/1/1.

Responses to Filasṭīn's Suspension

ʿĪsā al-ʿĪsā responded to this 'fraud' (*muġālaṭa*) with a load of sarcasm, publishing under the wings of a colleague, Iskandar Ḥalabī from the Jaffa based newspaper *al-Aḫbār* ('The News').[452] ʿAlī Riḍāʾ's evaluation of *Filasṭīn* was surely proof of his 'lack of understanding of Arabic', ʿĪsā scoffed, and affirmed his loyalty to the 'Unionists' (*al-ittiḥādīyūn*). Surely, the suspension would be lifted soon, since 'we already have been threatened with suspension several times' by Governor Māǧid Bek, because 'we reminded him of his duty to implement the resolutions ... and settle the conflict between us, the local citizens, and the Orthodox Patriarchate'.[453]

When *al-Aḫbār* was also temporarily suspended, the ʿĪsās switched to the Jerusalemite newspaper *ad-Dustūr* ('The Constitution'), newly established under the aegis of Ǧamīl al-Ḫālidī, who was, along with the ʿĪsās and Sakākīnī, one of the founders of the Constitutional School. Al-Ḫālidī established *ad-Dustūr* as a protest forum against the suspension of *Filasṭīn* und published it via the editorial office of the Constitutional School with Yūsuf al-ʿĪsā as editor-in-chief.[454] The first issue followed the standard structure of *Filasṭīn*; it gave extensive cover to the intra-Orthodox conflict under the title 'Danger to the Constitution' (*al-ḫaṭr ʿalā ad-dustūr*) to equate the censorship of newspapers with absolutist rule.[455] In addition, the first issue consisted of two special editions. The first addressed the governor in an open letter that was printed under the standard *Filasṭīn* masthead, to emphasize that they were being censored for their engagement in the Arab Orthodox cause, claiming that Māǧid Bek had 'annulled our newspaper *Filasṭīn* because it has driven campaigns in defense of the rights of this miserable *millal*.[456] The second page of this special edition was completely blank to show that they were silenced by the government. The ʿĪsās confidently demonstrated that they did not view the governor as a responsible person and announced that they would sue Māǧid Bek for compensation in the sum of 25 lira for each issue of *Filasṭīn* whose publication was banned from the date of its suspension.[457] The ʿĪsās had announced the same to vice *qāʾimaqām* ʿAlī Riḍāʾ, while they asked the readership for solidarity, 'in the age of the suspension of newspapers without a court ruling' (*ʿaṣr taʿṭīl al-ǧarāʾid bi-lā muḥākama*).[458]

452 *Al-Aḫbār*, 15 November 1913: 495/3/2. According to the ʿĪsās, Iskandar Ḥalabī approached them and explicitly asked them to publish on the pages of his newspaper. See *Filasṭīn*, 24 December 1913: 293/2/4–3/1.

453 *Al-Aḫbār*, 15 November 1913: 495/3/2.

454 Thus Ǧamīl al-Ḫālidī announced in the first issue. See *ad-Dustūr*, 27 November 1913: 1/1/1.

455 *Ad-Dustūr* 27 November 1913: 1/1/1–5.

456 'ʿ*Aṭala ǧarīdatunā Filasṭīn li-mā la-hā min al-ḥamlāt ad-difāʿīya ʿan ḥuqūq hāḏihi al-milla at-taʿisa.*' See *ad-Dustūr*, 27 November 1913; First Special Edition: 1/1.

457 *Ad-Dustūr*, 27 November 1913; First Special Edition: 1/1.

458 *Al-Aḫbār*, 19 November 1913: 496/1/1; 496/3/4.

Filasṭīn's suspension was received in Palestine with 'general discontent' (*ʿāmmat al-istiyāʾ*) among the intellectuals, stated reformer Ḥabīb Ḫūrī Ayūb from Gaza. He called *Filasṭīn* 'the social resistance fighter' (*al-fidāʾīya al-iǧtimāʿīya*) that 'takes on sacrifices in the service of its loyal Ottoman patriotism'.[459] The only 'bias' (*taḥāmul*), *Filasṭīn* could be accused of, he said, was 'its growing fanaticism (*taʿaṣṣubihā*) for Ottomanism, and its zeal (*ġayratihā*) for everything Ottoman'.[460] In Ayūb's view, *Filasṭīn* was one of the rare newspapers that managed to build 'solidary with the people over the government' *and* 'solidary with the government over the people'.[461] In Jaffa, the intellectuals organized resistance against press censorship. The Beirut newspaper *Lisān al-Ḥāl* reported that 'the progressive young Muslims and Christians' (*al-farīq ar-rāqī min šubbān al-muslimīn wa-l-masīḥīyīn*) of Jaffa had founded a committee to protest against the authorities and inform other press organs. In Jaffa's New Bar, journalists organized a discussion group on the 'freedom of the press' (*ḥurrīyat aṣ-ṣiḥāfa*).[462]

In the Arab press, too, the wave of solidarity with *Filasṭīn* was overwhelming. *Al-Aḫbār* documented a long series of protest telegrams from various cities to Jerusalem in protest against its suspension,[463] and journalists also petitioned Istanbul, reported *al-Karmil* in Haifa.[464] After *Filasṭīn* was revived in December 1913, it was full of reprinted articles from other newspapers that had expressed their solidarity and discussed press freedom in the Empire. Among these reports were voices from *Lisān al-Ḥāl* (Beirut), *al-Mufīd* (Beirut), *al-Qabas* (Damascus), *an-Naṣīr* (Beirut), *al-Ḥawādiṯ aṭ-Ṭarābulsīya* (Tripoli), *Abābīl*, *al-Iḫāʾ al-ʿUṯmānī*, *al-Murāqib*, *al-Muhaḏḏib*, *ar-Raʾy al-ʿĀmm*, *al-Ahrām* and *al-Ǧarīda* (Cairo), *al-Karmil* (Haifa), *al-Barq* (Tripoli), *Maǧallat an-Nafāʾis*, *Maǧallat al-Ḥikma*, *Maǧallat al-Iḫāʾ* and *al-Quds aš-Šarīf* (Jerusalem), among others.[465]

ʿĪsā and the Royal Commission of ʿAzmī Bek

While all this was happening, a royal commission arrived at the Jaffa port at the end of November 1913. It was headed by ʿAzmī Bek, advisor to the Ministry of Justice and Religious Affairs (*niẓārat al-ʿadlīya*), to investigate the Council's annulment.[466] As he had been governor of the Jerusalem District at the time when the 1910 Resolution was passed, he was familiar with the central conflict issues.

459 *Ad-Dustūr*, 27 November .1913: 1/1/5
460 *Ad-Dustūr*, 27 November 1913: 1/1/5.
461 '*Al-wuqūf maʿ aš-šaʿb ʿalā l-hukūma wa-l-wuqūf maʿ al-ḥukūma ʿalā aš-šaʿb*'. *Ad-Dustūr*, 27 November 1913: 1/2/1.
462 *Al-Aḫbār*, 19 November 1913: 496/3/4.
463 Reprinted from *Lisān al-Ḥāl* in *Filasṭīn*, 17 December 1913: 292/2/1.
464 Reprinted from *al-Karmil* in *Filasṭīn*, 17 December 1913: 292/2/1.
465 *Filasṭīn*, 17 December 1913: 292/2/1–3/5; 24 December 1913: 293/2/2–3 and 3/2–3; 27 December 1913: 294/2/4–5; 31 December 1913: 295/4/2.
466 *Ad-Dustūr*, 27 November 1913: 1/2/5.

Assisted by Māǧid Bek and ʿAbd al-Ḥamīd Pasha, military governor of Jerusalem, ʿAzmī Bek received petitions and delegations from the parties to the conflict from various cities.[467] In *Ad-Dustūr*, ʿĪsā addressed ʿĀzmī Bek in an open letter and claimed that '*Filasṭīn* is to be silenced (*tuḫras*) for the duration of your stay in Palestine because, for three years it has uncovered (*tafḍaḥ*) their [the clergy's] hidden actions … and shown the nation and the rulers how bad their [the clergy's] behavior is.'[468] ʿĪsā pleaded with ʿAzmī Bek to act according to the principle of 'equality' (*al-musāwāt*) and reminded him of former Grand Vizier Fuʾād Pasha who is quoted to have said to Sultan Abdülaziz in the 1860s:[469]

> For the wellbeing of the Christians, our policy should be limited to their liberation from the rule of the clergy as our political interests require us to make efforts to keep the Greeks far from the other Christian citizens under our rule because the spirit of the Greek element will permanently run counter to our interests (*rūḥ al-ǧins al-Yūnānī sa-tabqā ʿalā ad-dawām muḍādda li-maṣlaḥatinā*).[470]

Indeed, ʿAzmī Bek was remembered by Arab Orthodox activists for his unfulfilled promise to push through a lay majority in the Mixed Council. ʿĪsā quoted from his own speech at the opening of the Mixed Council when he had allegedly said to the local Orthodox, 'I give you the promise of a free man that it will not take one year for you to occupy eight seats in the Mixed Council and the monks only four. Thus, the majority will be on your side and you will be able to reform your *umma*.'[471] Under his successors, everything stagnated. During the office of Ǧawdat Bek (1911), the Ministry of Justice and Religious Affairs affirmed by Resolution 139 the formation of the trustees' councils, which did not materialize.[472] Muhdī Bek had to withdraw from his post in November 1912; the next governor, Ṭāhir Bek, stayed only two weeks in the District, and Māǧid Bek, in office from March 1913, could not do anything because of what he called 'difficult circumstances'.[473] ʿĪsā asked ʿAzmī Bek to restore 'all the legitimacy' (*ǧamīʿ aṣ-ṣalāḥīya*) of the Council, and to enforce the transfer of the budget to the Council and the electoral system for the trustees' councils to the dioceses.[474]

467 *Filasṭīn*, 17 December 1913: 292/4/5.
468 *Ad-Dustūr*, 27 November 1913; Second Special Edition: 2/1/1.
469 On Fuʾād Pasha, see Bölükbaşı 2009, 225.
470 *Ad-Dustūr*, 27 November 1913; Second Special Edition: 2/1/1.
471 *Ad-Dustūr*, 27 November 1913; Second Special Edition: 2/1/2.
472 *Ad-Dustūr*, 27 November 1913; Second Special Edition: 2/2/1.
473 *Ad-Dustūr*, 27 November 1913; Second Special Edition: 2/2/2.
474 *Ad-Dustūr*, 27 November 1913; Second Special Edition: 2/2/1–2.

Ottomanism versus an Arab Orthodox Proto-Nationalism?

At the end of 1913, when the Arab Orthodox had lost faith that the local authorities could be helpful in resolving the intra-Orthodox conflict, there were noticeable discursive turns in *Filasṭīn.* While the central state underwent a legitimacy crisis (faced by the Balkan crisis, the impact of Arab decentralization and the First Arab Congress, and the rise of other 'national questions' in Anatolia), the ʿĪsās became aware of an increasing 'Turkification' in bureaucracy and that the state was becoming gradually alienated from its non-Turkish elements. They also were aware that political separatist tendencies were fostered by the imperial powers, who presented themselves as protectors of the Empire's 'minorities', and that proto-nationalist arguments were starting to gain legitimacy in the political discourse in the Arab East. Thus, ʿĪsā consciously played with proto-nationalist terminology, which could be understood in various ways. When addressing ʿAzmī Bek, he defined the Arab Orthodox as an *umma waṭanīya*, a 'national community', that was currently at a 'critical point' (*markaz ḥariğ*) in its history. From here, there were two ways potential futures, ʿĪsā affirmed. Either the Orthodox youth would benefit from being protected under 'the shadow of the Constitution', or, if they continued in 'slavery' (*ʿubūdīya*) to the Patriarchate, they would leave the Ottoman homeland. ʿĪsā stressed that, to prevent Christian emigration from Palestine, it was not necessary to give the Arab Orthodox 'all the rights that are due to us as a national community' (*laysa kull al-ḥaqq allaḏī lanā ka-umma waṭanīya*), a term that might be understood here in the sense of 'minority'. It was merely necessary, ʿĪsā continued, to implement the official resolutions in order to remove the great misunderstanding among foreign nations who thought 'that there is neither justice nor just treatment in Turkey' (*lā ʿadl wa-lā inṣāf fī Turkiyā*).[475]

Here, ʿĪsā obviously played with the image of Turkey as the 'sick man' under 'despotic rule', which was widespread in the Western press in order to put pressure ʿAzmī Bek. This supports my former observation (in Chapter I) that the Ottoman discourse presented in *Filasṭīn* during the Young Turk era was a very 'instrumental patriotism' that was supposed to provide stability, and mainly to support the implementation of reforms on the local level. I take ʿĪsā's argumentation as a sign of two things. First, as the Empire approached World War I, Ottoman Christians were gaining in confidence to defend their interests vis-à-vis the central state by applying the imperialist discourse on the protection of 'minorities'. Second, in the context of the Council's annulment around the turn of 1913–14, the Ottomanism of the ʿĪsās in particular was increasingly becoming a thin layer of official political rhetoric.

475 *Ad-Dustūr*, 27 November 1913; Second Special Edition: 2/2/2.

The Reopening of Filasṭīn and the Mixed Council: Back to Neutrality?

Meanwhile, the matter of the suspension of *Filasṭīn* went to court and attracted many curious onlookers.[476] The ʿĪsās were accused because of their editorial 'What is seen and what is not seen', referred to above, and the court fined ʿĪsā al-ʿĪsā 25 lira for 'insulting the municipality and the gendarmerie forces' (*ḏamman wa-qadḥan fī hayʾat al-baladīya wa-anfār al-ǧāndarmeh*). ʿĪsā announced that he would appeal.[477] When, in the middle of December 1913, their newspaper finally reappeared under the old title, the ʿĪsās were triumphant. In the first editorial, entitled 'A High Building Collapses' (*Ṣurūḥ tanhāru*), Yūsuf said that the court had established that *Filasṭīn* was 'no traitor to the homeland' (*laysat ḫiyāna li-l-waṭan*), and he enthusiastically thanked his supporters who had been, during this time, the 'greatest comfort' (*akbar taʿziya*).[478] Upon *Filasṭīn*'s revival, people 'ripped it from the hands of the distributers with expressions of joy on their faces that touched us very much and motivated us to continue on our way', the editors euphorically claimed.[479]

However, despite of this euphoria on the part of Jaffa readers, the reopening of *Filasṭīn* was also accompanied by the end of the ʿĪsās' leadership of the anti-clerical campaign. While the royal commission mediated in the negotiations on the future of the Mixed Council during *Filasṭīn*'s suspension, ʿAzmī Bek was obviously in a position to press for a change of its agenda: after *Filasṭīn*'s revival, the ʿĪsās set a completely new conciliatory tone towards the Patriarchate, which was the most radical turnabout they had taken in their publication history during the Second Constitutional period. Suddenly, they rehabilitated Māǧid Bek and declared, with the help of ʿAzmī Bek, that they had understood that his 'hands were tied' without orders from Istanbul. The editors affirmed that *Filasṭīn* did not follow the custom of others to 'flatter the governors' but was 'at the service of truth, not at the service of interests' (*fī ḫidmat al-ḥaqīqa lā fī ḫidmat al-aġrāḍ*). Thus, their role was merely to mediate and present the voice of the people to the government and vice-verse. Never before, the ʿĪsās concluded, had there been such misunderstanding between them and the government as in the context of the Orthodox question.[480] They pledged that they would renounce any political agenda in the conflict and leave the solution to ʿAzmī Bek, in whom they had 'child-like' trusted and he had asked them to abstain from using 'the pen of war

476 *Ad-Dustūr*, 27 November 1913: 1/2/5. The case was first brought to court in Jaffa, which transferred it to the Court in Jerusalem whose further judgment was awaited. See ibid., First Special Edition: 1/1.

477 *Filasṭīn*, 17 December 1913: 292/4/5.

478 *Filasṭīn*, 17 December 1913: 292/1/1–3.

479 *Filasṭīn*, 24 December 1913: 293/2/5.

480 *Filasṭīn*, 24 December 1913: 293/3/1–2.

and opposition' (*qalam al-ḥarb wa-l-mudāfaʿa*) so as not to jeopardize negotiations.[481]

Did *Filasṭīn* lose its sting through the intervention of ʿAzmī Bek? Indeed, while the ʿĪsās were entangled in legal problems, they might have thought that the future of *Filasṭīn* was in jeopardy, or ʿAzmī Bek might have pressured them into believing that the reopening of the Council depended on them. Furthermore, they had not only supporters but also influential opponents, and during the court case, five (unknown) rivals brought cases against them for personal insults. In addition to the 25 lira fine, the editors were to pay a further 15 lira for insulting the municipality, plus 50 lira as compensation for personal insults, 10 lira to each of their accusers. This amounted up to 90 lira. The ʿĪsās declared this as 'an honorable wound the soldier obtains in the battlefield of jihad' (*al-ǧirāḥ aš-šarīfa allatī yanāluhā l-ǧundī fī mīdān al-ǧihād*), to demonstrate that they had not lost their combative spirit.[482]

Meanwhile in Jerusalem, ʿAzmī Bek tried to find a solution for the Council.[483]. In January 1914, *Filasṭin* presented the resolution of the royal commission, issued on 30 December 1913, without comment, and the ʿĪsās declared that they would abstain from further dispute on the Orthodox case so as not to put 'obstacles' (*ʿarāqīl*) in the way of the commission.[484] The first article ordered the reopening of the Council, and in January 1914, its doors opened again. Yūsuf al-ʿĪsā exulted that the Council had now attained 'extensive competence and complete independence of action', and the Orthodox were now to enjoy the fruits of victory after all their sacrifices.[485] Yūsuf euphorically announced, 'God has crowned our work with success' (*kallala allāhu ʿamalanā bi-n-naǧāḥ*), although 'more than 30 petitions' had previously demanded the Council's abolition.[486] Finally, he declared, he was willing to practice 'Christian forgiveness' (*at-tasāmuḥ al-masīḥī*) towards 'our spiritual fathers' and forget all former dissent and continue on a course of 'good intentions' (*ḥusn an-niya*).[487] An article in *Filasṭīn* by an anonymous Christian stressed the positive effect of the Orthodox *nahḍa* as a *cultural* movement on the 'Muslim brothers' in Jerusalem, claiming that, under its impact, they were about to work out an agenda for reforming the Islamic *awqāf*:

> May the hands perish (*tabbat yadā*) of anyone who claims that the nahḍa that the Christian citizens of Palestine (*aš-šaʿb al-masīḥī l-waṭanī fī Filasṭīn*) have been un-

481 *Filasṭīn*, 24 December 1913: 293/4/2.
482 *Filasṭīn*, 31 December 1913: 295/3/2–3.
483 *Filasṭīn*, 27 December 1913: 294/3/3; 21 January 1914: 300/3/2–3.
484 *Filasṭīn*, 24 December 1913: 293/4/2; 17 January 1914: 299/1/2.
485 *Filasṭīn*, 17 January 1914: 299/1/2–3.
486 *Filasṭīn*, 17 January 1914: 299/1/4.
487 *Filasṭīn*, 17 January 1914: 299/2/1.

dertaking was not the result of a national vitality (*ḥayāt qawmīya*) that has spread in the body of the umma… Those like him might come and see how our Muslim brothers have been motivated by the blessed and glorious phenomenon that has spread from us to them. The High Commission that gathered in Jerusalem has been able to… remove the misunderstandings. The Orthodox umma has reconciled with the Patriarchate and has eventually been able to convince it that the people who follow it in religion only want to progress in their cultural issues and in teaching their children in order to empower themselves to be able to compete with other nations in the struggle of life. And after the Commission issued its decision… our Muslim brothers also thought about the matter of their awqāf. Their scholars and notables gathered and issued a petition to the governor.[488]

Effects of the New Resolution after the Reopening of the Council

It is not known how ʿAzmī Bek managed to put pressure on the patriarch, but he achieved the reopening of the Council. After staying for almost two months for negotiations in Jerusalem, ʿAzmī Bek left by ship from Jaffa, and promised to keep an eye on the Mixed Council. What did the new resolution implement apart from the Council's reopening? It was not all victory, although the Council implemented some quick changes on the local scale, but without explaining the decision-making processes. First of all, the delegates from Salṭ and Jaffa, Mulkī and ʿĪsā, had to leave to make way for new delegates from Gaza and Beit Jala, as was ordered in the second article of the resolution.[489]

Second, the resolution enforced the election of trustees (which was only implemented in Jaffa), the appointment of a new school board and the election of new delegates. It is important to note that, since Yūsuf al-ʿĪsā had been deprived of his membership on the Council, he could no longer document the debates, and *Filasṭīn* now merely reported the results, not the negotiations.

Under the impact of the new resolution, the regulations for the election of trustees, in line with what the Council had already decided in spring 1911, were sent to the dioceses; and in February 1914, the patriarch finally transferred the long awaited document (*manšūr*).[490] A 'monitoring committee', quickly appointed to oversee the voting, announced that six trustees would be elected in Jaffa, and called on 'every Orthodox person over 20 years old to put his card into the ballot box, which will be open until sunset'.[491] The election result stated that Yūsuf al-ʿĪsā had received 'the most votes', but he resigned without explanation.

488 *Filasṭīn*, 24 January 1914: 301/1/1–3.
489 *Filasṭīn*, 17 January 1914: 299/1/4–2/1.
490 *Filasṭīn*, 14 February 1914: 307/3/5–4/3.
491 Voting was to take place in the hall of the Orthodox convent in Jaffa. Ḫalīl Efendi, commander of the gendarmerie, Nimr Efendi, secretary of the *qāʾimaqāmīya*, and the clergy and Orthodox notables would gather to observe the voting. *Filasṭīn*, 21 February 1914: 309/3/3–4; 25 February 1914: 310/2/3–4.

The six trustees for Jaffa were Ḥannā al-Malik, Ǧurǧī Dabbās, Yūsuf (ʿAbdallāh) Mitrī, Yūsuf Bartaqš, ʿĪsā al-ʿĪsā, and Ilyās Sālim al-Bartaqš.[492] In July 1914, in line with to the governor's order, the Patriarchate announced the trustees for Jaffa, who were now eight instead of six: Ǧirǧis Manṭūreh, Ǧurǧī Dabbās, Ḥanā al-Malik, Yūsuf (ʿAbdallāh) Mitrī, Mīnā Dabbās, Ibrāhīm al-Qudsī, Yūsuf Bartaqš and Yūsuf al-ʿĪsā.[493] I have found no explanation for this change, and there are no reports of election of trustees in other cities before the collection of *Filasṭīn* stopped in August 1914.

In January 1914, the Council confirmed the appointment of a school board in line with the new resolution: Archimandrite Dosithios, still a delegate in the Council, Archimandrite Bandalamion, Ǧurǧī Zaḫariyā, former Jerusalem delegate on the Council, and Sulṭī Ibrāhīm, the al-Ḥisn delegate.[494] In March 1914, the school board delivered its first report on reforms regarding two boarding schools, in Jerusalem and Jaffa. It ordered the acceptance of pupils from poor families (to be restricted to 40) free of charge, from middle-class families (restricted to 20 students) who would pay half fees, and students from rich families (restricted to 20 students), who would pay full fees. For the management of these schools, a 'monitoring committee' (*hayʾat al-idāra al-ʿāliya*) was appointed, comprising two clergy, two lay people from Jerusalem and one 'foreigner' (*aǧnabī*) from the dioceses, who was head of the boarding school in Jerusalem. The schools were open to every Orthodox, and taught in Turkish, Greek and Arabic, in addition to English or French as voluntary languages.[495]

As required by the royal commission, elections for new delegates took place in Beit Jala in January 1914. Ǧibrān Maṭar reported that serious dissent split the population between the two candidates, Yaʿqūb Maḫlūf and ʿAwdeh. As the atmosphere was heated, the local government wanted to resolve the matter and confirmed ʿAwdeh Ḫalīl as the new delegate, which provoked protests by the supporters of Yaʿqūb Maḫlūf. ʿAzmī Bek sent the ʿĪsā cousins (!) to Beit Jala to reach a compromise between the parties. The Orthodox of Beit Jala were then given a 24-hour deadline to work out a solution. First, the problem seemed solved when ʿAwdeh Ḫalīl resigned for unknown reasons and the local government confirmed Yaʿqūb Maḫlūf as new delegate.[496] Then, the ʿĪsās and the Orthodox notables reached another compromise to 'keep the peace' (*ḥifẓan li-s-salām*) between the two families: ʿAwdeh Ḫalīl would be delegate for Beit Jala in the first year, and another member of the Maḫlūf family, Ǧirǧis, in the second.[497]

492 *Filasṭīn*, 25 February 1914: 310/2/3–4.
493 *Filasṭīn*, 4 July 1914: 333/5/4.
494 *Filasṭīn*, 7 February 1914: 305/2/4.
495 *Filasṭīn*, 18 March 1914: 316/3/4–5.
496 *Filasṭīn*, 21 January 1914: 300/3/2–3.
497 *Filasṭīn*, 20 June 1914: 329/4/1.

Regarding the delegates from Kerak, al-Ḥiṣn and Jenin, ʿAzmī Bek insisted that their term would end in August 1914 in order to establish a proper system of rotation. This meant that their term in office was very short because it only started in 1914. At the end of June 1914, *Filasṭīn* reported that the Council had been sent on holiday, again without orders for the election of new delegates being sent to the dioceses.[498] We have no further information about what happened to the delegates, as the issues of *Filasṭīn* at my disposal end with August 1914.

7.7. From Polarization to Self-Censorship

The effect of the new resolution on *Filasṭīn*'s role as a 'mouthpiece' of the Arab Orthodox cause was that it made a total discursive change to 'neutrality', or rather, self-censorship. Through ʿAzmī Bek's intervention, Yūsuf al-ʿĪsā, the former leader of the lay opposition, was deprived of his role on the Council and was out of Damianos's way. The minutes of the Council debates, which recorded the statements of each speaker, was a stage on which the laity could perform their reform agenda and export it into the public discourse, and they now disappeared completely from *Filasṭīn*. Since Yūsuf no longer attended the sessions, he could not know the details of the debates and did not seem to have an informer in the Council. It may be that his interest in the Council's debates decreased when he was deprived of his platform. Did he engage in documenting the chronology of each speaker's statements while he was unable to present himself as a pioneer of Orthodox reforms? We do not know. What is sure is that the style of his reporting on Orthodox matters changed completely from January 1914 onwards. Coverage on Orthodox matters became rare, and ʿĪsā now abstained from provoking of the governor or the patriarch. Short reports presented the Council's decisions in a neutral style, without giving insight into the minutes of the debates and shifted to the presentation of results alone, without giving further comment.

Most reports on Orthodox matters from 1914 onwards dealt with Orthodox cultural activities on a local scale, charity events, cinema festivals and the like.[499] Church news, such appointments of clergy into certain positions, was presented with neutral vocabulary,[500] and the combative tone of the Jerusalem correspondent was also censored. In a short informative style, he noted that the Convent did not want to open the Orthodox boarding school in Jaffa this year as planned since 'the revenues are lacking and the Convent's financial situation is

498 *Filasṭīn*, 24 June 1914: 330/3/4.

499 *Filasṭīn*, 04 February 1914: 304/3/3; 07 February 1914: 305/3/5; 11 March 1914: 312/3/4; 01 April 1914: 320/3/1; and 04 July 1914: 333/5/5.

500 *Filasṭīn*, 08 July 1914: 334/5/3.

not healthy'.[501] He also reported, without any emotion, that a new committee had been formed to investigate the case of the Jerusalemites' allowances for places that were now defined as 'houses belonging to the *waqf*' (*dūr al-waqf*).[502] Coverage on Orthodox matters was now even occasionally positive about Patriarchal initiatives. The Jerusalem correspondent reported that the results of students in the Orthodox schools of Bethlehem were 'all successful and progressive' (*kull taqaddum wa-nağāḥ*).[503] Ğibrān Maṭar reported from Beit Jala that Damianos had started to send a Greek medical doctor weekly to Beit Jala to treat the poor.[504] It is obvious that, in *Filasṭīn*, Orthodox matters were no longer a 'national' matter. *Filasṭīn*, it seems, was forced to self-censor so as not to jeopardize its existence, and the ʿĪsās were from 1914 no longer central actors in the Movement.

The End of Filasṭīn as a Protest Forum in Orthodox Matters

This dramatic shift of *Filasṭīn*'s agenda regarding Orthodox matters caused irritation. Yūsuf al-ʿĪsā was aware that he was about to lose his credibility in the eye of the public and announced that 'we will not break the pen' (*lā nukassir al-qalam*) but stay on track concerning the Council's activities and gave assurance that 'we have already installed a great telescope that is pointing its barrel at the hall where the Council gathers to observe (*nurāqib*) what the lay members are doing, every one of them'.[505] But this was empty talk. Yūsuf al-ʿĪsā was cut off from information, and the change was perceived with utter amazement. Numerous letters reached the editorial department, asking for an explanation. From the perspective of Orthodox activists, *Filasṭīn* had simply disappeared from the battlefield. An anonymous Jerusalemite inquired about what had happened *Filasṭīn*'s former role as defender of Orthodox rights in Palestine, and expressed his irritation, asking:

> Why have you dropped Orthodox matters? Why have you forgotten your promise to observe the Council's activities? Have you lost hope in the continuation of the Jihad? Or are you possessed by the delusion that we have already received everything we had hoped for? Or are you in fear that the government might silence your paper as the the Convent desires? I impose on you... to persist in love for this unfortunate milla. So, point the telescope's barrel at the hall in which the Council gathers, observe what the lay members there do and give us news of it on the pages of your newspaper. It is astonishing to me that you keep silence ... Important matters are happening this week as the Council will decide on a school program and appoint the monitoring committee. The lay members should know beforehand that, if they decide against the resolution ... we

501 *Filasṭīn*, 15 July 1914: 336/2/5.
502 *Filasṭīn*, 15 July 1914: 336/2/5.
503 *Filasṭīn*, 15 July 1914: 336/2/5.
504 *Filasṭīn*, 04 July 1914: 333/5/2.
505 *Filasṭīn*, 17 January 1914: 299/2/1.

> will do all it takes ... We will not be satisfied with a patched up reconciliation (*lā narḍā ṣulḥan muraqqaʿan*) that is taken from our dignity and does not bring benefits.[506]

Yūsuf al-ʿĪsā confessed to the readers who had been sending letters that he was cut off from the Council, but that it 'is not our fault' (*lā yakūn aḏ-ḏanb ḏanbanā*).[507] How, he asked, 'could we know in Jaffa what is happening 87 kilometers away and inside a hall that is locked' (*qāʿa muġlaqa*)? He stressed that he was not giving up his demands for the Council to be accountable; he had called on the royal commission to ensure that the Council should publish its activities (*takūn ʿalānīya*) and ask the lay members to provide him with first-hand information; yet 'they refuse' (*yarfuḍūna*), he explained.[508] He sarcastically attacked the anonymous author who was better informed about the Council's activities better than himself to persuade the Jerusalem delegate to provide them with 'just a little bit' (*bi-qalīl al-qalīl*) of what was going on in the sessions, and pleaded with Jerusalem readers to find out about what was happening 'behind the walls of the Council' (*ḍimna ǧudrān al-maǧlis*).[509]

Saving Legitimacy: the Shift towards Anti-Zionism as a New Protest Field

After *Filasṭīn* was deprived of its political role in the Orthodox Movement, its character as a 'dispute forum' and a 'mouthpiece of the people' was put at risk, and the shrinking reports of Orthodox news created a gap in its coverage. How was it filled? The answer was a shift to an anti-Zionist campaign. By 1914, the Zionist movement had become a welcome enemy against which *Filasṭīn* could direct its traditional protest role. During the latter half of 1913, opposition to Zionist purchases of land in the District grew dramatically and anti-Zionism became accepted in the public discourse. After January 1914, *Filasṭīn* dropped its attacks on the clergy, the patriarch and Māǧid Bek, and the ʿĪsās found a new target in political Zionism, which had started to be perceived as a new national question. I propose that government pressure, censorship and fear of suspension, which made *Filasṭīn* give up its anti-clericalism, served as a catalyst for its shift towards anti-Zionism as the new main target of political protest. The way for this had already been prepared through growing resistance to Zionist migration during 1913, as will be outlined in the chapter on Zionism. Since Yūsuf did not have a single ally in the Council and could not access information about the sessions, *Filasṭīn* completely dropped out of the Orthodox activist scene, while the Movement also seemed increasingly internally fragmented. Around the same time, Sakākīnī, another leading figure in the Movement, withdrew from his en-

506 *Filasṭīn*, 4 March 1914: 312/3/4.
507 *Filasṭīn*, 4 March 1914: 312/3/5.
508 *Filasṭīn*, 4 March 1914: 312/3/5.
509 *Filasṭīn*, 4 March 1914: 312/3/5.

gagement, which may have been connected with a major confrontation he had with the patriarch towards the end of 1913 after he published a political pamphlet that encouraged the Palestinian youth to overthrow the clerical domination of the Patriarchate, as I discuss elsewhere.[510]

For the ʿĪsās, the time was ripe for a new enemy. From 1914 onwards, they presented themselves as pioneers of anti-Zionism in the Palestinian press and thus saved the reputation of *Filasṭīn* as a protest forum and 'resistance fighter'.

510 See Sakākīnī's pamphlet on the Orthodox Renaissance (1913), Sakākīnī 2004, vol 2, 47; and idem 1982, 57f, Bawalsa 2010a, 11, and my article 'The Appropriation of Political Concepts in Ḫalīl as-Sakākīnī's 'Orthodox Renaissance' (1908–14)' (forthcoming 2020).

IV. The Press Debate on Zionist Immigration: Driving Force or Obstacle to Local Development?

1. Framing the Topic

This chapter investigates the Palestinian debate on the 'Zionist question' (*al-mas'ala aṣ-ṣihyūnīya*), based on 362 articles or items published in *Filasṭīn* between July 1911 and August 1914. It identifies its central content issues and spectrum of actors, its communicational features, controversial elements and main discursive shifts. It also looks at how the world view of the contributing authors and their set of values were related to their argumentation regarding Zionism, shedding some light on the culture of debate in Palestine before World War I. As already explained, the ʿĪsās made their newspaper a forum for debating issues of public interest, and alongside the promotion of the Arab Orthodox Renaissance, Zionism was another hot topic in *Filasṭīn* that for many people in late Ottoman Palestine raised open questions and ambivalent feelings. In 1911, the editors acknowledged that the impact of the 'Zionist movement' (*al-ḥaraka aṣ-ṣihyūnīya*) on Palestine was an issue of public interest. In November 1911, they initiated a debate about its benefits and harms, declaring that they would 'provide for the authors' pens the space for criticism or approval of Zionist colonization' (*li-yattasiʿ li-aqlām al-kataba al-maǧāl fī ḏamm aw taḥbīḏ istiʿmār aṣ-ṣihyūnīyīn*).[1]

As a term, 'Zionism' was introduced by Nathan Birnbaum in his magazine *Selbstemanzipation* ('Auto-Emancipation'), and made the assumption that the necessary precondition for a free social, cultural and political Jewish life could only to be realized within the framework of a nation.[2] Starting as a European emancipatory renaissance movement that aimed at the liberation of Jews as a collective, 'Zionism' was a pool of spiritual, cultural and political trends that sought to foster a revival of Jewish life in various ways that were not united. Being rooted in the failure to implement civic equality which prevented the integration,

1 *Filasṭīn*, 4 November 1911: 83/2/1.
2 Reinkowski 1995, 21f.; Krämer 2002, 129f.

or assimilation, of European Jewry into the modern nation state, 'Zionism' as a reform movement was also accompanied by a movement for the enlightenment and secularization of Jewish life, the *Haskala*. As such, 'Zionism' was also a response to the rise of European ethnic nationalism during the nineteenth century and political anti-semitism, linking the ideals of modern European civil society with the concept of the Jews as a nation.[3] In its theoretical fundaments, Zionism can be defined as a national ideology deriving from European nationalism that aimed at the creation of a center for the Jews outside Europe.

The international Zionist movement included manifold concepts that were sometimes contradictory, and the main goals of 'Zionism' can be summarized as followed. First, 'cultural Zionism' aimed at the revival of Palestine as a spiritual center for the Jews. It was not a national project and not necessarily connected with migration but supported a spiritual Jewish revival in Palestine from 'exile' (Hebr.: *ġalūt*). Second, 'practical Zionism' came into being from the 1880s onwards and focused on the revival of a new Jewry in 'Eretz Israel', the land of the forefathers, through the establishment of Jewish colonies in Palestine. Inspired by Eastern European messianic movements, it saw the spirit of Judaism as threatened by the physical persecution of the Jews on the one hand, and secularist trends of the *Haskala* on the other. Third, 'political Zionism' defined the 'Jewish question' as national one and claimed to speak for world Jewry. Instead of building Jewish colonies that were isolated from each other and financed by philanthropic associations from the *ġalūt*, this was a secular nationalist movement that stood for the construction of a Jewish sovereign nation state in the modern sense.[4] Political Zionism was institutionalized in the World Zionist Organization (WZO), which claimed to be the international representative of the Jews. Its official agenda was the creation of a national home for the Jews in Palestine and this received international acknowledgement.[5] Theodor Herzl (1860–1904), considered the pioneer of this movement, introduced its program in his work 'The Jewish State' (*Der Judenstaat*, 1896). He opposed the 'infiltration' of Palestine through isolated colonies and philanthropic support from outside, and thought that the WZO should work out a political solution for the 'Jewish question' in the Middle East through diplomatic negotiations. In his view, Western European Jewish elites should have the leading role in the creation of the Jewish state, while Eastern European Jews, as the labor force, would be the

3 Schöps 1983, 14.
4 See Volkov (2001) on 'old' and 'new' elements of Jewish nationalism.
5 That was the central aim defined by the WZO in the 'Baseler Program', worked out at the first International Zionist congress in Basel (1897). See Reinkowski 1995, 21.

'practical material' for building up the state. This was, he thought, the solution for the misery of the oppressed Jews in Eastern Europe ('Judennot').[6]

The authors who discussed Zionism in *Filasṭīn* did not care about its internal ideological differences but discussed it as a *foreign*, not necessarily Jewish, migration movement from Europe into the Jerusalem District. They were not concerned with religious sentiments but with the very practical consequences of foreign immigration.

Since Jaffa was the center of the WZO in Palestine, the local middle and upper classes were concerned with the possible economic and cultural impact of a new generation of Jewish migrants on the urban context and speculated about the possible effects of Zionist colonization for the Palestinian Arab villages in the area. It should be noted here that the concept of 'colonization' (*istiʿmār*) presented in *Filasṭīn* did not necessarily have negative connotations but implied a notion of 'civilizational progress'. While in 1911 and 1912, the coverage on Zionism in *Filasṭīn* focused on possible economic rivalries resulting from foreign migration, the debate switched in 1913 and 1914 to the suspected political aspirations of the Zionists in Palestine as an Ottoman province. In the context of other political crises that the Ottoman Empire faced, the notion of Zionism as a political 'danger' (*ḫaṭr*) became dominant. In 1914, *Filasṭīn* gave wide coverage to resolutions of the Zionist congresses in Europe and the political strategies of the WZO, and very closely observed the initiatives of prominent Zionist figures like Baron Rothschild, the representative of the British Jewish community, and the Jewish National Fund (JN); the Zionist association that purchased land for Jewish settlement in Palestine as to systematically build up the 'New Yishuv' (*ha-yišuv ha-ḥadaš*), a term that describes the Jewish community in Palestine and is associated with the Zionist national project.

Relevance of the Topic and State of the Art

There is little qualitative evaluation of the early Arab Palestinian press coverage on Zionism. In this respect, *Filasṭīn* is one of the rare sources available for the years before World War I and provides rich insight into local attitudes to Zionism during the Second Constitutional era when Arab journalism was outstandingly controversial. During these years, the Arab press discovered Zionism as a topic of public concern and worked out its main arguments until, in the lead-up to World

6 For the development of the Zionist movement in Europe and its genesis as a national project in Palestine, see Brenner 2005 and Rahe 1988. For an overview of Zionist migration into Palestine since the nineteenth century and the development of the 'New Yishuv', defining the Jewish community in Palestine, until World War I, see Krämer 2002, 122–146. For a categorization of ideological trends within Zionism, see Schöps 1983, 75–95; and for the interrelation of European nationalism, Jewish defenses against anti-Semitism and Zionism as a national ideology, see idem 1996, 273–363.

War I, it was articulating an outspoken anti-Zionist position that would have considerable influence on Arab political discourse for decades.[7] This study looks at the beginnings of this process when a spectrum of authors established through controversial debating in *Filasṭīn* a discourse on the impact of Zionist migration into Palestine, and when local positions on Zionism were quite indecisive and contradictory.

Early Arab responses to Zionism through the press have received scholarly attention before. The first to show that Zionist migration into Palestine received early attention was the comprehensive study of Neville Mandel (1976) on Arab reactions to Zionism before World War I. Through the impact of the acquisition of large plots of land near al-Fūla in the Nazareth Subdistrict during 1910/11 by the JN, Arab opposition to Jewish colonization was increasingly articulated in the Arab press, which became a driving force in the establishment of anti-Zionist arguments. As early as 1911, the Jaffa-based Palestine Office, the WZO organ in Palestine to coordinate the building of the New Yishuv, started to systematically document anti-Zionist articles in about 25 Arab Palestinian, Beirut and Damascene newspapers. This was the basis for the study by Mandel, who evaluated a great number of articles and also quoted from *Filasṭīn*.[8] However, the weak point in Mandel's analysis is his selection of sources. Because of a lack of Arab sources, as Mandel claimed, he based his study on articles from the Arab press that had been translated into Hebrew and preserved in the archives of the Jewish Colonization Association (JCA), the Alliance Israélite Universelle (AIU), the Zionist Central Office (ZCO), in the Central Zionist Archives (ZCA) and the Israeli States Archives (ISA). But since only the antagonistic articles are collected in theses archives, Mandel did not pay attention to neutral or positive local reactions to Zionism. Besides this bias, Mandel depended on the selection of anti-Zionist articles translated into Hebrew or German and he never accessed the original Arabic material; a rather problematic position for a survey of Arabic media. Classifying the newspapers *Filasṭīn*, *al-Karmil* (Haifa) and *al-Mufīd* (Beirut) as the pioneers of anti-Zionism before World War I, many later studies continued to use Mandel's categorization of Arab press responses on Zionism.[9]

7 Mandel 1976, xix.
8 Mandel 1976, 130–132.
9 See Muslih 1988 and Tessler 2009. There is an interesting contradiction in Mandel's categorization. Mandel claimed that there was a relation between the attitude of a newspaper towards Zionism and its editor's religious confession and political affiliation. He stated that newspapers that adopted an anti-CUP stance were mainly published by Muslims and in general anti-Zionist, anti-Christian and anti-European. Pro-CUP newspapers were in general published by Christian Arabs and their stand towards Zionism was a neutral or even positive (Mandel 1976, 130–132). However, this categorization contradicts Mandel's description of *al-Karmil* and *Filasṭīn* as the Palestinian press pioneers of anti-Zionism, since both papers were

Another comprehensive investigation of Arab responses to Zionism in the press before World War I is provided by Rashid Khalidi, who analyzed articles on the topic in 22 newspapers between Cairo and Damascus. For the years 1911–1914, he analyzed 10 newspapers, including *Filasṭīn.*[10] According to his 1981 study, Khalidi identified more than 600 articles on Zionism in about 10,000 issues, categorizing them according to their attitude as anti-Zionist, neutral or pro-Zionist. He produced a quantitative analysis for each newspaper, except *al-Muqtabas* (Damascus) and *Filasṭīn.*[11] In spite of this comprehensive approach, Khalidi's results reveal inconsistences. His monograph on the genesis of a modern Palestinian identity (1997) is a rich study on 'overlapping identities and conflicting loyalties' in late Ottoman Palestine but includes a chapter on Arab press responses to Zionism that in general reproduces the results of his study from 1981 but less transparently. Comparing his studies, it turned out that his survey of *Filasṭīn* is based on articles reprinted in other press publications. Khalidi never systematically investigated *Filasṭīn*'s stance on Zionism through *Filasṭīn* itself, and judged *Filasṭīn*, here following Mandel, to be the pioneer of anti-Zionist coverage, articulating the political arguments that were picked up by other Arab newspapers up to World War I.[12] Another weak point in his evaluation regarding the coverage on Zionism in the Arab press is the fact that it is a quantitative analysis. Apart from very occasional quotations, Khalidi does not reveal the actual content, or the identity of authors contributing to the debate.

Zionism as a Driving Force for the Palestinian Press and Nationalism

The Zionist movement significantly stimulated the development of a controversial Arab press in Palestine. First, European-Jewish migration and Hebrew press production in Palestine inspired Arab journalistic enterprises. Second, Zionist colonization challenged local intellectuals to discuss its future impact on Palestine, and the stimulating effect of Zionism on the Palestinian press has been

---

edited by Christians and *Filasṭīn* was clearly pro-CUP, while Nağīb an-Naṣṣār's *al-Karmil* took a clear stand against the CUP.

10 Among them were *al-Karmil* (Haifa), *Filastīn* (Jaffa), *al-Mufīd*, *Lisān al-Ḥāl*, *al-Ittiḥād al-ʿUṯmānī*, *al-Ḥaqīqa* and *al-Iqbāl* (all of them Beirut), *al-Muqtabas* (Damascus), *al-Muqaṭṭam* and *al-Ahrām* (Cairo). For a short categorization of these papers, see Khalidi 1997, 119–144.

11 See Khalidi 1981, 22–26. Khalidi's later studies on Zionism in the Arab press (published between 1982 and 1997) no longer follow this categorization, but he now assessed all papers as anti-Zionist, apart from the Egyptian *al-Muqaṭṭam* (Khalidi 1997, 123–125). Nevertheless, Khalidi does mention occasional shifts. In 1913, there were negotiations between the Zionist Committee and the leadership of the Decentralization Party to work out a political strategy towards the Ottoman authorities. According to Khalidi, the antagonistic coverage on Zionism in the Arab press came to a halt during these months so as not to endanger the negotiations. Khalidi 1997, 140; Mandel 1976, 148f.

12 Khalidi 1997, 126f.

noted by many scholars,[13] and the incentivizing role of the Arab press in the emergence of an Arab Palestinian (proto-)national identity has also been stressed. Mandel considered the press as *the* vehicle that systematically formulated anti-Zionist paradigms (initiated by *Filasṭīn* and *al-Karmil*), which consolidated in the Palestinian public, were picked up by newspapers throughout the Middle East and later dominated the Arab political discourse on Zionism.[14] In contrast to Mandel, Khalidi stressed the 'bottom-up-effect' in the Palestinian controversy on Zionism, which, in his view, was not initiated by the press. Rather, Khalidi considers the revolts against land sales to Zionist organizations in rural areas as the driving force that brought Zionism as a political issue to Palestinian public awareness and motivated the Arab press to pick up the topic.[15]

Several other scholars have seen in the anti-Zionism presented by *Filasṭīn* before World War I the genesis of a distinct Palestinian national identity.[16] Naǧǧār claims that the 'national resistance against Zionism', especially in *al-ʿAṣmaʾī*, *al-Karmil* and *Filasṭīn*, was the driving force behind the rise of the Arab press in Palestine. Here, Naǧǧār identifies the motivation of the Arab press to 'unmask' Zionist ambitions (*faḍḥ aṣ-ṣihūnīya*) as a driving force for the emergence of Palestinian national awareness before World War I.[17] Ḥaǧǧū's thesis is a similar example. He investigated the perception of the 'Zionist danger' in the early Arab press to prove that Arab newspapers 'foresaw' later historical developments.[18] However, in my opinion, these views limit the factors stimulating press activity in post-revolutionary Palestine to the 'conflict perspective' and ignore other factors in journalistic creativity.

Khalidi, Tadros and Tamari also stress the anti-Zionism of the ʿĪsās as a major focus in *Filasṭīn*, based on quotations from the unpublished memoirs of ʿĪsā al-ʿĪsā, which have been accessed by a limited range of scholars but were not available to me.[19] In these memoirs, ʿĪsā recalls that, apart from the Arab Orthodox cause, anti-Ottomanism and the battle against Zionist aspirations were

---

13 Ayalon 1995, 66.

14 Mandel 1974, 12; and 1976, 127.

15 See Khalidi 1997, 93–117. He examined early anti-Zionist clashes between peasants from the village of Yahūdīya and settlers of Petaḥ Tikva in 1886 (pp. 99f.); local resistance to the sale of more than 60,000 *dunam* in the Tiberias region by the Sursuqs, a Beiruti merchant family, to Jewish settlement bodies from 1901 onwards; notables' protests against the transfer of land in northern Palestine to the JN in 1911 and the impact of the so called 'al-Fūla affair' on the Palestinian elites (pp. 107f.). He argues that these events established an early 'pattern of interaction between rural resistance and urban opposition to Zionism' (p. 115.).

16 The study by Bracy falls into this category; however, as proven by Beška, in Bracy's *Printing Class* (2011), plagiarisms from Khalidi and Mandel were found, and so Bracy's results on *Filasṭīn* cannot be considered here. See Beška 2012, 113–119.

17 Naǧǧār 2005, 41–52.

18 Ḥaǧǧū 2007, 146–230.

19 Khalidi 2009; Tadros 2009, 2011; and Tamari 2014b.

the main political agendas in his newspaper from the very beginning.[20] In this manuscript, written after 1948 under the strong impression of the Nakba and his exile in Beirut, ʿĪsā looks back more than 30 years later on the history of *Filasṭīn*. Presenting his political stance during the late Ottoman era, ʿĪsā al-ʿĪsā declares that he was very skeptical about the Second Constitutional period and had little hope in 'Arab Turkish unity', as stressed by Tamari, who quotes ʿĪsā as saying he had regarded the CUP as 'basically a Turkish nationalist party with strong Zionist sympathies'.[21] Khalidi also picks up the anti-CUP quotation in ʿĪsā's memoirs, taking it as evidence for his thesis that *Filasṭīn*, together with *al-Karmil*, was *the* advocate of early anti-Zionism during the late Ottoman period. Khalidi states that 'in fact, much more attention was devoted to Zionism than to the Orthodox cause, or indeed to any other matter, in the pages of *Filasṭīn*, almost from its inception in 1911 until its closure in 1967';[22] yet, without having conducted a qualitative survey of *Filasṭīn*. This treatment of ʿĪsā's memoirs as a source to evaluate the coverage of *Filasṭīn* during the late Ottoman era should be regarded critically since it is a an autobiographical narrative written under the influence of the evolution of the political situation after World War I and a re-evaluation of the Ottoman past, fired by the disappointment of Palestinian national hopes during the Mandate, and the Nakba. ʿĪsā's reflections on the Ottoman past were expressed even in the post-Mandate period and *after* full-blown Palestinian nationalism had consolidated into an ideology that rejected a positive evaluation of the Ottoman era. However, Khalidi, Tadros and Tamari have ignored this gap in time and the ideological gap between the post-Nakba period and the Ottoman era.

I suggest that ʿĪsā *corrected* in his late memoires his earlier past, which certainly do not comply with his political position as presented in *Filasṭīn* between 1911 and 1914. The systematic analysis of *Filasṭīn* in this period revealed three important points. First, anti-Zionism was *not* the main motivation in *Filasṭīn* from its inception. Zionism was certainly an important issue in the *Local News* section, but it was not the central issue covered in the newspaper, although it steadily increased in importance until it became a major issue after the turn of the year 1913/14. Second, the ʿĪsās were outspoken defenders of the CUP until 1914. Yūsuf al-ʿĪsā was active in the local party branch and rented out a room for the CUP in the editorial office, and the ʿĪsās had no motivation to spread anti-Ottoman views in *Filasṭīn*. On the contrary, regular demonstrations of Ottoman patriotism were an integral part of *Filasṭīn*'s coverage, even if it was an 'in-

20 Also noted in Robson 2011, 87, 189, n. 35 who took this from Nuwayhiḍ (1981, 30) who quoted from an unknown speech of ʿĪsā. Probably Nuwayhiḍ also commented on this manuscript.

21 From ʿĪsā's 'Memories of the Past' (*Min Ḏikrayāt al-Māḍī*, 14) as quoted in Tamari 2014b, 16–17.

22 Khalidi 2009, 91.

strumental patriotism', as was pointed out in chapter I. Third, the ʿĪsās's main focus was on fostering the Arab Orthodox campaign, and the major part of *Filasṭīn*'s coverage revolved around the Orthodox cause from its inception. Of course, as part of the overall agenda, the modernization of Palestinian infrastructure, education and agriculture received similar attention.

Relational Studies on Arab and Jewish Responses to Zionism

There have been other studies that address Jewish and Arab responses on Zionism before World War I taking a relational approach. Michelle Campos's detailed study on the constitutional discourses of Mizrachi and Sephardi Jews in post-revolutionary Palestine puts the emphasis on the concept of a multi-confessional 'Ottoman Brotherhood' as propagated in the Hebrew and Ladino press. She also evaluates the contemporary controversy on Zionism in the 'press battles' between Arab Palestinian Christian and Jewish intellectuals through the Hebrew-Palestinian press, as well as debate on the Zionist movement in Palestine in the Jewish press in Istanbul. In this respect, she filters out three outstanding models of identity among Jewish intellectuals: a 'universal Ottomanism' in so far as Ottomanism was the only accepted national identity, an 'Ottoman Zionism' as an attempt to harmonize Ottomanism and Zionism, and a 'Palestinian Zionism' as a form of Palestinian-Jewish Zionism that claimed that the impact of Zionism would only benefit Palestine.[23] Valuable insights into Jewish discourses during the Second Constitutional era are also provided by Abigail Jacobson, who has investigated the political identities of Sephardi intellectuals in late Ottoman Palestine based on memories of Palestinian Jews. Specifically, she analyzes a circle of Sephardi Palestinians who tried to include Zionism into their concept of Ottoman brotherhood and promoted Zionism to their fellow citizens as a form of local patriotism. She also investigates statements of Ashkenazi migrants on the 'Arab Question' in Palestine and their views on possible Zionist cooperation with local Palestinian Arabs.[24] Another innovative approach is Jonathan Gribetz's survey, which is systematic investigation of the semantics of the 'self' and the 'other' among Arab and Jewish intellectuals. He analyzes the Muslim-Palestinian intellectual perspective in the writings of Rūḥī al-Ḫālidī on the history of the Jewish people and Arab discourses on 'Jewishness' in Arab magazines, namely in Ǧūrǧī Zaydān's *al-Hilāl* ('The Crescent', Cairo), Yaʿqūb Ṣarrūf's and Fāris Nimr's *al-Muqtaṭaf* ('The Selection', Cairo), and Rašīd Riḍā's Islamic-Reformist

23 See Campos 2003b, 280–236; and 2011, 197–244. For the concept of Ottomanism in the Hebrew press, see Ben-Bassat 2009b, 461–475.

24 See Jacobson 2001, 23–35; 2003, 105–130; 2004, 41–48; 2008, 69–88; 2009, 73–92; 2011a; 2011b, 165–182.

magazine *al-Manār* ('The Lighthouse', Cairo). In addition, he interprets the discourse on 'Arabness' and Islam in the Hebrew-Zionist press of Jerusalem.[25]

Several surveys by Ben-Bassat on relational Palestinian history also provide valuable insight on early Arab–Zionist encounters as reflected in petitions from Palestine to Istanbul during the late nineteenth and early twentieth centuries. Here, he analyzes correspondence sent by Arab Palestinians villagers and Zionist settlers to the Grand Vizierate regarding land issues and the sale of land to Jewish colonies, and investigates the first violent encounters with Zionist settlements in rural areas and the contradictory interpretations of the parties to the conflict.[26] Finally, the most detailed and recent studies of Arab reactions on Zionism before World War I have been published by Beška. He has investigated the attitudes to Zionism of prominent Palestinian Muslims and Christians, such as Yūsuf Ḍiyāʾ al-Ḫālidī (a Muslim notable from Jerusalem and descend of the prominent al-Ḫālidī family), Šukrī al-ʿAsalī (a born Damascene, *qāʾimaqām* in the *qaḍāʾ* of Nazareth, Member of Ottoman Parliament in 1911, and an outspoken anti-Zionist), Naǧīb al-Ḫūrī Naṣṣār (editor of the anti-Zionist newspaper *al-Karmil* in Haifa) and Ḫalīl as-Sakākīnī (a Jerusalemite Greek Orthodox intellectual and leading figure in the Arab Orthodox Movement before World War I).[27] Beška also has investigated the effect of the 'al-Fūla affair' in the *qaḍāʾ* of Nazareth in 1910/11 on the public discourse on Zionism in northern Palestine,[28] analyzed the attitudes of the editors of *Filasṭīn* to Zionism, Judaism and anti-Semitism before World War I,[29] and worked out the major shifts in their attitude towards Zionism.[30]

My own investigation into the coverage on Zionism in *Filasṭīn* complements Beška's work but applies a different approach by considering the newspaper not as a private forum of the ʿĪsās but as a platform for debate between a pool of publishing authors. As far as possible, I reconstruct the communication networks between the disputing authors and set the coverage on Zionism in relation to dominant discourses used in other contemporary debates. I also consider how far discursive changes on Zionism were accompanied by the reconstitution of local inter-confessional relations on the ground.

25 Gribetz 2014.
26 Ben-Bassat 2009a; 2013a; 2013b; 2013c; 2013d.
27 Beška 2007; 2010; 2011; 2014; 2015.
28 Beška 2014, 54–67.
29 Beška 2016a, 99–108; 2016c.
30 Beška 2016c.

Main Thesis and Methodology

I propose that the coverage on Zionism during the years before World War I was much more controversial than former evaluations on *Filasṭīn* have noticed, and that it underwent several ideological shifts and varied in the positions it took. The debate on Zionism included a spectrum of authors with contradictory views and left space for an exchange of opinions. Inspired by the notion of 'dispute' (*al-munāẓara*) in the work of Glaß, I focus on the *controversial elements* in my investigation on *Filasṭīn*'s coverage on Zionism. I explore the spectrum of views on the topic and the 'order of what to say or not to say' in the debate, and I filter out its *dialogical elements* through a process of transmitting, receiving, interpreting and responding to messages. It is important to note that the coverage on Zionism oscillated between 'debate' and 'campaign'. A debate would include a circle of actors, not only the editors, who negotiated personal views on a topic in the newspaper using a dialogical approach, thus shaping and negotiating the discourse on the topic discussed and the whole publication process. On the other hand, a campaign would represent the editors' systematic intention to present a certain perspective on Zionism to the reader and spread their agenda; it was thus a monologue. I find both elements in *Filasṭīn* and identifying the space between debate and campaign is an aspect of the present study. The central questions are: how far did *Filasṭīn* serve as a platform for an anti-Zionist campaign by its editors, or as a forum that allowed the exchange of controversial views, and what limits were imposed to restrict the debate. The other central aspect of my survey is the oscillation between opposition to and cooperation with Zionism. In my opinion, the ambivalence of the newspaper reflected the mixed feelings of the population regarding Jewish migration. On the one hand, Jewish, generally European, migration was met with high hopes for the modernization of Palestine, and successful Jewish settlements were considered a driving force for progress. On the other, Jewish colonization created economic rivalries for local resources and fears of the political aspirations of Zionism. Mandel remarked in one sentence that the attitude towards Zionism in *Filasṭīn* was 'not fixed' during 1911–12 and that Jewish authors also used to publish in it, but he did not go into detail or incorporate this in his survey.[31]

Finally, as a contribution to this gap in research, I look at where the editors defined a position for or against the Zionist movement in Palestine and at how far they demonstrated a neutral attitude; what were the crucial criticisms they made, how far was there a sense of a 'Zionist threat' among the population, how far did the dispute on Zionism bring about new discourses on local interconfessional relations, how did the success of Zionist colonization influence these relations

31 Mandel 1976, 128.

and, finally, where do we find the authors participating in *Filasṭīn*'s debate working towards mutual understanding and where towards polarization?

2. Historical Context

2.1. Zionist Immigration before World War I

In 1881/82, pogroms in Tsarist Russia led to the beginning of modern Jewish, or Zionist, migration into Palestine. The academic literature has divided this modern Jewish immigration (Hebr.: *ʿaliyya*, pl. *ʿaliyyot*) into three stages (this study will use the term Aliya): the First Aliya (1882–1903/4), the Second Aliya (1904–1914) and the Third Aliya (1919–1923). In fact, these waves of migration were not clearly separate from each other and took place in the form of rather diffuse movements. Be that as it may, this immigration into Palestine constituted the New Yishuv which was associated with a national project, as explained before. Establishing the term, Zionist immigrants created a mental distance from the indigenous Palestinian-Jewish communities, which they called the 'Old Yishuv'. For this modern Zionist immigration, the term 'Aliya' was applied in the sense of 'rising up' – originally, the word meant to climb up to the Temple Mount in Jerusalem, situated in the upper town – since, in Zionist ideology, Jewish migration was related to the idea that the return to Palestine as the land of the forefathers would lead a debased exiled Jewish nation towards a new cultural and moral ascent.[32]

The Old Yishuv was very heterogenous in its composition. It consisted of Sephardi and Ashkenazi Jews of manifold origins, although the Sephardi Jews dominated Palestinian Jewry. They were culturally and socio-economically integrated into local Arab society, used Arabic as their daily language and, like their Muslim and Christian fellows, were Ottoman citizens.

The Ashkenazi Jews among them were of European origin and had migrated to Palestine since the sixteenth century. A lot of them had come for spiritual reasons and as part of messianic-revivalist sects or as followers of Orthodox charismatic leaders during the eighteenth and nineteenth centuries. They dedicated their life to religious study and were economically dependent on donations from diaspora communities (Hebr.: *ḥaluqqa*). They generally did not acquire Ottoman citizenship, did not speak Arabic and were not culturally integrated, although they were not officially acknowledged as a separate religious community. As a matter of fact, only the Sephardi community enjoyed the status of an

32 Krämer 2002, 127.

acknowledged *millet* before the authorities, and importantly, as non-Ottomans, Ashkenazi Jews enjoyed the protection of European states in the Empire.

The tremendous ethnic and cultural heterogeneity of the Yishuv further increased through the new Zionist migration from Europe.[33] Not all Jewish migrants of the modern period were ideological Zionists, however. Those who arrived with the First Aliya in particular mostly came for economic reasons or to escape anti-Semitism. Moreover, the distinction between the 'New' and 'Old' Yishuv was not always clear. Jewish migrants who might have come during one of the Aliyyot were perhaps not even secular or revolutionary in any respect and did not identify with the Zionist movement[34] and Jewish migration into Palestine was for decades not specifically related to political Zionism. Before the WZO formulated their political aims, there was Jewish-Zionist settlement of a different kind: followers of the 'Lovers of Zion' (Hebr.: *Ḥovevei Tzion, Ḥibbat Tzion*) founded the first agricultural colonies (Hebr.: *mošavot,* sing. *mošav*). The 'Lovers of Zion' were a coalition of groups from Russia, Romania and the Ukraine that emerged in response to anti-Semitic persecution in Eastern Europe; they were rooted in a religious tradition of desire for Zion ('Zionssehnsucht') and spiritually motivated. A group of them, the 'Biluim', founded the first Zionist settlements of Rishon le-Tzion (Hebr.: 'The First in Zion') in 1882 and Gedera in 1884.[35] These settlements were not economically self-sufficient but were dependent on donors such as Baron Rothschild. They also received financial help from colonization associations of the Lovers of Zion Movement and other Jewish philanthropic but non-Zionist organizations, such as the French Alliance Israélite Universelle (AIU), which was a rival of the Zionist WZO.[36] Another sponsor of Jewish colonization in Palestine was the non-Zionist Jewish Colonization Association (JCA), founded in 1897 by Baron Maurice de Hirsch.[37]

The WZO pursued a legal and political solution for the 'Jewish question' on an international humanitarian basis, and initially opposed the practical 'infiltration' of Jews into Palestine through partial colonization. However, during the eighth

33 Apart from Sephardi and Ashkenazi Jews, there were Jews of Yemeni, Bukhari, Indic or Iranian origin, who might have been Orthodox or secular, and differed in terms of political affiliation: they might have been socialist, Zionist or pro-Ottoman. They had different mother tongues, including Arabic, Ladino, Yiddish or Hebrew and different citizenships; according to Campos, about two-thirds of the New Yishuv were of foreign nationality. Campos 2003, 283–298.

34 Krämer 2002, 127.

35 'Biluim' is an abbreviation, formed from a phrase from Isaiah 2:5, where it says 'House of Jacob, get going' (*Bet Ya'aqov lekhu we-nelkha*). See Brenner 2005, 55.

36 For the rivalry between the AIU and the WZO, see Benbassa 1992, 225–251.

37 Krämer 2002, 136. There were also other German philanthropic societies that fostered Jewish settlement in Palestine that were not Zionist and were rivals of the WZO, such as the *Allgemeine Jüdische Kolonizationsgesellschaft* and the *Hilfsverein der Deutschen Juden.* See Reinkowski 1995, 22.

Zionist Congress (1907), it adopted a synthetic strategy to continue to pursue diplomatic efforts towards a political solution but at the same time create facts on the ground through practical settlement. As stated in the 'Ruppin-Memorandum' (1907), the WZO decided to focus on the colonization of a coherent agricultural area, situated between Jaffa and Tiberias, in order to counter Ottoman legal obstacles against foreign Jews acquiring land in Palestine.[38] Meanwhile, the principle of 'Hebrew Labor' (Hebr.: *'avoda 'ivrit*) was promoted and the idea of a 'conquest' of Palestine through work (Hebr.: *kibbuš ha-'avoda*). To secure expanding markets in Palestine for Jewish labor, the *ha-Po'el ha-Tza'ir* ('The Young Worker'), a Jaffa based Zionist newspaper with strong socialist orientation affiliated to the labor movement, demanded the systematic exclusion of Arabs from job opportunities in Jewish settlements and the transfer of these jobs to Jewish workers.[39] At the same time, some WZO organs were to become central pillars for the colonization of Palestine: the London-based Zionist Anglo-Palestine Bank (APB) was established as the main instrument to finance Jewish settlement. From 1903 onwards, there was a branch in Jaffa, then later others in Jerusalem, Hebron and Beirut. The JN, founded in 1901 on Herzl's initiative, was a Zionist foundation that collected worldwide donations from Jewish communities for the New Yishuv and, from 1907, focused on land purchase. The trade union of Jewish workers, the *Histadrut*, was secure the 'conquest' of the market for Jewish labor. In 1907, the Palestine Office was opened in Jaffa as the official representative of the WZO in Palestine. Under the leadership of Arthur Ruppin, a German Jew, it was to coordinate the establishment of the New Yishuv and implement WZO policies in Palestine.[40]

Krämer points out that, until World War I, Jewish migration did not really make a deep impact of demographic, economic or political balances in Palestine.[41] Apart from centers of Jewish settlement in the Galilee, an exceptions were Jerusalem as the only Palestinian city with Jewish majority, and the district of Jaffa as the center of Zionist organizations. In 1914, there were 47 Jewish colonies

38 See Shilony 1998, 18; Shafir 1996, 43; Reinkowski 1995, 23.

39 Shafir 1996, 46f., 59f. In Zionist ideology, 'conquest' also meant 'conquest of the self' (*kibbuš 'atzmi*), the 'activation' of the Jews and their reconnection to the soil of *Eretz Israel* through agricultural work and physical labor. The idea was that strengthening Jewish 'muscles' would result in a 'regeneration' of Jewish mental strength. For more meanings of *kibbuš* in Zionism, see Shafir 1996, 58–69.

40 Thanks to the archives of these organizations, the development of the New Yishuv is well documented in academic research, but local actors remain invisible in the process as if the Zionist project developed in isolation from the socio-economic conditions of its environment. Arab Palestinian villages are nameless in these documents or mentioned only in cases of conflict. Then, local actors are simply called 'Arab-tenant-farmers' or 'the former cultivators', as in Katz 1990, 29–45; Shilony 1997.

41 Krämer 2002, 122.

in the district with about 12,000 inhabitants. About 100,000 Jewish migrants came to Palestine during the First and Second Aliya, but half of them had left by 1914.[42] Most academic studies quote the census by Ruppin, who estimated the number of Jewish inhabitants at 85,000 in 1914, although McCarthy gives a much lower figure. According to him, Ottoman and foreign Jews together amounted up to 60,000, among a total population of 722,000.[43]

2.2. Local Responses on Zionist Migration up to World War I

Previous research has assessed that there were hardly Arab responses to Zionism until the Balfour Declaration (1917) became known in the Arab East,[44] but Mandel has shown that there were in fact early reactions to Zionist migration and settlement from the Ottoman government and the local population.[45] In 1882, the authorities restricted Zionist migration into Palestine and Syria to pilgrims only. The government regarded Zionist groups settling in Palestine as migrants with foreign citizenship and not primarily as Jews. This was sensitive especially in the case of Jews migrating from the Russian Empire as the Porte was constantly involved in military conflicts with the Tsar. From 1892 onwards, it was forbidden for Jews of foreign citizenship to purchase land in Palestine and, in 1909, this ban was imposed on all foreigners. What was problematic here was that the attitude of the authorities towards foreign migration was inconsistent. Ottoman officials were oscillating between imposing a strict migration embargo and lifting the restrictions on foreign diplomatic intervention and diplomats in the Empire who acted as protective powers on behalf of minorities.[46]

Apart from legal restrictions on Jewish land purchase and migration, there was also resistance from local people. Occasional tenant revolts against Jewish agricultural colonies and German Templar settlements occurred from the 1880s. This conflict paradigm was to consolidate during the Second Aliya, when the concept of the 'conquest' of Palestine through 'Jewish labor' made Arab tenants lose their jobs after the land they worked and also often resided on was transferred to Jewish landowners who replaced them with Jews; this had not necessarily been

42 Reinkowski 1995, 24.
43 McCarthy 1990, 19–22; cf. Krämer 2002, 164f.; Reinkowski 1995, 24–25.
44 The Balfour Declaration was not an official government document but a letter from British Foreign Minister Lord Balfour to Baron Rothschild, and published in Britain in *The Times*. It promised British support for the establishment of a 'national home for the Jews' while protecting the 'civil and religious rights of existing non-Jewish communities' in Palestine. On the asymmetry in the document concerning the recognition of both communities as 'nations', see Krämer 2002, 178–180; Reinkowski 1995, 36.
45 Mandel 1974; 1976, xvii–xxiv.
46 Reinkowski 1995, 27f; Mandel 1976, 1–26.

the case during the First Aliya, when ownership officially changed but Arab tenants continued to cultivate the land for Jewish colonies.[47] From the 1890s, resistance to Zionist migration was organized by Palestinian notables and, in 1897, the Jerusalemite intelligentsia, headed by the mufti of Jerusalem, handed in petitions.[48]

It is also to be noted that the First Zionist Congress in Basel (1897) was met with reactions from Palestinian notables. In 1899, the prominent Muslim Jerusalemite Ḍiyāʾ al-Ḫālidī, who had some knowledge of Hebrew, initiated a correspondence with the Chief Rabbi of France, Zadok Kahn, in which he elaborated on a solution for the 'Jewish question'. He expressed his empathy with the aims of the Zionist movement and acknowledged that the Jewish question was a national one, as long as Palestine as a territory was left out of play.[49] Outside Palestine too, Arab elites became engaged with the Jewish question.[50]

The political ambitions of Zionism triggered suspicions among Ottoman Turks and Arabs; especially when they observed the resolutions of the Zionist Congresses. The Seventh Congress (1905) defined Palestine as the targeted territory, whereas before, leading Zionists also discussed a possible land purchase in Uganda or South Africa. While the Ottomans faced the rise of separatist movements in the Balkans and Armenia, they feared that Zionism could evolve to another 'national question', similar to the 'Armenian question' and the 'Greek question'.[51] However, during the era of the Young Turks, it was the issue of land sales that raised Zionist colonization in the consciousness of local people and made it a hot topic in the Arab press. In this respect, the 'al-Fūla affair' was a cornerstone and created a resounding echo among Arab notables from Palestine and Lebanon. In 1910, Ilyās Sursuq, a trader from Beirut and one of the large-scale landowners in the Galilee, sold the land belonging to the Arab villages of al-Fūla in the Nazareth subdistrict to the JN. This transaction provoked a protest from Arab notables in Haifa and Nazareth, who sent collective petitions against

47 The clashes between Arab villagers and Jewish settlers from Petaḥ Tikva in 1886 were an early example of what would during the Second Aliyya become 'routine conflicts' in the countryside, according to Khalidi. See his chapter on peasant revolts against Jewish settlements in Khalidi 1997, 89–117.

48 Beška 2007, 24–26.

49 Theodor Herzl personally responded to Yūsuf al-Ḫālidī's letter to Zadok Kahn. See Beška 2007, 26–31.

50 For example, Muslim reformer Rašīd Riḍāʾ criticized political Zionism in his journal *Al-Manār* as early as 1902. The early Arab nationalist Naǧīb ʿAzūrī, in his pamphlet 'The Arab Awakening' (1905), attacked not only Zionism as a movement, but also the Jews as a felt universal threat. See Muslih 1988, 69–87. For responses of Palestinian elites and prominent Arabs, see Beška 2007, 22–44; Mandel 1976.

51 See Khalidi 1997, 105f., 120f.; Kayyali 1978, 18. For the Ottoman-imperial perspective on Zionist activities in Palestine, see Fishman 2011, 103–123.

the sale of this land.[52] The matter also led to in diplomatic involvement. Šukrī al-ʿAsalī, a former delegate to the Ottoman Parliament, and at that time *qāʾimaqām* of Nazareth, refused to pass the title deeds to the JN after the deal had taken place. He refused payment from an agent of the APB and stationed military personnel on the land to prevent its transfer, but this ultimately failed.[53] Reverberations from this incident raised the topic of Zionism in the press and a major anti-Zionist protest campaign developed in northern Palestine and in the press in Beirut.[54] In May 1911, the shock of this affair motivated the Jerusalem District delegates, Rūḥī al-Ḫālidī and Ḥāfiẓ as-Saʿīd, to deliver fierce speeches against Zionist aspirations in Parliament and complain about the government's neglect of the 'Zionist question'.[55]

The al-Fūla affair also made a strong impression on Naǧīb an-Naṣṣār. Inspired by the anti-Zionist speeches of the Palestinian delegates in Parliament, he published a series of articles in *al-Karmil* from March to June 1911 on the WZO's political strategies in Palestine.[56] An-Naṣṣār, a Lebanese-born Greek Orthodox who had moved to northern Palestine in his youth and converted to Protestantism, had worked as an estate agent for the JCA until he turned against the organization and left it on bad terms.[57] He became an outspoken anti-Zionist, which was his main motivation for starting a journalistic career. An-Naṣṣār started editing his newspaper *al-Karmil* in Haifa from 1908 onwards as an anti-Zionist organ. In the course of the al-Fūla affair, his campaign spread to other newspapers, which picked up sentiments against land sales to Zionist associa-

52 See Beška 2010, 241f.

53 On al-ʿAsalī, see Beška 2014, 240–247. In 1910, an anti-Zionist attack under the name of Ṣalāḥ ad-Dīn al-Ayūbī was published, whose author was afterwards identified as al-ʿAsalī. See Beška 2014, 243f.; Mandel 1976, 83f.

54 It should be noted that, in the available issues of *Filasṭīn*, starting in July 1911, this affair was not discussed at all, which, again, underscores the administrational and cultural division between the two Palestinian districts.

55 See Beška 2014, 248f., and the treatment of the Parliamentary speeches in Fishman 2011, 103–123. Prätor has documented that these protests were not taken seriously by the other delegates in Parliament. The elaborations of Rūḥī al-Ḫālidī about the spiritual inspirations and historical factors leading to the emergence of Zionism as a national trend, designed as an extended scholarly lecture, aroused the anger of his colleagues, who tried to calm him. Al-Ḫālidī nevertheless insisted on speaking out as an Ottoman representative of Muslims, Christians 'and maybe also … of Jews, of many Jews. Because, a lot of Jews are against the Zionists'. Quoted in Prätor 1993, 101.

56 The series appeared in the same year as a book titled 'Zionism: Its History, Aims and Relevance' (*Aṣ-Ṣihyūnīya: Tāʾrīḫuhā, ġaraḍuhā, ahamīyatuhā*), a translation and commentary on the article by Richard Gottheil, an American Zionist and Semitic Studies scholar, in the *Jewish Encyclopedia* (1905). An-Naṣṣār particularly criticized the Grand Vizier for cutting off the two delegates' anti-Zionist speeches. He acknowledged the success of the WZO and thought that the Palestinians were in need of 'loyal leaders' like Herzl, who put the 'public good' above personal interests. See an-Naṣṣār 1911, 64; Khalidi 1997, 125; Mandel 1976, 108f.

57 For more biographical details, see Beška 2011, 167–168.

tions.[58] This development worried the WZO and, from 1911 onwards, the Palestine Office started to document anti-Zionist coverage in the Arab press. Mandel and Khalidi both stress the importance of the anti-Zionist campaigns in the Arab press during the Second Constitutional era as a political force that significantly helped to establish discourses on different models of group identities.[59]

3. Framing the Debate on Zionism in the Local Press

3.1. Central Elements of the Debate on Zionism

After *Filasṭīn*'s inception in 1911, the debate on Zionism underwent several shifts, which will be considered here, and political Zionism as a topic started to fill a vacuum in *Filasṭīn*'s reporting after the newspaper ceased to be a leader of the Orthodox campaign at the beginning of 1914. In general, especially during 1911–1912, ambivalence was a central part of *Filasṭīn*'s coverage on Zionism as a movement of foreign migration that was not exclusively Jewish. In this respect, the potential of the Zionist movement for integration into local society was one of the main questions in the press debate on Zionism.

Ambivalence

The attitude of the Palestinian population towards Zionist migration and settlement was dominated by ambivalent emotions during the years before World War I. On the one hand, people speculated about how far Zionism could push technological, economic and cultural development for the benefit of local Arabs. On the other, there was suspicion about the possible damage to local social and economic structures that would be caused by Zionist migrants – typical concerns in any debate on foreign migration. In 1911, Albert Antébi (1873–1919), a prominent Sephardi Jew who will be introduced later, noted that the protest speeches of Palestinian delegates in Parliament had created a greater awareness of the Zionist movement among the Arab population, and that it fostered suspicion of Jews that sometimes led to absurd rumors. For instance, a Palestinian farmer had asked Antébi if the Jews in Jerusalem had already appointed a 'king' for their kingdom and if he was a 'foreigner' or had knowledge of Arabic.[60] Also

58 Beška 2014, 167–171. For his analysis of the anti-Zionist coverage in *al-Karmil* during 1914, see pp. 174–191.

59 For 'overlapping identities' in late Ottoman Palestine, see Khalidi 1997, 63–88.

60 Antébi was in general worried about growing hostility against the Jews in Palestine and saw the Arab Christians as the main initiators of these antagonistic feelings. He claimed that 'in all eyes, the Jew is becoming the anti-Patriot, the traitor prepared to plunder his neighbour to

Ḥāfiẓ Bek as-Saʿīd, an influential merchant from Jaffa and a Jerusalem delegate in Parliament, expressed his believe that the Zionist movement had the twofold potential to be either 'damaging' or 'beneficial' to Palestine.[61]

This ambivalence revealed in the statement of as-Saʿīd is very well reflected in *Filasṭīn* and, in my opinion, it was this ambivalence that defined the central questions of the debate. In this respect, I do not agree with the judgment of Mandel and Khalidi, who categorize *Filasṭīn* as *the* anti-Zionist pioneer from the beginning of its publication history, but want to stress that there was initially a very indecisive attitude towards Zionism among the population, which created the need among educated Christians, Muslims and Jews to debate its potential benefits or damage in public. *Filasṭīn* bears witness to this process.

A 'Migration Debate' in the Context of 'Modernization' and Economic Rivalries

In general, Zionism was discussed in the press as a foreign, rather than specifically Jewish, migration movement into the region. Therefore, the debate in *Filasṭīn* was strongly linked with the terms 'colonization' (*istiʿmār*), 'settlements' (*mustaʿmarāt*) and 'migration' (*muhāǧara*). In this light, the controversy on Zionism in *Filasṭīn* was one about 'integration', and was characterized by the typical questions of a 'migration debate'. It should be noted that the terms 'colonization', 'settlement' and 'migration' did not have negative connotations. On the contrary, the idea of settlement was also strongly linked with concepts of 'development' and 'civilization' that were in line with *Filasṭīn*'s overall agenda. Thus, and as a matter of the global *zeitgeist*, the debate on Zionism was naturally one about 'modernization' and was in line with the superimposed terminological frame and the 'set of modernist values' that were presented. As will be shown, the achievements of Jewish pioneers in agriculture and the consequent benefits for the *qaḍāʾ* from the settlements' vital economy were positively associated with 'progress' (*taqaddum*), which was the ideal to be pursued by all means. Thus, the debate mainly revolved around the questions of how far the Zionist presence could be a driving force for or an obstacle to the modernization of Palestine, and how far Zionist migrants would be able to become socially, economically and politically integrated into Arab Palestinian society. On the other hand, it was asked how far Zionism was *per se* an integrative or an exclusive movement, and how far the promotion of Zionist migration was compatible with or contradictory to Ottoman loyalty and local patriotism.

It is noteworthy that the controversy in *Filasṭīn* over Zionist migration was based not on religious considerations but on economic factors related to *rivalries*

take possession of his goods. The Christian excels in these accusations, but the Muslim follows on his heels'. See Mandel 1976, 121.

61 Quoted in Mandel 1976, 183.

for local resources in a shared economic space – for instance, on the impact of Zionist migration on access to the water of the Yarkon River, real estate, agricultural land and the labor market. Zionist acquisition of land was a heated topic when the concept of 'Jewish labor' was strongly promoted by leading Zionists, and the transfer of landownership to Jewish colonies was followed by the replacement of Arab tenants with newly 'imported' Jewish workers from places such as Yemen. The central question in dispute was whether Zionism was trying systematically to establish an exclusive economic system.

Sectarian Dimensions of the Debate on Zionism

Although the debate on Zionism was in its essence economic, it included a growing tendency to sectarianism, which had started to play a role between certain parties since 1913, when Zionism became a factor for the reconstitution of local inter-confessional balances, and especially led to a worsening of relations between Christian and Sephardi citizens in the Jaffa region. Meanwhile, the concept of Ottomanism also underwent substantial changes and was challenged by competing national identities before World War I. While 'national questions' (of the Armenians, Greek and Kurds) were arising in the heartland of the Empire and at the Balkans (1912–1913), Zionism was being increasingly perceived as a political threat to the Ottoman model, and the loyalty of Palestinian-Ottoman Jews, called 'Israelites' in the jargon of the contemporary Arab press, was more and more suspect. In the view of Christians and Muslims publishing in *Filasṭīn*, the Ottoman 'Israelite brothers' were at risk of being politicized by ideas of Zionism as a foreign nationalism. In the light of national questions and military threats, authors in *Filasṭīn* urgently called for inter-confessional unity and loyalty to the concept of Ottoman brotherhood, as we saw in chapter I, and clearly saw Zionism as a threat to this unity. Thus, Sephardi Jews were increasingly blamed for betraying Ottomanism by working for the WZO as agents in Zionist land purchase. On the other hand, Christian authors in *Filasṭīn*, especially the ʿĪsās, were judged harshly by Sephardi Jewish defenders of the Zionist movement for fostering rising anti-Semitism among Palestinian Arabs, as we shall see.

Geographical Scope of the Debate

The geographical focus of the coverage on Zionism in *Filasṭīn* was the areas around Jaffa, Ramla, Lod and Jerusalem, and the majority of texts focused on the Jaffa District. Thus, the debate was linked to a great extent with Jaffa's economic relations with the Jewish settlements in the near surroundings, identified in the jargon of *Filasṭīn* with the Arabic name of the villages the land belonged to before its transfer to a colony, especially ʿUyūn Qāra (Hebr. Rishon le-Tzion), Mulabbas or Mulabbis or Umm Labbis (Hebr. Petaḥ Tikva), and Dayrān or Dārān (Hebr.

Reḥovot).[62] It is sometimes difficult to identify the geographic position of these villages or to identify present-day Israeli places with the names used in *Filasṭīn*, since research on the New Yishuv is based on Zionist sources that use the Hebrew names.[63] There were also reports on Tel Aviv – the only Jewish settlement called by its Hebrew name in *Filasṭīn* and referred to as 'the colony Tel Aviv' (*mustaʿ-marat Tall Abīb*) to stress the Jewish exclusiveness of the place.[64] However, Tel Aviv was presented as a part of Jaffa when the article intended to stress the economic interconnectedness of the two places. For instance, in an advertisement for a tailor in Tel Aviv, one Madame Malāmīd who placed regular advertisements in *Filasṭīn* from 1913, Tel Aviv was called 'the new neighborhood' (*al-maḥalla al-ǧadīda Tall Abīb*) and thus was presented as an integral part of Jaffa.[65]

The mental map of the debate on Zionism in *Filasṭīn* mostly ends outside the Jerusalem District and south of Jerusalem; Hebron, Beersheba and Jericho are hardly mentioned. Northern Palestine and the district of Acre were rarely presented, although the concentration of Zionist colonies was especially high in the Galilee, which is evidence that there was a north–south division of late Ottoman Palestine in a cultural sense, too. *Filasṭīn*'s coverage on Zionist settlements essentially ends north of the settlements of Mulabbis (Petaḥ Tikva) and Dayrān (Reḥovot), both situated in the north of the Jaffa *qaḍāʾ*.[66] Only once was the prominent al-Fūla affair mentioned.[67] Here, the mental map of *Filasṭīn* differed from that of *al-Karmil*, which focused on northern Palestine, south Lebanon and Syria. One the other hand, *Filasṭīn* was also interested in reporting about Jewish communities abroad, such in New York.[68] In particular, Salonika, the only Eu-

62 The settlements of Ḥaḍīra, ʿĀqir and Wādī Ḥanīn were also mentioned. Sometimes, the newspaper slightly changed names or made mistakes. For instance, it often changed *ta marbūṭa* to *ha*; or confused between *ta* and *ṭa*. With regard to the Arab villages mentioned, the focus was on those that were affected by Jewish settlements or were about to be sold to Zionist organizations, such as for instance water mills at Ǧarīša, the lands of Biyar ʿAdas, Abū Šūša, Kafr Urīya, al-Muḥayzin and Nabī Rūbīn.

63 In this respect, the work of Walid al-Khalidi (1992) can shed some light on the geographical history of Palestine and the webpage www.palestineremembered.com.

64 This in the context of a report that Jewish community leaders had decided to bar traffic from the main street leading from Jaffa over Manšīya into Tel Aviv on Shabbat. *Filasṭīn*, 20 January 1912: 104/3/4.

65 *Filasṭīn*, 18 January 1913: 205/4/4.

66 There is only one article about a land sale in Caesarea (*Filasṭīn*, 13 April 1912: 127/4/1f.) and only twice is Haifa mentioned (both articles are reproduced from *al-Karmil*). Twice, land sales of the northern villages of Karkūr and Baydūs/Bīdūs are mentioned. See *Filasṭīn*, 21 December 1912: 199/3/5f.; 25 December 1912: 200/4/2.

67 *Filasṭīn*, 25 December 1912: 200/ 4/2.

68 See for instance an article about Jewish lobbying in Amerika and the high number of Jewish migrants to New York, which allegedly made it a 'Jewish city' (*madīna yahūdīya*). *Filasṭīn*, 14 December 1912: 197/4/1–2.

ropean city with a Jewish majority and called in the literature 'Jerusalem of the Balkans', was of interest to the editors.[69]

3.2. Communicational Aspects of the Coverage on Zionism

Participants in the debate in *Filasṭīn* on the Zionist question included Greek Orthodox Christian, Muslim and Sephardi Jewish Palestinians, all of them Ottomans, as well as Ashkenazi settlers and urban migrants with foreign nationalities. This shaped the controversial character of the debate, which left some space for the exchange of contradictory views. Participants either expressed support for the achievements of the Zionist movement or criticized its exclusive aspects, and condemned the displacement of Arab tenants from their land and the political separatist goals of the Zionists. The Jewish participants in the debate, both Sephardi and Ashkenazi, had a more positive opinion of Zionism then the other protagonists.

It should be stressed that the debate in *Filasṭīn* on Zionism was a *collective* publishing process by a spectrum of authors who came from different confessional and ethnic affiliations but were all from privileged Palestinian middle- and upper-class circles and shared similar educational backgrounds and cosmopolitan horizons. My study of *Filasṭīn*'s coverage of Zionism should therefore not only demonstrate the attitudes of the ʿĪsās but also pursue the scope of the debate among the Palestinian public by demonstrating the flow of communication between the contributing authors and how their controversy was accompanied by shifts in inter-confessional relations in the District; as far as this is evident in *Filasṭīn*. Here, it should be stressed that the character of the discussion as an 'elite debate' means that it did not necessarily reflect the attitude of the 'general people' (*al-ʿāmma*), the lower segments of Palestinian society, whose views on Zionism are not known. The contributors in *Filasṭīn* should be considered as individuals who helped to establish discourse on Zionism, but not necessarily as representatives of their communities in this matter, even though they might be claiming to speak in the name of a group.

There was without doubt space for free debate in *Filasṭīn*, but with limits. In the context of internal and external factors, the space for open debate on Zionism

69 In October 1912, during the Balkan War, Salonika was conquered by the Greeks, which brought its Jewish population under Greek rule. As becomes clear from *Filasṭīn*, rumors circulated in Palestine that the Jewish population of Salonika was suspected of being involved in a plot against the Ottoman government. *Filasṭīn*, 23 November 1912: 19/2/3f.; 27 November 1912: 192/2/1f.; 07 December 1912: 195/2/3f.; 15 January 1913: 204/2/5. For the administrational annexation of Saloniki's Jewish community under Greek rule, see Molho 1988, 391–403.

narrowed during 1912. By the middle of 1913, an anti-Zionism view was circulating in *Filasṭīn* that certainly echoed the opinions of the Palestinian intelligentsia. The aim of this communicational study is not to attribute to the authors who published in *Filasṭīn* a particular liberal attitude towards Zionism but to investigate what took place in an exchange of opinions, and to filter out the central shifts and the factors that made the exchange become an anti-Zionist campaign by 1913–1914.

Supporters of Zionism

Most supporters of Zionism in *Filasṭīn* were Palestinian Sephardi Jews who were, in terms of language and culture, integrated into local society, held Ottoman citizenship and adopted the discourse about Ottoman unity. At the same time, they maintained close relations with Zionist organizations. It was often they who purchased land around Jaffa and Jerusalem for these institutions; an example are the Moyals, a prominent Jaffa Sephardi family of Moroccan origin. Outstanding in the promotion on Zionism in *Filasṭīn* was a circle of Sephardi intellectuals affiliated with the Jerusalemite Hebrew newspaper *ha-Ḥerut*, published between 1909 and1917 and edited by Ḥaim Ben ʿAṭṭār; it was the mouthpiece of the Sephardi community in Palestine. Its authors were drawn from the Sephardi intelligentsia of Jerusalem, and also included Shimon Moyal and Nissim Malul, both residents of Jaffa.[70] This circle were strong advocates of Zionist activity in Palestine and stressed its economic and cultural benefits to the region. Their arguments were influenced by European Zionist terminology, which differed from the jargon of the Arab Christian and Arab Muslim protagonists publishing in *Filasṭīn*, as seen in the case studies. When referring to the New Yishuv, they spoke of the 'Jewish people' (*al-umma al-yahūdīya*) or 'the Israelite nation' (*al-shaʿb al-isrāʾīlī*) and did not distinguish between Jews of Ottoman and foreign citizenship.[71] Their contributions were designed as apologetics directed against the critics of Zionism, whom they accused of inciting 'hatred against the Jews' (*karh al-yahūd, buġḍ al-yahūd*) and anti-Semitism.[72] The arguments of the Sephardi contributors strongly fostered the sectarian tendency in the debate and they usually equated anti-Zionism with anti-Semitism.

Ashkenazi Jewish migrants, who will be introduced later, also participated in the debate, including Abraham Ludvipol, a Jewish journalist in France before his migration to Palestine, and S. Frumkin, a member of the Russian-Jewish Frumkin family based in Jerusalem, both pioneers of Hebrew journalism. An outstanding

70 For a more detailed discussion of the political and cultural agendas of *ha-Ḥerut* and its writers, see Jacobson 2001, 23–34; especially 25f.; 2003, 105–130; especially 13–15, 18–25.

71 *Filasṭīn*, 5 June 1912: 142/1/2.

72 *Filasṭīn*, 5 June 1912: 142/1/2–3.

contribution is a column in *Filasṭīn* written by the Ukranian Jew and co-founder of Rishon Le-Tzion Menashe Me'irovitch, a Zionist migrant who had adopted Ottoman citizenship and maintained good networks with the local Muslim and Christian elites. He published under the pseudonym Abū Ibrāhīm, presenting himself as an Arab farmer and spokesman for the rural population, and complained about the hardship of a local farmer's life. To set a contrast, he praised the sophisticated standards in the Jewish settlements as a symbol of progress and prosperity, and his column is an example for the Ashkenazi idealization of the 'civilization' of Palestine through Zionist activity.[73]

It was not only Sephardi and Ashkenazi Jews stressed the potential of Zionist settlements and their role as the economic motor of the region but also Ottoman officials. It is obvious from *Filasṭīn* that the Jerusalem governors paid a lot of attention to the Jewish colonies of the *qaḍāʾ* of Jaffa. In their annual round trips through the District, they focused much more on the Zionist settlements, and their schools, wineries and agricultural projects in the region, than on the Arab villages. As an example, Muhdi Bek, the Albanian governor of the Jerusalem District in 1912, portrayed Zionist colonies as an inspiration that should help the neighboring Arab villages to overcome their 'backwardness'.[74]

Critics of Zionism

Among the critics of the Zionist movement in *Filasṭīn* were its editors, at least from the turn of 1912/13, as well as a number of Arab Palestinian Muslim and Christian authors of readers' letters, often local traders or representatives of local tenants in the Jaffa *qaḍāʾ*. What triggered their anti-Zionism was mainly the concern that the Zionists would in the future control resources (land, water and the labor market). After 1913, political Zionism came to the fore in the debate, and Palestinian authors increasingly stressed the threat of possible future Zionist autonomy in Palestine. The editors of *Filasṭīn* blamed Jewish migrants for upsetting local social balances by promoting 'exclusive (*ḫāṣṣa*) neighbourhoods, markets and practices'.[75] In general, however, they considered 'Israelite colonization' (*istiʿmār al-isrāʾīlīyīn*) as beneficial for the advancement of Jaffa as long as migrants integrated themselves into local socio-economic structures.[76] Numerous anonymous authors were critical of the Zionists' economic or political exclusiveness, among them a 'retired broker' (*simsār mutaqāʿid*) who condemned the sale of large plots of land near Ramla to the JN around the turn of 1912/13, although a regulation prohibited Jews from acquiring agricultural land

73 His first letter appeared in *Filasṭīn* on 23 September 1911: 71/1/1f., and his last on 24 August 1912: 165/1/1–4.
74 *Filasṭīn*, 17 August 1912: 163/1/5.
75 *Filasṭīn*, 29 May 1912: 140/1/3.
76 *Filasṭīn*, 5 June 1912: 142/2/1.

in Palestine – a case that raised considerable disquiet in the District and was met with protests by ʿĀrif al-ʿĀrif, a young historian and son of the mayor of Gaza.[77] Another critic of the Zionists was ʿAbdallāh Ḫalaf from Gaza, who blamed tribal leaders in Beersheba for selling land to the Zionists out of greed.[78] Among the critical authors were also figures from the middle classes, such as Muṣṭafā Tamar, a secondary teacher from Jerusalem, who presented Zionism as an imperialist instrument that France, England and Russia had installed in the Middle East, revealing their 'political agenda and meanness' (*min ayāt as-siyāsīya wa-makāʾidihā*) and, especially with regard to the Russians, demonstrating their 'right to interfere into the policies of the Porte' (*ḥaqq at-tadāḫul fī siyāsat ad-dawla*).[79]

3.3. Terminological Elements

As explained, the term Zionism was used to refer to 'Zionist colonization' (*al-istiʿmār aṣ-ṣihyūnī*) in *Filasṭīn*, and its ideological or internal differences were of no consequence for this debate. The focal point of the debate was the socio-economic changes caused by the Zionist settlers in the Jerusalem District, and especially the Jaffa *qaḍāʾ*, with its successful colonies Rishon le-Tzion, Reḥovot and Petaḥ Tikva. As the argument in the debate corresponded with the superimposed discourse on modernization presented in *Filasṭīn*, the main question was whether the Zionists would serve the infrastructural, economic and cultural development of Palestine and if so, how. In this respect, no differentiation was made between organizations related to the WZO and those related to other Jewish associations, such as the JCA and the philanthropic AIU, both explicitly not Zionist. In *Filasṭīn*, all of these actors were subsumed under the term 'Zionists'.

However, the terminological differentiation between Palestinian (Ottoman) and Ashkenazi (foreign) Jews was clear. Muslim and Christian authors in the debate divided the Yishuv by nationality into 'Ottomans' and 'foreigners'. Applying the discourse of Ottoman 'unity' (*ittiḥād*), they spoke of local Jews as 'the Israelites' (*al-isrāʾīlīyūn*), or the 'Israelite community' (*al-milla al-isrāʾīlīya*), sometimes using the term 'confession' (*ṭāʾifa*, *umma*). When addressing Palestinian (Sephardi) Jews, they often added the expression 'our Israelite brothers' (*iḫwānunā l-isrāʾīlīyūn*) in order to stress their citizen status. The 'Israelite brothers' were regularly greeted in the *Local News* section on Jewish feasts. For instance, *Filasṭīn* wished 'all the best' for the Jewish New Year, Rosh ha-Shanah.[80]

77 *Filasṭīn*, 30 November 1912: 193/3/3–4; 22 January 1913: 206/2/5; 25 January 1913: 2074/1–2; see also Mandel 1976, 139.
78 *Filasṭīn*, 28 October 1911: 81/2/5.
79 *Filasṭīn*, 22 July 1911: 53/2/3.
80 *Filasṭīn*, 14 September 1912: 171/3/4.

Muslim and Christian authors publishing in *Filasṭīn* would never usually apply the Arabic word 'Jew' or 'Jewish' (*yahūdī*) to Palestinian and Ottoman Jews, but would only use it to refer to Jews *outside* the Empire and non-Ottoman citizens, as in the 'Jews of America' (*yahūd Amrīkā*), the Russian Jews or the Jews of Salonika.[81]

On the other hand, the (Ashkenazi) Zionist migrants in Palestine were referred to as foreigners, mostly called 'the Zionists' (*aṣ-ṣihyūnīyūn*), and occasionally 'the Israelite migrants' (*al-muhāǧirūn al-isrāʾīlīyūn*).[82] With regard to Jewish colonies, the terms 'Zionist' or 'Israelite settlements' (*al-mustaʿmarāt aṣ-ṣihūnīya* or *al-isrāʾīlīya*) were applied.[83] Only in individual cases was the term 'Jews' (*al-yahūd*) applied to Zionist migrants to stress their foreign status.[84] As an illustration of this terminological distinction, the *Local News* section once reported that the Jaffa police caught three thieves who were foreigners, among them one French and two 'Tunisian Jews' (*yahūd Tūnis*) who were clearly conmen who had cheated an elderly Jewish woman from Jerusalem who wanted to marry off her daughters; she was referred to as 'Israelite woman' (*imraʾa isrāʾīlīya*).[85]

This distinction was relevant insofar as several authors expressed the principle that Zionism was not to be confused with Judaism, nor 'Zionists' with 'Israelites'. This applied especially to the ʿĪsās, who always stressed their good relations with the local Jewish community and their impartiality towards all religious communities. They repeatedly condemned 'fanaticism' (*taʿaṣṣub*) and 'extremism' (*taṭarruf*) in relation to any confession. Following their principle of distinguishing Zionists from local Jews, they confirmed the necessity to differentiate between anti-Zionism and anti-Semitism, and distanced themselves from the latter. In their opinion, anti-Semitism was a European phenomenon dating back to the Middle Age, and incompatible with the modern age.[86] When criticizing Zionism, they emphasized that this was not to be confused with anti-Semitism. At the same time and as a matter of principle, they refused to apply the concept of 'nation' (*šaʿb*) or 'ethnic group' (*ʿunṣur*) to the Jews, whether Ottoman or foreign, in contrast to the Ashkenazi authors who argued in *Filasṭīn* in favour of Zionism. Being constantly afraid of igniting sectarianism, the ʿĪsās were terrified whenever they sensed that disputes between authors of different confessions were open to

81 For example, see *Filasṭīn*, 14 December 1912: 197/4/1–2.
82 *Filasṭīn*, 5 June 1912: 142/1/2.
83 *Filasṭīn*, 2 November 1912: 185/1/5–2/3.
84 *Filasṭīn*, 22 July 1911: 53/2/2–5.
85 *Filasṭīn*, 20 November 1912: 190/3/2.
86 Anti-Semitism was judged by them to be the 'shame of the twentieth century' (*maʿarrat al-qarn al-ʿišrīn*). See *Filasṭīn*, 25 October 1913: 283/1/1f.

being interpreted as 'religious conflict' (*ǧadal dīnī*)[87] and reminded them to follow the 'principle of neutrality' (*ḫiṭṭat al-ḥiyād*).[88]

A significant difference is notable in the terminology applied by both the Sephardi and Ashkenazi authors. The Sephardim adopted the term 'Jews' for all members of the Yishuv, referring to it as *one* collective group, regardless of nationality. Fostering a Jewish national renaissance in Palestine on the one hand and being culturally rooted in the Arab community on the other, the Sephardim were torn between Palestinian patriotism, Ottomanism and Zionism and, in the debate in *Filasṭīn*, they appeared as basically apologetic, defending the Zionist movement and usually interpreting any form of anti-Zionism as 'anti-Semitism' (*karh al-yahūd*). While it is clear that the editors of *Filasṭīn* used the term *umma* in the context of *milla* and both terms as equivalent to 'religious community', the Sephardi and Ashkenazi authors used the term in the sense of 'people' or 'nation' in the context of a national unity as propagated by the WZO. They also used the terms 'Israelites' and 'Jews' with greater flexibility than Muslim and Christian authors, depending on whether they wanted to stress the Ottoman citizenship of the Jews or their affiliation to the Jewish (national) community. In individual cases, they also spoke of a 'Jewish nation' (*aš-šaʿb al-yahūdī*) or an 'Israeli people' (*aš-šaʿb al-isrāʾīlī*), as we shall see.

4. Negotiating Zionist Exclusiveness versus Inclusiveness

The following sections illustrate two examples of press disputes fought on the pages of *Filasṭīn* during 1912 over the question of how far Jewish migrants in Jaffa had established an exclusive way of life or were ready to mingle with the local population in economic matters and social customs. The first dispute took place in early summer 1912 between Yūsuf al-ʿĪsā and the Ashkenazi migrant and journalist Abraham Ludvipol (1865–1921) and basically revolved around the question of whether Zionist migrants had established a parallel economic system in the urban context of Jaffa.[89] The second dispute took place during late summer and autumn 1912 was about the confessional policy of the Jewish Mikve Yisra'el School, situated four kilometers south-east of Jaffa, and the question of whether it integrated non-Jewish students into its training program or discriminated against them. The ʿĪsās initially opened the controversy about this agricultural school of the AIU to put pressure on Governor Muhdī Bek to establish an Arab

87 For instance, see *Filasṭīn*, 11 June 1913: 244/1/1–2.

88 *Filasṭīn*, 30 March 1912: 124/1/1–4.

89 See also how Beška discussed the case, which he identified as the first shift in *Filasṭīn*'s position regarding Zionism 'from neutrality to criticism'. Beška 2016c, 39–42.

agricultural school in the *qaḍā*ʾ, criticizing the exclusivist agenda of Mikve Yisra'el. They were supported in this position by two former Arab Muslim students of the school and rebuked by the Sephardi journalist Nissim Malul from Jaffa.

4.1. The Integration of Zionist Migrants in Jaffa

In May and June 1912, a dispute unfolded between ʿĪsā and Ludvipol about the exclusiveness or inclusiveness of Zionism, which should be seen in the context of the rapid demographic and urban growth that Jaffa had faced during the past decades. After the turn of the twentieth century, Jaffa's market area spread outside the Old City, surrounding the Muslim cemetery. In 1907, the Greek Orthodox convent built about 200 new warehouses there and rented them to Jewish migrants. From the 1890s, most shops in the Bustrus Market, where the editorial office of *Filasṭīn* was situated, had been rented out to Jews, as well as the flats on the upper floors.[90] The ethno-confessional composition of Jaffa's traders gradually shifted, as was observed by Yūsuf al-ʿĪsā, who blamed a new generation of Jewish-Zionist immigrants for establishing a separate economic system in the city from which the local Christian and Muslim Arabs were excluded.

Abraham Ludvipol was one of the Ashkenazi immigrants attacked by ʿĪsā, and he had a wholly different worldview, shaped by the Jewish experience in Europe. Ludvipol was director of the London-based Grisham life insurance company, which maintained a branch in Jaffa and regularly advertised in *Filasṭīn*, so the editors probably knew him personally. From the late 1880s, he had been active in the *Hibbat Tzion* Movement in Odessa, having started a career as a journalist in Paris, published in French and Yiddish, and gained a reputation in the Hebrew press in the aftermath of the Dreyfus Affair (1894). After his migration to Palestine in 1907, Ludvipol regularly published in the Hebrew press[91] and, after World War I, he became one of the editors of the Hebrew daily *Haaretz*.[92] In his dispute with ʿĪsā about the exclusiveness or integration of the Zionist movement in Palestine, Ludvipol took the opposite view and claimed that Jewish migrants were the driving force for Jaffa's development. The debate also included na-

90 Kark 1990b, 260f.

91 For instance, in 1911, he disputed with a circle of Sephardi journalists the foundation of a Jewish-Arabic newspaper in Palestine that should respond on anti-Zionism in the Arab press, represent the agenda of Palestinian Jews towards Zionism and address Arab Muslims and Christians in favor of the Zionist movement; an idea that Ludvipol opposed. See *Filasṭīn*, 28 October 1911: 81/3/4.

92 See 'Ludvipol, Abraham', in *Encyclopaedia Judaica*. See http://www.encyclopedia.com (accessed 18 Oct. 2017), and Kressel 2007, vol. 13, 251.

tionalist arguments, brought various models of collective identity into the dispute and, as is illustrated here, developed over different stages.

Initiating the Dispute

Initiating the debate, ʿĪsā elaborated in an editorial entitled 'The Migrants and the Rise in the Cost of Living' (*al-Muhāǧirūn wa-Ġalāʾ al-Maʿīša*) on economic difficulties in Jaffa, saying:

> We think that the main reason for impoverishment is the permanent and rising number of Israelite migrants. Surely it will be noted that we did not say the 'foreign migrants' but the 'Israelite migrants'!... Readers must not think that we intent a hostile attack towards this community (*šann al-ġāra ʿalā hāḏihi l-umma*). No! We are the first to acknowledge their right to reside and live in whatever country they want. One does not have to complain about them but one has to watch out and defend one's case... It is a fact that it is only through the effect of those many migrants to our city... that we have noticed a rise in the cost of living. At the same time, it is a fact that the rise in population is beneficial for the city (*mufīda li-l-balda*), and proof of its civilizational progress (*taqaddumihā l-ʿumrānī*).[93]

According to ʿĪsā, the essential problem was not migration as such, or the rise in prices resulting from migration. On the contrary, he considered this process to be an engine of the Jaffa's urbanization. ʿĪsā explained that rises in the cost of living and income functioned like a natural scale and they would simultaneously balance each other out, provided that all segments of the population participated in local economy. The crucial difference between former migrants and the New Yishuv was the Zionists unwillingness to mix with the local people in socio-economic matter, he claimed. Before, migrants had not lived separately from their Arab Palestinian environment but had blended with the locals into 'one block' (*kutla wāḥida*). Now, ʿĪsā criticized, 'we see that our brothers, the Israeli migrants (*iḫwānanā l-isrāʾīlīyīn al-muhāǧirīn*) have established for themselves exclusive residential areas, markets and customs' (*aḥyāʾ ḫāṣṣa wa-aswāq ḫāṣṣa wa-iṣṭilāḥāt ḫāṣṣa*).[94] On top of that, they meanwhile 'occupied most of the city markets and warehouses' (*iḥtallū akṯar aswāq al-balda wa-stāʾṯarū bi-maḫāzinihā*), he said.[95] This forced the locals to buy their goods from Jewish traders while the Jews only consumed goods sold by their own people. Thus they experienced both the rise in costs and the rise in rewards. However, they did not share the benefits with the local people, who had to deal with price rises without

93 See *Filasṭīn*, 29 May 1912: 140/1/2–3. The term *ʿumrānī* can be translated as 'civilizational', 'cultural' or 'urban', and incorporates the sense of a highly developed and sophisticated urban culture.

94 *Filasṭīn*, 29 May 1912: 140/1/3.

95 *Filasṭīn*, 29 May.1912: 140/1/3.

enjoying a higher income, and this resulted in an 'imbalance in the scales of urban life' (*ʿadam at-takāfūʾ fī kaffatai mīzān al-ʿumrān*), ʿĪsā said.[96]

Ludvipol's Response

ʿĪsā's article caught Ludvipol's attention – obviously as one of the migrants criticized for their exclusive practices – although he was not able to read Arabic, and his response (probably in French) was translated for publication in *Filasṭīn*. Ludvipol admitted that the rapid growth of Israelite immigration had played a part in the price rises in Jaffa. However, the claim that the Israelites had established exclusive markets was, according to Ludvipol, a 'fairytale' (*min qabīl al-ḫurafāt*), resulting from 'the prejudices that were fixed in [people's] minds' (*fikrat at-taḥāmul taṣallabat fī l-ʿuqūl*).[97] Ludvipol claimed that the Israelites did not gain the 'slightest economic privilege', unless the same could be said of the Christians in their 'exclusive neighborhood' of al-ʿAǧamī,[98] and the Jews (*al-yahūd*) limited their economic intercourse to Jewish warehouses as little as the Christians limited it to Christian shops.[99] Ludvipol blamed ʿĪsā for making an anti-Semitic attack on the Jews in Palestine, saying:

> The author mentioned that he does not intend to make a hostile attack on the Israeli people (*aš-šaʿb al-isrāʾīlī*) and was humble enough to acknowledge the right of this nation (*ḥaqq hāḏa š-šaʿb*) to reside where and how it wants to reside. Nevertheless, we can only conclude that the motive for this article was hatred towards Jews (*karh al-yahūd*).[100]

Ludvipol stressed the benefit for the local economy that derived from Jewish migration, referring to the successful Jewish colonies in the *qaḍāʾ*, Mulabbas (Petaḥ Tikva), ʿUyūn Qāra (Rishon le-Tzion) and Dayrān or Dārān (Reḥovot), where a significant number of Arabs worked. Petaḥ Tikva alone employed more than 3,000 non-Jewish workers, and the wages for Arab workers in the settlements amounted to 30,000–40,000 piasters a day going into the hands of non-Israelites (*ġayr isrāʾīlī*). He lamented that, even so, Jewish migrants were held responsible for the price rises in Jaffa, which were caused by the presence of all groups of migrants, 'European or not'. According to Ludvipol, 'hatred towards the Jews and the idea of anti-Semitism' (*buġḍ al-yahūd wa-hāḏihi fikrat al-antī ǧuwīf*) followed the Jews everywhere they went, and ʿĪsā too was obsessed by anti-Semitism.[101]

96 *Filasṭīn*, 29 May 1912: 140/1/3.
97 *Filasṭīn*, 5 June 1912: 142/1/2–3.
98 *Filasṭīn*, 5 June 1912: 142/1/2.
99 *Filasṭīn*, 5 June 1912: 142/1/3.
100 *Filasṭīn*, 5 June 1912: 142/1/2.
101 *Filasṭīn*, 5 June 1912: 142/1/3.

Sectarian Arguments

Ludvipol's hostile statement was commented on by ʿĪsā in an unexpectedly sarcastic response and inter-sectarian polemics and the debate turned into a dispute over group identities. Claiming that Ludvipol's accusation of anti-Semitism resulted from his lack of understanding (*ǧahl*) the Arabic text of *Filasṭīn*, ʿĪsā assumed that mistakes in his translation must have led to such a misinterpretation.[102] Tetchily reacting to what ʿĪsā thought was the Israelites' hypersensitivity to criticism, he did not hold back: 'Some of our brothers, the Israelites', he wrote, 'are sitting in ambush' all the time and, as soon as anyone dares to express the slightest criticism, they 'rampage around'. ʿIsā sarcastically asked if he, as a journalist, should 'dip the pencil into the rivers of the garden of Eden' when writing about the Israelites, or if people should 'wear a hat' and 'take off their shoes' when approaching them, as the prophet Moses had done on Mount Sinai when receiving the Ten Commandments.[103] ʿĪsā continued:

> They [the Israelites] want to make the whole world understand that their community (*ummatuhum*) is in its cultural interaction with the nations (*min ǧihat ʿalāqatihā l-adabīya maʿ aš-šuʿūb*) and its civilizational existence on this earth sanctified, beyond any suspicion (*muqadassa ʿan kulli rayb*) of ethnical fanaticism (*taʿaṣṣub ǧinsī*) and impeccable (*maʿṣūma*) when it comes to any fault in social behavior (*kull ġalaṭ iǧtimāʿī*).[104]

The identity models promoted by Ludvipol also came into conflict with ʿĪsā's understanding of loyalty to Ottoman unity in Palestine. He rejected Ludvipol's concept of the Jews as a 'nation' and stressed that nationality based on confessional affiliation was not in compliance with the needs of the present age:

> We were not full of hatred against the Jewish race (*buġḍ al-ʿunṣur al-yahūdī*) because we do not know of the existence of a Jewish race. We only know that there is an Israelite religion (*diyāna isrāʾīlīya*) that we appreciate and respect as much as we respect the other religions, and that the sons of this religion belong to the (ethnic) groups (*ʿanāṣir*) of the Turks, Indians, Russians and Arabs – as much as the Bulgarians, Serbs, French and Americans belong to the Christian religion. We believe that religious socialization (*al-ǧāmiʿa ad-dīnīya*) is not in compliance with the needs of the contemporary age.[105]

ʿĪsā furthermore explained the situation at the market of Jaffa as close to a 'civilizational struggle' (*ʿirāk ʿumrānī*). In order to avoid the danger that people would misinterpret the situation as a 'religious struggle' (*al-ʿirāk ad-dīnī*), ʿĪsā

102 *Filasṭīn*, 5 June 1912: 142/1/3.

103 Using more Biblical references, Yūsuf quoted from the Psalms of David to exaggerate the sensitivity of some Jews, saying ironically 'Do not touch my anointed ones and do not double-cross my prophets'. *Filasṭīn*, 5 June 1912: 142/1/1.

104 *Filasṭīn*, 5 June 1912: 142/1/1.

105 *Filasṭīn*, 5 June 1912: 142/1/3.

claimed that he had not spoken his mind.[106] As he no longer saw any reason to mince matters, ʿĪsā described the rivalry in the markets of Jaffa, predicting total ruin for local merchants and continued:

> All the time we keep discovering a new Israelite warehouse that opened on one of the big market places in town. So, we said 'peace be upon the warehouse' in which exactly the same stuff is being sold [as in the others]. It will be only one or two more years until our prediction comes true that the local merchant (*al-waṭanī*) closes his warehouse for another migrant to rent it and until anyone strolling around on the city markets finds them deserted on Saturdays. We have seen that the Israelite walks a distance of 500 meters to get his purchases from his brother. And we have seen that the rest of the population also walks a distance of 500 meters to buy from a warehouse that is one or two piasters cheaper. This is what we have seen and this was it what we wanted to say.[107]

ʿĪsā emphasized that they were not against Jewish immigration but against an exclusive economic system in an urban context, because it caused impoverishment and stimulated the emigration of Palestinians:

> We have always said and still say that we do not believe that there is any danger arising from Israelite colonization... Rather, we see in this some advantages. The increase of Israelites surrounding the Arab villages does not mean the end of progress, because the prosperity of one village does not interrupt the prosperity of a neighboring village. But the opposite is the case in a city where part of the population establishes a city within the city (*madīna ḍimna madīna*). In this case, the mutual advantage is lost and, after a short period of time the strong eats the weak... And then the original residents (*as-sukkān al-aṣlīyūn*) become frightened and will emigrate to foreign lands.[108]

The emigration of Palestinians to countries outside the Empire worried the editors and was a topic that was given considerable attention in *Filasṭīn* and was perceived as a serious problem. Peasants fled from hardship and heavy debts. Youth of all denominations tried to escape Ottoman military service, especially after the fall of Tripoli and the Balkan Wars, a fact much criticized in *Filasṭīn*, and went to seek their fortune in the New World. Impoverished Palestinians knew about the high living standards in Europe and tempting stories were in circulation about a wealthy life in America. In fact, the coverage on this topic in *Filasṭīn* should be explored more fully but can only be referred to briefly here. In several articles, patriotic arguments encouraged the local youth to work for the progress of Palestine from home and not to betray the Ottoman homeland.[109]

106 *Filasṭīn*, 5 June 1912: 142/1/3.

107 *Filasṭīn*, 5 June 1912: 142/1/4.

108 *Filasṭīn*, 5 June 1912: 142/2/1.

109 For instance, in a letter, Ǧurǧī al-Ḫūri Yaʿqūb, an Orthodox from Beit Sahour, complained about the increase in Palestinian emigration to America, particularly by Christians from Bethlehem and Mount Lebanon, but also by Bedouins, he claimed, to avoid Ottoman military service. In a 'message to the sons of the homeland' (*risāla ilā banī al-waṭan*), Yaʿqūb

Critical articles on the difficult situation of Palestinians and Syrians in exile were published. To discourage emigration from Palestine, Yūsuf al-ʿIsā published an editorial entitled 'Rubbing Salt into the Wound' (*Darr al-Milḥ ʿalā l-Ǧurḥ*), in which he elaborated on the misery of exile. Once blinded by the idea of quick fortune, emigrants were isolated, exploited and, against their expectations, drifted into deep poverty, ʿĪsā said, using the example of a Syrian emigrant who had failed in Liverpool.[110] The emigration of the Arab middle and lower classes from the Empire to Europe and America has so far received too little attention, and would be an interesting topic for future research.[111]

Hebrew Labor and the 'Yemeni Experiment'

The issue of 'Hebrew labor' as a premise of the Zionist Movement started to emerge at a later stage in the dispute between ʿĪsā and Ludvipol. ʿĪsā mocked the thesis that the local population benefitted from job possibilities in the nearby Jewish settlements as the 'usual compensation' (*at-taʿwīḏ al-muʿtād*), the usual argument that the Zionists 'pulled out' like a 'trump card' when justifying Zionist immigration by claiming that it promoted the progress of Palestine. ʿĪsā responded to Ludvipol that there were no non-Israelite workers in these settlements (*mā fīhā min al-ʿummāl ġayr al-isrāʾīlīyīn*). On the contrary, ʿĪsā claimed, a Zionist agency brought Yemeni Jews daily by bus from Jerusalem to the settlement of ʿArtūf (Hebr.: Hartuv) in the area of Ramla to replace 'the local farmers' (*al-fallāḥīn al-waṭanīyīn*).[112] Sometime later, ʿĪsā addressed a report to 'Sir Ludvipol' in the *Local News* section, stating that Yemeni Jewish migrants arrived at Jaffa's harbor for the third time in June 1912to become future Jewish

---

appealed to the citizens to avoid the 'humiliation' and 'bitterness' of life in exile and accept the honorable duty of serving the Ottoman homeland. *Filasṭīn*, 24 January 1912: 105/1/4–2/1.

110 *Filasṭīn*, 25 November 1911: 89/1/1–3.

111 This gap in the scholarship is correctly criticized by Fishman (2007). However, his own treatment of the issue is out of context. In the light of Zionist land purchase and Ottoman corruption, Fishman refers to 'an exodus of Palestinian peasants from their country' (p. 51). He concludes that this emigration 'created a sort of practical nationalism among the Palestinian peasants' and that they (the peasants) 'discovered the connection ... with the land ... and Palestine in general ... strengthened by the infusion of nationalist ... terminology through which they found expression' (p. 52). The extent to which farmers deprived of their livelihood adopted nationalist terminology is not clear. This quotation might prove Fishman's claim about early Palestinian nationalism apart from two petitions: one by village *muḫtārs* protesting against the violence of Jewish settlers of Reḥovot in 1913 (pp. 58–60), the other by Jerusalem notables asking the government to take measures against Zionist migration (pp. 65–71.).

112 *Filasṭīn*, 5 June 1912: 142/2/1 f. In 1883, the London Society for the Promotion of Christianity Amongst the Jews bought the land of ʿArtūf, settled Jews in the village and tried to get them to convert to Christianity. The experiment failed and was abandoned. In 1895, the settlement of ʿArtūf was revived by Zionist settlers from Bulgaria. For the history of the village, see Khalidi 1992, 268–269; Morris 2004, xx, 334.

labor in the settlements, while 'the goal behind acquiring them [the Yemenis]' is to let go of the indigenous farmers (*muzāriʿūn*) in the Israelite settlements'.[113] Indeed, it was a strategy of the WZO during the Second Aliya (1904–14) to expand the Palestinian market through the acquisition of Hebrew labor (Hebr.: *ʿavoda ʿivrit*), and the idea of achieving the 'conquest' of Palestine through work (Hebr.: *kibbuš ha-ʿavoda*) became part of Zionist ideology. However, despite this strategy, Jewish settlements did continue to employ Arab Palestinians as agricultural workers for simple reasons of economic viability.[114] To counteract this reality on the ground, Ruppin, director of the Palestine Office and a leading European Zionist agronomist, saw the solution in the recruitment of Jews from Yemen to replace Arab Palestinians in the settlements. The assumption was that Yemeni Jews, being Arabs as well as Jews, would manage with the same 'frugality' as Arab Palestinian farmers. They would allegedly survive on low wages, being used to simple living conditions, hard physical labor and a hot climate which was a problem when it came to European immigrants in the settlements who had difficulties coping with the harsh conditions of agricultural work and demanded a higher income and days off. It seems that another assumed benefit in the recruitment of Yemeni Jews was the fact that they spoke Arabic and were Ottoman citizens, which avoided legal problems since the authorities imposed restrictions on the immigration by foreign Jews.[115]

From 1911 onwards, the so-called 'Yemeni experiment' began. The Zionist Shmuel Warshawsky travelled as an envoy to Yemen to recruit Jews. He convinced about 2,000 of them to come to Palestine where they became employed in the agricultural branches of the settlements.[116] The 'Yemeni experiment' as a Zionist strategy was noted in *Filasṭīn*, too. In October 1912, an article reprinted from the British *Manchester Guardian* reported the suggestions of the German Zionist agronomist Felix Warburg, who proposed the settling and 'provisioning' of at least 1,000 more Yemeni Jews for the expansion of Jewish economic activities in Palestine, especially in agriculture and the textile industry. They should be trained in new training centers to work in the weaving factories in Jerusalem and Lod.[117] However, contrary to the theory of Zionist agronomists, the Yemenis could not deal with the harsh working conditions and the climate. They suffered

113 '*Wa-l-ġāya min ǧalbihim al-istiġnāʾ fī l-mustaʿmarāt al-isrāʾīlīya min al-fallāḥīn al-waṭanīyīn*'. *Filasṭīn*, 12 June 1912: 144/3/5.

114 The Zionist Moshe Smilansky stressed the lack of education of the 'Arab worker' as one if his virtues. Because the Arabs were not organized in labor unions and knew nothing about their rights, they were quite humble and willing to work for low wages on a daily basis. Shafir 1996, 56f.

115 Shilony 1998, 302–309.

116 Krämer 2002, 139f.

117 *Filasṭīn*, 9 October 1912: 178/3/1f.

from inadequate accommodation and health care and many of them became ill and died. The settlement of Petaḥ Tikva released reports of high mortality rates, stating that 40 percent of the 'imported' Yemeni Jews died, so that the management of the settlement complained about the high funeral costs.[118]

The issue was picked up in the *Local News* section in *Filasṭīn*. In November 1911, ʿĪsā reported the departure of 50 Yemeni Jewish migrants from the harbor on a Russian steamship. He wrote that they had decided to leave Palestine because of 'bad treatment, demands for excessive work and low wages' (*sūʾ al-muʿāmala kuṯra mā yafriḍūnahu ʿalayhim min al-ašġāl wa-qillat mā yadfaʿūnahu lahum min ar-rawātib*).[119] In 1913, the experiment was declared a failure and came to an end.[120]

Conflicting Concepts of Group Identity

Here, we should return to the sectarian arguments that unfolded between ʿĪsā and Ludvipol about the exclusiveness versus integration of Jewish migrants. This is a crucial point in the dispute as it demonstrates that the two protagonists promoted conflicting concepts of group identity. Ludvipol generally used nationalist terminology shaped in Europe. Borrowed from European nationalist discourse, the terms he applied to the New Yishuv carried a notion of ethnical identity to address the 'Israelite nation' (*aš-šaʿb al-isrāʾīlī*). As an Ashkenazi Jew, he was influenced by manifestations of political anti-Semitism, and had been personally affected by the Dreyfus-affair (1894) in France. Thus, it is not very surprising that he introduced accusations of 'hatred towards Jews' (*karh al-yahūd*) and 'anti-Judaism' (*fikrat al-antī-ǧuwīf*) in the controversy with ʿĪsā.[121]

ʿĪsā's vision was shaped by the concepts of patriotism in the Ottoman context. Thus, he spoke of the Jewish community as the followers of a 'religion' (*diyāna*), denying their existence as a national community. His concept of the Israelite community (he applied the term *umma*) was restricted to confessional affiliation and equivalent to *milla*, and he refused any kind of national socialization or political collective identity based on ethnicity or confessional bonds.[122] Ludvipol's understanding of the 'Israelites' as a 'nation' (*šaʿb*) was sharply rejected by ʿĪsā with the argument, that a 'Jewish (ethnic) group' (*al-ʿunṣur al-yahūdī*) did

118 Shafir 1996, 106.

119 *Filasṭīn*, 9 November 1912: 187/3/2–3.

120 For the 'Yemeni experiment', see Shafir 1996, 91–122.

121 *Filasṭīn*, 5 June 1912: 142/1/2. The Dreyfus affair also made a mark on other prominent figures in the Zionist movement, such as Theodor Herzl. It was through the impact of this affair that he declared the assimilation of Jews in Europe as having failed. See Brenner 2005, 29f. For the impact of the Dreyfus affair on Sephardi Jews in the Arab world, see Levy 2012, 145f.

122 *Filasṭīn*, 5 June 1912: 142/1/3.

not exist, as is seen in the quotation above. The term *šaʿb* (nation) used by Ludvipol was changed by ʿĪsā to *ʿunṣur*, the term for 'ethnic group' in the Ottoman context, with the various ethnicities and confessions that co-existed in the Empire, and this was not in line with what Ludvipol meant.[123] As a feature of an *ʿunṣur*, ʿĪsā pointed to a language, such as the Turks, Serbs and Arabs had. But, in this view, the bonds of language and ethnicity did not give a group the right to constitute a nation. The only legitimate 'nation' for the ʿĪsās was the 'Ottoman Homeland' (*al-waṭan al-ʿuṯmānī*), which united a plurality of confessions and ethnicities under the umbrella of Ottoman citizenship and constitutional rights. In line with this view, other features of group identity were not denied but they were not meant to challenge Ottoman integrity. In order to demonstrate that national socialization on confessional grounds was 'old-fashioned' and not compliant with modernity, ʿĪsā pointed to the hostilities between the Bulgarians and Serbs to reconfirm that this led to never-ending strife in the Empire.[124]

4.2. The Jewish Netter School and its Confessional Policy

The controversy over the Jewish Mikve Yisra'el Agricultural School and the question of whether it integrated non-Jewish students into its training or discriminated against them, also demonstrates how much the debate on Jewish migration in Palestine before World War I revolved around the question of the extent to which it was exclusivist or integrative. It also shows the centrality of the topic of the modernization of local agriculture, since Palestine was an agricultural province and its market depended on agricultural exports. Authors in *Filasṭīn* expounded on the urgency of agricultural reform, the privatization of land, the dissolution of feudal ownership, the provision of state grants to small peasants and tax relief for tenants who faced the dilemma of constant debts. The successful agricultural training center, the 'Netter School' (*Madrasat Nītar*), as the Mikve Yisra'el School was called in *Filasṭīn*, was considered an important institution in the *qaḍāʾ* and it maintained a secondary school and a teaching college in Jaffa, an agricultural experimental station in ʿAtlit, an art school in Jerusalem and a technical school in Haifa.[125]

In 1860, the AIU was founded in Paris to 'work for the emancipation and the moral progress of Jews'. It should be noted that it was not a Zionist organization and did not share the agenda of political Zionism but later became a rival of the WZO. Its emergence should be seen in the context of other European Jewish

123 For the role of the term *ʿunṣur* in the Ottoman context after the 1860s, see Zurcher 2000, 153.
124 *Filasṭīn*, 5 June 1912: 142/1/4.
125 Mandel 1976, 137.

efforts against political anti-Semitism, encouraging the foundation of several Jewish organizations and international networks.[126] The principle of the AIU was to foster Jewish education on a universal basis, and especially, to 'raise' Oriental Jewry and boost networks between Ottoman Jews and European Jewish communities. After the 1870s, the AIU established several educational and cultural institutions for Jews, from Istanbul to Baghdad, where the French education system was followed and which were considered local institutions that did not seek the protection of foreign powers but encouraged reforms and Ottomanism, and were promoted by the authorities. In fact, many members of the Ottoman bureaucratic elites were AIU graduates and tended to be pro-CUP.[127] In 1870, the 'Netter School' near Jaffa was established by Charles Netter, a Jewish a trader, philanthropist and a co-founder of the AIU from Strasbourg, who obtained a license from the sultan for its foundation.[128]

In 1912, *Filasṭīn* printed the text of the sultan's edict (Ar.: *firmān*, Tur.: *fermān*) to inform readers of the conditions of the contract between the AIU and the government. Officially, the school was founded on behalf of the 'children of the Mosaic confession' (*aṭfāl al-milla al-mūsawīya*), and for that purpose land was obtained land that belonged to the Arab farming village of Yāzūr.[129] As an Ottoman institution, the school was subject to the Ministry of Education, and required 'to accept students from other confessions' (*tuqbal fīhi talāmiḏa min sāʾir al-milal wa-l-maḏāhib*) provided that they held Ottoman citizenship (*bi-šarṭ an yakūnū ǧamīʿuhum min at-tabʿa al-ʿuṯmānīya*).[130] However, as is seen from the dispute, the Netter School was not too eager to educate children of other denominations although it did accept sons of the local Muslim and Christian elites. After Governor Muhdī Bek visited all the Jewish settlements in the *qaḍāʾ* in

126 See Brenner 2008, 16–18; Wilke 2011, 42–50. Often, the foundation of the AIU is explained as a reaction to anti-semitic outbursts during the nineteenth century. Examples in this context are the 'Damascus affair' (1840) – when the Jews of Damascus were accused of ritual murder after a Christian monk had disappeared and several Jews were imprisoned, tortured and killed – and the 'Mortara Affair' (1858) – the kidnapping of a Jewish boy, Edgaro Mortara, in Bologna, obviously through intervention of the Catholic Church. However, Arnold has put the foundation of the AIU in a wider context and also considered its rivalries with other regional Jewish associations. See Arnold 2010, 43–69, especially 43–50.

127 Levy 1992, 113–117.

128 Because of the difficult local conditions, Netter was against the 'infiltration' of Jews into Palestine; however, through the influence of the British Baron de Rothschild, he came to Palestine to boost the settlement of Mikve Yisraʾel, but soon fell ill and died. See Klausner and Catane 1994, vol. II, 991.

129 As Schölch knows, the farmers of Yāzūr strongly protested against the transfer of their land to the AIU. In 1870, during a visit with the governor of Damascus, Charles Netter saw the farmers clinging to the governor's trouser legs, lamenting that the Jews had taken their land from them. The governor simply chased them away with his riding whip. Schölch 1986, 109, 262.

130 *Filasṭīn*, 2 October 1912: 176/1/3–5.

Figure 21: Children in a classroom in Miqve Yisra'el/Netter School, between 1898 and 1934. From the G. Eric and Edith Matson Photograph Collection. (Source: Library of Congress)

the summer of 1912 and promised to establish an Arab agricultural school at Nabī Ruben along the lines of the Netter School, the ʿĪsās, who doubted the governor's motivation, raised the matter of the Netter School, which they cricitized for excluding and discriminating against non-Jewish students; they were supported by two authors who were former students of the school, Fāʾiz Efendi Ḥaddād from Jaffa and ʿAlī Muḥammad aṭ-Ṭāhir. Arguing for the other side, the Sephardi journalist Nissim Malul (1892–1959) intervened, rejecting these accusations and, as proof, he published the numbers of former non-Jewish graduates of the Netter School in the press.

Muhdī Bek's Tour of the Jewish Settlements

A flashpoint was the new Governor Muhdī Bek's introductory tour of the Jerusalem District in August 1912, during which he visited Jaffa, the Arab village of Nabī Rūbīn near Ramla, and the Jewish settlements in the *qaḍāʾ*, including Mikveh Yisra'el. *Filasṭīn*'s coverage of his tour gives the impression that he paid much more attention to the Jewish settlements than to the Arab villages in the *qaḍāʾ*,[131] indicating that he considered them significant for its economy and progress, which caused controversies in Jaffa that were picked up by the ʿĪsās. According to them, 'puplic opinion' in Jaffa was divided between 'pessimists' (*farīq yatašāʾim*) and 'optimists' (*farīq yatafāʿil*). While the former feared that Muhdī Bek's attention would be to the 'great benefit of the Zionist settlements' (*min fāʾida kabīra li-l-mustaʿmirīn aṣ-ṣihyūnīyīn*), the latter assumed that the governor had paid this much attention to the Jewish settlements to find out about its new technologies, which they hoped would benefit of the local population since he had announced the construction of an agricultural school in Nabī Rūbīn to be run according to 'modern standards' (*ʿalā aṭ-ṭarz al-ǧadīd*).[132] The editors took the governor's visit to Mikveh Yisra'el as an opportunity to point out that the Netter School, as an Ottoman institution, was obliged to integrate Arab Muslim and Christian students into their program. They criticized the school for rejecting non-Jewish enrollment and violating this law, and they sarcastically called on the governor to give his attention to this irregularity.[133]

The Intervention of Nissim Malul

The ʿĪsās' charges against the Netter School drew the attention of the Sephardi journalist Nissim Malul, correspondent for the Egyptian magazine *al-Muqaṭṭam*, who published his response in the Beirut newspaper *An-Naṣīr*. Born in 1892 in Safed and based in Jaffa, Malul came from a Tunisian religious family that had migrated to Palestine during the seventeenth century. Having received his education in Egypt, he was the first lecturer in Hebrew at Cairo University, and he was a member of the Party for Arab Decentralization, established in Cairo in 1912. In Palestine, Nissim belonged to the *Ḥerut* circle; he published in Hebrew and Arabic, and was both a Zionist and a cultural Arabist who promoted the revival of Arabic as a daily language in the Yishuv.[134] Since 1911, Malul documented anti-Zionist articles in Arabic newspapers for the Jaffa Palestine Office under the leadership of Ruppin, and responded to accusations against Jewish individuals and institutions in the Arab press. Picking up the case of the Netter School in *an-Naṣīr*, Malul published the names of 11 Christian and Muslim Palestinians who graduated from it, including two from well-known Jaffan families: Ḥilmī Aḥmad, the son of Ḥāfiẓ Bek as-Saʿīd, and Fāʾiz b. Maḥmūd Efendi. He addressed ʿĪsā as follows:

> If his excellency [Yūsuf al-ʿĪsā] still does not see in their [the students'] names [proof] enough to convince the population that the story in Filasṭīn is purely fabricated out of

131 *Filasṭīn*, 10 August 1912: 161/3/2.
132 *Filasṭīn*, 10 August 1912: 161/3/4.
133 *Filasṭīn*, 10 August 1912: 161/3/4.
134 See Jacobson 2004, 42–43; 2011a, 165–169.

> lurking prejudice, fanaticism and personal interests, we can produce the names of hundreds of others who have graduated from this school since its foundation.[135]

Malul's article was reprinted and commented on with a great deal of hostility by the ʿĪsās, who considered it 'full of distortions' (*malūʾuhā muġālaṭāt*) and unprofessional, and its author an inexperienced 'boy' (*šābb*). The ʿĪsās mocked Malul, claiming that he had previously tried his luck as a correspondent for various newspapers but that his articles turned out to be mere 'defenses of Zionism and the Zionists', who were aware that he was an 'ignorant lawyer' (*muḥāmī ǧāhil*) 'lacking knowledge of the law'. His article proved that Malul had no idea of public opinion (*bi-raʾy al-ǧumhūr*) about the school, the ʿĪsās claimed triumphantly, saying they had proofs that the Netter School had committed 'the greatest faux pas' (*aʿẓam al-ʿaṯrāt*) towards enrolled non-Israelite students.[136]

Regarding the two non-Jewish students Malul had mentioned, the editors claimed that they had only been accepted because they came from influential families with positions in bureaucracy. Ḥilmī was the son of Ḥāfiẓ Bek as-Saʿīd, a prominent Muslim merchant from Jaffa who owned several water mills beside the Yarkon River and in 1908 had been elected as a member of Parliament for the Jerusalem District.[137] The other, Fāʾiz Efendī, was the son of a government official, Maḥmūd, who had a leading position in the Jaffa land registry office (*raʾīs at-taḥrīrāt*). In addition, the ʿĪsās stressed, the Netter School had been founded 43 years ago as an Ottoman institution but the list presented by Malul contained only 11 non-Jewish graduates since then, for which the ʿĪsās saw no plausible explanation. They added: 'We cannot imagine that the obstacle was the lack of desire for knowledge among the population' (*lā naẓunn anna al-māniʿ kāna qillat ruġbat al-ahālī fī t-taʿlīm*).[138]

The Reaction of Fāʾiz Efendī

This polemical attack on Malul attracted the attention of two former non-Jewish students of the Mikveh Yisra'el School. Fāʾiz Efendi, now secretary (*bāškātib*) at the court of appeal (*maḥkamat al-istiʾnāf*) in Jerusalem, added to the attack on Malul, whom he called a 'flatterer of the Zionists'. Recalling his time as a student in the Netter School, Fāʾiz reported that, after he had received basic instruction in French, the director of the school refused to allow him to move up to the next level, arguing that it was not necessary for him to continue with agricultural

135 '*Wa-law lam yara ḥaḍratuhu fī asmāʾihim al-kifāya li-iqnāʿ al-ǧumhūr ʿalā anna riwāyat Filasṭīn maḥḍ iḫtilāq yanṭawī warāʾuhā at-taḥāmul wa-t-taʿaṣṣub wa-l-ġāya aš-šaḫṣīya latānā bi-asmāʾ miʾāt ġayr hāʾulāʾ mimman taḫarraǧū fī tilka al-madrasa munḏu taʾsīsihā.*' *Filasṭīn*, 4 September 1912: 168/1/3.

136 *Filasṭīn*, 4 September 1912: 168/1/2.

137 Buessow 2011, 222, 223, 504.

138 *Filasṭīn*, 4 September 1912: 168/1/4.

training as he was to become 'an official, not a farmer' (*mā ʾmūran lā zāriʿan*). Unfair treatment was also handed out to other non-Jewish colleagues, Fāʾiz continued. The above-mentioned Ḥilmī as-Saʿīd, after being enrolled in the school, was soon discredited and kicked out of class. Another Muslim comrade, a certain Ḥasan, was even more detested in this school because he was lazy, the 'rural type' and of 'rustic' character, Fāʾiz claimed, but, because Ḥasan's father had an important government position, his presence in the school was accepted for two years, during which 'he neither studied nor learned anything'.[139] Fāʾiz bitterly recalled the humiliating treatment he suffered at the school, which he linked to the fact that he was not Jewish, and he felt alienated. Being the only non-Jewish student among 300, he felt he was an outsider because the others avoided contact with him. Fāʾiz recalled his thoughts as a pupil, thus:

> This land is ours, this water and this air is ours. This school is Ottoman as we are too. Why, among this whole crowd of students, are there are no students belonging to the other non-Israelite confessional groups, so that I could find familiarity among them and avoid the contempt of those … among the Israelite community? Back then, I also wondered with my tiny mind why our Arabic language was so neglected and disregarded (*muhmala muḥtaqara*). As soon as just one word was spoken [in Arabic], and this in an Arab country, we were sharply chastised.[140]

Although Fāʾiz presented this as his thoughts when he was a child at the school, his description of patriotic feelings seems to have sprung from the mind of the intellectual adult, not a boy. Fāʾiz contrasted his outsider experience in a Jewish school with what he remembered about the treatment of the Jewish minority in a Jerusalemite secondary school where he used to teach – memories that he drafted as encounters with an inter-confessional harmony and Muslim generosity towards minorities. He recalled this time, saying:

> I had one Israelite student among hundreds of Muslim ones. This student was the object of sympathy and high esteem (*mawḍūʿ maʿazza wa-ikrām*) of all pupils and teachers likewise. So, I was very surprised about this contrast in moral behavior (*hādā t-tanāquḍ fī l-aḫlāq*).[141]

The Response of Muḥammad ʿAlī aṭ-Ṭāhir

A second response came from a young Muslim called Muḥammad ʿAlī aṭ-Ṭāhir from Jaffa, who had read Malul's article and wrote a letter in support of the ʿĪsās, to 'cut off the tongues' of those who tried to 'conceal the sunlight with their hand'.[142] He recalled, that in 1907, when aṭ-Ṭāhir was 13 years old, he was refused

139 *Filasṭīn*, 11 September 1912: 170/2/1–2.
140 *Filasṭīn*, 11 September 1912: 170/2/2.
141 *Filasṭīn*, 11 September 1912: 170/2/2.
142 *Filasṭīn*, 25 September 1912: 174/2/5.

access to the Netter School, which was justified by the director with the claim 'that the school system does not allow the acceptance of non- Israelites' (*anna niẓām al-madrasa lā yasmaḥu bi-qubūl ġayr al-isrāʾīlīyīn*).[143] However, since the father of aṭ-Ṭāhir was familiar with the said system, he protested against these 'illegal methods' (*ṭuruq ġayr mašrūʿīya*) for banning his son from the school because of his confession.[144] Thereupon, the director invented other excuses, saying that aṭ-Ṭāhir was too young, although the edict explicitly stated that students should be aged between 13 and 16 years, or that he could not speak Hebrew although the official language in the Netter School was French.[145]

From the statements of Fāʾiz Efendi and aṭ-Ṭāhir, it is obvious that the Mikve Yisra'el School as an Ottoman institution did accept non-Jewish students in its program but, at the same time, its policy was to limit the number of non-Jewish students to the sons of the local elites, who had access to political power. It is to be noted that the fact that the Netter School, as an AIU institution, was non-Zionist, did not play any role in the dispute; the crucial point was its perceived confessional exclusiveness.

On the other hand, there were Zionist associations that actively promoted an exclusivist Jewish education system. *Filasṭīn* observed these policies, and in May 1913, reprinted a report from *Ḥerut* on a Jewish 'Association for School Resistance' (*Ǧamaʿīyat Muqāwamat Madāris*), which pressured Sephardi Jews to send their children to Jewish institutions and sent a protest letter, signed by the Chief Rabbi, to Albert Antébi, a Sephardi of Damascene origin and a very influential figure in the District, because Antébi's children were enrolled in the Christian St Joseph School in Jerusalem. Antébi, known for his short temper, had beaten up the Jewish courier who delivered the letter; an incident commented on by the editors of *Filasṭīn*, who titled their article 'Extremism on Both Sides' (*Taṭarruf ʿinda al-Farīqayn*) and harshly criticized the agenda of the Association for School Resistance as 'a infringement of personal freedom' (*taʿaddū ʿalā l-ḥurrīya aš-šaḥṣīya*) and 'despotism' (*istibdād*). The ʿĪsās sarcastically asked the 'Jewish community' (*al-umma al-yahūdīya*) that 'lives among us... if this fanaticism fits the civilization of the twentieth century' (*iḏā kāna hāḏā t-taʿaṣṣub yalīq bi-madanīyat al-qarn al-ʿašrīn*)?[146]

143 *Filasṭīn*, 25 September 1912: 174/3/1.
144 *Filasṭīn*, 25 September 1912: 174/3/1.
145 *Filasṭīn*, 25 September 1912: 174/3/1.
146 *Filasṭīn*, 14 May 1913: 236/1/5–2/1.

5. Promoting Zionism in *Filasṭīn*

In compliance with the 'modernization and progress' imperative presented in *Filasṭīn*, the central questions in the Palestinian debate on Zionism before World War I was whether the Zionist Movement would advance regional development. The ambivalence on the matter among the Palestinian population during the Second Constitutional era has already been mentioned. The promoters of Zionism heavily relied on this modernist discourse and sought to prove the potential of Zionist colonization to be a 'pacesetter' for the modernization of Palestine. According to them, Jewish settlements would generate job opportunities for Arab farmers and workers and serve as positive role models for neighboring Arab villages, and its cultural imprint would 'raise' the civilizational level of Palestinians. The promoters of Zionism portrayed the traditional lifestyle of the local people, especially the rural population, as backward, and a relic from Biblical times. In contrast, the higher living standards in the Jewish settlement was the discursive counterpart, and described as healthy, reasonable and prosperous. Indulging in the dualist 'East–West paradigm', as explained in the introduction, the promoters of Zionism in *Filasṭīn* presented a European 'standard set of modernity' that was accepted by the Arab Palestinian elites of all communities. They heavily relied on the dichotomous world view of an 'unchanging' and 'lethargic' East that would only benefit from an 'enlightened' and 'activist' West, as we shall see in the following examples from *Filasṭīn*. Even the critics of Zionism could not escape the dichotomous comparison between East and West and, at times through clenched teeth, expressed admiration for the pioneering success of the Zionist movement in Palestine.

5.1. Zionism as a Stimulating Force for Development

S. Frumkin and the Backwardness of Palestine

Among the Ashkenazi migrants who stressed the civilizational superiority of the Zionists was S. Frumkin, probably a member of the prominent Jerusalemite Russian-Jewish Frumkin family, pioneers of early Hebrew journalism. He published an article in *Filasṭīn* about two Arab Palestinian greengrocers from Ramla who had sold vegetables in Rishon le-Tzion using inaccurate weights.[147] The

147 According to the article, the weights that were in use were light by one *wuqīya* per *raṭl* (approximately one pound). *Filasṭīn*, 22 July 1911: 53/3/4. In the Arab provinces, the *wuqīya* as a weight unit was not the same everywhere. In Jerusalem, it was 240 grams, according to Wehr's dictionary. According to Seikaly, the *wuqīya* in the southern region of Jerusalem was 37 grams, following the Egyptian *wuqīya*. In northern Palestine, it amounted to about 213 grams, following the measuring unit of the Beirut District. Seikaly 2007, 197, n. 100. I assume

settlement's judicial body, the House of Commission, imposed a a fine of a quarter *maǧīdī* on them[148] and announced that there would be heavier fines in case of a repetition. The editors of *Filasṭīn* commented on the financial penalty issued by a Zionist court, which in their opinion undermined the Ottoman judicial authority and criticized the fact that Ottoman citizens' money was going into the pockets of foreigners. This attracted Frumkin's attention and he responded with a long letter to present the case in the 'light of the truth' (*bi-nūr al-ḥaqq*).[149] In his view, the penalty was a light 'compensation' (*taʿwīḍ*) for the financial harm caused by the two grocers.[150] As they had supposedly deceived the settlers many times before, a quarter *maǧīdī* was a 'great mercy' (*marḥama kabīra*) in a country where 'no weight inspected by the municipality is correct' (*lā awzān ṣaḥīḥa turāqibuhā l-baladīya*) and 'all measure units are inadequate' (*al-ʿiyārāt kulluhā nāqiṣa*.[151] If the case had not arisen in a Jewish settlement but in an Arab village, the penalty would have been much more cruel, he declared, and the villagers would have given the criminals a severe beating, while the commission of Rishon le-Tzion was 'known for its dignity and righteousness' (*maʿrūfūn bi-šarafihim wa-stiqāmihim*). The Arab population should be grateful for the economic drive of those flourishing settlements, he said and claimed that the orange exports of Rishon le-Tzion came second in quantity to the orange exports of Jaffa in the *qaḍāʾ*, and the export taxes paid by the settlement were much higher than the taxes paid by the Arabs. Using Biblical images, Frumkin described the *qaḍāʾ* before the arrival of the settlers as dreary and desolate, and not cultivated for agrarian use. Rishon le-Tzion, south of Jaffa, was built on 'empty and neglected sand' (*arḍ ramlīya ḫālīya muhmala*), which had turned through the efforts of the settlers into a 'blooming paradise' (*ǧanna zāhira*).[152] For him, the progress of the region achieved through the settlers was tremendous; especially since he considered Palestine as a backward country in which 'knowledge is little' (*qalla fīhā l-ʿilm*), 'ignorance rules' (*sāda al-ǧahl*), and the educated ele-

that the region of Ramla used the Egyptian unit. Otherwise, the difference in weight would have been too big and the deception too obvious. For more information on Islamic measure units and weights, see Hinz 1970.

148 One *maǧīdī* was an Ottoman silver coin, named after Sultan ʿAbd al-Maǧīd, worth 20 piasters. For currencies and price levels in late Ottoman times, see Buessow 2011, 563f.

149 See *Filasṭīn*, 26 July 1911: 54/1/3. One cannot be completely sure about the author's identity as the name Frumkin was not unusual. The above-mentioned Frumkin family emigrated during the 1850s from Russia to Jerusalem. The father, Israel Dov Frumkin (1850–1914), was a pioneer of Hebrew journalism and, from 1869, edited the newspaper *Ḥavazelet* ('The Lily'), targetting the conservative Ashkenazi audience of the Old Yishuv. See Ben-Bassat 2009b; Slutsky 2007, 301–2.

150 *Filasṭīn*, 26 July 1911: 54/1/2.

151 *Filasṭīn*, 26 July 1911: 54/1/3.

152 *Filasṭīn*, 26 July 1911: 54/1/3.

ments created 'more damage than benefit'.[153] This argumentation was typical for the promoters of Zionism and in line with the famous Zionist theme that the settlers made the desert bloom.

The Settlers as Cultivators of the Desert

Shimon Moyal (1866–1915), a Sephardi from Jaffa, also stressed the 'civilizing effect' of European-Jewish immigration on Palestine. Moyal was a member of a prominent family of Moroccan origin and belonged to Jaffa's economic and intellectual elites. Born in Jaffa in 1866, Shimon was the son of Josef Moyal and the grandson of Aharon Moyal, who had brought his family from Rabat to Jaffa in 1853. Shimon Moyal received a cosmopolitan education and, like the ʿĪsās, studied in Beirut, and later at the al-Azhar University in Cairo, where he became part of the circle around the Muslim reformer Muḥammad ʿAbduh. He translated the Babylonian Talmud into Arabic, was active as a journalist in the Hebrew press (especially *Ḥerut*) and the Arabic press and was clearly also a doctor.[154] Moyal's wife, Esther, originally from Beirut, also published in Arabic. She edited a women's journal named *al-ʿĀʾila* ('The Family'), and encouraged the publishing activities of Arab women in Syria and Palestine.[155]

In *Filasṭīn*, Moyal stressed the settlers' potential contribution to the development of Palestine. In a letter, an author from Gaza, ʿAbdallāh Ḫalaf pointed the Gazan *qāʾimaqām* and the Jerusalem governor to the 'flame of the Zionist colonization' (*lahīb al-istiʿmār aṣ-ṣihyūnī*) blazing in Beersheba. Through the help of Sephardi intermediaries (*bi-wāsiṭat al-isrāʾīlīyīn*) from Gaza, who, he claimed, did not care for the 'ruin of the country' (*ḫarāb al-bilād*) or the 'misery of people' (*šaqāʾ al-ʿubbād*), Zionist settlers bribed tribal leaders who sold their land 'out of love for the ringing sound of gold' which 'the Bedouin loves more than his wife and his children'.[156] In fact, the Moyal family was active in purchasing real estate in Jaffa and land in the *qaḍāʾ*, which they sold to Zionist organizations, and Shimon Moyal responded to Ḫalaf's accusation with a counterattack. The notables of Beesheva who had previosly 'grabbed up' large

153 *Filasṭīn*, 26 July 1911: 54/1/3.

154 There is no information in the literature that Moyal practiced as a doctor. However, in 1913, *Filasṭīn* reported that he had been appointed community doctor of Ramla and Lod. *Filasṭīn*, 22 February 1913: 215/3/3–4.

155 On biographies of Shimon and Esther Moyal, see Jacobson 2011, 166–167. For a portrait of Esther Moyal as Jewish modernist and representative of the Arab *nahḍa* and Arab feminism as well as of Sephardi Zionism, see Levy 2012, 128–164. For Esther Moyal's correspondence with the editor of the Egyptian newspaper *al-Fatāt* ('The Young Lady'), Hind Nawfal, see Levy 2012, 128f.

156 '*Wa-tahāfat al-ʿurbān ʿalā at-taḫalluṣ min arāḍihim ḥubban bi-l-aṣfar ar-rannān allaḏī yuḥibbuhu l-badawī akṯar min imraʾtihi wa-awlādihi.*' *Filasṭīn*, 28 October 1911: 81/2/5.

pieces of land, Moyal said, were too lethargic to invest in its cultivation.[157] The Jews, against whom Ḫalaf 'stirs up public opinion' because of 'a couple of *dunam*', Moyal said, invested in modern agricultural machines to exploit the capacity of the soil, and the settlers change dry dirt into 'gardens with flowing rivers', thus, inspiring the locals to imitate them, which would boost the technological modernization of Palestine. Moyal explained, that

> in this way, the country will be cultivated and the yield among the subjects will increase. The planter will start to make profit, the trader will start to work and everyone will live in continuous prosperity.[158]

The Impression of Zionist Parades

In addition, the appearance of Zionist organizations and the military character of their parades were portrayed as progressive by both promoters and critics of Zionism. In 1912, *Filasṭīn* reported on a 'feast of flowers' in Tel Aviv that was an 'overwhelming joy', with 3,000 visitors and Arabs from Jaffa, and Zionist associations parading through the streets and putting on gymnastic performances that made an impression, as did the sports competitions in the Hebrew Gymnasium.[159] Another event that made a great impression was the annual 'great Zionist parade' (*al-istiʿrāḍ aṣ-ṣihyūnī l-kabīr*) that was held in Reḥovot and documented by *Filasṭīn* with lively interest. It is not clear whether the editors themselves followed the event or sent one of their correspondents or engaged a contact person in Reḥovot to cover it.[160] Whoever the observer was, he reported that the parade of 1913 was 'even greater' than the year before. Each product was displayed on a dedicated market stall, decorated with Zionist flags, and the agricultural exhibition of settlement products surprised the reporter with its high quality and a variety that was a 'sign of progress and growth'. In comparison to that, he said, the agricultural products of the 'local, poor and miserable farmer' looked 'puny'.[161] He also stressed how well the event, the performances and a special transport system that was arranged for the day between Jaffa and Jer-

157 '*Kasal baʿḍ aḏ-ḏawāt al-muḥtakirīn li-l-masāḥāt al-kabīra.*' *Filasṭīn*, 1 November 1911: 82/3/2.

158 '*Fa-tuaʿmmar al-bilād wa-tazīd ṯarwat al-ʿubbād fa-yuṣbiḥ al-muzāriʿ yastaġill wa-t-tāǧir yaštaġill wa-l-kull fī naʿīm muqīm.*' *Filasṭīn*, 1 November 1911: 82/3/2. For the rivalry between different urban actors in their relations to the Bedouins of Beersheba, see Buessow 2011, 429f.

159 *Filasṭīn*, 25 May 1912: 139/3/3–4.

160 *Filasṭīn*, 3 May 1913: 233/3/2f.

161 '*Taʿǧūb lahu an-nāẓir li-dalālatihi ʿalā taqaddum wa-irtiqāʾ taṣġur fī ǧānibihi kull al-maḥṣūlāt az-zirāʿīya allatī yastanbituhā l-fallāḥ al-waṭanī l-faqīr al-miskīn.*' *Filasṭīn*, 3 May 1913: 233/3/2.

usalem had been organized.[162] In particular, the athletic contests and the military 'discipline' (*tartīb*) of the parade made a great impression on the observer: a festive march of Zionist organizations through the settlement with flags, accompanied by the applause of cheering crowds, was filmed and provided the 'a very awesome sight' (*manẓar muhīb ǧiddan*) to the visitor, he reported.[163] Later, the author witnessed competitions on the sports field in Reḥovot and praised the Jewish athletes who seemed to him as a 'most disciplined army' and were, in the sequences of their motions, 'perfectly trained' in the 'military arts'.[164] He also commented on a horse race, in which Jewish men and women participated, dressed in traditional Bedouin costume, so that he almost considered them 'Arab horsemen' (*fursān al-ʿarab*).[165]

These portrayals of Jewish nationalism were rooted in European populist-nationalist traditions of the late nineteenth century and were much influenced by chauvinistic tendencies and ideals of very physical masculinity and fitness. Zionism as a national ideology integrated this masculine ideals as well as European anti-Semitic stereotypes. The image of the traditional 'studious Jew' ('Studierjude') became a symbol of a mental, physical and social alienation from Jewishness in its authentic form that had arisen through life in exile. As a countertype to the Jew of the exile, the 'new Hebrew' was created. Combative Jewish figures and heroes from an ancient Biblical tradition were incorporated into the Zionist narrative, which constructed the ideal of the modern 'muscular Jew'. By creating positive images of Jewish heroes, it was thought that the youth would be attracted to engage in Zionist sports clubs and associations.[166] Taking 'discipline' as a feature of modernity, it is no wonder that the appearance of Zionist parades, with their sporty character, combative spirit and military style, impressed passionate Arab modernists such as the ʿĪsās and their fellow countrymen.

162 The newspaper wrote of 'hundreds of special trains' (*al-qiṭārāt al-ḫuṣūṣīya al-miʾāt*), which sounds somewhat exaggerated. *Filasṭīn*, 3 May 1913: 233/3/3.

163 It is mentioned that the 'cinematograph' was used to film the event.

164 '*Ǧayšan munaẓẓaman aḥsan tanẓīm wa-mudarraban aḥsan tadrīb limā fī ḥarakātihim min al-funūn al-ʿaskarīya.*' *Filasṭīn*, 3 May 1913: 233/3/3.

165 *Filasṭīn*, 3 May 1913: 233/3/2–3.

166 On the need to educate the 'degenerate' Eastern European 'ghetto Jew' through Western Jewry, see Max Nordau on the meaning of physical exercise for the new 'muscular Jew'. Nordau 1909, vol. II, 'Muskeljudentum', 219–224; and 'Was bedeutet das Turnen für uns Juden', 225–235. See also Reizbaum 2003. On the creation of the 'new Hebrew type', the 'Sabra', and his productivity and ability for defense, see Avineri 1999; Haumann 1998.

Muhdī Bek and the Potential of Jewish Settlements

Ottoman officials, too, saw the Jewish settlers as symbols of modernization that could help to implement reforms that the state in fact had to enforce. Governor Muhdī Bek was convinced that local government could benefit from an infrastructure built by the settlers.[167] He treated the Jewish settlements in the District with great benevolence and was on good terms with Zionist representatives. During his introductory trip in summer 1912, he paid more attention to the colonies than to the Arab villages in the *qaḍā'*, and was not the only governor to do so.[168] On this trip, Muhdī Bek was accompanied by the local political elites: the major of Jerusalem, Salīm Efendī al-Ḥusaynī,[169] the *qā'imaqām* of Jaffa and Albert Antébi, who had inspired Muhdī Bek to consider the settlements' potential for the District.[170] Muhdī Bek visited Reḥovot and Petaḥ Tikva, the successful winerie of Rishon le-Tzion and the Netter School to look for ideas for a future agricultural school that he promised to establish near the Arab village of Nabī Rūbīn. He visited the Hebrew Gymnasium in Tel Aviv and drank tea with its Jewish major, Dizzengoff, who organized a reception in his villa where the governor met with the Chief Rabbi and Arthur Ruppin, director of the Palestine Office.[171]

Special attention was paid to Rishon le-Tzion. *Filasṭīn* reported in detail about the sparkling reception given to Muhdī Bek there. In the presence of Jewish notables from Jaffa and other Jewish colonies in the region,[172] the governor was received in Rishon le-Tzion with the Ottoman anthem and even stayed there

167 He knew what the presence of settlers of foreign nationality meant in a juridical sense, as he was the author of a book on the capitulation treaties. See Mandel 1976, 134.

168 In May and June 1913, a series of newspaper reports appeared on the visit made by the new governor, Māğid Bek, around the district. Apart from meeting the elites in Gaza and Mağdal, he focused on the Jewish colonies of Rishon le-Tzion, Wadi Hanin, Reḥovot, Petaḥ Tikva and others, where he was met with impressive receptions and speeches in Arabic that praised Ottoman rule. Like his predecessor, Māğid Bek was greatly impressed by the striking differences in lifestyle between European settlers and the local rural population. He admired Zionist progress and supported the idea of creating a safe haven for the Jews in the Empire. He also was interested in Jewish educational institutions and inspected the Hebrew Gymnasium in Tel Aviv and the Netter School, as well as the Templar settlement Wilhelma. *Filasṭīn*, 31 May 1913: 242/3/1–4; 7 June 1913: 243/3/3–4; 11 June 1913: 244/3/2–3; and 14 June 1913: 245/3/2–3.

169 Salīm Efendī was the major of Jerusalem from 1910 to 1917. Jacobson sees him as one of the 'alternative voices' in late Ottoman Palestine who saw potential in Jewish-Arab cooperation and pleaded for peaceful inter-confessional coexistence, although I believe that her presentation of Palestinian 'alternative voices' is too romantic. See Jacobson 2004, 45f.

170 Mandel 1976, 134.

171 *Filasṭīn*, 10 August 1912: 161/3/1–2.

172 Besides representatives from the settlements of Mulabbis (Petaḥ Tikva), Dayrān (Reḥovot) and al-Ḫuḍaira (Ḥadera), 'Āqir und Wadi Ḥanīn were mentioned, whose Hebrew names I do not know. *Filasṭīn*, 17 August 1912: 163/1/4.

overnight. In an extended speech before the Jewish representatives, Muhdī Bek confirmed the government's good will towards the Jewish presence in the Jerusalem District, and his personal support. He discredited rumors 'that the government in principle opposes the Zionists' (*anna l-ḥukūma tuʿāriḍ dāʾiman aṣ-ṣihyūnīyīn*), referring to the Ottoman restrictions against Jewish immigration and land acquisition. Although he was a lawyer, Muhdī Bek tried to present Zionist migration as being in harmony with the Ottoman *millet* policy, applying a completely different discourse: the Ottomans never thought, Muhdī Bek argued, that the Jews had political intentions (*ġāyāt siyāsīya*) in Palestine but accepted that they were motivated by Jewish tradition, for it was the land of their forefathers (*bilād ābāʾihim wa-ǧdādihim*). Relations between the Empire and the Jews were, in the interpretation of Muhdī Bek, harmonious, and the Porte had always been a merciful patron of the Jewish minority in times of persecution, receiving them 'with open hearts and arms' (*ṣudūr raḥba wa-ḏirāʿ mamdūda*). Now too, he confirmed, the government was aiming not at harassment but at rapprochement (*lā tuʿākisuhum bal annahā tasʿī fī t-taqarrub ilayhim*).[173] Palestine was for the Jews a 'haven for your souls and your property' (*maʾman ʿalā arwāḥikum wa-amwālikum*), he said, giving assurance that not only did the Ottoman government appreciate the Zionist presence in the District, but the settlers were also an inspiration to the local population. He went on to say:

> You are like examples (*ka-miṯāl*) for the other Arab villages and like teachers (*asātiḏa*) and living books (*kutub ḥayya*) for its inhabitants – who are able neither to read nor write and greatly appreciate you for all of the good the country has received though your hands.[174]

To demonstrate his support, Muhdī Bek encouraged the settlers to establish an independent administration (*dāʾira baladīya*) and security apparatus, a gendarmerie and watchmen, who would be trained and provided with uniforms and 'the necessary weapons' (*al-asliḥa al-lāzima*) with government help.[175] Moreover, the settlements should be connected with the telecommunication services in Jerusalem and Jaffa, and last but not least, Muhdī Bek promised to provide Rishon le-Tzion with a title deed on a strip of sandy land for cultivation. He clarified that this was for the benefit of the state, the population and the settlements alike, since the settlers were undertaking developmental projects, and

173 *Filasṭīn*, 17 August 1912: 163/1/4–5.

174 '*Yuqaddirūn lakum kull al-ḫayr allaḏī nālathu al-bilād ʿalā aydīkum.*' *Filasṭīn*, 17 August 1912: 163/1/5.

175 '*Wa-taḫtārū lakum ḥurrāsan minkum … yakūnū bi-sifat ǧāndarma.*' *Filasṭīn*, 17 August 1912: 163/1/5.

thus, Muhdī Bek underlined his arguments, 'You will help the government as it helps you; and you will progress and live comfortably.'[176]

The claim that the European colonists were taking over development responsibilities for the public benefit was an argument frequently made by the promoters of Zionism, and it matched the modernist spirit of the 'new age'. However, Muhdi Bek was aware that his promises were not in accord with the official government line, which prohibited foreign Jews from acquiring land in Palestine. His open support for the settlements made a significant impact on relations between Rishon le-Tzion and Jaffa. The local people were not so grateful about the transfer of the strip of land to the settlement, which will be treated in the section below on the campaigns for the control of land, and Muhdī Bek's policy towards the Zionists aroused mistrust in Jaffa[177] and provoked the campaign against the Netter School.

5.2. The Column 'Letters of a Farmer' by a Russian-Zionist Immigrant

From 1911 to 1912, the Russian-Ukranian immigrant and Zionist settler Menashe Me'irovitch (1860–1949), a co-founder of Rishon le-Tzion, published in *Filasṭīn* under the pseudonym 'Abū Ībrāhīm' a regular column entitled 'Letters of a Farmer' (*Rasā'il Fallāḥ*) – a series of fictional narratives in which the author presents himself as an Arab Palestinian peasant and attorney for the Arab rural population. This publication was based on a temporary alliance between the ʿĪsās and Me'irovitch and promoted first, the modernization of Palestinian agriculture, infrastructure and education. Second, Me'irovitch used his series of development articles to portray Zionist immigration to the region as a 'pacesetter' for local development and, using the identity of an Arab Palestinian as a strategy, actively advertised the achievements of Rishon Le-Zion, presenting it as a symbol of progress, prosperity and success.[178]

Since the economy of the Jerusalem District depended on the agricultural sector, the modernization of Palestinian agriculture was among the top topics in *Filasṭīn*. Palestinian elites had a vital interest in the improvement of the peasants' living conditions: editors and authors of letters frequently commented on the misery of rural society, and Me'irovitch, who shared the 'educating mission' of the ʿĪsās, hit on a hot topic with his 'Letters'. Importantly, the column is an outstanding example of the deep ambivalence towards Zionism that existed until

176 *Filasṭīn*, 17 August 1912: 163/2/1.
177 *Filasṭīn*, 10 August 1912: 161/3/1–2, 4.
178 Dolbee refers to the tradition of using false identities in publishing for political purposes. Dolbee and Hazkani 2015a, 242 n. 11, 258.

1912. It proves that the common agenda for 'reform and progress' prevailed over conflicting political agendas and confessional affiliations among the elites in Palestine. During the years before World War I, this shared commitment to modernization overruled other differences and, specifically, led to this (secret) year-and-a-half collaboration between ʿĪsā and Me'irovitch, who were personally acquainted with each other.[179] The column also illustrates how 'trans-Ottoman modernity' was interpreted in Palestine, in this case by an immigrant from the Russian Empire, and how a somewhat globalized 'modernization outlook' was brought into the local debate on identity and ethno-confessional relations in Palestine. From spring 1911 to summer 1912, Me'irovitch published 17 articles in *Filasṭīn*,[180] of which I have been able to locate only 12, since the first six months of the publication of *Filasṭīn* are missing.[181] The agenda, contents and functions of his column will be introduced below.

The Uniting Agenda of the 'Modernization of Palestine'

I have documented more than 100 articles published in *Filasṭīn* between 1911 and 1913 on agriculture that are linked with my topic of investigation, but much more material is to be found. Investment in the modernization of local agriculture was portrayed as a form of patriotism, and this motif appeared in *Filasṭīn*. To give one example, the author Muḥammad al-ʿAfīfī, about whom I have no further information, pleaded for agricultural development in 'our country Palestine' (*bilādinā Filasṭīn*) as a patriotic service, calling for the establishment of agricultural schools to provide training for farmers and stressing that European colonists and Zionists had realized the potential Palestinian agriculture had for them. It was a mistake, in his view, that the farming as an occupation received so little esteem, and he urged teachers to convey a love for science and agriculture to the younger generation in school.[182] The 'Letters of a Farmer' also portrayed the modernization of Palestinian agriculture and education as a 'patriotic service' and even incorporated the Zionist settlers into the vision of 'Ottoman unity' in Palestine. The modernization of Palestine was the common denominator in the matrix of

179 This alliance for the sake of modernism has also been noted by Dolbee and Hazkani, who suggest reading newspapers to consider more closely the construction of press texts, which complicate stories of national differentiation and reveal other levels of the understanding of self and others. See Dolbee and Hazkani 2015a, 241–243; eidem 2015b, 27, 28.

180 The author himself claimed in his last letter that he had written 17 pieces. *Filasṭīn*, 24 August 1912: 165/1/1.

181 The accessible letters appeared in *Filasṭīn*, 5 August 1911; 57/2/4f.; 23 September 1911: 71/1/1f.; 14 October 1911:77/3/4–4/3; 18 November 1911: 87/1/1f.; 6 January 1912: 101/1/1f. + 4/1f.; 3 February 1912: 108/1/4–2/1; 22 May 1912: 138/1/3–4; 1 June 1912: 141/1/3–2/3; 8 June 1912: 143/1/1–4; 15 June 1912: 145/1/1–4; 3 August 1912: 159/1/1–4; 24 August 1912: 165/1/1–4.

182 *Filasṭīn*, 20 March 1912: 121/2/2–4.

cultural values of both critics and promoters of Zionism, this is clear from the '‘Īsā-Me'irovitch collaboration'. Although Me'irovitch's articles praised the achievements of the Zionists in the *qaḍā'*, his articles were mostly printed as editorials and received positive responses from readers.[183] Remarkably, the promotion of Zionism by Abū Ibrāhīm was never criticized by a single reader, and the editors repeatedly praised the efforts of 'our farmer (*fallāḥunā*) Abū Ibrāhīm'. A Zionist settler[184] supported his demands to lift the tithe (*‘ušr*) and abolish communal land ownership (*mušā‘*),[185] and saw the settlers as struggling in the same battle for modernization.

Agenda and Identities of Me'irovitch alias Abū Ibrāhīm

Each of the 'Letters of a Farmer' is a fictional narrative in which Abū Ibrāhīm argues from the perspective of a local farmer. Each 'Letter' is a passionate plea for enlightenment, often soaked with pathos, and containing harsh criticism of the government's neglect of reforms as well as passionate demonstrations of Ottoman patriotism and support for the Constitution. As a first-person narrator, Abū Ibrāhīm continuously lamented a famer's hardship in Palestine, demanding that the state implement reforms in the agricultural sector and improve living conditions for the rural population. To contrast the harsh conditions suffered by the local peasantry, he praised the sophisticated standards of the Zionist settlements, especially Rishon le-Tzion, as a symbol of technological effectiveness, economic prosperity and modern civilization that would 'spread' and benefit the neighboring Arab villages. First, this shows how much the author was influenced by a 'modernization utopia', the idea, that comprehensive modernization was a precondition and guarantee of wellbeing. Second, to legitimize the colonists' role in the local economy, Abū Ibrāhīm integrated them into the narrative of Ottoman Brotherhood. He portrayed the modernization of Palestine as a 'humanitarian mission' that was driven by Jewish colonists, who somehow compensated for the Ottoman state's neglect of the duty of development. In this argumentation, Zionism was portrayed as a form of patriotic developmentalism, and the Zionist settlers were presented as 'Ottoman compatriots'. Further, Abū Ibrāhīm clearly campaigned for the rights as citizens of the rural population, the majority of the Palestinians, who were neglected in terms of education and living conditions. Addressing the readership in the voice of a peasant who was not not submissive but actively demanding his rights, the author passionately set out concepts of social equality.

183 Positive reactions to the 'Letters of a Farmer' came from an Ottoman Jew in *Filasṭīn*, 7 February 1912: 109/4/1 f.; from one Abū Ḫatab from Maǧdal (13 January 1912: 102/3/1), and from the Palestinian emigrant in Chile Ǧurǧī Ḥazbūn (27 November 1912: 192/4/2 f.).

184 *Filasṭīn*, 7 August 1912: 160/1/4.

185 *Filasṭīn*, 23 December 1911: 97/1/1 f.

This column in *Filasṭīn* has been noted in previous research, but has been misinterpreted by Khalidi and Fishman, who have both assumed that Yūsuf al-ʿĪsā was the author of the 'Letters of a Farmer', noting his interest in the issue of agriculture.[186] They took the fact that 'a large number of articles in Filasṭīn were devoted to agricultural matters, and in particular to the state of peasantry' as proof of their thesis that the ʿĪsās were setting out an early form of Arab Palestinian nationalism during the Second Constitutional Era. This was related to their belief that, in the words of Khalidi, 'the struggle for Palestine would be decided at the level of the individual peasant and the individual Zionist settler'.[187] Accordingly, Khalidi interpreted the 'Letters of a Farmer' as an expression of Palestinian national identity and anti-Zionism.[188] Fishman takes up this view to support his own thesis of an early expression of Palestinian national identity in *Filasṭīn.* Referring to one of the 'Letters', printed in September 1911 as an editorial, he claims that it was a 'prime example' of how 'the urban educated class' sought to place 'a human face on the peasant' and worked towards 'creating an imaginary (and national) bond between the two disparate groups'.[189] It is to be concluded from this that neither of them read the content of this column systematically, since they overlooked the fact that one of its central functions was to advocate Zionism under the umbrella of the contemporary discourse on modernization and Ottoman patriotism applied in the post-revolutionary Arab press.

From reading the column, it is clear, that the ʿĪsās were not its authors, that Abū Ibrāhīm was a fictional character and that the person behind it was not a peasant but an intellectual with a special interest in agriculture and education. The identity of Me'irovitch as its author is confirmed by Arthur Ruppin, director of the Palestine Office, who knew Me'irovitch personally and corresponded with him. He recorded that *Filasṭīn* published the 'Letters of a Farmer' which 'originate from our friend Me'irovitch in Rishon le-Tzion and of which all are, of course, written in favor of the Jews'.[190] The Zionist archives reveal that Ruppin had a somewhat conflictual position on Me'irovitch's engagement in the Arabic press. In several items of correspondence with Ruppin towards the end of 1911, Me'irovitch asked for financial support from the Palestine Office for expenses he incurred form buying and reading *Filasṭīn* and *An-Nafīr* with the help of a

186 In 'The Iron Cage', Khalidi portrays the ʿĪsās as the pioneers of an early Palestinian national identity and fierce anti-Zionism in one. See Khalidi 2006, 90–104; Fishman 2007, 46f., 56–66.

187 Khalidi 2006, 103.

188 Khalidi 2006, 103 n. 106, 250; cf Khalidi 2009, 92 n. 35, 96.

189 Fishman 2007, 48; see also n. 28.

190 According to a remark made by Ruppin on 6 June 1912, in: CZA Zy/1448. I owe many thanks to Samuel Dolbee who shared this document with me! For reference to the real identity of Abū Ibrāhīm, see also Mandel 1976, 128 n. 52, and the correspondence in the Central Zionist Archives, mentioned in Dolbee and Hazkani 2015a, 261.

translator, and his tone became increasingly harsh when Ruppin did not support his engagement.[191]

Me'irovitch was an interesting and somewhat controversial character. He was Ukranian and emigrated in 1882 under the pressure of anti-Jewish pogroms in the Russian Empire, joining a group of Biluim under the leadership of David Levontin, later director of the Zionist Anglo-Palestine Bank (APB) in Jaffa.[192] In Istanbul, he attempted in vain to obtain a permit for Jewish settlement in Palestine as a member of a delegation, and consequently arrived alone in 1883. Facing problems entering the country upon arrival, he took Ottoman citizenship.[193] The Biluim, with support from the British Baron de Rothschild, founded Rishon le-Tzion in 1882 as the first Zionist settlement in Palestine, and Me'irovitch was among its co-founders. In 1899, Rishon le-Tzion had 270 settlers, who increased by 1914 to 1,300.[194] As a cultivator, Me'irovitch actively contributed to its growing success. An experimental agricultural station was later opened under his leadership, and he introduced viniculture to the settlement, which would become its main field of activity in the 1930s. Besides his engagement as agronomist, Me'irovitch was an editor and journalist; he published in Yiddish, Hebrew and Russian and had a good command of French.[195] Despite having contacts with high-ranking Ottoman officials, Me'irovitch was imprisoned in Jerusalem during World War I. Under British rule, he became a magistrate in the court system of the New Yishuv.[196]

However, although he had been living for 30 years in Palestine, Me'irovitch, by his own admission, had no command of Arabic, apart from some colloquial phases. When he started publishing the 'Letters of a Farmer', he depended on a translator, who was, according his own report, ʿĪsā al-ʿĪsā himself.[197] However that may be, it is certain that Me'irovitch did not write in Arabic and, in some of his handwritten drafts in French, preserved in the Zionist Archives, he mixed French with Arabic curses, to which he added French accents, as, for example, in the expression *Allah ihréb betum*, a common colloquial curse, meaning 'may God

191 Dolbee and Hazkani 2015a, 250f.

192 See Mandel 1976, 5–6.

193 This, according to his own statement in a newspaper article in the Hebrew newspaper *ha-Or* ('The Light') in 1913. See Dolbee and Hazkani 2015a, 246 and 260 n. 48.

194 Ṭarāwina 2000, 131–132.

195 Meʿirovitch published books about his experiments with silkworms, and edited an agricultural magazine that was published in Palestine in Yiddish and Hebrew (1893–1895). He also published articles in the Russian press. For Rishon le-Tzion, see Klausner 1994, vol. II, 945, 925; Orni 1994, vol. II, 1110, 1111.

196 For more biographical information on Me'irovitch, see Dolbee and Hazkani 2015a, 246–247.

197 This according to Me'irovitch regarding his publications in the Arab press before World War I in the magazine *Doar ha-Yom* (19 April 1935), and others, as cited in Dolbee and Hazkani 2015a, 249 n. 69, 242, 260.

destroy their house'.[198] Me'irovitch's drafts may have been translated into Arabic by Yūsuf or ʿĪsā al-ʿĪsā or by a Sephardi Jewish friend. In any case, the ʿĪsās could easily have omitted the pro-Zionist passages from the text without Me'irovitch having control over it, which they did not do, and neither do they say anything about their collaboration with the Zionist settler, but he referred to it later in the Hebrew press during the Mandate era. According to Me'irovitch, it was ʿĪsā who approached him because of his expertise in agronomy, asking him to publish something in *Filasṭīn* about the state of the peasants. Me'irovitch claimed that ʿĪsā flattered him for being such a high-profile writer and had to persuade him to agree, arguing that 'it is our duty to work hand-in-hand for the good of the Homeland'. ʿĪsā apparently offered to let him write in the language that was easiest for him and said he would convert his texts into Arabic.[199]

It was not unusual for authors to publish under fictional identities in the press. *Filasṭīn* was no exception to this and many authors assumed hidden identities or took nicknames. The pseudonym Abū Ibrāhīm that Me'irovitch chose for his role as an Arab peasant was, incidentally, the Arabic counterpart of his own name. He had a son named Avraham,[200] which in Arabic, made him 'Abū Ibrāhīm', the 'father of Avraham'. The pseudonym was also practical in other aspects since Ibrāhīm or Avraham was a universal figure and the father of the religious traditions in the Bible and the Qur'an, so the name was used by Jews, Christians and Muslims.

The idea of addressing the lower segments of society as a farmer might reflect Me'irovitch's belief that people would identify more easily with the character as an authentic Palestinian, and the fact that he, as an agronomist, also personally identified with peasantry. Me'irovitch also published in *an-Nafīr* ('The Horn'), a newspaper that was founded in Alexandria but moved to Jerusalem after the 1908 Revolution and was pro-Zionist, since most of its readers were Jews.[201] From 1911, Me'irovitch contributed a column in it called 'Letters of a Merchant' (*Rasāʾil Tāǧir*), which he signed as 'an Ottoman merchant' (*tāǧir ʿuṯmānī*).[202]

198 The text was published in *Filasṭīn*, 6 January 1912: 101/1/1f. – without the curse. Dolbee and Hazkani 2015a, 242 n. 67, 260; 2015b, 25, 26.

199 *Doar ha-Yom*, 19 April 1935, and others; see Dolbee and Hazkani 2015a, 249 n. 69, 260; 2015b, 29. However, Me'irovitch's statements give slightly contradictory versions of the beginning of his collaboration with ʿĪsā. In 1935, Me'irovitch described the meeting between them as taking place in Jaffa in 1911, while, in 1941, Me'irovitch stated that ʿĪsā approached him by coming to Rishon le-Tzion, as is documented in the Zionist Archives (CZA A322/28); cf. Dolbee and Hazkani 2015a, 249f. n. 70, 260.

200 See the 'Digital Family Album' of Rishon le-Tzion. http://www.gen-mus.co.il/en/person/?id=547 (accessed 29 May 2012).

201 Yehoshu'a 1974, 50–53.

202 The Zionist archives reveal his personal correspondence about that column with the editor of *an-Nafīr*, Elīyā az-Zakkā. See Dolbee and Hazkani 2015a, n. 114, 262; and 2015b, 35.

Figure 22: The Russian immigrant Menashe Meirovitch, co-founder of Rishon Le-Zion. (Source: Rishon Le-Zion Family Album)

Narrative Style Themes of the Column

The linguistic style of the 'Letters of a Farmer' differs markedly from that of the rest of the articles in *Filasṭīn.* Written as simple narratives, the articles were meant to reflect that Abū Ibrāhīm was a simple man from the lowest segments of society who expressed himself somewhat naïvely. As newspaper texts were read aloud in public places, coffeehouses, etc., these 'Letters' were produced to be listened to, not only to be read, and were also meant to address simple people and be an educational instrument for the rural population. Each letter focused on a selected reform issue related to the Jerusalem District or the Jaffa *qaḍāʾ:* local politics on health and hygiene, the lack of education, the cycle of debts that beset tenants who lacked state loans for agricultural investment, the ailing infrastructure and the harbor of Jaffa, sustainable land use, the desertification of land, and so on. Each article followed a standard pattern: the narrator Abū Ibrāhīm introduced his letter with an extended background based on personal observation before leading into the issue of the article. Swearing patriotic oaths to the Homeland, Abū Ibrāhīm mourned the current political crisis in the Empire. Then, he usually turned to a problematic issue that had been brought to him by a fellow farmer, trader, shop owner or Jewish settler, or something he had observed personally, and complained at length about the lack of state interest in this problem. Set against these grievances, Abū Ibrāhīm would then elaborate on a Jewish pioneer work achieved in the very same field. The motifs that Abū Ībrāhīm repeatedly used will be outlined below.

Motif I: The Post-Revolutionary 'Metamorphosis' of Abū Ibrāhīm

As farmers usually did not read newspapers or actively contributes to them, it was a curiosity that a farmer would express his views on local politics. Abū Ibrāhīm explained his personal transition from a simple-minded peasant to someone with a strong sense if community and citizen rights, and the ability to make the connection between local problems and imperial policies. He described this as a mental metamorphosis from someone in a state of ignorance to a 'thinking individual' with a 'new freedom' to express himself. Abū Ibrāhīm's transition was noticed by those around him, he claimed, which made him a learned man and 'scholar' (*ʿālim*) in the eyes of other farmers, so he started to be consulted by fellow tenants who approached him as an intermediary, asking him to explain the outside world to them and to write letters to the authorities or to the press on their behalf. In this way, Abū Ibrāhīm presented himself in a role traditionally occupied by local patrons, tribal leaders and urban notables, and as a petition-writer.[203]

Directly linked with Abū Ibrāhīm's metamorphosis was the Young Turk Revolution and the restoration of the Constitution. Like the ʿĪsās, Abū Ibrāhīm saw the constitution as having a sacred dimension and as a driving force in his transformation. He described life in the pre-revolutionary period as being in sharp contrast to his post-revolutionary existence: back then, he was merely busy working hard to feed his family, not knowing anything but the 'rubbish heaps of my village' (*mazābil qaryatī*). Nobody cared that 'we die as flies die' (*namūt kamā yamūt aḏ-ḏubāb*), he said, and also he himself had not previously known that he had rights to demand. But after comprehending through the effect of the 1908 Revolution that 'freedom makes everybody equal' (*anna al-ḥurrīya sāwat bayna al-ǧamīʿ*), he had started to consider his life.[204] Although he did not see any fruit from his critical articles in the press, which 'faded away like a cry in the desert' (*ḏahabat ka-ṣarḫa fī wādin*),[205] he could not return to his former naïve life of 'cows, sheep and flowering fields'. He became addicted to collecting knowledge. Like a 'crazy man' (*maǧnūn*), he absorbed newspapers from Cairo, Istanbul, Beirut and Palestine and, since he had 'learned to think and feel', he was now also able to comprehend his own misery and was 'screaming', as Abū

203 *Filasṭīn*, 14 October 1911: 77/3/4.
204 *Filasṭīn*, 5 August 1911: 57/2/4–5.
205 *Filasṭīn*, 14 October 1911: 77/2/4.

Ibrāhīm described his pain.[206] Although this kind of activism was unusual for a farmer, Abū Ibrāhīm insisted that he was an absolutely 'free individual' (*ḥurran muṭlaqan*), that his conscience 'belongs to me' (*ḍamīrī aṣbaḥ yaḫuṣṣunī*) and his love for the Homeland (*ḥubbī li-waṭanī*) was as valuable as the patriotism of the upper classes.[207] In addition, he said that his contributions in *Filasṭīn* received positive feedback and he believed in the 'tremendous cultural influence' of *Filasṭīn* on his fellow citizens.[208] Although it was considered a crime (*ǧināya*) when a farmer demanded something, Abū Ibrāhīm said, he insisted on his rights, which were upheld in the constitution (*fa-l-ḥaqq fī ḏālika ʿalā d-dustūr*).[209] Permanently criticizing the exploitation of the rural population, he lamented:

> We are still like a cow that is milked without being fed (*baqra tuḥlab bidūn an tuʿlaf*). When it is dead, they skin it (*yasluḫūn ǧildahā*) and make from it a whip (*sauṭ*) in order to … chase grazing animals. Are we not the neglected class (*aṭ-ṭāʾifa l-muhmala*) among all sorts of people (*bayna aṣnāf al-bašar*)?… Is it not like this that the sweat on our foreheads (*ʿaraq ǧabīninā*) keeps away the sweat of your foreheads? Is it not [that sweat] that feeds you… that is wrapping you in the best clothes and protecting you from the heat of the sun that has been roasting us? … Well, the world is divided into hierarchies (*ad-dunyā daraǧāt*).[210]

Motif II: The Hardship of the Rural Population and Government Neglect

A central element in the column was protest against the government's neglect of reforms in the local infrastructure, agriculture and education, and Abū Ibrāhīm's protest was not in contradiction to his patriotism. Rather, the calls for development were a way to demonstrate care for the Homeland. Abū Ibrāhīm had enough issues to complain about. What concerned him was the inescapable spiral of poverty from which the tenants suffered. In one story, he described the dilemma of a small-holder friend. Because of harvest losses, he was forced to take on loans at exorbitant rates in order to buy new seed. From the yield of the current year, he did not even have enough to get his family through the winter or to buy the seed for the coming spring, after deducting the cost of animal feed, debts, interest rates, the tithe (*ʿušr*), property tax (*wīrkū*), and all the other fees. Thus, he was forced to take on new loans, and was trapped in a vicious cycle of debts and poverty, year after year (*aḏyāl al-fuqr min sanna ilā sanna*).[211] Stressing that the poverty line lay along the border between urban and rural life, Abū Ibrāhīm asked:

206 *Filasṭīn*, 1 June 1912: 141/1/4–5.
207 *Filasṭīn*, 3 February 1912: 108/1/5.
208 *Filasṭīn*, 3 February 1912: 108/1/4–5.
209 *Filasṭīn*, 1 June 1912: 141/2/3.
210 *Filasṭīn*, 22 May 1912: 138/1/4.
211 *Filasṭīn*, 23 September 1911: 71/1/1–3.

> Are there perhaps two sorts of humans (*hal al-bašar nau'ān yā turā*)? The urban population and the rural population?... Tell me, where is this freedom?... They only think about us when it is about paying the tithe, the commercial taxes, the fees and and and ...[212]

Abū Ibrāhīm pleaded with the government to supply tenant small-holders with affordable loans so that they would not be forced to take on private loans at exorbitant rates. He reported that he had read in the Turkish newspaper *Tanīn* about the 'Turkish Bank for Investments in Agriculture and Industry' (*bank Turkīya li-tanšīṭ az-zirāʿa wa-aṣ-ṣināʿa*). Ottoman farmers with a title deed would be granted loans to purchase modern agricultural machines produced in the 'greatest factories of Europe'. Abū Ibrāhīm related that he had enquired about a branch in the Jerusalem District and found that there was none in Jerusalem, Gaza, Jaffa or Nablus, only in the Turkish provinces of the Empire.[213] Setting the technology used in Rishon le-Tzion in contrast to his own possibilities as an Arab peasant, Abū Ibrāhīm complained:

> I do not have the means to replace this plough... that is like a rusty nail (*miḥrāṯ... šibhu s-simsār*). And after ploughing comes harvesting and I will be reaping for several weeks together with my sons, wives and daughters, while my neighbors, the Israelites (*muǧāwirī l-isrāʾīlīyīn*), will be finished within one or two days with the help of their modern machines.[214]

Abū Ibrāhīm did not only criticize the lack of financial and technological means to advance local agricultural production but also promoted the privatization of land, in contrast to feudalism and state ownership of *mīrī*, which was auctioned off in regular intervals. He addressed the minister of agriculture, demanding that 'our land be set apart' (*ifrāz arḍinā*). The Ottoman Homeland could only be strong, Abū Ibrāhīm argued, if 'we farmers get strong' (*qawaynā naḥnu al-fallāḥūn*), and he predicted: 'Give to everyone the piece (*al-qiṭʿa*) he is entitled to (*allatī taḫuṣṣuhu*) and then see the wonder happening in your country.'[215]

Abū Ibrāhīm tackled the tradition of communal land use (*mušāʿ*) which stood against the privatization of agricultural areas. Agricultural production in late Ottoman Palestine was heavily based on *mušāʿ*. This applied to land registered as private property (*mulk*) and state land with the right to usufruct for a certain period (*mīrī*). A group of growers cultivated an area that was divided into small units, in a rotating system. The units rotated among the shareholders, who often also lived on the land but often did not have a title deed and could not prove ownership but made their claim as an inherited family right. It could be that the

212 *Filasṭīn*, 23 September 1911: 71/1/3.
213 *Filasṭīn*, 14 October 1911: 77/3/5–4/2.
214 *Filasṭīn*, 14 October 1911: 77/4/2.
215 *Filasṭīn*, 18 October 1911: 87/1/3.

Figure 23: Palestinian peasants reaping, between 1898 and 1946. From the G. Eric and Edith Matson Photograph Collection. (Source: Library of Congress)

land was registered in the name of an individual sheikh, tribal leader, notable or absentee landowner. Communal land use was also applied to uncultivated land that was commonly used for grazing by a nearby village or tribe. Whenever communal land was sold to a private owner, it conflicted with the inherited rights of the shareholders who mostly had neither a document nor a concept of private ownership.[216] The practice of *mušāʿ* had a bad reputation among Zionists. Whenever the colonists purchased land from local tax farmers or absentee landowners, shared ownership and the 'parceling' of land into tiny units clashed with the demands of private ownership and commercialization through mono-cultures, which was considered a precondition for the modernization of agriculture.[217] Abū Ibrāhīm shared this stance and defined *mušāʿ* as a 'disease' (*dāʾ*), the 'source of our misery' and a 'our incurable wound' (*ǧarḥunā l-ʿaḍāl*). He

216 For literature on the history of *mušāʿ* in the Middle East, see Gerber and Pellat: Mušāʿ, in *EI*[2]. On the practice of it, see Schaebler 2000, 241–307. For a defence of the *mušāʿ* system as 'efficient' in the Arab Levant and the damaging effects of the British land reforms following 1921, see Nadan 2003, 320–354; especially 326f. See also Krämer 2002, 100–105; LeVine 2004, 100–146.

217 LeVine 2004, 105.

Figure 24: Jewish colonists harvesting; between 1898 and 1920. From the G. Eric and Edith Matson Photograph Collection. (Source: Library of Congress)

described how he had discussed the issue with a Jewish settler acquaintance and enquired about the possibility of purchasing modern machines from them. The settler refused, arguing that investment in the agricultural sector was in vain as long as the *mušāʿ* system was followed.[218]

Motif III: The Settlers as Educators of their Arab Environment

Abū Ibrāhīm portrayed Jewish, and in general European, colonization as a precondition for the civilizational and educational advance of the region. Once, he recalled a night session in bright moonlight during which he had discussed with his imaginary Muslim friend, Hajj ʿAbdallāh, the issue of civilizing Palestine. ʿAbdallāh declared that, as long as Palestinian society believed in 'fairytales' and kept 'splitting into factions', nothing would change for the better.[219] Abū Ibrāhīm agreed, admitting that 'the majority of my brothers the farmers' were swimming in a 'sea of stupidity' (*baḥr al-ġabāwat*) and knew nothing of what the 'European farmer' had been learning. Instead of studying 'modern methods' (*aṭ-ṭuruq al-ǧadīda*), farmers hung on to their 'dirty way of life' (*maʿīšatihim al-qaḏira*). This

218 *Filasṭīn*, 18 October 1911: 87/1/2.

219 '*Muḥāfiẓīn ʿalā ḫurāfātinā wa-taʿaṣṣubinā tafarruqinā l-aḥzāb wa-tamazzuqinā l-aḥqād.*' *Filasṭīn*, 3 August 1912: 159/1/1.

was, Abū Ibrāhīm said, a result of a lack of education (*natīǧat ʿadam at-taʿlīm*). For instance, farmers used 'rusty tools' that they called a 'plough', they lived in dirty houses and applied dubious medical treatment, such as cauterizing wounds, Abū Ibrāhīm complained.[220] He said the rural population did not know the basic rules of hygiene, and reported the death of a young boy from an Arab village who died after he caught an infection from a fly. The villagers called the Jewish medical doctor from Rishon le-Tzion who appeared as the 'educator' in the story, explaining to them the health risks arising from dead animals lying around in the village and instructed them to bury the corpses to avoid the risk of infection. Here, Abū Ibrāhīm stressed the educational role of a Jewish doctor, although it was the state's responsibility: the accident would not have happened, Abū Ibrāhīm lamented, if the state had sent health advisors, but even in Jaffa, there were animal corpses at the side of the main streets, and in the middle of town dead camels, horses and dogs were lying around.[221]

To return to the discussion about educational standards between Abū Ibrāhīm and his imaginary friend ʿAbdallāh, stressing the difference in educational levels between the confessional communities, ʿAbdallāh quoted statistics. The lowest rate in the Jerusalem District was found among the Muslim majority: there were 142 pupils per 1,000 Israelites and 120 pupils per 1,000 inhabitants among the Christians, and only 4 pupils per 1,000 inhabitants among the Muslims.[222] And the considerable lead of the minorities over the Muslims in education was not only measurable in quantity. As a result of the poor quality of their education system, the Muslims were the 'neglected sector' in Palestine, ʿAbdallāh complained:

> Take (for example) the school in our village and compare it with the rest of the Muslim schools … and then tell me if you can compare it with the Christian and Israelite schools … which the government does not help or spend money on, as it does for the Muslim schools.[223]

220 *Filasṭīn*, 3 August 1912: 159/1/2.

221 *Filasṭīn*, 5 August 1911: 57/2/5–3/1.

222 According to his statistics, the population of the Jerusalem District (340,000 inhabitants) consisted of 226,000 Muslims, 70,000 Israelites and 44,000 Christians. The Muslims maintained about 242 schools with 10,000 pupils, the Israelites 40 schools, also with 10,000 pupils; and the Christians more than 100 schools with 5,200 pupils. See *Filasṭīn*, 3 August 1912: 159/1/2–3. However, it is not reasonable to assume that, in 1912 the Christians were the smallest group in the Jerusalem District, and the number given for Jewish inhabitants is too high. The census by Ruppin reported 85,000 Jews in all three provinces of pre-World War I Palestine, which is still too high. Krämer has noted the trend on the part of both Zionists and Palestinians to overestimate the number of Jewish inhabitants, which served both sides' political arguments. Krämer 2002, 154f., 165f.

223 *Filasṭīn*, 3 August 1912: 159/1/3.

Abū Ibrāhīm agreed with ʿAbdallāh. In a protest letter to Governor Muhdī Bek, written by a 'man of the general public' (*rağul min ʿāmmat aš-šaʿb*), Abū Ibrāhīm stressed that the Arab rural population benefitted from being educated by the Israelites in their area. The reason for his protest was the governor's announcement of the opening of an Arab agricultural school in Nabī Rūbīn, a plan that Abū Ibrāhīm approved but did not believe in its realization. For years, he had been hearing 'empty promises' about such a school and nothing happened.[224] Because of the lack of schools, he explained, the children spent their days in the alleys and playing on rubbish heaps; and apart from those villages that benefitted from neighborhood and nearby Jewish settlements, the district was a complete disaster.[225] Here, Me'irovitch alias Abū Ibrāhīm did not explicitly mention the Jewish Netter School about whose confessional policy the editors started a dispute at about the same time, indirectly stressing the model function of these institutions, which achieved something that was the responsibility of a state that was failing.

Motif IV: The Settlers as the Cultivators of Palestine – Palestinian Patriots?

The economic significance of the *qaḍāʾ* for the Jerusalem District was an important issue in Me'irovitch's column. Like the ʿĪsās, he made passionate demands for the modernization of the harbor and infrastructure as a precondition for urban development. In one letter, Abū Ibrāhīm reported a conversation with his friend ʿAbdallāh, who stressed that the *qaḍāʾ* was so successful because of the 'large number of Israelite migrants' (*kuṯrat al-muhāğirīn ilayhā min al-isrāʾīlīyīn*). Without these German and Israelite colonists, there would not be 'millions of trees' that turned into 'extended orchards' (*ġābāt wāsiʿa*) that yielded 'millions of boxes of fruit'.[226]

The image of the colonist as a cultivator who was transforming Palestine into fertile land was an important motif in Me'irovitch's column. In one episode, Abū Ibrāhīm portrayed himself as the friend of a Jewish settler from Rishon le-Tzion, Abū Mūsā, who complained about the lack of government cooperation in the cultivation of land. Knowing that his advocacy for Jewish colonization could raise criticism among Palestinian readers, Abū Ibrāhīm justified his support for the Jewish colonists by referring to their 'practical patriotism' – by helping Palestine through cultivation. To exemplify his position, Abū Ibrāhīm recalled a visit to Rishon le-Tzion, where he found his friend Abū Mūsā planting eucalyptus trees on the west side of his farm, at the edge of Rishon le-Tzion bordering the sand

224 '*Samiʿnā munḏu sinnīn ʿadīda bi-madrasa zirāʿīya fī n-Nabī Rūbīn wa-kullamā ğāʾa mutaṣarrif aẓhar ruġbatahu bi-inšāʾihā wa-lakin ḏālika lam yakun illā wuʿūd fāriġa fī wuʿūd fāriġa.*' *Filasṭīn*, 24 August 1912: 165/1/1–2.

225 *Filasṭīn*, 3 August 1912: 159/1/2.

226 *Filasṭīn*, 6 January 1912: 101/1/1f.

dunes towards of the sea. The encroachment of sand from the coast made the settlers lose a couple of meters of arable land every year, Abū Mūsā explained. For years, Abū Mūsā had been laboriously planting trees along the border of his land as to stop this encroachment. Although Rishon le-Tzion had been asking for government approval for large-scale eucalyptus planting in the dunes as to protect the cultivated land, they never received permission to do so. As a contrasting example, Abū Mūsā described measures taken in Bordeaux. There, a patriotic farmer planted a ring of pines, thick as a wall, around the city as to save his town from erosion, proving by this his love for his country. The settlers intended to the same in Palestine, but the government prevent them.[227]

This letter sparked the reaction of an anonymous 'Ottoman Israelite' (*isrāʾīlī ʿuṯmānī*). Even though the Jewish settlers intended to offer a 'service free of charge' (*ḫidma maǧǧāniya*) for the Homeland and the 'public good' (*an-nafaʿ al-ʿāmm*), the author saw that they were discriminated against because migration restrictions were only applied to the Jews, not to Russians, Greeks or Germans. The law discriminated against the Jews although 'the land has seen nothing but benefits from them'. What else, he asked, 'has made the government accept all the [other] foreigners who could create another Tripolitanian problem every day and refuse the Jews!?'[228] Dolbee and Hazkani suggest that the 'Ottoman Israelite' was probably a false identity, fabricated by Me'irovitch and ʿĪsā together.[229] I do not think so. Instead, it was not unusual for Sephardi Jews to publish in *Filasṭīn* anonymously or under their real name, criticizing anti-Zionism.

The Patriotism of Me'irovitch alias Abū Ibrāhīm

It is true that patriotic support for the Homeland on the settlers' side was not only imaginary. Me'irovitch was a citizen and believed that, by his literary effort in support of the modernization of Palestinian agriculture, he was playing his part in demonstrating Ottoman loyalty. There were also settlers who fought in the military, and Me'irovitch, alias Abū Ibrāhīm, was a fierce critic of the Imperialist penetration of the Empire, the Capitulations and European Christian missionary activities on Ottoman territory.[230] He said, the Europeans

> to whom we have opened our hearts before and welcomed them to our Ottoman lands (*bilādinā l-ʿuṯmānīya*) and to whom we have granted privileges (*imtiyāzāt*), have invaded us with their ships and trading products. We have paved the way for their scholars and religious delegates, we have protected their monasteries and schools, we have

227 *Filasṭīn*, 3 February 1912: 108/2/1.
228 *Filasṭīn*, 7 February 1912: 109/4/1.
229 Dolbee/Hazkani 2015a, 255.
230 For the European influence in Palestine that was manifest in various foreign religious institutions and missionaries in the Holy Land, and especially in Jerusalem, from Russia, France and other countries, see Kushner 2005, 33–54.

> honored their monks and nuns ... How shall I understand the fact that they invaded Tripoli, attacked our Empire ... and captured our ships?[231]

In the context of the Ottoman defeat in Libya and as a member of a religious minority in Palestine, Me'irovitch sought to demonstrate his loyalty to the Homeland, and to educate the Arab reader, explaining the meaning of self-sacrifice for the Ottoman community:

> I am an old sheikh and unable to take revenge by my own hand for my community and my Homeland. That is why I have handed over my son Ibrāhīm ... to his Homeland, so he can take revenge for his country.[232] From my fellows farmers (*rifāqī l-fallāḥīn*), I have collected financial help for their government, which they paid with great enthusiasm (*bi-ḥamās šadīd*) ... And they told me that you can find the same zeal (*ġayra*) among the Christians and Israelites too. And this is no wonder since we are all sons of this Ottoman Homeland that the foreigner has been attacking.[233]

It is notable that, in the rhetorical style of the 'Letters', Me'irovitch never used polemic themes against local Christians as were frequently applied by the Sephardi Jews, and he never accused them of being anti-Semitic. Often enough, he referred to Christian and Jewish productivity in Palestine in the same sentence and limited his antagonism to foreign (Christian) Imperialism. We do not know if Me'irovitch's son Abraham really fought in the Ottoman army. However, the acquisition of Ottoman citizenship was not exceptional for migrants who arrived with the First Aliya. Citizen status made it much easier to acquire land and deal with the Ottoman authorities. Among the first wave of modern Jewish immigrants to Palestine were many 'Ottomanized' Ashkenazi Jews, and *Filasṭīn* reported some examples: the Ashkenazi migrant Eisenberg, one of the co-founders of the Zionist colony of Reḥovot, received the honorary title of a Ghazi (*ġāzī*) – traditionally a term used to describe an honorable Islamic fighter, for his actions in the Ottoman military, the ʿĪsās noted.[234]

We do not know how far the discourse on Ottoman brotherhood by Me'irovitch alias Abū Ibrāhīm was strategic or represented his personal views. However that may be, his patriotism is not contradictory to his identity as a settler and, during the late Ottoman years, he also published articles in the constitutional Ottomanist discourse in the Hebrew press.[235] He was no exception: the Jewish-Ottoman press in general supported the concept of imperial citizenship,

231 *Filasṭīn*, 18 October 1911: 87/1/1.

232 '*Laysa fī imkānī an antaqim bi-yadī li-ummatī wa-waṭanī wa-liḏālika ... waladī Ibrāhīm ... sallamtuhu li-dawlatihi li-yaʾḫuḏ bi-ṯār waṭanihi.*' *Filasṭīn*, 18 October 1911: 87/1/1.

233 '*Fa-ǧamīʿnā abnāʾ hāḏā l-waṭan al-ʿuṯmānī allaḏī iʿtadā ʿalayhi al-ġarīb. Filasṭīn,*' 18 October 1911: 87/1/1.

234 See *Filasṭīn*, 28 December 1912: 201/3/3.

235 Dolbee and Hazkani 2015a, 247.

as did Jewish organizations of the post-revolutionary period, such as the Society of Ottoman Jews.[236] Me'irovitch is an example of an integrated migrant who presented a 'Zionist Ottomanism', the idea that Zionist colonization worked for the Homeland as a kind of 'patriotic developmentalism' in support of the central state.

The End of the Column 'Letters of a Farmer'

For Me'irovitch, belief in the virtual virtual sanctity of modernization overruled the antagonism that often characterized Christian–Jewish relations in pre-World War I Palestine, ʿĪsā's belief in it overcame his anti-Zionism, and Me'irovitch's strategy to advocate Zionism under the umbrella of the contemporary reform discourse was not prevented by the ʿĪsās. Their modernist agenda brought them together for a while and both promoted cooperation for the sake of the 'neglected' Muslim majority in the Jerusalem District. Also, Me'irovitch's commitment to local farmers was not just lip service. He firmly believed in the potential of Jewish colonization in terms of agricultural industrialization and progress for the Palestinians. However, he fell prey to the Ashkenazi idealization of 'civilizing' Palestine – the illusion that a Western-style modernization was the remedy leading to comprehensive well-being and harmony between all groups. However, from the end of 1912, rivalries over control of local resources in the *qaḍāʾ* led to inter-confessional confrontations.

It is not certain exactly why Me'irovitch refrained from publishing in *Filasṭīn* after late summer 1912. Maybe he came to the conclusion that his appeals for reforms were going unheard and he was disappointed. What is more likely is that his positive portrayal of Zionist settlements brought him into conflict with the editors of *Filasṭīn*. It was around the same time that Me'irovitch's version of Jewish colonization as a driving force for modernization must have lost its credibility among the readership because of growing rivalries between villagers and settlers in the *qaḍāʾ*. Around this time, Governor Muhdī Bek demonstrated his comprehensive good will for the settlers of Rishon le-Tzion and promised the transfer of a large piece of land to the settlement for cultivation. This created a campaign driven by the ʿĪsās against the transfer of this land and, as a consequence, a chilly atmosphere between Jaffa's residents and Rishon le-Tzion from September 1912 onwards, as is demonstrated in the next section. It is also possible that Abū Ibrāhīm kept silent because he came into conflict with the campaign in *Filasṭīn* against the policy of the Netter School. However, it seems more likely to me that the conflict between Jaffa and Rishon le-Tzion over the 'sand dunes' (see next section) made Me'irovitch refrain from publishing after September 1912.

236 See Campos 2011, 146–148; see also Campos 2005a.

In parallel, the Balkan Wars broke out in the autumn of 1912, which increased anti-European resentment. While in other parts of the Empire this led to growing antagonism towards Arab Christians, in Palestine, opposition to European-Zionist migration strengthened Muslim–Christian relations. Antébi reported outbursts of a 'chauvinist nationalism' among Muslims and Christians against the Zionists and Me'irovitch adopted the same position. During a conversation between the settler and Antébi in October and November 1912, Me'irovitch complained that Palestinian Christians and Muslims approached the Jerusalem governor together in order to 'damage and slander us'[237] – a tone contradictory to his conciliatory rhetoric applied in *Filasṭīn*. Other articles published in the Hebrew newspaper *ha-Or* and the Arabic *an-Nafīr* in late 1912 and 1913 show that Me'irovitch had changed his opinion of the ʿĪsās when he wrote (under various pseudonyms) against *Filasṭīn* as an organ, inciting feelings against the Jews with 'extremely poisonous' articles, as Dolbee and Hazkani have shown.[238]

6. Campaigns for the Control over Land and Water

This chapter illustrates the issue of Jewish land purchase as part of the debate on Zionism by portraying selected campaigns for the control over land and water in the Jerusalem District that were fought on the pages of *Filasṭīn*. This was a crucial topic, since, in the context of growing rivalries for local resources from the turn of 1912–1913 onwards, Jewish land purchases led to increasing conflicts between Arab Palestinians and Jewish settlers. First, essential legal aspects regarding Jewish migration and land acquisition in Palestine and some particularities concerning property rights will be outlined. Then, I shall present selected cases concerning this issue that were discussed by various actors in *Filasṭīn* : the transfer of a stripe of sand dunes to the settlement of Rishon le-Tzion, and the transfer of land of to the Jewish National Fund, the campaign over the sale of a cluster of water mills on the Yarkon River near Jaffa to Jewish colonists, and finally, a campaign driven by notables against the sale of Palestinian 'Crown Lands'.

237 Meirovitch to Antébi as recorded in the JCA archives. Cited in Mandel 1976, 139 n. 108.
238 Dolbee and Hazkani 2015a, 256–257 n. 118, 262.

6.1. Jewish Land Purchase as a Dispute Issue

In *Filasṭīn*, the majority of articles regarding land transactions to Jewish colonies harshly criticized the Ottoman authorities, corrupt officials and Sephardi Jews, who were accused of acting as stooges for the Zionists and were portrayed as traitors. Often, these were complaints by readers who addressed the governor or other prominent figures in an 'open letter' (*kitāb maftūḥ*). Usually, Palestinian landlords were accused of selling off their land to the Jews out of greed for money, and Bedouins, tenants and small holders who sold land to rid themselves of debts, were described as too 'ignorant' (*ǧāhil*) to recognize the consequences, being seduced by the prospect of a 'quick profit' (*ar-ribḥ aẓ-ẓāhir*).[239] The hard facts concerning these land transactions were often not stated in the articles: the names of those who bought the land, as well as its locations, remained unspecified.

Legal Contradictions in Terms of Jewish Migration and Land Acquisitions

Legal inconsistencies concerning Jewish land acquisition automatically led to conflicts between Arab Palestinians and Zionists. The Ottoman state had imposed restrictions on Jewish migration and land acquisition from 1882 onwards, but these were enacted rather randomly. The state first prohibited Ottoman Jews from acquiring land classified as *mīrī* in Palestine in 1892, but this restriction was never effectively implemented. In 1901, a new law allowed all Ottomans, including Jews with a long-term residence in Palestine to acquire *mīrī*. Although it had been illegal to sell land to foreign Jews since 1892, those settlers were now in practice treated as Ottoman citizens.[240]

Since the restrictions concerning Jewish immigration and land acquisition contradicted other regulations defined in the Capitulations, these restrictions were never effective. The Capitulations (*imtiyāzāt*) granted foreign citizens in the Ottoman realm the privilege of being able to travel and engage freely in trade and excluded them from Ottoman legal prosecution, as explained in the introduction, but this contradicted Ottoman laws on Jewish immigration that limited to three months the residency of foreign Jews in Palestine, be it for pilgrimage or trade. The Ottoman authorities had initially restricted Jewish immigration to Palestine in 1882 as a response to the 'Biluim'. However, European pressure made this restriction ineffective and, from 1901 onwards, Jewish pilgrims and traders had to exchange their passport upon arrival for a 'Red Paper' (*al-waraqa al-ḥamrā'*), a document that granted residency for a maximum of three months.[241]

239 *Filasṭīn*, 25 January 1912: 207/4/1.
240 See Mandel 1976, 1–31.
241 Mandel 1976, 15f.

The legal framework was also ambivalent regarding Jewish land acquisition. The Ottoman Land Law, introduced in 1867, explicitly permitted foreigners to acquire *mīrī*, which was intended to encourage foreign investment and thus speed up cultivation of land. So the 1892 prohibition of land acquisition in Palestine by foreign Jews contradicted the Land Law, which created many conflicts. European diplomats constantly protested against this restriction as a violation of the Capitulation treaties, and were regularly successful.

As a standard pattern, ambassadors in Palestine intervened on behalf of their Jewish fellow-citizens and pressed the Porte until it withdrew the restrictions. When officials enacted the restrictions on foreign Jews, the latter sought support from their national consulates until the governor lifted the restrictions. Here, the governors were in an awkward position. Pressured by local opposition to Jewish land acquisition, they sought to preserve stability in the District; however, as Kushner notes, they were also aware of the difficulties that might be caused by tensions in relations between the Porte and the Great Powers.[242] Further, the Jerusalem governors were usually only in power in the District for a short time. Being unfamiliar with the legal anomalies concerning Palestine as a special case and overstretched by the high number of protest letters regarding Jewish land purchases, they requested instructions from the Porte in individual cases. Mandel has explained the paradox that the Ottoman authorities' desire to prevent Jewish migration and settlement in Palestine was matched by their failure to apply their rules.[243]

There was also inconsistency in the implementation of the ban on Palestinian Jews acquiring land. This restriction was enacted in 1892 and repeated in 1904, 1910 and 1912, even though Sephardi Jews were Ottoman citizens, since they often acted as agents for Zionist organizations in the purchase of land. This ban arouse fierce protests among local Jews, who denounced it as a violation of their citizenship and interpreted it as anti-Semitism, especially since Christian foreigners were able to acquire land in Palestine under the Capitulations.[244] Even so, the ban on Jewish citizens acquiring land was only randomly implemented, and through the engagement of influential figures, such as the Sephardi Albert Antébi, restrictions were repeatedly lifted.

242 Kushner 1986, 314. For disputes over the application of the Capitulations in Palestine between the governors and foreign consuls in general, and, in specific, in terms of Jewish migration, see Kushner 1986, 309–319.

243 Mandel 1976, 3–18.

244 Note the outraged letter of an anonymous 'Ottoman Israelite' who referred to the patriotism of Jewish settlers and complained about Ottoman restrictions on Jews while foreign Christians acquired land, enjoying the protection of their nations. *Filasṭīn*, 7 February 1912: 109/4/1–2.

Inconsistent Property Rights

Another factor that had the potential to cause conflict over the sale of land to Zionist settlements was that land ownership in Palestine was often not transparent and those who farmed the land were not its legal owners in the eyes of the Ottoman state. Here, a crucial role was played by the land reforms of 1858 and 1867, by which the Porte had intended to break the spread of *mušāʿ*, the communal use of land, its division into small parcels and the rotation of this parcels among a farming community. The law of 1858 allowed individuals to acquire title deeds for land, which was meant to encourage privatization, limit *mušāʿ*, make land more profitable, and make property rights transparent for the state in order to guarantee a steady flow of levies to the center.[245] The Land Law of 1867 gave foreigners the right to acquire title deeds on land, which opened the way for European investment.[246]

However, as the registration of title deeds was linked to military service and taxation, many small holders registered land for which they held traditional cultivation or ownership rights (and which sometimes circulated within a community) in the name of local tribal leaders, sheikhs or notables, who, overnight, officially became major land owners. In practice, the farmers continued cultivating the land as they had traditionally and often lived on it. Legally, however, they became tenant farmers without registered property rights. This made land use and legal ownership not transparent but more obscure. Moreover, registration was insufficient. In 1925, 75 percent of the area of Palestine was not registered with the land registry; and if it was, exact information about borders was often missing.[247]

Since the law allowed the acquisition of large areas, agricultural land became a favorite target for investment. Strongmen, churches, Arab merchants and foreign diplomats acquired large areas, which created a new type of landowner, the 'absentee landlord'.[248] These large-scale landowners included wealthy Christians from Lebanon and Syria, foreign officials, diplomats, traders and Zionist organizations. Local perceptions regarding traditional (communal) land use and shared ownership collided with the private ownership of European settlers who

245 Property tax (*wīrkū*) was imposed on private property (*mulk*), be it land or real estate. The tithe (*ʿušr*) was imposed on *mīrī*, whose owner was guaranteed the right of usufruct for some years, after which it reverted to the state. The Land Law also permitted individuals to acquire title deeds for uncultivated or waste land (*māwāt*), desert areas used for grazing, sand dunes and swamps. Krämer 2002, 100–105.

246 Krämer 2002, 100–105.

247 Krämer 2002, 102. For the land reforms, see Krämer 2002, 100–112; Gerber 1987, 67–82; Mundy 2007, 44–48.

248 Krämer 2002, 100–105.

had acquired legal property rights.[249] This created violent conflicts, especially after the second Aliya, between foreign settlers and Palestinian tenants when the former cultivators of the land who also lived on it were replaced by Jewish labor.[250] By 1914, according to Khalidi, 58 percent of land purchased by Zionists had been sold by absentee landlords, 36 percent by Palestinian absentee landlords, and only 6 percent by locals and small tenants.[251]

6.2. Muhdī Bek and the Sand Dunes of Rishon le-Tzion

A dispute about the transfer of a piece of land to Rishon le-Tzion in 1912 demonstrates the rivalry for resources between the settlers and their neighbors. The settlers had been trying for years to negotiate with the authorities over the acquisition of this coastal stripe in order to prevent the sand from advancing onto their farm land.[252] It appears that they had offered 6,000 lira for the land to former Governor Kāẓim Bek,[253] since the silting up of agricultural land was a problem in coastal regions and the settlers had tried to overcome it by planting eucalyptus trees, which grow very fast.[254] During a visit to Rishon le-Tzion in August 1912, Governor Muhdī Bek, who supported the presence of Jewish colonies in the *qaḍā'*, promised to transfer the strip of sand dunes along the coast to Rishon le-Tzion for cultivation.[255] The editors of *Filasṭīn* started a campaign against this transaction, reminding the governor that the inhabitants whose land bordered the dunes had traditional rights on it. They declared that the dunes were categorized as wasteland (*mawāt*); its transfer to the settlement contradicted the laws regarding property rights and, under the Land Law, the land was available for public use, and the surrounding villages used to collect firewood on it.[256]

249 For the contradiction between pre-capitalist and capitalist conceptions of ownership, see Shafir 1996, 201f.

250 For the 'conquest of labor', see Shafir 1996.

251 Khalidi 1997, 112, 113.

252 It was the same strip that bordered the farm of Rishon le-Tzion towards the coast, a topic that Abū Ibrāhīm discussed in one of his letters with his Jewish friend, Abū Mūsā. See *Filasṭīn*, 3 February 1912: 108/2/1.

253 *Filasṭīn*, 17 August 1912: 163/3/2–3.

254 Eucalyptus was first discovered in Australia in 1777 by Captain Cook and apparently introduced in Palestine by the Templar colonists of Sarona in 1871. In order to dry out the swamps, they planted eucalyptus, which absorbed the water from muddy ground, grew quickly and could reach a height of 11 meters within seven years. Eucalyptus was imported soon after by the Jewish Mikveh Yisra'el colony and later became a famous symbol of Zionist achievements in Palestine. In 1920, about 80 percent of the trees planted by the JN were eucalyptus. See Glenk, Blaich and Haering 2005, xix; Tal 2013, 78.

255 *Filasṭīn*, 17 August 1912: 163/1/5–2/1.

256 *Filasṭīn*, 17 August 1912: 163/3/2–3.

The editors declared that it was not the planting of eucalyptus on this land that they opposed, but the conversion of land that was available for communal use to private property, which would prevent local people from accessing it. It should be mentioned that the juridical point made by *Filasṭīn* is not correct, since the Land Law of 1858 permitted the conversion of *mawāt* to *mulk*, that is, private property. Legally, what was not allowed was only the sale of land to foreign Jews. Mandel posits that Muhdī Bek (a CUP supporter) was not provided with clear instructions concerning Zionist settlement before he arrived because of the political upheaval at the center – the opposition LU had gained power in Istanbul in summer 1912.[257] However that may be, the governor's promise to the settlers brought letters of protest and he soon received an order from the Grand Vizierate that prohibited the sale of land in Palestine to foreign *and* Ottoman Jews. Muhdī Bek ignored this and quickly confirmed the right of Ottoman Jews to acquire property, provided it was real estate in the cities, not agricultural land.[258] According to Mandel, it was due to the intervention of Albert, who reached a compromise with Muhdī Bek, that land transfer to Ottoman Jews was permitted as long as they did not act as middlemen for Zionist organizations. In any case, in the summer of 1912, Rishon le-Tzion received the title deed to the sand dunes. Moreover, other large plots of agricultural land were transferred to the JN while Muhdī Bek was in power in the District, despite warnings from the Grand Vizierate. Muhdī Bek was not able to quell protests against him in the District, but he remained as governor until December 1912 through the support of pro-CUP notables from Jerusalem – while the opposition LU governed in Istanbul – until he was relocated during the Balkan Wars, making way for speculation in Jerusalem.[259]

257 Mandel 1976, 136–138.

258 *Filasṭīn*, 2 November 1912: 185/1/5–2/3.

259 For information on Muhdī Bek, see Mandel 1976, 134–138. In Jerusalem, there was speculation about Muhdī Bek's removal. *Filasṭīn*'s Jerusalem correspondent reported rumors that this was an act of revenge by the Zionists since he had partly interrupted land sales to the Zionists, though the correspondent maintained that the governor had never really enacted restrictions against Zionist purchases. See *Filasṭīn*, 11 December 1912: 196/2/5–3/1. The Sephardi newspaper *Ḥerut* accused *Filasṭīn* of 'fueling' rumors that the Jews had 'bought the governor' and 'blackened his reputation in Istanbul' (*sawwadat sumʿatahu fī l-Istāna*). See *Filasṭīn*, 18 December 1912: 198/3/1–2. The editors of *Filasṭīn* stated that the reason for Muhdī Bek's removal was the Balkan War, since he was Albanian. See *Filasṭīn*, 21 December 1912: 199/3/4.

6.3. The Transaction of Abū Šūša and Kafr Urīya

The more rivalries over local resources increased, the more readers' letters in *Filasṭīn* complained about government neglect concerning the legal restrictions on Jewish land acquisition, corrupt officials and Sephardi Jews or Palestinian notables, who were accused of being 'stooges' for Zionist organizations. This criticism dramatically increased around the turn of the year 1912–1913 in the light of the transfer of land belonging to the villages of Abū Šūša and Kafr Urīya, situated near Ramla, which was conducted with the help of officials and Ottoman Jews.

The 'Retired Broker'

In November 1912, an anonymous author who signed himself 'a retired broker' (*simsār mutaqāʿid*) responded to an Ottoman Israelite who, in the Egyptian newspaper *al-Muqaṭṭam*, had complained about the 'prohibition of land sales to Israelite colonies' (*manaʿ bayʿ al-arāḍī li-l-mustaʿmarāt al-isrāʾīlīya*), and specifically about Muhdī Bek, who had allegedly refused to agree to a sale of a mere three *dunam* to the 'Israelites'.[260] We do not know the identity of this Jewish author but it was possibly Ḥaim Ben ʿAṭṭār, since *Ḥerut* was at that time discussing the same case.[261]

The 'retired broker' declared that it was not colonization that he opposed, but the swindles of the 'Israelite Brothers' who 'always throw dust in [people's] eyes' (*dāʾiman ḏarr ar-rumād fī l-ʿuyūn*). While complaining about three *dunam*, the Jewish author did not mention that 6,000 *dunam* belonging to Kafr Urīya had recently been transferred to the 'Israelite settlements', that is the JN,[262] with the governor's permission, as was announced on the public noticeboards in Jaffa and Jerusalem; according to the retired broker's argument, this was an illegal transfer. He declared that part of the land was *maḥlūl*, meaning currently uncultivated *mīrī* that had to revert to the state to be sold off at public auction, so that the old owner would be able to buy it back. But it seemed that Muhdī Bek had issued a title deed on the land to the JN instead of putting up for auction or heeding local people who held property rights on it.[263]

260 *Filasṭīn*, 30 November 1912: 193/3/3.

261 Ben ʿAtar had obviously interviewed Muhdi Bek about why Yosef Elyashar, a Sephardi Jew, had been refused the purchase 'three *dunam*' of land from the Našāšībīs. The governor responded that the local Jews were traditionally not farmers and it was likely that they acquired land as intermediaries 'for others'. Since Istanbul had just reconfirmed a regulation from 1904 that prohibited the sale of land to Ottoman Jews in Palestine, Muhdī Bek sought to avoid further complaints against him. Campos 2003, 345f.

262 Cf. Mandel 1976, 139.

263 *Filasṭīn*, 30.11.1912: 193/3/4.

The 'broker' was clearly an activist against the sale of land to Jews. Two months later, he wrote that he had been publicly attacked for his involvement by some local Jews,[264] and explicitly asked 'Muslim and Christian readers' to take note of another land sale at Abū Šūša, a village near Ramla and close to Kafr Urīya, that had already been registered[265] In January 1913, the JN had managed to purchase an area of 6,700 *dunam* there.[266] The broker complained that, although the land at Kafr Urīya and Abū Šūša came under the land registry in Jaffa, the transaction had been settled in Jerusalem as to conceal the deal from Jaffa officials, who would only know about it after it was concluded.[267]

The Intervention of Albert Antébi

Another letter appeared regarding this affair and confirmed the statement of the 'broker' that the transaction had been conducted in Jerusalem to keep it secret from the Jaffa land registry.[268] He presented further details about the committee that discussed the case in Jerusalem and the intervention of Antébi, who often acted as an intermediary on behalf of the New Yishuv, while at the same time supporting Jewish-Arab coexistence, and who was known for his short temper. Albert Antébi (1869–1919) was a Sephardi Jew of Damascene descent who had close relations with the Ottoman authorities and the governor, Zionist organizations and local elites of all denominations. He was director of the AIU and active for the JCA in Palestine. Together with Muslim notables from Jerusalem, he founded the Palestine Trading Bank to secure concessions for public projects and was a member of the Jerusalem Chamber of Commerce.[269] Antébi observed the situation in the New Yishuv for the AIU and the JCA, both non-Zionist institutions, but also functioned as advisor to the Palestine Office on strategies for Zionist settlement. After 1911, he complained about growing anti-Semitism in the District and blamed this on the radical methods of the Zionists, as well as on the local Christians and Muslim notables, such as the Jerusalemite Našāšībīs. In 1912, he complained about mass anti-Semitic petitions that he saw initiated by a Muslim-Christian alliance against the Jews. As an Ottoman citizen, he also criticized the lack of will among Zionist migrants to integrate into local structures and considered that the ideological priorities of the Second Aliya encouraged Arab anti-Semitism. In practice, however, he was one of the strongest supporters of the WZO in Palestine and, apart from the Moyals, the most active intermediary in the transfer of land to foreign Jews in the region of Jaffa and Jerusalem; and he

264 *Filasṭīn*, 22 January 1913: 206/2/5.
265 *Filasṭīn*, 22 January 1913: 206/2/5.
266 Mandel 1976, 139.
267 *Filasṭīn*, 22 January 1913: 206/2/5.
268 *Filasṭīn*, 29 January 1913: 208/3/1.
269 Campos 2011, 173–180.

was as influential as he was unpopular. Campos mentions that he was almost 'excommunicated' by the Zionists for his pro-Ottomanism. And because of his engagement on behalf of Zionist organizations, he was frowned upon by his Arab Palestinian fellow citizens.[270]

Back to the land transaction in Jerusalem, where Antébi suddenly appeared before the committee as 'the settler's agent' (*wakīl al-mustaʿmirīn*) and with a member of the Jaffa municipality, although neither was the buyer or the seller. The official, a member of the committee, opposed the sale: since the land was communal property, and one of the owners had died, he said, his share could not be sold off but should pass to his heir. Another shareholder from a village near Jaffa had also not approved the sale. Moreover, the official argued that 2,000 *dunam* of the land was apparently to be sold off to a 'foreign Israelite', a sale that could only be conducted by special permission of the Porte. Antébi was reported to have rampaged around and threatened the official until the committee approved the transaction and ordered the Jaffa land registry office to issue the title deeds, the *qawāšīn*.[271]

The Intervention of ʿĀrif al-ʿĀrif

The protest of the 'broker' also provoked an open letter addressed to Ṭāhir Ḫair ad-Dīn at-Tūnisī, who had replaced Muhdī Bek as governor of Jerusalem in January 1913. It was written by ʿĀrif al-ʿĀrif, a young intellectual and historian and son of the mayor of Gaza, who condemned the 'weakness' of the authorities in failing to prevent Zionist migration.[272] ʿĀrif al-ʿĀrif would later pursue a career in state bureaucracy during the Mandate era and, after 1948, in the Jordanian administration. He also became a prominent scholar of modern Palestinian history.[273]

Since Governor at-Tūnisī had previously edited the Istanbul newspaper *ʿAlamdār*, ʿĀrif reminded him of the time when, as a student in Istanbul, he had been impressed by at-Tūnisī's 'patriotic campaigns' (*al-ḥamlāt al-waṭanīya*) against the Zionists in his newspaper. Now, as governor of this 'miserable district', at-Tūnisī had been 'seduced by the Zionists from all sides' and might have forgotten his patriotism. To remind him, ʿĀrif quoted from a patriotic anti-Zionist article in *Filasṭīn* that had been published in the past in the Turkish

270 The Hebrew newspaper *ha-Zvi* labeled him an 'Oriental despot', while the Arabic *al-Munādī* called him an 'agent of the colonizers' (*wakīl riǧāl al-istiʿmār*). See Mandel 1976, 64, 78, 121, 139; Campos 2003, 294–297, 342f.

271 *Filasṭīn*, 29 January 1913: 208/3/2.

272 *Filasṭīn*, 25 January 1913: 2074/1–2.

273 Before 1948, he was chief secretary to the Jordanian government, and 1950–1955 mayor of Jerusalem. In the late 1950s, he published *An-Nakba* ('The Disaster'), a work in six volumes on the 1948 war. For ʿĀrif al-ʿĀrif, see Fischbach 2000, 81; Mandel 1976, 139.

newspaper *Hadaf* – co-edited by *ʿAlamdār* under the leadership of at-Tūnisī.[274] The article complained about the impact (*nufūḏ*) of the Zionist movement in Palestine through their pamphlets, flags, parades and military training, and called for the implementation of the restrictions regarding Zionist immigration and land purchase so as to build a 'dam against those who want to play with the rights of this Homeland' (*saddan manīʿan fī waǧh kull man arāda al-ʿabṯ bi-ḥuqūq haḏā l-waṭan*).[275] Because of corrupt officials and 'evil brokers (*samāsirat as-sūʾ*), the author of the article said, the Zionists were able to receive title deeds to land as private property, and rising prices seduced the local farmers into getting rid of their land for 'empty profit' (*ar-ribḥ al-fāriġ*).[276] ʿĀrif quoted approvingly from the article a passage that complained of government neglect of the restrictions against Zionist migration and land acquisition:

> And what measures did the government take to encounter this devastating flow (*at-tayyār al-muhlik*)? Nothing… although it said: I do not allow the Zionists to settle in the Palestinian lands (*lā asmaḥ li-ṣ-ṣihyūnīyīn bi-l-iqāma fī l-bilād al-filasṭīnīya*). I only allow them to visit as long as it does not exceed a duration of three months!!! It would be a wonder if this government was able to know the number of visitors and kick them out since it is unable (*ʿāǧiza*) even to know the current number of students in its schools![277]

This was open mockery of the government, which was unable to control (and document) the arrival and departure of Jews through the 'Red Paper' (*al-waraqa al-ḥamrāʾ*) system, which the authorities were meant to use to produce monthly statistics on illegal residencies in Palestine. However, as *Filasṭīn* several times complained, the Red Paper was subject to abuse and corruption, and foreign diplomats put pressure on officials at the Jaffa port to fake the documents.[278] Since the Red Paper was not effective, it was abolished in 1913.[279]

It was true that, at this time, the central government had other problems than Zionist immigration to Palestine. After Muhdī Bek left in December 1912, the District was without a governor for more than a month. Ṭāhir Bek at-Tūnisī arrived in January 1913 and remained in office for only 11 days. After the manipulated parliamentary elections in summer 1912, when the opposition LU had taken power in Istanbul, the CUP took power again in January 1913 and removed Ṭāhir Bek, an LU-supporter. He had been too short a time in the District to do anything against the transfer of the Abū Šūša land. His successor, Māǧid Bek, arrived in March 1913 but several transfers of land to the JN had taken place while

274 *Filasṭīn*, 25 January 1913: 207/3/5.
275 *Filasṭīn*, 25 January 1913: 207/4/1.
276 *Filasṭīn*, 25 January 1913: 207/4/1.
277 *Filasṭīn*, 25 January 1913: 207/4/1–2.
278 *Filasṭīn*, 16 September 1911: 69/1/1f.; 2 November 1912: 185/1/5–2/3; 18 October 1913: 281/1/3f.; 27 December 1913: 294/1/5–2/3. See also Mandel 1976, 15f.
279 *Filasṭīn*, 2 August 1913: 259/3/4; 15 October 1913: 280/3/4.

the District had been without a governor.[280] This political vacuum that existed in the Jerusalem District between November 1912 and March 1913 marked a crucial point for Zionist land acquisition, and dramatically changed the discourse on Zionism in *Filasṭīn*.

6.4. *Filasṭīn, Ḥerut* and the Water Mills at the Yarkon

Another example for rivalries over local resources between Arab Palestinian locals and the Zionist settlers in the Jaffa *qaḍāʾ* was a dispute about the use of water from the Yarkon River. The Yarkon, in Arabic *Nahr al-Aʿūǧa* ('the Meandering') was considered crucial for the vitality of local agriculture and, besides the plantations in the Jaffa region, there were numerous water mills along the river, which were a profitable investment until their monopoly was broken by combustion engines, run by steam and petroleum. In *Filasṭīn*, they were called 'river mills' (*ṭawāḥīn an-nahr*) or 'grinding mills' (*maṭāḥin*). They could be wheels to draw water for irrigation, or mills for grinding grain or sesame or for pressing olives, or they could be used to provide power to run other machines. In 1908, 21 water mills were operating in Jaffa, plus 29 olive presses and 11 sesame presses.[281] Between December 1912 and February 1913, *Filasṭīn* disputed the rights concerning particular water mills, situated in the villages of Ǧarīša, seven kilometers from Jaffa, and al-Farūḫīya.[282] At al-Ǧarīša in particular, the mills were situated at a strategic point near the junction of the road leading to Nablus. When plans for the sale of these mills to Zionist settlers leaked out, the editors of *Filasṭīn* initiated a campaign against the transaction.[283] The main actors in this case were the ʿĪsās and a group of notables and landowners from Jaffa, pitted against the Sephardi newspaper *Ḥerut*. The ʿĪsās feared that Jaffa's landowners' and peasants' usage rights were at stake and suspected a Muslim Jerusalemite notable of act as a stooge for the Zionists. On the other side, *Ḥerut* interpreted the involvement of the ʿĪsās as anti-Jewish incitement and called on Palestinian Jews

280 See Mandel 1976, 120f., 139.

281 In 1896, Ḥāfiẓ Bek as-Saʿīd from Jaffa, a parliamentary delegate for the Jerusalem District, bought eight mills at once, situated by the bridge at al-Ǧarīša. Buessow 2011, 222, 223.

282 For the history of the village of al-Ǧarīša, see Khalidi 1992, 246, 247. I have not been able to find any information about al-Farūḫīya.

283 In the context of this affair, another case was picked up regarding the installation of a pump on the Yarkon by the settlers of Petaḥ Tikva. *Filasṭīn* reported that they had installed a 12hp 'steam engine' (*wābūr*) at the riverside to irrigate their land. After protests, the Chamber of Commerce sent an engineer to inspect the machine and its effect on the collective water rights. In February 1913, the editors happily reported that the central authorities had permitted the local government to decide upon the pump and was free to remove it at any time. *Filasṭīn*, 11 December 1912: 196/3/3; 22 February 1913: 215/3/3; 26 February 1913: 216/3/4.

to boycott *Filasṭīn*. The case demonstrates that rivalries over local resources reached a peak around the turn of the year 1912–1913 and that this rivalry really closed the space in the debate about the question of whether Zionism could be understood as a positive force for modernization in Palestine.

In December 1912, *Filasṭīn* on a plan by the Jerusalemite Muslim notable Yūsuf Wafā to buy the water mills at the al-Ǧarīša junction. Wafā, as president of the Chamber of Commerce, was a prominent figure in Jerusalem, and he enjoyed relations with investors of all confessions. Among them was Antébi, who, together with Wafā, was co-founder of the Palestine Trading Bank (*bank Filasṭīn at-tiǧārī*), set up to encourage local investment and secure concessions, and who was also member of the Chamber of Commerce.[284] For the ʿĪsās, two factors proved that something in Wafā's intention to buy the mills was not right. First, the Administrative Council in Jerusalem, which assessed the request for the purchase of the mills, did not issue a public tender but treated it confidential. Second, the close relationship between Wafāʾ and Antébi, who worked for the Zionists, was known.[285] For the ʿĪsās, Antébi was the 'instigator' (*muḥarrik*) of the planned transaction and was using Wafā as a stooge. They warned readers that whoever bought the mills would also own the 'hidden forces' (*al-quwā l-maknūna*) of the river, and pleaded with the population to participate in the auction 'lest the most vital source in their country (*aʿẓam mawrid ḥayawī fī bilādihim*) might get into external hands and after the greatest part of its water was lost to the settlement of Mulabbis'.[286]

Jaffa's Notables against the Sale of the Mills

The news about Wafā's intention to buy the water mills (as a stooge) raised attention in Jaffa. Residents sent a protest telegram to the central authorities in Istanbul, and local landowners and merchants forwarded a petition (*ʿarīḍa*) to the municipality in which they stressed the Jaffa's dependency on the Yarkon for its urban development and protested against the sale of the mills to a private investor. The petition was signed by 48 persons of whom 33 were landowners who cultivated plantations and depended on water for irrigation; there were also six merchants, one lawyer, one doctor, one pharmacist and six individuals whose occupation was not stated.[287] In making their case, the petitioners argued for a participatory concept of citizenship and the representative function of governance, and called the municipality a 'downsized picture' of Jaffa society:

284 The Palestinian delegates Rūḥī l-Ḫālidī und Saʿīd Bek al-Ḥusaynī held considerable shares in this bank. Because it could not raise enough capital from local investors, it later merged with the APB. Campos 2011, 173–180.

285 *Filasṭīn*, 4 December 1912: 194/3/3.

286 *Filasṭīn*, 4 December 1912: 194/3/3–4.

287 *Filasṭīn*, 7 December 1912: 195/3/3–4.

> Of course, this river is the soul of our city (*rūḥ baldatinā*) and the success of future economic projects depends on it. The progress of this city (*taraqqī hāḏihi al-balda*) and its urban development (*sayrahā fī ṭarīq al-ʿumrān*) are expected [to derive] from its water. And of course, the one who has the power over these mills will also control the river (*aʿinnat an-nahr*) and direct its waters as he likes. However, the members of the municipal council are a downsized picture of the social body (*ṣūra muṣaġġara min maǧmūʿ al-umma*). Each member is responsible to the population of his city, to every individual. This is why we came to warn you through this urgent petition that we will protest with all our might against the sale of the mentioned mills, whether he [the buyer] be a foreigner or an Ottoman (*kāna aǧnabī au ʿuṯmānī*). We will make you [the members of the municipal council] responsible to the community (*amām al-umma*) for the fatal consequences for the city that will result from that step. We instruct you (*nufawwiḍukum*) to protest to every high authority against this destruction … and to use the authority (*as-sulṭa*) given to you by the city to represent it (*li-tumaṯṯilūhā*) and to defend its rights.[288]

The Jaffa municipality reacted quickly. In the next issue, the editors happily reported that the notables' involvement had borne fruit and, as a result of their protests, the municipality had decided to purchase the mills for the 'public benefit' (*li-l-manfaʿa al-ʿāmma*), that is, as public property.[289] *Filasṭīn* reminded the municipality of the law concerning public property (*qānūn al-istimlāk li-l-manfaʿ al-ʿāmma*) and wished it success in this 'national service' (*al-ḫidma al-waṭanīya*).[290] The economic value of the mills was evident from the way the price rose during the public auction. *Filasṭīn* reported that the price for the mills at al-Ǧarīša had gone up to 317,000 piasters, and at al-Farūḫīya to 72,050.

Ḥerut and the Sephardi "Boycott" of Filasṭīn

The campaign against the purchase of the mills on the Yarkon brought the Jerusalemite Sephardi newspaper *Ḥerut* into the dispute. In December 1912, *Filasṭīn* reproduced and commented on two articles from *Ḥerut* that reported on the campaign against the sale of the mills. According to *Ḥerut*, *Filasṭīn* 'harasses the Jews and attacks us … through articles that are completely untrue, in order to stir up the Muslim element against us'.[291] Pointing to the threat to inter-confessional relations in Palestine, *Ḥerut* pleaded for a boycott of *Filasṭīn:*

> After all, we do not doubt that every single Israelite (*kull fard isrāʾīlī*) sees the need to establish an Arabic newspaper that defends the Jews (*tudāfiʿ ʿan al-yahūd*) and fosters the good relations (*al-ʿalāʾiq al-ḥasana*) that exist between them and the Muslims, especially after the Italian war and the present war. Filasṭīn found the right moment to

288 *Filasṭīn*, 7 December 1912: 195/3/2.
289 *Filasṭīn*, 11 December 1912: 196/3/3.
290 *Filasṭīn*, 18 December 1912: 198/3/3.
291 '*Tuʿākis al-yahūd wa-tatahaǧǧam ʿalayhum … bi-maqālāt laysat min al-ḥaqīqa fī šayʾ wa-ḏālika li-kay tuhayyiǧ al-ʿunṣur al-islāmī ḍiddanā.*' *Filasṭīn*, 18 December 1912: 198/3/1.

> deceitfully collude against the Jews (*li-takīd li-l-yahūd*) by alleging that they have stolen the water of the river al-ʿAūǧā[292] and that they have bought the governor so that his reputation was ruined in Istanbul and he, in consequence, was removed; and more such poisonous statement … So, nothing else remains but to ask our brothers, the Israelites: How long do they want to continue to tolerate the hand of him who beats them?[293]

This paragraph reflects the dramatic deterioration in Sephardi–Christian relations in the Jerusalem District by the end of 1912 when *Ḥerut* was trying to stabilize the Sephardi–Muslim coalition – a phenomenon that should be seen in the context of international tensions. In the Tripoli war (1911), the Empire lost Libya to the Italians. When, at the end of 1912, Serbia, Montenegro, Bulgaria and Greece forced the Ottomans out of the Balkans, and Muslim refugees arrived in the Empire, an anti-Christian atmosphere developed while Muslim–Jewish relations stayed stable. In Palestine, however, the trend was the opposite as anti-Jewish sentiment increased in response to Zionist migration. *Ḥerut* saw the resistance to the sale of the mills as initiated by the local Christians, and it is true that most of the petitioners were Christians from Jaffa. *Ḥerut* further blamed *Filasṭīn* for the unpopularity of Muhdī Bek in the District who, after complaints about his benevolence towards Zionist settlements, was removed from his post in December 1912. *Ḥerut*, which from the end of 1912 became a fierce enemy of *Filasṭīn*, claimed in another article that the success of *Filasṭīn* rested mainly on Jewish capital: a large part of the newspaper's revenue allegedly came from Israelites who subscribed *Filasṭīn* or regularly advertised in it. Moreover, the Zionist APB rented a room in the ʿĪsās' house on ʿAǧamī Street and they paid, according to *Ḥerut*, 'many times over' the regular rent.[294] *Ḥerut* addressed Muslim–Jewish solidarity and demanded compelling consistency from the Israelites:

> The newspaper Filasṭīn is an enemy of the Jews (*ʿadūw li-l-yahūd*) and especially of the Zionist organization. Every Israelite is out of respect for our honor obliged to boycott it and not advertise in it anymore – as also many Muslims are boycotting it.[295] … Otherwise we would be like one who puts the sword into the hand of his enemy so he can fight him with it.[296]

The editors of *Filasṭīn* reacted to this with sharp sarcasm. The ʿĪsās responded that such a call for a boycott was 'the best kind of publicity' (*aḥsan ṭarīqa li-l-*

292 Here, another spelling was used; the usual spelling was *al-Aʿūǧa*.
293 *Filasṭīn*, 18 December 1912: 198/3/1–2.
294 *Filasṭīn*, 18 December 1912: 198/3/2.
295 *'Fa-min al-wāǧib ʿalā kull isrāʾīlī iḥtirāman li-šarafinā an yaqṭaʿ ištirākahu bihā wa-lā yuʿlin fīhā kamā qaṭaʿ kaṯīrūn min al-muslimīn ištirākahum bihā.'* *Filasṭīn*, 18 December 1912: 198/3/2.
296 *Filasṭīn*, 18 December 1912: 198/3/2.

iʿlān) for their newspaper,[297] and corrected *Ḥerut:* The APB paid less rent than the Ottoman Bank had previously offered them, but they claimed they were not greedy. Second, the ʿĪsās declared that only 20 of the 1,121 persons who subscribed *Filasṭīn* were Israelites, and ten of those had not yet paid their annual fee. In an unusually pointed manner that was not in line with their usual mantra of inter-confessional brotherhood, the ʿIsās announced that, from now on, the issues of *Filasṭīn* would only be delivered to those who paid their annual fee in advance![298]

This episode revealed intense hostility between the Christian ʿĪsās and the Sephardi *Ḥerut* circle, and their dispute became known beyond the borders of the District. In an unusual sign of support of *Filasṭīn*, the Christian editor of the Haifan *al-Karmil*, Naǧīb an-Naṣṣār, who did not seem to be a friend of the ʿĪsās but was famous for his anti-Zionism, called on the readership for solidarity with *Filasṭīn*, and used the case to rail against Sephardi support for Zionism as a foreign power that undermined the Ottoman frame as a Muslim Empire:

> What an impudence (*qiḥa*) of Ḥerut! It is a newspaper that lives under the firmament of Ottomanism while [at the same time] it serves the Zionist principle (*al-mabdāʾ aṣ-ṣihyūnī*) which aims to create a nationalism (*qawmīya*) and a foreign rule (*ḥukūma aǧnabīya*) in the heart of the Ottoman Sultanate! This is what we [shall] draw the government's attention to, and we encourage patriots (*al-waṭanīyīn*) to support the newspaper Filasṭīn, which serves its government and defends its existence and unity as a society as well as its economic interests.[299]

Triumph for the Petitioners and the ʿĪsās

To return to the dispute about the mills: the decision of the Jaffa municipality to reject their sale to a private investor and instead to make them public property led to protests and disputes in the Administrative Council in Jerusalem, and Governor Muhdī Bek raised objections to the ban. *Filasṭīn* accused the supporters of the Zionists of encouraging dissent *(taḥrīḍ)* in the Council, although it is unclear whether this remark was aimed at Antébi, who had excellent relations with Muhdī Bek and the Jewish members of the Council. Nevertheless, the ban on the sale was confirmed by the central authorities. In February 1913, after Muhdī Bek had been removed from his post, an order arrived from Istanbul that prohibited the sale of the mills, and the ʿĪsās proudly triumphed and attributed the credit for this success to themselves:

> Concerning these orders and [the fact] that the central government was awakened up to this case, the praise partially belongs to the newspaper Filasṭīn (*nālat Filasṭīn qisman*

297 *Filasṭīn*, 18 December 1912: 198/3/1.
298 *Filasṭīn*, 18 December 1912: 198/3/1f.
299 *Filasṭīn*, 28 December 1912: 201/3/3.

> *minhu*), in spite of the complaints the Administrative Council has filed against it, incited by Muhdī Bek and the henchmen of the Zionists (*aḏnāb aṣ-ṣihyūnīyīn*) among the Council members.[300]

6.5. Notables against the Sale of the 'Crown Lands'

In the summer of 1913, a campaign against the sale of the Palestinian Crown Lands took off in *Filasṭīn* that was driven by notables from the Jerusalem and Nablus region. During his reign, the former sultan, Abdülhamid II, had acquired about 56,000 million *dunam* of land in the Arab Ottoman provinces. This was the sultan's private land, categorized as *Ciftlik*, and included 211,261 *dunam* in the Jerusalem District.[301] In Palestine, Abdülhamid owned 832,222 *dunam* of *Ciftlik*, divided into 115 tracts. After the Young Turk Revolution, his private land was confiscated by the state.[302] In *Filasṭīn*, these private estates were called 'Circulated Lands' (*al-arāḍī l-mudawwara*) or 'State Lands' (*arāḍī amīrīya*), in the sense of land 'transferred' back to the state. The financial crisis caused by the ongoing wars motivated the Ottoman government to sell Abdülhamid's private lands in Iraq, Syria, Lebanon and Palestine. These lands were given various names, including *Sannīya* or 'Crown Lands' (*al-arāḍī l-amīrīya*), which were categorized as *mīrī*, state land. Later, these estates were renamed Circulated Lands and sold off, which created confusion and was followed by protests by the holders of shares in these *mīrī* lands in the Arab provinces.[303]

After the government of the Jerusalem District was informed by Istanbul in the summer of 1913 that the Palestinian Circulated Lands were to be sold at auction, notables from Nablus and the Jordan Valley organized resistance against this move, fearing that the land would be sold to Zionist organizations or European investors. The ʿĪsās and the editor of the Haifan *al-Karmil*, Naǧīb an-Naṣṣār, also participated in the campaign, calling for the shareholders in these lands to receive title deeds. It is mportantto note that this protest was driven by Palestinian notables from the Jerusalem and the Nablus District. For the first time, the debate on Zionism in *Filasṭīn* extended beyond the geographical borders of the District. In addition, the dispute over the Crown Lands contained proto-national arguments. Securing the Crown Lands for local farmers was equated with patriotism and it was openly stated that relations between Palestinian citizens and the Ottoman state were being disturbed by the ʿĪsās.

---

300 *Filasṭīn*, 22 February 1913: 215/3/3.
301 Fischel and Kark 2008, 146.
302 Kark and Frantzman 2010, 52–54.
303 Maghdid 2016, 2031. For the different names for these lands used in Iraq, see Issawi 1988, 289.

A Call from Nablus for 'Jihad' through a 'National Company'

An anonymous letter from Nablus, clearly from a Muslim notable, informed the readers of *Filasṭīn* that Jerusalemite notables had called upon the elites of Nablus for a meeting in Jerusalem to organize resistance to the sale of the Crown Lands. In unusually combative language, the author called for united opposition against Zionist land acquisition from the urban elites of Jerusalem, Jaffa, Gaza, Nablus and Haifa. The *banī Isrāʾīl*, as he called the Zionists, a term used in Islamic tradition for Jews, 'are attacking us with money, knowledge, activism, national fanaticism and other things that are necessary to win on the battlefield'.[304] In an alarmed tone, he called for great caution towards 'this dynamic, hardworking and stubborn nation' (*tilka al-umma an-našīṭa al-ʿāmila al-ʿanīda*) that was working for the realization of their national project in Palestine. If they managed to buy the Crown Lands, he warned, 'all our political, social and economic vitality will be destroyed'. He called for the 'defense' (*difāʿ*) of the Crown Lands by the only ones who 'owned weapons' (*arbāb as-silāḥ*) in Palestine: the journalists. They should raise awareness that political organization was necessary. He called for the 'foundation of a national Palestinian company' (*taškīl šarika waṭanīya filasṭīnīya*) by the 'rich of Nablus, Jerusalem, Jaffa, Haifa and Gaza', which should apply at the Ottoman government for a concession to invest (*imtiyāz istiṯmār*) in the Crown Lands. He supposed that it was possible to collect 50,000–60,000 lira and borrow the same amount from the banks, and thus the 'true jihad' (*al-ǧihād al-ḥaqīqī*) would be accomplished.[305] However, he stressed the right of the *Banī Isrāʾīl* to settle in other fertile provinces of the Empire such as the 'land between the two rivers' (Mesopotamia), on condition that they became Ottomans.[306]

Two Authors on Zionist Colonization and the Question of Iraq

A response to the debate over the Palestinian Crown Lands and the call for the foundation of a 'National Company' beyond the District borders came in three letters from an anonymous anti-Zionist author, who titled his contribution 'Beware of the Sudden Danger' (*Tadārakū al-ḫaṭr ad-dāhim*), and was among the first writers in *Filasṭīn* to apply a specifically nationalist discourse by referring to the inhabitants of the various districts as 'the Palestinian people' (*aš-šaʿb al-filasṭīnī*), calling upon them to develop their patriotism. He defined European immigrants in Palestine, using the historical term 'Franks' (*al-afranǧī*), as those who headed material progress, industrial production and international economy and with whom local traders could not compete. The Zionists embodied a 'na-

304 *'Inna banī Isrāʾīl yuhāǧimūnanā bi-l-māl wa-l-ʿilm wa-n-našāṭ wa-l-ʿaṣabīya al-qawmīya ilā ġayr ḏālika min mūǧabāt al-fawz fī mīdān al-ʿirāk.'* *Filasṭīn*, 12 July 1913: 253/1/3–4.

305 *Filasṭīn*, 12 July 1913: 253/1/4–5.

306 *'In kāna Banū Isrāʾīl yurīdūna at-tawaṭṭun fī l-bilād al-ʿuṯmānīya fa-naḥnu lā narfuḍuhum wa-hā amāmahum bilād bayna an-nahrayn wāsiʿa muḫṣiba.'* *Filasṭīn*, 12 July 1913: 253/1/5.

tion' that made profits by applying 'scientific standards' (*umma... tazraʿ ʿalā qawāʿid al-ʿilm*) while Palestinian farmers still worked in 'the way of Noah' (*uslūbihim an-nūḥī*), without generating any surplus.[307] The local economy was doomed to 'stagnation' (*ǧumūd*) since Palestine, the author complained, 'has no industry and the foreigner has control' (*al-aǧnabī yamluku nāṣiyatahā*).[308] Palestine could only be competitive he thought, if Palestinians developed a sense of community. In the light of the Zionists' seizure of Crown Lands, he saw the country in mortal danger and defined two obligations for the Palestinians. Every Palestinian district and city was to 'raise its voice in a call for help and protest to the government' and send 'a lot of telegrams' to Istanbul. Like the first author who engaged in this matter, he also called for the establishment of a 'national company' (*šarika waṭanīya*) by the urban elites of Jaffa, Haifa, Nablus, Jenin and Acre that would raise half a million lira, and buy the Crown Lands from the government. The author made it clear that this was not supposed to be a 'charity project' but a 'great business enterprise that will yield enormous profit if smart and creative hands engage in it'.[309]

Sometime later, 'an Arab notable' (*min faḍīl ʿarabī*) of unknown origin, who currently resided in Istanbul, responded. Showing solidarity with the local farmers, he feared that 'the Zionist's superiority in colonization' (*tafawwuq aṣ-ṣihyūnī bi-l-istiʿmār*) and the sale of the Crown Lands would cause severe damage to Palestine. 'If our people were more progressive and stronger' (*law kāna šaʿbunā arqā wa-aqwā*), they would be able to stand up to the feudalist enslavement of the local farmer, European interests and the Zionists, he said, but he criticized the advice of the first author who had suggested that the Zionists should colonize the uncultivated areas of Iraq, and was outraged, because he saw Palestine and Iraq as connected:

> Know that Iraq and Palestine are twins (*ṣinwān*). The misery of the first and the second will return to us. We are happy about the benefit for both one and the other. If Palestine is affected by damage, may God forbid, then Iraq will cry about it. And if the first one is joyful, then the second one comes alive, too; and vice versa.[310]

The ʿĪsās commented on the possible extension of Zionist colonization to Iraq in a calming tone. Arguing for the 'modernization imperative', they linked colonization to cultivation and progress, while insisting on the distinction of Iraq and Palestine as Ottoman provinces and stressing the special danger Zionism posed for Palestine:

307 *Filasṭīn*, 30 July 1913: 258/1/5.
308 *Filasṭīn*, 30 July 1913: 258/1/4.
309 '*Mašrūʿ tiǧārī ʿaẓīm iḏā taʿahhadathu aydin ʿālima fannīya yaʿūdu minhu al-arbāḥ aṭ-ṭāʾila.*' *Filasṭīn*, 30 July 1913: 258/2/1.
310 *Filasṭīn*, 23 August 1913: 265/2/2.

> We see it this way: Iraq and Palestine are not the same in terms of Zionist colonization. Because there [in Iraq], the whole Israelite community (*al-umma al-isrāʾīlīya bi-aǧmaʿihā*) could get settled without throttling the local population as would be the case at our end [in Palestine].[311] What is concluded from this letter is that its author considers the migration of Israelites to the Ottoman Empire as one of the greatest plagues (*āfa min al-āfāt*). But this is neither compatible with the opinion of the first author... nor with our opinion. What we fear is that the extraordinary powers that Zionism concentrates in Palestine mirror the interest that lies behind [it], since its name 'Zion', and Palestine, are the same province.[312]

Notables' Engagement for the Crown Lands in the Jordan Valley

There was local engagement in directing the sale of the Palestinian Crown Lands. A group of notables from Nablus became active in the acquisition of these lands and were described by the ʿĪsās as patriots 'the homeland can be proud of' (*yaḥuqqu li-l-watan an yufāḫir bi-him*).[313] These notables inquired from the governor of Beirut about the conditions for buying Crown Lands in the Baysān Valley (*Ġūr Baysān*), situated west of the River Jordan, where Abdülhamid had acquired extensive properties during the 1880s.[314] Since they did not receive a response from either Beirut or Istanbul, the press picked up the case. The ʿĪsās promoted the organization a 'national conference' (*muʾtamar waṭanī*) in Nablus to discuss how local people could buy Crown Lands,[315] and considered the initiative from Nablus to purchase the Baysān Valley an example of patriotism, unlike the attitude in other Palestinian cities in the District,

> in which the number of Zionist stooges multiplied so that even the trader, state official, teacher, attorney and farmer are among those who will tomorrow betray his brother, the farmer, out of greed for dirhams gained from the brokerage business.[316]

The ʿĪsās contributed suggestions about what should be the practical outcome of a national conference in Nablus, which they seem to have picked up from *al-Karmil*. An 'action committee' (*laǧna ʿāmila*) with branches in other cities was to represent local interests in the purchase of the Crown Lands, communicate with

311 '*Inna al-ʿIrāq huwa ġayr Filasṭīn bi-izāʾa al-istiʿmār aṣ-ṣihyūnī fa-hunāka tastaṭīʿ al-umma al-isrāʾīlīya bi-aǧmaʿihā an taḥull dūna an tuḍayyaq al-ḫanāq ʿalā ahālī l-bilād kamā huwa al-ḥāl ʿindanā.*' *Filasṭīn*, 23 August 1913: 265/2/2.

312 *Filasṭīn*, 23 August 1913: 265/2/2.

313 *Filasṭīn*, 2 August 1913: 259/1/2.

314 For a map of the Baysān district and the Arab tribes that were settled there, see Kark and Frantzman 2010, 53. For the properties acquired by Abdülhamid in the Baysān Valley during the 1880s, see Fischel and Kark 2008, 161–165.

315 *Filasṭīn*, 2 August 1913: 259/1/2.

316 '*Kaṯurat fīhā samāsirat aṣ-ṣihyūnīyīn ḥattā daḫalat ʿadādahum at-tāǧir wa-l-maʾmūr wa-l-muʿallim wa-l-muḥāmī wa-l-fallāḥ allaḏī ġadan yaḫūnu aḫāhu al-fallāḥ ṭamʿan bi-darāhim as-samsara.*' *Filasṭīn*, 2 August 1913: 259/1/3.

the financial elites who were able to invest money, raise public attention by talking to the press, and send protest telegrams to the authorities. In the view of the ʿĪsās, the central government had failed in its loyalty towards the people since it wanted to sell off of the Crown Lands 'in one piece' (*ṣafqa wāḥida*), without splitting it into smaller units so that local people would be able to buy it. On the other hand, the Palestinians had not proven their patriotic intentions because they had not asked for a 'domestic credit' (*qarḍ dāḫilī*).[317] ʿĪsā also called on the Grand Vizierate to order all governors to cooperate with the local elites in collecting capital to buy the Crown Lands from the state.[318] Since the governor of Beirut did not respond to the request from Nablus, notables and tribes from the Baysān Valley joined the campaign, sending letters to newspapers in Beirut, the Haifa-based *al-Karmil*, and others. In August 1913, *Filasṭīn* published a telegram signed by Bedouin leaders of the aṣ-Ṣaqr, al-Bašātwah and al-Ġuzzawīya tribes and the representative of the Christians in the Baysān Valley. It urgent the Palestinians 'in the name of mutual solidarity and patriotism' (*bi-sm at-taḍāmun wa-l-waṭanīya*) to join the campaign.[319] However, this initiative from Baysān did not have a wider effect on Palestinian networks. The first anonymous author again expressed his anger about the lack of patriotism among the economic elites in Palestine. He complained that, apart from a notable from Jenin, Salīm ʿAbd al-Hādī, nobody had approached the local government about the purchase of Crown Lands.[320]

However, the elites tried to cooperate on a local basis. In Nablus, a 'public meeting' (*iğtimāʿ ʿāmm*) was held in August 1913. It was not a 'national conference', however, attended by 'thousands of inhabitants' (*ulūf muʾallifa min al-ahālī*), and its outcome was a petition that was published in *Filasṭīn* and signed by the 'social committee in Nablus'.[321] Apart from delivering 'protest speeches' (*ḫiṭab iḥtiğāğīya*), this committee addressed the authorities, demanding

> that the government definitely abstain from the public auction (*al-mazād al-ʿalanī*) and instead, give the said divided lands to those who have the right to usufruct and cultivate it (*li-l-mutaṣarrifīn wa-l-muzāriʿīn fīhā*), who lost it in a despotic manner (*bi-ṭuruq istibdādīya*) and who, if the government takes it away from them, will have nothing to resort to and will fall into distress and misery, which will force them to take measures

317 *Filasṭīn*, 2 August 1913: 259/1/3.

318 *Filasṭīn*, 2 August 1913: 259/1/4.

319 Salīm Ṣāliḥ signed on behalf of farmers and tenants. Others who signed were the leader of the Ġazawīya tribe Bašīr, the leader of the al-Bašātwah tribe Sulaymān, the leader of the aṣ-Ṣaqr tribe ʿAbdallāh, and Ḥannā, the head of the Christians of Baysān. See *Filasṭīn*, 6 August 1913: 260/2/2–3.

320 *Filasṭīn*, 9 August 1913: 261/1/4–2/1.

321 The members who signed the petition were mentioned as: Ibrāhīm ʿAbd al-Hādī, ʿAbd al-Fattāḥ Ṭūfān/Ṭawfān, Ḥasan Ḥamād Nimr an-Nābulsī and Kāmil Hāšim. *Filasṭīn*, 9 August 1913: 261/3/1.

> that lead to punishment. Because this sale in this manner means in reality that we are being sold and our country (*hāḏā l-bayʿ… bi-l-ḥaqīqa bayʿ la-nā wa-li-baladinā*). So, we protest in the sharpest way and with all our power against the sale, asking that the government might pay attention to the material, ideational and political damage arising from it.[322]

This was the end of the campaign against the sale of Palestinian Crown lands in *Filasṭīn.* Further, we do not know, how active the elite network really became. Clearly, the affair kicked up a lot of dust in all three Palestinian provinces, provoked discussions about political organization on a regional level and brought about lively resistance by notables in Nablus and Baysān. However, this initiative was far from stimulating united action on a 'national level', although elements of national discourse infiltrated the debate on Zionism at this point.

Last but not least, there was success on the practical level. In August 1913, *Filasṭīn* reported (in an article reprinted from the newspaper *Iṣlāḥ*) that the Ottoman government intended to take a loan of 40 million lira from French banks 'to be dispersed' for the Crown Lands so they could be sold to Ottoman citizens.[323] In September, *Filasṭīn* reported (via the newspaper *Turǧmān*) the foundation of an Ottoman society that wanted to acquire the Palestinian Crown Lands for 300,000 lira in advance, with the rest to be paid in installments, and afterwards sell the lands off to Palestinian farmers.[324] The last report on the case was printed in September 1913 and informed potential buyers residing in the Jerusalem District that it was possible to pay 'by installment' (*bi-t-taqsīṭ*).[325] After this, the matter was never mentioned again. While in *Filasṭīn*, the affair was covered in 12 articles, it was much more extensively reported in the northern Palestinian press. As Beška notes, *al-Karmil* in Haifa, being more closely connected to Baysān than the Jerusalem District through the railway line, published more than 70 articles on the affair.[326]

The Disturbed State–Citizen Relationship

It is worth mentioning that the subdued interest of Palestinian notables in the purchase of the Palestinian Crown Lands caused the ʿĪsās to critically re-evaluate Ottoman citizen–state relations. The success of any state depended on mutual solidarity, cooperation and trust, wrote Yūsuf al-ʿĪsā. Elaborating on concepts of patriotism, he quoted Victor Hugo (1802–1885), a French author from the ro-

322 *Filasṭīn*, 9 August 1913: 261/3/1.

323 *Filasṭīn*, 20 August 1913: 264/3/2.

324 *Filasṭīn*, 3 September 1913: 268/2/2.

325 Interested investors were to contact Naḫleh Kattan in Jerusalem or his deputy in Jaffa, Šukrī Fayʿānī. *Filasṭīn*, 17 September 1913: 272/3/3–4.

326 Beška 2016c, 91; for Beška's discussion of the affair about the Palestinian Crown Lands, see also 87–92.

mantic age who defined patriotism as 'stronger than love' (*aqwā min ʿišq*) and as the 'soul of the people' (*rūḥ aš-šaʿb*).[327] Yet, according to ʿĪsā, the neglect of the Crown Land affair revealed that state–citizen relations had reached a disastrous state of mutual mistrust. The citizens watched the authorities with 'skepticism' (*naẓar ar-rība*) which caused serious moral damage that was like 'a disease that is gnawing at the bone of this Empire' (*ad-dāʾ allaḏī yanḫur ʿaẓm hāḏihi al-mamlaka*).[328] In the light of this dilemma, ʿIsā demonstrated his deep concern about the 'misunderstandings' in intra-Ottoman relations, complaining that, on both sides, the regime and the population, there was a lack of identification with the 'Ottoman nation'. He elaborated:

> Oh God, our heart has broken with grief witnessing this situation ... what arrow could be more bloody for the heart (*admā li-l-qalb*) than the sight of a nation (*šaʿb*) that does not comprehend the meaning of patriotism (*maʿnā l-waṭanīya*) and deprives its government of support. And what [could be worse[than a government that sees its nation like the living dead (*mayyit bayna aḥyāʾ*) and does not offer him the bread of life? Because the Ottoman nation and the Ottoman government are made of the same soil and its majority belongs to the same religion. So, how could this comprehensive trust and mutual loyalty get lost, and reach the point where one sees the other as a stranger?[329]
>
> Is it not [so] since hearts have grown apart and there is strife in [people's] minds, and in practical life there are bad intentions? And is it not [so] that the nation (*aš-šaʿb*) does not comprehend the meaning of patriotism and the government fears for the loyalty of the nation? And both forget that a government that does not mix (*lā yamtaziǧ*) with the nation and a nation that does not mix with the government to constitute one single body (*ḥattā yaṣīrān kullahumā ǧasadan wāḥidan*) will not be successful (*lā naǧāḥ lahā*)?![330]

This was the first time that *Filasṭīn* openly discussed the idea that relations between the center and the Palestinian provinces were too distant. The quotatione further reflects ʿĪsā's comprehensive disappointment at the population's lack of self-identification with the Ottoman state, which he saw as precondition for a united national body.

327 *Filasṭīn*, 2 August 1913: 259/1/2.
328 *Filasṭīn*, 2 August 1913: 259/1/4.
329 *'Min ṭīna wāḥida wa-akṯarīyatuhumā min dīn wāḥid fa-limma faqadat min baynihimā aṯ-ṯiqa at-tāmma wa-l-iḫlāṣ al-mutabādil ḥatā ṣāra aḥaduhumā yanẓur li-l-āḫira ka-ġarīb ʿanhu'.* *Filasṭīn*, 2 August 1913: 259/1/1.
330 *Filasṭīn*, 2 August 1913: 259/1/2.

7. The Impact of Zionism on Christian-Jewish Relations

The following section investigates how the Zionist question redefined inter-confessional coexistence in the Jerusalem District during the years before World War I, and specifically, tackled relations between Christian and Sephardi intellectuals in the Jaffa-Jerusalem region and their visions of Ottoman brotherhood and unity. It illustrates where the actors who disputed Zionism in *Filasṭīn* worked for a harmonization of Christian–Jewish relations, or towards polarization. It outlines in specific the role of the Christian editors of *Filasṭīn* in the debate, while considering their socio-economic and personal networks with the 'Israelite brothers' and with Zionist immigrants in Jaffa, and how they distinguished between 'good' Israelites and the 'black sheep' among them.

7.1. Strategies for Conflict Management

In the debate on Zionism, the ʿĪsās and other participating authors used various strategies to work towards de-escalation and conflict management in local inter-confessional relations. Since religious 'fanaticism' (*taʿaṣṣub, taṭarruf*) and sectarian 'partisanship' (*taḥāmul*) were perceived as a serious threat to Ottoman unity, especially in the light of the political crisis the regime faced before World War I, Palestinian authors constantly warned against partisanship in the press. The ʿIsās (as CUP-supporters) distanced themselves from rumors circulating in the 'political clubs' about alliances between the Young Turks and the Zionist Movement, which they perceived as unreasonable conspiracy theories, invented by the political opposition.[331] Instead, one should know 'what is our duty now' (*māḏā yulzamnā al-ʿān*) as 'real compatriots' (*ka-waṭanīyīn ḥaqīqīyīn*) and 'humanists' (*ka-insānīyīn*), ʿĪsā reminded readers during the Libya crisis, and documented mutual Muslim, Christian and Jewish demonstrations of solidarity with the Ottoman military in Beirut as good example.[332] Further, and as part of their stand for 'neutrality' (*ḥiyād*), the ʿĪsās constantly insisted on differentiating between 'Israelites' and 'Zionists', and on a strict separation of anti-Zionism from

331 The 'alliance' between Zionists and Young Turks was a frequent argument used by critics of the regime. For conspiracy theories in the late Ottoman Empire and the myth of the influence of the Freemasons and Jews on the Young Turks, see Mandel 1976, 83f.; Reinkowski 1995, 28f., and 2011, 93–104. According to the ʿĪsās, such statements were dangerous and should be silenced. *Filasṭīn*, 23 August 1911: 62/1/4.

332 There, as ʿIsā described it, Muslims, Christians und Israelites came 'in swarms' to donate money and make sacrifices for the Ottoman cause. See *Filasṭīn*, 7 October 1911: 75/1/2–3. The recruitment of young Ottoman Jews was a major issue discussed in the Hebrew press. Many Hebrew newspapers pleaded passionately with young Jewish men to join the Ottoman army and do their civil duty. See Campos 2011, 152–157; Ben-Bassat 2009b, 467f.

anti-Semitism, condemning the latter as an outdated relic from the Middle Ages. In the light of the debate on Zionism, Palestinian Jews also worked for conflict management in inter-confessional relations in order to affirm their credibility as loyal Ottomans, as will be seen. Further, as a phenomenon of political crisis and multiplied demonstrations of Ottoman loyalty in the press, even Zionist settlers, who mostly possessed foreign citizenship, were sometimes included in the concept of a multiple ethno-confessional unity in Palestine, as will be shown by reports in *Filasṭīn.*

Separating Israelites from Zionists and anti-Zionism from anti-Semitism

In the summer of 1912, the ʿĪsās reminded readers that, in 1911, they had established the 'Section of the Addressee' (*Bāb al-Ilā*) and the 'Section of the Sender' (*Bāb al-Min*) to initiate an exchange of opinions on the Zionist question, on condition that participants would 'consider the ethnic and religious feelings' of others (*yurāʿī l-ʿawāṭif al-ǧinsīya wa-d-dīnīya*) and 'not dip their pen into the inkwell of bias' (*lā yuġiṭṭ qalamahu fī miḥbarat at-taḥāmul*).[333] An anonymous Israelite author who called himself 'someone who loves just treatment' (*muḥibb inṣāf*) commented critically that he saw nothing but an 'occasional rebuke' in this section 'concerning the Israelite question' (*fī masʾalat al-isrāʾīlīyīn*), urging the editors to bring positive news about the Israelites to prove their 'principle of moderation' (*mabdaʾuhā l-muʿtadal*). The ʿĪsās corrected the author, insisting on a separation of Israelites from Zionists. The section had been established to take a stand on 'towards the Israelites', the ʿĪsās said, but 'towards the Zionist question alone' (*illā li-l-masʾalat aṣ-ṣihyūnīya*) and should provide authors with 'the space for rebuke or approval of Zionist colonization' (*al-maǧāl fī ḏamm aw taḥbīḏ istiʿmār aṣ-ṣihyūnīyīn*), and they affirmed that they knew that the Israelite *umma* included many honorable people who understood 'the meaning of humanism' (*maʿnā l-insānīya*).[334]

Further, and as a matter of principle, the ʿĪsās insisted on separating anti-Zionism from anti-Semitism, and warned readers against confusing them. While anti-Zionism was in their opinion legitimate in so far as the Zionist movement was considered a threat to their environment with its economic and political exclusivism, anti-Semitism was unacceptable. While the Sephardi circle around the Hebrew newspaper *Ḥerut* interpreted anti-Zionist critique in the Arab press in general as anti-Semitism, the ʿĪsās categorically distanced themselves from anti-Semitism. In 1912, they accused a Muslim Sheikh from Beirut, Yūsuf an-Nabahānī, verbally derailing Christians and Jews. Nabahānī had published a booklet of poetry that was, according to the ʿĪsās, an unacceptable 'defamation of

333 *Filasṭīn*, 22 July 1912: 53/2/2.
334 *Filasṭīn*, 4 November 1911: 83/2/1.

Jews and Christians' and a 'devaluation of their religion and honor'.[335] Nabahānī had cursed the Jews, whose character he defined as 'malicious' and the worst group among all infidels.[336] To demonstrate the opposite example of a Muslim with a 'noble soul who disapproves of trading in religion' (*muslim āḫar ḏū nafs kabīra tastankir al-mutāǧara bi-d-dīn*), the ʿĪsās quoted another Muslim Sheikh, Muḥammad al-Qalqīlī. He had published in the Lebanese press a counter statement to Nabahānī's anti-Semitic attack, which he called a 'disaster for the Ottomans' (*min maṣāʾib al-ʿuṯmāniyīn*), considering how much effort they were giving to 'harmonizing' (*tawfīq*) between the groups in the Homeland. The ʿĪsās approved Qalqīlī's call for Nabahānī's arrest and the confiscation of his book so that his 'poison will not circulate in the body of the Syrian people'.[337]

At another point in 1913, while anti-Zionist sentiments in the Arab press were already in full swing, the editors published another editorial on the phenomenon of anti-Semitism, which they called 'the shame of the twentieth century' (*maʿarrat al-qarn al-ʿašrīn*),[338] picking up the issue in the context of a trial against a Jew, Menachem Mendel Beilis from Kiev who was accused to have committed the ritual murder of a Christian boy.[339] The case resounded powerfully in Palestine, and not only made headlines in the Hebrew press but was also covered in several articles on the front page of *Filasṭīn*. In Jaffa, rabbis issued a prayer of lamentation dedicated to Beilis that was published in *Filasṭīn*,[340] Jews demonstrated in the synagogue in Manšīya,[341] and in Tel Aviv, Russian-Zionists protested, and attacked Jewish and Turkish representatives.[342] The Russian Consulate, which prohibited demonstrations and tried to prevent public mobilization with the help of the *qāʾimaqām*'s forces but failed because of the overwhelming presence of Zionist youth, faced a night time attack by Russian Jews.[343] When Beilis, after a trial that lasted over a month, was declared innocent, he received

335 '*Waqīʿa fī l-yahūd wa-n-naṣārā wa-taḥqīr dīnihim wa-l-ḥaṭṭ min ʿirḍihim.*' *Filasṭīn*, 11 May 1912: 135/1/1–2.

336 *Filasṭīn*, 11 May 1912: 135/1/2–3.

337 '*Ḥattā lā tasrī samūmuhu fī ǧism aš-šaʿb as-sūrī.*' *Filasṭīn*, 11 May 1912: 135/1/3.

338 *Filasṭīn*, 25 October 1913: 283/1/1 f.

339 The accusation that Jews murdered Christian children to use their blood for religious rituals has a long history in Europe that goes back to the Middle Ages, but the accusation of ritual murder in the modern Russian Empire caused a shock in the international press. The 'Beilis affair' is well covered in scholarly literature. See Beška 2016a, 99–101, and 2016c, 131–133; Costin 2004, 69–93; Leikin 1993; Rogger 1993, 1257–1273; Weinberg 2013.

340 *Filasṭīn*, 22 October 1913: 282/2/4.

341 *Filasṭīn*, 25 October 1913: 283/1/3–5.

342 Zionists disturbed a celebration in the Hebrew Gymnasium to enforce public mourning over Beilis's case – which the editors judged to be a 'living example for mutual solidarity, unity and national feelings' (*miṯāl ḥayy ʿan at-taḍāmun wa-l-ittiḥād wa-aš-šuʿūr al-ǧinsī*). *Filasṭīn*, 22 October 1913: 282/1/3–4.

343 *Filasṭīn*, 25 October 1913: 183/1/3–5.

warm compliments and donations from the Jewish communities all over Palestine.[344] After the affair, Beilis left Russia for Palestine, where he lived until he emigrated to New York in 1921.[345] Upon his arrival in Jaffa in February 1914, Beilis, once a 'simple worker' (*ʿāmil basīṭ*), was now famous and was welcomed by a crowd.[346] The editors published an interview with him by a friend, the correspondent of the Lebanese *Lisān al-Ḥāl*, ʿAzīz ʿArīḍeh. ʿArīḍeh politely approached him in Tel Aviv with a translator, assuring to him that the 'progressive Palestinian youth, despite of their different confessional affiliations, were affected by what happened to you and do not believe the accusation against you'.[347]

It was also in the context of the 'Beilis affair' that Yūsuf al-ʿĪsā issued a severe warning against accusations of blood libel, as one of the 'fairytales' that had spread among the simple-minded since the early days of Christianity and was simply not in compliance with 'an age in which the light of knowledge (*nūr al-ʿilm*) has been spread'. He called the rumors of blood libel 'a shame' (*maʿarra*) that is (still) 'sticking to the twentieth century'.[348] Again, ʿĪsā criticized the 'Israelites' for their exclusivist customs and declared his fierce opposition to the political aspirations of the Zionist movement in Palestine, but insisted on a strict separation of anti-Zionism from anti-Semitism and condemned anti-Jewish or discriminatory arguments in the debate on Zionism, as well as the defamation of the Jews. He declared:

> What is attributed to the Jews (*al-yahūd*), that they shed blood during the performance of religious rituals, is a fairytale (*ḫurāfa*); and, for those who believe it and those who spread it, it is an abomination (*saǧāma*). It is a shame [still] attached to this twentieth century, and if the spirits will not be able to detach from the chains of ignorance, God will not release them forever.[349]

> Whoever follows what this newspaper has been writing, knows that we have spared no efforts in criticizing the Israelites as a community that isolates itself from other communities, and in fighting those who we call 'Zionists', since among them is a faction that seeks our material destruction and our cultural enslavement in this Palestinian land. But God forbids us to sacrifice the truth on the altar of [personal] goals or to keep silent over the allegation of lies, false witness and defamation, even it is related to one of our

344 *Filasṭīn*, 12 November 1913: 288/3/4; 15 November 1913: under the aegis of *al-Aḫbār*, 495/3/1.
345 Beška 2016a, 100–101.
346 *Filasṭīn*, 14 February 1914: 307/1/3–5.
347 *'Bi-anna aš-šabība al-filasṭīnīya ar-rāqiya ʿalā iḫtilāf maḏāhibihā kānat mutaʾaṯṯira bi-mā ǧarā laka wa-ġayr muṣaddiqa mā ittahamta bihi.' Filasṭīn*, 18 February 1914: 308/2/1.
348 *Filasṭīn*, 25 October 1913: 283/1/2–3.
349 *Filasṭīn*, 25 October 1913: 283/1/1. ʿĪsā here mixes the terminology about 'Jews' and 'Israelites', referring to the Jews as a global religious community and the followers of Judaism by using the term *yahūd*. When later referring to the 'Israelites', he addressed the Jewish *milla* in Palestine, the 'brothers' in Ottoman citizenship.

> opponents, because we honor the Jews as followers of a revealed religion who are exonerated from committing such an atrocity that a sound mind cannot accept.[350]

> It is possible that there are those among the Jews, as among all communities, murderers, blood shedders, monsters and religious extremists, who hate those who do not follow it to death. It is also possible that blindness is driving some of their individuals to the point of calling for the killing of someone who does not belong to their community … However, tarnishing the honor of the Israelite religion with this stigma and claiming that its worship could not be performed without drinking human blood, is an insanity – may God protect the minds of this century from paying attention to it.[351]

The ʿĪsās' response to the 'Beilis affair' befitted their general rejection of sectarian tendencies or anything that would discredit the narrative of Ottoman brotherhood. Since the affair led to violent encounters between Zionists and the local government, and the Russian consulate in Jaffa and Tel Aviv, the ʿĪsās made efforts to calm people's minds. As always, they were terrified that inter-sectarian violence could provide the European powers with the excuse of 'Eastern fanaticism' to interfere in the Empire's affairs on behalf. Until 1914, they held on to the distinction between (foreign) Zionists and (Ottoman) Israelites, Zionism and Judaism, and (legitimate) anti-Zionism and (unacceptable) anti-Semitism. In July 1914, when the coverage in *Filasṭīn* had turned into a full blown anti-Zionist campaign, the ʿĪsās published a prayer written by the famous Jewish scholar, philosopher and physician Moses Maimonides (1135/38–1204), the doctor of Sultan Saladin in Cairo, that was meant to be an inspiration for modern doctors, and wise guidance for readers.[352]

Demonstrations of Inter-Confessional Coexistence

Filasṭīn also reported on demonstrations by Palestinian Jews in favor of inter-confessional Ottoman unity and coexistence in Palestine. In August 1911, the editors conducted an interview with Jaacov Me'ir (1856–1939), *ḥāḫāmbāšī* of Salonika, but originally from Jerusalem. Me'ir was personally acquainted with the ʿĪsās, who appreciated him as 'meritorious scholar' (*ʿālim fāḍil*).[353] When asked

350 '*Lam naʾlu ǧuhdan fī intiqād al-isrāʾīlīyīn ka-umma muʿtazila ʿan baqiyat al-umam wa-muḥāraba man nadʿūhum ṣihyūnīyīn baynahum ka-fiʾa ṭāmiḥat al-ʿayn li-ihlākinā mād-dīyan wa-stiʿbādinā adabīyan fī hāḏihi al-buqʿa al-filasṭīnīya wa-lākin yaʾbī llāh an nuḍaḥḥī l-ḥaqq ʿalā maḏbaḥ al-ġāya aw naskut ʿan tafnīd zūr wa-buhtān wa-law kāna fī ḥaqq ḫaṣm lanā innanā nuǧill al-yahūd ka-aṣḥāb dīn munazzal ʿan al-ityān bi-miṯli hāḏihi al-faẓāʿa allatī lā yaqbuluhā ʿaql salīm.*' *Filasṭīn*, 25 October 1913: 283/1/1.

351 *Filasṭīn*, 25 October 1913: 283/1/1–2.

352 *Filasṭīn*, 29 July 1914: 340/2/2–3.

353 Jaacov Meʾir had previously been a rabbi in Jerusalem. Der Matossian has presented the struggles over the Chief Rabbinate in Jerusalem as an example of inter-ethnic Jewish rivalries in Jerusalem after the Young Turk Revolution in 1908. While the Chief Rabbi of Istanbul and the Zionists backed their own candidate, Elyahu Panigel, Albert Antébi, the AIU liberals and

about Zionist aspirations in Palestine, Me'ir decried the WZO agenda, and called the creation of a 'Zionist Empire' 'gossip' with which simple people sought distraction. He affirmed, only the 'redeemer' would be able to bring about the 'kingdom of Israel', but Zionism was trying to 'collect the scattered Israelites in one place' (*ǧamʿ šatāt al-isrāʾīlīyīn fī buqʿa wāḥida*), where they could coexist with other groups.[354] Further, Me'ir called on the Zionists to abstain from 'gossiping' so as 'not to hurt the feelings of their brothers of other confessions'.[355] Me'ir's statements can be considered as part of the usual 'rhetoric of conflict management' that was applied by representatives of religious minorities during public celebrations and when addressing government officials, and it remains unknown how far Me'ir approved of Zionism's political goals.

As outlined before in chapter I, this public rhetoric of conflict management was a phenomenon that appeared all the more during times of political crisis. When the Ottoman troops temporarily reconquered Tripoli in November 1911, the population of Lod held a public celebration with fireworks. It was attended, as *Filasṭīn* stated, by Ottomans 'without consideration of their ethnic or confessional affiliation and the surrounding Bedouins and the Israelite settlers of Bayt Ṭarīf'.[356] Shortly after, *Filasṭīn*'s correspondent in Lod reported on an event even more surprising. As a 'sign of affection and intimate friendship' (*dalāla ʿalā wuǧūd al-maḥabba wa-l-ulfa*) between 'the different elements' (*al-ʿanāṣir al-muḫtalifa*), he stressed, 'our Israelite brothers in Bayt ʿArīf' (*iḫwānunā l-isrāʾīlīyūn fī Bayt ʿArīf*) reciprocated the former invitation and invited the 'Muslims and Christians of Lod' to join a celebration. While the first article mentioned the settlement of 'Bayt Ṭarīf', the second called it 'Bayt ʿArīf', which is apparently the correct spelling.[357] Anyway, *Filasṭīn*'s correspondent reported that there was a

Sephardi groups (Yemenites, Bukharites, Persians) supported Me'ir, an AIU graduate, as their candidate. When Me'ir won, the Ashkenazi community, which had boycotted the election, complained to the Chief Rabbinate in Istanbul. Me'ir was in good terms with Governor Rašīd Bek, and did not leave his post until the arrival of the new governor, ʿAlī Akram Bek, after which he left for Salonika where he served as Chief Rabbi from 1908 to 1919. Der Matossian 2009–10, 22–24, and 2014, 81–87. Me'ir told the ʿĪsās that, in 1911, he had received a call from the Jerusalemite community but could not leave his community in Salonika. *Filasṭīn*, 12 August 1911: 59/1/3–2/2. Under the British Mandate, Me'ir was the first to be elected to the newly established Chief Rabbinate of Palestine (1921), bearing the title Rishon le-Tzion ('The First in Zion'). See also https://www.jewishvirtuallibrary.org/rabbi-jacob-meir (accessed 23 February 2018).

354 *Filasṭīn*, 12 August 1911: 59/2/1.

355 *Filasṭīn*, 12 August 1911: 59/2/1–2.

356 '*Wa-tuwārid al-ʿuṯmānīyūn ʿalā iḫtilāf ʿanāṣirihim maʿ al-ʿurbān al-muǧāwirīn wa-l-isrāʾīlīyīn al-mustaʿmirīn Bayt Ṭarīf.*' *Filasṭīn*, 4 November 1911: 83/4/2.

357 With regard to the first version 'Bayt Ṭarīf', there was an Arab village near Lod and Ramla named Dayr Ṭarīf that should according to Khalidi, be identified with a Roman settlement called Bayt ʿArīf. No early Jewish settlement called 'Bayt Ṭarīf' is mentioned in either in Khalidi's study on Arab villages depopulated in 1948 or in Ṭarāwina. A Jewish Moshav called

friendly reception and that people spent a 'brilliant night' (*layla zāhira*) together.[358] The fact that the settlers of Bayt ʿArīf were called 'our Israelite brothers' suggests that some of them were Ottoman citizens. It is to be assumed that they naturally met their material needs at the markets of Lod and Ramla and occupied Arab cultivators. However, a mutual celebration of that kind was a rare occasion for social interaction between settlers and Palestinians, caused by political circumstances that erased for a moment existing ethno-confessional borders between the urban population, nomads and Jewish-European colonists.

How short this moment of harmony was is demonstrated by an article of another kind on Bayt ʿArīf in March 1913; after a violent clash in the settlement, now called the 'Israelite Company of Bayt ʿArīf' (*qumbānīyat Bayt ʿArīf al-isrā ʾīlīya*), when an Arab farmer was fatally injured after he entered Bayt ʿArīf's land with his sheep and got involved in a fight with the guard. The case was investigated by the authorities, but the guards escaped and the police were unable to solve the case. The editors left a mocking remark, saying that the result of the investigation would have been different 'if the criminal was Ottoman' (*law kāna al-muǧrim ʿuṯmānīyan*).[359] This suggests that some of the settlers had retained their foreign citizenship, which always entailed complications in criminal cases, and that the honeymoon between the settlers of Bayt ʿArīf and the Arab villagers around was over as a result of conflicts about access to grazing. Back to the 'brilliant night' in Bayt ʿArīf in 1911: the fact that representatives of all groups ostentatiously showed off their loyalty to Ottomanism was more a sign of their fear of tension than of stable friendship and was an established strategy in conflict management. How international politics influenced local balances is documented by the establishment of an inter-confessional committee in Jaffa during the Balkan War of 1912 in Jaffa, which contained representatives from all confessions, and the qadi, the mufti and the rabbi, who were reminded to give

Bayt ʿArif was founded by Bulgarian immigrants only in 1949 on the ruins of the depopulated village of Dayr Ṭarīf (see Ṭarāwina 2000, 112; Khalidi 1992, 378f.). No Jewish settlement called 'Dayr Ṭarīf' or 'Bayt Ṭarīf' during Ottoman times is documented anywhere. The 1922 British census by Barron records a total Muslim population of 836 souls for Dayr Ṭarīf, and no Jews or Christians (Barron 1923, 22). The 1931 British census by Mills reports a Muslim population of 1.246 souls for Dayr Ṭarīf (Mills 1932, 20). As for the second version called in *Filasṭīn*, 'Bayt ʿArīf', I suppose that this was the correct name of the settlement. Jaffa's Sharia court records documented in 1904 the village 'Mazraʿat Bayt ʿArīf', situated north-east of Lod. Although it was registered as an Arab village, Ṭarāwina reports that, by 1904, most agricultural areas there were owned by Jews (Ṭarāwina 2000, 106). In 1913, 'Bayt ʿArīf' was mentioned in *Filasṭīn* for a second time in the context of a violent clash between the settlers and an Arab farmer. *Filasṭīn*, 15 March 1913: 221/3/3.

358 *Filasṭīn*, 15 November 1911: 86/3/3.

359 *Filasṭīn*, 15 March 1913: 221/3/3.

patriotic 'advice' to their followers.[360] In general, during the crises of 1911, 1912 and 1913, calls for inter-confessional solidarity in the Arab and Hebrew press were repeated to a degree that seems exaggerated, but it demonstrates how motivated Muslim, Christian and Jewish actors were to stabilize group relations in Palestine.

7.2. Towards Polarization: the 'Black Sheep' among the Israelites

This section outlines how the Zionist question spurred conflicts and confrontations in Palestinian group relations before World War I; especially in Christian–Jewish relations. This is a relevant aspect of the press debate in *Filasṭīn* that was to a considerable degree conducted between the Christian editors and Jewish authors from the Jaffa-Jerusalem region, and included polemic tendencies. As much as the ʿĪsās insisted on their 'neutrality' (*ḥiyād*) towards every *millet* and condemned sectarian 'partisanship' (*taḥāmul*),[361] so much they also attacked individual Jews whom they viewed as the 'black sheep' among the Israelites who spoiled the reputation of the local Sephardi community with their practical support of the Zionist movement. The ʿIsās unashamedly let off steam against them, which contributed to conflicts in local Christian–Sephardi relations. There were three categories of 'black sheep', as I call them, identified by the ʿĪsās: the Sephardi *Ḥerut* circle, the Sephardi 'stooges' in Zionist land acquisition, and the Ashkenazi migrants who came during the Second Aliya and were more associated with Zionist ideology and more radical then the first generation of Jewish migrants, especially in terms of their agenda for a conquest of Palestine through 'Hebrew labor'. In the following, we shall investigate how far the Zionist question created tension between these groups of actors and the ʿĪsās, as far as is visible in *Filasṭīn*.

Black Sheep I: Ḥerut, the ʿĪsās and anti-Semitism

The *Ḥerut* circle were identified by the ʿĪsās as troublemakers per excellence and the agitators of the Sephardi community in the Jerusalem District. To this circle belonged the editor of *Ḥerut*, Ḥaim Ben ʿAṭṭār from Jerusalem, and Shimon Moyal and Nissim Malul from Jaffa. *Filasṭīn* closely followed the coverage in *Ḥerut*, and often commented on *Ḥerut* reports and reprinted them, although it is not known who translated the Hebrew articles into Arabic for the ʿĪsās. As

360 Its members were Yūsuf al-ʿĪsā, Ḥāfiẓ Bek as-Saʿīd, Shaykh Darwīš ad-Daǧǧānī, Yaʿqūb Abū l-Hudā, Ǧirǧī Kassāb, Ilyās Ǧallād, Ǧirǧī Būǧūṣ, Boris Rabbinowitch and David Mizrakhi. *Filasṭīn*, 9 October 1912: 178/3/4f.

361 *Filasṭīn*, 7 December 1912: 195/1/1–4.

Jacobson states, *Ḥerut* saw itself as a 'Zionist-national paper for the entire Jewish population in the Yishuv', but specifically it spoke for the Sephardi community in Palestine. One of its focal points was the revival of Hebrew, and it was involved in the 'language struggle' in the Yishuv in 1913 between supporters of Hebrew and supporters of German. Second, it strongly promoted Zionism among Arab Palestinian citizens, and Sephardi authors in the *Ḥerut* circle published pro-Zionist articles in the Arab press. Third, *Ḥerut* promoted Ottoman loyalty and Arab–Jewish coexistence in Palestine, and fostered the integration of foreign Jews, encouraging them to adopt Ottoman citizenship.[362] One of *Ḥerut*'s major concerns was the 'Arab question': the position of the Yishuv towards the Arab population and the question of how far Zionist immigrants should adapt to their environment. The Sephardi Jews were confronted with a dilemma. Being Arab Jews *and* Palestinians, they were forced to find a balance between a Jewish-national identity, Palestinian patriotism and Ottomanism. As Ottomans, Arab Palestinians and members of a universal Jewish community, they tried to harmonize between all of these identity layers. The result was, according to Jacobson, a Sephardi 'integrative Zionism', a fusion between Zionism and Ottomanism that differed from the exclusivist Ashkenazi vision of the Zionist Yishuv.[363]

The Sephardi intelligentsia sought to spread their vision of an inclusive Palestinian Zionism by addressing both the Arab Palestinians and the Yishuv. In the Arab press, they made an effort to convince the Arab local population of the benefits they would receive as a result of Zionism while trying to preserve an alliance with the Muslim majority in Palestine. At the same time, they appeared before the Arab collective as defenders of Zionism, reacted highly sensitively to anti-Zionist critique and identified the Christian intelligentsia as the main agitators of hatred against the Jews. At the core of this was, in their view, an anti-Semitic campaign run by *al-Karmil* and *Filasṭīn*, which they defined as the archenemies of the Jews.[364] Addressing their Ashkenazi coreligionists in the Hebrew press, the Sephardi intelligentsia put the same energy into encouraging the idea of Jewish–Arab coexistence in Palestine. They called on Zionist immigrants to integrate culturally into their new environment, learn Arabic, adopt Ottoman citizenship and serve in the military. For Jacobson, this was an extraordinary stand for Jewish–Arab coexistence at a time of growing inter-confessional polarization,[365] which gave consideration to partnership with the Arabs and stood against the 'exclusive Zionism' of the Ashkenazi Jews, who excluded

362 Jacobson 2001, 25f., and 2003, 13–15, 18–25.

363 Jacobson 2011, 97f., and 82–116; Campos 2003, 280–312, and 2016, 310–325.

364 For the Sephardi interpretation of Arab Christian anti-Semitism in *Ḥerut*, see Jacobson 2001, 26, 29, 30.

365 Jacobson 2004, 42–44, and 2011a, 165–182.

Arabs from their vision of Palestine.[366] Regarding Jewish–Arab coexistence, Jacobson and Campos have discussed the involvement of Nissim Malul,[367] who propagated the idea that Zionism should return to its Semitic elements. As a precondition for merging with the 'people of the country', Malul called on immigrants to adopt Arabic as a first language in which the Jews of the New Yishuv should 'think and feel' – according to him, the key for mutual understanding. Malul also suggested the foundation of a Jewish–Arab Teachers' Union and a Jewish-Arabic journal to 'fortify ourselves through the Arabic language'.[368] Malul got into conflicts with other Jewish journalists over this language policy,[369] and declared that his purpose was 'pure and simple: to strengthen the internal foundations of the Yishuv by bolstering it from outside'.[370]

As was seen from the press disputes over the Netter School and the water mills on the Yarkon, both involved Sephardi intervention and led to a call for a boycott of *Filasṭīn*. From the end of 1912 onwards, the *Ḥerut* circle constituted the main opponents of the ʿĪsās in the debate on Zionism. The ʿĪsās from time to time forgot their principle of moderation and gave way to hostile sarcasm directed against *Herut*, and ridiculed Jewish oversensitivity to criticism, as illustrated above. Malul and Moyal particularly provoked the ʿĪsās, and they were all personally acquainted with each other. Malul collaborated with the Palestine Office in the monitoring of the anti-Zionist coverage in the Arabic press. He frequently responded to anti-Zionist articles in Arabic newspapers from Palestine to Lebanon and was a correspondent of the Egyptian *Muqaṭṭam*,[371] though the ʿĪsās ridiculed his journalistic skills. Moyal also closely observed the debate on Zionism in the Palestinian press and actively contributed there with pro-Zionist articles. In *Ḥerut*, he published translations from the Arab press.[372] Moyal and Yūsuf al-ʿĪsā in particular must have met personally quite often through their activities as elected delegates for the Jaffa *qaḍāʾ*,[373] and their memberships in the

366 Jacobson 2011b, 97f.; cf Gribetz 2014, 126–130.

367 Campos 2003, 355f.

368 Behar and Ben-Dor Benite 2013, 65.

369 Malul's attitude was in this point not shared by *Ḥerut*'s editor, Haim b. ʿAṭṭār, who championed Hebrew as the first language in the Yishuv and thought that Arabic should be only a secondary language. Jacobson 2004, 43.

370 This in a press dispute with Ya'acov Rabinowitz, who 'expressed bitterness' at Malul's suggestions in *Ha-Po'el ha-Za'ir*, a Zionist newspaper published in Jaffa. See Behar and Ben-Dor Benite 2013, 64–69, here 67.

371 Jacobson 2004, 42f.

372 Actually, he also sought to translate the anti-Zionist booklet by the *al-Karmil* editor Naǧīb an-Naṣṣār. It is not known whether Moyal was one of the Sephardi authors working for the Palestine Office in monitoring the anti-Zionist coverage in the Arab press. He does not appear on the payroll of the Palestine Office but he was wealthy and did not depend on payment from the Zionists. See Gribetz 2014, 11, 191f.

373 Buessow 2002, 93.

local CUP branch and the Freemasons' Barkai Lodge in Jaffa.[374] Moyal had a reputation for being a troublemaker. He founded a new lodge in his house that was not recognized by the Barkai Lodge, which brought a case against him.[375] After the Young Turk Revolution, Moyal, his wife Esther and Malul became active in several Jewish associations. In 1909, Moyal founded the National Israelite Society in Jaffa, an organization of 27 members, to educate the Jews according to the constitutional values and defend it from inside against 'betrayal'; this was the official agenda. In practice, it was to defend the interests of the Sephardi community in Palestine.[376]

The defense of Sephardi interests in Palestine was a central issue for Moyal and Malul during the years before World War I. In 1909, Moyal opened the discussion about the foundation of an Arabic-Jewish newspaper that was to draw a positive picture of Zionism for Arab readers. This idea saw lively discussion in *Ḥerut,* and Ashkenazi Jews in particular criticized it.[377] In 1912, the Moyals and Malul founded the 'Arabic Printing Society' (*aš-Šarika aṭ-Ṭibāʿīya al-ʿArabīya*), which was to raise funding for a Jewish-Arabic printing press, counter anti-Zionist articles in the Arab press and remind local people about 'how the Jews have worked for the good of the Homeland'.[378] In 1913 or 1914, the Moyals and Malul established with other Jews from Jaffa *ha-Magen* (Hebr. 'the Shield'), another society to monitor anti-Zionist articles in Arabic newspapers and translate them into Hebrew.[379] The younger Malul was particularly active after World War I in the foundation of the Arabic newspapers *al-Aḫbār* and *as-Salām*, which were funded by the Zionist movement.[380]

374 The number of members of the Barkai Lodge increased greatly after the 1908 Revolution and a number of branch lodges were founded. Kark 1990b, 162.

375 Campos 2011, 185, n. 70, 293. On Moyal see also Ben Hanania, Yehoshu'a 1944. Dr. Shimon Moyal and the Jewish-Arab Problem. In *Hed ha-Mizrach* 3, 25 (in Hebrew).

376 Campos 2011, 201.

377 The dispute about the foundation of such a newspaper would occupy the Hebrew press for years until in 1914, the Moyals and Malul collaborated in publishing the short-lived *Ṣawt al-ʿUṯmānīya* ('The Voice of Ottomanism'). See Campos 2003, 305–311. *Filasṭīn* was at odds with *Ṣawt al-ʿUṯmānīya* from the beginning. See the discussion on hostilities in *Filasṭīn* against this newspaper in Beška 2016, 65f.

378 Levy 2007, 241f.; Campos 2011, 163.

379 According to Jacobson, its members were prominent Sephardi families form Jaffa. Apart from Nissim Malul, and Shimon and Esther Moyal, they were Avraham Elmalech, David Moyal, Yosef Amzalek, Yosef Eliyahu Chelouche, Ya'akov Chelouche, Moshe Matalon, David Hivan and Yehoshu'a Elkayam. Their aim was, in the words of Elmalech, to 'defend by all kosher and legal means our status in the land'. See Jacobson 2011, 171–173.

380 He also participated in the Arabic journal *Ittiḥād al-ʿUmmāl* ('The Workers' Union'), published by the Jewish Workers' Union, the *Histadrut.* See Jacobson 2011, 167–168, 173–174. According to Malul, its editorial board also maintained contacts with the Hashemites, King Faisal and Emir ʿAbdallāh during the post-war years. For more biographical details on Malul, see Levy. 2007, 218f.; here 220.

The editors of *Filasṭīn* observed the Sephardi initiatives with interest, including, for instance, the 'war of pens', as they called it, between Moyal and Ludvipol in *Ḥerut* about the sense or nonsense of a Jewish-Arabic newspaper. Ludvipol thought that an Arabic newspaper would not have credibility among the Palestinians as soon as it was known as Jewish enterprise.[381] Moyal responded to *Filasṭin*'s coverage of the topic, saying that he rejected any interference.[382] The ʿĪsās countered that it was their right as journalists to inform readers about disputes in the Hebrew press that were not accessible to Arabic speakers, while the 'Israelite brothers' were well informed about anything going on in the Arabic press.[383] On their part, the ʿĪsās complained about the Jewish Arabic Printing Society circulating pamphlets in which the ʿIsās were insulted as 'morons' and 'low life' (*ṭaġām*), they reported.[384]

Doubtless, the *Ḥerut* circle were trying to motivate Ashkenazi immigrants to integrate culturally into their new surroundings. Confronted with an identity dilemma as Arab Palestinians and Zionists, they tried to solve it by developing an overlapping identity concept that Jacobson calls 'integrative Zionism', and Campos 'harmonization' between Zionism and Ottomanism. What is seen from the Sephardi contributions to the debate on Zionism in *Filasṭīn* is that they were mainly apologetic: their role was to defend and they hardly got involved in the contents of anti-Zionist articles. In general, they interpreted anti-Zionist critique as anti-Semitism, and focused on presenting the progressive power of Zionism. Jacobson's view that the Sephardi 'alternative voices' were working for mutual understanding is rather romantic and ignores the fact that the central element in the Sephardi contribution to the Arab debate on Zionism was apologetics. However that may be, the hostility in the disputes between the ʿĪsās and the *Ḥerut* circle indicates that relations between the Christian and Sephardi intelligentsia in the Jaffa-Jerusalem region were deeply disturbed after late 1912.

Black Sheep II: Israelite 'Stooges' for the Zionists

Ideologically, the Sephardi Jews promoted Zionism in the Arab press; in practice, they supported it as sponsors and intermediaries to bypass the legal ban on foreign Jewish land purchases. In Jaffa, the Moyals, the Chelouches and the Amzaleks were much involved in these transactions; in Jerusalem, it was the Yellins and Albert Antébi. Avraham Moyal was until his death in 1885 the local representative of the Ḥovevei Tzion Society in Jaffa; his brother Yosef helped the Biluim to purchase land in the region from the Jewish community. In the 1890s,

381 *Filasṭīn*, 28 October 1911: 81/3/4.
382 *Filasṭīn*, 1 November 1911: 82/3/1–2.
383 *Filasṭīn*, 1 November 1911: 82/3/2–3.
384 *Filasṭīn*, 18 December 1912: 198/3/2.

Aharon Chelouche, Haim Amzalek and Yosef Moyal bought the vineyards north of Jaffa, which later became the new Jewish neighborhoods of Neve Tzedek, Neve Šalom, Maḥane Jehuda, Maḥane YoseFilasṭīn, Šeḥunat Aharon und Maḥane Yisra'el.[385]

The Sephardi involvement in Zionist land acquisition often led Arab notables to demand the extension of the ban to Ottoman Jews, which was from time to time confirmed by the authorities but never really enforced because of the active protests of prominent Sephardis such as Antébi.[386] It is noticeable from the debate in *Filasṭīn* that public opinion in Palestine started to be biased against the Sephardi Jews because of their role as intermediaries. When Shimon Moyal was rewarded for his voluntary military service with the post of community physician for Ramla and Lod, the editors of *Filasṭīn* commented on it mockingly. Under the title 'There is no Greater Broker' (*Mā Akṯar as-Samāsira*), the ʿĪsās reported that Moyal was currently trying to buy 'one quarter' of the village al-Kanīsa for 1,200 lira; and an additional area for 5,000 lira. As Moyal was rather wealthy, they remarked that he was to be rewarded, like the Ashkenazi Eisenberg before him, with the title of a *ghazi* (*ġāzī*), an honorable title for a fighter in the Islamic army or the Ottoman troops. But the ʿĪsās said scornfully that Moyal was actually to receive this title from the Zionists because he was 'snapping up the lands of Palestine' for them.[387] In 1890/1, Aharon Eisenberg, one of the co-founders of Reḥovot, had established a cooperative settlement south-east of Jaffa as a moshav; he was an influential entrepreneur and director of the Zionist Labor Association (*Agudat Neṭaʿim*) and had become an Ottoman.[388] Because of his engagement in the army, Eisenberg's son received the exceptional honorific title of *ghazi*.[389]. *Filasṭīn* admitted that only five other persons in the Empire had been rewarded with this title, but this did not make the Eisenbergs 'real' Ottomans. A letter accused Eisenberg of being one of those 'Zionists adopting Ottoman citizenship' (*riǧāl aṣ-ṣihyūnīyīn al-mutaʿaṯmānīn*) for tactical reasons and 'to snap up the lands of Palestine'.[390]

Black Sheep III: Zionists Boycotting the Citizens

On the intra-confessional level, too, community life between Sephardi and Ashkenazi Jews in Jaffa became quite conflictual during the years before World War I. The bulk of Zionist organizations in Palestine were concentrated in Jaffa,

385 Campos 2003, 344f.; Kark 1990b, 247f.
386 Campos 2003, 347.
387 *Filasṭīn*, 22 February 1913: 215/3/3–4.
388 According to Shafir, he was among the first Zionists to plead for the 'import' of Yemeni Jews who could replace Arab workers in agriculture. Shafir 1996, 96f.
389 *Filasṭīn*, 28 December 1912: 201/3/3.
390 *Filasṭīn*, 21 December 1912: 199/4/1.

and they exposed local Jews to pressure from all sides – from their Arab fellow countrymen, to demonstrate loyalty to Ottomanism, and from the Zionists, to take an active stand for the Jewish national project. The Director of the Palestine Office in Jaffa, Arthur Ruppin, actually complained about the lack of passion for Zionism among Jaffa's Sephardi Jews, for they rejected Zionist symbols and annoyed him with ostentatious demonstrations of Ottomanism. According to him, they were Jews only in confession but not in terms of national feeling.[391]

On the other side, Arab Palestinians blamed the Zionists for having a bad influence on the Sephardi Jews and working towards a split in Jaffa society. From *Filasṭīn*, it is clear that, from 1913 onwards, the Sephardi stance on Zionism had become an *anchor point* in Jaffan Jewish–Christian relations. The ʿĪsās called on their fellow 'Israelite brothers' to distance themselves from the Zionist agenda. In an article in September 1913, entitled 'The Zionists Boycott the Citizens' (*aṣ-Ṣihyūnīyūn Yuqāṭiʿūn al-Waṭanīyīn*), they complained about aggressive Zionist youth organizations that threatened the Jewish subscribers to *Filasṭīn* and imposed the principle of 'Hebrew Labor' on the 'patriotic sons of the country' (*abnāʾ al-bilād al-waṭanīyīn*), the Israelite citizens, and they reported about two examples. After members of the Sephardi family of Dāwūd Ẓarīfeh had purchased of a piece of real estate situated behind Bustrus Market that belonged to the Muslim Abū l-Hudā family, the Zionists pressed a rabbi in Jaffa to issue a 'ban' that forbade every Israelite to buy or rent this land since they wanted to buy it themselves. Another Sephardi, Yūsuf Ǧamīl, had a Zionist boycott imposed on him: a large message in Hebrew on the walls of his property forbade Jews from renting a place in his building.[392] For the ʿĪsās, this policy amounted to instigating social unrest in Jaffa, and they criticized the local Jews for conceding victory to the Zionists, saying:

> We know that the Israelite compatriots (*al-isrāʾīlīyīn al-waṭanīyīn*) do not watch the actions committed by those that we call 'the Zionists' with a satisfied eye (*bi-ʿayn ar-riḍā*). But their [the Zionists'] power (*saṭwatuhum*) has already defeated them (*qad taġallabat*) and their hearts are filled with fear. They surrendered (*fa-staslamū*) to the tricks of those who will not rest until the people begin to merge Zionism with Jewry (*ḥattā ṣāra an-nās yamzuġūna aṣ-ṣihyūnīya bi-l-isrāʾīlīya*).[393]

The ʿĪsās claimed that the Zionists intended to equate 'Jewry' with the Zionist national project, and also asked sarcastically if it was this what the Zionists called the 'peaceful conquest of Palestine' (*fatḥ Filasṭīn as-silmī*).[394] The accusation that the 'Israelites' had already 'surrendered' to Zionism reveals the deep rift in

391 Campos 2003, 291.
392 *Filasṭīn*, 20 September 1913: 273/2/4–5.
393 *Filasṭīn*, 20 September 1913: 273/2/5.
394 *Filasṭīn*, 20 September 1913: 273/2/5.

Sephardi–Christian relations, and indicates that the atmosphere in Jaffa was becoming increasingly anti-Jewish by 1913. The above quotation suggests that the ʿĪsās, until World War I, did differentiate between Jewish co-citizens and the exclusivist Zionist immigrants of the Second Aliya who were stigmatized for causing cleavages in local society. It also reveals the ʿĪsās's personal dilemma, because it is obvious from the quotation that the 'Israelites' of Jaffa were under pressure to explicitly and publically distance themselves from the policies of the Zionists, although, in the socio-economic environment in the small town of Jaffa, all groups were in fact somehow interconnected – an issue that will be discussed further in the last section.

Apart from the Zionist strategy of 'Hebrew labor', conflicting Jewish agendas about which language, German or Hebrew, should be the official language in the Yishuv, broke lose in 1913 – the 'war of languages'.[395] The issue was the subject of controversy in the Hebrew press and the *Ḥerut* circle supported a language policy in favor of Hebrew.[396] This internal Jewish dispute was observed by *Filasṭīn*, where the Hebrew faction were declared 'extremists'.[397] The 'war of languages' also led to violent conflicts in Jaffa and Tel Aviv, and to boycotts against Jews who supported other languages then Hebrew in education, culture, etc. The region was the center of modern Hebrew life and national culture in the Yishuv, but it was also home to Ashkenazi immigrants who stuck to Yiddish as their daily language and the reference point of their cultural identity. For the ideological Russian-Zionist immigrants of the Second Aliya, this symbolized Jewish exile and a humiliation to be overcome; an agenda that they even pursued by violence.

395 The German 'Hilfsverein der Deutschen Juden' (the 'Benevolent Society of German Jews' or the Ezra Society) encouraged German as the language of instruction and modern sciences and as the 'most cultured language', as declared the Technicum in Haifa, a technical institute with a secondary school established by the Ezra Society. On the Zionist side, the Hebrew Teachers' Association, founded in 1903, stood in opposition to this and promoted Hebrew as the official language of the Yishuv. Since different European powers competed with each other in support of Christian and Jewish educational institutions in Palestine, the opposition to German was also a stand against imperialist interference in the Yishuv. The Teachers' Association declared a ban on the Technicum, and intimidated members of the Hilfsverein – a conflict that was finally won by the Zionists. See Bentwich 1965, 12–15; Friedmann 1977, 171–188. See also Friedmann on 'Language War', in *Encyclopedia Judaica*, vol. 12, 482–483.

396 Jacobson 2001, 25.

397 For instance, *Filasṭīn* reported on the case of the 'Lämel School', a Jewish school in Jerusalem whose policy was to push the introduction of Hebrew as the language of education. The Lämel School received funding from a German charity and was part of the 'Hilfsverein' network, but under the leadership of the school's deputy head, David Yellin, the 'extremist teachers' (*al-muʿallimīn al-mutaʿaṣṣibīn*), as *Filasṭīn* called them, went on strike and demonstrated with 300 pupils, who chanted 'Hebrew or death' (*ima al-luġa al-ʿibrānīya wa-ima al-mawt*) in the streets of Jerusalem. *Filasṭīn*, 27 December 1913: 294/3/3–4. For the 'war of languages' and the role of the Lämel School, see Beška 2016c, 115–123.

In April 1914, such Russian Zionists distributed flyers in Arabic, Hebrew and French in Jaffa, warning 'the Israelite Community' (*al-ṭā'ifa al-isrā'īlīya*) against attending a literary performance 'in Yiddish' (*bi-l-luġa aš-šaknāzīya*) in the house of Feingold at Yefe Nof, a Jewish neighborhood situated west of Neve Shalom at Manšīya.[398] Despite the warning, the performance was well attended and Feingold's salon was packed. Zionist protesters demonstrated in front of it and finally burst in and threw 'stink bombs' at the audience (*mādda kīmawīya ḏāta rā'iḥa karīha muz'iğa aḏarrat al-mutafarriğīn*). The situation escalated into a riot. The Russian consul intervened and the police forcibly removed the protesters, who responded by throwing stones, until the police opened fire and dispersed the crowd. *Filasṭīn* thanked them for maintaining public order. Under a headline 'Not every Israelite is a Zionist' (*Laysa Kull Isrā'īlī Ṣihyūnīyan*), they reaffirmed that 'not all of our Israelites brothers share the ill-fated Zionist principle' (*al-mabda' aṣ-ṣihyūnī al-maš'ūm*), but 'the followers of the Zionists' (*aḏnāb aṣ-ṣihyūnīyīn*) werer trying to 'mislead' the people and deny this distinction.[399] This is another example of the way in which the nationalist agenda of the Zionists of the Second Aliyya split the Jews of Jaffa into parties, and damaged the reputation of Jewish immigrants, who became stigmatized as troublemakers.

7.3. *Filasṭīn*'s Networks with Jews and Zionists

The principle of 'social separation' and simultaneous 'economic interconnectedness' in Jaffan inter-confessional life, outlined in chapter II, also applied to relations between Jews and other confessions. Moreover, the separation of Israelite citizens from foreign Zionists was practically impossible in Jaffa's economic life. The Sephardi community was tightly interwoven with the Ashkenazi Jews, who dominated the Jewish 'Town Committee' (Hebr.: *va'ad ha-qehilla*) and Zionist institutions. And local Arabs, too, maintained profitable relations with the Zionists. On the one hand, anti-Zionism was growing, while on the other, Christian and Muslim notables had established profitable economic networks with these immigrants. The 'Īsās were part of these networks, and they enjoyed profitable personal or economic relations with Sephardi entrepreneurs, Ashkenazi immigrants and representatives of Zionist institutions. They tried to protect these relations but feared that the boycott policy of a new generation of Zionists who worked for 'Hebrew labor' could spoil these ties for good and, by 1913, the 'Īsās were confronted with a serious dilemma.

398 In 1904, Feingold had built the Hotel Bella Vista there, containing a salon and a concert hall. I am grateful to the architect and independent scholar Samuel Giler for this information.

399 *Filasṭīn*, 20 September 1913: 273/2/5; 24 June 1914: 330/5/3.

The ʿĪsās' Personal Ties

Filasṭīn was read regularly by Sephardi Jews in Jaffa and beyond and, according to the ʿĪsās, there were 20 Jews paid an annual subscription.[400] In addition, the ʿĪsās rented out the ground floor of their house on ʿAǧamī Street to the Jaffa branch of the APB, the Zionist credit institution established to finance the establishment of the New Yishuv. Since its founding in 1903, the APB had built close ties with Arab Christians and Muslims, and provided loans to local notables such as the Muslim Ḥusaynī family from Jerusalem.[401] The ʿĪsās stated that they had let their place to the APB, although they would have received more money had they let it to the Ottoman Bank, while their enemy, *Ḥerut*, claimed that the Zionist bank paid 'many times over' the regular rent.[402] Whether this was true or not, the ʿĪsās enjoyed profitable relations with Jaffa's APB and they were on extraordinarily good terms with its director Goldenberg, an Ashkenazi immigrant. The editors praised his liberal character, good morals and excellent relations with local companies and the Christian community; they admired his professional competence and his Arabic language skills. Despite being an Ashkenazi immigrant, he was referred to as a 'compatriot' (*waṭanī*).[403] The ʿĪsās also enjoyed socio-economic contacts with Ashkenazi students in Jerusalem, to whom Yūsuf al-ʿĪsā apparently taught Arabic.[404]

The section for advertisements on the last page of *Filasṭīn*, which Jewish traders and institutions frequently used, was an important source of income for the ʿĪsās. In 1911, the 'Commission of the Israelite Comunity' (*Qūmisīyūn al-Milla al-Isrāʾīlīya*) advertised for weeks under 'Lost Jewellery' (*ḥallī mafqūda*) in *Filasṭīn* that they were looking for the owner of some deposited jewels.[405] Other regular Jewish advertisers in *Filasṭīn* were the successful Sephardi construction company of the Chelouche Brothers (*Šlūš Iḫwān*), who owned a tile factory and maintained various businesses with local Christian merchants and Muslim wood suppliers, and Bedouins from Beersheva and Gaza.[406] The international Grisham life insurance company, directed by the Ashkenazi immigrant Abraham Ludvipol who was involved in the dispute about the price rise in Jaffa, regularly put an-

400 *Filasṭīn*, 18 December 1912: 198/3/1f.

401 On APB relations in the District, see Mandel 1976, 43. On the intercommunal loan network of the APB, see Campos 2003, 181–191, and 2011, 171–183.

402 *Filasṭīn*, 18 December 1912: 198/3/2.

403 *Filasṭīn*, 16 April 1913: 230/3/5; 3 May 1913: 233/3/4; 7 May 1913: 234/3/3; 20 September 1913: 273/2/4.

404 Yehoshua 1974, 23; cf. Ayalon 1995, 197.

405 *Filasṭīn*, 19 July 1911: 52/1/1.

406 Abraham Chelouche trusted his business partners among the Bedouins from Beersheba and Gaza enough to receive their payments 'blindly', without checking their receipts. For the Chelouche family and their relations with other groups, see the memoires of Yosef Eliyahu Chelouche in Buessow 2011, 238–256.

nouncements in *Filasṭīn*. And several medical doctors also used it to promote their services, many of them apparently foreigners. From 1911 to 1914, Dr Nissim Braun, a Jewish dentist who ran a laboratory on Jaffa's Iskandar Street, advertised in every single issue of *Filasṭīn* with an illustration of false teeth. Braun had migrated to Jaffa in the end of the nineteenth century and, according to Delmaire, his qualities as an intermediary in disputes between Arabs and Jews were well known.[407] In 1913, a Jewish dressmaker one Madame Malāmīd, of 'Lilienblumstraße' in the 'Tel Aviv neighborhood' (*maḥallat Tall Abīb*), as it was called, started regularly to advertise her modern fashion styles.[408] *Filasṭīn*'s Jerusalem correspondent, an outstanding anti-Zionist, actually promoted in the newspaper the fashions of Madame Rachel, a Jewish dressmaker who opened a 'workshop' (*mašġal*) for fashion female in the 'Israelite school' in Jerusalem in 1913 and was, according to the correspondent, 'very famous in Jaffa and Haifa'.[409]

APB Director Goldenberg: a Zionist of a Different Kind?

The good relationship between the editors and APB director Goldenberg is an example that deserves attention here, and shows the extent to which the Palestinian debate on Zionism before World War I was linked to the question of the inclusiveness or exclusiveness of immigrants' behaviour. Goldenberg was well integrated in Jaffa and, according to *Filasṭīn*, local Christian and Muslim businessmen enjoyed profitable dealings with him. Although he was an Ashkenazi immigrant and represented a Zionist institution, the ʿĪsās referred to him as a 'compatriot' or 'citizen' (waṭanī), distinguishing him from the other Zionists of the Second Aliya generation. Unfortunately, I could not find background information about Goldenberg, but the articles in *Filasṭīn* suggest that he adopted Ottoman citizenship, was fluent in Arabic and maintained excellent relations with Jaffan residents of various denominations. The ʿĪsās knew Goldenberg personally and thought he was very competent in his profession and spoke Arabic 'like the best sons of the Arabs'.[410] When he was appointed director of the APB branch in Beirut, the editors congratulated him warmly,[411] and when it later turned out that Goldenberg would not take the post but was about to withdraw from the APB for good, the editors expressed their deep regret. Goldenberg's resignation was a 'painful blow' to local merchants and the population, who had

407 I saw his advertisements in *Filasṭīn* during 1911–1914, not knowing from the Arabic script (*Brūn*) if he was German or English. An issue in April 1914 showed that he was Nissim Braun, who had run his laboratory on Iskandar Street for the past 15 years. See *Filasṭīn*, 1 April 1914: 320/4/4–5. On Nissim Brawn, see Delmaire 1999, 126.

408 *Filasṭīn*, 18 January 1913: 205/4/4.

409 On Madame Rachel, see *Filasṭīn*, 8 October 1913: 278/2/5.

410 *Filasṭīn*, 16 April 1913: 230/3/5.

411 *'Min ar-riğāl al-ḫabīrīn wa-l-mālīyīn al-muḥannakīn.' Filasṭīn*, 16 April 1913: 230/3/5.

found 'an open heart' in Goldenberg as he always tried to 'ease' financial matters.[412] Having left the APB, Goldenberg took a new post as director of the American company Vacuum Oil, and *Filasṭīn* congratulated him some time later.[413]

Goldenberg seems to have been extraordinarily popular in Jaffa, not only because of his good contacts with local merchants but also because of his polite behavior towards local people and his involvement in Christian charity initiatives.[414] *Filasṭīn* praised him as an individual who united 'European courtesy' and the well-educated behavior and 'tolerance' of the Arabs.[415] Specifically, the editors gave approved his employment of local craftsmen, both Muslims and Christians, in the construction of his new house in Tel Aviv, although Zionist organizations generally gave priority to the principle of 'Hebrew labor'.[416] Goldenberg, an Ashkenazi and representative of a Zionist institution, was portrayed by the ʿĪsās as a shining example of an immigrant who was well-integrated into local structures. In their view, it was this willingness to cooperate with the local people that distinguished him from other Zionists.

Goldenberg's collaborative ways apparently made him a traitor in the eyes of Zionist activists. As *Filasṭīn* presented it, Goldenberg became a victim of Zionist boycott policies in Jaffa. In spring 1913, the ʿĪsās reported an act of violence against Goldenberg, apparently committed because he employed Arab workers on the constructing his Tel Aviv house. During a Zionist celebration in that city, organized by the surrounding Jewish settlements and including parades, sports and fireworks 'blazing up to the sky', Goldenberg's house was set on fire. The editors commented on this act as the 'final highlight' of the Zionist games. For them, it was an 'act of revenge' (*intiqām*) against Goldenberg, 'for he was not a Zionist as they want him to be' (*li-annahu laysa ṣihyūnīyan kamā yurīdūn*).[417] Soon after, the editors reported that Goldenberg had left the APB because of his differences with Zionists of another kind. The fact that he dealt with Arab companies and workers was for those Zionists the 'height of impudence' (*muntahā l-waqāḥa*), and the ʿĪsās claimed that they had intrigued against

412 '*Hāḏihi l-istiqāma waqaʿat ʿalā t-tuǧǧār ka-ḍarba muʾlima limā kānū yaǧidūna ʿinda haḏā ḏ-ḏāt min aṣ-ṣadr ar-raḥib wa-ḥusn al-muʾāmala wa-tashīl al-aʿmāl.*' *Filasṭīn*, 3 May 1913: 233/3/4.

413 *Filasṭīn*, 7 May 1913: 234/3/3. Vacuum Oil had previously been referred to positively in *Filasṭīn* for its policy of employind people for their qualifications, not for their national or confessional affiliations. *Filasṭīn*, 30 September 1911: 73/2/3–4.

414 *Filasṭīn*, 20 September 1913: 240/2/4.

415 '*Kāna l-Ḫawāǧā Kūldenbarġ … raǧulan ǧamaʿ ilā riqqat al-ūrubīyīn wa-tahḏībihim ṭibāʿ al-ʿarab wa-tasāhulahum.*' *Filasṭīn*, 20 September 1913: 273/2/4.

416 '*Bannāʾīn wa-tuǧǧār min al-waṭanīyīn al-muslimīn wa-l-masīḥīyīn.*' *Filasṭīn*, 20 September 1913: 273/2/4.

417 *Filasṭīn*, 28 May 1913: 240/3/5.

Goldenberg until he resigned.[418] The ʿĪsās' solidarity with the influential Ashkenazi Goldenberg, for them a model of a well-integrated Jewish immigrant, is an example of the distinction they made between 'Jews' and 'Zionists', a principle that they upheld until the end of their publication period before World War I.

8. The Debate Ends: Towards a Political Campaign against the 'Zionist Danger'

This section demonstrates, using various examples from what authors published in *Filasṭīn*, the shift that took place during 1913 in the press debate on Zionism, which was quite open to controversial views, and its final turn into a full blown campaign against the 'Zionist danger', which was now perceived as a serious political threat on various levels. The debate on the mills at al-Ǧarīša on the Yarkon River around the turn of the years 1912–1913 had a direct impact on relations between the Sephardi and Christian elites in the Jerusalem District, as has already been noted. It particularly changed the relationship between *Filasṭīn*'s editors and the Sephardi *Ḥerut* circle. Furthermore, the matter of the transfer of the lands at Kafr Urīya and Abū Šūša in the end of 1912 had a deep effect on the Palestinian debate on Zionism and opened the way for a campaign against Zionist policies from the first half of 1913 onwards. A contributing factor was the absence of a governor in the District around the same time, which enabled the JN to purchase considerable plots of land in Palestine between November 1912 and March 1913. The influence of these land transactions *and* the echo of the Balkan Wars as a threat to the Empire's integrity changed the tone of the press debate on Zionism dramatically. Since the coverage on Zionism during 1913–1914 has been thoroughly documented in detail in the latest work by Beška (2016), what follows here will only briefly explain where I see the main shifts during 1913 and 1914 and the underlying reasons that I have identified.

The Discursive Shift from Economic Rivalry to Political and Demographic Danger

As a consequence of the offensive against the Ottomans by Serbia, Montenegro, Bulgaria and Greece in Macedonia and Thrace in 1912, the Empire lost all of its Balkan territories. The policies of the Zionist Movement in Palestine were reconsidered in the context of these losses, and this pushed the debate in *Filasṭīn* to another dimension. More letters than before linked Zionism with a movement of political separatists at the heart of the Empire, who were simply waiting for a chance to obtain national sovereignty. While the Zionist Movement had pre-

418 *Filasṭīn*, 20 September 1913: 273/2/4–5.

viously been discussed in the context of rivalries over local economic resources, it started to be portrayed as a political threat. From 1913 onwards, Zionism was increasingly presented as a form of European nationalism with territorial claims in the Middle East. In the Balkans, the 'national hopes' (*āmāl qawmīya*) of the Serbs and other nations had come to fruition since they had developed in a political 'vacuum', one author said (in an article reprinted from *al-Muqtabas*) and he warned that Zionism might pursue the same goal in Palestine.[419] A growing number of articles in *Filasṭīn* now stressed the *political* dimension of Zionist immigration and land purchases. The systematic seizure of Palestine was discussed, some authors even fearing the expulsion of the local Arab population. Authors predicted a future struggle for political hegemony in Palestine with consequences for the Empire. In the context of the transfer of land at Kafr Urīya und Abū Šūša to the JN and a vacuum caused by the absence of a governor in the Jerusalem District during winter of 1912–1913, ʿĀrif al-ʿĀrif from Gaza predicted the Zionist seizure of Palestine, which he compared to the Ottoman territorial losses in Northern Africa and the Balkans:

> Am I dreaming or am I awake? Is it true what I am hearing, or is it fantasy and pipe dreams (*aḍġāṯ al-aḥlām*)?[420] Yesterday, the land of Kafr Urīya was sold, today the village of Abū Šūša. It will not be long before the Zionists take possession of our land, village by village, city by city (*qaryatan qaryatan baldatan baldatan*). Tomorrow, all Jerusalem and the whole of Palestine will be sold off (*tubāʿ al-Quds bi-aǧmaʿihā wa-Filasṭīn bi-kullīyatihā*), and if we don't pay attention to the issue, the Porte will be exposed to what it experienced in Tripoli or the Balkans.[421]

Another author predicted, in an article reprinted from *al-Mufīd*, that the Zionists were about to 'seize Palestine, village by village' (*al-istīlāʾ ʿalā Filasṭīn al-qarya baʿd al-qarya*), while the authorities ignored what was happening.[422] Being impressed by the loss of the Balkans, he announced a real struggle for survival in Palestine as part of the Ottoman realms:

> Is Palestine not part of the Ottoman homeland (*laysat ǧuzʾan min al-waṭan al-ʿuṯmānī*)? Does the Zionist seizure not harm the Porte in general and the Arabs in particular? Why don't you raise your voices and protest to stand against this devastating flow (*haḏā at-tayyār al-muhlik*)? I am surprised and I wonder how you [dare] on the one hand to demand life and, on the other, put up with this worm that is gnawing on the body of the homeland (*tataḥammalūn as-sūs allaḏi yanḫur fī ǧism al-waṭan*). If the homeland is gone, what kind of life do we have?... Will you stay silent until you become a minority in Palestine (*ḥattā taṣīrū fī Filasṭīn aqallīya*) and until what happened in Macedonia happens to you? Wake up, you Ottomans (*afīqū ayyuhā l-ʿuṯmānīyūn*)... if you demand

419 *Filasṭīn*, 25 December 1912: 200/4/2.
420 The phrase *aḍġāṯ al-aḥlām* is quoted from Sūrat Yūsuf in Quran 12: 44.
421 *Filasṭīn*, 25 January 1913: 207/3/4.
422 *Filasṭīn*, 21 December 1912: 199/4/1.

> life. Otherwise, there will be no longer be any life under the occupation of the foreigner (*iḥtilāl al-ağnabī*).[423]

Another author also predicted a struggle for survival in Palestine since the Zionists were seeking to make it a 'Jewish country'. He announced that the Zionists aimed to

> dissolve the country out of the hands of its rightful inhabitants and bring it into the hands of the settlers, so the original, lazy and simple [local] will disappear in favor of the immigrant and the active worker, so that Palestine will become again, as it was once, a Jewish country from which Muslims and Christians are forced to depart, struggling to survive.[424]

Several other authors, at this point, started to discuss the shifting demography caused by Zionist immigration to Palestine. An unknown author stated that 'one-fifth of the land' was already in the hands of Zionists who constituted 'one-seventh of the population'.[425] In 1914, the population of all three Palestinian provinces was about 722,000. Assuming that one-seventh of them were Zionists, they would have numbered more than 100,000, which exceeds by far the actual number of Ottoman *and* foreign Jews in pre-World War I Palestine. It also must be stressed that not all the Jews in Palestine, whether Ottomans or foreigners, were Zionists. Thus, this statement was exaggerated, but it did follow a general trend among Palestinians and Zionists alike, who tended to give inflated figures for the number of Jews of late Ottoman Palestine in order to highlight the fact that the Jewish population was about to gain considerable political weight.[426]

Palestine as a 'Jewish Country' and an Extension of Western Imperialism in the Middle East

The ʿĪsās, too, changed their tone dramatically after the spring of 1913. They stopped merely providing a forum of debate and actively contributed to the anti-Zionist campaign. In April 1913, Yūsuf al-ʿĪsā claimed that, including the prov-

423 *Filasṭīn*, 21 December 1912: 199/4/1.

424 '*Yuḥāwilūn taḫlīṣ al-bilād min īday ahlihā aṣ-ṣādiqīn ilā īday al-mustaʿmirīn li-yafnī l-aṣīl al-ḫāmil al-basīṭ fī daḫīl al-ʿāmil an-našīṭ wa-tarğaʿ Filasṭīn kamā kānat fī awwal amrihā bilādan yahūdīyan yuḍṭarr ilā hağrihā bi-ḥukm tanāzuʿ al-baqāʾ al-muslim wa-l-masīḥī.*' *Filasṭīn*, 25 December 1912: 200/4/2.

425 *Filasṭīn*, 25 December 1912: 200/4/2. The article, written in the context of the sale of lands belonging to the villages of Karkūr and Bīdūs, was reprinted from the Damascene newspaper *al-Muqtabas*, published by Muḥammad Kurd ʿAlī (1876–1953) in cooperation with Šukrī al-ʿAsalī (1868–1916), the anti-Zionist and former *qāʾimaqām* of Nazareth, who had initiated a protest campaign against the sale of the lands of al-Fūla in 1911.

426 Krämer has observed a tendency among historians to overstate the number of Jews who lived in pre-World War I Palestine. Among the 722,000 people living in 1914 in Palestine, according to the census by Metzer, 602,000 were Muslims (83 percent), 81,000 Christians (11.2 percent) and 39,000 Ottoman (!) Jews (i.e. 5 percent). Krämer 2002, 165, n. 21, 395.

inces of Acre and Nablus, there were '100,000 Zionists of different nationalities who possessed great knowledge and competences', an unrealistic number, like those referred to above.[427] In the light of the demographic threat felt from the Zionist presence, ʿĪsā predicted that, if another 20,000 Zionists adopted Ottoman citizenship, they would achieve dominant status as a result of their property ownership, and 'gain the majority' (*iktisāb al-akṯarīya*) in the city councils. He feared that, if the Zionists dominated the political institutions, 'Palestine will in practice become Jewish in the most powerless way' (*fa-tuṣbiḥ Filasṭīn yahūdīya fiʿlan ʿalā ahwan sabīl*).[428]

This quotation demonstrates that the space for open debate closed during the first half of 1913. Public opinion consolidated in the belief that a serious demographic, political and territorial threat to Palestine came from Zionism, and this was also reflected in shifts in terminology. Zionism was frequently equated with a 'danger' (*ḫaṭr*); thus, the Empire was 'in danger' from what had happened in the Balkans, and people felt that Palestine was put into danger by the Zionist seizure. This is reflected in the titles of articles in *Filasṭīn*, as a range of examples demonstrate.[429] In May 1913, when Zionist settlers purchased land that had been available for communal use near the village al-Muḫayzin in the Ramla region,[430] the ʿĪsās pleaded for the courts to have 'empathy' (*ḥusn wiǧdān*) and protect local farmers, complaining about the monopolization of Palestine by the Zionists, who were doing everything 'to seize power over the land and its economic resources' (*li-qabḍ ʿalā aʿinnat al-bilād wa-mawāridihā l-iqtiṣādīya*).[431]

With growing public awareness for the political impact of Zionism on Palestine, *Filasṭīn*'s articles on the issue started to compare the Zionist Movement to a European nationalist movement in the heart of the Empire, and, from the first half of 1913 onwards, portrayed it as the arm of imperialist states extended into the Middle East. The ʿĪsās were especially critical of German policies in the Middle East. They complained that German newspapers promoted emigration to Syria and Palestine, portraying them as a 'run-down' and 'empty' area that would

427 *Filasṭīn*, 19 April 1913: 231/1/3.

428 *Filasṭīn*, 19 April 1913: 231/1/4.

429 See the editorial 'The Homeland Is in Danger' (*al-Waṭan fī l-Ḫaṭr*), in *Filasṭīn*, 15 February 1913: 213/1/1–3. See also the poem entitled 'The Zionist Danger' (*al-Ḫaṭr aṣ-Ṣihyūnī*) by Sulaymān at-Tāǧǧī, which included anti-Semitic elements, in *Filasṭīn*, 8 November 1913: 287/2/3–4, and the article 'The Works of the Zionists' (*Aʿmāl aṣ-Ṣihyūnīyīn*), focusing on Zionist immigrants with foreign citizenship who, as their countries' protégés, enjoyed 'privileges' (*imtiyāzāt*) in Palestine, and the new dimensions of these privileges in the light of the 'Zionist danger', in *Filasṭīn*, 17 December 1913: 292/4/3. See too a letter from a Muslim in Jaffa, entitled 'The Zionist Danger for Palestine' (*al-Ḫaṭr aṣ-Ṣihyūnī ʿalā Filasṭīn*), referring to increasing Zionist immigration through Jaffa's port. *Filasṭīn*, 27 December 1913: 294/1/5–2/3.

430 For the case of al-Muḫayzin, see Khalidi 1992, 398; Beška 2016c, 79–80.

431 *Filasṭīn*, 28 May 1913: 240/3/2–3.

rise from lethargy through German settlement. This was translated from the German press and the ʿĪsās warned that Germany was seeking to make Palestine 'a European colony under German influence'.[432] They warned several times that the German government was instrumentalizing the WZO to secure influence in the Holy Land, and promoting the Zionists to make them 'pioneers of its interests' (*ruwwādan li-maṣāliḥihā*), and they also observed that German institutions were encouraging the use of German as a leading language in the New Yishuv, which caused conflicts in the context of the Jewish 'language struggle'.[433]

The Reception of the 'Crown Lands Sale' and the Zarnuqa Incident

The fact that, from 1913 onwards, Zionism was perceived not only as an economic rival but also as a serious political threat on a national level was demonstrated in the campaign by Palestinian notables against the sale of the Crown Lands in the summer of 1913. The 'national conference' that was called for as a united political initiative by the economic elites of all the Palestinian districts did not take place in the form that authors had demanded in *Filasṭīn*. However, a conference that was organized in the fall of 1913 by a group of notables in Nablus and attended by many visitors, indicates that there were attempts to establish regional cooperation against the sale of land to Zionist organizations. The echo of the 'Crown Lands' Affair' in *Filasṭīn* indicates that Zionist settlement and land purchases were perceived as a political matter of 'national' importance and that resistance to Zionism now extended across the borders of the various Palestinian districts – which had not previously been the case in the debate over Zionism in *Filasṭīn*. While the al-Fūla affair of 1911, a cornerstone in early Arab responses to Zionism, left no echoes in *Filasṭīn*, the Crown Lands Affair was met with intense interest in the Jerusalem District and was extensively covered in *Filasṭīn*. I conclude from this that the resistance to the sale of land to Zionists started to connect anti-Zionists beyond the former geographical borders. At this point, the Zionist Congress in Vienna, held in the fall of 1913, was covered by six pieces in *Filasṭīn*, including articles reprinted from the Jewish press and readers' comments.[434] The Zionist movement was now perceived as a political actor with a nationalist agenda and international networks.

Another turn in the debate on Zionism that was maybe even more important, occurred in the context of the 'Zarnuqa incident', during the summer and fall of 1913. It involved an escalation of violence between rural Palestinians and Zionist

432 *Filasṭīn*, 30 November 1912: 193/1/4–2/2. For the ambivalent relations between German colonists and the Palestinian population, see Carmel 1973, 238–258, and 1975, 446–455.

433 *Filasṭīn*, 24 September 1913: 274/2/2–3.

434 *Filasṭīn*, 10 September 1913: 270/3/1–2; 13 September 1913: 271/1/3–5; 1 October 1913: 276/2/2; 4 October 1913: 1913: 277/3/4–5; 5 November 1913: 286/2/1–2; and 8 November 1913: 287/2/1–3.

settlers and was sparked by a fight between Arab camel drivers and the *ha-shomer* (Hebr. 'the Guardian'), an organization of Jewish-Russian guards known for their harsh behavior towards the local people, on the road between Rishon le-Tzion and Reḥovot over a handful of grapes stolen from the colony's vineyards.[435] The incident has been evaluated by Beška through *Filasṭīn*, and by Ben-Bassat and Alroey using different narratives on the incident,[436] who have interpreted it as a 'milestone in the annals of Zionist–Arab relations'.[437] Most historical sources on Arab–Jewish encounters leave the researcher with the difficulty that they do not represent the views of all the actors involved.[438] The accounts on the Zarnuqa incident are outstanding as they include the narratives of colonists, hired guards, travelers, the Jewish and Arab press, and Arab villagers.[439] Alroey examines the incident in the context of the policy of the *ha-shomer*, who called for the 'conquest of guardianship' (Hebr. *kibbush ha-shmira*) through a 'blood and honor' rhetoric and saw in the revenge for the Arab theft an act of national defense.[440] Alroey argues that the *ha-shomer* had imported 'terrorist' behavior that characterized defense patterns of the revolutionary underground socialist cells in Tsarist Russia during the anti-Jewish pogroms,[441] and explains the mentality of the guards as one reason for the escalation. Afterwards, the colony ended the contract with the *ha-shomer*, who were expelled from Reḥovot.[442]

The Zarnuqa incident led to the involvement of local and central authorities, representatives from Zarnuqa and Ramla, and David Moyal from Jaffa, the Mufti of Gaza and Albert Antébi from Jerusalem, and Jewish and Arab journalists.

435 The *ha-shomer* was established as an organization in 1909 in Kfar Tavor; it was based on Bar Giora, a secret organization of young motivated Russian-Jewish watchmen from Tsarist Russia, who dedicated themselves to protecting Jewish colonies in Palestine. Shafir explains the *ha-shomer* as being the 'vanguard in the conquest of labor' that demanded from the Moshavot and Kibbutzim that their Jewish workers take part in guarding Jewish settlement. Up to 1912, the *ha-shomer* spread from the Galilee to the Jerusalem District and was invited into most settlements, where it replaced former Arab watchmen and took over the armed protection of the colonies' fields and vineyards. It remained an autonomous organization until 1920, when it was absorbed into the defense force of the Histadrut, the Haganah (Hebr. 'Defense'), the main defense forces during the British Mandate. See Shafir 1996, 135–145, and especially 136, on the 'identity of soldier and settler, 1907–14'.

436 Beška 2016, 96–100; Ben-Bassat and Alroey 2016d, 787–803.

437 Ben-Bassat and Alroey 2016, 787.

438 See Ben-Bassat 2009a, 43–44, and 2016d, 788.

439 That is, accounts from the *ha-shomer* archives, reports from the Hebrew newspapers *Ha-Poel ha-Tza'ir*, *Ha-Ahdut* and *Ha-Tzfira*, and the notes of the colonist and historian Moshe Smilansky from Reḥovot. Ben-Bassat and Alroey 2016d, 788–792.

440 According to Alroey, the history of the *ha-shomer* has an important status in Zionist historiography and has been interpreted as the revolutionary core of the Israeli Defense Forces (IDF). For the history of the Bar Giora, the *ha-shomer* and their status in Zionist historiography, see Goldstein 1998; Alroey 2013, 31f.

441 See Alroey 2013, 31–60.

442 Alroey 2013, 38f.

Filasṭīn covered the event in 19 articles from July 1913 until August 1914.[443] The case reveals the deep rupture between Arab villagers and a new generation of ideologically motivated colonists. It all started when an Arab caravan, coming from the direction of Jaffa, passed the road between Rishon Le-Tzion and Nes Ziona that leads towards Reḥovot. One camel driver, apparently from Zarnuqa, was caught by a Jewish guard stealing grapes from a vineyard belonging to Rishon Le-Tzion or Nes Tziona, which led to a 'small fight' (*maʿraka saġīra*) between them, as *Filasṭīn* called it.[444] In the course of the event, the camel driver took the the guard's pistol and escaped southwards, and the guard sent for help from watchmen from Rishon le-Tzion, Nes Zionah and Reḥovot, who chased the camel drivers. Near Reḥovot, the guards were approached by farmers from Zarnuqa (where the camel drivers had clearly taken refuge) and Bedouins. The encounter escalated into fighting with sticks and shooting between the two parties, which ended with several injured and one dead on each side. After the incident, the Mufti of Gaza, Aḥmad ʿĀrif al-Ḥusaynī, Jewish representatives, the *ḥāḫāmbāšī* of Jaffa and Albert Antébi met in an effort to prevent further escalations.[445] There was also immediate reaction from Arab villagers: on 29 July, dozens of villagers from the Gazan *qaḍāʾ* and a semi-nomadic group who were settled near the Yarkon sent a joint petition to the Grand Vizierate in Istanbul, complaining about the danger to the public from Jewish hired guards in the settlements since they were illegally equipped with guns and pistols, controlled the roads, and threatened, robbed or even murdered local people who passed by. The courts in Gaza and Jaffa had already sentenced some guards but the wanted men had escaped 'to Russia or Europe', the petitioners claimed. They asked for the confiscation of illegal weapons from the settlers, complaining that they 'do whatever they want, as if they have a little government of their own inside the country'.[446]

As an echo of the 'Zarnuqa incident', a press dispute that included several actors evolved in *Filasṭīn*. From Ramla, Fāris an-Naʿāma commented dramatically on the incident, blaming all the aggression on the Jewish colonists who 'flocked together' against the village of Zarnuqa.[447] Naʿāma complained that this act of aggression abused the hospitality of the 'sons of the country and real owners of the land' (*abnāʾ al-waṭan al-aṣlī wa-mullāk al-bilād al-ḥaqīqīyīn*). In Naʿāma's version, the Jewish immigrants had come like wolfs who tore apart the sons of the country like sheep, and he called Reḥovot the 'key of strife and evil' (*miftāḥ al-fitna wa-bustūs aš-šarr*).[448] The Sephardi lawyer David Moyal from

443 Beška 2016, 96.
444 *Filasṭīn*, 26 July 1913: 257/3/4.
445 *Filasṭīn*, 9 August 1913: 261/3/1–2.
446 Ben-Bassat 2013d, 223–225; Ben-Bassat and Alroey 2016d, 792–793.
447 *Filasṭīn*, 30 August 1913: 267/2/1 f.
448 *Filasṭīn*, 2 August 1913: 259/2/3–3/1.

Jaffa responded to Naʿāma's accusation with a counter-narrative according to which it was the Arabs who had started the aggression while the Jews had tried to prevent violence by peaceful negotiation.[449] Moyal said that the Jewish victim, Shmu'el Friedman from Reḥovot, had been killed at the border between Reḥovot and the Arab village of Qubayba, more than half an hour from Zarnuqa, where more than a hundred villagers and Bedouins had attacked the Jewish guards, and the murder could not be seen as an act of self-defense. People from Reḥovot had only arrived later to help the guards after the emergency bell had been rung when Friedman was found. At this point, the editors brought the dispute between Moyal and Naʿāma to an end, saying that the legal aspects were to be judged by the court, not the press.[450] An anonymous Jew from Jaffa intervened, accusing the teacher of the Muslim school Dār al-ʿUlūm ('House of Science'), Musṭafā Mağdī, of inciting the people of Zarnuqa during a school feast to 'slaughter' the Jews. The ʿĪsās reacted angrily. They responded to the author, saying that 'the Zionist intruders' had exploited 'our tolerance' (*tasāhulinā*): first, they arrived in Palestine 'expelled, barefoot and humiliated' (*maṭrūdīn muhāfīn uḏalāʾ*) and then they behaved as if they were 'our masters' and claimed that 'we were fanatical, brutal and hateful' in order to attract European attention by claiming that 'we want to slaughter them'.[451] This was, by the way, the only time, the ʿĪsās took a stand with regard to the Zarnuqa incident; they did not take an active role or initiate a campaign against Reḥovot.[452]

In November 1913, *Filasṭīn* reported that a reconciliation (*ṣulḥ*) between Reḥovot and Zarnuqa had been reached. After the mediation of Ḫalīl and ʿUṯmān al-ʿIzza from Jaffa, a delegation of forty members from Reḥovot arrived in Zarnuqa and brought five sheep, five *raṭl* (pounds) of clarified butter (*samn*) and a sack of rice as a peace offering. Now, the parties agreed that there were 'Maghrebis as well as Bedouins' among the guards who were responsible for the shooting. At least with regard to the Maghrebis, we have already seen that they were social outsiders, so it was definitely a convenient compromise for all the parties to the conflict to attribute the crime to them.[453] Although the ʿĪsās did even not take an active role in the press dispute about the Zarnuqa incident, it is also a mile stone in *Filasṭīn*'s debate on Zionism since, after this incident, Jewish

449 *Filasṭīn*, 20 August 1913: 264/3/2f.

450 *Filasṭīn*, 30 August 1913: 267/2/1f.

451 *Filasṭīn*, 27 August 1913: 266/2/3–4.

452 In contrast, Sulaymān at-Tāğğī al-Fārūqī, a merchant and landowner, directed an open letter to the governor in which he spoke out against Jewish land acquisition, claiming to speak for 'Palestinian public opinion' (*ar-raʾy al-ʿāmm al-filasṭīnī*), and he interpreted the theft of grapes as a desperate act of protest by the people of Zarnuqa against the usurpation of their land by Reḥovot. See *Filasṭīn*, 30 August 1913: 267/2 – Supplement *Mulḥaq*/1–4.

453 *Filasṭīn*, 1 November 1913: 285/3/1–2.

authors, as far as I saw it, ceased to publish their comments in *Filasṭīn*. I can not tell if this was a direct reaction of the violence that occurred in the Zarnuqa incident or not. However, in the end of 1913, Jews simply disappeared from the pool of authors who had contributed before to make *Filasṭīn* a shared project.

January 1914: the Zionist Movement Seen as the 'External Enemy'

The last and the most important discursive turn before World War I occurred at the beginning of 1914, when the ʿĪsās lost their role as leaders of the local Arab Orthodox in the anti-clerical campaign against the Patriarchate, outlined in chapter III. It was explained there that the ʿĪsās' initial agenda was to support the Orthodox Renaissance and win the public over to its cause in *Filasṭīn*. From 1914, the anti-Zionist opposition in *Filasṭīn*, which had increased since 1913, burst into a full-blown anti-Zionist campaign driven by the editors from the moment they were forced by the Ottoman authorities to step down from the Orthodox campaign. I have identified 362 articles or items on Zionism published in *Filasṭīn* between 1911 and 1914, of which 122 were published from January to August 1914 and the other 250 during the years 1911 to 1913, which show how much reporting on Zionism in *Filasṭīn* increased during 1914.

I have concluded that the anti-Zionist campaign in *Filasṭīn* from 1914 onwards was a side effect rather than calculated. The ʿĪsās always presented *Filasṭīn* to its readers as 'the mouthpiece of the people' in general, and 'the mouthpiece of the Orthodox' in particular. The ʿĪsās were proud to have built up a well-known forum for exchange and debate between Palestinian intellectuals of different confessions. At the beginning of 1914 and after a legal case and the temporary closure of *Filasṭīn*, a serious confrontation with the authorities – especially with Governor Māǧid Bek and ʿAzmī Bek, head of the Royal Commission from Istanbul to intervene in the Arab-Orthodox conflict – forced the ʿĪsās to implement a 180 degree turn in their coverage of the Orthodox cause, and so they almost completely avoided the subject. *Filasṭīn* published 407 items on it from 1911 to 1913, but 45 in 1914, and they were written in a dry informative style and without personal statements. This complete turn-around put them at risk of losing their credibility as 'educators of the nation' and as the combative activists for the Orthodox Renaissance that they had been before. Their withdrawal from the Arab Orthodox campaign meant that the ʿĪsās faced a vacuum to fill in terms of content in *Filasṭīn* and the challenge of maintaining the newspaper's former combative character and their own credibility as serious journalists.

Meanwhile, the Zionist movement was coming to be perceived as a political enemy in Palestine. Thus, the ʿĪsās could freely express their opposition to Zionism without being censored, and without risking provoking another confrontation with important local political players or the authorities, such as the Jerusalem governor, the *qāʾimaqām* of Jaffa or the Patriarch. The Zionist movement as an external, and therefore 'safe, enemy', provided the ʿĪsās with a new and welcome campaign cause. An anti-Zionist discourse was consolidating during the same period among the Palestinian public, and the issue of Zionism was, in terms of domestic politics, a 'safe battlefield' where the ʿĪsās' struggle for reform and emancipation in Palestine could be continued.

The Full Blown anti-Zionist Battle during 1914

How was this 'safe battle' fought in *Filasṭīn*? From the beginning of 1914, *Filasṭīn* started carefully to observe the political strategies of the Zionist movement as a powerful international actor. Before 1914, the hot topics of the debate were the 'economic exclusiveness' of Zionist settlements, especially Rishon le-Tzion, Reḥovot and Petaḥ Tikva, and the sale of land to Zionist organizations, and they were debated by a spectrum of authors from different confessional backgrounds and positions, and without the ʿĪsās necessarily interfering. From 1914 onwards, the coverage on the issue was now an anti-Zionist battle, driven by anti-Zionist authors alone, while the defenders and supporters of Zionism disappeared from this point on. It is not clear why they did so; they either boycotted *Filasṭīn* or their contributions were refused.

Now, latest developments in the international Zionist movement were covered weekly in *Filasṭīn* and Zionist activities in Palestine dominated the 'Local News' section. In April 1914, the editors apologized that 'the great part, especially the Local News, revolves around Zionism and the Zionists', declaring that, since they found themselves in Jaffa surrounded by the Zionist movement, they thought it was 'our journalistic mission to report on its news and activities'.[454] To underscore this, they reprinted a telegram that the 'progressive youth' (*aš-šabība ar-rāqiya*) had written to the Grand Vizier, in which they complained that the Zionists in Jaffa 'are a government within a government' (*ḥukūma ḍimna ḥukūma*).[455] The coverage on Zionism was now dominated by articles reprinted from other newspapers that documented the network of Zionist leaders in Europe, the WZO's budget strategies, the situation of world Jewry, foreign Zionist delegations' meetings with Jewish representatives in Palestine, and the financial resources that the Zionist movement was investing in the building of the New Yishuv.[456] In this context, the Zionist donors' support for the Yishuv was closely observed. From February–April 1914, at least 14 articles reported on Baron

454 *Filasṭīn*, 4 April 1914: 321/3/2.

455 *Filasṭīn*, 4 April 1914: 321/3/3–4. This telegram was written in the context of the 'Tel Aviv Incident', when an Arab Palestinian farmer, who became involved in a dispute with a Jew while selling coal in Tel Aviv, was 'kidnapped' by Jewish guards and detained inside the Hebrew Gymnasium. *Filasṭīn*, 21 February 1914: 309/3/2; *Filasṭīn*, 28 February 1914: 311/3/3. See also the evaluation of the case in Beška 2016, 103–106.

456 See examples in *Filasṭīn*, 11 February 1914: 306/3/4; and 14 February 1914: 307/1/3–4.

Rothschild's donations and his meetings with delegations in Jewish settlements, schools and associations, etc. were published.[457] Rothschild also donated for non-Jewish institutions. Interestingly, he gave Jaffa's Muslim 'Society for Piety and Welfare' (*Ǧamaʿīyat al-Birr wa-l-Iḥsān*) 250 lira and donated 2,000 francs through the Jaffa branch of the JCA for the Ottoman fleet.[458]

Filasṭīn also investigated Zionism in new ways and translated Jewish leaders' statements on Zionism as a national ideology; for instance, the article 'An Appeal and a Beginning for the Jewish Nation in the World' (*Nidāʾ wa-Stibdāʾ li-l-Umma al-Yahūdīya fī l-ʿĀlam*), reprinted from a Zionist newspaper, addressed the national pride of the Jewish individual and the Jews as a collective.[459] The ʿĪsās also interviewed local notables on their personal views regarding Zionism; for instance the MP Ḥāfiẓ as-Saʿīd from Jaffa, and the pedagogue Ḫalīl as-Sakākīnī from Jerusalem, who thought that the real goal of the Zionist movement in its geographical focus on Palestine was to split the 'Arab nation' (*al-umma al-ʿarabīya*) in two halves, since Palestine was situated between the Arabian Peninsula and Africa.[460] In a special edition in April 1914, the editors mocked the 'contradictions' in a speech by Rothschild, in which he elaborated on peaceful coexistence between Zionists and Muslims in Palestine and criticized boycotts of the Zionists.[461] In a special eleven-page edition in June[462] dedicated to the Zionist question, the ʿĪsās reprinted at length contributions from the Arab press that commented on the latest developments in the Zionist movement or compared official statements of Zionist leaders with the current situation in Palestine.[463]

In July-August 1914, the ʿĪsās dedicated extensive space to the political program of Menachem Ussishkin (1863–1941), the chair of the Hovevei Zion Committee since 1906 and a leader of political Zionism in Russia, which he had

457 For instance, see *Filasṭīn*, 7 February 1914: 305/3/3; 11 February 1914: 306/3/4; 14 February 1914: 307/2/5; 18 February 1914: 308/2/1–2; 18 February 1914: 308/3/2; 21 February 1914: 309/3/2; 4 March 1914: 312/3/1; 7 March 1914: 313/3/3; 8 April 1914: 322/2/4; 11 April 1914 – Mulhaq (special edition) – 323/2/1.

458 *Filasṭīn*, 4 March 1914: 312/3/1; 7 March 1914: 313/3/3.

459 *Filasṭīn*, 1 April 1914: 320/2/1–2.

460 *Filasṭīn*, 4 April 1914: 321/1/1–4.

461 *Filasṭīn*, 11 April 1914: 323 – Mulḥaq (special edition) 323/2/1–5.

462 This, according to the appendix in Beška 2016, 148. I only had nine pages of this issue from 6 June 1914 at my disposal.

463 To give a few examples from this special edition: A long contribution of more than one-and-a-half pages by one Ibrāhīm Salīm an-Naǧǧār elaborated on the latest results of Jewish immigration into Palestine and was reprinted from *Al-Ahrām*. *Filasṭīn*, 6 June 1914: 325/3/1–4/4. One Rafīq al-ʿAẓm wrote an extended comment on 'The Zionists and the Arabs', quoting Zionist leader Nachum Solokov, in an article reprinted from the Egyptian *al-Muqaṭṭam*. *Filasṭīn*, 6 June 1914: 325/4/3–5/2. A long editorial by Naǧīb an-Naṣṣār entitled 'Zionism Is Either a Great Danger or a Good Example' was reprinted from *al-Karmil*, in *Filasṭīn*, 6 June 1914: 325/6/2–5.

published in 1904 under the title 'Our Program'.[464] They published Ussishkin's program in five chapters – the first systematic Arabic translation of the political program of the Zionist movement in the Arab press since Naǧīb an-Naṣṣār's booklet 'Zionism', which was published as a series of articles in *al-Karmil* in 1911 and was a translation and commentary on Gottheil's article in the Jewish Encyclopedia (1905).[465] In July 1914, *Filasṭīn* published on the front page 'A Bedouin of Palestine' (*Badawī Filasṭīn*), a patriotic poem by an anonymous author opposing the 'Zionist danger'.[466] I assume that this contribution was not from a Bedouin but probably from the editors, who would have meant to send a signal that awareness of the Zionist 'danger' had reached the lower segments of Palestinian society. Whoever was the author, the poem shows that the opposition to political Zionism was a central starting point for the development of a distinct Palestinian patriotism just before the outbreak of World War I. It is also a signal that the debate on Zionism in *Filasṭīn* was over by the beginning of 1914. Now, there was only space for contributions that re-asserted that the Zionist question put Palestine economically, demographically and politically under a serious threat. The following quotation by the Orthodox Ǧūrǧī al-Ḫūrī Ayūb demonstrates that the space for approving Zionism was closed by summer 1914:

> Those who applaud the Zionist movement in Palestine and say that it is for the benefit [of Palestine] are of two kinds: The first is stupid and does not realise the dreadful consequences for citizens and the economic, social and political damage that would result from it. The second is bad and mean without knowing it. However, his meanness makes him support those who seek to seize his country and the home of his ancestors for money. The first needs to be warned, and the second needs to be battered.[467]

To conclude from this that, by 1914, the 'modernization imperative' was no longer a credible argument that could be used by promoters of Zionism in the Arab press. The public discourse had turned against the Zionist movement as a power undermining local development, and as a serious political danger. In 1914, the debate ended for good. It is also striking that *Filasṭīn*'s coverage of the Zionist question now very heavily depended on articles reprinted from other newspapers, translations of political programs, and readers' contributions. However, and interestingly, the ʿĪsās personally hardly contributed to it anymore! What had happened to the character of *Filasṭīn* as a protest forum? This question remains unsolved. It is clear that, in 1914, *Filasṭīn* was at the forefront of the anti-Zionist battle and had established itself as a leading newspaper in Palestinian

464 *Filasṭīn*, 15 July 1914: 336/3/3f.; 18 July 1914: 337/3/3f.; 22 July 1914: 338/3/3f.; 25 July 1914: 339/3/3f.; 1 August 1914: 341/3/3f.

465 See the evaluation and comparison between both by of Beška 2016, 107–114.

466 *Filasṭīn*, 15 July 1914: 336/1/4–5.

467 *Filasṭīn*, 6 June 1914: 325/5/2–3.

journalism. However, the passion and personal engagement of the ʿĪsās that was seen with regard to the Orthodox cause, or the question of the Maghrebi outsiders, is missing in this full-blown anti-Zionist coverage, which, from 1914 onwards, seems very static and definitely not creative.

V. Conclusion

This study has explored how identity and ethno-confessional relations were negotiated in late Ottoman Palestine, with a geographical focus on the Jerusalem District, particularly the region between Jaffa and Jerusalem. Based on 1,895 articles or items extracted from *Filasṭīn*'s coverage from 1911–1914, this micro-study analyses local debates on 1. the social cohabitation of groups in the Jaffa *qaḍāʾ*, 2. the socio-economic integration of Zionist immigrants into the Jerusalem District, and 3. the political participation of Arab Palestinian Orthodox Christians in the Greek Orthodox Patriarchate of Jerusalem. In the light of these press debates in *Filasṭīn*, it looks at how 'late Ottoman modernity' was translated in Palestine during the years before World War I, when central concepts regarding politics and society-building throughout the Ottoman realms were deeply transformed. This is relevant since this moment in time may be seen as a little 'saddle period' (Sattelzeit) of its own, to use Kosellek's concept, in the reshaping of group relations in the Arab East generally and in Palestine in particular, in the context of the late Ottoman world between the age of modernity and 'Cataclysm', the end of the Ottoman world during the 1910s which has been considered as a decade of 'catastrophic change'.

Central for this study has been the analysis of communication patterns observed in *Filasṭīn*'s coverage. *Filasṭīn* may be seen as a platform for intellectual exchange, not as the personal platform of its editors, in which a pool of publishing authors from different communities controversially discussed and contributed to new discourses on group relations. Thus, I have explored *Filasṭīn* as a 'communication channel' between editors and readers, between government and readers, and between readers and readers. This approach has helped to distinguish between different actors' levels, and to follow the 'communication flow' in a debate. This means discerning who was speaking and who was addressed and considering whether an issue discussed in *Filasṭīn* was part of a campaign driven by the editors, or a controversy between different actors.

With regard to the discourse applied in a debate, the 'order of what to say or not to say', the study picked out central concepts conveyed through *Filasṭīn* by looking into the 'mindset' of the contributing authors: the set of moral values reflecting their ideals. It has been pursued how these concepts were reflected in forms of language, and how they overlapped in different fields of debate, which has given an insight into how concepts 'travelled' between regions or content issues. In this way and in the frame of the three specific fields mentioned above, the study has analyzed chronologically the major shifts that occurred in the debates from 1911 to 1914 as a 'saddle period', while taking into account the impact of broader trends on local relations. Further, it was relevant in the press debates to distinguish between 'discourse' and the 'reality' of group relations where this was possible. The contributing authors in *Filasṭīn* were individuals primarily representing themselves, although they might have claimed to speak for a certain community. It should be borne in mind that, behind their argument, there was an agenda influenced by practical considerations such as political networks and economic dependencies. On the other hand, a lot of information about social cohabitation or conflicts in the Jerusalem District was diffused through articles without having a direct voice from the actors; for example, the pro-clerical spectrum did not contribute to the debate on the Orthodox cause in *Filasṭīn*.

Chapter I analyzed how a circle of authors from different confessional but similar social and educational backgrounds who published in *Filasṭīn* sought to 'educate the nation' in the 'spirit of the age' (*rūḥ hāḏā al-ʿaṣr*). They promoted, above all, reform and modernization, constitutionalism, Ottoman unity and brotherhood, and notions of the public sphere. Chapter II framed the Jaffa region as an 'ethno-confessional contact zone' and the context from which *Filasṭīn* emerged, with regard to patterns of socio-economic interrelations and ethno-social conflicts. It explored the 'hot topics' in Jaffa's politics: the modernization of infrastructure and the expansion of state control over 'public security' (*al-amn al-ʿāmm*); a debate that included campaigns for the expulsion of outsider groups from the social fabric, especially the Maghrebis who were regarded as 'dangerous elements'. Chapter III explored the campaign of the 'Orthodox Renaissance Movement' (*an-nahḍa al-urṯūḏuksīya*) for cultural reforms in the Greek Orthodox Patriarchate of Jerusalem and local participation in its financial affairs. It analyzed the negotiations between the Orthodox laity and the clergy in the Mixed Council, their entanglement of the Ottoman government and the mobilization of the Orthodox congregation; all of which included the vast exploitation of the contemporary Ottoman constitutionalist discourse by the Orthodox. The chapter provided the local perspective on the intra-Orthodox conflict which has not yet received scholarly attention, at a time when the Renaissance Movement was articulating its major political arguments. Chapter IV investigated how the 'Zionist question' was controversially debated by Arab Muslims, Christian and Sephardi Palestinians and Ashkenazi migrants. Under the premise of 'development and progress' as the overall imperative to be accomplished, it was discussed if Zionist migration was beneficial or detrimental for Palestine. The chapter explored the chronological shifts in the press coverage on Zionism and its turning points from an ambivalent controversy to a full-blown anti-Zionist campaign in 1914.

In the following, I revise the main arguments and results of the study, I outline overlapping conclusions, and conclude with an outlook on possible further research topics.

1. Central Terminology and Concepts in *Filasṭīn*

Chapter I portrayed the emergence of *Filasṭīn* in the light of its social and cultural background and the general ability of the post-revolutionary Arab press to access markets and generate a readership. *Filasṭīn* strongly promoted the ideals of Western-style modernization, in particular with regard to the field of education. Culturally, it supported the ideals of the Arab *nahḍa*. Politically, it promoted concepts of Ottoman unity and brotherhood, against the background of the political crisis prior to World War I. This particularly applied to the editors as unwavering supporters of the CUP, since they viewed the Young Turks as the only guarantee of stability and development in Palestine. In terms of content priorities, the main goal of the ʿĪsās was to generate public support for the Arab Orthodox Movement: the driving force for the foundation of *Filasṭīn* in 1911. Apart from that, Zionist immigration, Jaffa's infrastructure and public security in the Jaffa and Bethlehem regions were central issues in the Local News.

While previous research has treated *Filasṭīn* as a private enterprise of its editors, this study has approached it as a 'collective enterprise' that depended on networks and alliances. In this respect, the editors particularly benefitted from close links with influential personalities in Jaffa, such as *qāʾimaqām* Hāšim al-Atāsī and police commander Ḫalīl Efendi, director of the Anglo Palestine Bank Goldenberg and the local CUP branch, and their bonds to the Orthodox communities of Jaffa, Jerusalem and Bethlehem. They encouraged readers' contributions to the newspaper's production through 'dialogical sections' and columns, and each issue was a joint publication, produced by a 'pool of publishers'. Beside reproducing items from local and international press organs and news agencies' reports, *Filasṭīn* depended on a network of regular correspondents. These were Muslims and Christians who reported from cities in the Jerusalem District, the Arab provinces, major Ottoman urban centers and international metropolises. Apart from the ʿĪsās' contributions (editorials and local news), notables of diverse backgrounds from the Jerusalem, Bethlehem, Jaffa and Gaza regions extensively published in *Filasṭīn*. They addressed the readership passionately, in the dichotomous rhetorical style of 'praising or defaming' and used the press to spread a modernist 'mindset' rather influenced by European modernity. The function of the press was, in their view, to create a 'public opinion' (*raʾy ʿāmm*) and spread knowledge. As authors, they saw themselves as 'educators of the nation', drawing the line between themselves and the general people (*al-ʿāmma*), who were to be educated in line with the 'spirit of the age', the constitutional era. The concept of 'the new age' was taken by these authors as equivalent to everything that belonged in their view to the Western-style set of modernity: progress, patriotic values, civic rights and active citizenry.

On the top level of the newspaper's discourse was the sacralized notion of 'modernization and progress' as 'overall imperative'. It was imposed on every issue reported on, and terms such as growth, progress, civilization and urbanization, were key slogans in *Filasṭīn*. The precondition for the modernization of society was, in the view of these authors, the reformation of Palestinian education in line with progressive standards. The reading of *Filasṭīn*, that previously was categorized mostly as *the* anti-Zionist pioneer of the pre-World War I Arab press, revealed the centrality of 'education' (*tarbiya*) as part of its reform agenda, which included articles on infrastructural, technical, economic and cultural development.

The great hope of the authors publishing in *Filasṭīn*, a lot of them teachers, lay in the young generation. A bi-product of this study has been the discovery that the education of the 'new youth' (*an-nāšiʾa al-ǧadīda*) as target group who should be prepared to become mature and free thinkers, upright men and patriots, was at the top agenda of *Filasṭīn*; an agenda that fostered female education and chauvinistic images of a new masculinity at the same time. The articles on the modernization of education could not be systematically registered in the framework of this study because there were so many, but the centrality of the concept of the 'new youth' was obvious in many contributions. Liberal and interactive teaching methods, as applied by Sakākīnī in his Constitutional School and in American schools, were strongly promoted. As much as concepts of modernization and progress were praised, the authors equally addressed Eastern 'backwardness', 'lethargy' and 'decline', motifs that derived from concepts of modernity that took the West as the main benchmark. From reading *Filasṭīn*, it became clear that the image of Eastern decline, as developed by Western authors, was widely circulating among Arab intellectuals and reproduced by them. The circle of *Filasṭīn* publishers belonged to a generation that accessed modern knowledge and followed global developments with curiosity. They were frustrated by the constant comparison between Western standards and the 'Eastern type', which reveals the increasing alienation of the Arab middle and upper classes from local society during this period.

Second in importance in the mindset promoted in *Filasṭīn* was the imperial discourse in line with the political culture of the Second Constitutional Era; here, the main elements were praise of constitutionalism (*dustūrīya*) and the condemnation of 'despotism' (*istibdād*). This dichotomy was strongly exploited by Arab Orthodox activists, who portrayed their cause as a repetition of the Ottoman 'Constitutional Revolution' in the Jerusalem District. Ottoman 'unity' (*ittiḥād*) was a most strongly defended concept in *Filasṭīn*, both as a matter of principle and out of pragmatic considerations. The members of the Palestinian elites who published in *Filasṭīn* believed that the Ottoman government, although far away and much criticized for its ineffectiveness in implementing reforms in the Jerusalem District, was the only political power capable of maintaining stability, which was the precondition for development. Ottoman unity was the only option. This ambiguity, the passionate defense of Ottoman patriotism and its vast instrumentalization for the sake local reform goals, applied especially to the ʿĪsās. Under the influence of the Arab Congress in Paris in 1913, they feared that the influence of the Decentralization Party might undermine political stability in the Arab provinces and they harshly criticized the Beirut Reform Committees, who sought to generate support from Palestinian notables. They confirmed their unlimited loyalty to the CUP as long as it supported the Constitution and stood for 'reform'. However, under the impact of the changing political discourse in Istanbul and growing conflicts between the Young Turks and Arab activists, new talk of 'Arabs' versus 'Turks' was slowly introduced. Further, from the summer of 1913, a concept of 'minority' (*aqallīya*) started to circulate in *Filasṭīn* and was applied when discussing the proportional confessional quota policy in the Jerusalem Provincial Council.

The non-negotiable Ottomanist discourse applied in *Filasṭīn* found its strongest expression with regard to inter-confessional group relations in Palestine. In contrast to the ideal of Ottoman unity and brotherhood, ethnic partisanship and nationalist models based on confessional affiliations were stigmatized as the counter-concepts that would cause a cataclysm in the Arab East. During the years before World War I, the Palestinian elites had an overwhelming fear of inter-religious conflict. As members of a religious minority, the ʿĪsās repeatedly affirmed their impartial approach to all confessions and their loyalty to multi-confessional Ottomanism. Part of this was their strict separation of anti-Semitism from anti-Zionism and their separation of (Ottoman) Israelites from (foreign) Zionists. It is important to note that the distinction between Zionists and Israelites was strictly upheld until 1914. The 'unity imperative' as the precondition for stability and development did not allow the editors to stigmatize 'Jews' in general. In this respect, the strongly promoted concept of Ottoman unity was a very instrumental patriotism, often motivated by fear of inter-confessional strife.

In *Filasṭīn*, this patriotism was most passionately demonstrated by the minorities, the Ottoman Christian and Jewish authors: a phenomenon that increased during political crises, as during the Tripoli War or sudden eruptions of violence between Muslims and Christians, such as during the 'Ramla incident' in November 1911. The response to this incident by the ʿĪsās is an example of how desperately they held on to the Ottoman model. For example, they accused the Christians of Ramla, who left their houses and hid overnight in the Franciscan monastery out of fear of attack by a Muslim mob, of having betrayed their Muslim brothers by seeking protection in a foreign institution, which they viewed as a scandal. These demonstrations of loyalty were typical for minorities in societies with fragile ethno-confessional balances during times of sectarian and political crisis.

In the Arab press, sentiments against foreign influence in the Empire and European military hegemony in the Arab East rapidly increased under the impact of the Ottoman territorial losses in North Africa (1911) and the Balkans (1912/13). The writings of the ʿĪsās demonstrate a great ambivalence towards Europe. On one hand, Western-style modernization and education were strongly promoted, and culturally, the ʿĪsās were fond of European literature and philosophy. On the other, their fierce opposition to the *imtiyāzāt* of the foreigners in the Empire and European imperialism was a major factor in their own discussion of Muslim-Christian cohabitation in the East. The ʿĪsās were the fiercest enemies of images of 'Muslim fanaticism' in the Arab East that was conveyed by the Western press. For the ʿĪsās, the Western press was a 'market of lies' in the service of European colonial agendas that aimed to break multi-confessional Ottoman unity. The extent to which the ʿĪsās wanted to preserve Muslim-Christian alliances in Palestine is seen in their repeated references to traditional Muslim-Christian harmony in Islamic history.

With regard to collective identities, the texts in *Filasṭīn* presented a diversity of models. Apart from commitment to Ottoman unity and brotherhood, the paper presented notions of a Palestinian identity, in the sense of a cultural rather than a political identity and of local patriotism. The notion of Palestine as a geographical unit was internalized among the local population before World War I, but with fluid borders. Various proto-national concepts and nationalist terminologies circulated in *Filasṭīn*, but the authors applied them quite freely, as the terms *umma* and *šaʿb* also defined confessions or populations of cities, and not necessarily a national collective in the modern sense of 'nation'.

Third in the newspaper's discursive hierarchy, I have identified strong notions of the public sphere and civic society, and of the 'public opinion' as a political power. Authors usually underpinned their different reform agendas by claiming to be engaging in the 'public interest' (*al-maṣlaḥa al-ʿāmma*) or for the 'public benefit' (*an-nafaʿ al-ʿāmm*) whenever addressing the authorities. The impact of the political culture of the Second Constitutional era on the Arab press is also seen in the promoted notions of civic society and 'citizenship' (*muwāṭana*) that were conveyed through *Filasṭīn*. The ʿĪsās explained concepts of transparency and the 'accountability' (*muḥāsaba*) of political institutions to the public, and they addressed the people as 'the citizens' (*al-muwāṭinīn*) or 'the nation' (*aš-šaʿb*). Political legitimacy was to be guaranteed through 'representative' rule in distinction from illegitimate 'despotic' rule not backed through elections. It was expected that the function of any government was to be 'at the service of people' (*fī ḫidmat aš-šaʿb*), to develop the region and maintain order and security by controlling the public space. This was most relevant in the Jaffa *qaḍāʾ* where due to high crime rates the authorities were much criticized for not being able to do so.

2. Jaffa as an 'Ethno-Confessional Contact Zone'

Chapter II portrayed developments in the Jaffa region from the *Tanzimat* until World War I with regard to rapid spatial expansion, demographic diversity and the mobility of people and goods. It focused on Jaffa as a port city, an agricultural agglomeration, a magnet for global immigration, and a showcase model of Ottoman modernity in the Jerusalem District. Given that the region was an 'ethno-confessional contact zone', the relationalities of space and society-building in the Jaffa *qaḍāʾ* were outlined; the links between urban and agricultural spaces, between the city and the rural hinterlands. This was relevant since these conditions shaped the socio-cultural and political background of *Filasṭīn*. In contrast to nostalgic images of late Ottoman Jaffa as 'Bride of the Sea', as in the Palestinian post-*nakba* narrative, or its stigmatization as Tel Aviv's 'back yard', as in the Zionist national narrative in which Tel Aviv occupied an outstanding position as the 'White City' emerging 'out of the sands', the relationalities of the region were central in this chapter, which relies extensively on the works of Kark and Ṭarāwina, and on *Filasṭīn*.

The rapid development of Jaffa from a 'fortress' to a 'boom town' within fifty years during the second half of the nineteenth century was accompanied by its rise as the administrative center of the *qaḍāʾ*, the massive cultivation of land and the quick transition of the Jaffa environs into an agricultural agglomeration consisting of gardens and citrus plantations (*bayyārāt*). A network of roads connected the export hit of local industry, the 'Jaffa Orange', with the port, and new workers' residences, situated in the fields, with Jaffa town. This development stimulated international migration from Egypt, Morocco, Tunisia, Algeria, Afghanistan, Iran and India, which transformed the region into a 'globalized space'. Sephardi Jews migrated from North Africa, and German Protestants and Ashkenazi Jews from Eastern Europe settled in the area, making the Jaffa *qaḍāʾ* a center of Jewish settlement, and Jaffa the center of Zionist activity and Hebrew culture. All these groups made Jaffa highly diverse and, although provincial, the most cosmopolitan place in Palestine, integrating dozens of nationalities, ethnicities and confessions, each which maintained its own places of worship, schools, clubs, social welfare, etc. With regard to ethno-confessional cohabitation, social division and economic interaction was the general principle.

As far as spatial relationalities were concerned, the rapid expansion of Jaffa through the 'plantation fever' and the 'building boom' of the 1880s and 1890s fostered the quick integration of suburbs as neighborhood into the urban fabric. *Filasṭīn* articles confirm awareness of new Jewish quarters north of the town as parts of the expanding city, calling Tel Aviv a 'neighborhood' (*maḥalla*). Moreover, the expanding citrus industry connected city center, suburbs and gardens through commercial ties and roads while the harvesting, boxing and packing took place in the fields, where the workers also lived. It should be stressed that the economic success of the Jewish settlements paid for the *qaḍāʾ*. With regard to the production and export of wine from Rishon le-Tzion, Jaffa's municipality raised the wine tax in 1913.

Unlike in other Palestinian regions and the highlands, villages in the Jaffa *qaḍāʾ* were not fortified against Bedouin tribes. Relations between city dwellers and the tribes settled north-east of Jaffa at the Yarkon River, south-east of town or elsewhere in the further hinterland, were rather good, and *Filasṭīn* very rarely reported clashes involving Bedouins. Occasionally, exclusivist Zionist institutions were criticized, such as the House of Government that was established in Tel Aviv despite the fact that Jaffa was the administrative center of the *qaḍāʾ*. The importance of Jaffa as a port and the center of modern communication technologies in the Jerusalem District explains the tight links between Jaffa and the capital Jerusalem, which were much stronger than Jerusalem's links with Nablus, Gaza or Hebron. The image of the *qaḍāʾ* presented in *Filasṭīn* was that of a 'showcase model' for Ottoman-Palestinian modernity, and Jaffa town as a symbol of cultural cosmopolitanism and religious moderation. Stressing the Jaffa-Jerusalem connection, *Filasṭīn* extensively covered the visits by Jerusalem governors in the region who viewed the *qaḍāʾ* as a drawing force for the cultural and economic development of the Jerusalem District, also especially through the presence of foreign colonies. As seen from many *Filasṭīn* reports, the Templar village of Sarona, the factories of Rishon le-Tzion, the farms of Petaḥ Tikva and Reḥovot, the training center of the Netter School and the Hebrew Gymnasium in Tel Aviv were favorite destinations for Ottoman officials and were considered as positive raw models for local development.

In terms of 'cohabitation patterns', the social climate in Jaffa was fragile before World War I, and the usual peaceful coexistence was interrupted by occasional eruptions of ethno-confessional violence. Zionist organizations were known for their policies of boycotting local Muslims, Christians and Jews as to enforce an exclusive market for Hebrew labor. Sephardi 'Israelites' and Ashkenazi Jews competed in Jaffa for community leadership in the Jewish Town Committee. Conflicts about the Zionist agenda on Hebrew culture and language provoked riots between Ashkenazi immigrants of different origins. On the intra-confessional level, the intra-Orthodox conflict found its expressions in Jaffa through boycott actions against the abbot of the Orthodox monastery who was sent by the Patriarchate but not accepted by the local community and was locked out of his church. In terms of ethno-confessional cohabitation, the Templar colonies were almost a blank spot on the mental map of *Filasṭīn*. They very rarely appeared in the local news although they were economically very successful. However, they lived an enclosed life and did not provoke debates in the local Arab press since they had no demographic weight in the *qaḍāʾ* and they also did not constitute a political threat in the local perception, unlike the Jewish colonists since 1913.

Further, institutional power in Jaffa's economic and political life was strong, both through governmental institutions, including the role of the *qāʾimaqām*, and through activities undertaken by communal associations and Zionist organizations. 'Pressure groups' with special influence in the local economy and politics were the merchants (*at-tuǧǧār*), the land owners (*al-mallākūn*) and the guards (*an-nawāṭīr*), who were employed in the urban area and the citrus fields and perceived as a tremendous danger to public security. The points at the top agenda of Jaffa's merchants and landowners in local politics were the development of Jaffa's infrastructure to expand trade through a road network and a modernized deep-water port, and the improvement of public order and security. Transportation roads became 'swamps' in winter; cargo was dashed in storms since the steamships had to anchor in the open sea and bring their goods to the beach via small boats. Importantly, Jaffa's rivalry with Haifa made local merchants fear that Palestinian trade would in future be handled through Haifa, which was connected to the Hijaz Railway. Then, Jaffa would be cut off from trade routes, which is what happened during the Mandate.

In *Filasṭīn*, there was a strong notion of urban space as a 'public law and order space'. In the view of the local elites, this space should be in control of the state and defended against dangerous 'elements'. A steep rise in crime during the years before World War I, this impression is conveyed through *Filasṭīn*, put the business of Jaffa's merchants and landowners at risk and revealed that local government was too weak to control either the urban space or the countryside. The lack of public security was interpreted as a 'disease' (*dāʾ*) and discussion on how to provide security for traders and their goods was a top topic in *Filasṭīn*. Readers were outraged at the inability of the police to defend Jaffa's businessmen from robbery, kidnapping, murder and blackmailing, all committed by the guards, who were armed. These guards were Muslim migrants of Moroccan, Algerian and Afghan origin, and the issue was discussed as a 'Maghrebi problem'. The guards were organized in gangs; they ambushed travelers, transport and postal services, and especially land owners. They vandalized fields when their owners refused to pay protection money and, although the *qāʾimaqām* made efforts to get a grip on the problem, he failed. The ʿĪsās, supported by merchants of Sūq al-Balābisa, initiated a campaign against the guards, stigmatizing them as dangerous strangers. The traders refused to pay 'security taxes' and started to organize private armed forces to protect their shops. The ʿĪsās demanded the eviction of the Maghrebis from Jaffa to 'where they came from', and, later, they pressed upon the enforcement of the Islamic Sharia penalties on them. The Ottoman juridical system was too soft, and the Muslim 'divine penal law is greater than the civil law', the ʿĪsās argued, despite being Christian, and generously ignoring in this case the constitutional values they usually stood for. This case is provides more evidence of the instrumental patriotism of the local elites and the ambivalent application of concepts in *Filasṭīn* before World War I. Other regions, including Bethlehem, also had a 'Maghrebi problem', but the question of how the integration or exclusion of these Muslim migrants was discussed in other parts of Palestine or the Arab East cannot be covered in this study.

3. The Arab Orthodox Renaissance

Chapter III explored how the 'Orthodox Renaissance Movement' (*an-nahḍa al-urṯūḏuksīya*) negotiated local political participation in the Greek Orthodox Patriarchate of Jerusalem. Promoting the Orthodox cause in *Filasṭīn* was on the ʿĪsās' main agenda from the inception of their newspaper. The foundation in December 1910 of the Mixed Council, consisting of six clerics and six lay delegates, gave the final impetus for the establishment of *Filasṭīn* as a 'mouthpiece' for the Orthodox in Palestine and a central platform for Palestinian Orthodox activists to spread their reform agenda and generate public support. The engagement of the ʿĪsās in this cause is well known. However, *Filasṭīn*'s extensive coverage of this matter has not been studied and scholarship has rather tended to emphasize its leading role in spreading anti-Zionism and an early Palestinian national identity. A thorough reading of *Filasṭīn* from 1911 to 1914 has shown that its coverage of Zionism, although certainly noteworthy, was less extensive than that dedicated to Orthodox matters. Orthodox activities received a lot of attention, and these years were decisive for the Orthodox Movement in the articulation of political arguments, the mobilization of the public and the elaboration of a program that was pursued until the Mandate period. The coverage on the Orthodox cause in *Filasṭīn* was designed from the beginning as a full-blown political anti-clerical campaign that sought to delegitimize the Convent. Yūsuf al-ʿĪsā, who represented the diocese of Jaffa in the Council, published in *Filasṭīn* the debates in the Mixed Council in form of detailed records of the speeches, documenting the course of each session in the chronological order of each speaker, and extensively used the records to portray himself as *the* defender of Orthodox rights in the Council.

The Orthodox Movement exploited the post-revolutionary discourse extensively to portray their cause as a struggle between Ottoman Constitutionalism and Greek despotism (*istibdād*). As they argued it, their campaign for local participation in the administration of the Patriarchate was a revolution for the 'constitutional rights' (*ḥuqūq dustūrīya*) of the 'Orthodox people' (*aš-šaʿb al-urṯūḏuksī*) in Palestine. They used very combative language and sanctified their cause by equating the Orthodox *nahḍa* with a 'jihad'. The Greek clergy were portrayed as a gang of foreign strangers who ruled through mismanagement and corruption and usurped the property of Ottoman Orthodox citizens so as to turn Palestine into a 'Greek colony' (*mustaʿmara yūnānīya*).

In the course of the anti-clerical rebellion, the Orthodox activists occupied churches and Holy Sites, most importantly the church of Mār Yaʿqūb (Engl.: St. James) in Jerusalem. There, Arab lay people affiliated with the Renaissance Movement, gave sermons, organized demonstrations after church service, stirred up the congregation, and motivated them to boycott religious ceremonies conducted by the Patriarch. Another method used by the Movement was intense petitioning to the Ministry of Justice and Religious Affairs and the Grand Vizier in Istanbul, and the strong involvement of the Jerusalem governors by sending them countless open letters and protest delegations.

The controversies between the lay and the clerical members of the Mixed Council, which was the first experiment in democratic negotiation in the Orthodox Patriarchate of Jerusalem, illustrated the way in which intra-confessional political bodies functioned during the late Ottoman era and what the major points of conflict were. Here, the role of the 'local trustees' in the dioceses was a key conflict that dominated the Mixed Council for three years. The enforcement of these 'trustees' councils' was a precondition for further reforms in the dioceses, which was prevented by the Patriarch since he sought to prevent Orthodox notables, especially in Jerusalem but also elsewhere in the dioceses, to lay their hands on the extensive Church properties. Both parties, the clergy and the lay delegates, argued for their 'constitutional rights' to legitimize their cause. They pointed to contradictory articles in the Fundamental Law and to a number of resolutions issued by the imperial government. The lay delegates stressed articles that stipulated participatory rights and equality, while the clergy argued for the Patriarchal *berat*s confirmed in other articles of the Constitution. The laymen used rhetoric that tried to put the 'privileges' of the clergy on level with the *imtiyazāt* granted to foreigners, thus equating Greek clerics with colonial powers. Importantly, each conflict party tried to expand its sphere of influence in a way that undermined the *status quo* embodied in the 1910 Resolution, by quoting contradictory articles in Ottoman Law as to legitimize their cause as 'constitutional', which shows the extent to which the Constitution was instrumentalized by all parties in the intra-Orthodox conflict.

Another key conflict between the Patriarch and Jerusalem's Orthodox notables were the rent allowances, a traditional payment that the Jerusalemite Orthodox community received annually from the Patriarchate. This question caused a major confrontation between the clergy and the Jerusalemites and led to several instances of government involvement. In the Mixed Council, this led to escalations between the Patriarch and the Jerusalemite delegates, as well as to increasing rivalry between Jerusalem and the dioceses, where reforms could not be implemented since the constant conflicts over the competence of the Jerusalemite trustees and their role in obtaining the rent allowances was the underlying reason why the Patriarch continued to prevent the establishment of the trustees' councils in the dioceses.

Further main points of contention debated in the Council were educational reforms in matters such as the competences and the composition of the School Board which constantly changed, leading to further conflicts between the Orthodox delegates in the Council, and specifically between ʿĪsā and the Jerusalemite delegate. Another substantial controversy was the allocation key of the social budget, which was to be assigned by the Patriarchate to the Mixed Council and distributed to the various dioceses. This controversy was at some point interrupted, leaving the reader in the dark as to what finally happened about the budget. Another matter of dispute was the rotation of the Mixed Councils' delegates: under the 1910 Resolution, half of the delegate from each side should be replaced by lot each year. In the three new dioceses, that were to have lay representatives on the Council, the Orthodox populations should elect them, while the three new clerical delegates would be appointed by the Patriarchate.

However, the rotation of delegates in 1911 was suspended since the Council was busy with the matter of the 'trustees' councils'. In 1912, it was decided that, of the six dioceses represented on the Council, Acre, Nazareth and Bethlehem were to be replaced by Nablus, al-Ḥisn and Kerak. There were irregularities during the election of the new candidates, and the clerical side constantly postponed the appointment of the monitoring committee that was meant to oversee new elections in the dioceses. Thus, the new delegates from the dioceses on the Council were not in place after the summer break of 1912. The Orthodox in the dioceses conveyed their anger by sending petitions and letters of protest to *Filasṭīn*, but the Patriarchate did not send the monitoring committee to the dioceses until June 1913. When the Council reopened after the 1913 summer break, the candidates from Ḥisn, Kerak and Jenin (instead of Nablus) who had been elected in the meantime were absent since they had not been invited by the Patriarch. The Council was incomplete and thus, unable to act. Behind this lay an ultimatum from the Patriarch, who threatened that the Council would never be reopened unless the Arab Orthodox rebels handed over the occupied churches to the Patriarchate.

Debates in the Mixed Council were increasingly dominated by Yūsuf al-ʿĪsā and his personal conflicts with the Patriarch and, after summer 1912, these debates escalated into personal feuds between ʿĪsā and Damianos or his deputy Malatios. The Patriarch opened several court cases against ʿĪsā in 1912 and tried to excommunicate him. ʿĪsā's firm supporter, the delegate from Bethlehem Ḥazbūn, left the Council in summer 1912, and ʿĪsā increasingly portrayed himself as a solitary fighter against the Patriarch, surrounded by traitors. Since the new delegates did not arrive from the dioceses, the Council was incomplete and approached a new level of crisis in its history. In the winter of 1912/13, it completely lost its credibility in the eyes of the Orthodox public. After Orthodox Christmas at the beginning of 1913, the Patriarch no longer attended and the Council could not be officially reopened. Malatios, representing Damianos, refused to take decisions in his absence. At the same time, rumors popped up in Jerusalem that the Patriarchate was planning to abolish the Council unilaterally. From the 'annulment affair' onwards, the Council was in the crossfire of public criticism, as is clear from the intensity of readers' comments in *Filasṭīn*.

In June 1913, a new level of tension was reached when the Patriarch's deputy refused to publish of the Council's meeting minutes, which led to a major confrontation between ʿĪsā and Malatios about the accountability of political bodies to the congregations they represented. With regard to the unilateral abolition of the Council by the Patriarchate, and since the Council's credibility with the public had been destroyed, a flood of delegations, petitions and telegrams from various Orthodox communities (Jerusalem, Bethlehem, Beit Jala, Nablus) addressed the governor in Jerusalem. During fall 1913, Archimandrite Dosithios was on a tour of the dioceses, trying to persuade Orthodox community leaders to call on the authorities for the abolition of the Mixed Council, and the public campaign of Arab Orthodox activist circles in the District against the Patriarchal establishment as the illegitimate rule of foreign despots over the indigenous Orthodox Ottoman citizens had reached at its peak.

The local government became much more entangled in the affair than it wished and it seemed rather helpless. Governor Māgid Bek did not get involved and so the ʿĪsās declared in *Filasṭīn* that, since the government did not feel responsible for the intra-Orthodox conflict, the Patriarchate was 'not Ottoman anymore' and they openly portrayed Māǧid Bek as a man unable to govern. This had consequences. In November 1913, *Filasṭīn* was temporarily suspended following fierce government criticism of the Orthodox cause. The ʿĪsās initiated a solidarity campaign for the reopening of *Filasṭīn* under the headings *ad-Dustūr* and *al-Aẖbār*. This raised a debate over press freedom in the neighboring Arab press, and the ʿĪsās received tremendous support from fellow journalists in and outside Palestine, who portrayed them as resistance fighters.

At the same time, in November 1913, a government commission from Istanbul, headed by former Jerusalem Governor ʿAzmī Bek, arrived in the district to mediate in the conflict about the 'annulment or revival' of the Mixed Council. Suddenly, there was a radical turn: the ʿĪsās halted from their anti-clerical campaign in *Filasṭīn*, massively pressured by ʿAzmī Bek not to endanger the work of the arbitration commission. In January 1914, the Council was officially reopened, the suspension of *Filasṭīn* rescinded, and the editors published the regulations of the new resolution regarding the future of the Mixed Council, which was released by the commission in the '1913 Resolution'.

This Resolution declared that the Orthodox trustees, now called *wukalāʾ*, representatives, were to be elected immediately in the various towns and cities. *Filasṭīn* reported in February 1914 on their election in Jaffa, but not in other places. Regarding educational reforms, two new boarding schools were to be opened, one in Jaffa and one in Jerusalem. A new school board was set up and, in March 1914, delivered its first report on reforms to be implemented in the new schools in Jaffa and Jerusalem. The dioceses of Salṭ, Kerak and Nablus were to be replaced on the Council by Jerusalem, Gaza and Beit Jala. *Filasṭīn* reported on elections in Beit Jala during the first half of 1914, where the ʿĪsās had been sent to mediate between conflicting parties, but not in other places. The rent allowances for the Jerusalemites were restricted to 8,000 lira a year. The Resolution declared that the occupied churches were to be reopened, and Mār Yaʿqūb was given up by the activists.

In January 1914, the ʿĪsās adopted a completely new discourse on the Orthodox cause which was a radical 180-degree turn. They praised the work of the arbitration commission of ʿAzmī Bek and the new Resolution as a success and struck a strikingly conciliatory tone towards 'our spiritual fathers', the clergy, whom they had previously compared to insects and microbes. Yūsuf withdraw from his leading role as driver of the anti-clerical campaign, leaving Orthodox readers confused by this radical turn around. Yūsuf al-ʿĪsā was no longer a delegate on the Mixed Council and did not have access to what was negotiated there. After presenting himself for three years as the leading actor in the Orthodox campaign and the Patriarch's main opponent, he seems surprisingly to have had not a single ally among the new lay delegates on the Council and was completely deprived of access to information.

Filasṭīn's coverage of Orthodox matters became rare after January 1914; only short points of news were presented, without any sense of personal interest or even comment. The reader, at this point, loses any insight into the negotiations that took place in the Mixed Council. *Filasṭīn* had simply dropped out of the Movement, which irritated the readership. The ʿĪsās, as leaders of a medium that they had presented throughout the past three years as the 'educator of the nation', the 'mouthpiece' of the Orthodox in Palestine, and the 'shaper of public opinion' and a protest forum, faced a serious credibility crisis.

In order to rescue its legitimacy as a protest forum, *Filasṭīn* shifted its focus to the anti-Zionism campaign as its new cause, and found fertile ground because sentiment against the aspirations of the Jewish settlers in the Jerusalem District were already high. Although *Filasṭīn* had published anti-Zionist articles before, it was obvious that the editors were not nearly as personally engaged in that issue as in the anti-clerical campaign; and the most hostile anti-Zionist contributions came from other authors, not the ʿĪsās. The anti-Zionism views expressed in *Filasṭīn* in 1913 did also not reach the level of aggression of the anti-clerical campaign. In fall 1913, when other authors were emotionally deeply involved in the 'Zarnuqa affair', which left its mark in the District, the ʿĪsās personally did not even interfere. They were at this point fully engaged in the campaign against the annulment of the Council by the Patriarchate and focused on furious attacks against the local authorities because of they did not pressure the Patriarchate.

We do not know what exactly made the ʿĪsās withdraw so completely from their role in the Orthodox Renaissance. It is open to speculations whether it was due to their ruined relations with the Jerusalem governor and the Jaffa *qāʾimaqām*, who threatened them. Whatever the case may be, the Patriarch had won. For three years, he had successfully blocked the Council from implementing reforms, culminating in not installing the new lay delegates in fall 1912 and preventing the Council's official reopening in 1913. At the turn of 1913/14, the Orthodox Movement had worked out their political arguments, however it was deeply fragmented and unable to present a united agenda to the authorities. When the Council underwent its legitimacy crisis in 1913, the Movement lost some of its spirit, it seems. And, apart from the Patriarchal strategies of blocking the Council, it transpired that the lay delegates had not overcome their rivalries, especially those between Jerusalem as the center and the dioceses on the periphery. All of this had greatly weakened the Orthodox Movement by 1914.

4. The Debate on Zionist Migration

Chapter IV discussed the controversial debate on the Zionist question in *Filasṭīn*, to which authors from different confessional backgrounds and political spectrums contributed, including the ʿĪsās, Ottoman citizens from the Christian, Muslim and Sephardi spectrum, and Ashkenazi migrants. Importantly to note:

all of them shared the same modernist 'mindset'. They discussed Zionism mainly as an immigration movement of *foreigners*, and not necessarily as a Jewish movement, and through the spectacles of 'Ottoman modernity'. The general call for 'modernization and progress' strongly circulated in this debate, which from the beginning ranged around the question of whether Zionist migration was beneficial or damaging to the economic, technological and cultural development of Palestine. Thus, the debate on Zionism was embedded in the wider debate on development and was influenced by the 'modernization imperative' proposed by Palestinian intellectuals of all faiths in *Filasṭīn.*

The debate was characterized by ambivalence, which reflects the indecisive attitude of the Palestinian public towards the Zionist movement during 1911 and 1912. The defenders of Zionism were the Sephardi circle around the newspaper *Ḥerut*, especially Shimon Moyal, who published extensively in *Filasṭīn*, and Ashkenazi European authors such as Abraham Ludvipol, who all tried to convince the Arab Palestinian readership that Zionism would be an engine of local development. This was particularly emphasized in the column 'Letters of a Farmer', contributed by the Zionist Menashe Me'irovitch. Up to the late summer of 1912, he openly promoted the progressive power of Zionist settlement in *Filasṭīn*, especially highlighting Rishon le-Tzion's civilizing role in its rural Arab environment which was an attractive topic for *Filasṭīn* readers, since the modernization of Palestinian agriculture was at the top of the agenda of the Palestinian elites and an interest also shared by the ʿĪsās. The supporters of Zionism made extensive use of *Filasṭīn* as a platform, promoting their pro-Zionist agenda until the late summer of 1913. Importantly to note, the Jewish contribution in the press debate ceased for good after the 'Zarnuqa incident' in the fall of 1913, making it a cornerstone in the debate on Zionism in the Jaffa *qaḍāʾ*.

The critics of Zionism were the Muslim and Christian contributors in the press debate who opposed the exclusive character of the Zionist movement, whether on the social, economic or political level, although they admired the Zionists' economic and cultural achievements and called on Palestinians to learn from their ambitious agenda.

The role of the ʿĪsās, who had established *Filasṭīn* as a forum for debate on the Zionist question, oscillated during the period investigated. In 1911 and the first half of 1912, they were ambivalent about Zionism, acted as neutral mediators in the debate, and usually closed a debate when the opponents slid into 'extremism'. In May/June 1912, in a dispute with Ludvipol, they criticized the exclusive socio-economic structures of Zionist immigrants in Jaffa. While former immigrants had blended into 'one bloc' with Jaffa's population, the new generation of Jewish migrants ruined business for Jaffa's traders by establishing a 'city within the city', they claimed, although they approved of migration as beneficial for the urban progress. In line with this developmentalism, the ʿĪsās actively approved the Zionist column *Letters of a Farmer.*

During 1911–14, I identified five major discursive shifts in the press debate. The first occurred in the late summer of 1912, brought on by the support of governor Muhdī Bek for Rishon le-Tzion. During an extensive round trip in the Jaffa *qaḍāʾ*, he announced his support for an autonomous administration and security forces for the Jewish settlements and also promised the transfer of a piece of communal *mawāt* land, a strip on the coast, to Rishon le-Tzion for cultivation. The response to this was fierce local opposition to the growing autonomy of Jewish settlements in the region, and the ʿĪsās sponsored campaigns against the policy of the Jewish Netter School in Mikveh Yisra'el, which clearly discriminated against non-Jewish students, despite being an Ottoman institution, and against the transfer of communal *mawāt* to Rishon le-Tzion as a violation of the Ottoman land law. It is striking that, at this time, Me'irovitch from Rishon le-Tzion ceased publishing his Letters of a Farmer in *Filasṭīn.*

The second shift occurred at the turn of 1912/13, when economic rivalries between the Jewish colonies of the region and Jaffa's economic elites reached a high point. This is illustrated in the campaign run by landowners and merchants from Jaffa against the sale of mills on the Yarkon River to Jewish settlers, a campaign in which the ʿĪsās massively engaged. This contributed to growing hostility between *Filasṭīn* and *Ḥerut:* the Zionist-Palestinian competition for resources became from 1913 a trigger for Christian-Sephardi hostilities. In the light of the Sephardi role in Zionist land acquisition in the *qaḍāʾ* and the Zionist principle of creating exclusive Hebrew markets, the position of Jaffa's Sephardi Jews for or against Zionism became an anchor point in local Christian-Sephardi relations. Thus, a side effect of the impact of Zionism on Palestine was the deterioration of the relations between the Ottoman Christian and 'Israelite brothers' in the region between Jaffa and Jerusalem.

This third shift in the debate on Zionism was influenced by the impact of the sales of large areas at Abū Šūša and Kafr Urīya to the JN in the winter of 1912/13 during a time when there was no governor in the District, which erupted in public protests against the land transactions as illegal. Opposition to Zionism also increased under the psychological impact of the Balkan Wars 1912/13 which illustrates an important shift in the public opinion about Zionism in pre-World War I Palestine, in so far as measurable through the press as a dispute forum for the educated segments of society. The opinion of Palestinian notables on the Zionist movement changed from seeing it as a local economic rival to believing it to represent a serious political danger. From the first half of 1913 and through the impact of these wider events mentioned, Zionist immigration was increasingly discussed as a demographic and political threat to Palestine; now perceived as a

European nationalist movement in the Ottoman domain, as a consequence of the Balkan Wars.

A fourth shift was to be observed in summer 1913 following the affair of the Palestinian 'Crown Lands' and the 'Zarnuqa incident'. Protests against the sale of the Crown Lands occurred beyond the borders of the Districts of Nablus and Jerusalem, accompanied by the first test of trans-regional cooperation between notables against Zionist land acquisition. Even more importantly, the Zarnuqa incident, that led to political interventions on the local, regional and imperial levels, was also a turning point in the perception of Zionism within the Jerusalem District. In *Filasṭīn*, it marked the end of Sephardi and Ashkenazi contributions to the press debate on Zionism during fall of 1913. However, it is to be stressed that the editors did not engage personally in the campaign against Reḥovot, although the affair marked a turning point in pre-World War I Jewish-Arab relations. It was other authors in *Filasṭīn* who interpreted the 'Zarnuqa incident' as an omen of the disaster that would befall local people as a result of Zionist migration, while the editors were in late summer and early fall of 1913 preoccupied with attacks on the Patriarchate and the governor because of the escalation in the intra-Orthodox conflict.

The final turn in the discussion of Zionist migration in *Filasṭīn* occurred at the beginning of 1914, when the coverage burst into a full-blown anti-Zionist campaign driven by the editors. This happened when, and also because, the editors were deprived of their leading role in the anti-clerical battle after the suspension of their newspaper following their confrontations with the Jerusalem governor and Jaffa's *qā ʾimaqām* and the radical intervention of Azmi Bek, who put a stop to their further personal engagement in the Orthodox cause. Suddenly, there was a vacuum in the paper's content, especially in the Local News, and it was filled with an anti-Zionist campaign, a 'safe' enemy for the ʿĪsās who were fearful of a possible suspension of their newspaper.

This study has proposed that the radical turn towards the Zionist movement as main enemy was a side effect of the loss of the editors' leading role in the Arab Orthodox *nahḍa*. The Zionist movement was a 'safe' enemy for the ʿĪsās with regard to state censorship, since, by the end of 1913, the Zionist movement was discussed in the Arabic press of Jerusalem, Beirut and Damascus as a foreign national movement and territorial threat in the Ottoman realms, as is clear from many articles reprinted in *Filasṭīn*. It was therefore easy for the ʿĪsās to take up and reproduce the image of the Zionists as an 'external' enemy undermining Ottoman unity, an image that was meanwhile circulating in the press discourse in the Palestinian provinces and beyond.

With regard to the ʿĪsās' personal anti-Zionist sentiment, it is to be stressed that they were far more hostile to the Muslim Maghrebis residing in the *qaḍā ʾ*, whom, in 1913, they wanted expelled from the region. Further, from the inception of *Filasṭīn*, the ʿĪsās' rhetoric was by far more aggressive with regard to the Patriarchal establishment than it was regarding the Zionists. Form the beginning of their anti-clerical campaign, they equated the monks with 'parasites' and stigmatized the Patriarchate as the illegitimate 'rule of strangers', ethnically and culturally.

In the debate on Zionist migration, the editors were much more careful. They could not afford to ground their opposition on an ethnical or religious argument, since the 'Israelite brothers' were conceptually part of the 'Ottoman unity', which was, in the view of the ʿĪsās, essential for stability and development in the Jerusalem District. And practically speaking, the Israelites *and* the Zionists were both successfully involved Jaffa's trade and political networks. The debate on Zionism in *Filasṭīn* was clearly not a religious dispute but a debate over the control of local recourses, although this debate on the Zionist question became a key issue in inter-confessional relations in the Jerusalem District from 1913 onwards. Both, Palestinian Christians and Sephardi Jews, sought to stabilize their alliances with the Muslims, while the rivalry between the two minorities radically increased. This is at least evidenced with reference to Sephardi-Christian intellectuals between Jaffa and Jerusalem, as demonstrated in the hostilities between *Filasṭīn* and the *Ḥerut* circle, and the boycott campaign against *Filasṭīn* initiated by the latter.

In the context of the boycott actions implemented by Zionist immigrants against local Muslims, Christians and Israelites as to enforce 'Hebrew labor', the gap between Sephardi Jews and Christians in the Jaffa region increased. In September 1913, the ʿĪsās called on local Israelites to explicitly distance themselves from the Zionist movement to prove their loyalty to the local society, which indicates that the debate on Zionist migration had started to cause inter-confessional tension. In Jaffa, a provincial environment were people were forced to deal with each other economically and could not even avoid each other personally, it was fundamental to distinguish between Sephardi Israelites, old-established and financially significant Ashkenazi Jews, and a new generation of Russian Jewish immigrants who were influenced by a more revolutionary Zionist ideology of the Second Aliyya and the anti-Jewish pogroms occurring in Tsarist Russia and who sought to enforce an exclusivist economy and thus, upset local economic balances in Jaffa. These Zionists were the declared enemy in *Filasṭīn*, stigmatized as troublemakers and the ones who were about to ruin Ottoman Palestinian unity and socio-economic stability in the *qaḍāʾ* and create chaos.

The distinction between Zionists and 'other Jews' was strictly maintained during the whole period investigated in this study. This firm principle of the ʿĪsās is demonstrated in their regard for Goldenberg, a well-established and integrated Ashkenazi and director of the Zionist APB in Palestine. The editors were on extraordinarily good terms with him and praised him for his respectful attitude towards Muslims and Christians and his goodwill to local investors. Thus, the approval or criticism of Zionist immigration was in the local perception intertwined with the question of whether it was a driving force for or an obstacle to local development.

By the second half of 1913, the mistrust of the Palestinian public in the Jerusalem District towards the Zionist movement as a purely exclusivist movement had overwhelmed the earlier argument that the Zionist immigrants would stimulate progress and local development. The debate was over. However, the principles of 'unity and stability' were imperative: the ʿĪsās were in personal contact and economically involved not only with Jews but also with Zionists, and they benefitted from these involvements. The stigmatization of Jews who were potential investors would be contrary to this principle. Jews who contributed to local development were easily included in the 'unity paradigm', and the Ashekanzi Goldenberg, for example, was even portrayed by the ʿĪsās as 'compatriot' (*waṭanī*).

The anti-Zionist campaign in *Filasṭīn* in 1914 focused on the portrayal of the Zionist movement as a national movement that was seeking to lay its hands on Palestine and was backed by imperialist powers that supported foreign Jewish migration in order to expand their influence through the protection of minorities. The 'Cataclysm' was beginning to be felt, and the Zionist movement was seen as a puppet, installed by the imperialist powers in the Middle East. The coverage of Zionism in 1914 took the form of a 'static' and not very creative campaign. It was dominated by documentaries of the activities of the WZO, decisions taken at Zionist congresses, articles reprinted from other newspapers, and the publication of political 'programs'; a new trend. In the summer of 1914, *Filasṭīn* published an extensive translation of Menachim Ussishkin's program of political Zionism. Reports on the Zionist movement became increasingly inflammatory and focused on the observation of their activities on an international scale. A lot of these reports were reprinted or translated from elsewhere, however, personal comments of the editors were totally missing.

Filasṭīn's character as a 'protest forum' had surprisingly ceased during 1914. At the same time, the amount of advertisement rose dramatically in *Filasṭīn*, sometimes covering three pages in a six-page issue. It is left to speculations on the exact reasons behind this shift and the identity of the actors commissioning these ads. Interestingly, a whole new range of foreign products appeared on the advertisement page during 1914, mostly promoting European luxury hygiene and medical products.

5. General Conclusions and Outlook

This micro-study on the changing ethno-confessional relations in the Jerusalem District from 1911–14 through the spectacles of *Filasṭīn* as a local medium for public debate has identified three cases of prime importance that reflect how the parameters of Ottoman modernity were translated into local Palestinian group relations: the intra-Orthodox conflict between local Arab Orthodox and the Patriarchate, the potential impacts of Zionist migration on the District, and the improvement of public security in the Jaffa *qaḍāʾ*, including the exclusion of Maghrebi migrants. These cases were controversially discussed by a 'pool of publishers' that *Filasṭīn* as a joint production strongly depended on. They all derived from the rising Palestinian middle or upper classes and were of different confessional and ethnic backgrounds but shared a very similar 'mindset' of moral values that was shaped by the 'modernization imperative', the concept of 'Ottoman unity', as the guarantee for political stability, and notions of the 'public sphere'. This primary mindset was the immovable 'template' that emanated into all the issues debated in *Filasṭīn* whereas the authors presented themselves as 'mouthpiece' of their communities and as 'educators' of the people and the government alike. However, it belongs to the ambivalence of Arab-Palestinian modernity in the years World War I years as an era of rapid transformation that political key concepts were rather fluid, as seen from the flexible application of national terminology (*šaʿb, umma, waṭan*), and the circulation of new concepts, such as of 'Turks versus Arab' and 'minorities' – elements of the post-War order that emerged during 1913–14 within a very brief incubation period, or a 'saddle period' before the outbreak of the War.

In reference to paradigms for alliances or segregation between groups, it was shown that this was not related to 'confession' or 'ethnicity' but strongly linked with the aims of economic 'development' and political 'stability'. In the region of Jaffa, the Maghrebis were excluded from the 'unity paradigm' and stigmatized as 'stranger elements' who were to be evicted from the Jaffa *qaḍāʾ* since they were a danger to security and trade while residing in the region as long as many other group in globalized Jaffa, being Arabic speakers *and* Muslims.

The controversy of Zionist migration to the region was to be approved or opposed was also strongly linked to the question if it was to be considered a driving force or an obstacle for local development, and supporters of Zionism contributed to the debate as long as the 'progressive power of Zionism' as an argument enjoyed some credibility in the public discourse. The increasing opposition to Zionism brought local Christian-Sephardi relations in the Jerusalem-Jaffa region into a crisis; and Sephardi contributions in *Filasṭīn* ceased in 1913 after the violent 'Zarnuqa incident' between Jewish settlers and Arab villagers.

The 'Arab Orthodox cause' in the Jerusalemite Patriarchate, the driving force behind the journalistic engagement of *Filasṭīn*'s editors, was a cultural reform movement with aspirations to access the Patriarchates economic resources. However, the 'Orthodox Movement' vastly exploited the constitutional discourse as to delegitimize the clerical establishment as the 'despotism' of a minority and 'Greek strangers' over a majority of indigenous 'citizens'. The conflict was ruled from the beginning by asymmetric power relation whereas the locals did not have legal means to pressure the Patriarchate, as seen from the Mixed Council as a platform for both conflict parties to negotiate reforms in the Orthodox dioceses. In the local perception, the Council was a sequence of failures with led to the outbreak of a political struggle and its suspension in fall 1913 until central governmental intervention revived it.

After that crisis, *Filasṭīn*'s editors and other leaders of 'dropped out' of the Movement due to government pressure. The content vacuum in *Filasṭīn* was filled with an anti-Zionist campaign in 1914 whereas the Zionist movement had meanwhile changed in the discourse of the Arab press from 'economic rival' to a 'political threat'; this under the impact of the Balkan Wars 1912/13 and the rise of other 'national questions' in the Empire. In 1914, it is to be observed that *Filasṭīn* was economically well established as an enterprise, belonged to the leading newspapers of the region. The prize, the editors paid for this success was partially the decline for *Filasṭīn* as a forum for open controversy and protest. Meanwhile, anti-Zionism had manifested in the public discourse and in 1914, the ethno-confessional balances had become more become fragile and certain groups had dropped out of the vision of Ottoman unity. The main interest of the editors, it seemed was the protection of the alliance with the Muslims.

Regarding further conceptual changes on group relations and the transformation of local alliances in Palestine during and right after World War I when the vision of 'Ottoman brotherhood' finally ceased, much is still left in the dark and could be subject of future research on the era of the Ottoman Cataclysm.

VI. Glossary and Appendices

1. Appendix I: Resolutions on the Arab Orthodox Case

1.1. Summary of the 1910 Resolution

The following paragraphs treat the demands handed in by the Orthodox laity to the Imperial Commission and its responses, defined in the 1910 Resolution, based on Ḫūrī's account, which I have translated and summarized in so far as it concerns the intra-Orthodox conflict and the debates in the Mixed Council between 1911 and 1914.

The First Demand: Communal Councils

The first demand formulated by the laity was the creation of 'communal councils' (*maǧālis ǧamāʿa*) in each *qaḍāʾ* to be entrusted with the administration of 'local' or 'communal' *waqf*s and their revenues, as pointed out article 111 of the Fundamental Law. The government respond admitted that this request was 'in line with the Fundamental Law when, in the future, a system for the election and obligations of the mentioned councils will be enacted by the High Porte'. However, it added that this was to take place 'in line with the conditions of the *awqāf* in Jerusalem, its surrounding areas and all the other regions and communities'.[1] Bertram and Luke mention that the acceptance of this first demand was 'merely nominal' as there was practically 'no communal *waqf* to administrate'.[2]

The Second Demand: the Mixed Council

The second demand of the laity was the formation of a Mixed Council analogous to the model of the Council in the Patriarchate of Constantinople. This Council was to be headed by the patriarch and would consist of 'one third monks and the

1 Ḫūrī and Ḫūrī 1992, 262–263.
2 Bertram and Luke 1925, 265.

other two-thirds laymen elected by the local people'. It would have 'authority to supervise schools, places of worship and all *awqāf* and to regulate and administer the various incomes'. Further, it would be the 'authority over all matters concerning the dioceses belonging to the Patriarchate'.[3] The government response to the second demand was in favor of the 'sublime and high *berats* (*al-baraʾāt aš-šāhānīya al-ʿāliya*) granted to patriarchs of Jerusalem since the olden times', which contradicted the right of the laity to have a say in the administration of church property. It was confirmed that the patriarch had the right to 'regulate and dispose of what belongs to the Patriarchate, like the patriarchs before him';[4] and it was confirmed that nobody could oppose these inherited rights 'by any means',

> because the monasteries and pilgrimage sites in Jerusalem are not local in character but belong to the citizens and all Ottoman Orthodox; and since the formation of such councils in Jerusalem and the participation of the local laity in the administration of the monasteries and shrines attached to it, is against the old customs undermining the sublime berats mentioned; and since the patriarchal system complies with the exceptional nature particular to the Patriarchate mentioned, which has been established since the olden times on the ground that it is a monastic body – and because of that character it receives some donations that other spiritual churches do not receive; and since this system … guarantees benefits for the local Orthodox in all aspects – the demand to modify the system is not grounded on [legal] right or true need.[5]

The government permitted the formation of a 'joint committee' for the administration of the Patriarchate on condition that it was only responsible for *social matters*, although it was admitted by the government that a state of disorder

3 '*Taʿdīl niẓām baṭrakḫānat al-Quds ʿalā asās niẓām baṭrakḫānat al-Istāna wa-taškīl maǧlis muḫtalaṭ bihā taḥta riʾāsat al-baṭrīark yakūn ṯulṯahu min ar-ruhbān wa-ṯ-ṯulṯāni al-āḫirāni min al-ʿawāmm yantaḫibuhum al-ahālī l-maḥallīyūn …. ʿalā an yakūn lahu ḥaqq al-munāẓara ʿalā l-madāris wa-l-maʿābid wa-ǧamīʿ al-awqāf wa-ḍabṭ wa-idārat al-wāridāt al-muḫtalifa wa-an yakūn ilayhi marǧaʿ ḫuṣūṣīyāt al-abrašīyāt at-tābiʿa li-l-baṭrīarkīya.*' Ḫūrī and Ḫūrī 1992, 263.

4 '*Li-l-baṭrīyark an yaḍbuṭ wa-yataṣarraf bi-mā yaḫtaṣṣ li-l-baṭrīyarkīya ka-mā ǧarā ʿalā ḍabṭihi wa-t-taṣarruf al-baṭārika salafāʾuhu.*' Ḫūrī and Ḫūrī 1992, 263. Here, various categories of real estate are referred to, such as vineyards, gardens, farms, mills, fields, grazing lands, houses and stores, trees, holy springs, monasteries with all their belongings, including animals, and everything dedicated to the Church. See Ḫūrī and Ḫūrī 1992, 263–264.

5 '*Al-adyura wa-z-ziyārāt bi-l-Quds aš-šarīf laysa lahā ṣiffa maḥallīya bal hiya mutaʿalliqa bi-l-waṭanīyīn wa-ʿumūm al-urṯūḏuks al-ʿuṯmānīyīn wa-bimā anna taškīl maǧālis ka-hāḏihi bi-l-Quds wa-štirāk al-ʿawāmm fī idārat al-adyura wa-l-mazārāt al-mutaʿalliqa bihā muḫālif li-l-ʿawāʾid al-qadīma wa-limā taṣraḥ bi-hi al-baraʾāt al-ʿāliya ka-mā anna hāḏā al-amr muḫīll bi-mtiyāzāt al-baṭrīyarkīya al-maḏkūra wa-bimā anna niẓām al-baṭrīyarkīya huwa muwāfiq li-l-mawqiʿ al-istiṯnāʾī al-muḫtaṣṣ bi-l-baṭrīyarkīya al-maḏkūra al-muʾassasa munḏu al-qadīm ʿalā hayʾat dayr wa-taḥṣul bi-hāḏihi aṣ-ṣiffa ʿalā baʿḍ al-musāʿadāt lā taḥṣul ʿalayhā ġayruhā min al-kanāʾis ar-rūḥānīya wa-bimā anna niẓāmahā hāḏā yatakaffal bi-taʾmīn manāfiʿ al-urṯūḏuksīyīn al-waṭanīyīn bi-kull al-wuǧūh kāna ṭalab taʿdīl an-niẓām ġayr mustanad ʿalā ḥaqq wa-ḥtiyāǧ ḥaqīqī.*' Ḫūrī and Ḫūrī 1992, 264.

reigned in the educational and welfare system as a result of neglect by the Patriarchate. The report specified:

> It was discovered from the complaints that the elementary schools and hospitals founded and run by the Patriarchate are not in a state of order and the sums that are required to be assigned to the poor are at risk of misuse and waste (muʿarraḍa li-sūʾ al-istiʿmāl wa-t-taṣarruf). Based on that – and in compliance with the first article of the patriarchal system, which states that the Patriarchate is obliged to take care of the schools and hospitals attached to the monasteries; to take care of the poor according to the extent of the monasteries' revenues; and to guarantee that these duties are accomplished in an appropriate manner; to reform the local people's hospitals and schools established to treat the poor and to spread knowledge – it is necessary to establish a joint committee (hayʾa muḫtalata) under the presidency of the patriarch or his deputy, consisting of twelve members of whom six members shall be clerics together with the president and who are to be appointed by the Patriarchate; and the other six (members) shall be elected by local notables on the basis of an electoral system to be decided on by the Patriarchate and representatives of the community (muʿtabarī l-milla).
>
> By the end of the first year after the establishment of the committee, one half of each team will be renewed and replaced by drawing lots (bi-l-qarʿa). Then after the second year, the other half of it will be renewed and replaced systematically. The local government will be informed officially by the Patriarchate about its composition; once at the beginning [of its formation] and then each time when it is annually renewed.[6]
>
> The obligations of this committee are: to investigate and examine (al-baḥṯ wa-t-tadqīq) what is happening among the population and what is transmitted by the Patriarchate (yuḥāl min) with approval of the Synod about everything concerning marriage and the setting of expenses; and to inform the Patriarchate through a report about the amount. to supervise (al-munāẓara) the administration of all the finances and properties bequeathed to it [the Patriarchate] and dedicated to meet the needs of the poor and needy ones, as well as their hospitals and churches, villages and towns in a manner that complies with the sublime regulations stipulated in the Constitution on Ṣafar 7 of 1278.[7] Further, to supervise the schools of the local Orthodox and its administration, direct its education system and reform it along with the reformation of the hospitals according to the needs of the population. Moreover, to supervise the distribution of alms to the poor and needy people and [to supervise] their housing and to spend it on them in a just manner (bi-ṣūra ʿādila).[8]
>
> One-third of the Patriarchate's revenues, but not less than 30,000 lira, which is according to the present amount of revenues, and if there are no circumstances that for some reasons prevent this, are to be dedicated to and made available for this committee every year, and in installments appropriate for the Patriarchate; to be spent on the hospitals

6 Ḫūrī and Ḫūrī 1992, 265.
7 Ḫūrī and Ḫūrī 1992, 265–266.
8 Ḫūrī and Ḫūrī 1992, 266.

and schools dedicated to the local people and the housing of the poor and their other needs.

Concerning the administration of the churches, schools and all the other institutions in the villages, as well as the properties belonging to the Patriarchate that concern the locals, and the administration of their income and expenditure, it is necessary to transfer it to trustees who are to be elected by the local people, whose electoral system must be set up by the mixed committee and who are under the authority of the spiritual leaders, known as the Ighoumenos.[9]

The Third Demand: Access of Local People to the Fraternity and Clerical Ranks

In the third demand, the laity demanded 'access for local Orthodox to the monastic order' (*ad-duḫūl fī silk ar-rahbana*) to 'preserve the principle of equality between them and other monks' (*murāʿāt qāʿidat al-musāwāt baynahum wa-bayna sāʾir ar-rahbana*) and to 'allow them into spiritual ranks' (*tarqiyatahum ilā l-marātib ar-rūḥīya*). Further, it was demanded that candidates accepted into the monastic order would be confirmed by the Mixed Council, so nobody would be able to access the Convent without approval from the Council.[10] Here, the government referred to the patriarchal claim that the monastic body had never refused access to the Fraternity to locals who possessed the necessary qualifications.[11] The government therefore announced that this matter was to be put in the hands of the Patriarchate to deal with it in a just manner, but also pointed out that the appointment of monks had, in line with the sublime *berats*, to be performed by the spiritual leaders only. To conclude, it was 'unacceptable' and 'not valid to take the opinion or approval of councils composed of laymen', as this was not practiced in any other Orthodox patriarchate.[12]

9 '*Ammā idārat al-kanāʾis wa-l-makātib wa-sāʾir al-muʾassasāt al-mawǧūda fī l-qurā wa-l-aṭyān al-mansūba ilā al-baṭrīyarkīya wa-l-mutaʿalliqa bi-l-waṭanīyīn wa-kaḏālika idārat wāridātihā wa-maṣārīfihā fa-min al-muqtaḍā iḥālatihā ilā mutawallīn yantaḫibuhum al-ahālī l-maḥallīyūn ʿalā an yuʿayyanū ṣūrat intiḫābihim min qibal al-hayʾa al-muḫtalaṭa wa-yakūnū taḥta riʾāsat ar-ruʾasāʾ ar-rūḥānīyīn al-maʿrūfīn bi-l-Īġūminūs.*' Ḫūrī and Ḫūrī 1992, 266.

10 Ḫūrī and Ḫūrī 1992, 266–267.

11 This had been granted in the *Katastikon* by Patriarch Ierotheos in 1875 and was reconfirmed by Damianos. The situation on the ground was different. Until today, local people in the Convent are a minority. Panzer 1998, 26, n. 44.

12 '*Ammā amr inḍimām raʾy al-maǧālis al-mušakkala min al-ʿawāmm wa-muwāfaqatihim fa-ḏālika ġayr marʿī l-iǧrāʾ wa-lā fī baṭrīyarkīya min baṭrīarkīyāt ar-rūm fa-ʿalā ḏālika wuǧida istidʿāʾ al-waṭanīyīn al-mutaʿalliq bi-hāḏā al-amr ġayr qābil li-l-iǧāba.*' Ḫūrī and Ḫūrī 1992, 267.

The Fourth Demand: Patriarchal Elections and the Holy Synod

The fourth demand of the laity was for the modification of the system for patriarchal elections and to 'create and expand the sphere of the right for the population to become involved ... in the electoral process'. The demand was also to 'limit the functions of the Synod to spiritual matters' and 'admit clergy recognized as priests to the Synod'.[13] The government pointed out that there was no reason at all to adjust the patriarchal electoral system. The involvement of local people in the electoral process was rejected, and seats on the Synod were restricted to bishops (*maṭārina*) and archimandrites as was the case in all Greek Orthodox patriarchates. Thus, the demand for priests to have seats on the Synod 'is of course not compatible with the regulations of the [patriarchal] system or with common practice'.[14]

The Fifth Demand: Residential Duty for Bishops Elected by the Local People

The fifth demand was for bishops to reside in their dioceses, and for all bishops, archimandrites, priests and deacons (*šammās*) to be elected by the local population.[15] The government refused both, explaining that the position of bishops in the dioceses of the Jerusalemite Patriarchate was merely 'nominal' as they, unlike in other patriarchates, did not enjoy sublime *berat*s or receive any income from the local people (*laysa lahum ʿāʾidāt min al-ahālī wa-maʾmūrīyatuhum hiya ʿalā nawʿ mā iʿtibārīya*). Furthermore, the election of bishops, archimandrites, priests and deacons by the local people was not compatible either with the privileges or with the custom of the Greek Orthodox Church.[16]

The Sixth Demand

The sixth demand was that monks be prohibited from taking up secular occupations according to the principle of equality and in order not to privilege one nation over another. The government responded that it was self-evident that this point was to be implemented in line with the measures mentioned before.[17]

The Seventh Demand

The seventh demand was for the removal of all monastic privileges and for the prohibition of access to the monastic order for non-Ottomans. The government replied that, as the monastic privileges were stipulated in the fifth article of the

13 '*Taškīl wa-tawzīʿ niṭāq al-ḥaqq bi-tadāḫul ahālī ... fī l-muʿāmalāt al-intiḫābīya wa-yaḥṣir waẓāʾif maǧlis as-Sīnūdis fī l-umūr ar-rūḥānīya wa bi-idḫāl al-ḫawārina al-maʿrūfīna bi-l-qusūs bi-s-sinūdis.*' Ḫūrī and Ḫūrī 1992, 267–268.

14 Ḫūrī and Ḫūrī 1992, 268–269.

15 Ḫūrī and Ḫūrī 1992, 269.

16 Ḫūrī and Ḫūrī 1992, 269–270.

17 Ḫūrī and Ḫūrī 1992, 270.

Fundamental Law, it was 'self-evident' (*min al-badīhī*) that this was no subject for discussion. As for the second aspect, it was assured that this was in compliance with article 15 of the patriarchal system that all bishops had to be of Ottoman citizenship.[18]

The Eighth Demand

This demand was that the patriarch should only be deposed for a serious reason and if it was approved by Orthodox representatives and priests. The response to this was that the election of the patriarch as stipulated in the patriarchal system, and his removal or the participation of the locals in it was not a subject for discussion.[19]

The Ninth Demand

This demand asked for the unification (*tawḥīd*) of revenues from several sources and the publication of an annual balance sheet of income and expenditure. The government rejected this as there was no need to abolish the division of the Patriarchate's revenues. Concerning an annual balance sheet, the government recommended it, in order to remind the Patriarchate to work in compliance with the third article of the patriarchal system and to implement 'sound administration' (*ḥusn idāra*).[20]

The Tenth Demand

This demand was for the formation of an Arab choir (*ǧawq*) to sing in Arabic in every church, including the Church of the Holy Sepulcher, although the prayers were to be conducted in Greek. The government refused and considered it necessary to keep the status quo in the holy places. Moreover, the way of conducting prayers in Greek in churches and shrines 'shared by Greek Orthodox and other confessions' (*muštaraka bayna ar-rūm wa-sā'ir aṭ-ṭawā'if*) was based on regulations fixed in the *Katastikon*, which could not be changed. In addition, prayers in the churches of Jerusalem belonging to locals only, and in the villages and towns, were already conducted in Arabic 'since olden times'.[21]

The Eleventh Demand

This was a demand to 'register the pious endowments in the name of the Orthodox community' (*qayd al-awqāf ʿalā ism aṭ-ṭā'ifa*). The government response did not exclude this for the future but in practice retained the status quo, clar-

18 Ḫūrī and Ḫūrī 1992, 270–271.
19 Ḫūrī and Ḫūrī 1992, 271–272.
20 Ḫūrī and Ḫūrī 1992, 272.
21 Ḫūrī and Ḫūrī 1992, 272–273.

ifying that the registry of endowments in the name of Orthodox communities depended on a modification of the law for the disposal of property (*taʿdīl al-qawānīn al-ḥāḍira al-mutaʿalliqa bi-t-taṣarruf bi-l-amlāk*). The government explained:

> When these necessary modifications are implemented, then endowments can be registered in the name of whoever they go back to or belong to (ʿāʾida ʿalayhi). And when they go back to the monasteries and the shrines and the churches, then they can be registered under their names. And when they are bound to the benefit of the people they can be registered under the name of the communities. But for now, there is no need to undertake [such] measures. End.[22]

1.2. Summary of the Regulations Concerning the Local Trustees

As the 1910 Resolution admitted that Orthodox institutions in the dioceses were open to 'misuse and waste' by the Patriarchate, trustees elected by local people were to manage schools, churches, hospitals, poor houses and other Orthodox institutions in the villages and towns outside Jerusalem classified as 'local' (*mutaʿalliqa bi-l-waṭanīyīn*). They were to supervise the expenditure and revenues of these institutions under the authority of the spiritual head in the dioceses, the 'Ighoumenos'.[23]

The regulations concerning the election of local trustees were passed by the Mixed Council in spring 1911 and published in *Filasṭīn* in February 1914. It was fixed that the management of pilgrimage sites and churches of monasteries considered as *waqf* were to be excluded from the remit of the trustees, and that their functions concerning the schools were still to be defined by a board of experts for the 'management and synchronization' of education. The Mixed Council decided that, first, the patriarch was to send a document (*manšūr*) to all dioceses ordering their elections.[24] Then, the parish priests were to gather with local community leaders (*wuǧahāʾ aš-šaʿb*) to function as a monitoring committee for the elections in which every 'individual Orthodox above the age of twenty' should have the right to vote.[25] Second, the election was to be conducted as a 'general vote' (*at-taṣwīt al-ʿāmm*). If problems arose from this in some places, the vote there was to be be conducted in line with local custom (*bi-mūǧab aṭ-ṭarīqa al-maʿlūfa fīhā*). In case of dissent (*iḏā ḥaṣala ḫilāf*), the majority of votes would be decisive.[26] Third, the trustees were to be elected only by Greek Orthodox

22 Ḫūrī and Ḫūrī 1992, 273–274.
23 Ḫūrī and Ḫūrī 1992, 265–266.
24 *Filasṭīn*, 14 February 1914: 307/3/5.
25 *Filasṭīn*, 14 February 1914: 307/4/1.
26 *Filasṭīn*, 14 February 1914: 307/4/1.

who were registered as Ottomans, came from the Jerusalemite Patriarchate, and were assumed to be 'righteous people of good morals', registered in the Greek Orthodox community (*asmāʾuhum muqayyada fī siǧill millat ar-rūm al-urṯū-ḏuks*) and able to read and write. Fourth, the number of trustees elected was not to exceed six persons in the cities, and three in the villages. The trustees were to be elected for a two-year term.[27] Fifth, the monitoring committee for the elections was to deliver a report (*maḍbaṭa*) that contained the names and signatures of all voters to the patriarch, who would transfer it to the Mixed Council. The Council was to confirm it and investigate irregularities regarding it (*li-l-muṣādaqa ʿalayhā wa-taḥqīq kull iʿtirāḍ bi-šaʾnihā*). The Council was also the principal contact for the local trustees in any case (signed by the council's secretary: Ǧarīs Saʿīdeh, on 1 April 1911).[28]

1.3. Summary of the Resolution of 30 December 1913

The first article of the resolution, issued in December 1913 by the royal commission headed by ʿAzmī Bek, stipulated that the Mixed Council should be reopened. Second, the new delegates elected in Salṭ, Kerak and Nablus were to replace those who had finished their term, and elections for the new delegates from Jerusalem, Gaza and Beit Jala wre to be conducted immediately. In the future, the persons allowed to vote were to pass a report on the elections and have it confirmed by the local government to avoid contradictory reports being in circulation. For this, the representatives in the dioceses were to reform the electoral regulations.

Third, the budget the Council was to administer was to be locked in an iron safe. One clerical member and one lay member were to hold a key. Every amount spent from this budget had to be decided within the Council and the head of the Council was to give the order for its expenditure. Fourth, regarding the Jerusalemites, it was decided that the Patriarchate had already spent a lot of money on the poor and that a housing allocation of 8,000 lira per year was sufficient. A committee of three monks and three Jerusalemites was in charge of a register of Orthodox households that were to receive allocations and was to present it to the Council for confirmation before the money was distributed. The government would mediate if conflicts over the division of the budget or its distribution should occur. Fifth, the patriarch would chair the Mixed Council or appoint a representative. Sixth, the Council's decisions would be taken on the basis of a majority vote, as defined earlier, and the government would intervene if a deci-

27 *Filasṭīn*, 14 February 1914: 307/4/2.
28 *Filasṭīn*, 14 February 1914: 307/4/2.

sion so taken was not implemented. Seventh, based on the earlier resolution, the 'representatives' (*wukalāʾ*), as the trustees were now called, to watch over the administration of institutions in various cities classified as local were to be elected immediately according to the electoral system previously established by the Council. Eighth, regarding school reforms, one school should be opened in Jerusalem and one in Jaffa, as a 'florishing town' (*balda ʿāmira*). Each should have a boys' and a girls' department and a boarding school for 40 pupils, who should be accepted from all dioceses in numbers proportionate to its population. In each school, 'competent teachers' were to be appointed as an administrative school board, which was not open to members of the Mixed Council. However, the Council was to appoint specialists (*iḫtiṣāṣīyīn*) to oversee the schools' administrational and educational matters. Ninth, the churches and schools closed during the Orthodox conflict were to be quickly reopened. For this, the local people were to elect representatives. Tenth, since many people who rented houses or shops from the Patriarchate did not pay their rent, they were required to hand them over or legal steps would be taken.[29]

2. Appendix II: Chronology of the Orthodox Movement, 1908–14

Year	Event and Further Information
1908	A delegation of Orthodox notables from Jerusalem handed in demands to the Patriarch, announcing the formation of a local council of 40 members in compliance with article 111 of the Fundamental Law.
1908	Outbreak of violence in Jerusalem.
1908	Occupation of the church of *Mār Yaʿqūb*, situated in the center of the Patriarchate.
1909	On July 13th 1909, a lay delegation from the Jerusalem District arrived at Istanbul for negotiations and handed in their demands to the government until it returned on October 12th 1909.
1910	The 1910-Resolution as a Governmental Response on Orthodox lay demands was issued by a governmental commission and sent by the Council of Ministers' in Istanbul to Jerusalem.
1910	Formation of the Mixed Council in December 1910 with 12 delegates from Jerusalem and the dioceses (six clerics, six lay Orthodox).
1911	Release of the Resolution of the Ministry of Justice – regarding the demand of the Jerusalemites to exclude their traditional rent allowances from their share of the social budget assigned to the Mixed Council.
1911	Issue of Resolution 139 by the Ministry of Justice and Religious Affairs (*niẓārat al-ʿadalīya wa-l-maḏāhib*) on 30 Hazayran 327 (June 1911) regarding the local trustees' issue (published in FILASṬĪN, 25. 11. 1911).

29 *Filasṭīn*, 17 January 1914: 299/1/1–2.

(Continued)

Year	Event and Further Information
1912	Release of the 1912 Resolution by the Grand Vizierate *(aṣ-ṣadāra al-ʿuẓmā)* in February 1912.
1913	Suspension of the Mixed Council due to the Patriarchs' strategy of 'delay'.
1913/ 14	Release of a new resolution by the High Commission, headed by ʿAzmī Bek on December 30th 1913 in Jerusalem
1914	Reopening of the Mixed Council in January 1914
1914	Enactment of local trustees' councils in the dioceses, at least in Jaffa

3. Appendix III: Persons Engaged in the intra-Orthodox Conflict, 1910–14

Lay Delegates in the Mixed Council

Name	Further Information
Ḫalīl Baydas	Delegate for Nazareth in the Mixed Council, 1910–13; editor of the reform magazine an-Nafāʾs al-ʿAṣrīya; changing in his affiliation
Ilyās al-Ḥalabī	Delegate of Jerusalem in the Mixed Council, 1911–13; first enemy of the Patriarch, then affiliated with him
ʿĪsā Yūsuf Ḥazbūn	Delegate for Bethlehem in the Mixed Council, 1910–13; usually affiliated with Yūsuf al-ʿĪsā and his supporter in the opposition to the Patriarch
ʿAwdeh Ḫalīl	Delegates for Beit Jala in the Mixed Council, 1914, affiliation not known
Yūsuf al-ʿĪsā	Delegate for Jaffa in the Mixed Council, 1911–13; leading oppositional against the Patriarch
Yaʿqūb Efendī Maḫlūf	Delegates for Beit Jala in the Mixed Council, 1914, affiliation not known
Šawqī al-Malikī or Mulkī	Delegate for Acre in the Mixed Council, 1910–13, changing in his affiliation
ʿAwdeh as-Sālim	Delegate for Salṭ in the Mixed Council, 1910–13, not very much present in the meeting minutes
Ǧurǧī Zaḫariyā	Delegate of Jerusalem in the Mixed Council, 1910–11; enemy of the Patriarch

Orthodox Activists or Supporters of the Arab Orthodox Cause

Name	Further Information
Miḫāʾīl Aṭlīl	Author of readers' letter from Jerusalem
Iskandar Niqūlā Badar	Latin Orthodox, correspondent of *Filasṭīn* in Beit Jala

(Continued)

Name	Further Information
Iskandar (al-Ḫūrī) al-Baytǧālī	Pedagogue, poet and journalist from Beit Jala with reformist and moralist agenda, author of the column *Lilies in the Field (zanābīq al-ḥaql)* in *Filasṭīn* from 1911–13/14
Ḥanā᾽ Miḫā᾽īl Buyūk,	Palestinian emigrant from Bethlehem, agent of *Filasṭīn* in Chile, La Calera
Salīm Buyūk	Member of the Buyūk family in Chile
Salīm Ǧurǧī al-Ḫaml	Author of readers letter, teacher at the Orthodox *Mār Ǧirǧis School* for boys in Jerusalem
ʿĪsā Yūsuf Ḥazbūn	Author of readers' letters and delegate for Bethlehem in the Mixed Council, 1910–13; strongly affiliated with Yūsuf al-ʿĪsā
Ǧurǧī Ḥanā Ḥazbūn	Member of the Orthodox Ḥazbūn family from Bethlehem, migrated to Chile, readers' letters from there
Bandalī al-Ḫūrī	Journalist and writer from Bethlehem
Ǧibrān Maṭar	Writer and activist from Beit Jala
Ḫalīl Naṣr	Author of readers' letter from Haifa
Būlos Šahādeh	Protestant, Journalist and activist from Jerusalem, editor of *Mir᾽āt aš-Šarq*
Ḫalīl as-Sakākīnī	Pedagogue, writer and activist from Jerusalem, director of the Ottoman *Constitutional School*, engaged in the modernization of Orthodox education
Ḥanā Abū ṣ-Ṣawf	Palestinian emigrant in Mexico and author of readers' letters
Ḫalīl Qazāqīh	Activist in the Orthodox Community in Bethlehem
Ǧurǧī al-Ḫūrī Yaʿqūb	Pedagogue from Beit Sahour, articles for the modernization of Palestinian education

Supporters of the Greek Orthodox Clergy or the Patriarch

Archimandrite Dosithios	Delegate in the Mixed Council
Archimandrite Eftimios	Delegate in the Mixed Council
Archimandrite Makarios	Delegate in the Mixed Council
Archimandrite Yūsuf	Delegate in the Mixed Council
Muṭrān Malatios	Deputy of the Patriarch in the Mixed Council
Muṭran Sofronios	Delegate in the Mixed Council

Members of the New School Board, 1914

Archimandrite Bandalamion
Archimandrite Dositios (clerical delegate in the Mixed Council)
Ǧurǧī Zaḫariyā (former Jerusalemite lay delegate for Jerusalem)
Sulṭī Ibrāhīm (Jerusalemite Orthodox)

Secretary in the Mixed Council

Ǧarīs Sa ʿīdeh	Secretary of the Council in Spring 1911
Īsīdrūs aš-Šammās	Secretary of the Council later in 1911

4. Appendix IV: Glossary of Terms

Hebrew Terms

ʿaliyya (Pl. *ʿaliyyot*)	literally „rise"; Jewish migration to Eretz Yisra'el/Palestine.
ʿavoda ʿivrit	Hebrew labor.
Eretz Yisraʿel	Land of Israel.
ġalūt	Jewish Exile.
haskala	Movement for Jewish Enlightenment.
ḥalukka	Donations for the Jewish Communities in Eretz Yisra'el/Palestine.
kibbuš ha-ʿavoda	Conquest of Labor.
mošav (Pl. *mošavot*)	Jewish cooperative settlement.
šomer (Pl. *šomrim*)	Jewish guard.
yišuv	literally „settlement", Jewish population of Eretz Yisra'el/Palestine.

Arabic Terms

abrašīya	diocese.
afandī	"gentlemen", (Engl.: Efendi), honorary title.
archimandrite	episcopal rank in the hierarchy of the Greek Orthodox church below the bishop *(muṭrān)*, also applied to an abbot in charge of a group of monasteries, or a priest who was member of the monastic order.
badal ʿaskarī	(Tur.: *bedel-i askeri*) a tax, paid by Christians and Jews in lieu of Ottoman military service.
dūnam	(Engl.: dunam), square measure, 919 square meters.
ḏimmī	non-Muslim (under Muslim rule and protection).
ġāzī	(Engl.: ghazi), fighter.
ḥāḫāmbāšī	chief rabbi, honorary title for head of Ottoman Sephardi Jewish community.
ḫān	(Ottoman) household.
ḫawāǧa	„Mister", honorary title for non-Muslim dignitaries and Europeans.
Ighoumenos (Hegumenos)	Orthodox spiritual rank, similar to a bishop.

imtiyāzāt	"Capitulations", bilateral treaties between the Empire and European states that guaranteed their foreigner extraordinary privileges.
katastikon	literally „constitution" (Greek: *kata stikon* "by line"), the 1875-resolution, issued by Patriarch Ierotheos on imperial pressure, permitting lay participation in the Patriarchate of Jerusalem, including the establishment of a Mixed Council, which was never implemented.
līra	(Engl.: Lira), Ottoman pound.
liwāʾ	literally „banner", Ottoman district.
maǧīdī	silver coin of 20 piaster (see Buessow 2011, 563).
maǧlis baladī	Ottoman municipality council.
maǧlis idāra	Ottoman administrative council of a district or a subdistrict.
maǧlis ʿumūmī	Ottoman provincial council.
maǧlis al-wukalāʾ	(Tur.: *Meclis-i Vükela*), the Council of Ministers in Istanbul.
maḥlūl	literally „released", *mīrī* land of lapsed ownership that fell back to the state as not cultivated for three years.
matrūk	literally „left over", communal land, open areas (streets, village places, etc.) used by all inhabitants and freely to access.
mawāt	„uncultivated land" or land not in regular agricultural use. Since the *Tanzimat*, *mawāt* could be aquired also as *mulk* which was not restricted to agricultural use.
milla	(Tur.: *millet*), religious group, acknowledged community in the late Ottoman context.
mīrī	(Engl. *miri*), „state land" for which one could acquire from the Ottoman state the right to usufruct, for which taxes had to be paid, the *ṭābū*, and which was restricted to agricultural use. If *mīrī* was not cultivated for three years, it fell back to the state as *maḥlūl*.
muftī	(Engl.: mufti), Islamic jurist who is authorized to give juridical advise *(fatwa)* on the Islamic law and value system *(šarīʿa)*.
muḫtār	representative of a community, village, tribe to the Ottoman government.
mulk	(also: *milk*), private ownership of land and property.
mušāʿ	communal land ownership which is shared by the residents of a village and rotates among them regularly.
mutaṣarrif	governor of an Ottoman district.
mutaṣarrifīya	Ottoman district (see also, *liwāʾ*).
muṭrān	hierarchical rank in the Greek Orthodox Church which included metropolitans, archbishops and bishops.
nahḍa	literally „rise, Renaissance", modern Arabic movement as cultural Renaissance.
nakba	literally "catastrophe", meaning the Arab defeat in the Israeli War of Independence, 1948
niẓāra	Ottoman Ministry or supervising authority.
niẓārat al-ʿadlīya	the Ministry of Justice and Religious Affairs in Istanbul.

qaḍā'	subdistrict within an Ottoman district.
qāḍī	(Engl: qadi), judge and notary.
qāʾimaqām	Ottoman governor of a subdistrict.
qurūš (Sg. *qurš)*	Piaster.
riyāl	Ottoman silver coin.
šayḫ	(Engl: sheikh), honorary title for Islamic scholars, heads of families and tribes.
šūrā ad-dawla	State Council
aṣ-ṣadāra al-ʿuẓmā	Grand Vizierate.
tanẓīmāt	(Engl. *Tanzimat*), literally 're-organization', Ottoman reform period (1839–1976).
ṭābū	Ottoman title deed and name for taxes to be paid for land and property, also used for the Ottoman land registration office.
wālī	Ottoman governor of a province.
waqf (Pl. *awqāf*)	religious foundation.
wilāya	Ottoman province.
wīrkū	Ottoman property tax.

VII. Bibliography

Arabic Newspapers Consulted

Filasṭīn newspaper. Jaffa. 1911–14.
Al-Karmil newspaper. Haifa. 1914.

Reference Works

EI^2: Encyclopedia of Islam 1960 ff: Leiden.
EJ: Encyclopedia Judaica 1971: Jerusalem.
Wehr, Hans 1998: Arabisches Wörterbuch für die Schriftsprache der Gegenwart. Arabisch – Deutsch. 5. Edition. Wiesbaden.

Books and Articles

Abujaber, Raouf 2012: Arab Christianity and Jerusalem. A History of the Arab Christian Presence in the Holy City. London.
Abu-Manneh, Butrus 1999: The Rise of the Sanjak of Jerusalem in the Late Nineteenth Century. In: Pappé, Ilan (ed.): The Israel – Palestine question. London; 41–52.
Ágoston, Gábor; Masters, Bruce (eds.) 2009: Encyclopedia of the Ottoman Empire. New York.
Agmon, Iris 2004: Recording Procedures and Legal Culture in the Late Ottoman Shari'a Court of Jaffa, 1865–1890. In: Islamic Law and Society 11, no. 3; 333–377.
Agmon, Iris 2006: Family and Court, Legal Culture and Modernity in Late Ottoman Palestine. Middle East Studies beyond Dominant Paradigms. Syracuse, New York.
al'Āmirī, Su'ād 2003: 'Imārat qurā l-karāsī. Min tārīḫ al-iqṭā' fī rīf Filasṭīn fī l-qarnayn aṯ-ṯāmin wa-t-tāsi' 'ašar. Ramallah.
Allen, Phillip 2000: The Last Despot: Ethnic Consciousness, Power Politics, and the Orthodox Church in Late Ottoman Syria. PhD diss. Princeton University.

Alroey, Gur 2013: The Russian Terror in Palestine: The Bar Giora and Ha-Shomer Associations, 1907–20. In: Horowith, Brian; Ginsburg, Shai (eds.): Bounded Mind and Soul: Russia and Israel, 1880–2010. Bloomington; 31–60.

Altheide, David; Schneider, Christopher (eds.) 2013: Qualitative Media Analysis. 2nd edition. Los Angeles.

Anderson, Benedict 1996: Die Erfindung der Nation: zur Karriere eines folgenreichen Konzepts. Frankfurt/Main.

Anderson, Perry 1986: Agendas for Radical History. In: Radical History Review 36; 32–37.

Antonius, George 1979: The Arab Awakening: The Story of the Arab National Movement. (First published in 1938) New York.

al-ʿAqqād, Aḥmad Ḫalīl 1967: aṣ-Ṣiḥāfa al-ʿarabīya fī Filasṭīn. Damascus.

Aref, el-Aref 1974: Bedouin Love, Law and Legend: Dealing Exclusively with the Badu of Beersheba. (English Version of the Arabic 1944 edition) Jerusalem.

ʿĀrif, ʿĀrif al- 1934: Tārīḫ Biʾr as-Sabʿ wa-qabāʾilihā. Jerusalem.

ʿĀrif, ʿĀrif al- 1943: Tārīḫ Ġazza. Jerusalem.

Arnold, Rafael 2010: Das nationale und internationale Engagement französischer Juden: Die *Alliance Israélite Universelle*. In: Wyrwa, Ulrich (ed.): Einspruch und Abwehr. Die Reaktion des europäischen Judentums auf die Entstehung des Antisemitismus (1879–1914). Frankfurt/Main, New York; 43–69.

Aṣleh, Fādī 2012: Ǧarīdat Filasṭīn bayna al-hawīya al-ʿuṯmānīya wa-l-filasṭīnīya, 1911–14. http://fadyasleh.blogspot.de/2012/07/1911-1914_8304.html (accessed 30.08.2017).

Avineri, Shlomo 1999: Die Anfänge des Zionismus im historischen Kontext. In: Brenner, Michael; Weiss, Yfaat (eds.): Zionistische Utopie, israelische Realität: Religion und Nation in Israel, München; 18–38.

Avcı, Yasemin 2011: Jerusalem and Jaffa in the Late Ottoman Period: The Concession-Hunting Struggle for Public Works Projects. In: Ben-Bassat, Yuval; Ginio, Eyal (eds.): Late Ottoman Palestine. The Period of Young Turk Rule. London, New York; 81–102.

Avneri, Arieh 1984: The Claim of Dispossession: Jewish Land-Settlement and the Arabs, 1878–1948. Ramat Efal, Israel.

Auji, Hala 2016: Printing Arab Modernity. Book Culture and The American Press in Nineteenth-Century Beirut. Leiden.

Ayalon, Ami 1995: The Press in the Arab Middle East: a History. New York.

Ayalon, Ami 1998: Sihafa: The Arab Experiment in Journalism. In: Middle Eastern Studies 28, no. 2; 258–280.

Ayalon, Ami 2002: Modern Texts and their Readers in Late Ottoman Palestine. In: Middle Eastern Studies 38; 17–40.

Ayalon, Ami 2004: Reading Palestine. Printing and Literacy, 1900–1948, Austin.

Ayalon, Ami 2008: Private Publishing in the Nahda. In: International Journal of Middle East Studies 40, no. 4; 561–577.

Ayalon, Ami 2010: Arab Booksellers and Bookshops in the Age of Printing. 1850–1914. In: British Journal of Middle Eastern Studies 37, no. 1; 73–93.

Ayalon, Ami 2016: The Arab Print Revolution. Cultural Production and Mass Readership. Cambridge University Press.

Ayaß, Ruth (ed.) 2006: Qualitative Methoden der Medienforschung. Reinbek.

Baedeker, Karl 1875: Palästina und Syrien. Handbuch für Reisende. Verfasst von Albert Socin. Leipzig.

Baedeker, Karl 1912: Baedeker's Historical Palestine: Handbook for Travelers. 5th edition. Leipzig (reprint New York. 1985).
Baldensperger, Philip 1913: The Immovable East: Studies of the People and Customs of Palestine. Edited by Frederic Lees. London.
Barkey, Karen 2006: Changing Modalities of Empire. A Comparative Study of Ottoman and Habsburg Decline. In: Esherick, Josef; Kayali, Hasan; Van Young, Eric (eds.): From Empire to Nation: Historical Perspectives on the Making of the Modern World. Lanham Boulder; 167–197.
Baron, Beth 1991: Mothers, Morality and Nationalism in Early Twentieth-Century Egypt. In: Khalidi, Rashid; Anderson, Lisa; Muslih, Muhammad; Simon, Reeva (eds.): The Origins of Arab Nationalism. New York; 271–288.
Baron, Beth 2005: Egypt as a Woman: Nationalism, Gender, and Politics. Berkeley.
Barron, J. (ed.) 1923: Palestine: Report and General Abstracts of the Census of 1922. Government of Palestine.
Başak Kale 2014: Transforming an Empire: The Ottoman Empire's Immigration and Settlement Policies in the Nineteenth and Early Twentieth Centuries. In: Middle Eastern Studies, 50, no. 2; 252–271.
Bauer, Thomas 2007: Arabische Kultur. In: Ueding, Gerd (ed.): Historisches Wörterbuch der Rhetorik, vol. 8. Tübingen 1992f; 111–137.
Bauer, Thomas 2016: Ambiguität in der klassischen arabischen Rhetoriktheorie. In: Auge, Oliver; Witthöft, Christiane (eds.): Ambiguität im Mittelalter: Formen zeitgenössischer Reflexion und interdisziplinärer Rezeption. Berlin; 21–45.
Bawalsa, Nadim 2010a: Unpacking the Modern, National Self. The Diary of Khalil al-Sakakini. A Master Thesis, submitted to Georgetown University.
Bawalsa, Nadim 2010b: Sakakini Defrocked. In: Jerusalem Quarterly 42; 10–13.
Bawwāb, ʿAlī Ḥasan 2003: Mawsūʿat Yāfā al-ǧamīla. 1st edition. Beirut.
Bayly, Christopher 2004: The Birth of the Modern World 1780–1914. Global Connections and Comparisons. Oxford.
Behar, Moshe; Ben-Dor Benite, Zvi 2013: Modern Middle Eastern Jewish Thought. Writings on Identity Politics and Culture 1893–1958. Waltham, Massachusetts.
Ben-Artzi, Yossi 1990: Changes in the Agricultural Sector of the Moshavot, 1882–1914. In: Gilbar, Gad (ed.): Ottoman Palestine, 1800–1914: Studies in Economic and Social History. Leiden; 131–15.
Ben-Artzi, Yossi 1997: Early Jewish Settlement Patterns in Palestine, 1882–1914. Jerusalem.
Bentwich, Josef 1965: Education in Israel. London.
Bernstein, Deborah 2000: Constructing Boundaries. Jewish and Arab Workers in Mandatory Palestine. New York.
Bertram, Anton; Luke, Harry 1921: Report of the Commission appointed by the Government of Palestine to inquire into the affairs of the Orthodox Patriarchate of Jerusalem. London.
Bertram, Anton; Young, Jacob 1926: Report of the Commission Appointed by the Government of Palestine to Inquire and Report upon Certain Controversies between the Orthodox Patriarchate of Jerusalem and the Arab Orthodox Community. London.
Beška, Emanuel 2007: Responses of Prominent Arabs Towards Zionist Aspirations and Colonization Prior to 1908. In: Asian and African Studies 16, no. 1; 22–44.

Beška, Emanuel 2010: Šukrī al-ʿAṣalī, an Extra-Ordinary Anti-Zionist Activist. In: Asian and African Studies 19; no. 2; 237–254.

Beška, Emanuel 2011: Anti-Zionist Journalistic Works of Najīb al-Khūrī Nassār in the Newspaper al-Karmal in 1914. In: Asian and African Studies 20, no. 2; 167–192.

Beška, Emanuel 2012: Polemikos. 'Isa al-'Isa and Printing Class: Too Much Borrowing? In: Jerusalem Quarterly 50; 113–119.

Beška, Emanuel 2014: Political Opposition to Zionism in Palestine and Greater Syria: 1910–1911 as a Turning Point. In: Jerusalem Quarterly 59, no. 1; 54–67.

Beška, Emanuel 2015: Khalil al-Sakakini and Zionism before WWI. In: Jerusalem Quarterly 63/64; 40–53.

Beška, Emanuel 2016a: "The Disgrace of the Twentieth Century": The Beilis Affair in the Filastin Newspaper. In: Jerusalem Quarterly 66; 99–108.

Beška, Emanuel 2016b: ʿĪsā al-ʿĪsā's Defence Speech at the May 1914 Trial in Jaffa. In: Studia Orientala Victori Krupa Dedicata. Bratislava: Slovak Academy of Sciences; 27–36.

Beška, Emanuel 2016c: From Ambivalence to Hostility: The Arabic Newspaper Filasṭīn and Zionism, 1911–1914. Bratislava.

Benbassa, Esther 1992: Zionism and the Politics of Coalitions in the Ottoman Jewish Communities in the Early Twentieth Century. In: Rodrigue, Aron (ed.): Ottoman and Turkish Jewry. Community and Leadership, Bloomington; 225–251.

Ben-Bassat, Yuval 2009a: Proto-Zionist Arab Encounters in Late Nineteenth-Century Palestine: Socioregional Dimensions. In: Journal of Palestine Studies 38, no. 2; 42–63.

Ben-Bassat, Yuval 2009b: Rethinking the Concept of Ottomanization: The Yishuv in the Aftermath of the Young Turk Revolution of 1908. In: Middle Eastern Studies 45, no. 3; 461–475.

Ben-Bassat, Yuval; Ginio, Eyal (eds.) 2011: Late Ottoman Palestine. The Period of Young Turk Rule. London, New York.

Ben-Bassat, Yuval 2013a: Conflicting Accounts of Early Zionist Settlement: A Note on the Encounter between the Colony of Rehovot and the Bedouins of Khirbat Duran. In: British Journal of Middle Eastern Studies 40, no. 2; pp. 139–148.

Ben-Bassat, Yuval 2013b: Beyond National Historiographies: Reflections on the Ottoman Background of Proto-Zionist – Arab Encounters in Fin de Siècle Nineteenth Century Palestine. In: Ginio, Eyal; Kasr, Karl (eds.): Ottoman Legacies in the Contemporary Mediterranean: The Balkans and the Middle East Compared. Jerusalem; pp. 93–118.

Ben-Bassat, Yuval 2013c: Rural Reactions to Zionist Activity in Palestine before and after the Young Turk Revolution of 1908 as Reflected in Petitions to Istanbul. In: Middle Eastern Studies 49, no. 3; pp. 349–363.

Ben-Bassat, Yuval 2013d: Petitioning the Sultan: Justice and Protest in Late Ottoman Palestine. London.

Ben-Bassat, Yuval 2015: Bedouin Petitions from Late Ottoman Palestine. Evaluating the Effects of Sedentarization. In: Journal of the Economic and Social History of the Orient (JESHO) 58; 135–162.

Ben-Bassat, Yuval; Alroey, Guy 2016: The Zionist–Arab Incident of Zarnuqa 1913: a Chronicle and Several Methodological Remarks. In: Middle Eastern Studies 52, no. 5; 787–803.

Biger, Gideon 2004: The Boundaries of Modern Palestine, 1840–1947. New York.

Bliss, Frederick Jones 1972: The Religions of Modern Syria and Palestine. Lectures Delivered before Lake Forest College on the Foundation of the late William Bross. [Faks.-T.] New York.
Bloom, Etan 2011: Arthur Ruppin and the Production of Pre-Israeli Culture. Leiden.
Boogert, Maurits H. van den 2005: The Capitulations and the Ottoman Legal System: Qadis, Consuls, and Beraths in the 18th Century. Leiden, Boston.
Bosworth, C. E. 1982: The Concept of Dhimma in Early Islam. In: Braude, Benjamin (ed.): Christians and Jews in the Ottoman Empire. The Functioning of a Plural Society, vol. 1. New York; 37–51.
Bracy, Michael 2010: Printing Class: 'Isa al-'Isa, Filastin, and the Textual Construction of National Identity, 1911–1931. Lanham, MD.
Braude, Benjamin 1982: Foundation Myths of the Millet System. In: Braude, Benjamin; Lewis, Bernard (eds.): Christians and Jews in the Ottoman Empire: The Functioning of a Plural Society, vol. 2. New York; 69–88.
Braude, Benjamin 2000: The Strange History of the Millet System. In: Kemal Çiçek (ed.): The Great Ottoman-Turkish Civilization, vol. 2. Ankara; 409–418.
Brenner, Michael 2005: Geschichte des Zionismus, München.
Brosius, Bernd; Koschel, Friederike; Haas, Alexander 2009 (eds.): Methoden der empirischen Kommunikationsforschung: eine Einführung. Wiesbaden.
Bucher, Hans-Jürgen 1986: Pressekommunikation. Grundstrukturen einer öffentlichen Form der Kommunikation aus linguistischer Sicht. Tübingen.
Buessow, Johann 2002: Die osmanische Elite Palästinas im Spiegel der Zeitung Filasṭīn, 1911–1914. Master Thesis, Berlin University (unpublished).
Buessow, Johann 2010: Mental Maps: The Mediterranean Worlds of Two Palestinian Newspapers in the Late Ottoman Period. In: Kolluoğlu, Biray; Toksöz, Meltem (eds.): Cities of the Mediterranean: From the Ottomans to the Present Day. London; 100–115.
Buessow, Johann 2011: Hamidian Palestine. Politics and Society in the District of Jerusalem, 1872–1908. Leiden.
Buessow, Johann 2011b: Children of the Revolution: Youth in Palestinian Public Life, 1908–14. In: Ben-Bassat, Yuval; Ginio, Eyal (eds.): Late Ottoman Palestine: The Period of Young Turk Rule. London, New York; 55–78.
Buessow, Johann 2012: Geschichtsort Jaffator. Osmanische Kommunalverwaltung und bürgerschaftliches Engagement in Jerusalem 1867–1917. AphorismA, Berlin.
Buessow, Johann 2014: Ottoman Reform and Urban Government in the District of Jerusalem, 1867–1917. In: Freitag, Ulrike; Lafi, Nora (eds.): Urban Governance under the Ottomans. Between Cosmopolitanism and Conflict. London; 97–141.
Buessow, Johann 2015: Re-Imagining Islam in the Period of the First Modern Globalization: Muhammad 'Abduh and His *Theology of Unity*. In: Kozma; Liat, Schayegh; Cyros, Wishnitzer; Avner (eds.): A Global Middle East: Mobility, Materiality and Culture in the Modern Age, 1880–1940. London, New York; 273–320.
Buheiry, Marwan 1981: The Agricultural Exports of Southern Palestine, 1885–1914. In: Journal of Palestine Studies 10, no. 4; 61–81.
Bulliet, Richard 1987: Medieval Arabic Tarsh: A Forgotten Chapter in the History of Printing. In: Journal of the American Oriental Society 107, no. 3; 427–438.

Campos, Michelle 2003: A 'Shared Homeland' and Its Bounderies: Empire, Citizenship and the Origins of Sectarianism in Late Ottoman Palestine, 1908–13. Ph.D. dissertation. Ann Arbor, Mich.

Campos, Michelle 2005a: Between Beloved Ottomania and the Land of Israel: The Struggle over Ottomanism and Zionism among Palestine's Sephardi Jews, 1908–1913. In: International Journal of Middle East Studies 37; 461–483.

Campos, Michelle 2005b: "Freemasonry in Ottoman Palestine." In: Jerusalem Quarterly 22/23, 37–62.

Campos, Michelle 2011: Ottoman Brothers. Muslims Christians and Jews in Early Twentieth Century Palestine. Stanford.

Campos, Michelle 2015: "The Ottoman Sickness and Its Doctors": Imperial Loyalty in Palestine on the Eve of World War I. In: Kieser, Hans-Lukas; Öktem, Kerem; Reinkowski, Maurus (eds.): World War I and the End of the Ottomans: from the Balkan Wars to the Armenian Genocide. London; 92–103.

Campos, Michelle 2016: Zionism in the Era of Ottoman Brotherhood. In: Isom-Verhaaren, Christina; Schull, Kent (eds.): Living in the Ottoman Realm: Empire and Identity, 13th to 20th Centuries. Bloomington; 310–325.

Canaan, Taufik 1914: Aberglaube und Volksmedizin im Lande der Bibel. Hamburg.

Canaan, Taufiq 1927: Mohammedan Saints and Sanctuaries in Palestine. Jerusalem.

Canaan, Taufiq 1929: Dämonenglaube im Lande der Bibel. Leipzig.

Canaan, Taufiq1960: Vom arabisch-palästinischen Familienleben. Studia Orientala 25, vol. 2. Helsinki.

Carmel, Alex 1973: Die Siedlungen der württembergischen Templer in Palästina 1868–1918: ihre lokalpolitischen und internationalen Probleme. Stuttgart.

Carmel, Alex 1975: The German Settlers in Palestine and Their Relations with the Local Arab Population and the Jewish Community, 1868–1918. In: Ma'oz, Moshe (ed.): Studies on Palestine During the Ottoman Period. Jerusalem.

Carmel, Alex 1983: Palästina-Chronik, vol. 2. 1883 bis 1914. Deutsche Zeitungsberichte von der ersten jüdischen Einwanderungswelle bis zum Ersten Weltkrieg. Ausgew., bearb. u. erl. von Alex Carmel. Ulm.

Clogg, R. 1982: The Greek Millet in the Ottoman Empire. In: Braude, Benjamin (ed.): Christians and Jews in the Ottoman Empire. The Functioning of a Plural Society, vol. 1. New York; 185–207.

Çiçek, M. Talha 2014: War and State Formation in Syria. Cemal Pasha's Governorate During World War I, 1914–1917. London, New York.

Çiçek, Talha 2015: Martyrs/Separatists, Syrian and Lebanese, in: 1914–1918-online. International. Encyclopedia of the First World War, ed. by Ute Daniel, Peter Gatrell, Oliver Janz, Heather Jones, Jennifer Keene, Alan Kramer, and Bill Nasson, issued by Freie Universität Berlin, Berlin 2015-04-10. DOI: http://dx.doi.org/10.15463/ie1418.

Cohen, Hillel 2008: Army of Shadows. Palestinian Collaboration with Zionism, 1917–1948. Berkeley.

Çolak, Hasan 2012: Relations between the Ottoman Central Administration and the Greek Orthodox Patriarchates of Antioch, Jerusalem and Alexandria. dissertation (e-thesis). University of Birmingham.

Costin, Rebekah Marks 2004: Mendel Beilis and the Blood Libel. In: Garber, Robert (ed.): Jews on Trial. Ktav, Jersey City, New York; 69–93.

Cragg, Kenneth 1992: The Arab Christian. A History in the Middle East. 1st publ. London.
Cust, L. G. 1980: The Status Quo in the Holy Places. Jerusalem.
Dabbāġ, Muṣṭafā Murād 1965–1976: Bilādunā Filasṭīn. 11 Volums. Beirut.
Dalman, Gustaf 1925: Hundert deutsche Fliegerbilder aus Palästina. Gütersloh.
Dalman, Gustaf 1928–41: Arbeit und Sitte in Palästina. 7 Volums. Gütersloh.
Daǧǧānī, Aḥmad Zakī ad- 1989: Madīnatunā Yāfā wa-ṯawrat 1936. Cairo.
Daǧǧānī, Sa'd Yūsuf 1991: Kay lā nansā Yāfā. Amman.
Davison, Roderic 1968: The Advent of the Principle of Representation in the Government of the Ottoman Empire. In: Polk, William; Chambers, Richard (eds.): Beginnings of Modernization in the Middle East. The Nineteenth Century. Chicago; 93–108.
Davison, Roderic 1973: Reform in the Ottoman Empire 1856–1876. 2nd. print. New York.
Davison, Roderic 1982: The Millets as Agents of Change in the Nineteenth-Century Ottoman Empire. In: Braude, Benjamin (ed.): Christians and Jews in the Ottoman Empire. The Functioning of a Plural Society, vol. 1. New York; 319–337.
Davison, Roderic: Tanẓīmāt. In: Encyclopaedia of Islam. 2nd edition.
Dawn, Ernest 1973: From Ottomanism to Arabism. Essays on the Origin of Arab Nationalism. Urbana.
Dawn, Ernest 1991: The Origins of Arab Nationalism. In: Khalidi, Rashid (ed.) The Origins of Arab Nationalism. New York.
de Bellaigue, Christopher 2001: Turkey's Hidden Palace. In: The New York Review of Books. (http://www.nybooks.com/articles/2001/03/08/turkeys-hidden-past/#fnr1, 28. 10.2017).
Delmaire, Jean-Marie 1999: De Jaffa Jusqu'en Galilée: Les Premiers Pionniers Juifs (1882/ 1904). Lille.
Der Matossian, Bedross 2009/2010: The Young Turk Revolution: Its Impact on Religious Politics of Jerusalem (1908–1912). In: Jerusalem Quarterly File 40, vol. 4; 18–33.
Der Matossian, Bedross 2011: Administrating the Non-Muslims and the 'Question of Jerusalem' after the Young Turk Revolution. In: Ben-Bassat, Yuval; Ginio, Eyal (eds.): Late Ottoman Palestine. The Period of Young Turk Rule. London, New York. 211–239.
Der Matossian, Bedross 2012: Formation of Public Sphere(s) in the Aftermath of the 1908 Révolution among Armenians, Arabs, and Jews. In: 'L' ivresse de la Liberté': la Révolution de 1908 dans l'Empire Ottoman. Paris; 189–219.
Der Matossian, Bedross 2014: Shattered Dreams of Revolution. From Liberty to Violence in the Late Ottoman Empire. Standford, California.
Dierauff, Evelin 2015: Global Migration into Late Ottoman Jaffa as Reflected in the Arab-Palestinian Newspaper Filasṭīn (1911–1913). In: Kozma, Liat; Schayegh, Cyrus; Wishnitzer, Avner (eds.): A Global Middle East: Mobility, Materiality and Culture in the Modern Age, 1880–1940. London, New York; 165–174.
Dierauff, Evelin 2020a: Performances of Late Ottoman Modernity: Culture, Entertainment and Leisure Activities in Pre-World War I Jaffa. In Ben-Bassat, Yuval and Johann Buessow (eds.). From the Household to the Wider World: Urban Governance in Late Ottoman Bilad al-Sham. Tuebingen (forthcoming).
Dierauff, Evelin 2020b: The Appropriation of Political Concepts in Ḫalīl as-Sakākīnī's 'Orthodox Renaissance' (1908–14). In Dierauff, Evelin; Dierks, Dennis; Henning, Barbara; Leber, Taisiya and Anie Sargsyan (eds.). Circulating Knowledge. Goettingen (forthcoming).

Divine, Donna 1994: Politics and Society in Late Ottoman Palestine: The Arab Struggle for Survival and Power, Boulder.

Dolbee, Samuel 2010: Mandatory Bodybuilding: Nationalism, Masculinity, Class, and Physical Activity in 1930s Syria. Master Thesis. Georgetown University. Washington.

Dolbee, Samuel 2012: Seferberlik and Bare Feet: Rural Hardship, Citied Dreams, and Social Belonging in 1920s Syria. In: Jerusalem Quarterly 51; 21–35.

Dolbee, Samuel; Hazkani, Shay 2015a: "Impossible is not Ottoman": Menashe Meirovitch, 'Isa al-'Isa, and Imperial Citizenship in Palestine. In: International Journal of Middle East Studies 47, vol. 2; 241–262.

Dolbee, Samuel; Hazkani, Shay 2015b: Unlikely Identities: Abu Ibrahim and the Politics of Possibility in Late Ottoman Palestine. In: Jerusalem Quarterly 63/64; 24–39.

Doumani, B. Beshara 1992: Rediscovering Ottoman Palestine: Writing Palestinians into History. In: Journal of Palestine Studies 21, no; 5–28.

Dowling, T. E. 1913: The Orthodox Greek Patriarchate of Jerusalem. London: 1913.

Dumper, Michael 2007: Jaffa. In: Dumper, Michael; Stanley, Bruce (eds.): Cities of the Middle East and North Africa. A Historical Encyclopedia. ABC CLIO; 199–202.

Eisenstein, Elizabeth 1980: The Printing Press as an Agent of Change: Communications and Cultural Transformations in Early-Modern Europe. Cambridge.

Eisenstadt, Shmuel 2000: Multiple Modernities. In: Daedalus 129; 1–29.

Eisler, Jakob 1997: Der deutsche Beitrag zum Aufstieg Jaffas 1850–1914: zur Geschichte Palästinas im 19. Jahrhundert. Wiesbaden.

Elden, Stuart 2007: There is a Politics of Space because Space is Political. Henri Lefebvre and the Production of Space. In: Radical Philosophy Review 10, no. 2; 101–116.

Embaló, Birgit; Neuwirth, Angelika; Pannewick, Friederike (eds.) 2001: Kulturelle Selbstbehauptung der Palästinenser: Survey der modernen palästinensischen Dichtung Würzburg.

Ergınbaş, Vefa 2014: Enlightenment in the Ottoman Context: İbrahİm MüteferrİKa and his Intellectual Landscape. In: Roper, Geoffrey (ed.) 2014: Historical Aspects of Printing and Publishing in Languages of the Middle East: Papers from the Third Symposium on the History and Printing and Publishing in the Languages and Countries of the Middle East, University of Leipzig. Leiden; 54–100.

Fakhr Eldin, Munir 2008: Communities of Owners: Land Law, Governance, and Politics in Palestine, 1858–1948. PhD dissertation. New York University.

Farah, Irmgard 1993: Die deutsche Pressepolitik und Propagandatätigkeit im Osmanischen Reich von 1908–1918 unter besonderer Berücksichtigung des „Osmanischen Lloyd". Beirut.

Ferree, Deanna 2014: Syrian Protestants & the Case of the Beirut Church: Re-imagining the American Missionary Encounter in Ottoman Syria. In: Syrian Studies Association Bulletin, vol. 19, no. 1.

Fischbach, Michael 2000: al-'Isa, 'Isa. In: Mattar, Philip (ed.), Encyclopedia of the Palestinians, Chicago, London; 190.

Fischbach, Michael 2000: Arif al-Arif. In: Mattar, Philip (ed.), Encyclopedia of the Palestinians, Chicago, London; 81.

Fischel, R. S.; Kark, R. 2008: Sultan Abdülhamid II and Palestine: Private Lands and Imperial Policy. In New Perspectives on Turkey, no. 39; 146.

Fishman, Louis 2005: The Haram al-Sharif Incident. Palestinian Notables Versus the Ottoman Administration. In: Journal of Palestine Studies 135, no. 3; 7–22.
Fishman, Louis 2007: Palestine Revisited: Reassessing the Jewish and Arab National Movements, 1908–1914. Ph.D. dissertation: University of Chicago.
Fishman, Louis 2011: Understanding the 1911 Ottoman Parliament Debate on Zionism in Light of the Emergence of a 'Jewish Question'. In: Ben-Bassat, Yuval; Ginio, Eyal (eds.): Late Ottoman Palestine. The Period of Young Turk Rule. London, New York; 103–123.
Fortescue, Adrian 1920: The Orthodox Eastern Church. 3. thousand. London.
Foucault, Michel 1991: Die Ordnung des Diskurses. Frankfurt/Main.
Frantzman, Seth 2010: The Arab Settlement of Late Ottoman and Mandatory Palestine. New Village Formation and Settlement Fixation, 1871–1948. Ph.D. dissertation. Hebrew University of Jerusalem.
Freitag, Ulrike 2008: Arabische Visionen von Modernität im 19. und frühen 20. Jahrhundert: Die Aneignung von Universalien oder die Übernahme fremder Konzepte? In: Barberowski, Jörg; Kaelble, Hartmut; Schriever, Jürgen (eds): Selbstbilder und Fremdbilder. Repräsentation sozialer Ordnungen im Wandel. Frankfurt; 89–117.
Friedmann, Isaiah 1977: Germany, Turkey, and Zionism: 1897–1918. Oxford.
Ġarbīya, ʿIzz ad-Dīn 1987: Qiṣṣat madīnat Yāfā. Tunis.
Gelvin, James 2005: The Israel-Palestine Conflict: One Hundred Years of War. Cambridge.
Gerber, Haim 1985: Ottoman Rule in Jerusalem: 1890–1914. Berlin: Schwarz.
Gerber, Haim 1987: The Social Origins of the Modern Middle East. Boulder Col.
Gerber, Haim; Pellat, Ch.: Mu<u>sh</u>āʿ. In: Encyclopaedia of Islam 2nd edition.
Glaser, Barney; Strauss, Anselm (eds.) (2010): Grounded Theory: Strategien qualitativer Forschung. 3rd edition. Bern.
Glaß, Dagmar 2004: Der Muqtaṭaf und seine Öffentlichkeit: Aufklärung, Räsonnement und Meinungsstreit in der frühen arabischen Zeitschriftenkommunikation, 2 Volumes. Würzburg.
Glenk, H.; Blaich, H.; Haering, M. (eds.) 2005: From Desert Sands to Golden Oranges: the History of the German Templar Settlement of Sarona in Palestine 1871–1947. Victoria.
Goldschmidt, Arthur 2000: Biographical Dictionary of Modern Egypt. Boulder, Col.
Goldstein, Yaacov 1998: From Fighters to Soldiers: How the Israeli Defense Forces Began. Portland.
Grallert, Till 2012: To Whom Belong the Streets? Investment in Public Space and Popular Contentions in Late Ottoman Damascus. In: Bulletin d'études Orientales 61; 327–359.
Gribetz, Jonathan Marc 2014: Defining Neighbors. Religion, Race, and the Early Zionist-Arab Encounter. Princeton, Oxford.
Grossman, David 2011: Rural Arab Demography and Early Jewish Settlement in Palestine. Distribution and Population Density During the late Ottoman and Early Mandate Periods. New Brunswick, New York.
Gunn, Simon 2011: The Spatial Turn: Changing Histories of Space and Place. In: Gunn, Simon; Morris, Robert (eds.): Identities in Space: Contested Terrains in the Western City since 1850. Burlington.
Habermas, Jürgen 1981: Theorie des kommunikativen Handelns. 2 Volums. Frankfurt/Main. Vol. 1: Handlungsrationalität und gesellschaftliche Rationalisierung. Vol. 2: Zur Kritik der funktionalistischen Vernunft.

Hackeschmidt, Jörg 1997: Von Kurt Blumenfeld zu Norbert Elias: Die Erfindung einer jüdischen Tradition. Hamburg.

Haddad, Mahmoud 1994: The Rise of Arab Nationalism Reconsidered. In: *International Journal of Middle East Studies (IJMES) 26*; 201–222.

Ḥāǧǧ, Samīr Fawzī 2004: Yāfā. Baiyārat al-ʿiṭr wa-š-šiʿr. Tawṯīq antūlūǧī. Beirut.

Ḥaǧǧū, Munā Muḥammad 2007: al-Ḫaṭar aṣ-ṣihyūnī ʿalā Filasṭīn wa-ṣadāhu fī mirʾāt aṣ-ṣiḥāfa al-ʿarabīya fī bilād aš-Šām wa-Miṣr: (1897–1917). Risālat māǧistar fī t-tā'rīḫ. Master thesis. St. Yosef University. Beirut.

Haiduc-Dale, Noah 2013: Arab Christians in British Mandate Palestine. Communalism and Nationalism, 1917–1948. Edinburgh.

Hamzah, Dyala 2012: From 'Ilm to Sihafa or the Politics of the Public Interest *(Maslaha):* Muhammad Rashîd Rida and his Journal *al-Manar* (1898–1935). In: Hamzah, Dyala (ed.): The Making of the Arab Intellectual, 1880–1960: Empire, Public Sphere and the Colonial Coordinates of Selfhood. London; 90–127.

Hanania, Mary 2007: Jurji Habib Hanania: History of the Earliest Press in Palestine, 1908–1914. In: Jerusalem Quarterly File 32; 51–69.

Haumann, Heiko (ed.) 1998: Der Traum von Israel: die Ursprünge des modernen Zionismus, Weinheim.

Häussermann, Hartmut; Siebel, Walter (eds.) 2004: Stadtsoziologie. Eine Einführung. Frankfurt, New York.

Hawārī, ʿIrfān Saʿīd Abū Ḥamad 1979: Aʿlām min arḍ as-salām. Haifa.

Heikal, Yousef; El-Haj, Imad 1984: Jaffa… as It Was. In: Journal of Palestine Studies 13, no. 4; 3–21.

Hepp, Andreas 2010: Cultural Studies und Medienanalyse: eine Einführung. 3. überarbeitete und erweiterte Aufl. Wiesbaden.

Hermann, Rainer 1990: Kulturkrise und konservative Erneuerung. Muḥammad Kurd ʿAlī (1876–1953) und das geistige Leben in Damaskus zu Beginn des 20. Jahrhunderts. Frankfurt/Main.

Herzog, Christoph (ed.) 1995: Presse und Öffentlichkeit im Nahen Osten. Heidelberg.

Rachel Heuberger 2006: Die revidierte DIN-Norm zur Umschrift des hebräischen Alphabets. In: Zeitschrift für Bibliothekswesen und Bibliographie 53; 185–187.

Hinz, Walther 1970: Islamische Masse und Gewichte. Umgerechnet ins metrische System. Leiden, Köln.

Hobsbawm, Eric 1990: Nations and Nationalism since 1780. Cambridge.

Hopwood, Derek 1969: The Russian Presence in Syria and Palestine 1843–1914. Church and Politics in the Near East. Oxford.

Hourani, Albert 1968: Ottoman Reform and the Politics of Notables: In: Polk, William; and Chambers, Richard (eds): Beginning of Modernization in the Middle East; 41–68.

Hörning, Karl 2004: Kultur als Praxis. In: Jaeger, Friedrich (ed.): Handbuch der Kulturwissenschaften. Vol 1 of 3. Stuttgart; 139–154.

Hughes, Bettany 2017: Istanbul. A Tale of Three Cities. Hachette.

Ḥūt, Šafīq al- 2007: Bayna l-waṭan wa-l-manfā: min Yāfā badaʾa al-mišwār. Beirut.

Hüttermann, Jörg 2006a: Islamische Symbole und „avancierende Fremde". Konfliktkommunikation in Stadt und Gesellschaft. In: Salden, Adelheid (ed.): Stadt und Kommunikation in bundesrepublikanischen Umbruchzeiten, Wiesbaden; 285–305.

Hüttermann, Jörg 2006b: Das Minarett. zur politischen Kultur des Konflikts um islamische Symbole. Weinheim, München.

Ḫūrī Šaḥḥāda; Ḫūrī Niqūlā 1992: Ḫulāṣat tārīḫ kanīsat Ūrušalīm al-urṯūḏuksīya. Ta'līf ŠihādaḪūrī wa-Niqūlā Ḫūrī bi-l-iḍāfa ilā nubḏa 'an tārīḫ al-qaḍīya al-urṯūḏuksīya fī Filasṭīn wa-l-Urdun bayna 1925 wa 1992 bi-qalam Ra'ūf Sa'd Abū Ǧābir. (Reprint of the Jerusalem edition of 1925. Place of Publication and Publisher not Identified).

Ḫūrī, Yūsuf 1976: aṣ-Ṣiḥāfa al-'arabīya fī Filasṭīn. 1876–1948. Beirut.

Ilyās, Yūsuf 1982–83: Taṭawwur aṣ-ṣiḥāfa as-sūrīya fī mi'at 'āmm (1865–1965). Vol I of two Vol. Beirut.

Issawi, Charles 1988a: The Trade of Jaffa, 1825–1914. In: Nashabe, Hisham (ed.): Studia Palaestina. Studies in Honour of Constantine K. Zurayk. Beirut; 42–51.

Issawi, Charles 1988b: The Fertile Crescent, 1800–1914. A Documentary Economic History. New York.

Issawi, Charles 2006: An Economic History of the Middle East and North Africa (Reprint ed.). Taylor & Francis.

Jacobson, Abigail 2001: The Sephardi Jewish Community in Pre-World War I Jerusalem. Debates in the Hebrew Press. In: Jerusalem Quarterly 14; 23–34.

Jacobson, Abigail 2003: Sephardim, Ashkenazim, and the 'Arab Question' in Pre-First World War Palestine: A Reading of Three Zionist Newspapers. In: Middle Eastern Studies 39, no. 2; 105–130.

Jacobson, Abigail 2004: Alternative Voices in late Ottoman Palestine: a Historical Note. In: Jerusalem Quarterly 21; 41–48.

Jacobson, Abigail 2006: Sephardic Zionism in the Ottoman Empire: 'The Time is Here', Ha-Herut, 1 April 1915. In: Amin, C.M.; Fortna, B.C.; Fierson, E.B. (eds.): The Modern Middle East: A Sourcebook for History. Oxford New York; 350–352.

Jacobson, Abigail 2008: Negotiating Ottomanism in Times of War: Jerusalem During World War I through the Eyes of a Local Muslim Resident. In: International Journal of Middle Eastern Studies 40, no. 1; 69–88.

Jacobson, Abigail 2009: A City Living through Crisis: Jerusalem During World War I. In: British Journal of Middle Eastern Studies 36; 73–92.

Jacobson, Abigail 2011a: Jews Writing in Arabic: Shimon Moyal, Nissim Malul and the Mixed Palestinian/Eretz Israeli Locale. In: Ben-Bassat, Yuval; Ginio, Eyal (eds.): Late Ottoman Palestine. The Period of Young Turk Rule. London, New York; 165–182.

Jacobson, Abigail 2011b: From Empire to Empire. Jerusalem between Ottoman and British Rule. New York.

Jawhariyah, Wasif 2014: al-Quds al-'uthmanīya fī l-muḏakkirāt al-Ǧawharīya (in English). The Storyteller of Jerusalem. The Life and Times of Wasif Jawhariyyeh 1904–1948. Edited and Introduced by Salim Tamari and Issam Tamar; Translated by Nada Elzeer with a Foreword by Rachel Beckles Willson. Northampton, Mass.

Jäger, Siegfried 2004: Kritische Diskursanalyse: Eine Einführung. 4th edition. Münster.

Kahl, Thede (ed.) 2009: Christen und Muslime. Interethnische Koexistenz in südosteuropäischen Peripheriegebieten. Wien, Berlin, Münster.

Kaleel, Mousa 1920: When I was a Boy in Palestine. London (edition of 1914).

Kark, Ruth 1986: The Contribution of the Ottoman Regime to the Development of Jerusalem and Jaffa, 1840–1917. In: Kushner, David (ed.): Palestine in the Late Ottoman Period: Political, Social and Economic Transformation. Jerusalem; 46–58.

Kark, Ruth 1990a: The Rise and Decline of Coastal Towns in Palestine. In: Gilbar, Gad (ed.): Ottoman Palestine: 1800–1914. Studies in Economic and Social History. Leiden; 69–90.

Kark, Ruth, Jaffa 1990b: Jaffa: A City in Evolution. 1799–1917. Jerusalem.

Kark, Ruth; Frantzman, Seth 2010: Bedouin, Abdül Hamid II, British Land Settlement and Zionism: The Baysan Valley and Sub-district 1831–1948. In: Israel Studies 15, no. 2; 49–79.

Karlinsky, Nahum 2005: California Dreaming. Ideology, Society, and Technology in the Citrus Industry of Palestine, 1890–1939. Albany.

Karsh, Efraim 2002: Fabricating Israeli History. The 'New Historians'. London.

Kasaba, Reşat 2006: Dreams of Empire, Dreams of Nations. In: Esherick, Josef; Kayali, Hasan; Van Young, Eric (eds.): From Empire to Nation: Historical Perspectives on the Making of the Modern World. Lanham, Boulder; 198–227.

Katz, Yossi 1994: The "Business" of Settlement. Private Entrepreneurship in the Jewish Settlement of Palestine, 1900–1914. Jerusalem.

Katz, Yossi 2005: The Battle for the Land. The History of the Jewish National Fund (KKL) before the Establishment of the State of Israel. Jerusalem.

Katz, Itamar; Kark, Ruth 2005: The Greek Orthodox Patriarchate of Jerusalem and Its Congregation: Dissent over Real Estate. In: Journal of Middle Eastern Studies 37; 509–534.

Katz, Itamar; Kark, Ruth 2007: The Church and Landed Property: The Greek Orthodox Patriarchate of Jerusalem. In: Middle Eastern Studies 43, no. 3; 383–408.

Katz, Yossi; Neumann, Shoshana 1990: Agricultural Land Transactions in Palestine, 1900–1914. A Quantitative Analysis. In: Explorations in Economic History 27, no. 1; 29–45.

Kayalı, Hasan 1997: Arabs and Young Turks: Ottomanism, Arabism, and Islamism in the Ottoman Empire, 1908–1918. Berkeley.

Kayalı, Hasan 2014: Cemal Paşa, Ahmed. In: 1914–1918-Online. International Encyclopedia of the First World War. Daniel, Ute; Gatrell, Peter; Janz, Oliver; Jones, Heather; Keene, Jennifer; Kramer, Alan; Nasson, Bill. Issued by Freie Universität Berlin.

Kayyali, Abdul-Wahhab 1978: Palestine: A Modern History. London.

Kechriotis, Vangelis 2005: Greek-Orthodox, Ottoman Greeks or just Greek? Theories of Coexistence in the Aftermath of the Young Turk Revolution. In: Études Balkaniques 41; 51–71.

Khalidi, Rashid 1977: Arab Nationalism in Syria. The Formative Years, 1908–1914. In: Haddad W.; Ochsenwald W. (eds.): Nationalism in a Non-National State. Columbus, Ohio; 207–237.

Khalidi, Rashid 1980: The Question of Zionism in the Arab Press, 1908–1914. In: The Third International Conference on The History of Bilad al-Sham. 19.–24- April 1980, University of Jordan: Amman; 1–25.

Khalidi, Rashid 1982: The Role of the Press in the Early Arab Reaction to Zionism. In: Peuples Méditerranéens 20; 105–123.

Khalidi, Rashid 1984: Social Factors in the Rise of the Arab Movement in Syria. In: Arjomand, Said Amir (ed.): From Nationalism to Revolutionary Islam. Albany, New York.

Khalidi, Rashid 1991: Ottomanism and Arabism in Syria Before 1914: A Reassessment. In: Khalidi, Rashid; Anderson, Lisa; Muslih, Muhammad; Simon, Reeva (eds.): The Origins of Arab Nationalism. New York.

Khalidi, Rashid 1992: All that Remains: The Palestinian Villages Occupied and Depopulated by Israel in 1948. Institute for Palestine Studies. Washington D.C.

Khalidi, Rashid 1997: Palestinian Identity. New York, Columbia.

Khalidi, Rashid 2001: Palestinian Peasant Resistance to Zionism before World War I. In: Said. E.; Hitchens, C. (eds.): Blaming the Victims: Spurious Scholarship and the Palestinian Question. London, New York.

Khalidi, Rashid 2006: The Iron Cage. The Story of the Palestinian Struggle for Statehood. Boston, Mass.

Khalidi, Rashid 2009: Anti-Zionism, Arabism and Palestinian Identity: ʻIssa al-ʻIssa and Filastin. In: Seikaly, Samir (ed.): Configuring Identity in the Modern Arab East. Beirut; 83–96.

Khalidi, Walid 1984: Before Their Diaspora: A Photographic History of the Palestinians. Washington.

Khoury, Shahadeh; Khoury, Nicola; Abujaber, Raouf Sa'd (eds.) 2002: A Survey of the History of the Orthodox Church in Jerusalem. Amman.

Kieser, Hans-Lukas; Öktem, Kerem; Reinkowski, Maurus 2015 (ed.): World War I and the End of the Ottomans: from the Balkan Wars to the Armenian Genocide. London.

Kildani, Rev. Hanna 2010: Modern Christianity in the Holy Land. Ph.D. thesis. Bloomington.

Kießling, Rolf 2001: Kommunikation und Region in der Vormoderne. Eine Einführung. In: Hoffmann, Carl; Kießling, Rolf (eds.): Kommunikation und Region. Konstanz; 11–39.

Kozma, Liat; Schayegh, Cyrus; Wishnitzer, Avner 2015 (ed.): A Global Middle East: Mobility, Materiality and Culture in the Modern Age, 1880–1940. London, New York.

Klausner, I. 1994: Meirovicz, Menashe. In: Wigoder, Geoffrey (ed.), New Encyclopedia of Zionism and Israel, 2 Volums. Madison (a.o.), vol. 2; 924–925.

Klausner, I.; Catane M. 1994: Netter, Charles. In: Wigoder, Geoffrey (ed.), New Encyclopedia of Zionism and Israel, 2 Volums. Madison (a.o.), vol. 2; 991.

Klein, Menachem 2014: Lives in Common. Arabs and Jews in Jerusalem, Jaffa and Hebron. London.

Kollmeier, Kathrin 2011: Begriffsgeschichte und historische Semantik. In: Docupedia-Zeitgeschichte, 29.10.2012.

Koselleck, Reinhart 2006: Begriffsgeschichten: Studien zur Semantik und Pragmatik der politischen und sozialen Sprache. Mit zwei Beiträgen von Ulrike Spree und Willibald Steinmetz sowie einem Nachwort zu Einleitungsfragmenten Reinhart Kosellecks von Carsten Dutt. 1st edition. Frankfurt/Main.

Krämer, Gudrun 2002: Geschichte Palästinas. Von der osmanischen Eroberung bis zur Gründung des Staates Israel. München.

Kressel, Getzel 2007: Ludvipol, Abraham. In: Skolnik, Fred; Berenbaum, Michael (eds.): Encyclopaedia Judaica 13, vol. 2. Detroit, New York; 251.

Kuruvilla, Samuel 2011: Church-State Relations in Palestine: Empires, Arab Nationalism and the Indigenous Greek Orthodox, 1880–1940. In: Holy Land Studies 10, no. 1; 55–72.

Kushner, David 1986: The "Foreign Relations" of the Governors of Jerusalem Toward the End of the Ottoman Period. In: Kushner, David (ed.): Palestine in the Late Ottoman Period: Political, Social and Economic Transformation. Jerusalem; 309–319.

Kushner, David 2005: To be Gouverneur of Jerusalem. The City and District During the Time of Ali Ekrem Bey, 1906–1908. Istanbul.

Lauzière, Henri 2016: The Making of Salafism: Islamic Reform in the Twentieth Century. Columbia.
Layish, Aharon 1970: The Sijill of the Jaffa and Nazareth Sharīʻa Courts as a Source for the History of Ottoman Palestine. Jerusalem.
Layish, Aharon 1975: The Sijill of Jaffa and Nazareth Shari'a Courts as a Source for the Political and Social History of Ottoman Palestine. In: Ma'oz, Moshe (ed.): Studies on Palestine During the Ottoman period. Jerusalem.
Lefebvre, Henri 1991: The Production of Space. Oxford, Cambridge, Mass.
Leikin, Ezekiel (ed.) 1993: The Beilis Transcripts. The Anti-Semitic Trial that Shook the World. Jason Aronson, Northvale NJ.
LeVine, Mark 2004: Land, Law and the Planning of Empire: Jaffa and Tel Aviv During the Late Ottoman and Mandate Periods. In: İslamoğlu, Huri (ed.), Constituting Modernity. Private Property in the East and West. London, New York; 100–146.
LeVine, Mark 2005: Overthrowing Geography: Jaffa, Tel Aviv and the Struggle for Palestine, 1880–1948. Berkeley.
Levy, Avigdor 1992: The Sephardim in the Ottoman Empire. Princeton, New Jersey.
Levy, Avigdor 1994: Millet Politics: The Appointment of a Chief Rabbi in 1835. In: Levy, Avigdor (ed.): The Jews of the Ottoman Empire. Princeton; 425–438.
Levy, Lital 2007: Jewish Writers in the Arab East: Literature, History, and the Politics of Enlightenment, 1863–1914. University of California: Berkeley.
Levy, Lital 2012: Partinioned Pasts. Arab Jewish Intellectuals and the Case of Esther Azharī Moyal (1873–1948). In: Dyalah, Hamzah (ed.): The Making of the Arab Intellectual (1880–1960): Empire, Public Sphere and the Colonial Coordinates of Selfhood. Routledge; 128–164.
Lockman, Zachary 1996: Comrades and Enemies. Arab and Jewish Workers in Palestine 1906–1948. Berkeley.
Lockman, Zachary 1999: Railway Workers and Relational History. Arabs and Jews in British-Ruled Palestine. In: Pappé, Ilan (ed.): The Israel – Palestine question. London; 99–128.
Löw, Martina 2001: Raumsoziologie. Frankfurt/Main.
Luhmann, Niklas 1984: Soziale Systeme. Grundriss einer allgemeinen Theorie. Frankfurt/Main.
Luke, Harry 1927: Prophets, Priests and Patriarchs. Sketches of the Sects of Palestine and Syria. London.
Maghdid, Rekurd 2016: Early Iraqi Arab Nationalism against the Turkish Nationalism and the Westernization (1905–1918). In: International Journal of Science and Research (IJSR) 5, no. 1; 2027–2034.
Makdisi, Ussama 2008: Artillery of Heaven: American Missionaries and the Failed Conversion of the Middle East. Ithaca.
Makdisi, Ussama Samir 2000: The Culture of Sectarianism. Community History and Violence in Nineteenth Century Ottoman Lebanon. Berkeley.
Malak, Ḥannā 1996: al-Ǧuzur al-Yāfīya. Jerusalem.
Mandel, Neville 1974: Ottoman Policy and Restriction on Jewish Settlement in Palestine: 1881–1908 – Part I. In: Middle Eastern Studies 10, no. 3; 312–332.
Mandel, Neville 1976: The Arabs and Zionism before World War I. Berkeley.

Mannāʿ ʿĀdil al- 1995: Aʿlām Filasṭīn fī awāḫir al-ʿahd al-ʿuṯmānī. 1800–1918. 2nd ed. Beirut.
Ma'oz, Moshe 1982: Communal Conflict in Ottoman Syria During the Reform Era: The Pole of Political and Economic Factors. In: Braude, Benjamin; Lewis, Bernard (eds.), Christians and Jews in the Ottoman Empire: The Functioning of a Plural Society, vol. 2. New York; 92–95.
Ma'oz, Moshe 2002: Changing Relations between Jews, Muslims and Christians During the Nineteenth Century, with Special Reference to Ottoman Syria and Palestine. In: Levy, Avigdor (ed.): Jews, Turks, Ottomans. A Shared History, Fifteenth through the Twentieth Century. New York; 108–118.
Masters, Bruce 2001: Christians and Jews in the Ottoman Arab World. The Roots of Sectarianism. 1st publ. Cambridge.
Masters, Bruce 2013: The Arabs of the Ottoman Empire, 1516–1918. A Social and Cultural History. Cambridge.
Masʿūd, ʿAlī al-Milīǧī 1946: Yāfā: mašrūʿ taḫṭīṭ al-madīna. Cairo.
Matthews, Weldon 2006: Confronting an Empire, Constructing a Nation. Arab Nationalists and Popular Politics in Mandate Palestine. London.
Matuz, Josef 1985: Das Osmanische Reich. Grundlinien seiner Geschichte. Darmstadt.
Mayring, Phillip 2008: Qualitative Inhaltsanalyse: Grundlagen und Techniken. Weinheim.
McCarthy, Justin 1990: The Population of Palestine: Population History and Statistics of the Late Ottoman Period and the Mandate. New York.
McCarthy, Justin 2002: Population History of the Middle East and the Balkans. Istanbul.
Meier, Andreas 1994: Der politische Auftrag des Islam. Programme und Kritik zwischen Fundamentalismus und Reformen; Originalstimmen aus der islamischen Welt. Wuppertal.
Mehren, August 1853: Die Rhetorik der Araber: nach den wichtigsten Quellen dargestellt und mit angefügten Textauszügen nebst einem Literaturgeschichtlichen Anhang versehen. Kopenhagen.
Merten, Kai 2013: Untereinander, nicht nebeneinander. Das Zusammenleben religiöser und kultureller Gruppen im Osmanischen Reich des 19. Jahrhunderts. Marburg.
Metzer, Jacob 1998: The Divided Economy of Mandatory Palestine. Cambridge.
Mills, Eric 1932: Census of Palestine 1931. Population of Villages, Towns and Administrative Areas. Jerusalem: Government of Palestine.
Mißfelder, Jan-Friedrich 2010: Religiöse Koexistenz im urbanen Raum – Konzeptionelle Überlegungen und begriffliche Parameter. In: Schmauder, Andreas (ed.): Kaftan, Kreuz und Kopftuch. Religiöse Koexistenz im urbanen Raum (15. – 20. Jahrhundert). Ostfildern; 7–20.
Molho, Rena 1988: The Jewish Community of Salonika and Its Incorporation into the Greek State, 1912–19. In: Middle Eastern Studies 24, no. 4; Routledge; 391–403.
Monterescu, Daniel 2005: Spatial Relationality: Urban Space and Ethnic Relations in Jewish-Arab Mixed Towns, 1948–2004. Ph.D. thesis, University of Chicago.
Monterescu, Daniel; Rabinowitz, Dan 2007 (ed.): Mixed Towns, Trapped Communities: Historical Narratives, Spatial Dynamics, Gender Relations and Cultural Encounters in Palestinian-Israeli Towns. Burlington.
Morris, Benny 2007: The New Historiography. Israel confronts Its Past. In: Morris, Benny (ed.): Making Israel. Michigan; 11–28.

Mundy, Martha; Smith Richard (eds.) 2007: Governing Property, Making the Modern State. Law Administration and Production in Ottoman Syria. London, New York.

Muslih, Muhammad Muslih 1988: The Origins of Palestinian Nationalism. New York.

Nadan, Amos 2003: Colonial Misunderstanding of an Efficient Peasant Institution: Land Settlement and Musha' Tenure in Mandate Palestine, 1921–47. In: Journal of the Economic and Social History of the Orient 46, no. 3; 320–354.

Naǧǧār, 'Āida an- 2005: Ṣiḥāfat Filasṭīn wa-l-ḥaraka al-waṭanīya fī niṣf qarn: 1900–1948. Beirut.

Naṣṣār, Naǧīb al-Ḫūrī an- 1911: aṣ-Ṣihyūnīya. Tāʾrīḫuhā – ġaraḍuhā – ahamīyatuhā. Mulaḫḫaṣan ʿan al-ansīklūbīdīyā al-yahūdīya. Haifa.

Nimr, Iḥsān an- 1937–1975: Tārīḫ Ǧabal Nāblus wa-l-Balqaʾ. 4 Volums. Nablus.

Nordau, Max 1909: Max Nordau's Zionistische Schriften, hrsg. vom Zionistischen Aktionskomitee, 3 volums. Vol. 2. Köln, Leipzig.

Norris, Jacob 2013: Land of Progress: Palestine in the Age of Colonial Development, 1905–1948. Oxford.

O'Mahony, Anthony 2000: Palestinian-Arab Orthodox Christians: Religion, Politics and Church-State Relations in Jerusalem, c. 1908–1925. In: Chronos: Revue d' Histoire de l'Universite de Balamand 3; 61–91.

O'Mahony, Anthony (ed.) 2003a: The Christian Communities of Jerusalem and the Holy Land. Studies in History, Religion and Politics. Cardiff.

O'Mahony, Anthony (ed.) 2003b: The Christian Communities of Jerusalem and the Holy Land: A Historical and Political Survey. In: O'Mahony, Anthony (ed.): The Christian Communities of Jerusalem and the Holy Land. Studies in History, Religion and Politics. Cardiff; 1–37.

O'Mahony, Anthony (ed.) 2004: Eastern Christianity. Studies in Modern History, Religion and Politics. London.

O'Mahony, Anthony 2009: Christianity and Jerusalem. Studies in Modern Theology and Politics in the Holy Land. Leominster.

Orni, E. 1994: Rishon le-Tzion. In: Wigoder, Geoffrey (ed.): New Encyclopedia of Zionism and Israel, 2 volums. Vol. 2. Madison (a.o.); 1110–1111.

Osterhammel, Jürgen 2004: Die Vielfalt der Kulturen und die Methoden des Kulturvergleichs. In: Jaeger, Friedrich (ed.): Handbuch der Kulturwissenschaften. Vol. 2. Stuttgart, Weimar; 50–65.

Osterhammel, Jürgen; Petterson, Niels 2003: Geschichte der Globalisierung: Dimensionen – Prozesse – Epochen. München.

Osterhammel, Jürgen 2005: „The Great Work of Uplifting Mankind": Zivilisierungsmission und Moderne. In: Barth, Boris; Osterhammel, Jürgen (eds.): Zivilisierungsmissionen: Imperiale Weltverbesserung seit dem 18. Jahrhundert. Konstanz; 363–426.

Oswald, Ingrid 2007: Migrationssoziologie. Konstanz.

Öztürk, Fatih 2009: The Ottoman Millet System. In: Güneydoğu Avrupa Araştırmaları Dergisi, Band 16; 71–86.

Panzer, Regina 1998: Identität und Geschichtsbewusstsein. Griechisch-orthodoxe Christen im Vorderen Orient zwischen Byzanz und Arabertum. Hamburg.

Panzer, Regina 1998b: Die politische Identifikation griechisch-orthodoxer Christen im Vorderen Orient. In: Orient 39, no. 2; 235–249.

Papadopoulos, C. 1924: Les Privilèges du Patriarcat Oecuménique (Communauté Grecque Orthodoxe) dans l'Empire Ottoman. Ph.D. thesis. Paris.
Papastathis, Konstantinos und Kark, Ruth 2014a: Orthodox Communal Politics in Palestine after the Young Turk Revolution (1908–1910). In: Jerusalem Quarterly 56 & 57; 118–139.
Papastathis, Konstantinos und Kark, Ruth 2014b: Colonialism and Religious Power Politics: The Question of New Regulations within the Orthodox Church of Jerusalem During the British Mandate. In: Middle Eastern Studies 50, no. 4; 589–605.
Pappé, Ilan 1999: Introduction. In: Pappé, Ilan (ed.): The Israel/Palestine Question. London New York; 1–7.
Pappé, Ilan (ed.) 2005: The Modern Middle East. London.
Pappé, Ilan 2007: The Ethnic Cleansing of Palestine. Oxford.
Pappé, Ilan 2010: The Rise and Fall of a Palestinian Dynasty. The Husaynis 1700–1948. London.
Philipp, Thomas 1971: The Role of Jurjī Zaidān in the Intellectual Development of the Arab Nahda from the Beginnings of the British Occupation of Egypt to the Outbreak of World War I. Dissertation. Los Angeles.
Philipp, Thomas 1973: Language, History and Arab National Consciousness in the Thought of Jurji Zaidan (1861–1914). In: International Journal of Middle East Studies 4, no. 1; 3–22.
Philipp, Thomas 1979: Ǧurǧī Zaidān: his Life and Thought. Wiesbaden.
Philipp, Thomas 2010: Progress and Liberal Thought in al-Hilāl, al-Manār and al-Muqtaṭaf before World War I. In: Schumann, Christoph (ed.): Nationalism and Liberal Thought in the Arab East: Ideology and Practice. London; 133–143.
Philipp, Thomas 2011: Jurji Zaydan's Role in the Syro-Arab Nahda: a Re-Evaluation. In: Beshara, Adel (ed.): The Origins of Syrian Nationhood. Histories, Pioneers and Identity. Abingdon; 79–90.
Plank, Peter 1999: Archimandrite. In: Fahlbusch, Erwin (ed.): Encyclopedia of Christianity. Vol. 1. Grand Rapids; 118.
Prätor, Sabine 1993: Der arabische Faktor in der jungtürkischen Politik. Eine Studie zum osmanischen Parlament der II. Konstitution (1908–1918). Berlin.
Qalyūbī, Ṭāhir Adīb 2006: ʿĀʾilāt wa-šaḫṣīyāt min Yāfā wa-qaḍāʾuhā. Beirut.
Rabinowitz, Dan; Monterescu, Daniel 2008: Reconfiguring the "Mixed Town": Urban Transformations of Ethnonational Relations in Palestine and Israel. In: International Journal of Middle East Studies 40; 195–226.
Rahe, Thomas 1988: Frühzionismus und Judentum. Zur Programmatik und historischem Kontext des frühen Zionismus bis 1897. Frankfurt/Main.
Ram, Hana 1996: ha-Yishuv ha-yehudi be-Yafo: me kehilla sefardit le-merkaz tzioni (The Jewish Community of Jaffa: from Sephardi Community to Zionist Center). Jerusalem.
Reinkowski, Maurus 1995: Filasṭīn, Filistin und Eretz Israel. Die späte osmanische Herrschaft über Palästina in der arabischen, türkischen und israelischen Historiographie. Berlin.
Reinkowski, Maurus 2011: Zionismus, Palästina und Osmanisches Reich. Eine Fallstudie zu Verschwörungstheorien im Nahen Osten. In: Gall, Lothar; Willoweit, Dietmar (eds.): Judaism, Christianity and Islam in the Course of History: Exchange and Conflicts. Oldenburg; 93–104.

Reizbaum, Marilyn 2003: Max Nordau and the Generation of Jewish Muscle, Jewish Culture and History, 6:1, 130–151.

Robertson, Roland 1995: Glocalization: Time, Space and Homogeneity-Heterogeneity. In: Featherstone, Mike; Lash, Scott; Robertson (eds.): Global Modernities. London; 25–44.

Robson, Laura 2011a: Colonialism and Christianity in Mandate Palestine. Austin.

Robson, Laura 2011b: Communalism and Nationalism in the Mandate: The Greek Orthodox Controversy and the National Movement. In: Journal of Palestine Studies 41, no. 1; 6–23.

Rogger, Hans 1993: The Beilis Case. Anti-Semitism and Politics in the Reign of Nicholas II. In: Strauss, Herbert (ed.): Hostages of Modernization. Studies on Modern Antisemitism, 1870–1933/39, vol. 2: Austria, Hungary, Poland, Russia. Berlin; 1257–1273.

Rohdewald, Stefan 2005: „Vom Polocker Venedig." Kollektives Handeln sozialer Gruppen in einer Stadt zwischen Ost- und Mitteleuropa (Mittelalter, Frühe Neuzeit, 19. Jh. bis 1914). Stuttgart. Zugleich Dissertationsschrift Universität Zürich.

Rohdewald, Stefan; Frick, David; Wiederkehr, Stefan 2007: Transkulturelle Kommunikation im Großfürstentum Litauen und in den östlichen Gebieten der Polnischen Krone: Zur Einführung. In: ibid. (ed.): Litauen und Ruthenien. Studien zu einer transkulturellen Kommunikationsregion (15. - 18. Jahrhundert). Wiesbaden; 7–33.

Rohdewald, Stefan; Fuess, Albrecht; Riedler, Florian and Stephan Conermann 2019: "Wissenszirkulation". In: Rohdewald, Stefan, Conermann, Stephan and Albrecht Fuess (eds.). Transottomanica - Osteuropäisch-osmanisch-persische Mobilitätsdynamiken. Perspektiven und Forschungsstand. V&R unipress, 83–103.

Roper, Geoffrey 2007: Printing Press and Change in the Arab World. In: Baron, Sabrina (ed.), Agent of Change: Print Culture Studies after Elizabeth L. Eisenstein. Amherst: Univ. of Massachusetts; 250–267.

Roussos, Sotiris 1994: How Greek, how Palestinian? The Patriarchate of Jerusalem in the Mid-War Years. In: Sobornost: Incorporating Eastern Churches Review 17, no. 1; 9–18.

Roussos, Sotiris 2003: The Greek Orthodox Patriarchate and Community of Jerusalem: Church, State and Identity. In: O'Mahony, Anthony (ed.): The Christian Communities of Jerusalem and the Holy Land. Studies in History, Religion and Politics. Cardiff; 38–56.

Roussos, Sotiris 2004: Patriarchs, Notables and Diplomats: the Greek Orthodox Patriarchate of Jerusalem in the Modern Period. In: O'Mahony, Anthony (ed.): Eastern Christianity. Studies in Modern History Religion and Politics. London; 372–387.

Roussos, Sotiris 2005: Eastern Orthodox Perspectives on Church–State Relations and Religion and Politics in Modern Jerusalem. In: International Journal for the Study of the Christian Church 5, no. 2; 103–122.

Said, Edward 1978: Orientalism. Pantheon Books, New York.

Sakākīnī, Ḫalīl as- 1913: an-Nahḍa al-urṯūduksīya fī Filasṭīn. Jerusalem.

Sakākīnī, Ḫalīl as-; Sakākīnī, Hāla as- 1982: Kaḏā anā yā dunyā. Beirut.

Sakākīnī, Ḫalīl as-; Musallam, Akram 2004 Yawmīyāt Ḫalīl as-Sakākīnī. Yawmīyāt, rasāʾil, taʾammulāt. Edited by Akram Musallam, 8 volums, 2003–2010. Vol. 2: al-Nahḍa al-urṯūḏuksīya, al-ḥarb al-ʿuzmā, an-nafī ilā Dimašq, 1914–1918. Ramallah: Khalil Sakakini Cultural Center.

Sanbar, Elias 1994: Les Palestiniens Dans le Siècle. Paris.

Salten, Felix 1986: Neue Menschen auf alter Erde: eine Palästinafahrt. Königstein.

Schaebler, Birgit 2000: Practicing Musha': Common Lands and the Common Good in Southern Syria under the Ottomans and the French. In: Owen, Roger (ed.): New Perspectives on Property and Land in the Middle East. Harvard; 241–307.

Schaefer, Karl 2006: Enigmatic Charms: Medieval Arabic Block Printed Amulets in American and European Libraries and Museums. Leiden.

Schölch, Alexander 1986: Palästina im Umbruch 1856–1882: Untersuchungen zur wirtschaftlichen und sozio-politischen Entwicklung. Stuttgart.

Schölch, Alexander 2001: Der arabische Osten im 19. Jhd. (1800–1914). In: Haarman, Ulrich (ed.): Geschichte der arabischen Welt. München.

Schöps, Julius 1983: Zionismus: Text zu seiner Entwicklung, Wiesbaden.

Schöps, Julius 1996: Deutsch-Jüdische Symbiose oder die mißglückte Emanzipation, Darmstadt.

Schmelz, U. 1990: Population Characteristics of Jerusalem and Hebron Regions according to Ottoman Census of 1905. In: Gilbar, Gad (ed.): Ottoman Palestine: 1800–1914. Studies in Economic and Social History. Leiden; 15–68.

Schmidt, Volker 2006: Multiple Modernities or Varieties of Modernity? In: Current Sociology 54; 77–97.

Schwarz, G. 1880: Jaffa und Umgebung. Erläuterung zu Tafel III. In: Zeitschrift des Deutschen Palästina-Vereins (ZDPV) 3; 44–51.

Schulze, Reinhard 1997: The Birth of Tradition and Modernity in 18th and 19th Century Islamic Culture - The Case of Printing. In: Culture and History 16; 29–72.

Shafir, Gershon 1996: Land, Labor and the Origins of the Israeli-Palestinian Conflict, 1882–1914. Berkeley, Los Angeles, London.

Shapira, Anita 1992: Land and Power. The Zionist Resort to Force, 1881–1948. New York.

Shaw, Stanford J.; Shaw, Ezel Kural 1977: History of the Ottoman Empire and Modern Turkey, vol. 2. Cambridge.

Shlaim Avi 1988: Collusion Across the Jordan. King Abdullah, the Zionist Movement, and the Partition of Palestine. Oxford.

Shomali, Qustandi 1995: Palestinian Christians: Politics, Press and Religious Identity, 1900–1948. In: O'Mahony, Anthony (ed.): The Christian Heritage in the Holy Land. London.

Segev, Tom 2007: Es war einmal ein Palästina: Juden und Araber vor der Staatsgründung Israels. 4th edition. München.

Seikaly, May 2002: Haifa at the Crossroads: An Outpost of the New World Order. In: Fawaz, Leila; Bayly C.A. (eds.): Modernity and Culture from the Mediterranean to the Indian Ocean. Columbia; 96–111.

Seikaly, Samir 1981: Damascene Intellectual Life in the Opening Years of the 20th Century: Muhammad Kurd 'Ali and Al-Muqtabas. In: Buheiry, Marwan (ed.): Intellectual Life in the Arab East: 1890–1939. Beirut; 125–153.

Seikaly, Sherene 2007: Meatless Days: Consumption and Capitalism in Wartime Palestine, 1939–1948. Ph.D. dissertation. Departments of History and Middle Eastern and Islamic Studies, University New York.

Selaiha, Nehad 2011: Oedipus in Egypt. In: Nelis, Jan (ed.): Reception of Antiquity. Gent; 153–160.

Sheehi, Stephen 2000: Inscribing the Arab Self: Buṭrus al-Bustānī and Paradigms of Subjective Reform. In: British Journal of Middle Eastern Studies 27, no. 1; 7–24.

Sheehi, Stephen 2004: Foundations of Modern Arab identity. Gainesville, Fla.

Sheehi, Stephen 2011: Butrus al-Bustani: Syria's Ideologue of the Age. In: Beshara, Adel (ed.): The Origins of Syrian Nationhood. Histories, Pioneers and Identity. Abingdon; 57–78.

Shilony, Zvi 1998: Ideology and Settlement. The Jewish National Fund, 1897–1914, Jerusalem.

Slutsky, Yehuda 2007: Frumkin, Israel Dov. In: Skolnik, Fred; Berenbaum, Michael (eds.), Encyclopaedia Judaica, vol. 7. Detroit, New York; 301–2.

Smith; Anthony 1998: Nationalism and Modernism: a Critical Survey of Recent Theories of Nations and Nationalism. London, New York.

Somel, Selcuk Aksin 2010: The A to Z of the Ottoman Empire. A to Z Guide Series, no. 152. Lanham, Toronto, Plymouth.

Sonyel, Salahi Ramadan 1993: Minorities and the Destruction of the Ottoman Empire. Ankara.

Stein, Rebecca; Swedenburg, Ted 2004: Popular Culture, Relational History, and the Question of Power in Palestine and Israel. In: Journal of Palestine Studies 33, no. 4; 5–20.

Sternhell, Zeev 1998: The Founding Myths of Israel. Nationalism, Socialism, and the Making of the Jewish State. Princeton.

Stock, Kristina 1997: Warum so viele Worte? Ein Annäherungsversuch an arabische Stilnormen. In: Zeitschrift der Deutschen Morgenländischen Gesellschaft 147, no. 2; 266–302.

Stock, Kristina 2005: Arabische Stilistik. Wiesbaden.

Sulaymān, Muḥammad 1987: Tā'rīḫ aṣ-ṣiḥāfa al-Filasṭīnīya. 1876–1976, vol. 1. Nicosia.

Suleiman, Mohammed Basil 2009: Early Printing Press in Palestine: A Historical Note. In: Jerusalem Quarterly 36; 79–91.

Šūmalī, Qusṭandī 1992: Ǧarīdat Filasṭīn, 1911–1967. Dirāsa naqdīya wa-fihris tā'rīḫī li-n-nuṣūṣ al-adabīya wa-ṯ-ṯaqāfīya. Jerusalem.

Šūmalī, Qusṭandī 1996: Ǧarīdat al-Karmil, 1908–1941. Dirāsa naqdīya wa-fihris tā'rīkhī. Jerusalem.

Swedenburg, Ted 1995: Memories of Revolt. The 1936–1939 Rebellion and the Palestinian National Past. Minneapolis.

Tadros, Noha Khalaf 2009: Les Mémoires de 'Issa al-'Issa. Journaliste et Intellectuel Palestinien (1878–1950). Saint-Denis.

Tadros, Noha Khalaf 2011: Falastin versus the British Mandate and Zionism (1921–1931): Between a Rock and a Hard Place. In: Jerusalem Quarterly 45, no. 1; 6–24.

Tal, Alon 2013: All the Trees of the Forest: Israel's Woodlands from the Bible to the Present. Yale, New Haven, London.

Taki, Victor 2015: Limits of Protection: Russia and the Orthodox Coreligionists in the Ottoman Empire. In: The Carl Beck Papers in Russian and East European Studies 2401. University of Pittsburgh; 1–79.

Tamari, Salim; Hammami, Rema 1998: Virtual Returns to Jaffa. In: Journal of Palestine Studies 27, no. 4; 65–79.

Tamari, Salim 2000: Jerusalem's Ottoman Modernity: The Times and Lives of Wasim Jawhariyyeh. In: Jerusalem Quarterly 9; 5–27.

Tamari, Salim 2002: The Last Feudal Lord. In: Jerusalem Quarterly 16; 27–42.

Tamari, Salim 2003: A Miserable Year in Brooklyn: Khalil Sakakini in America, 1907–1908. In: Jerusalem Quarterly 17; 19–40.

Tamari, Salim 2009: City of Riffraff: Crowds, Public Space, and New Urban Sensibilities in War-Time Jerusalem, 1917–1921. In: Kamran Asdar Ali; Martina Rieker (ed.): Comparing Cities: The Middle East and South Asia. Oxford; 23–48.

Tamari, Salim 2011a: Year of the Locust: a Soldier's Diary and the Erasure of Palestine's Ottoman Past. Berkeley.

Tamari, Salim 2011b: Confessionalism and Public Space in Ottoman and Colonial Jerusalem. In: Diane E. Davis (ed.): Cities & Sovereignty. Identity Politics in Urban Spaces. Bloomington; 59–84.

Tamari, Salim 2013/14: A "Scientific Expedition" to Gallipoli: The Syrian-Palestinian Intelligentsia and the Ottoman Campaign Against Arab Separatism. In: Jerusalem Quarterly 56 & 57. Winter/Spring 2013/14; 6–28.

Tamari, Salim 2014b: Issa al Issa's Unorthodox Orthodoxy: Banned in Jerusalem, Permitted in Jaffa. In: Jerusalem Quarterly 59; 16–36.

Ṭarrāzī, Fīlīb dī 1913–14: Tāʾrīḫ aṣ-ṣiḥāfa al-ʿarabīya: yaḥtawī ʿalā aḫbār kull ǧarīda wa-maǧalla ʿarabīya ẓaharat fī l-āʿlam šarqan wa-ġarban maʿa rusūm aṣḥābihī wa-l-muḥarrirīn fīhā wa-tarāǧim mašāhīrihim. 4 Volums. Beirut.

Ṭarāwina, Muḥammad Salīm al- 2000: Qaḍāʾ Yāfā fī l-ʿahd al-ʿuṯmānī. Dirāsa idārīya iqtiṣādīya iǧtimāʿīya, 1281–1333 h/1864–1914m. (The Subdistrict of Jaffa during the Ottoman Period: Administrative, Economic and Social Studies, 1281–1333 h/1864–1914m). Amman.

Tessler, Mark 2009: A History of the Israeli-Palestinian Conflict. Bloomington, Indianapolis.

Tolkowsky Samuel 1924: The Gateway of Palestine: A History of Jaffa. London.

Tonkiss, Frank 2005: Space, the City and Social Theory: Social Relations and Urban Forms. Cambridge.

Tsimhoni, Daphne 1978: The Greek Orthodox Patriarchate of Jerusalem During the Formative Years of the British Mandate in Palestine. In: Asien and African Studies 12, no. 1; 77–121.

Tsimhoni, Daphne 1984: The Status of the Arab Christians under the British Mandate in Palestine. In: Middle Eastern Studies 20, no. 4; 166–192.

Uhl, Heidemarie 2001: Modernisierungstheorie und Geschichtswissenschaft. In: Newsletter Moderne. Zeitschrift des SFB Moderne, Sonderheft 1: Moderne – Modernisierung – Globalisierung; 10–15.

Ullrich, Peter 2008: Diskursanalyse, Diskursforschung, Diskurstheorie. Ein- und Überblick. In: Freikamp, Ulrike; Matthias Leanza; Janne Mende; Stefan Müller; Peter Ullrich, and Heinz-Jürgen Voß (eds.): Kritik mit Methode? Forschungsmethoden und Gesellschaftskritik. Berlin: Karl Dietz Verlag, 19–31.

Ursinus, Michael 1989: Zur Diskussion um „millet" im Osmanischen Reich. In: Südost-Forschungen 48; 195–207.

Vatikiotis, P. J. 1994: The Greek Orthodox Patriarchate of Jerusalem between Hellenism and Arabism. In: Middle Eastern Studies 30, no. 4; 916–929.

Volkov, Shulamit 2001: Reflexionen zum modernen und uralten jüdischen Nationalismus. In: Das jüdische Projekt der Moderne: zehn Essays. München; 32–48.

Wansbrough, J., İnalcık, Halil; Lambton, A.K.S.; Baer, G.: Imtiyāzāt. In: Encyclopaedia of Islam, 2nd edition.

Watenpaugh, Keith 2006: Being Modern in the Middle East: Revolution, Nationalism, Colonialism, and the Arab Middle Class. Princeton.

Weber, Wolfgang 2001: Die Bildung von Regionen durch Kommunikation. Aspekte einer neuen historischen Perspektive. In: Hoffmann, Carl; Kießling, Rolf (eds.): Kommunikation und Region. Konstanz; 43–67.

Weinberg, Robert 2013: Blood Libel in Late Imperial Russia: The Ritual Murder Trial of Mendel Beilis. Bloomington.

Wilke, Carsten L. 2011: Alliance Israélite Universelle. In: Diner, Dan (ed.): Enzyklopädie jüdischer Geschichte und Kultur (EJGK), vol. 1. Metzler, Stuttgart, Weimar; 42–50.

White, Benjamin Thomas 2011: The Emergence of Minorities in the Middle East. The Politics of Community in French Mandate Syria. Edinburgh.

Wittrock, Bjön 2000: Modernity: One, None or Many? European Origins and Modernity as a Global Condition. In: Daedalus 129; 31–50.

Wittrock, Björn; Heilbron, Johan; Magnusson, Lars 1998: The Rise of the Social Sciences and the Formation of Modernity. Conceptual Change in Context, 1750–1850. Dordrecht.

Yacobi, Haim 2003: Urban Ethnocracy: The Building of a Town and the Construction of Identity: The Case of Lod. Ph.D. dissertation. Jerusalem: Ben-Gurion University.

Yacobi, Haim 2016: From 'Ethnocracity' to Urban Apartheid: The Changing Urban Geopolitics of Jerusalem\al-Quds. In: Cosmopolitan Civil Societies Journal 8, no.3; 100–114.

Yazbak, Mahmoud 1999: Templars as Proto-Zionists? The "German Colony" in Late Ottoman Haifa. In: Journal of Palestine Studies 28; 40–54.

Yehoshu'a, Ya'acov (Yehošuʿ, Yaʿqūb) 1974: Taʾrīḫ aṣ-ṣihāfa al-ʿarabīya fi Filasṭīn fī-l-ʿahd al-ʿuṯmānī, 1909–1918. Jerusalem.

Yiftachel, Oren; Yacobi, Haim 2003: Urban Ethnocracy: Ethnicization and the Production of Space in an Israeli 'Mixed City'. In: Environment and Planning D: Society and Space 21; 673–693.

Zachs, Fruma 2011: Pioneers of Syrian Patriotism and Identity: a Re-Evaluation of Khalil al-Khuri's Contribution. In: Beshara, Adel (ed.): The Origins of Syrian Nationhood. Histories, Pioneers and Identity. Abingdon; 91–107.

Zeine, Zeine 1973: The Emergence of Arab Nationalism, 3rd edition. New York. First published in 1958.

Zerubavel, Yael 1995: Recovered Roots. Collective Memory and the Making of Israeli National Tradition. Chicago.

Zurcher, Erik-Jan 2000: Young Turks, Ottoman Muslims and Turkish Nationalists. Identity Politics 1908–1938. In: Karpat, Kemal (ed.), Ottoman Past and Today's Turkey. Leiden; 150–179.

Zurcher, Erik-Jan 2004: History of Modern Turkey. London, New York.

Websites Consulted

Palestinian Destroyed Villages

www.palestineremembered.com (29 May 2012).

Ottoman 'Cataclysm' Project/University of Basel

https://nahoststudien.unibas.ch/forschung/projekte/laufende-projekte/ottoman-cataclysm/ (17 August 2017).

Blogspot Aṣleh Fadi on *Filasṭīn*

http://fadyasleh.blogspot.de (30 August 2017).

Jrayed – Arabic Newspaper Archive of Ottoman and Mandatory Palestine

https://web.nli.org.il/sites/nlis/en/Jrayed (15 August 2019).
https://web.nli.org.il/sites/nlis/en/jrayed/pages/Mirat-al-Sharq.aspx (15 August 2019).

Palestine: Information with Provenance (PIWP database)

http://cosmos.ucc.ie/cs1064/jabowen/IPSC/php/journal.php?joid=2079 (20 November 2017).

New York Review of Books

http://www.nybooks.com/articles/2001/03/08/turkeys-hidden-past/#fnr1 (28 October 2017).

Unesco – White City of Tel Aviv

http://whc.unesco.org/en/list/1096 (2 August 2017).

Palestine Remembered

http://www.palestineremembered.com/Jaffa/Jaffa/ (20 November 2017).

Maronites of the Holy Land

https://now.mmedia.me/lb/en/reportsfeatures/546588-maronites-of-the-holy-land (6 June 2017).

Archnet, Hayy al-Agami

https://archnet.org/sites/3552 (6 June 2017).

Throne Villages Palestine

http://www.riwaq.org/qura-al-karasi-throne-villages-palestine (10 October 2017).

Ottoman Constitution – Boğaziçi University, Atatürk Institute of Modern Turkish History

http://www.ata.boun.edu.tr (17 November 2017).
http://www.anayasa.gen.tr/1876constitution.htm (17 November 2017).

Enyclopedia Judaica

http://www.encyclopedia.com (18 October 2017).

Digital Family Album Rishon le-Tzion

http://www.gen-mus.co.il/en/person/?id=547 (29 May 2012).

Jewish Virtual Library

https://www.jewishvirtuallibrary.org/rabbi-jacob-meir (22 February 2012).

Website of the Khalidi Library

http://www.khalidilibrary.org/indexe.html (14 May 2019).